THE GOVERNMENT OF CANADA

CANADIAN GOVERNMENT SERIES

General Editors

R. MacG. Dawson, 1946–58/J. A. Corry, 1958–61/C. B. Macpherson, 1961–

The Government of Canada

R. MacGREGOR DAWSON

Fifth edition, revised by NORMAN WARD

University of Toronto Press

Preface to first edition

IT IS A DISTURBING FACT that until a year or two ago no comprehensive book on the government of Canada had ever been written. The nearest approach had been a few slim and dreary volumes on Canadian "civics" for use in the high schools, some excellent work on Canadian constitutional history, and several collections of government documents and allied material dealing with constitutional questions. The great obstacle in the way of preparing a more ambitious account of Canadian government has been the dearth of specialized studies on various phases of the subject which would provide a fund of secondary material and ease the burden of research among the primary sources. Progress along these lines during the past twenty years has been slow, but by no means negligible, and as a result the task, while still formidable, has been greatly lightened. Several years ago Professor Clokie took the plunge, and appeared with what may fairly be called the first descriptive account of the government of Canada. This volume is the second. Even so, this does not attempt to cover, except incidentally, anything more than the Canadian federal or central government and its relations with the provinces.

The absence of an adequate supply of secondary sources has not only entailed research, it has also led me to rely heavily on many of my friends and acquaintances for suggestions and for the checking of material. I have, indeed, been quite inconsiderate in the immoderate demands which I have made on both their knowledge and good nature, and it is difficult to overstress the substantial assistance which they have rendered. It is one of the most pleasing and satisfying sides of academic life that help of this kind can invariably be taken for granted and is always given cheerfully and without stint whenever required. From this host of advisers and critics I wish to thank especially the following, although the list given is by no means exhaustive. Dr Eugene A. Forsey leads by a substantial margin. He has struggled through almost the entire manuscript, and his exceptional knowledge and frank expressions of opinion have been, quite literally, of incalculable benefit to me. Professor J. A. Corry, Pro-

fessor Chester Martin, and Mr A. D. P. Heeney have within more limited
fields given help of equal value. Dr Arthur Beauchesne and Mr L. C. Moyer
of the parliamentary staff, Ottawa, Mr R. B. Bryce and Mr J. W. Pickersgill of
the Dominion civil service, Mr Harry Johnson, Toronto, and Professors F. C.
Auld, H. A. Innis, and V. W. Bladen have read various chapters and have contributed many useful suggestions and criticisms. Finally, I desire to acknowledge the aid given by the Library staff of the University of Toronto and the
editorial staff of the University of Toronto Press. They have combined unfailing
courtesy and understanding with a most painstaking efficiency and have helped
in no small measure to lighten my task.

R. MacG. D.

UNIVERSITY OF TORONTO
September 1947

Preface to fourth edition

WHEN R. MacG. DAWSON FINISHED the first edition of this book in 1947, he referred to "the dearth of specialized studies on various phases of the subject which would provide a fund of secondary material and ease the burden of research among the primary sources" as an obstacle in the way of writing such a book as *The Government of Canada*. Since that time, a number of valuable studies have appeared which have immeasurably lightened the task of describing and commenting on various Canadian institutions, and indeed it can now be said that although there are still many gaps, particularly in the field of political theory, a small but respectable literature on Canadian politics now exists. The great bulk of that literature is pragmatic rather than philosophical, and most of what is useful in it is still, as it was with Dr Dawson's own books, the work of academics. With occasional exceptions for which we should all be grateful, neither politics nor journalism in Canada has attracted many people with a contemplative or analytical mind that naturally turns to writing; and even when such people can be found, their demanding professions commonly do not allow them sufficient leisure to write much anyway.

One of the interesting adventures of revising Dr Dawson's work has centred around the extent to which his earlier generalizations, based on research which he himself considered somewhat haphazard in a few areas, have stood the test of time. In an impressive majority of instances his conclusions have needed little correction, but only qualification or updating, if that. There were none the less three general areas where the text, without being inaccurate, seemed to me to need strengthening. Almost the whole of the earlier text could have been read without giving the reader an adequate appreciation of the third of the country that is French-speaking, and the impact of that fundamental fact of Canadian politics on the country as a whole; the book was, in short, an English-Canadian version of Canadian government, and while I cannot pretend to have made it any less so, I have where possible amended the text to include references to the rest of us. Secondly, Dr Dawson's approach to the public service generally, because of his own earlier work, concentrated on the rather old-fashioned and negative problems of preventing abuses in the public service, rather than on the positive aspects of devising a public service that is an instrument for achieving certain desirable goals. And finally, parts of his chapters on political parties paid more attention to the democratic facades which the parties present than seemed realistic in the light of the parties' actual roles in Canadian society.

I do not claim in one revision to have satisfactorily solved all the particular problems that concerned me, let alone problems that may concern others. My main problem was the intimidating one of taking a book which I knew was good, written by a man whom I greatly admired, and trying to make it even better for the chief purpose for which it was devised – teaching; while at the same time, in deference to the expressed wishes of the publishers and the Dawson family, retaining the original form and character of the book as conceived by Dr Dawson. That latter task at least was simple: many of my alterations are in the direction in which Dr Dawson's own plans for further revision were travelling, and in any event the general structure of the book which he developed was so sound for its purpose that it could hardly be improved. The rest of the task was also simplified, though lengthened, by the admirable books and articles which have appeared in recent years, to which acknowledgments are made in footnotes and in the bibliography. The manuscript was completed in the autumn of 1962, and I have been able to make only passing references to works which have appeared since then, including monographs and the report of the Royal Commission on Government Organization.

Any revision of a large book requires the assistance of a large number of people, and I have been extraordinarily fortunate in those to whom I turned for help. It would be impossible to list them all and describe their contributions; and when I add that there is one paragraph in the book on which the combined views of three prime ministers have been brought to bear, the reader will be able to conclude, and rightly, that I sowed my inquiries freely and reaped a good crop. I do not say that all sections of the book received attention at the summit; I addressed my requests for information to those most likely to have it, and as a result I am indebted to a host of politicians, public servants, professional colleagues and others, who donated their time and talents generously. I should particularly like to acknowledge the help given by Mr E. A. Driedger, deputy minister of Justice; Mr J. A. Murray of the Civil Service Commission, who read chapters XII and XIII; Professor E. A. Tollefson of the University of Saskatchewan, who read chapter V; Mr R. J. Batt, assistant parliamentary counsel, who through the offices of Mr Speaker Michener prepared for me a valuable memorandum on the office of parliamentary secretary; Professor John Meisel, Queen's University, who read chapters XXI, XXII, and XXIII; the offices of the attorney general in Ontario and Saskatchewan; and Mr R. I. K. Davidson, associate editor, University of Toronto Press, who wrestled successfully with the editorial problems which I sent him on a fairly systematic basis. None of these people are of course responsible for anything in the book; in accordance with an ancient and discomforting tradition, the author in that regard stands alone.

A special mention must be made of that tireless analyst of manuscripts, Dr Eugene Forsey. The original author of this book said not once but frequently that anybody who published a book about government in Canada without having it dissected by Eugene Forsey was asking for trouble, and with this conclusion I entirely concur. Trouble, as a matter of fact, is what you get if you *do* have Dr Forsey read your manuscript, for his uncannily sharp eye misses no shaky generalization, and treats all allegations of fact as being created equal in the sense that they are born to be challenged. I honestly do not know how to thank Eugene Forsey adequately for his dozens of pages of critical commentary and supporting briefs; but I should like to publicize in unequivocal terms the affection and admiration I have for him and his works. Long may he flourish!

And so, too, my wife, who behaved throughout the preparation of the following pages exactly as a wife is supposed to behave when her husband is revising for a fourth edition a mighty manuscript from the pen of a man who was a good friend to both of us.

NORMAN WARD

SASKATOON
May 10, 1963

Preface to fifth edition

IN THE PREFACE to the fourth edition I explained the nature of the changes I had made in Dr Dawson's text, and I must now explain changes made in the material for which I am myself responsible. So much has happened in Canadian government and politics in the past few years, including extensions of the information and understanding available, that a justification of change in a general text may hardly seem needed. But this edition is so much longer than the fourth (though the pages are fewer) that the publishers were moved to suggest tentatively that the book be divided into two, a notion well calculated to put any author-editor on the defensive.

I have, to begin with, eliminated facts and concepts that seemed no longer necessary or relevant to a comprehension of the governmental process in Canada; what remains is what, on the basis of twenty-five years in the business, I still consider necessary. I have also attempted not merely to record, but to assess, the substantial changes that have been taking place in Canadian institutions in recent years. These have been greatest in party affairs, where the deposing of Mr J. G. Diefenbaker as head of the Progressive Conservatives may yet develop into a genteel Canadian parallel to the beheading of Charles I. But in almost every other major aspect of Canadian politics there have been changes too, and even the House of Commons has effected the first fundamental amendments in its rules since Confederation. Bodies which have not yet been altered, such as the Senate and the Supreme Court, are none the less on the agenda for reform, as is the British North America Act itself. That agenda is not merely long but, it must be admitted, contains sections which are getting old.

The fourth edition of this book was ably criticized by a number of reviewers, and I have done my best to take account of their opinions. Unfortunately several of them were based in part on the premises that the book should have been an entirely different one, that I should accept views which I reject for what I consider excellent reasons, and that the kind of institutional material on which

Dr Dawson based his first edition is becoming obsolete. I should be the first
to agree that there are other approaches to the study of Canadian government
than that employed in what follows, and that the institutional route needs to
be supplemented by the sociological, the behavioural, and probably any other
that may be available; I use other approaches myself. But it is also true that
other approaches cannot ignore the institutional, and indeed I cannot conceive
how one could understand the government of Canada without having at least
some understanding of its main institutions: a belief supported by the reading,
for this edition, of a variety of works by authors who appear to have attempted
that daring feat.

I am still deeply indebted to the people who assisted me with the fourth
edition, and to them I must gratefully add more names. Professor E. A. Tollefson again read the sections on constitutional law; Stanley Knowles the chapter
on procedure in the House of Commons; Mr Arthur Harnett and Mr Jack
Heath, respectively of the Ontario Progressive Conservative and Liberal parties, the sections on party organization; and Mr J. G. Lane, of the Saskatchewan
Attorney General's Office, the passage on the hierarchy of courts. Mr A. R. K.
Anderson, director general of Staffing Branch, Public Service Commission of
Canada, read the chapters on the public service, and Professor David E. Smith
bravely read the entire manuscript, as did the indefatigable Eugene Forsey, my
obligation to whom, in the fourth edition, I tried to express. Many others helped
in correspondence and interview, and if I have inadvertently omitted to name
any I should have, I offer not only my gratitude but my apologies. The University of Toronto Press, of course, offered all its excellent facilities.

It is a particular pleasure to add that help from my family this time included,
as usual, one indispensable wife, but also a Mrs Robert Enright, whom I knew
for twenty-one years as Nora Ward. Nora was my research assistant at the
start of the fifth edition, and an indexer at the end; it seems somehow relevant
she was born in the same year as the first edition of R. MacGregor Dawson's
The Government of Canada, and Dr Dawson thought at the time that of the
two projects I had got the better deal.

NORMAN WARD

UNIVERSITY OF SASKATCHEWAN
Saskatoon, June 9, 1970

Contents

Part I CONSTITUTIONAL DEVELOPMENT

1 Representative and responsible government

THE CHARACTER OF A GOVERNMENT, like that of an individual, is shaped by the two primary forces of heredity and environment; and the study of a government, again like that of an individual, must perforce devote some attention to parentage and the special associations which have had direct contact with each particular institution. Discussions along these lines will appear in the following chapters as occasion warrants. But there are also other influences of a similar though more general nature to be considered – influences which can be traced beyond the immediate family to the more remote ancestors or which flow in from the broader milieu in which the institution has developed. Thus while the government of Canada came into existence on July 1, 1867, and its features were to a material degree determined by the British North America Act, a very significant part of the new government was contributed by the practices of the component provinces which, in turn, were associated with the political experience of other areas on the continent. The greater part of the government was also profoundly affected by British law, traditions, and habits of mind, and by precepts and example in the United States, and these influences have never ceased to operate during the ensuing years. Similarly, Quebec's adherence to the French language, which greatly influenced the government created in 1867, has influenced the course of Canadian government ever since. This and the two chapters following will, therefore, be primarily concerned with certain broad lines of political and constitutional development and they will endeavour to supply a general background for the more particular and detailed studies which follow.

The early colonial governments in what later became the Dominion of Canada acquired their importance for the most part after the American Revolution when England began to rebuild her shattered empire. Three of these colonies, however, were in existence at the time the revolution and held aloof from it, and to these might be added a number of small colonies in the West Indies. But while Quebec had been a British possession and Prince Edward

Island a separate colony for only a few years before the Declaration of Independence, Nova Scotia (excluding Cape Breton) had finally come under the British Crown as early as 1713, and the continuous British connection with the West Indies was of far longer standing. The rebellious American colonies, Nova Scotia, Quebec, Prince Edward Island, and the British West Indies, despite the widest differences in population and origins, were thus to a degree the beneficiaries of one tradition and for a short period had a common if not a uniform experience as subordinate governments under the British Crown.

The first permanent English settlement on the Atlantic seaboard was Virginia, 1607, and twelve years later the first representative government in the Americas was constituted when the governor of that colony, acting in accordance with his instructions, secured the election of "two burgesses out of every town, hundred or other particular plantation" to assist the appointed Council of State. In the year following, 1620, two other representative bodies appeared: Bermuda set up a legislature which included a number of elected members; and the Pilgrim Fathers established a completely self-governing colony at Plymouth. The Massachusetts Bay Company, because its charter happily omitted to specify where the company's headquarters were to be located, was able to follow the Plymouth example and to found in 1630 another self-governing community. It was about this time that the Crown, which despite the above events had not hitherto definitely favoured representative institutions, began a practice which gave representation an explicit though indirect support and thereby greatly advanced its general adoption. When the Crown granted a charter and extensive economic and political rights to a lord proprietor it inserted a clause which compelled him to secure the approval of the people of the colony to all proposed laws. Thus in 1627 when the Earl of Carlisle was granted most of the Lesser Antilles, his charter stated that the laws were to be made "with the Consent, Assent and Approbation of the freeholders of the said Province, or greater part of them thereunto to be called,"[1] and the charter issued to Lord Baltimore in 1632 contained a similar provision concerning the government of Maryland. From then on, while local conditions might furnish the cause or excuse for occasional lapses, representative institutions in the British colonies became the established practice, although the exact legal rights of the colonists to these institutions remained in doubt for some time. This uncertainty was dispelled during the eighteenth century by decisions of the British courts which declared that a colony's rights to self-government depended primarily on whether the Crown had acquired the colony by settlement or by conquest.

The courts held that in a colony which was acquired by settlement British subjects were assumed to have taken with them all English laws and liberties

1/As a result of this provision in the charter, Barbados, Antigua, St Kitts, Nevis, and Montserrat had each its little representative Assembly as early as 1663. At the time of the American Revolution no less than twelve governments in the West Indies (including Bermuda) had representative institutions. H. Wrong, *Government of the West Indies* (Oxford, 1923), pp. 22–52, 80–1.

so far as they were compatible with local conditions. When legislation was to be enacted in the colony (and this included taxation) it could be passed only with the consent of the local inhabitants or their representatives. In short, the right to participate in legislation was an inalienable right of a British subject which could not be lost merely by crossing the Atlantic and establishing a settlement on another continent. On the other hand, the inhabitants of a colony acquired by conquest from, or cession by, a civilized power were held by the courts to possess no such right under the common law. Here the Crown (the King-in-Council or the Governor-in-Council in the colony) had an unfettered right to legislate without consulting the original inhabitants or any British subjects who might happen to be there. Such a lack of political rights, however, was clearly not apt to attract British settlers, and in practice the Crown, in order to encourage immigration to the colony, would frequently promise or grant representative institutions. The courts decided[2] that if this promise or grant was once made it was irrevocable and the Crown would have to abide by its gift, although there was, of course, nothing to prevent the British Parliament (as distinguished from the executive power, the Crown) making any change it desired. Representative institutions were therefore the inherent right of all settled colonies and even, when once granted or promised, the right of colonies acquired by conquest or cession. Thus, all the American colonies save one[3] had representative government by right of settlement; the exception was New York, which was captured from Holland, but secured it by virtue of a grant by the Crown.[4] The precise form which this government assumed, however, varied greatly in different colonies.

Nova Scotia, although it had been captured from the French not once but four times, and although the French had unmistakable priority of permanent settlement, was conveniently considered to be a settled English colony. An early statute of 1759 recited that the province "did always of Right belong to the Crown of England, both by Priority of Discovery and ancient Possession"[5] and the courts showed the same splendid disregard of the historical facts.[6] Nevertheless the colony was ruled in the first instance (following its cession by France in 1713) by a military governor and an appointed Council, although in 1727 a representative Assembly was promised as soon as local circumstances warranted. There was also some uncertainty as to whether the final

2/The ruling case was *Campbell* v. *Hall* (1774), 1 Cowper, 204.

3/Strictly speaking, there were three, for Spain ceded East and West Florida to England in 1763, and these were promised representative institutions in that year (see *infra*, p. 6n). But Florida was at this time of little consequence and reverted to Spain in 1783.

4/The treaty of cession in 1664 guaranteed representative government to "the town of Manhatans," and this constituted a moral though probably not a legal obligation on the Crown. The distinction between settled and conquered colonies was of no significance in this very early period.

5/*N. S. Statutes*, 33 Geo. II, c. 3.

6/*Uniacke* v. *Dickson*, 1 N.S. Reports, 287; C. J. Townshend, *History of the Court of Chancery in Nova Scotia* (Toronto, 1900), pp. 4–19.

government was to be modelled on that of Virginia or of Massachusetts.[7] When systematic settlement began with the founding of Halifax in 1749 the commission issued to Lord Cornwallis clearly indicated that the decision had been given in favour of the Virginia or "royal" type, for the governor was empowered to appoint a Council of his own choosing and "to summon and call General Assemblys of the Freeholders and Planters within your Government according to the usage of the rest of our Colonies and Plantations in America." For a few years conditions in the new settlements made an elected body undesirable, but soon agitation by British and particularly by New England immigrants, combined with repeated instructions from the home authorities, forced the issue. In 1758 Governor Lawrence summoned the first Assembly, a step which marked the explicit beginning of representative government in Canada.

Prince Edward Island was given by the Crown in 1769 a separate government which was at first composed of only a governor and Council; but four years later it too secured a representative legislature. In 1784 New Brunswick was divorced from Nova Scotia and the Crown authorized the governor to appoint a Council and summon an Assembly of its own.[8] The origin of all three Maritime legislatures was therefore a summons by the Crown, an exercise of the prerogative[9] and not a statute of the British Parliament. Despite many vicissitudes these three provincial governments still rest on that foundation.[10]

Quebec was legally, as well as in fact, a conquered colony; but almost as soon as the cession was completed, Governor Murray received instructions[11] which not only required him to establish a Council but also stated that "so soon as the Situation and Circumstances of Our said Province will admit thereof, You shall, with the Advice of Our Council, summon and call a General Assembly of the Freeholders of Our said Province; You are, therefore, as soon as the more pressing Affairs of Government will allow to give all possible attention to the carrying this important Object into Execution." But before these intentions were implemented the British government changed its mind.

7/The government of Virginia was the "royal" type composed of an appointed governor and Council and an elected Assembly; Massachusetts after 1691 had the "charter" type with an appointed governor and an elected Council and Assembly. Rhode Island and Connecticut were also "charter" colonies, but they elected their governors as well as the Council and Assembly.

8/In the same year Cape Breton Island was separated from Nova Scotia and given its own governor and Council, but no Assembly. It was reunited to Nova Scotia in 1820.

9/Infra, pp. 147–9.

10/See C. A. Stuart, "Our Constitution outside the British North America Act," Canadian Bar Review, Feb. 1925, pp. 69–79.

11/Dated Dec. 7, 1763. An earlier proclamation (Oct. 7, 1763) had also contained a similar statement of intention. The proclamation covered not only Quebec but also East and West Florida and Grenada, and referred to the calling of Assemblies "in such Manner and Form as is used and directed in those Colonies and Provinces in America which are under Our immediate Government." A. Shortt and A. G. Doughty, eds., Documents Relating to the Constitutional History of Canada, 1759–1791 (Ottawa, 1918), pp. 163–8, 181–205.

The overwhelming preponderance of French-speaking subjects in Quebec, and the friction between them and the few but very aggressive British merchants, gave little encouragement to proceed; the growing difficulties with the American colonies, which found their chief spokesmen and leaders in the Assemblies, made the British government look upon colonial popular chambers with active distrust; while there were some people (Guy Carleton, the second governor of Quebec, for one) who desired to use the colony as a base of operations against the Americans in the event of the growing tension culminating in war. There was, moreover, some doubt whether the Québécois really wanted so novel an institution as an Assembly, and a further question arose whether an Assembly could be used by the Roman Catholic members who might not be allowed to sit unless they had first taken the oath of supremacy and had made a declaration against transubstantiation.[12] But the regrets and misgivings of the British cabinet were of themselves insufficient to bring about a change, for the Crown had no power to revoke the representative institutions which it had in an unguarded moment so freely promised. Such action could be taken only by Parliament.

The result was the passage of the Quebec Act of 1774. This greatly extended the western limits of the colony so that it included the hinterland between the Ohio and the Mississippi. It also declared that Roman Catholics were to enjoy freedom of religious worship (thus confirming and even perhaps amplifying the terms of the Treaty of Paris) and that the French-Canadian civil law was to be retained until altered by the colony. Interestingly enough, in view of later developments, the act contained no specific guarantees for either the French or the English languages.[13] The criminal law was to remain that of England. The act explicitly repealed the Proclamation of 1763 because it was "found upon Experience to be inapplicable to the State and Circumstances of the Province," and inasmuch as the calling of an Assembly was "at present inexpedient," provision was made for an appointed Legislative Council. The Council was given, however, no power of levying general taxes, this being exercised by the British Parliament. Finally, a special oath was provided for Roman Catholics so that they could accept seats in the Council.[14]

The Quebec Act was warmly approved by the French Canadians who not unnaturally saw in it a great charter of their liberties; partly for the same reason, a number of English colonists opposed it. It is difficult not to consider it

12/This same barrier, however, had been overcome in Grenada without much difficulty. The pre-Confederation story of qualifications and disqualifications for candidates and electors is admirably recounted in John Garner, *The Franchise and Politics in British North America, 1755–1867* (Toronto, 1969).

13/See Norman Ward, "Parliamentary Bilingualism in Canada," *Parliamentary Affairs,* x, no. 2 (Spring 1957), pp. 154–64. The several dozen research reports prepared for the Royal Commission on Bilingualism and Biculturalism provide a library of studies relevant to the two official languages.

14/See W. P. M. Kennedy, *The Constitution of Canada, 1534–1937* (2nd ed., London, 1938), pp. 50–70.

in other respects a reactionary measure, for it completely reversed the principle of representative government and political self-expression which had hitherto marked out British colonies as distinct from those of any other nation. "It is not right," said Fox, "for this country to originate and establish a constitution in which there is not a spark or semblance of liberty ... To go at once and establish a perfectly despotic government, contrary to the genius and spirit of the British constitution carries with it the appearance of a love of despotism and a settled design to enslave the people of America, very unbecoming this country."[15] The autocratic government, the extension of the western boundaries, which was an obvious challenge to American expansion, and the association of all this with other coercive measures passed by the British Parliament about this time, could not fail to arouse both resentment and suspicion in the American colonies, and there can be no doubt that the act was an important contributory factor to the débâcle which was only a few months distant.[16] On the other hand, when the war did break out the act was instrumental in keeping Quebec fairly cold to American blandishments (although the habitant showed little enthusiasm for either side)[17]; and Canada never tried to avail herself of article XI in the Articles of the American Confederation which provided for her admission as the fourteenth state.

Whatever the impact of the American Revolution on subsequent British colonial policy, it had one immediate effect on Canadian development. The revolution brought a great exodus of loyalist stock to the Maritime provinces[18] and to the western part of Quebec around Lake Ontario and Lake Erie. These people had grown up in an atmosphere of political freedom and they had long enjoyed representative institutions, so that settlement and a demand for political reform took place almost simultaneously. Those who came to Quebec lost no time in objecting to the restrictions of the Quebec Act, and they insisted on their right to enjoy the British civil law, habeas corpus, trial by jury, and, above all, representative government.[19]

The solution was not long delayed and was embodied in the Constitutional Act of 1791. Quebec was to be divided into two parts, Upper and Lower Canada, and each province was thereupon to be given its own governor, nom-

---

15/Sir Henry Cavendish, ed., *Debates in the House of Commons in the Year 1774* (London, 1839), pp. 61–2.

16/See Sir Reginald Coupland, *The Quebec Act* (Oxford, 1925); Chester Martin, *Empire and Commonwealth* (Oxford, 1929), pp. 94–147.

17/See S. D. Clark, *Movements of Political Protest in Canada, 1640–1840* (Toronto, 1959), especially pp. 75–102.

18/Resulting in the creation of the new province of New Brunswick in 1784. See *supra*, p. 6.

19/See petition of Nov. 24, 1784, in Shortt and Doughty, *Documents Relating to the Constitutional History of Canada*, pp. 742–52. Interestingly enough, large numbers of the immigrants were technically aliens. See Garner, *The Franchise and Politics in British North America*, pp. 162–76.

inated Council, and elected Assembly. The act thus restored the rights of representation which had been denied Quebec seventeen years before and marked a return to the overseas practice of the British constitution. In another respect, however, the acts of 1774 and 1791 were not contradictory but complementary, for they combined to preserve and consolidate the status of the French-speaking in British North America: the former provided many essential guarantees; the latter protected them from possible conflict, absorption, and subordination, and recognized both English and French for the taking of oaths of allegiance by legislative members. By 1840, when the two provinces were again united, the half-century of segregation and self-government had done its work and French Canada was too firmly entrenched to be seriously threatened. Lord Durham's expectation that Quebec might come to be another weak French outpost like Louisiana, which was being assimilated into the United States, proved to be a startling miscalculation in a report conspicuous for the shrewdness of many of its judgments.[20]

The first half of the nineteenth century witnessed the steady economic and political development of British North America, and as the colonies increased in importance and virility so their dissatisfaction with their government increased also. In this they acted in accordance with the best traditions on the continent and, it might be added, in accordance with the best traditions of the British people as well. "It is the genius of the English race in both hemispheres," said Robert Baldwin, "to be concerned in the government of themselves."[21] The form of representative government in British North America was not only a copy of that previously existing in the American colonies, but it was reproducing with unhappy accuracy many of the identical problems and sources of friction which had appeared in those colonies before the revolution. Quarrels between governor and legislature, for example, were as common – and crucial – in British North America as they had been fifty or a hundred years before, and the outcome (as in the earlier struggles) was largely determined by the degree of financial independence which the governor could command. Thus in Lower Canada, where the Crown enjoyed a substantial independent revenue derived in large measure from land and from the imposts of the Quebec Revenue Act (passed by the British Parliament in 1774 before a representative legislature existed in Quebec), the governor was able successfully to hold out against the Assembly and carry on the executive government with or without its co-operation.[22] In Nova Scotia, on the other hand, the independent revenue of the Crown was small. The income from land was comparatively unimportant, and the indirect taxes, imposed (as in Quebec) on

20/*Infra*, pp. 12–15.
21/Quoted in Martin, *Empire and Commonwealth*, p. 50.
22/D. G. Creighton, "The Struggle for Financial Control in Lower Canada, 1818–1831," *Canadian Historical Review*, XII, no. 2 (June 1931), pp. 120–44.

articles of trade and commerce, were for the most part paid into the general provincial fund over which the legislature and not the governor had control.[23] Frequently the Assembly showed its vigilance and its determination to maintain its advantage intact,[24] for it fully realized the great value of this financial weapon in its contest with the governor for supreme power. The weapon was, none the less, often used ineptly, and none of the colonies developed effective financial controls over the executive before Confederation.[25]

The discouraging feature of the struggle in British North America over self-government was not only its similarity to an earlier experience, but the apparent inability of the home government to learn anything from its first failure. For if the British had drawn any moral from the American Revolution, it was apparently the exact opposite of the correct one. They were confident that the key to the disaster was excessive freedom and too much power in the popular Assembly, and they were therefore disposed to increase and not diminish the pressures on that body and to support the power of the governor and the social classes in the colony on which he relied. Some, indeed, took an even gloomier view, and held that no effort to hold the colonies could in the nature of things be successful, but that in a few more years the inherent centrifugal forces would gain control and the colonies would once again declare their independence.

In truth the similarity of organic growth between the first Empire and the second is borne in upon one at every point. Not only are the local problems the same but with the exception of Nova Scotia the process of colonial government begins again almost *de novo*; and if the second Empire, like the first, came to the brink of disaster it was not because it had not a fair chance ... All the approved specifics for making the officials of government "independent of the factious will and caprice of an assembly" are tried again. The same catchwords of "due subordination" and "the rights and liberties of British subjects" appear on either side. The same bitter struggle ensues, a struggle wholly indigenous to Canadian soil but complicated by false analogies drawn from the results of the earlier conflict. Within fifty years the same malignant disease had run its course. Fortunately there was no recourse to surgery, though the poisoning of mutual confidence threatened the same dissolution. Governor Bernard never vilified his political opponents in Massachusetts more heartily than Sir Francis Head berated the "republicans" of Upper Canada. Before the struggle was over, men as staunchly British as Robert Baldwin and Joseph Howe had become very nearly as desperate as Washington in 1774. Baldwin solemnly warned Lord Durham in 1838 that without responsible government "England will continue to retain these Colonies by means of her troops alone." Howe advised Charles Buller as late as 1846 that if men like those who "drove the old Colonies to separation" had their way, the problem would

---

23/Under the Colonial Tax Repeal Act of 1778 the imperial Parliament declared its policy of relinquishing from this time forward its own colonial taxing powers (save for the regulation of commerce) and provided that the net proceeds of any tax raised in any colony should be spent there as a part of the general revenue for use of that colony.

24/See H. A. Innis, *The Cod Fisheries* (rev. ed., Toronto, 1954), pp. 269–71.

25/Norman Ward, *The Public Purse: A Study in Canadian Democracy* (Toronto, 1962), chap. II.

be "discussed in a different spirit, ten years hence, by the Enemies of England, not by her friends."[26]

The crux of the matter was the control of the executive power. All the colonies, it is true, had representative government through the elected Legislative Assembly, but the latter's control in any real sense was frustrated by other elements in the government which held no popular mandate whatever. Even the legislative power was shared by the Assembly with an appointed Legislative Council, but this was of small importance when compared with the exclusive executive authority wielded by the governor and the Executive Council, the members of which he appointed. The lack of popular control in this arrangement was greatly aggravated by the social, religious, and cultural factors involved. The Council in all colonies was drawn from a small and exclusive group representing wealth, education, government, church, and society, who frequently used their official positions to advance their own interests through the direction of policies and the distribution of patronage. Even the governor found it to his interest to propitiate the "Chateau Clique" of Lower Canada, the "Family Compact" of Upper Canada, and similar groups in the other provinces. A letter of Joseph Howe's still presents an unrivalled account of the governor's predicament:

He may flutter and struggle in the net, as some well-meaning Governors have done, but he must at last resign himself to his fate; and like a snared bird be content with the narrow limits assigned him by his keepers. I have known a Governor bullied, sneered at, and almost shut out of society, while his obstinate resistance to the system created a suspicion that he might not become its victim; but I never knew one who, even with the best intentions and the full concurrence and support of the representative branch, backed by the confidence of his Sovereign, was able to contend, on anything like fair terms, with the small knot of functionaries who form the Councils, fill the offices, and wield the powers of the Government. The plain reason is, because, while the Governor is amenable to his Sovereign, and the members of Assembly are controlled by their constituents, these men are not responsible at all; and can always protect and sustain each other, whether assailed by the representatives of the Sovereign or the representatives of the people.[27]

The attacks of the reformers went to the centre of these difficulties, and they demanded the right to control the advisers of the governor. Let the governor call to his Executive Council those who have the confidence of the Assembly, they argued, and let these advisers be changed whenever the Assembly indicates that it wishes a change to be made, and at one stroke the friction and quarrelling between the executive and the legislature will disappear. *Representative* government would then be transformed into *responsible* government. The solution had been discovered in England years before, although many im-

26/Martin, *Empire and Commonwealth*, pp. 48–50.
27/Joseph Howe, Letter to Lord John Russell, Sept. 18, 1839, in J. A. Chisholm, ed., *Speeches and Public Letters of Joseph Howe* (Halifax, 1909), I, pp. 230–1.

portant implications of the general principle were slow to be worked out by empirical methods, as was to be the case in Canada. But the colonial situation presented one important difference. If this innovation took place, how would the governor be able to follow the advice of a Council responsible to the Assembly, and at the same time obey instructions from London? How could he serve two masters with no assurance or even likelihood that they would agree? This dilemma became a most useful argument in the hands of the reactionaries and for years it remained also an insurmountable barrier to many sincere reformers.

The story of the fight for responsible government in the provinces in all its aspects, the rebellions in Upper and Lower Canada, the more restrained yet equally effective tactics in Nova Scotia, the agitation in other provinces, the devices resorted to by the Assemblies to enforce their demands, the personalities involved, and many other details cannot be discussed in these few pages. The immediate sequel, as is well known, was the dispatch in 1838 of Lord Durham as governor-in-chief of all five provinces (and Newfoundland) with authority to restore order and tranquillity, to inquire into the causes of the rebellion, and to suggest measures for the future.

The result of Lord Durham's mission was the presentation of his report, the greatest constitutional document in British colonial history. In substance, he found the complaints of the critics of the existing system amply justified. The situation in Lower Canada, while bearing a strong resemblance to that in other provinces, was complicated and endangered by the clash between the English- and French-speaking elements. "I expected to find a contest between a government and a people," wrote Durham in a famous passage, "I found two nations warring in the bosom of a single state: I found a struggle, not of principles, but of races; and I perceived that it would be idle to attempt any amelioration of laws or institutions until we could first succeed in terminating the deadly animosity that now separates the inhabitants of Lower Canada into the hostile divisions of French and English."[28] To this situation in Lower Canada were added all the problems and difficulties which were found in the other colonies as well. The governor had never been free to follow his own judgment; for he was hampered by his advisers in the colony and tied down by instructions from, and constant supervision by, the secretary of state and British civil servants. He was therefore too prone to refer all matters to London; but neither minister, Parliament, nor civil servant had sufficient knowledge of local conditions to give adequate guidance, and, as a result of this ignorance, neither Parliament nor the British people had ever been able to maintain any more than a sporadic interest in colonial affairs. The governments in the colonies had become confused and increasingly incompetent. The governor was the central figure; but there were no heads to the important departments, and the members of the

28/Lord Durham, *Report on the Affairs of British North America,* ed. Sir C. P. Lucas (Oxford, 1912), II, p. 16. The report is now available in the Carleton Library, no. 1, ed. Gerald M. Craig (Toronto, 1963).

Executive Council took an equal part in all matters which came before them. This Council, with no special legal qualifications, also sat in each colony as a court of appeal. Municipal institutions either did not exist at all or were extremely ineffective, and nowhere was there an adequate system of municipal taxes. A part (and, until recent years in some colonies, a very large part) of each government's revenue and expenditure was not dependent upon the annual vote of the legislature and hence was administered under executive and not legislative control. The English system of securing the consent of the Crown before introducing financial measures into the legislature was not followed, and as a result a wild scramble annually ensued over any surplus funds that were available for public works in the constituencies. But the fundamental weakness common to all the governments was their failure to meet the elementary political needs of their communities for the control of their own affairs through the subordination of the executive to the legislative authority.

It was a vain delusion to imagine that by mere limitations in the Constitutional Act, or an exclusive system of government, a body, strong in the consciousness of wielding the public opinion of the majority, could regard certain portions of the provincial revenues as sacred from its control, could confine itself to the mere business of making laws, and look on as a passive or indifferent spectator, while these laws were carried into effect or evaded, and the whole business of the country was conducted by men, in whose intentions or capacity it had not the slightest confidence. Yet such was the limitation placed on the authority of the Assembly of Lower Canada; it might refuse or pass laws, vote or withhold supplies, but it could exercise no influence on the nomination of a single servant of the Crown. The Executive Council, the law officers, and whatever heads of departments are known to the administrative system of the Province, were placed in power, without any regard to the wishes of the people or their representatives; nor indeed are there wanting instances in which a mere hostility to the majority of the Assembly elevated the most incompetent persons to posts of honour and trust. However decidedly the Assembly might condemn the policy of the Government, the persons who had advised that policy retained their offices and their power of giving bad advice. If a law was passed after repeated conflicts, it had to be carried into effect by those who had most strenuously opposed it. The wisdom of adopting the true principle of representative government and facilitating the management of public affairs, by entrusting it to the persons who have the confidence of the representative body has never been recognized in the government of the North American Colonies.[29]

The two major recommendations of the report were the reunion of Upper and Lower Canada and the immediate grant of responsible government. So far as the two Canadian colonies were concerned these proposals were interdependent; for Durham considered that only union could eliminate the racial conflict in Lower Canada and thus make it possible for responsible government to function effectively. His expectation (already noted) was that this would result in the absorption of the French by the combined British elements in the two colonies, and hence his idea of a union was not at all along federal lines but was

29/*Ibid.* (Lucas ed.), II, pp. 76–7.

one of fusion, "a complete amalgamation of peoples, races, languages, and laws."[30] Durham also looked forward to a wider union of all the British North American colonies, but he considered that the time for so ambitious a project had not yet arrived.

His endorsement of responsible government as a comprehensive cure for many of the troubles of the colonies was whole-hearted and explicit. Moreover, as he pointed out, this change would involve no legislation and no radical innovation of any kind, but simply a consistent application of the principles of the British constitution, where the same change had occurred in the same informal way:

Every purpose of popular control might be combined with every advantage of vesting the immediate choice of advisers in the Crown, were the Colonial Governor to be instructed to secure the co-operation of the Assembly in his policy, by entrusting its administration to such men as could command a majority; and if he were given to understand that he need count on no aid from home in any difference with the Assembly, that should not directly involve the relations between the mother country and the Colony. This change might be effected by a single despatch containing such instructions.[31]

The above passage also suggests Lord Durham's answer to the question of how colonial autonomy and British supremacy were to be reconciled, how the governor was to be spared the dilemma of having to follow two masters who offered conflicting advice. Durham believed that the key to the difficulty was the division of subjects between the imperial and colonial governments. The governor as head of the colonial administration would follow the advice of his Council in matters of colonial concern; but as the agent of the British government, he would be expected to see that the allotment of authority was kept intact and that the local cabinet and Assembly did not trespass on the field of his principal. There would be few if any occasions for conflict, and these would properly be brought to the attention of the imperial authorities. "The matters which so concern us, are very few. The constitution of the form of government – the regulation of foreign relations, and of trade with the mother country, the other British Colonies, and foreign nations – and the disposal of the public lands, are the only points on which the mother country requires a control."[32] The list of reserved subjects named by Durham was somewhat odd, and much more comprehensive than at first appears. Presumably "foreign relations" included the control over all the armed forces of the colony; "the disposal of public lands" certainly involved matters of local revenue which Durham stresses elsewhere in the report as being essential to self-government; and reasonable implication would suggest that the clause affecting trade would cover a wide area. But Durham's central idea that a line of division was practicable was the solution adopted some years

30/Sir C. P. Lucas in *ibid.*, I, p. 124.
31/*Ibid.*, II, pp. 279–80.
32/*Ibid.*, II, p. 282.

later, although events were to demonstrate that such a distinction was neither easy to draw nor easy to maintain.

The report also offered a number of minor recommendations which need only be mentioned here. It urged the creation of strong municipal governments in each colony. All Crown revenues (except those derived from the sale of public lands) were to be placed at the disposal of the colonial governments in exchange for a civil list. All financial bills should originate in the Assembly and should receive the consent of the Crown before being introduced, that is, they should be initiated only by a member of the cabinet. Durham did not recommend an elected Legislative Council, a measure frequently advocated by the reformers, for he felt that in such an event it would cease to act as a check on the lower house, but he expressed dissatisfaction with its existing composition. The responsibility of the cabinet was unmistakably to be to the Assembly and not to the Legislative Council. Finally, the independence of the judiciary was to be ensured by giving its members a secure salary through the civil list and a tenure during good behaviour.

The first major recommendation of the report as well as a number of the minor ones were implemented by the Union Act of 1840 which brought Upper and Lower Canada together once more. The act provided for a governor, a Legislative Council, appointed for life by the Crown,[33] and an elected Legislative Assembly of eighty-four members, each of the two former colonies being given forty-two members. This favoured Upper Canada, which at the moment had the smaller population; but after some years, when the favours began to fall the other way, Upper Canada with a suddenly awakened conscience protested the unfairness of the arrangement and demanded inconsistently but none the less vehemently "Rep. by Pop." The Union Act made English the official language of record, but the restriction on French proved unworkable and it was altered eight years later when both languages were placed on an equality for all official purposes.[34] Revenues were consolidated and independent Crown income was surrendered in exchange for a permanent civil list; but bills dealing with Crown lands and religion were to be reserved by the governor for the consideration of the home authorities. All money bills were to originate with the governor, and then be introduced into the Assembly.

The Union Act thus made no mention of responsible government, and even if it had done so this would not have affected any of the other provinces. In fact, neither the colonial governors nor the British government had been converted to the proposal, although an increasing emphasis was laid in despatches from the Colonial Office on the desirability of admitting to the governor's Council and to the public service "those persons, who by their position and character,

33/This was changed in 1856 by making the members submit to election for an eight-year term.
34/Ward, "Parliamentary Bilingualism in Canada," pp. 154–64; "The National Political Scene" in Mason Wade, ed., Canadian Dualism/La Dualité canadienne (Toronto, 1960), pp. 260–76.

have obtained the general confidence and esteem of the inhabitants of the province."[35] But this was far removed from an absolute obligation being placed on a governor to shed the old advisers and take on the new ones whenever the Assembly indicated its desire for a change. Various half-way measures were tried during the next few years, and although some met with a temporary success and the members of the Assembly received more consideration than before the Durham report, responsible government was still far from being achieved. The governor during this transitionary period was forced by circumstances to become a politician; for since he could not ignore the Assembly and have any Council he chose, the obvious and perhaps the only alternative to responsible government was to try to persuade the Assembly that those who followed his leadership deserved its support. The governor thus became his own first minister and endeavoured to build up, usually from the moderate element, his own party. Governors in more than one colony plunged into the political battles and devoted their utmost efforts, sometimes successfully, though as a rule for only short periods, to secure the election of those whom they favoured. At other times the governor's necessities would compel him to organize a coalition Council, although the very nature of its personnel and the fact that only the governor's adroitness and resource had brought it into existence, made cohesion difficult and stability almost impossible.

The transitionary period was brief; indeed, the unhappy consequences of the half-way policy could scarcely have continued for long without threatening once again to tear the structure to pieces. Fortunately a change of government in Great Britain in 1846 brought Earl Grey to the Colonial Office, and Grey was prepared to give the Durham proposal a fair trial. "This Country," he wrote some six years later, "has no interest whatever in exercising any greater influence on the internal affairs of the Colonies, than is indispensable either for the purpose of preventing any one Colony from adopting measures injurious to another, or to the Empire at large, or else for the promotion of the internal good government of the Colonies, by assisting the inhabitants to govern themselves."[36] The appointment of two exceptionally able and liberal-minded governors opportunely prepared the way on the other side of the Atlantic. Sir John Harvey was made governor of Nova Scotia shortly before Grey came to office, and a few months after the latter event Lord Elgin, Durham's son-in-law, was

35/Lord John Russell to C. Poulett Thomson (Lord Sydenham), Sept. 7, 1839, in W. P. M. Kennedy, *Statutes, Treaties, and Documents of the Canadian Constitution, 1713–1919* (Toronto, 1930), p. 417. Hereafter *Constitutional Documents*. Lord John Russell (colonial secretary, 1839–41) was one of those who considered that responsible government placed the governor in an impossible position between the British and colonial authorities. His statement to the British House of Commons on responsible government was the occasion for Joseph Howe's four open "Letters to Lord John Russell," which are not unworthy of a place beside Lord Durham's report. See *Speeches and Public Letters of Joseph Howe*, I, pp. 221–66.

36/Earl Grey, *The Colonial Policy of Lord John Russell's Administration* (2nd ed., London, 1853), I, p. 17.

appointed governor of the Province of Canada. Grey's despatches from the Colonial Office laid down the lines on which he felt the change to responsible government should be made; and, as Durham had foreseen, no other action, save the cordial and unreserved support of the governors and the colonial governments, was necessary to bring the new system into operation. The acid test to determine the existence of responsible government was, of course, not merely a governor's Council supported by the Legislative Assembly (that condition had already occurred repeatedly during the transition) but the immediate changing of that Council when it had lost the confidence of the popular body. The first test of this nature was applied in Nova Scotia when, following a general election, a direct vote of want of confidence in the administration was carried by the Assembly on January 25, 1848, the first effective vote of its kind to be taken outside the British Isles. The Executive Council resigned on the 27th, and the new premier, J. B. Uniacke, was asked to form a government the following day.

In March of the same year a similar defeat on a vote of want of confidence and an immediate change of government took place in the Province of Canada. The same principle was asserted almost simultaneously in New Brunswick, and three years later it was conceded in Prince Edward Island. Newfoundland, which had been given representative government by the governor's exercise of the prerogative in 1832, achieved responsible government in 1855.

British Columbia and Vancouver Island had a more varied history, and their isolation and small white population delayed the growth of self-government. They were governed first by a governor and Council, from 1849 to 1856, but in the latter year a small Assembly (seven members elected by about forty freeholders) was added.[37] The discovery of gold on the Fraser and the resulting influx of miners led in 1858 to the passage of a British statute which made the mainland of British Columbia a separate Crown colony without an Assembly. In 1866 another act was passed reuniting the two colonies and setting up only one government composed of a governor and a Council. Although the latter contained some elected members, they were in a minority, so that the change took from Vancouver Island the popular control of her legislature. In 1870 the British government by order-in-council gave the Council a majority of elected members, and this latter body proceeded to set up an elected Assembly. In the next year British Columbia entered Confederation, and (in accordance with the terms of union) instituted responsible government.[38]

The Province of Manitoba was created after Confederation by Dominion statute in 1870, and it obtained at once the usual governor, Council, and elected Assembly with a responsible cabinet. To complete the story, Alberta

37/Garner, *The Franchise and Politics in British North America,* p. 119.
38/For about a year longer, however, the governor and not the premier ruled. See W. N. Sage, "The Position of the Lieutenant-Governor in British Columbia," in R. Flenley, ed., *Essays in Canadian History* (Toronto, 1939), pp. 178–99; John T. Saywell, *The Office of Lieutenant-Governor* (Toronto, 1957).

and Saskatchewan, after being governed as federal territories by the Dominion government assisted by a territorial legislature, were set up as provinces in 1905 with a governor, an Assembly, and a cabinet responsible to the latter;[39] in 1949 Newfoundland entered Confederation with a similar provincial constitution. The possibility of creating an eleventh province in the Yukon and Northwest Territories is now often discussed, but the sparse population, combined with the enormous differences and distances between settlements, is a powerful argument against it in the mind of every federal government.

In none of the provinces has responsible government been given statutory recognition: the governor is simply empowered to summon an Executive Council, and no mention is made of the necessity for members of the Council to have seats in the Assembly or to enjoy its confidence. In fact, responsible government in every province of Canada rests on the same airy foundation. Whether the provincial constitution is that of one of the three Maritime provinces, which were called into existence by the prerogative; or that of one of the Prairie provinces which were explicitly created by a Dominion statute; or that of Newfoundland created *de novo* in 1949; or that of one of the other provinces, responsible government receives the same treatment: it is denied any explicit description and is found entirely in custom and usage. Lord Durham's simple and convenient device for introducing cabinet government proved so simple and so convenient that for a century it seemed likely to remain indefinitely; but constitutional discussions in the late 1960s early began to include proposals for a more specific recognition of responsible government.[40]

The achievement of the fundamental conditions necessary to responsible government in 1848 (by a coincidence, the same year in which the English and French languages acquired official equality in the Province of Canada) concluded a critical chapter in a long development that began with the granting of representative institutions to Virginia in 1619, or, if Canadian antecedents only are considered, to Nova Scotia in 1758. The American struggle to extend popular control ended in independence. The loyal colonies were at that time either so alien or so small and undeveloped that the process had to begin anew under almost identical conditions, yet with the enormous advantage of having the American Revolution constantly in the background as a warning to official intransigence. Had these colonies been of greater consequence or even, in Quebec, of Anglo-Saxon stock, they might have been able to restate and to assert with some weight and to their own advancement the true lesson to be drawn from the revolution. For in a very short time it again became evident that representative institutions alone – as the American colonies had discovered and, one might have thought, had unmistakably proved – were but a stage in the

39/See L. H. Thomas, *The Struggle for Responsible Government in the North-West Territories, 1870–1897* (Toronto, 1956).
40/See, for example, Pierre Elliott Trudeau, *The Constitution and the People of Canada* (Ottawa, 1969), pp. 28–34.

evolution of self-government. A limited control over legislation was merely an irritant to a people imbued with British political traditions; and no peace was possible until the next logical step was taken and executive power was either given to those directly chosen by the people (as was done in most of the United States) or was brought under the authority of the popular legislature.[41] But responsible government within the empire, as Durham and others clearly realized, could only be conceded at that time if it was placed squarely upon a separation of imperial and local affairs. Experience was soon to demonstrate, however, that responsible government on these terms contained elements almost as unstable as any representative institutions which tried to stop with the exercise of legislative powers alone. The line of demarcation between imperial and local affairs proved in the event to be neither clear-cut nor obvious, and the desire for more and more autonomy began immediately to widen the local area and narrow that which had been reserved in general terms for the imperial authorities. This was, however, a gradual process, which was possible in large measure because of the comparative unimportance and immaturity of British North America in international affairs, the temper of the people, and the very nature and vagueness of the disputed area. For the practice of responsible government based on the idea of allocation not only permitted further adventures in self-government, but it facilitated an advance which proceeded step by step and which could be made with little friction or ill-feeling. These developments were eventually to affect many aspects of Canadian government, and they did not reach their logical destination until 1926 and 1931 when the full equality of the United Kingdom and the dominions was formally declared.

41/In this struggle, as Dr Garner has shown in *The Franchise and Politics in British North America,* the franchise itself was a relevant factor.

2 Confederation

THE DOMINION OF CANADA was the legal creation of the British North America Act, which became effective on July 1, 1867. This great climacteric in Canadian history demands far more space than can be given here. All that will be attempted, therefore, is a general account of the leading events and a brief statement of some of the constitutional provisions, many of which will receive more detailed treatment in later pages.

The possible union of the colonies in British North America was mooted almost as soon as the American colonies had won their independence, and the project was put forward repeatedly as time went on by both visionaries and men of affairs.[1] It was mentioned, as noted above, by Lord Durham in 1839, but was dismissed as inopportune. The establishment of responsible government, however, and the almost simultaneous abandonment of the old colonial system of Great Britain gave a new impetus to the proposal: the one produced a greater virility in provincial governments and institutions by giving the training and responsibility which were an essential preparation for the venture; the other disrupted provincial trade and forced the provinces both to seek their own solutions to their problems and to strengthen their position as best they might in a highly competitive and even dangerous world. No two colonies had identical difficulties, but the success of the federation movement was largely due to the discovery that many difficulties could be met through one common solution.

There were, of course, common difficulties as well, such as the general trade problem, mentioned above, which the British had precipitated in 1846 by their repeal of the navigation laws and the abandonment of the preferential tariff on

---

1/R. G. Trotter, *Canadian Federation* (Toronto, 1924), pp. 5–10. See also G. P. Browne, ed., *Documents on the Confederation of British North America* (Toronto, 1969), a compilation based on Sir Joseph Pope's original work cited in n. 17 below; Donald Creighton, *The Road to Confederation* (Toronto, 1964); W. L. Morton, *The Critical Years: The Union of British North America, 1857–1873* (Toronto, 1964). Canada's centennial in 1967 helped generate a considerable volume of relevant studies, and the list is too long to add here.

colonial goods.[2] There was also the many-sided menace from the United States which cast a shadow over all the colonies: the bellicose statements of many American politicians; the exceptional military power of a country engaged in a prolonged civil war; the danger, frequently apparent, of becoming embroiled in war through British-American quarrels; and the threat to the colony of Canada, although this in a sense was a common threat also, of having the United States isolate the whole northeastern corner of North America from the remainder of the continent by taking possession of all the empty western territory. The pre-Confederation period, moreover, was also a time of disturbing changes in the economic world, and the different colonial economies were finding great difficulty in adjusting themselves to the new technological and industrial conditions.[3] "The shift from wood to iron," writes Professor Creighton, "from water-power to steam, from canals to railways and from sailing-ships to steamboats became virtually an accomplished fact. All these changes fell with jarring force upon provincial economies which were unprepared to sustain the tremendous and expensive adjustments involved."[4]

Each province also had its particular problems to meet, some of which were exclusively its own while others were special manifestations of more general questions in which all might have some share. It was evident from the first that the colony of Canada had most to gain from some form of union both because of the seriousness of its existing difficulties and the possibilities of profitable development under the new regime. In the decade before the beginning of the negotiations which eventually led to federation, the government of the colony was hopelessly deadlocked as a result of a balance created by political and racial differences, and several attempts at constitutional tinkering[5] had failed to yield any substantial improvement. From 1841 to 1867 there were no less than eighteen different cabinets in office. Portfolios were divided equally between Canada East and West; some government departments, such as education, were run in two separate sections with approximately equal expenditures, and appropriations in one section were always balanced against appropriations in the other.[6] A perpetual source of dissatisfaction in Canada West was the fact that although she had a much greater population than her partner[7] and surpassed her in wealth and importance and in the payment of taxes, the two

2/D. G. Creighton, *The Commercial Empire of the St. Lawrence, 1760–1850* (Toronto, 1937), pp. 358–70.

3/H. A. Innis, *Problems of Staple Production in Canada* (Toronto, 1933), pp. 17–23.

4/D. G. Creighton, "British North America at Confederation," *Report of the Royal Commission on Dominion-Provincial Relations* (Ottawa, 1940) (*Rowell-Sirois Report*), Appendix no. 2, p. 11.

5/Such as: an elected upper house; an increase in the number of members in the Assembly, although retaining an equal number from Canada East and West; the "double majority" convention which endeavoured unsuccessfully to ensure that a cabinet should retain a majority in both sections of the province.

6/Creighton, "British North America at Confederation," p. 21.

7/In 1861 this excess of population was 284,525 and by 1864 was well over 300,000.

sections still retained equal representation in the Legislative Council and in the Assembly. Economic embarrassments in the colony were also acute, one of the chief troubles centring about the pending expiration of the reciprocity treaty between Canada and the United States. If, as seemed likely, the United States were unwilling to renew the treaty, the Canadian producers would face a serious loss of markets, and one obvious answer for this and other economic difficulties was an enlargement of political and economic boundaries. The province had been engaged for over two decades in a strenuous and costly endeavour to develop a transportation system of canals and railroads which could hold the trade of the Great Lakes region against American competition; but the financial burden was becoming excessive and the harvest of traffic had been disappointing. The Canadian effort was thus gradually working towards a more restricted national east-to-west economy built about the existing and projected means of transportation, and this necessarily involved expansion westwards into the territory of the Hudson's Bay Company. The French in the Province of Canada could scarcely be expected to support a development of Canada West which would yield such one-sided returns, but an expansion under federal or other auspices was not nearly so objectionable and might, indeed, yield very substantial returns to French Canada as well.[8] Both sections of Canada also favoured a winter outlet to the Atlantic coast which would make them independent of the favour of either a sister colony or a foreign government.[9]

Many in Nova Scotia and New Brunswick also felt they had something to gain by federation, although their eyes were at first fixed upon a smaller and less ambitious Maritime union with Prince Edward Island. Their limited population made these provinces conscious of their isolation and weakness, and they therefore put in the forefront of their demands for the larger federation the construction of an intercolonial railway. Nova Scotia and New Brunswick had, indeed, been urging this project upon the British authorities for years past, and, failing to obtain sufficient support, had begun to build short segments on their own responsibility. But the financial drain had been heavy, and both provinces looked to the proposed federation to supply the capital to complete the project. Nova Scotia and New Brunswick also expected other economic benefits from union: a common tariff; a sale in the Canadian provinces for certain of their natural products such as coal and fish; and also a market for those manufactured articles which they confidently expected to produce as a result of the availability of coal. Maritime shipbuilding, shipping, and commerce, which had been for years past major activities, were not unnaturally expected to profit greatly by this anticipated expansion of trade.

8/Creighton, "British North America at Confederation," pp. 14–21.
9/"He would defy any one to take a map of the world and point to any great nation which had not seaports of its own open at all times of the year. Canada ... was shut up in a prison, as it were, for five months of the year in fields of ice which all the steam engineering apparatus of human ingenuity could not overcome." Sir E. P. Taché, in *Confederation Debates*, 1865, p. 6.

Prince Edward Island did not have the same inducements as the two main-land provinces. The Island would in any event be able to make use of the inter-colonial railway, if built; and it had not the diversity of resources which could hope to find an extensive market in Canada. Its great hope was that the federa-tion might give substantial assistance in buying out the rights of absentee landed proprietors whose grip on the Island had been its greatest single handicap since its settlement. Maritime union had virtually nothing to offer, for this almost inevitably meant the extinction of the Island as a separate political entity, al-though the smaller union might conceivably become a first step to the wider federation.[10] The advantages of a federal scheme to Newfoundland were prob-ably even more doubtful than to Prince Edward Island, although the possibili-ties of increased trade were somewhat more alluring. However, Newfoundland was interested in the outcome of the federation negotiations, and her entry into the union was regarded both by herself and others as a real possibility.

Canadian federation began to be a matter of practical politics in the spring of 1864 when Dr Charles Tupper, the premier of Nova Scotia, introduced a resolution into the legislature of that province[11] requesting that delegates should be appointed "to confer with delegates who may be appointed by the Govern-ments of New Brunswick and Prince Edward Island for the purpose of con-sidering the subject of the union of the three provinces under one Govern-ment and Legislature." The resolution was unanimously passed, and similar resolutions were carried in the legislatures of the two other Maritime colonies. Arrangements were thereupon made to hold a conference of delegates at Char-lottetown in September. On June 30 a new coalition government was formed in the Province of Canada, pledged to use its best efforts to bring about con-federation in the British North American colonies. Believing that the Charlotte-town meeting was most opportune for the consideration of the wider union, the Canadian government inquired if it might also send representatives to join in the discussion. The request was granted, although the Maritime governments cautiously pointed out that their authority was formally limited to proposals for a Maritime union.

The Charlottetown Conference was not the first interprovincial meeting, for others had been called on occasion to discuss postal services, tariffs, railway lines, and other matters of common concern. But these gatherings had been

10/W. M. Whitelaw, *The Maritimes and Canada before Confederation* (Toronto, 1934), pp. 196–207, 254–6.
11/There were numerous harbingers of federation which preceded the Nova Scotia resolution. There was an earlier resolution of the Nova Scotia Assembly in 1861 which had advocated consultation on the feasibility of both general and Maritime union; an in-terprovincial conference at Quebec in 1862 had discussed among other things political union, and had shelved it; the governor of New Brunswick in a despatch to the colonial secretary, Dec. 31, 1862, had proposed Maritime union, and henceforth (with Colonial Office approval) became its ardent advocate; and in 1863 the legislature of Prince Edward Island had passed a resolution stating that it was "prepared attentively to consider" any proposal for union which might come from its neighbours. For still earlier references, see Browne, *Documents*.

rare, and this was the most ambitious conference which had been attempted up
to that time. Indeed, one of the most awkward obstacles in the way of co-operation was the lack of previous contact and understanding among the delegates, who were virtually unknown to one another; and even such leaders as
Charles Tupper and Leonard Tilley had not met John A. Macdonald before
the Charlottetown Conference.[12] "We don't know each other," stated a Halifax
newspaper in 1866. "We have no trade with each other. We have no facilities,
or resources, or incentives, to mingle with each other. We are shut off from
each other by a wilderness, geographically, commercially, politically, and so-
cially. We always cross the United States to shake hands."[13] A special tour of
Canadians to the Maritime colonies was arranged in the summer of 1864 for
the purpose of increasing knowledge and mutual understanding, and the experiment was generally considered to have been most successful. The conditions
of the time, however, are indicated by two significant facts: first, the need
for organizing such a trip; and second, that the route followed by the party was
the usual one whereby travellers went from Montreal to Saint John by way of
Portland, Maine.[14] It is evident that, while provincial isolation and lack of
knowledge of one another were two of the greatest barriers to federation, they
constituted at the same time two of the strongest arguments in its support.

The conference at Charlottetown was made up of twenty-three delegates:
Canada sent eight, and Nova Scotia, New Brunswick, and Prince Edward
Island, five each.[15] All delegations contained representatives from different
political parties; but that from Canada, representing a coalition government,
spoke with one voice, whereas the Maritime delegations represented not only
three colonies, but frequently divergent views in each colony. The advent of
the "unofficial" Canadian delegation completely altered the original agenda of
the conference, and discussion on Maritime union was temporarily pushed to
one side. The Canadian representatives put forward their proposals for a comprehensive union; and each of five speakers gave an exceptionally able presentation of some particular aspect of the general plan and then submitted to cross-
questioning by the other members of the conference. Finally, after some days'
discussion the Maritime delegates met alone to consider what had been the
main purpose of the meeting; but in the face of Prince Edward Island's quix-
otic determination both to preserve its own legislature and to have any new
capital located on the island, little progress was made in the direction of Maritime union. The conference adjourned its sessions to convene again at Halifax,
Saint John, and Fredericton, where general meetings of all delegates and spe-

12/Sir Joseph Pope, *Memoirs of the Right Honourable Sir John A. Macdonald*
(Ottawa, 1894), I, p. 271.
13/Quoted in Creighton, "British North America at Confederation," p. 36.
14/Trotter, *Canadian Federation*, pp. 88–90.
15/John A. Macdonald, Brown, Cartier, Galt, and McGee were the outstanding
Canadian delegates; Tupper and Tilley the leading delegates from the Maritime provinces.
Joseph Howe was unable to be present.

cial meetings of Maritime delegates were again held. All sessions were secret, and while advisability of such a procedure could scarcely be questioned, it served to arouse suspicion and distrust in some quarters. The decision was reached that a formal conference of all delegations (and Newfoundland) should reassemble at Quebec in October, and the Maritime representatives decided that the proposed smaller union should be held in abeyance awaiting the results of the Quebec Conference.[16]

The Charlottetown Conference had thus made substantial progress in bringing the delegates together and making them known to one another, and also in breaking the ground for federation and familiarizing the political leaders in all colonies with the major issues involved. Its informal and tentative character forbade explicit resolutions and commitments, but it had nevertheless brought many of the issues to the point of general agreement and a large part of the framework of the new federation had begun to take shape. It was, however, a somewhat embarrassing circumstance, as disclosed by the sparse records of the Quebec Conference, that at times the delegates differed widely in their ideas as to what had actually been agreed upon at Charlottetown, for the absence of definite resolutions at the earlier meeting made varied and conflicting understandings possible.[17]

That the union should be one of a federal character – that the legislative residuum should be in the central Parliament – that Parliament's powers should be general and provincial powers local – that there should be an Upper and a Lower House – that there should be three districts in the Confederation, each equally represented in the Upper House – that the Commons representation should be based on population – that there should be a system of executive government and a judiciary and proper arrangements concerning property, assets, and finance – that the Confederation was to be British in system and practice – was all easily settled, not at Quebec, but at Charlottetown, before the Quebec Conference was ever called. Even detail was to some extent disposed of at Charlottetown, Halifax, Saint John and Fredericton, before the Conference met at Quebec. If the *principles* of union had not been settled in advance it is evident that Union would not at that time have been discussed through to conclusion – that there would not have been any Quebec Conference. Thus we find the Quebec Conference concerning itself, principally, with the completion of matters of detail, already largely settled, and the *recording* of matters of principle. The task of applying already admitted general principles to practical and political facts was, however, found to be the really difficult part of constitution building.[18]

The same representatives who had been at Charlottetown appeared also at Quebec, although all the colonies except Nova Scotia increased the size of their

16/Whitelaw, *The Maritimes and Canada before Confederation*, pp. 219–31.

17/See, for example, Sir Joseph Pope, ed., *Confederation: Being a Series of Unpublished Documents Bearing on the British North America Act* (Toronto, 1895), pp. 69–70, 84–5.

18/Senate of Canada, *Report on the British North America Act* (1939), Annex 4, pp. 32–3. See also, W. M. Whitelaw, "Reconstructing the Quebec Conference," *Canadian Historical Review*, XIX, no. 2 (June 1938), p. 131.

delegations. Canada had now twelve (its entire Executive Council); New Brunswick and Prince Edward Island, seven each; Nova Scotia, five; and Newfoundland, two. Both political parties were again represented on each delegation, but the conference was nevertheless essentially Conservative, for that party had the majority of delegates from every colony except New Brunswick, and even the Reformers in New Brunswick had never been very aggressive. Party clashes, in any event, were of no great consequence during the deliberations, for disagreements tended to follow other lines. Each colony had one vote, but for obvious reasons Canada was allowed to count as Upper and Lower Canada with one vote each, an arrangement which still gave the Atlantic colonies a majority of four to two. It is of some interest to observe that there is no record of any split in the Canada vote; that on only one recorded occasion did all four Atlantic votes go against the two from Canada; and that in fully half the recorded votes Prince Edward Island voted against all the others.[19] Here, as in all other proceedings of the conference, the record is by no means complete; for the meetings (following the Charlottetown precedent) were held in secret and no official minutes of the discussions were kept. The information which is available has thus been gathered from many sources and pieced together by careful historical investigation and reconstruction.

The fundamental principle accepted at Charlottetown was endorsed unreservedly at Quebec, namely, that the new government should be a federation and not a unitary government or, to use the current phrase, a "legislative union." All the delegates would doubtless have admitted, as many of them did, that they considered a legislative union a superior form of federation; but all would also have added that nothing but the latter would be able to find general acceptance. The peculiar position of Quebec with its different national origin, religion, language, educational institutions, laws, and culture would alone have made a large measure of local autonomy imperative, but Quebec was not the only colony with a strong local patriotism. "We had either to take a federal union," said George Brown, "or drop the negotiation. Not only were our friends from Lower Canada against it, but so were most of the delegates from the Maritime Provinces. There was but one choice open to us – federal union or nothing."[20] John A. Macdonald, for one, relinquished the idea of legislative union with regret,[21] and he chose the next best thing, a centralized form of federalism. This distribution of power between the Dominion and the provinces was the feature of the constitution greatly affected by American experience. The United States had been engaged for some years in a civil war which was attributed primarily to the constitutional emphasis on the rights and powers of the individual states, leading to the assertion of state sovereignty and eventually to armed conflict. British North America had the opportunity of

19/Whitelaw, *The Maritimes and Canada before Confederation*, pp. 237, 240.
20/*Confederation Debates*, 1865, p. 108.
21/*Ibid.*, p. 29.

profiting by the experience of her neighbour, and the conference believed that the outstanding lesson to be learned was the necessity of strengthening the centripetal forces in the proposed federation. Macdonald pushed the argument as far as he dared, and had the satisfaction of seeing the delegates accept a constitution along the lines he had suggested.

The true principle of a Confederation [he said with more conviction than accuracy] lay in giving to the General Government all the principles and powers of sovereignty, and that the subordinate or individual states should have no powers but those expressly bestowed on them. We should thus have a powerful Central Government, a powerful Central Legislature, and a decentralized system of minor legislatures for local purposes.[22]

The proposed constitution therefore aimed at building up the authority of the Dominion in a number of ways:

First, it granted the provinces a moderate, but only a moderate, list of powers, these being essentially of a local or private nature which would be best suited to the capacity and position of the provincial authority. Some powers, which in the United States had been left with the states, such as criminal law, marriage and divorce, were given in the Canadian constitution to the federation.[23]

Secondly, the new constitution was to grant to the Dominion all powers which were not explicitly given to the provinces. In any federal constitution an exhaustive enumeration of powers granted to the central and local governments is quite impossible, and hence it is customary to insert a blanket clause whereby all unallotted powers (the so-called residual powers) are vested in one party or the other. The United States' constitution had allowed the states to retain this residue and had thereby greatly enhanced their importance; the Quebec Conference decided to follow the other course and pass on the residue to the Dominion. And to make the matter quite clear, this comprehensive grant was illustrated by a long list of topics which were explicitly placed under Dominion jurisdiction. To quote Macdonald once more:

In framing the constitution, care should be taken to avoid the mistakes and weaknesses of the United States' system, the primary error of which was the reservation to the different States of all powers not delegated to the General Government. We must reverse this process by establishing a strong central Government, to which shall belong all powers not specially conferred on the provinces.[24]

We have strengthened the General Government. We have given the General Legislature all the great subjects of legislation. We have conferred on them, not only specifically and in detail, all the powers which are incident to sovereignty, but we have expressly declared that all subjects of general interest not distinctly and exclusively conferred upon the local governments and local legislatures, shall be conferred upon the General Government and Legislature. We ... make the Confederation one people and one government, instead of five peoples and five

22/*Ibid.*, p. 1002.
23/*Ibid.*, p. 41.
24/Pope, *Memoirs of Sir John A. Macdonald,* I, p. 269.

governments ... one united province, with the local governments and legislatures subordinate to the General Government and Legislature.[25]

Thirdly, the constitution stated that the Dominion government was to have the power of appointing and removing the lieutenant governors (styled superintendents in the initial draft of the British North America Act) in each province, thereby placing the Dominion in the position occupied up to that time by the imperial government in relation to the administration of the individual colonies. The Dominion would thus have an agent and a spokesman in each province; he was given the power of refusing assent to provincial bills or reserving them for the pleasure of the governor general; and while it was sometimes stated that the lieutenant governor would be an independent official,[26] there can be little doubt that the expectation was that his influence would be as important a factor in the future province as it had proved to be in the colony of the past.[27] The Dominion's appointment powers were also to extend to all judges in provincial courts above the local magistrates' courts, and to the senators whose duties in Ottawa were, in theory at least, to include representing the interests of the people of the provinces in Parliament, for matters under federal jurisdiction.

Fourthly, the Dominion government was given the right to disallow or set aside any provincial law within a year of its passage. This was another existing function of the British government, and one which would give the new Dominion the last word on all acts of all the provincial legislatures. "By vesting the appointment of the lieutenant governors in the General Government," said George Brown, "and giving a veto for all local measures, we have secured that no injustice shall be done without appeal in local legislation."[28]

The federation was thus intended to depart radically from the pure federal form in which the component local units are of equal or coordinate rank with the central government. The provinces were to be inferior bodies possessing little more prestige and authority than inflated municipalities. Even the sketchy records of the contemporary discussions which have come down to us contain scattered references to "municipal councils on a large scale," "local municipal parliaments," and the like, while the provincial legislatures are repeatedly described as "subordinate," "minor," and "inferior" bodies. "We propose," said Dr Charles Tupper in a revealing sentence, "to preserve the Local Governments in the Lower Provinces because we have not municipal institutions"; but he was also careful to state that while "we should diminish the powers of the Local Governments, we must not shock too largely the prejudices of the people in that respect."[29] It is noteworthy that the provinces were not given,

25/Confederation Debates, 1865, pp. 33, 41–2.
26/See Pope, Confederation Documents, p. 78.
27/Confederation Debates, 1865, p. 42. See also Saywell, The Office of Lieutenant-Governor.
28/Confederation Debates, 1865, p. 108.
29/Pope, Confederation Documents, pp. 85, 75–6.

either individually or collectively, any powers in relation to the Dominion, such as the Dominion's powers outlined above.

History was to prove, however, that the Dominion had not acquired, nor had the provinces relinquished, nearly as much as the Fathers of the Confederation had planned or the paper constitution suggested. The course of this development will be taken up in another chapter,[30] but the general trend may be indicated briefly here. The emphasis which was later laid by the Judicial Committee of the Privy Council on the plenary nature of provincial authority, the broad interpretation which they gave to the provincial jurisdiction over property and civil rights, and the narrow interpretation which they placed on the residual power of the Dominion, combined to render almost completely nugatory the intentions of the Quebec Conference on these matters. Moreover, the anticipated Dominion influence through the agency of the lieutenant governors, while at first of some use, proved in the long run to be of little consequence, and had Canada followed the practice (later adopted in Australia) of allowing the British government to continue its appointment of local governors, the final position of Dominion and province would have been virtually the same as it is today.[31] Dominion appointment of senators (particularly) and judges, has not proven to be a viable instrument that has strengthened the federal government as such. The remaining instrument of Dominion control, the power of disallowance, also failed to realize the original expectations. For many years after Confederation, it is true, the Dominion government frequently intervened on various grounds and disallowed provincial statutes, but in Laurier's day a shift in the grounds for using disallowance developed, and in due course the power began to be employed as an exceptional rather than a normal expedient. Sporadic revivals of disallowance have occurred during the past thirty-five years, but it is still far from being the active agent in assuring to the Dominion that oversight which was contemplated in 1864.[32] The combined trend of all these aids to Dominion predominance in the federation has been at least until recently to lessen and not to enrich Dominion authority. Such is the vanity of foresight in constitutional matters.

The detailed working-out of some of the ideas tentatively agreed upon at Charlottetown caused at times many difficulties and misgivings at Quebec. One of the most acute controversies centred about the composition of the two legislative houses proposed. The small provinces (knowing that representation by population would be adopted for the lower house) urged that they should each receive eight members in the upper chamber (or thirty-two) as against twenty-four for each of the Canadas (or forty-eight for Upper and Lower Canada combined). Curiously enough, there seems to have been only one suggestion (from

30/*Infra*, pp. 89–96.
31/See Saywell, *The Office of Lieutenant-Governor*.
32/*Infra*, pp. 213–17. G. V. LaForest, *Disallowance and Reservation of Provincial Legislation* (Ottawa, 1955).

a Prince Edward Island delegate) that representation in the upper chamber should be on the strictly federal basis of granting the same representation to each province, and even this was substantially modified by its proposer almost as soon as it was put forward.[33] The most likely explanation of this lack of assertiveness on the part of the small provinces is that the conference regarded this feature of the American constitution as one of the grave dangers implicit in the doctrine of states' rights. After a three days' struggle, which threatened to break up the meeting, a compromise was reached which was founded on the still extant proposal for Maritime union. This compromise gave to the three Maritime provinces (soon, perhaps, to be united) twenty-four members (Nova Scotia and New Brunswick, ten each; Prince Edward Island, four), to Newfoundland an additional four; while the two Canadas retained twenty-four each. The recent Canadian experience with an elected upper chamber had not impressed even the delegates from that province, and this was reinforced by the conviction that inasmuch as responsible government was necessarily identified with the lower house, it would be wiser not to risk a possible rival by calling into existence a second elected body. The conference therefore decided to have the members of the new Senate appointed for life by the Governor-General-in-Council. The original body, however, was to be filled wherever possible (except in the case of Prince Edward Island) from the members of the existing Legislative Councils in each province on the nomination of the provincial governments, who were to see that both political parties were fairly represented.[34] This proposal, while tending to destroy the federal character of the Senate, was clearly designed to facilitate the acceptance of the federation plan by the provincial legislatures. In both houses of the new Parliament, as in the legislature of the old province of Canada, and in the proposed new province of Quebec, English and French were to enjoy equality as official languages.

The apportionment of members in the House of Commons, unlike that in the Senate, was a simple problem, for Lower Canada had already conceded representation by population in this chamber (and it was the key concession that made Confederation possible) in exchange for equality with Upper Canada in the Senate. The same principle was accepted without demur by everyone except some of the delegates from Prince Edward Island. Quebec was to be given the constant number of sixty-five members (the same seats, in effect, as she had had in the Legislative Assembly of the Province of Canada), and the representation of each of the other provinces was to bear the same relation to its population as sixty-five bore to the population of Quebec. Inasmuch as the Newfoundland census on which its first representation was to be based was taken four years earlier than that of the others, Newfoundland was granted an

33/A. G. Doughty, ed., "Notes on the Quebec Conference" (A. A. Macdonald), *Canadian Historical Review*, I, no. 1 (March 1920), pp. 35–6.

34/Pope, *Confederation Documents*, pp. 62–6; Whitelaw, *The Maritimes and Canada before Confederation*, pp. 242–6. This preference to existing legislative councillors was eventually left out of the BNA Act.

additional member. The plea of Prince Edward Island to be allowed more than the allotted five members[35] was, however, not heeded, on the ground that the rule must be "rigid and unyielding" and apply equally to all.[36] The decision was not satisfactory to the Island delegates whose votes from this time on were cast steadily against the other votes of the conference.

The distribution of powers between Dominion and provinces seems to have occasioned surprisingly few difficulties of a serious nature, so convinced were the delegates of the necessity of creating a strong central government. A suggested distribution had been worked out previously in the Canadian delegation and this was agreed upon by the entire conference substantially as proposed. "Sea coast and inland fisheries" were to be left under federal jurisdiction but shared with the province;[37] "incorporation of private or local companies, except such as relate to matters assigned to the General Parliament" was added to the suggested provincial powers; and several other minor changes were made. Education was placed under provincial jurisdiction with the rider added that the rights and privileges as to denominational schools which were possessed by the Protestant and Catholic minorities in Lower and Upper Canada respectively were to remain undisturbed. Finance was one of the most controversial questions and it threatened for a time to stop the negotiations. The division of the taxing field won substantial agreement, but it left the provinces in a large measure dependent upon the Dominion for assistance. The Atlantic provinces, because of the rudimentary character of their municipal institutions and the meagre revenues and services which these provided, were accustomed to rely more upon the provincial government to supply various services than was the practice in Canada, and their delegates therefore demanded generous contributions from the Dominion to meet this need.[38] The Dominion assumption of provincial debts, however, supplemented by a system of subsidies and special grants,[39] eventually secured consent, although Prince Edward Island, whose financial sacrifices were relatively heavy, was far from satisfied and voted against these resolutions.

The conference proposals regarding the executive power were covered for the most part in one vague comprehensive clause stating that this power was vested in the sovereign and was to "be administered according to the well understood principles of the British Constitution by the Sovereign personally

35/One Island delegate stated that "not even two or three more members would induce me to give my assent to the scheme. I never understood that any proposition at Charlottetown was to be binding as to representation by population ... It was a mere suggestion then thrown out by Canada for consideration." Pope, *Confederation Documents*, p. 69.
36/The agreement reached was: Upper Canada, 82; Lower Canada, 65; Nova Scotia, 19; New Brunswick, 15; Newfoundland, 8; Prince Edward Island, 5. *Ibid.*, pp. 66–73.
37/*Ibid.*, pp. 22–30.
38/O. D. Skelton, *Life and Times of Sir Alexander Tilloch Galt* (Carleton Library, no. 26, Toronto, 1966), pp. 156–7; Whitelaw, *The Maritimes and Canada before Confederation*, pp. 253–6.
39/*Infra*, pp. 99–104.

or by the Representative of the Sovereign duly authorized." The feeling of the delegates was that the prerogative powers of the Crown could not be restricted by clauses relating to the composition and personnel of the cabinet, and that any explicit mention of responsible government was both improper and unnecessary. The resolutions dealing with the law and the judiciary were equally non-controversial and were easily settled, jurisdiction in these matters being divided between the two authorities. Provision was made for the possible creation by the Dominion of a general court of appeal.

The Maritime provinces obtained an undertaking that the Dominion would secure without delay the completion of the intercolonial railway. Another clause (a *quid pro quo* demanded by the Canadian delegates) stated that the conference regarded communication with the northwestern territory as of the highest importance, and that this should be prosecuted "at the earliest possible period that the state of the Finances will permit." Another clause made tentative and general provision for the later admission of the North-West Territory, British Columbia, and Vancouver, although it was stated that the exact terms and conditions would be decided at the time of entrance.

The Quebec Conference brought its labours to a close in the short period of three weeks, although after an interval of travelling and speech-making the delegates held a brief session at Montreal to make a few minor revisions. The recommendations were embodied in seventy-two resolutions. One of these suggested the next step which was contemplated, namely, that "the sanction of the Imperial and Local Parliaments shall be sought for the Union of the Provinces on the principles adopted by the Conference." Inasmuch as no legislature had formally authorized the conference (although that of Canada had been given a general statement of its government's federal intentions) some formal approval would seem to have been highly desirable. A general appeal to the people in an election for a mandate to proceed with the proposals was considered unwise by the conference, which also felt that such an expedient leaned too much towards the American rather than the British practice.

The sanction mentioned in the Quebec Resolutions, however, was never obtained. In March 1865 the legislature of Canada, after a long debate, accepted the seventy-two resolutions as recommended, and requested the imperial Parliament to implement them. But the other colonies thought otherwise. Prince Edward Island, the consistent rebel at the Quebec Conference, rejected the resolutions and even went on record as wishing to dissociate itself permanently from any kind of union with Canada or with any other colony. Newfoundland postponed any final decision for the time, but later repudiated federation. The premier of New Brunswick held a general election on the question, and he and his party sustained a decisive and humiliating defeat. The premier of Nova Scotia, mindful of the New Brunswick election results and influenced by Joseph Howe's opposition and his growing popular support, avoided a vote in the Assembly on the Quebec proposals by securing another which again expressed approval of Maritime union. Thus one of the five colonies at the Quebec Conference had approved of federation, one had side-stepped it because of increasing opposition, and three had virtually or explicitly repudiated the proposals.

A delegation composed of members of the Canadian cabinet nevertheless went to England to discuss, among other questions, the suggested federation. The British government proved to be extremely sympathetic and gave assurances that it would use all legitimate means to induce the Maritime provinces to agree to the proposal. This proved in the event to be no idle promise. A clear intimation to the governors in both Atlantic provinces that the British authorities were very desirous of having federation approved, the resulting activity of the none too scrupulous governor of New Brunswick,[40] a blunt refusal by the Colonial Office in 1865 to assist in any plan for Maritime union unless it were part of a wider scheme, a growing appreciation by New Brunswick of the benefits to be expected from the intercolonial railway, the threatened Fenian invasion from the United States in 1866 – all helped to turn public opinion in New Brunswick more and more in the direction of federation. On April 10, 1866, the government of New Brunswick resigned, being virtually pushed out of office by the governor,[41] and in the ensuing election, which was financed in large measure by contributions from Canada, the federation party secured a victory as complete as that of its opponents a year before. Dr Tupper, who had been carefully watching the progress of events, decided that the time for more decisive action had come; and he moved, and the Nova Scotia Assembly passed, a resolution in April 1866 expressing the desirability of general federation and authorizing the governor "to appoint delegates to arrange with the Imperial Government a scheme of union which will effectively ensure just provision for the rights and interests of this Province." The New Brunswick legislature passed a resolution in June in almost identical terms. Thus, although neither Nova Scotia nor New Brunswick had accepted the Quebec Resolutions, their legislatures had expressed a desire to have the whole federation question reconsidered and to work out a scheme of union in consultation with the British government. In December 1866 the new conference began its sittings in London.

Although the Quebec Resolutions had been in high disfavour in Nova Scotia and New Brunswick they were nevertheless used as the basis of discussion at the London Conference. A few important changes and a large number of comparatively minor alterations and additions were made, but in most essentials

40/A new governor was selected for Nova Scotia who would be more enthusiastic about federation than his predecessor.
41/See George E. Wilson, "New Brunswick's Entrance into Confederation," *Canadian Historical Review*, ix, no. 1 (March 1928), pp. 4–24. The governor of Canada, Lord Monck, considered the possibility of dragging New Brunswick into federation even against the wishes of the people. Why should the British Parliament, he asked Macdonald, "allow a majority in one branch of the Legislature in a small province to overbear the expressed opinion of the rest of b.n.a."? *Ibid.*, pp. 21–2.

the terms of the Quebec Resolutions were re-endorsed. There is, however, no doubt that the seven draft bills (resulting finally in the British North America Act) were founded in the immediate sense on the London and not on the Quebec Resolutions. This substitution of new resolutions for those drafted at Quebec was, indeed, essential. The provinces represented at London were not the same as those represented at Quebec, and the dropping-out of Prince Edward Island and Newfoundland might well have necessitated substantial changes or the cancellation of compromises which had been made on the assumption that these provinces were to enter. Moreover, the Quebec Resolutions had been approved by Canada only, and Nova Scotia and New Brunswick had reappointed delegates with the express intention of receiving terms more acceptable than those obtained at Quebec.[42] The Maritime provinces were therefore bound to insist on a reconsideration of the federation proposals, and this took place at London, where the basic scheme of the Quebec Resolutions none the less stood up strongly.

The changes made by the London Resolutions affected the Dominion and provincial powers, education, the Senate, the pardoning power, provincial subsidies, and the intercolonial railway, as well as minor matters. Full control over Dominion electoral machinery was vested in Parliament; jurisdiction over penitentiaries was transferred from the provinces to the Dominion; statistics became a stated Dominion topic; solemnization of marriage was given to the provinces; jurisdiction over sea-coast and inland fisheries ceased to be a concurrent power and was given to the Dominion alone. A greater protection of minority rights and privileges in education was extended to all provinces, and provision was made for an appeal to the Dominion government and, if need be, Parliament in the event of these rights or privileges being infringed. Nova Scotia and New Brunswick each received twelve senators instead of ten, although provision was made that in the event of Prince Edward Island entering Confederation, these would revert to ten and the Island would receive the four seats thus made available. The pardoning power of the lieutenant-governors was restricted. Additions were made to the provincial subsidies which improved somewhat the position of the Maritime provinces, and the provision regarding the intercolonial railway was altered by making its immediate construction mandatory. When the colonial delegates had consulted with the British authorities (who were responsible for remarkably few actual alterations) and the proposals were drafted in the form of a bill, other changes were made, the chief ones being the omission of the lieutenant governor's power of pardon, and a clause designed to overcome some of the rigidity in the total number of

42/When Dr Tupper reported back to the Nova Scotia Assembly in 1867, he said: "The position that we occupy ... is one of no little pride for we are able to say that we have not only obtained everything which was granted at Quebec, but that very important concessions have been made in the arrangements that are now being consummated, and that all these alterations are most favourable to the interests of these Maritime Provinces." *N.S. Assembly Debates*, March 18, 1867, p. 9.

senators by permitting a limited number of emergency appointments. The bill also contained skeleton constitutions for Ontario and Quebec; for these provinces, unlike Nova Scotia and New Brunswick, had no separate existence in 1867 and it was therefore necessary to substitute two provincial governments for the one which had been in existence since the Union Act of 1840.

The bill was introduced into the House of Lords by the colonial secretary, Lord Carnarvon, and passed both houses without arousing any great interest or enthusiasm. A. T. Galt was shocked by the English indifference to Confederation and attributed much of it to a fear that Canadian issues might involve England in a war with the United States; Sir John Macdonald caustically observed some years later that the bill was treated with no more concern than if it "were a private bill uniting two or three English parishes"; and a spectator, sitting in the gallery of the Commons, noted that when the House passed on to the next bill, which dealt with the imposition of dog taxes, there was a perceptible brightening of the interest of the members in the business before them. The British North America Act received the royal assent on March 29, was proclaimed on May 22, and came into effect on July 1, 1867.

Mention should be made of the fact that there was no general consensus of the authorities in British North America behind the written constitution as eventually enacted in 1867. Nova Scotia and New Brunswick may be considered as repudiating by inaction and by the implication of their later resolutions the terms which had been drafted at Quebec, although they both empowered their representatives to negotiate a new agreement at London. The legislature of Canada, on the other hand, had formally accepted the Quebec Resolutions, but it had not given its cabinet any authority to enter into further negotiations to draw up a new or modified agreement.[43] Both the Nova Scotia and New Brunswick delegates reported to their respective legislatures the sixty-nine London Resolutions as embodying the results of their labours; but the Canadian delegation apparently retained the fiction that the British North America Act rested on the resolutions agreed to at Quebec. No colony had any opportunity to pass upon the new federation either in a general election (until it was too late) or by a popular vote, an omission peculiarly aggravating to Nova Scotia where the federation proposals were notoriously unpopular. Lord Monck's suggestion that they should ignore the wishes of the people of New Brunswick had been applied, in effect, a few miles further to the south and east. Nova Scotia ushered in the new Dominion on July 1, 1867, by draping her streets in black; and the first Dominion election returned eighteen out of nineteen members pledged to repeal.

Even the general nature of the above account will indicate how many features of the British North America Act were shaped not only by the local constitutions and history but also by the immediate influences of Great Britain and

43/See Senate of Canada, *Report on the British North America Act* (1939), Annex 4, pp. 24–30, 36–47.

the United States. The Confederation debates of the Canadian legislature in 1865 are filled with references to the institutions of both these countries, and their experiences are freely called upon to serve either as a warning or an inspiration from which Canada should draw the appropriate lesson. There can be no doubt that the majority of the founders of the Dominion were anxious to maintain the British connection and the British stamp upon their political institutions, and the records, although scanty, breathe loyalty and admiration in almost every paragraph; the French Canadians, although Cartier spoke fulsomely, were generally more taciturn. Possible independence, which had many outspoken advocates in Britain, found no support at the constitutional conferences. The preamble to the British North America Act was therefore stating the simple truth when it proclaimed that the people of the provinces desired "a Constitution similar in Principle to that of the United Kingdom."

Thus the chief characteristics of the new Canadian government, with one important exception, bore the mark of their ancestry: the monarch (and governor general) as the chief executive officer; the central and dominant position of the Crown; the nominated Senate with a life tenure; the representative House of Commons; the treatment of financial measures, in both their initiation by the Crown and their introduction into the House of Commons; the privileges of the houses; the appointment of lieutenant governors; the disallowance of provincial legislation; the appointed judiciary holding office during good behaviour – these were all derived immediately or by direct descent from Great Britain. Even the nomenclature was affected by the contagion: the House of Commons, Her Majesty's Privy Council for Canada, and, if Macdonald had his way, the Kingdom of Canada, were striking examples. Some of the omissions are characteristically British also; and the failure to insert a specific bill of rights section (an omission which Parliament attempted to overcome in part by ordinary statute in 1960), the refusal to attempt any legal definition of the principles of responsible government, and perhaps the absence of an amending clause, are no less indicative of its derivation than are the explicit statements of the act.

The outstanding exception to the general rule of British influence was, of course, the part of the act dealing with the federal distribution of power. Here, as has been already indicated, the experience of the United States worked both to encourage and to dissuade. "It is the fashion now," said Macdonald in 1865, "to enlarge on the defects of the Constitution of the United States, but I am not one of those who look upon it as a failure. I think and believe that it is one of the most skilful works which human intelligence ever created; [it] is one of the most perfect organizations that ever governed a free people. To say that it has some defects is but to say that it is not the work of Omniscience, but of human intellect."[44] The American example, as this passage indicates, un-

44/*Confederation Debates*, 1865, p. 32. See Edgar McInnis, "Two North American Federations," in Flenley, *Essays in Canadian History*, pp. 94–118.

doubtedly served as a constant inspiration which encouraged the British North American colonies to seek their solution in some form of federalism; but in determining the balance of authority between the federalism and the provinces, the allotment of subjects, and the location of the residual power, they endeavoured to interpret American experience and profit by American mistakes. The same attitude is evident in other matters as well; indeed, on most questions there is a fairly strong bias against American practices. Certain "republican" manifestations were regarded with alarm by most of the delegates, despite the past tendencies of the Clear Grit party in Canada to copy some of the features of Jacksonian democracy. The election of judges was apparently not even mentioned at any of the conferences; a proposal of George Brown to abolish responsible government in the provinces and substitute an executive and legislature, popularly elected for fixed terms, could find no other supporters; and the terms of the judges, of the senators, and even of the members of the House of Commons show the same disregard for the Jacksonian principles of frequent elections and rotation in office. Nor was there much of the Jacksonian influence in the consistent reluctance to submit the question of federalism to any popular verdict. "The course of the New Brunswick Government in dissolving their Parliament, and appealing to the people," wrote John A. Macdonald, "was unstatesmanlike and unsuccessful, as it deserved to be . . . Whatever might have been the result in the legislature, the subject would have been fairly discussed and its merits understood, and if he [the premier] had been defeated, he then had an appeal to the people."[45] This desire to avoid an election or to hold any form of plebiscite was conveniently explained as being in accord with British ideas of the functions of a representative legislature; but it also sprang from a shaky belief in the solid virtues of popular government.

To these undoubted British and American influences can be added at least one exclusively Canadian: the guarantee that both English and French could be used in Parliament, Dominion courts, and the legislature and courts of Quebec. The principle behind this, indeed, showed an initial disposition to spread from the national arena and Quebec to new accretions to Canada. The extension of the boundaries of the Dominion and the realization of the ambition of the Fathers of Confederation to expand westwards to the Pacific were not long deferred, and with them, at first, went the two languages. The first new province to be admitted, Manitoba, was created in 1870 on the same bilingual basis as Quebec.[46] The British North America Act had provided for the admission of Rupert's Land and the North-West Territory into the union by imperial

45/Sir Joseph Pope, ed., *Correspondence of Sir John A. Macdonald* (Toronto, 1921), p. 23.

46/Because some doubts arose as to the power of the Dominion Parliament to create new provinces and provide for the government, the Manitoba Act was validated and the general power ensured for the future by the passage of an amendment to the BNA Act in 1871 (*Brit. Statutes*, 34–35 Vict., c. 28).

order-in-council in response to an address by the Canadian Parliament. Proceedings were initiated in 1867 to bring this about, and on July 15, 1870, these territories were formally annexed to the Dominion; their government too, when it was in due course organized, was established as bilingual, although the Dominion government had not originally intended it.[47]

The other areas admitted as provinces were not made officially bilingual, the Dominion ultimately coming to hold that the languages to be used locally were of provincial concern only.[48] In 1871, in compliance with addresses from the Canadian Parliament and the legislature of British Columbia as provided under the terms of the British North America Act, an imperial order-in-council admitted British Columbia to the Dominion, and two years later (1873) after similar addresses and under the same authority another order-in-council admitted Prince Edward Island. In 1905 two Dominion statutes transformed a large block of the western territory into the provinces of Alberta and Saskatchewan; the remainder of the territories, comprising an area that is nearly 40 per cent of the country, is still under federal jurisdiction. (The Yukon now has "representative but not responsible government" and the Northwest Territories, consisting of the districts of Franklin, Keewatin, and Mackenzie, have been progressing towards that limited goal.[49]) Finally, in 1949 Newfoundland entered the federation as the tenth province. The existing situation in Newfoundland made section 146 of the British North America Act inoperative, and the legal steps to bring about the union (after the island had held two referendums) were approval by the Newfoundland commission of government, a Canadian statute,[50] and a British statute which both accepted the plan of union and amended the British North America Act.[51]

The extension of English and French as equal official languages did not end with Canada's territorial expansion. Largely as a result of the work of the Royal Commission on Bilingualism and Biculturalism, set up by L. B. Pearson's government in 1963, and the disturbing situation that led to the appointment of the commission, both languages have again begun to find larger official use. New Brunswick has adopted both languages for provincial purposes, and Ontario appears to be working more slowly towards the same end; several other predominantly English-speaking provinces have reversed earlier trends and enlarged the use of French for educational purposes. Parliament in 1969 passed the Official Languages Act, which for matters under federal jurisdiction

47/See Thomas, *Struggle for Responsible Government in the North-West Territories*, p. 78.
48/Professor Frank Scott has argued that the abolition by the Manitoba legislature in 1890 of the use of French as an official language in Manitoba means that English has no security in Quebec. See F. R. Scott, *Civil Liberties and Canadian Federalism* (Toronto, 1959), p. 32.
49/See *Canada Year Book, 1968*, pp. 110–16; and *Report of the Advisory Commission on the Development of Government in the Northwest Territories* (Ottawa, 1966).
50/*Can. Statutes*, 13 Geo. VI, c. 1.
51/*Brit. Statutes*, 12–13 Geo. VI, c. 22.

provided for the creation of bilingual districts anywhere in Canada where the proportion of either English- or French-speaking persons, though in a minority, was at least 10 per cent of the population. It also created a language commission to investigate and report on alleged violations of language rights; provided for the limited use of the two languages in criminal proceedings in provincial courts; and forthrightly declared English and French to be Canada's official languages. To the overwhelming majority of members of Parliament who passed the bill, their work (judging from their speeches) struck them as one more step towards the rounding out of the Confederation begun well over a century ago.[52]

52/The act is *Can. Statutes*, 17–18 Eliz. II, c. 54. The bill was introduced on Oct. 17, 1968, and most of the parliamentary debate on it occurred between May 16 and July 7, 1969, inclusive.

3 Dominion and nation

THE UNIQUE INTERNATIONAL POSITION and powers of the self-governing dominions in the Commonwealth of Nations had their origin with the earliest colonial settlements. The problem of how much autonomy colonies should exercise was faced (though not solved) at that time, and it has not yet ceased to be a question of importance. It was a critical issue in the history of the American colonies; after the revolution it was scarcely less so, with the leadership in the movement for increasing powers of self-government still coming from the North American continent. A number of the important stages in this history have already been discussed under the origins of representative and responsible government. These two great advances were, indeed, far more vital to Canadian autonomy than any of the changes which have occurred during the past century; and without these preliminary steps, none of the later developments would have been possible. The creation of the Dominion of Canada marked another advance of a somewhat different kind, although this event made little immediate change in the aggregate powers of self-government of the federated colonies. It added enormously, however, to their prestige and importance; and when in later years the Dominion pressed for progressively greater powers, it was not only able to make its voice more clearly heard, but that voice also carried far greater authority and was much more difficult to ignore or to refuse.

Attention has already been called to the fact that the setting of definite boundaries to what were to be considered as local affairs and what was to be treated as the special province of the British government was, in the nature of things, impermanent,[1] but that the arrangement had the great advantage of yielding gradually to pressure whenever the occasion demanded. Material and far-reaching changes could thus be brought about not by sensational crises and bitter quarrels over great principles, but quietly, and as a rule temperately, through the settlement of minor problems arising in the day to day relationships

1/*Supra*, p. 19.

of the British and overseas governments. The Durham line of division between matters of imperial and local jurisdiction[2] was in fact partly abandoned almost as soon as it was stated. The "disposal of public lands" became at once a matter for the local authorities, and the disposal of the vexed question of the clergy reserves by the Canadian legislature as early as 1854 proved how intimately these matters were related to the local government and how necessary it was that government should make the settlement. The "constitution of the form of government," while to some small degree involving the British Parliament, was in practice also left to the colonies to determine. Thus British North America drew up its own terms of confederation, and the function of the imperial authorities at this time was primarily one of rendering technical advice and guidance after the essential articles of agreement had been debated and finally agreed upon.

There remained Durham's third and much more extensive area of imperial control, namely, "the regulation of foreign relations, and of trade with the mother country, the other British Colonies, and foreign nations." Some of these limitations on colonial authority were to persist for many years; but even here the barrier began to crumble some time before Confederation. Colonial leaders had at first unreservedly accepted the position that the British Parliament would determine the general outline of the empire's fiscal policies and would therefore be responsible for the enactment of tariffs both at home and throughout the empire. Even when British economic policy was radically altered in the late 1840s through the repeal of the corn laws and the navigation acts, and although the colonies were permitted under the Enabling Act of 1846 to repeal British duties in force in their territories, the colonial legislatures remained for a brief period under the old spell. In 1849, for example, Francis Hincks in introducing the Canadian budget expressed the view that a colonial tariff against Great Britain would be little short of a declaration of independence. But the following years witnessed a marked and speedy change. In 1859 the Canadian legislature passed a bill which raised the general tariff on manufactured articles, a step which caused a violent outburst from certain English manufacturing interests in Sheffield who insisted that British rights were being infringed. This protest was forwarded to Canada by the imperial government with an intimation that the Canadian act might conceivably be disallowed, a challenge which was quickly and successfully accepted in a memorandum drawn up by Alexander T. Galt, the Canadian Finance minister. Its interest lies not alone on the unequivocal statement of the rights of the colony, but also in the allied argument that the freedom of action which the memorandum demanded was an inescapable consequence of responsible government.

The Government of Canada acting for its Legislature and people cannot, through those feelings of deference which they owe to the Imperial authorities, in any manner waive or diminish the right of the people of Canada to decide for themselves

2/*Supra*, pp. 14–15.

both as to the mode and extent to which taxation shall be imposed. The Provincial Ministry are at all times ready to afford explanations in regard to the acts of the Legislature to which they are party; but, subject to their duty and allegiance to her Majesty, their responsibility in all general questions of policy must be to the Provincial Parliament, by whose confidence they administer the affairs of the country ... Self-government would be utterly annihilated if the views of the Imperial Government were to be preferred to those of the people of Canada. It is, therefore, the duty of the present Government distinctly to affirm the right of the Canadian Legislature to adjust the taxation of the people in the way they deem best, even if it should unfortunately happen to meet the disapproval of the Imperial Ministry. Her Majesty cannot be advised to disallow such acts, unless her advisers are prepared to assume the administration of the affairs of the Colony irrespective of the views of its inhabitants.[3]

Such restraints on Canadian autonomy as persisted from Confederation to the First World War operated within three broad fields: (1) Canadian internal affairs; (2) external affairs; (3) imperial relations. The restraining power was naturally the imperial government, and the constant trend of events was towards the partial or complete removal of all these restrictions.

INTERNAL AFFAIRS, 1867 – 1914

The British government, as indicated in the above pages, had relinquished, even before Confederation, all important controls over local affairs in British North America, although there were a number of opportunities still remaining for the exercise of influence in minor matters. These came, for the most part, through the governor general, who was the representative of the British government and who had the right to intervene in certain contingencies, even against the wishes of his cabinet. Many of these powers of intervention were, however, uncertain and vague, for they rested on law as interpreted by custom, and there was frequently no certain rule to decide on what occasions the governor was to act on his own responsibility and when he was expected to follow the advice of his Council. Even the governor's routine Instructions were far from constituting an infallible guide, for an accumulation of precedents might make some of these obsolete, and the governor might also refer to England for special instructions to cover a particular problem. But whether the British cabinet influenced affairs indirectly through the governor or whether the governor without any reference to London tried to exercise an independent power of his own, the result, so far as it touched on Dominion autonomy, was much the same: a non-Canadian authority was attempting to decide what was as a rule a purely Canadian question. Canadian cabinets, therefore, could be counted upon to resist any exercise of the governor's power on domestic issues whenever that

3/Kennedy, *Constitutional Documents*, p. 539.

action was not taken under the advice of his constitutional advisers; and if the precedents conflicted or if the British North America Act or the Instructions were ambiguous, the cabinet would almost invariably assert its own right to advise the governor as to what action should be taken. As late as 1876, nevertheless, Lord Dufferin was urging upon his prime minister, Alexander Mackenzie, that "within the walls of the Privy Council I have as much right to contend for my opinions as any of my Ministers"; earlier, he had advised Sir John A. Macdonald that the governor general's right to preside over his Council should not be allowed to fall into disuse.[4]

The most notable of the advances in Canadian powers at the governor general's expense was made in 1878 through Edward Blake, the Canadian minister of Justice, whose efforts secured material changes in the Commission and Instructions that were issued to the governor. These instruments for the delegation of the prerogative powers[5] had remained unchanged for many years and as a result a number of their provisions had become either obsolete or quite unsuited to the existing conditions. Thus the governor general had been instructed to reserve for the consideration of the British government any bill for divorce, any bill making paper money or other currency legal tender, any bill for imposing differential duties, and bills for other specified purposes; and, in fact, twenty-one bills had been so reserved by the governor between 1867 and 1878. The British government had suggested that the new instruments which it was proposing to issue should contain not only instructions such as the above, but also a clause authorizing the governor general to preside at Council meetings, another clause freeing him from the necessity of consulting with his cabinet in certain contingencies, and another allowing him on occasion to overrule his cabinet. Blake, with the uneasy and sometimes disputatious relations that existed between Lord Dufferin and Alexander Mackenzie no doubt in mind, pointed out that these instructions regarding reservation of bills were quite inapplicable to Canada. He argued that a Canadian governor had not for years sat with the cabinet except on ceremonial occasions, and that while under unusual circumstances he might not follow advice, such action was to be considered most exceptional and would be confined in almost every instance to those matters in which imperial interests were involved. These criticisms were effective, and very substantial modifications were made along the lines suggested. The broad principle of Blake's argument throughout was that Canada was no longer to be treated as a small dependency, and that practices which might be applicable to some parts of the colonial empire were quite unsuited

4/See Dale C. Thomson, *Alexander Mackenzie: Clear Grit* (Toronto, 1960), p. 290; W. E. D. Halliday, "The Privy Council Office and Cabinet Secretariat in Relation to the Development of Cabinet Government," *Canada Year Book, 1956*, pp. 62–70; Eugene Forsey, "Meetings of the Queen's Privy Council for Canada, 1867–1882," *Canadian Journal of Economics and Political Science*, XXXII, no. 4 (Nov. 1966), pp. 489–98.
5/*Infra*, pp. 146–9.

to a large nation, supposedly exercising comprehensive powers of self-government.

Canada is not merely a colony or a province: she is a Dominion composed of an aggregate of seven large provinces federally united under an Imperial Charter, which expressly recites that her constitution is to be similar in principle to that of the United Kingdom ... These circumstances, together with the vastness of her area, the number of her free population, the character of the representative institutions and of the responsible Government which as citizens of the various provinces and of Canada her people have so long enjoyed, all point to the propriety of dealing with the question in hand in a manner very different from that which might be fitly adopted with reference to a single and comparatively small and young colony.[6]

On a number of occasions specific issues raised what was broadly the same general problem as that discussed by Blake, namely, the power of the governor general to make his own personal decisions on Canadian questions. The British North America Act gave a number of powers to the Governor-General-in-Council, but it also frequently omitted to mention participation by the Council at all, and thus might be interpreted as giving certain powers to the governor acting alone. In many of the latter instances no difficulties occurred, for the governor tended to follow advice, but there were some powers which were questionable. The power of the governor to disallow provincial legislation, to dismiss a lieutenant governor, to make statements on public questions, to exercise the prerogative of mercy, to dismiss ministers, to refuse prorogation or dissolution, to reject appointments suggested by his cabinet – all these were at some time under discussion or were raised by concrete issues, and in the majority of cases the decision was in favour of the governor accepting the advice of his cabinet. The emphasis of the argument was not placed so much on the exact working of the British North America Act or of the prerogative instruments involved, but on the broad intent and on precedents in Canada, Great Britain, and the other dominions. The general effect by 1914 was to make the Canadian practice coincide with that in Great Britain and thus to emphasize the reality of Canadian autonomy in all aspects of its internal affairs.

EXTERNAL AFFAIRS, 1867–1914

Canadian control over external affairs in 1914 was, however, a different story; for although this had formed part of the same general trend, it had made much slower progress than the control over purely domestic matters. In some of the foreign or international fields Canada could do nothing whatever, but in others she had been able to make a moderate advance towards autonomy. She had

6/Memorandum of Edward Blake, Aug. 1876, in Kennedy, *Constitutional Documents*, p. 669.

gained ground steadily in her participation in the making of those commercial and political treaties in which she had an immediate concern, and she had also won limited recognition at a few international conferences as a nation with her own individual interests and opinions.

Canada had successfully asserted the right to control her own tariff (as indicated above) as early as 1859; and the practice was also well established before Confederation that the provinces would be allowed to send representatives abroad to discuss informally commercial relations with foreign countries. With this as a beginning, the Dominion was able to extend its power over commercial agreements and treaties through a series of gradual adaptations which proceeded *pari passu* with its growth in size and importance and its progress towards self-government in other fields. The first of these steps was taken when the Canadian agents were expressly recognized as associates of the British negotiators in an advisory capacity, even although the former did not sign the resulting agreement. The Canadian government was next permitted to have on such occasions its own representative, who was formally appointed a British plenipotentiary and formed a part of the British delegation. This was at first a subordinate position, but the Canadian high commissioner in London, Sir Charles Tupper, who served on several missions of this kind, soon became the dominant member, an advance which was made more rapidly because of his aggressiveness, his undoubted ability, and his special knowledge of the items under discussion. In 1884, for example, Tupper took the major role in negotiations with Spain, and had an agreement been concluded he would have signed the treaty as one of the British representatives. In 1892-3 Tupper again played the leading part in conducting negotiations with France, and the treaty was signed by him in company with the British ambassador. But the pace was apparently becoming too hot for the British government, and in 1895 Lord Ripon issued a reactionary dispatch which aimed at relegating the colonies to a definitely subordinate position in such matters. The principles of this dispatch were, however, never put into practice; and the earlier position of Tupper was formally and openly recognized by the British government in its instructions to its ambassador at Paris in 1907, which, indeed, went a step further by advising him that the Canadians would conduct the negotiations and "will doubtless keep you informed of their progress." The British ambassador merely signed the treaty in association with the Canadian plenipotentiaries. The British government's control over the negotiation of Canadian commercial treaties was from this time on no more than formal, although it continued to intervene at three stages in the proceedings: the British government (on the recommendation of the Canadian cabinet) appointed the plenipotentiaries, one of whom was always a British official; the latter, as well as the others, signed the treaty; and the ratification was given by the King upon the advice of the British cabinet. Even this nominal control was sometimes avoided by the

Canadian government negotiating informal agreements which were implemented by the two parties enacting reciprocal legislation, a device which
eliminated the British government completely.[7]

Canada had also acquired by 1914 other privileges in regard to commercial
treaties. She was no longer bound by new trade agreements made by the British
government unless she so desired, and if she later wished to withdraw separately
from such agreements, she could do so. She was also consulted by the British
government when the latter was considering new trade arrangements with
foreign countries, and she was gradually withdrawing from the scope of those
most-favoured-nation treaties which had been concluded by Great Britain
before Canada had been able to determine her own commercial obligations.

Control over political, as distinguished from commercial, treaties was not
relinquished by Great Britain so readily, although definite progress towards
greater dominion participation had been made by 1914. The origin and status
of the negotiations of any political treaty in which Canada was primarily
interested were much the same as with those dealing with commerce, except
that here the special British representative was expected to function, and did
function, as an active member. In one instance Canada had gone a bit further,
in setting up in association with the United States an International Joint Commission to settle disputes regarding boundary waters and other questions. All
three Canadian representatives were Canadians, nominated by Ottawa, but
appointed on the responsibility of the British government. Canada had also
acquired the right in some political treaties to adhere at her own discretion. The
rule, however, was that in all political negotiations of a general nature, which
might affect Canada only incidentally as part of the empire, the British government went its own way without any reference to or consultation with the
Dominion.[8] It should be observed that in all these formal commercial and
political treaties[9] the diplomatic unity of the empire was carefully preserved:
the British government was the channel through which all formal steps were
taken, and thus always had an opportunity of ensuring that its views were at
least given adequate consideration.

The dominions were also represented in their own right at a number of international conferences in which they had a special interest. In two instances
before 1914[10] they had even signed the resulting agreements on their own

7/A. G. Dewey, *The Dominions and Diplomacy: The Canadian Contribution*
(London, 1929) I, pp. 150–82. See also H. Gordon Skilling, *Canadian Representation
Abroad* (Toronto, 1945).

8/The British government in 1911 had cautiously committed itself to possible
consultation in the future.

9/The informal commercial agreements, implemented by reciprocal legislation, are
not included. Over these the British government exercised no control.

10/There was also a very early precedent in 1883 when Sir Charles Tupper not only
signed the protocols on behalf of Canada, but even on one occasion voted against all his
British colleagues, who eventually came over to his side. Sir Charles Tupper,
Recollections of Sixty Years in Canada (London, 1914), p. 175.

behalf and apart from the British delegates, who had signed for the remainder of the empire.

IMPERIAL RELATIONS, 1867–1914

Co-operation between Great Britain and the self-governing dominions was achieved in the early part of this period largely through the Colonial Office and the local governor, the contact being maintained through a constant exchange of dispatches. A notable advance was made in 1879, when Canada appointed Sir Alexander T. Galt as high commissioner in London, a position which, while consular rather than diplomatic, nevertheless gave the Dominion government a conveniently placed advocate and spokesman.

The great agency for occasional consultation and formal discussion was, however, the imperial conference. This began in 1887 as the colonial conference, and continued (with occasional lapses) to meet every four or five years. It was composed of the prime ministers and certain of their colleagues from the self-governing colonies and dominions, and leading members of the British cabinet. The conference was in no sense an executive or legislative body, for it could not bind its principals; it was essentially a conference of governments, meeting to consider matters in which all had a common concern. Thus while it would from time to time express an opinion in the form of advisory resolutions, these necessarily depended for their effectiveness upon the subsequent action of a number of autonomous parliaments.

The colonial and then the imperial conference usually avoided putting controversial measures to a vote, but it did not hesitate to discuss them; and imperial federation, empire defence, and reciprocal tariff preferences came up for frequent attention. The general attitude of the dominions (although this, like the personnel, varied somewhat from one meeting to the next) was as a rule opposed to any decided centralizing movement and in favour of maintaining the separate powers of each self-governing unit. The conference in its later sessions before the First World War gradually moved on from discussions of defence to foreign policy; and while the imperial government was quite explicit in asserting that it alone could be held responsible for that policy, the earlier ban on such discussions was being slowly removed. The 1911 conference, for example, listened to the foreign secretary submit a long and careful exposition of empire foreign policy, an unprecedented concession to the growing importance of the dominions. In the years immediately before the outbreak of war the dominion governments were given additional information from time to time concerning these and allied matters. It is doubtful if the dominions' spokesmen generally (with the possible exception of Sir Robert Borden) really desired anything more than this limited contact with foreign affairs and empire defence; for they felt that if they allowed themselves to be placed in a position where they offered advice, they could scarcely avoid accepting responsibility and backing up the joint decision with such forces as they had at their disposal.

Thus by 1914 Canada and the other dominions were completely self-governing in all their internal affairs, and they were also beginning to acquire substantial powers in external relations. So far as commercial treaties were concerned the realities of power had already passed over to the dominions, and with political treaties there had been some progress in the same direction. The dominions had even made a modest début at international gatherings of a minor nature. In empire matters affecting one another, each self-governing part tended to follow its own course, subject, however, to fairly continuous informal consultation with the United Kingdom and a general consultation from time to time through the imperial conference. But in formulating foreign policy the dominions had virtually no share; and in the more vital matters of declaring war, making peace, appointing diplomatic agents, and participating in major international gatherings the dominions had no share whatever.

On August 4, 1914, Canada found herself at war through the action of the British government. She had not been consulted; she had herself made no declaration of war; and she had in no way taken part in the diplomatic exchanges which had led to the final catastrophe. But although legally committed to the war, the extent of her participation was admittedly in her own hands; for this principle of autonomy had been stated time and again, and had received a practical demonstration during the South African War. The Canadian Parliament therefore made its own independent decision on how active a role Canada should play in the struggle.

The First World War began a new period in the development of dominion status, for while the events which followed were rooted in the past and might well be considered to be the natural outcome of earlier tendencies, the advance was extremely rapid and the results were both far-reaching and decisive. The drive behind this movement was the dominions' conspicuous war effort, which gradually built up in each a strong national consciousness of its individuality, its power, and its importance. For a year or two of war this feeling grew slowly, but it then rapidly mounted and remained at a high level. It found expression in a general conviction throughout the dominions that their efforts and sacrifices should be recognized as a fair measure of their maturity, and that they were therefore entitled to a far greater control of their own destinies than heretofore.

The first great concession to this demand was in 1917 when all dominion prime ministers were summoned to meet with the British war cabinet as an empire cabinet, which proceeded to discuss and decide questions of high policy and the general conduct of the war. Dominion representatives in the following months held other meetings of the same nature with the British cabinet; they later took part in the deliberations of the Paris Peace Conference; and they signed the peace treaties. When the League of Nations was created, the dominions became participating members.

The years following the peace conference were dotted with constitutional issues (raised for the most part by Canada) which served to test the powers of the dominions to participate actively in foreign affairs. A common empire foreign policy, enunciated by a meeting of the prime ministers of the empire, was tentatively tried in the immediate post-war years; but it broke down badly when submitted to sudden strain in the Chanak crisis in 1922. From that time on, issue after issue persistently emphasized the determination of most of the dominions to be their own masters, even although such a policy necessarily involved the abondonment of the diplomatic unity of the empire. Finally, after four years of Fabian tactics, several dominions brought the matter to an explicit decision at the Imperial Conference of 1926. This conference issued a formal statement proclaiming the complete equality in status of the United Kingdom and the dominions, an equality which was manifest not only in international affairs but also within the empire. The British Commonwealth was to remain united under a common King; and subordination, either in law or in practice, was to give way to association and co-operation among autonomous partners.

Their position and mutual relation [that is, of Great Britain and the dominions] may be readily defined. *They are autonomous Communities within the British Empire, equal in status, in no way subordinate one to another in any aspect of their domestic or external affairs, though united by a common allegiance to the Crown, and freely associated as members of the British Commonwealth of Nations ...*

It is an essential consequence of the equality of status ... that the Governor-General of a Dominion is the representative of the Crown, holding in all essential respects the same position in relation to the administration of public affairs in the Dominion as is held by His Majesty the King of Great Britain, and that he is not the representative or agent of His Majesty's Government in Great Britain or of any Department of that Government.[11]

The conference proceeded to discuss a number of the points implied in these statements in some detail. Disallowance of dominion legislation by the British authorities and reservation by the governor general were declared to be obsolete, it was desirable to repeal a number of British statutes which still applied to the dominions; the retention of judicial appeals to the Judicial Committee of the Privy Council should rest entirely with the dominion concerned; each dominion should possess complete treaty-making authority, acting through the sovereign, but on the advice of its own cabinet; neither Great Britain nor any dominion could be committed to active obligations in foreign affairs without the definite assent of its own government; all parts would profit by an exchange

11/R. MacG. Dawson, *The Development of Dominion Status, 1900–1936* (Toronto, 1937), pp. 331, 333. For a full discussion of the events of this period, see *ibid.*, pp. 36–103, 203–324.

of information, consultation, and, at times, co-operation in foreign affairs, and new arrangements for consultation and communication between one part of the empire and another should therefore receive special consideration. The long-cherished diplomatic unity of the empire in foreign affairs was thus tacitly abandoned; for the King might follow several contradictory policies depending on the different capacities in which he was called upon to act.

These declarations of the 1926 conference still left a number of legal inequalities untouched, and arrangements were made for a later meeting of experts to consider how these could best be removed. This body was accordingly set up as the Conference on the Operation of Dominion Legislation and Merchant Shipping Legislation, and it presented its report in 1929 along the lines suggested. The Imperial Conference of 1930 concurred in this report, and formally requested that the recommendations there made should be enacted by the British Parliament. In response to this request the British Parliament passed the Statute of Westminster in 1931.[12]

The Statute of Westminister thus endeavoured to augment the autonomy of the dominions as proclaimed in 1926 by removing certain legal handicaps which to some degree still hampered their powers. It provided that the Colonial Laws Validity Act (under which dominion statutes were void if they conflicted with statutes of the imperial Parliament) was no longer to apply to the dominions, that in the future no dominion statute was to be declared void because it was repugnant to the law of the United Kingdom, and that no act of the imperial Parliament was to extend to a dominion unless it declared that the dominion had requested and consented to its enactment. The statute also declared that a dominion Parliament had the power to enact laws having extraterritorial operation. The Colonial Courts of Admiralty Act, 1890, and the Merchant Shipping Act, 1894, were no longer to apply to the dominions. A special clause stated that the provisions of the Statute of Westminster were not to affect the position of the British North America Act and its amendments, a reservation inserted at the request of Canada in order that the whole British North America Act should not be amendable by an ordinary act of the Canadian Parliament. In 1949, as will be seen, Parliament was by formal amendment given the power to amend parts of the act, and lengthy negotiations between the Dominion and the provinces, aimed at domiciling the rest of the act in Canada, began about the same time.[13]

The action of the dominions on the outbreak of the Second World War in 1939 furnished an instructive contrast to the practice of 1914. Australia and New Zealand considered that the British declaration of war included them as well; while South Africa, Canada, and Eire deliberately made their own choice. South Africa thus declared war three days after the United Kingdom reached its decision; Canada did the same after a lapse of seven days; Eire remained

12/Appendix.
13/*Infra*, pp. 127–9.

permanently neutral. Subsequent constitutional developments have flowed steadily in the one direction. The war itself, the formation and activities of the United Nations, the North Atlantic Treaty Organization, the Colombo Plan, the Australia–New Zealand–United States Pacific Security Council, and the Korean War, to name but a few, have all furnished irrefutable evidence that the dominions are now independent nations in the fullest sense of the word and are everywhere recognized as such.

The mutual understanding and sympathy and the close co-operation which for so long characterized the relations of different members of the Commonwealth are nevertheless still maintained, though now they arise between autonomous powers dealing with one another as equals. Every day sees confidential communications pass from one capital to another; special missions are dispatched to acquire information or to discuss projects; officials are exchanged on subjects of common concern; meetings and consultations occur at different levels with an occasional conference of prime ministers to settle matters of great moment. Mr Lester Pearson, while still secretary of state for External Affairs, once explained the relations between Canada and the other nations of the Commonwealth in words undoubtedly acceptable to his successors in office:

Outwardly and inwardly Canada has come of age, but she has no desire to leave the Commonwealth family in which she has grown up. The last war and its aftermath have seen my country accept responsibilities in the international field which we would hardly have contemplated before 1939. We are no longer so much concerned with the assertion of a nationhood which we can now take for granted. We are more concerned with the search for ways by which, without jeopardizing what is essential to our own national freedom, we may share the international responsibilities which all free peoples must accept if liberty is to be maintained and security established ... The Commonwealth ... is capable of significant co-operation and collective action. Furthermore, there is in the Commonwealth always the desire to work together, to see each other's point of view, even when that desire does not express itself in immediate agreement ... When divisions rack the world, plain friendship between nation and nation is worth more than we often realise.[14]

The Commonwealth has changed in composition, however, since the Second World War, and in doing so has again demonstrated its extraordinary ability to adapt itself to a changing environment. Eire and South Africa have dropped out, the latter with assistance; yet they occupy an anomalous position, for although not in the Commonwealth they are nevertheless not treated by their old associates as foreign powers. India, Pakistan, Ceylon, Ghana, Malaysia, Nigeria, Cyprus, Sierra Leone, Tanzania, Jamaica, Trinidad and Tobago, Uganda and over a dozen other countries have become fellow members as free and autonomous nations. In 1949 when India decided to become an independent republic and expressed a desire to remain in the Commonwealth, she was allowed to do so. She thereby rejected the sovereign as head of government,

14/*Listener*, June 18, 1953.

but accepted him "as the symbol of the free association of its independent member nations and as such the Head of the Commonwealth." When South Africa withdrew from the Commonwealth in 1961 it was not because she had become a republic, but because of Commonwealth disapproval of her racial policies.[15] Rhodesia, when it declared its independence in 1965, did not apply to join.

When Elizabeth II became Queen in 1952 it was decided by a meeting of prime ministers and other representatives of the Commonwealth countries that the time was opportune to bring the Royal Style and Title into accord with current constitutional practice. Subject to the approval of the proper authority in each member country and duly confirmed by the Queen's proclamation, each country would henceforth use "for its own purposes a form of title which suits its own particular circumstances, but retains a substantial element which is common to all." In accordance with this understanding the Canadian Parliament approved the following: "Elizabeth the Second, by the Grace of God of the United Kingdom, Canada, and Her other Realms and Territories Queen, Head of the Commonwealth, Defender of the Faith."[16] This was formally proclaimed at Ottawa on May 29, 1953, four days before the Queen's Coronation.

Precisely what the Commonwealth and membership in it now mean to the great mass of Canadians is not easy to assess. French Canadians, though many of their elected representatives are among those who render lip service to the Commonwealth, none the less appear to view the institution not merely with detachment but with a fine Gallic scepticism. English Canadians unquestionably accept the Commonwealth as a highly satisfactory club for gentlemen; but those who find in the Commonwealth a nostalgic connection with the "old country" can hardly help but be nonplussed by the modern Commonwealth's predominantly non-white membership, a fact whose full implications are not as yet apparent. What is clear is that the vast majority of Canadians support, tacitly or overtly, the increasingly active part in international affairs that Canada has assumed in the past few decades, and membership in the Commonwealth is one of the most familiar of these. Canadians have become accustomed to reading about what their representatives have said at the United Nations, at NATO meetings, and at sundry Commonwealth conferences on many topics all over the globe. When in 1961 the prime minister of Canada played a leading role in the events that led up to the withdrawal of South Africa from the Commonwealth, Canadian commentators variously expressed approval and disapproval of Canadian policy. The same was true in 1962 when the Canadian prime minister led the way in expressing opposition to the United Kingdom's attempts to join the European Common Market. But on neither occasion did anyone express surprise that Canada assumed so leading a role.

15/See *Commonwealth Survey*, VII, no. 8 (April 11, 1961), pp. 362–6.
16/*Can. Statutes*, 1–2 Eliz. II, c. 9.

Recent developments involving Canada as a nation have been less concerned with her traditional role in international affairs than with more domestic matters, and in most of them a rapidly developing technology, including communication by satellite, has played a part. The discovery of oil in Arctic areas has raised questions about Canada's jurisdiction in waters surrounding her northern islands, and even on the islands themselves, few of which can be said to be effectively settled in a manner congruent with some modern theories of international law. In the settled parts of Canada, Quebec particularly (though not solely) has been testing the dimensions of the country's nationhood, and in 1968 Mr Daniel Johnson, the premier, addressed a federal-provincial conference in a brief which included: "the equality to be established between our two cultural communities depends not only on extending bilingualism territorially but even more on extending the jurisdictions of Quebec, the homeland of the French Canadian nation."[17] One of the jurisdictions Quebec wishes to extend turns on the province's role in international affairs, when dealing with subjects which within Canada are under provincial jurisdiction, and in the 1960s a number of incidents occurred which showed Quebec, representing one concept of a nation, as a rival to Canada, representing another. Clearly one constitutional decision Canada will sooner or later have to make concerns how many nations it is. The legal answer, at least, is clear: one.

17/*The Government of Quebec and the Constitution* (Quebec, 1968), p. 88. See also Mitchell Sharp, *Federalism and International Conferences on Education* (Ottawa, 1968); Bora Laskin, "The Provinces and International Agreements," in Ontario Advisory Committee on Confederation, *Background Papers and Reports* (Toronto, 1967), pp. 101–13; *Reference re Ownership of Off-Shore Mineral Rights*, 65 D.L.R. (2d) 353.

Part II THE CONSTITUTION

4 The nature of the constitution

ALEXANDER TILLOCH GALT, one of the most active of the Fathers of Confederation, was one of those who wanted a strong federal government. On the assumption that the three Maritime provinces would become one, the cabinet to which Galt belonged in 1864 favoured a local legislature for each of Upper and Lower Canada and the new Maritime province, "the powers of which should be carefully restricted to certain local matters to be specified and defined ... whilst all general Legislation should be dealt with by, and all undefined powers of legislation reside in, a central Legislature which should in fact be not only a federal assembly charged with the consideration of a few topics specially committed to its care, but the real Legislature of the country, whilst the local assemblies were to be allowed to sink to the position of mere municipalities." The lieutenant governor who reported those words shortly added in the same despatch:

Whilst however these very rational views are held by Mr. Galt and other members of the Canadian Government, I am bound to state that they are not those generally entertained, nor do they harmonize with the interpretation usually affixed to the word "Federation" in these provinces.

"A federal union" in the mouth of a lower Canadian means the independence of his Province from all English or Protestant influences – in the mouth of an inhabitant of the Maritime Provinces it means the retention of the machinery of the existing local executive government; the expenditure within each province of the revenue raised from it, except a small quota to be paid towards federal expenses; and the preservation of the existing Legislatures [;] a central Parliament to which the consideration of some few topics of general interest are to be confided under vigorous restraints, prompted by a jealous care for the maintenance of Provincial independence ...[1]

These varying views of the nature of the constitution that was to be estab-

1/Lieut. Gov. A. H. Gordon to Edward Cardwell, in Browne, *Documents,* pp. 42–3. For more modern statements of differing theories of the nature of the constitution, see *Report of the Royal Commission of Inquiry on Constitutional Problems* (Quebec, 1956); Ontario Advisory Committee on Confederation, *Background Papers and Reports*; J. Peter Meekison, ed., *Canadian Federalism: Myth or Reality* (Toronto, 1968).

lished in the 1860s are as relevant today as they were then. Their emphasis has altered in part, with divisions arising now between "have" and "have not" provinces; now between English-speaking and French-speaking; now between those who conceive of a constitution encompassing "one nation" and "two nations"; now between those who envisage Canada as a pact between races, and those who do not. But of the essential fact that Canadian theories of the nature of the constitution differ profoundly, there can be no doubt. This book, it must be frankly admitted, leans towards a "one nation" and centralist view of the constitution, a bias to be kept in mind by the reader, and especially in these opening chapters.

It is a convenient but far from accurate statement to say that Canada has a written constitution, for the written British North America Act and its amendments tend to overshadow those other constitutional principles and understandings whose nature and significance are not so clearly and obviously indicated. The written document has been, of course, historically and legally indispensable in that it created the Dominion by uniting the four original provinces, and it has since then formed the common tie which has bound together the ten provinces which today compose the federation. The act is thus undoubtedly of fundamental constitutional importance: it outlines in some detail certain parts of the central government; it gives the distribution of power between the Dominion and the provinces; it establishes Canada to a defined extent as officially bilingual; and because of the peculiar situation existing in 1867, it also provided an initial government for both Ontario and Quebec.

The British North America Act, however, does not pretend to be a comprehensive document, such as, for example, the constitution of the United States; and there is thus little of the well-rounded, balanced description and enumeration of authorities and functions which so frequently characterize those written constitutions which aim to cover all the essentials of government within a limited number of carefully articulated sections. There are many vital things about the government of Canada (to say nothing of the provincial governments) which are not stated or even hinted at in the British North America Act, and even those matters which are dealt with in some detail are frequently given in such fashion that they become ambiguous and sometimes misleading. Thus any earnest literal-minded student who would endeavour to learn about Canadian government by nothing more than a conscientious examination of the act would be shocked to discover that the Dominion is ruled as follows.

The executive government and authority of Canada is vested in the Sovereign, who is apparently[2] represented by a governor general (sections 9, 10). The latter is assisted by a Council, which he chooses, and summons, and removes (11), and which advises him in his work (12, 13). The Sovereign is commander-in-chief of all naval and military forces in Canada (15). The governor

2/There is a small gap here in the act which is filled by the issue of prerogative instruments by the Crown. *Infra*, pp. 147–9.

general appoints the Speaker of the Senate (34) and virtually all the judges (96). He appoints all the members of one house of the legislature (24). The other legislative body, the House of Commons, is called together by the governor (38) and this house can be dissolved by him at any time and a new election ordered (50). All money bills must first be recommended by the governor before they can be passed by Parliament (54). The governor may assent to legislation; he may refuse his assent; or he may reserve a bill for the consideration of the Queen-in-Council in Great Britain (55-7); and he may also disallow any provincial act or refuse his assent to any provincial bill reserved for the signification of his pleasure (55-7, 90). The same general powers are exercisable by the provincial lieutenant governors, who are appointed by the governor general, are accountable to him, and may be removed by him (58, 59, 90).

This is a careful and literal rendering of those parts of the British North America Act which deal with the executive power and its relations to the legislature. Canada would thus appear to suffer under a dictatorship, the autocratic rule of one central figure, acting in the place of the Sovereign, who governs the Dominion with little reference to or control by the people. The only popular element is apparently supplied by a House of Commons, which meets when the governor desires, considers financial legislation which he recommends, and can be forced into an election whenever he deems it desirable. While it is true that the governor is advised by his Council, the exercise of the above powers is vested in the governor alone. This was, indeed, substantially the nature of the executive government before 1848, and this part of the written constitution still wears garments more than a century old. It can be properly understood and interpreted today only in the light of the changes which have occurred since then, and these changes are to be found in large measure in the "unwritten" constitution – a misleading term used to cover parts of a constitution lying outside the fundamental documents, yet perhaps still written down.

The unwritten portion of the Canadian constitution thus includes such matters as the following, all (and more) of which are necessary to an understanding of the nature of the executive power: (1) that today on virtually all questions and virtually all of the time the governor general does not act according to his own judgment or on his own responsibility, but on the advice of his Council; (2) that this Council is not the Council mentioned in the British North America Act, but only a part of that Council acting in the name of the whole; (3) that this active part of the Council is the cabinet, a body not mentioned anywhere in the act; (4) that this part of the Council is chosen by the prime minister; (5) that there is such a person as a prime minister: the most important political figure in Canada does not appear in any part of the written constitution; indeed, he is mentioned only casually in one or two Canadian statutes; (6) that the prime minister and his cabinet must always have the support of the House of Commons, and that all members of the cabinet, including the prime minister, must have seats in that body or in the Senate; (7) that the cabinet stays in office largely because of its steady support from a political party; (8) that most of the cabinet members are heads of executive departments; (9) that almost all the above are reproduced in miniature in the provincial governments.

A large number of major omissions thus deal with the executive power. This peculiarity can be traced to the British government *via* the founders of the federation, who apparently believed that while the discretionary powers of the governor general were in many matters clearly comprehended and controlled, they should nevertheless be treated in a statute as though they still existed in all their pristine vigour. "We cannot limit or define the powers of the Crown in such respect," said John A. Macdonald. "See our Union Act. There is nothing in it about responsible government. It is a system which we have adopted. There is not even any resolution on our own journals as to the number of the executive. The Sovereign may have such number as she pleases."[3] It was, no doubt, a harmless idiosyncrasy, and in the result it proved to be highly beneficial; for a more explicit statement might conceivably have lessened the flexibility of the constitution and have caused greater friction and embarrassment in later years. On the other hand, both Australia and South Africa at a later date found it possible to be less reticent about one at least of these principles in their governments, and boldly stated that ministers within three months of their appointment must find seats in Parliament.

Even these few illustrations make it abundantly clear that the unwritten constitution is every whit as important as the British North America Act, and, indeed, that much of the latter is transformed and made almost unrecognizable by the operation of the former, which in all these instances consists of established customs and usages which have grown up over a long period of years. But the unwritten constitution includes very much more than these conventions. The term also embraces principles of the common law as defined by the courts; some British and Canadian acts of Parliament and orders-in-council; judicial interpretations of the written constitution and other laws; the rules and privileges of Parliament; and many other habitual and informal methods of government in addition to those noted above. All these, many of them (despite the term "unwritten") committed to writing, others in much more intangible and elusive form, exert a powerful influence on constitutional practice.

The English common law[4] and many parts of the statutes and the historic constitutional documents of England came to Canada (excepting Quebec) by direct inheritance. It has already been indicated how the common law determined the powers of self-government in both settled and conquered colonies,[5] and a subsequent chapter will indicate the way.in which many of the executive

3/Pope, *Confederation Documents*, p. 77.
4/*Infra*, p. 384.
5/*Supra*, pp. 4–6.

powers in Canada are still affected by the delegation from the Crown in Great Britain of those powers which it has for many centuries possessed under the common law.[6] The broad rule applied to the early colonies was that settled colonies (and to a small degree conquered colonies also[7]) were possessed of as much of the general English law, common and statutory, as was conveniently applicable to the colonial conditions.[8] The scope of the law so applied and the time when it was to be considered effective in the colony were decided either by the local courts or by formal enactment of the local legislative authorities.

The peculiar position of Quebec, a colony acquired by conquest, with an established and quite different legal system, led to the passage by the imperial Parliament of the Quebec Act, 1774, whereby the English criminal law was retained and the French civil law formally confirmed, both being subject to change by local ordinance.[9] Immediately following the separation of Upper and Lower Canada in 1791, Upper Canada (hitherto bound by the Quebec Act) seized the opportunity to adopt the English civil law, and the first act of the first session of its legislature declared that "in all matters of controversy relative to property and civil rights resort shall be had to the Laws of England," as of October 15, 1792. The second act of the same legislature introduced trial by jury.[10]

Nova Scotia, on the other hand, deeming herself a settled colony, and not being controlled by any special British statute like the Quebec Act, could and did allow the relevant English law to be selected and applied by the courts as the need arose, and she thus became possessed of the fundamental English liberties without any legislative action whatever. A legal commentator in Nova Scotia expressed the situation thus in 1832:

While it seems doubtful whether any English laws (except those in which the Colonies are expressly named) have any validity here, until they have been adopted into our local jurisprudence by distinct legislation or general recognition and usage; yet, what are generally esteemed the most valuable portions of British law, have been transplanted into our land, – the Habeas Corpus – the freedom of the Press – the trial by Jury – the Representative Branch of legislature, – the viva voce examination of witnesses; in fine all those branches of public law which have drawn the eulogium of the wisest and the best of men upon the British constitution, we possess. While we are freed from many that have formed the subject of constant objection in the mother country.[11]

6/Infra, pp. 147–8.

7/The extent of the political rights of the Crown, for example, was determined in conquered colonies by the common law. See supra, pp. 4–6. See A. B. Keith, The Governments of the British Empire (London, 1935), pp. 10–17.

8/See The Lauderdale Peerage (1885), 10 App. Cas. 692, at pp. 744–5.

9/Supra, pp. 6–9.

10/Upper Canada Statutes, 32 Geo. III, cc. 1, 2. A number of the other provinces have similar enactments which set a definite date for the application of the English law.

11/Beamish Murdoch, Epitome of the Laws of Nova Scotia (Halifax, 1832), I, p. 35. Cf. T. C. Haliburton, An Historical and Statistical Account of Nova Scotia (Halifax, 1829), II, pp. 343–7.

It should further be noted that legislation in England after 1774 did not apply to any colony unless it was expressly indicated in the English statute, and also that the colony was free to amend any part of the general law which had been declared to be the law of the colony.[12] The power to define, enlarge, or restrict these fundamental constitutional rights by legislation was later distributed between the Dominion and the provinces by the British North America Act, and the situation has thereby become extremely complicated. No attempt has been made by either the Dominion or the provinces to state the exact content of these rights in statutory form. They are still rights resting primarily on common law even though modified and defined in some particulars by legislation. For example, the provincial legislatures have enacted statutes regulating the administration of the jury system but not affecting substantially the right of trial by jury. The older provinces have enacted statutory provisions relating to habeas corpus in civil matters. Through their authority over "property and civil rights" the provincial legislatures have some power to modify the inherited common law rights. It would appear, however, that some at least of these rights, such as freedom of discussion and, perhaps, freedom to disseminate religious views, cannot be essentially restricted by the provincial legislatures but are solely under the jurisdiction of the Dominion Parliament.[13] Also, of course, the Dominion Parliament through its power to make the criminal law is able to define and limit personal rights. Thus the definitions of sedition and unlawful assembly in the criminal code define the outer limits of the rights of freedom of speech and assembly respectively.

The Canadian constitution also includes a number of British statutes expressly referring to Canada or to the empire. There are still in existence at least one hundred and thirty of these British statutes which apply to Canada;[14] but many of them are not constitutional in nature, and many are today of no importance whatever, such as, for example, those dealing with the slave trade; the status of all of them will presumably be altered when the British North America Act is "repatriated" to Canada. The Statute of Westminister, 1931,[15]

12/The essential provisions of the English Habeas Corpus Act, 1679, were adopted by local ordinance in Quebec in 1784. This was confirmed by the Constitutional Act, 1791, and all the English law, common and statutory, relating to habeas corpus in civil matters was applied to Upper Canada by the omnibus statute (already noted) of 1792. (Habeas corpus in *civil* matters was not introduced into Quebec until 1812.) The provisions of the English Habeas Corpus Act of 1816, on the other hand, did not apply to Upper Canada until specifically enacted by the local legislature.

13/*Alberta Press Bill Case*, [1938] S.C.R. 100; *Saumur* v. *City of Quebec*, [1953] 2 S.C.R. 299. The passage of a Dominion Bill of Rights in 1960 does not really clarify the doubts explicit in the above statement.

14/One hundred and twenty-nine are named in a list, furnished by the Department of External Affairs, which is reproduced in Maurice Ollivier, *Problems of Canadian Sovereignty* (Toronto, 1945), pp. 465–9. The minister of Justice gave the number as "about 150." *Can. H. of C. Debates*, March 19, 1937, p. 1941.

15/Appendix.

declared that certain British statutes[16] were to be no longer in force in the dominions and that the latter have now the general power to enact legislation which may run contrary to the provisions of an imperial act.[17] The surviving British statutes of major constitutional importance for Canada are thus very few indeed. They are, as of 1970, the British North America Act and its amendments (which may be conveniently allowed to remain in the separate category of the written constitution allotted to them above), and the Statute of Westminster,[18] together with any acts which may have been passed at the express request of the Canadian government. The Declaration of Abdication Act, 1936, for example, is in the last group.

Closely associated with the acts of the British Parliament are those British orders-in-council (passed under statutory authority) which form a small but by no means negligible part of the Canadian constitution. The orders-in-council admitting to the Dominion Rupert's Land and the North-West Territory, British Columbia, and Prince Edward Island (authorized by section 146 of the British North America Act) fall into this category.[19]

There is another group which may be called "constitutional statutes." These occupy a midway position between the British North America Act and a Canadian statute; for they are statutes of the Canadian Parliament, yet, once enacted, cannot be amended by it. Thus, the Alberta and Saskatchewan acts, which created the original constitutions for those provinces, were Canadian statutes in origin but thenceforward could be amended only by their respective provincial legislatures.[20]

Acts of the Dominion and provincial parliaments form in many instances other parts of the "unwritten" constitution. These statutes are what the French call *organic* laws, namely, laws which are looked upon as constitutional, not because of some special or formal method of enactment (which is the same as that used for ordinary statutes) but by their content – the fact that the subject material of these statutes is constitutional in its nature. Thus the Dominion Act of 1875 which created the Supreme Court of Canada, while passed in the same way as any ordinary public law, is by its purpose and content unmistakably a part of the constitution. The Dominion acts which have admitted new provinces, altered boundaries, established the franchise, adjusted the provincial subsidies,

16/The Colonial Laws Validity Act, 1865; the Merchant Shipping Act, 1894; and the Colonial Courts of Admiralty Act, 1890. *Supra,* pp. 49–50.

17/*Supra,* p. 50. The Foreign Enlistment Act, 1937, thus displaced for Canada the British Foreign Enlistment Act previously applicable.

18/It might be noted in passing that the security of full dominion legislative powers which is granted by the Statute of Westminister rests on the constitutional convention and assurance that no future law applicable to a dominion will be passed by the British Parliament except at the instance of the dominion, and this convention is set forth in the preamble of the statute.

19/*Supra,* pp. 37–9.

20/BNA Act, 1871, section 6.

created new government departments, provided for the trial of controverted elections, and a host of others are all organic laws. Inasmuch as large sections of the provincial constitutions are in the form of provincial statutes,[21] these parts fall entirely in this category. The Dominion and provincial governments may also from time to time pass orders-in-council concerning constitutional matters which will form further additions of a similar nature.

An entirely different category of documents has so frequently been asserted in recent years to be, in effect, part of the constitution, that it should be referred to here. Treaties made with, and about, Indians, severally transferring territory, guaranteeing Indians certain hunting and fishing rights, or permitting them to cross the Canadian-American boundary without paying customs duties, have often on the Indians' behalf been claimed to take precedence over acts of Parliament. The courts, however, have fairly consistently ruled otherwise, and an authority has written: "Federal legislative competence with respect to Indians is unfettered by treaties – either Indian treaties or international treaties – or by the Royal Proclamation of 1763."[22] While no doubt sound constitutionally, that point is one of whose validity it is not easy to persuade Indians, who not unnaturally find some inconsistency in a *de facto* situation in which treaties affecting Indian rights can be superseded, while those transferring Indian lands to whites are not.

Attention has already been directed to the function of the judiciary in creating part of the early unwritten constitution by its task of selecting those English laws and precedents which seemed applicable to the young colonies. "Our courts of justice are of necessity obliged to exercise to a certain extent powers of a legislative description, in adopting or rejecting different parts of the English law, on the apparent applicability to our circumstances, or the reverse."[23] But the activity of the courts in constitution-making did not abate after the early period of settlement, for they have continued to interpret and amplify the formal constitution, the common law, statutes, orders-in-council, etc. The necessity of applying the distribution of Dominion and provincial authority contained in the British North America Act has given the courts an especially prominent and effective place in moulding the Canadian unwritten constitution.[24]

Parliament provides another part of the unwritten constitution through its special privileges and its rules of order and procedure. The privileges of both the Dominion and provincial legislatures, while they rest on statutory authority,

21/The BNA Act provided, as already stated, for the constitutions of Ontario and Quebec, and Dominion statutes for those of Manitoba, Alberta, and Saskatchewan, but these provinces have the same power as the others to alter their constitutions by ordinary statute.

22/Kenneth Lysyk, "The Unique Constitutional Position of the Canadian Indian," *Canadian Bar Review*, Dec. 1967, p. 551. For an Indian commentary on treaty rights see Harold Cardinal, *The Unjust Society* (Edmonton, 1969).

23/Murdoch, *Epitome of the Laws of Nova Scotia*, I, p. 34.

24/*Infra*, pp. 82–98. For a survey of the history of judicial review, see B. L. Strayer, *Judicial Review of Legislation in Canada* (Toronto, 1968).

nevertheless trace their descent from and are referred to those long established in England by the law and custom of Parliament. The way in which the Canadian Parliament transacts its business is controlled by its own rules (with the exception of a few clauses in the British North America Act dealing with a quorum, majority vote, election of a Speaker, and the origination of money votes). These rules are not in statutory form – indeed, many of them are merely precedents – and they can be modified at any time by each house as it sees fit. The rules deal with such matters as parliamentary committees, conduct of debates, general procedure, and, to some degree, the relations between the two houses.

There are also the conventions of the constitution, the customs and usage which have supplemented, modified, and in some instances preceded many of the other parts.[25] Those which affect the executive power as outlined in the British North America Act have already been described, and while these furnish the best illustrations of the vital role played by the conventions, there are many more, similar in nature and equally pervasive in their influence, which occur in other fields of government. A number of illustrations follow.

The functioning of the legislature and the relations between the legislature and the executive are to a marked degree determined by usage. The English and French languages are legal equals in Parliament, for example, but English was for years the day to day working language, and French the language of translation; the use of the two languages has been altered considerably by simultaneous translation for spoken words, and a growing practice of publishing documents in both languages at the same time. The dependence of the cabinet on legislative support, the conditions under which the cabinet will resign, its responsibility to the House of Commons and not to the Senate, the insistence that all members of the cabinet who hold portfolios must (with rare exceptions) sit in the House, many of the rules of parliamentary procedure and the interpretations of these rules (as mentioned above) are largely or entirely based on usage.

The political parties furnish many other examples. Parties as such are all but unknown to federal law in Canada, though the Canada Elections Act recognizes the existence of opposing "political interests," and minor parties have been given statutory recognition in order that their leaders could be paid a special stipend;[26] but their activity is unceasing, and they reach into almost every part of the government and exert a decisive influence on very many activities of those who support and those who oppose the administration. The prime minister is the choice, not of the governor general alone, but usually of a

25/No attempt has been made to distinguish between custom, usage, and convention. A common distinction is to treat custom and usage as synonymous terms, and convention as a usage which has acquired obligatory force.

26/See *Report of the Committee on Election Expenses* (Ottawa, 1966), pp. 38–40. The committee recommended formal recognition of parties in order that they could be held accountable.

national party convention as well (a phenomenon discussed in a later chapter);
all the members of the House with a very few exceptions have been nominated
and elected as a result of party support; almost all the senators have been
appointed because of party services; and party affiliations colour the greater
part of the proceedings of both houses.

The former conduct of imperial relations, the accretion in dominion powers,
and the eventual development of national status have taken place through conventional rather than legal means. The correspondence between the governor
general and the home government, the decisions of special issues and disputes,
the assertions of power by the colonial or dominion authorities, the proceedings
of imperial conferences, the refusal of dominion governments to accede to the
wishes of Great Britain or their compliance therein – from these there was built
up through the years a set of principles which governed inter-imperial relations
and dominion powers without the necessity of changing the letter of the law.
Eventually, it was considered desirable to try to bring the law up to date and
into greater accord with the recognized practices, and the Statute of Westminster was the result. But these matters never stand still, and the same process
of gradual development by informal means immediately began again and has
continued steadily since that time.

To include certain general principles, ideas, and popularly held beliefs on
matters of government as other parts of the unwritten constitution may place
some strain upon what is usually included in the term. Yet these also form an
essential element of the conventional constitution and they will most assuredly
influence and often determine the way in which the forces of government will
be exerted. The mere fact that a constitutional doctrine is not explicitly enunciated and formally committed to writing may affect the external appearance but
not disturb the genuineness or force of that doctrine. Thus the broad tolerance
which will permit differences of opinion and will disapprove of punitive or
repressive measures against the dissenters is of as great constitutional significance and may conceivably under some circumstances afford an even more
assured protection than an explicit guarantee of freedom of speech, written into
a constitution, yet with no solid conviction behind it. "As in the creation of
law," wrote Sir Ivor Jennings, "the creation of a convention must be due to the
reason of the thing, because it accords with the prevailing political philosophy,"[27] and certain principles of this philosophy and certain observed
conventions become virtually indistinguishable. Thus the chief restraint on a
Canadian cabinet which prevents it from endeavouring to eliminate all
opposition activity and criticism is the prevalent popular belief (which the
cabinet itself shares, despite occasional evidence to the contrary) in fair play,
free speech, and open criticism, and the cabinet is therefore not disposed to use
measures of suppression. Fundamental attitudes respecting the liberty of the
citizen, whether those principles enjoy special protection in law or not, come

27/*The Law and the Constitution* (3rd ed., London, 1943), p. 131.

under this category and derive an enhanced prestige and sanction from the conviction with which they are generally held.

All these conventions, so varied in the manifestations and in their influence, obviously perform a most useful function in the government. The legal framework is bound by its very character to be stiff and unyielding, and changes in the law will come as a rule after much deliberation and many ponderous formalities. The conventions give life to the written words; they introduce a saving element of flexibility and enable the constitution to develop and adapt itself to demands and conditions which are of necessity continually changing. They vary widely, however, in authority. Some will represent merely acceptable procedures, while others are explicit and well-recognized practices; one may be trifled with on occasion or even, if necessary, ignored, while another may in its extreme form partake of the same rigidity as the written constitution itself. The number of members in the Canadian cabinet, for example, though largely customary, can be readily altered; the representation of the different provinces in the cabinet can be somewhat modified, but not abandoned; while the responsibility of the cabinet to Parliament is a custom more firmly entrenched than most of the British North America Act. As a rule, however, the conventions can be more readily submitted to the acid test of suitability to the purpose in hand, and they will respond more readily when their inadequacy is demonstrated. Written law and the conventions will normally complement one another, and each becomes necessary to the proper functioning of the other. To quote from the report of the 1929 Committee of the Imperial Conference:

The association of constitutional conventions with law has long been familiar in the history of the British Commonwealth; it has been characteristic of political development both in the domestic government of these communities and in their relations with each other; it has permeated both executive and legislative power. It has provided a means of harmonizing relations where a purely legal solution of practical problems was impossible, would have impaired free development or would have failed to catch the spirit which gives life to institutions. Such conventions take their place among the constitutional principles and doctrines which are in practice regarded as binding and sacred whatever the powers of Parliament may in theory be.[28]

Unlike the other parts of both the written and the unwritten constitution, conventions are rarely, if ever, legally enforceable.[29] Parliament is itself a court in one sense, of course, and can sit in judgment on its own members and

28/*Report of the Conference on the Operation of Dominion Legislation and Merchant Shipping Legislation* (London, 1929), section 56.

29/It is not necessary here to go into the question of the exact boundary line between law and convention, or, indeed, to consider whether any such line can always be drawn. In most instances the distinction is clear; but there are signs that occasionally the courts themselves are not above incorporating constitutional usages (as they did centuries ago) into the constitutional law of Canada. See Jennings, *The Law and the Constitution*, pp. 99–131; *Labour Conventions Case*, [1936] S.C.R. 461, at pp. 471–7; *Alberta Press Bill Case*, [1938] S.C.R. 100, at pp. 144–6.

practices.[30] But the regular courts recognize only the written constitution, the statute, the order-in-council, the common law, and the general scope of the privileges of Parliament; the conventions must look for support elsewhere. Thus the letter of the law is always carefully observed even although the actual conventional practice may be far different. Many things, for example, are done in the name and through the agency of the governor general, although the real power of decision rests with the governor's advisers. In some matters, this real authority has by convention been transferred a second time. When Canada, for example, took over the power to make her own treaties, the transaction continued to be conducted through the monarch, although his part had been long ago taken over by the British cabinet, and the new change simply involved a substitution of the Canadian for the British ministers as the actual treaty-making authority.

Conventions, being unable to rely on the law, must rest on their general acceptability and on the unfortunate consequences which are likely to ensue if they are disregarded. These consequences are political, or sometimes in the last resort legal, or even both. A cabinet, for example, will resign (or will fall back on a general election) when it has lost the support of the House of Commons, but this immediate relinquishment of power is not made necessary by the operation of any section of the written constitution. A retention of office under these circumstances would, however, be politically suicidal, for it would violate a cherished convention and would almost certainly be punished at the next election. A single defeat, of course, does not necessarily mean that the House of Commons has withdrawn its support;[31] but, as A. V. Dicey pointed out long ago, a cabinet which endeavoured to stay in office after unmistakable defeat would eventually run into legal difficulties as well, for, lacking a majority, it could not obtain parliamentary authorization for expenditures, and sooner or later the pressure on the cabinet would become intolerable.[32]

The practice of referring to the Canadian constitution as a written one is thus far from exact; for the constitutional material is so varied that such a description unduly emphasizes the one formal document and slurs over the equally important informal elements. The above discussion, has, however, served two useful purposes: it has indicated the unsatisfactory nature of the distinction (although it will nevertheless be found to be extremely convenient), and it has drawn

30/And also on others. See Norman Ward, "Called to the Bar of the House of Commons," *Canadian Bar Review*, May 1957, pp. 529–46.

31/See *Can. H. of C. Debates*, Feb. 19 to 28, 1968, pp. 6896–7078. Here the House first defeated a minority government 84 to 82 on a bill, then spent five days deciding 138 to 119 that it had not intended it to be a vote of non-confidence.

32/*The Law of the Constitution* (8th ed., London, 1915), pp. 441–6. A Canadian cabinet can of course govern temporarily with the use of governor general's warrants; but Parliament must be summoned at least once a year (even though a session could be a single day) so that the cabinet would soon be brought to account. See Eugene Forsey, "The Crown and the Constitution," *Dalhousie Review*, xxxiii, no. 1 (Spring 1953), pp. 31–49, and Ward, *The Public Purse*.

attention to the wide assortment of laws, decisions, and usages that enter into the structure and operation of the government. An attempt to fit the Canadian constitution into another classification, namely that of rigid and flexible, depending on the ease or difficulty of formal amendment, is not much better, for this again singles out the British North America Act as the sole criterion. This new classification, however, has the advantage that it stresses the hierarchical nature of the legal powers in Canada and the way in which these legal powers are ascertained, interpreted, and enforced.

The Canadian constitution may thus be labelled as rigid, in that its major provisions cannot be formally changed except by a process which differs from the passage of an ordinary statute of the Canadian Parliament,[33] namely, by an act of the Parliament of Great Britain, following a request from the Canadian Parliament. The British North America Act (and a few other significant British statutes and orders-in-council[34] which for the sake of convenience will be ignored in the following discussion) constitutes the supreme law of the Dominion, and therefore its provisions must control all government bodies in Canada – Dominion, provincial, and municipal. There exist, therefore, two kinds of law-making authorities, the constitution-amending authority, and the ordinary law-making authorities of various kinds; and, corresponding to these, two kinds of law, the law of the written constitution, and other laws of subordinate grade and of inferior validity. Inasmuch as the legislatures in the second group may in turn transmit authority to bodies subordinate to them, there appear additional lower orders in the legal hierarchy. Dominion and provincial legislatures must keep within the jurisdiction specified in the British North America Act (although, owing to the federal structure, they are broadly equal and not subordinate to one another), and the Dominion and provincial statutes must each comply with the terms of the supreme constitutional document. Dominion and provincial orders-in-council must likewise be passed in accordance with the terms of Dominion and provincial statutes respectively, as well as with the provisions of the British North America Act. Similarly, orders passed by inferior bodies within the Dominion or province, such as municipal by-laws, must keep within the scope specified by their statutes of origin and also by the more general provisions of the British North America Act.

The final arbiter which passes on the validity of these laws and which also sees to it that activities by various officials of government are kept within the powers allotted to them, is the judiciary. A Dominion or provincial statute or an enactment by a minor body may be challenged by any interested party (or a question may be referred to the court by the Dominion or provincial govern-

33/A flexible constitution is one which can be amended by an ordinary statute of the legislative body. Great Britain has a flexible constitution, and the Canadian provinces also in that they can amend the provincial constitution (save for the office of lieutenant governor) by an ordinary act of the provincial legislature. Some parts of the BNA Act are amendable by the Canadian Parliament. *Infra*, pp. 119–30.

34/*Supra*, pp. 62–3.

ments) and the court will hear arguments by the opposing parties and give judgment. If the suspected law is considered to be within the power of the body which sponsored it, the court will declare it valid or *intra vires* (within the powers of the enacting body); if otherwise, the court will declare the law to be void or *ultra vires* (beyond the powers of the enacting body). Indeed, in the latter event, the court will hold that the so-called law has never been a law at all, for as the enacting body had no legal power to create such a law, the measure was by that very fact void from the moment of its passage.[35]

Such action by the courts is a natural product of the milieu in which Canadian institutions have developed and it is, indeed, the same power which the British courts have long exercised in pronouncing on the validity of the acts of any inferior law-making body. The British North America Act was a British statute explicitly referring to Canada, and inasmuch as all legislation enacted by Dominion, province, or other governing body in Canada must conform to the terms of this and other applicable British statutes any law which did not so conform was necessarily void. The federal character of the Canadian government made the maintenance of the boundary lines between the Dominion and provincial authorities an unusually vital matter, and the fathers of the federation fully understood the important role to be played by the courts. "Hereafter we shall be bound by an Imperial Act," said the attorney general of Nova Scotia at the Quebec Conference of 1864, "and our judges will have to say what is constitutional under it as regards general or local legislation."[36] The function of the judiciary in Canada thus follows closely that of the judiciary in the United States, for in both countries the courts not only interpret the terms of the written constitution, but also set aside enactments from all sources which are repugnant to its provisions. The question does not arise, of course, in Great Britain. There the constitution is flexible; and any act of the legally omnipotent British Parliament is constitutionally valid.

The power of the courts to declare laws *ultra vires* has, however, never been as important in Canada as in the United States, for the British North America Act contains few of those limitations on the powers of government which are a conspicuous feature of the American constitution. Even the Canadian Bill of Rights, enacted in 1960 and being itself an ordinary act of Parliament, puts no fundamental limits on the powers of Parliament. The American constitution and its amendments not only forbid the federal government, the state governments, and sometimes both of them to exercise a number of common governmental powers, but they also abound in prohibitions designed to protect the rights of the citizen. Thus the American federal government cannot forbid freedom of religious worship, abridge freedom of speech or of the press or of assembly, abolish trial by jury or demand excessive bail, and it must respect a number of other privileges set forth in the so-called Bill of Rights clauses.

35/See Strayer, *Judicial Review of Legislation in Canada.*
36/W. A. Henry, in Pope, *Confederation Documents,* p. 87.

Neither federal nor state governments can enact any *ex post facto* law nor can they "deprive any person of life, liberty, or property without due process of law." The American courts must interpret and enforce all these constitutional guarantees, and some of them have led them far afield and given rise to innumerable cases affecting a wide variety of human relationships concerning which the courts have no certain or stable standards they can apply.

The few constitutional guarantees that occur in the British North America Act are designed to protect the rights of the French and Roman Catholic minorities in Canada and those of the English Protestants in Quebec. The guarantees given in identical terms to the English and French languages have already been mentioned. Further, the schools of sectarian minorities existing at the time of union or authorized later are to be maintained without any interference with their privileges.

But other rights of the citizen are left untouched by the act, although, following the English practice, they receive protection under various statutes and the common law, and the federal government has plans to extend substantially the written guarantees entrenched in the constitution.[37] For several years before 1960 there was a growing conviction in Canada that the constitutional and other guarantees of fundamental liberties were insufficient, a conviction amply justified by a number of events. The "padlock law" of Quebec (1937) which, aimed at communism, struck also at freedom of speech and other rights of the citizen; the persecution of the Jehovah's Witnesses in Quebec (1949–53) which attacked the freedom of religion; the "press bill" of Alberta, introduced in 1937 and later declared *ultra vires,* which endeavoured to control the press; the threatened deportation of Canadian citizens of Japanese descent (1945–6); and the arbitrary arrest, detention, and interrogation of citizens in the spy hunt of 1946, were all disturbing signs of a weakening concern by Dominion and provincial governments for personal rights and liberties. None of these, moreover, occurred during the war, when certain of these rights might conceivably have had to be temporarily relinquished.

The questionable nature of some of the measures cited may perhaps be more readily apprehended by a consideration of the following extract from a report by a committee of the Canadian Bar Association on the Quebec padlock law:

It gives the Attorney-General great powers, which he can exercise in the first instance without the slightest judicial restraint, and takes away all of the safeguards which even an ordinary criminal enjoys before conviction. Irrespective of whether one is a radical or not it is difficult to admit that legislation is good which gives any official the right to padlock anyone's home simply because he suspects that Communism is propagated from it. It is true that after the padlock is locked the owner may apply to the court for relief, but Communism is not defined by the Act, and there are probably very few people, including the judges, who can tell what Communism

---

37/See Trudeau, *The Constitution and the People of Canada,* especially pp. 14–22.

is. From the point of view of our jurisprudence, it might be as well to observe that possibly it is under laws such as this that in other lands the homes of respectable and law-abiding citizens are ransacked simply because their owners do not wear a brown or a black shirt.[38]

Among those disturbed by these invasions of citizens' rights was Mr J. G. Diefenbaker, MP, who in 1957 became prime minister after an election campaign in which further protection for rights was pledged. The result was the Bill of Rights of 1960, already mentioned, which recited a conventional list of freedoms which "have existed and shall continue to exist" in Canada, and further declared that "every law of Canada shall, unless it is expressly declared by an Act of the Parliament of Canada that it shall operate notwithstanding the Canadian Bill of Rights, be so construed and applied as not to abrogate, abridge or infringe ... any of the rights or freedoms herein recognized and declared." The bill, though an admirable step in the right direction, was criticized not only because it was not entrenched as part of the British North America Act, but also because it offered no protection against invasions of rights by the provinces.[39]

Many aspects of fundamental rights are thus still left to the discretion of provincial legislatures, rather as if rights were not the attributes of Canadian citizens but those of the inhabitants of a particular area. "No province," said Mr Justice Cannon in the Alberta Press Bill Case, "has the power to reduce in that province the political rights of its citizens as compared with those enjoyed by the citizens of other provinces of Canada," and this *obiter dictum* (although further confirmation by the courts is desirable before it can be accepted as definitely settled) would seem to apply to many rights other than those concerned with the freedom of the press. Yet even the Dominion Parliament has not at all times proved to be sufficiently zealous in upholding the rights and liberties of the individual. The people of Great Britain appear to have acquired a veneration for statutory and common law rights which is derived from many centuries of constant endeavour and stubborn resistance to abuses and which has made them jealous of any threatened encroachments; but the tradition in Canada is not nearly so strong or so deep-rooted and hence affords in itself an inadequate safeguard against attack. The fact that the Canadian Bill of Rights applies only to those fields of human activities under Dominion jurisdiction, and can itself be amended

38/Canadian Bar Association, *Reports of Committees, 1937,* pp. 36–7.
39/*Can. Statutes,* 8–9 Eliz. II, c. 44. See also *Can. H. of C. Debates,* July 1, 4, 7, Aug. 1–4, 1960. For a critique of the Bill of Rights see Scott, *Civil Liberties and Canadian Federalism;* and *Canadian Bar Review,* March 1959 (a special issue devoted to the Bill of Rights); and Walter Tarnopolsky, *The Canadian Bill of Rights* (Toronto, 1966). See also Douglas Schmeiser, *Civil Liberties in Canada* (Oxford, 1964); Edward McWhinney and Armand de Mestral, "The Provinces and the Protection of Civil Liberties in Canada: The Province of Quebec," in Ontario Advisory Committee on Confederation, *Background Papers and Reports,* pp. 37–73; W. R. Lederman, "The Nature and Problems of a Bill of Rights," *ibid.,* pp. 25–36; *Royal Commission Inquiry into Civil Rights* (Toronto, 1968–9).

by an ordinary act of Parliament, means that fundamental protection for all rights is still lacking. At the very least, however, the Bill of Rights has aroused interest in itself, and it is now a common occurrence for members of Parliament to draw the attention of their fellow parliamentarians to real and alleged violations of the law.

Another Canadian inheritance which is closely identified with some of these fundamental rights of the citizen is the rule or supremacy of law, a long-established principle of the British constitution. The exact meaning and implications of this principle are not readily stated,[40] but its essence is the restriction on arbitrary authority in government and the necessity for all acts of government to be authorized by "reasonably precise" laws[41] as applied and interpreted by the courts. The provision in the old Massachusetts constitution that "this shall be a government of laws and not of men" was clearly a vain hope, but it was an endeavour to state in one phrase substantially the same idea – the certainty of legal procedures, the absence of untrammelled official power, the protection of the citizen against unknown and unpredictable authority. The increasing complexity of modern government, the growing emphasis on the social rather than the individual good, and the resulting need for government intervention in almost all fields of human endeavour have inevitably resulted in far wider discretionary powers being given to executive and administrative officials, accompanied by a consequent narrowing of the rule of law. Thus the sweeping accountability of officials to the courts of law when the legality of their acts was in question has had its scope somewhat diminished by the grant of wider and more general legal powers, and this has tended to a limited degree to remove the acts of the officials from judicial scrutiny. Despite this modification, the rule of law remains a cardinal principle of the Canadian constitution and a sturdy bulwark against abuse of power. The following comment on the rule of law in Great Britain is equally applicable to Canada:

For a long time now, Parliament has been granting to officials special powers to take action not justified under the ordinary law, and it has been limiting the right of the citizen to have the actions of officials scrutinized by the judicial power. Yet there has been no general removal of officials from judicial surveillance, and it remains true in most cases that anyone who asserts that he has been wronged by the action of a government official can bring that official before the courts of law to answer for his conduct. The official may justify himself by pointing to an act of Parliament which gives him a special privilege to do what he has done. But he cannot turn aside the complaint merely by asserting an exalted official status and an inscrutable executive expediency in what he has done. This state can throw away the conscript's life but it cannot conscript him in the first instance on the plea of high policy or public expedience except as supported by law sanctioned by Parliament. The Rule of Law,

40/Dicey, *The Law of the Constitution,* pp. 179–409; Jennings, *The Law and the Constitution,* pp. 41–61.
41/Jennings, *The Law and the Constitution,* p. 47.

although qualified today by the grant of special powers to officials, remains an indispensable instrument for ensuring that government remains servant.[42]

It is evident from the historical account of the development of responsible government,[43] that Canada long ago accepted without reservation the British idea of the union of the executive and legislative branches of government. This was, of course, the antithesis of the system adopted in the United States which embodied the opposing principle of the division or separation of powers. The latter system was designed to prevent the exercise of despotic control by cutting the executive, legislative, and judicial authorities apart from one another and giving each its own powers to exercise to the almost complete exclusion of the others. Thus the president, the Congress, and the judiciary have their respective spheres set forth in the written constitution, and although this division (particularly as it affects the executive and legislative branches) may make a smooth and efficient government impossible, nevertheless, despite this possibility, a resultant of forces usually develops, decisions are reached, and action is taken.

The contrasting theory of union of powers brings the chief branches of government under the control of one of their number – in a democracy, this will be the legislature – and final direction and authority emanate from this source. The government of Great Britain, the outstanding embodiment of this principle, possesses in its Parliament the body which can dominate completely the two other branches. In practice, however, the British Parliament's control over the judiciary is virtually never exercised, not because this control is not available, but rather because it is universally recognized to be undesirable; for the nature of the judicial function is such that any suspicion of interference or domination would destroy the greater part of the usefulness of the courts. The executive or cabinet, on the other hand, is constantly responsible to Parliament, and it is through this relationship that the principle of union of powers finds its chief expression.

Canada, as stated above, has retained the British idea of the close sympathy between the legislative and executive branches, accomplished by the pre-eminence of the former, and the members of the cabinet thus sit in Parliament and are responsible at all times to the House of Commons. Both legislature and executive have, as in Britain, abandoned virtually all control over the judiciary; but the legal position in the two countries is not quite the same. The virtual independence of the judiciary in Great Britain exists legally[44] by virtue of voluntary parliamentary abstention and self-denial; but in Canada the ban on interference is in large measure imposed on Parliament by the provisions of

42/J. A. Corry and J. E. Hodgetts, *Democratic Government and Politics* (3rd ed., Toronto, 1959), p. 96.
43/*Supra*, pp. 9–19.
44/It should be noted that in Great Britain the tradition of an independent judiciary is, no doubt, even stronger than the statute. The statutory guarantee is found in the Act of Settlement (1701); but the tradition and practice antedate this by several centuries.

the written constitution which Parliament in itself has no power to change. The British North America Act, while stating that the judges (with a few minor exceptions) are to be appointed by the governor general, ensures the independence of all superior court judges by providing that they shall hold office (until the age of seventy-five[45]) during good behaviour, and can be removed by the governor general only after a joint address of both Houses of Parliament. This guarantee of the independence of the judiciary through formal constitutional provisions marks a limited acceptance of the principle of separation of powers, although in no wise disturbing the idea of union of powers as applied to the vital relationship between the executive and the legislative bodies.

45/The retirement age was set by constitutional amendment in 1960.

5 The distribution of powers

THE CONSTITUTION OF CANADA has now (1970) been undergoing careful scrutiny for several years, and for the past two of these continuing committees of ministers and officials from federal and provincial levels have been examining specific proposals for amendment. It is a noteworthy feature of these negotiations that while some of the provinces, with Quebec the most conspicuous, have been pressing for wider powers, the proposals of the federal government have not included any general realignment of the distribution set forth in the British North America Act.[1] That original distribution had of course as its main purpose the creation of the federation, and the provisions dealing with Dominion and provincial powers and relationships comprise a large and important section of the written constitution. Many of these provisions have also given rise to disputes and uncertainties, and they have furnished the material for the constant and doubtless inevitable struggle between the rival national and local authorities. Moreover, as these same provisions appear in the formally rigid constitution, they have not been readily amendable, even when the courts have read into them meanings which were never intended and which, in some instances at least, failed to coincide with the country's needs.

A federal system implies by its very definition an aggregation of local governing units, each exercising its own separate powers apart from those which are in the hands of the central or federal government. Local autonomy is thus an essential characteristic, although the degree and kind of self-government which the units enjoy can vary materially from one federation to another. The deliberate plan which was adopted in creating the Dominion of Canada was to form a federation of a highly centralized kind, and to that end certain special powers and functions were placed in the hands of the central government. The manner in which some of these have worked themselves out in practice has already been mentioned,[2] and the following pages will discuss some aspects of this development in greater detail.

1/See Trudeau, *The Constitution and the People of Canada.*
2/*Supra*, pp. 26–9.

A federal system may also imply (as it does in the United States) equal constitutional standing and privileges for all the component parts.[3] The Canadian federation only partially recognizes the idea of equality. The general powers of all the provinces are the same, but certain other elements in the provincial position and status depend not upon abstract and equal rights, but upon the terms under which a particular province entered the federation or even upon those which it has been able to conclude at a later date. This is obvious in the financial arrangements between the Dominion and the provinces; for although general principles have been enunciated and followed, these have often been circumvented by devious devices and substantially affected in the aggregate by the use of supplemental grants to overcome certain needs or alleged injustices.

The unequal position of the provinces is manifest, however, in other matters as well. The usual practice has been for the province to have vested in it the ownership of all public lands; but these were retained by the Dominion when Manitoba, Alberta, and Saskatchewan were created and joined the federation. The arrangement may have been wise at the time, but it was discriminatory; and even although the Dominion paid an additional annual grant as compensation,[4] it led inevitably to accusations of unfair treatment and the eventual transfer of these resources to the aggrieved provinces. The French language has constitutional protection in Quebec which it does not have in any other province, though other provinces are moving to extend its use.[5] The terms of admission of Newfoundland contained special clauses regarding education and the manufacture and sale of oleomargarine.[6] The provinces have never had the same representation in the Canadian Senate, and a strong case can be made against any doctrinaire equality of members; but there is not even an intelligible scheme or plan which provides equitable representation. Manitoba was given on entrance a flexible number of senators, increasing with population from two to four; British Columbia (admitted a year later) was given three; Saskatchewan and Alberta were on their admission each given a minimum of four which with increases in population might be raised to five or six. Even when the western membership in the Senate was altered in 1915, it bore little relation to the representation from the eastern provinces, which was broadly based on population tempered with ideas of equality.

3/In the United States, for example, Congress may endeavour to impose conditions on a new state as a condition of entrance, but these conditions cease to be binding the moment the state is admitted to the union.
4/Manitoba for years received neither land nor compensation. See Chester Martin, *The Natural Resources Question* (Winnipeg, 1920).
5/Manitoba was originally established as a bilingual province. French is, of course, widely recognized outside Quebec, in both Dominion law and practice (as in the Canada Elections Act and the Citizenship Act), and the Official Languages Act will mean much larger extensions. It is important to note that while within any one province both English and French may be used in a variety of matters under federal jurisdiction, the same will not necessarily be true of matters under provincial jurisdiction.
6/*Can. Statutes*, 13 Geo. VI, c. 1. Schedule sections 17, 46.

Leaving these occasional incongruities (and there are others) to one side, the provinces are of equal status, and they operate without any serious interference from the Dominion. The latter possesses, it is true, a certain potential control over the provinces through the lieutenant governors and the power of disallowance,[7] but although this cannot be entirely ignored, it is (as indicated elsewhere) used infrequently. Provincial powers are as full and as complete as those of the Dominion within the areas allotted by the British North America Act, and both Dominion and provincial legislatures may delegate their authority to other bodies of their own creation, but not to each other. "The powers of the legislature of the province," said Mr Justice Riddell, "are the same in intension though not in extension as those of the Imperial Parliament. The Legislature is limited in the territory in which it may legislate, and in the subjects; the Imperial Parliament is not – that is the whole difference."[8] The Dominion and provincial legislatures between them cover the entire field of legislation.[9] There are thus, as pointed out in the preceding chapter, few constitutional limitations of any consequence (save those of jurisdiction and the pragmatic problems that can arise when a field is divided between Dominion and provincial jurisdiction) to hamper the exercise of legislative power in Canada; and wisdom, justice, rights of property, and similar considerations restrict only so far as the legislature chooses to heed them. A provincial legislature can, if it wishes, confiscate property without compensation; it can take what belongs to A and give it to B; it can alter the wills of deceased persons; it can enact *ex post facto* laws. An attempt, however, to prevent the validity of its own legislation being challenged in the courts was declared *ultra vires* in 1937, on the ground that if such an attempt were upheld the legislature would have the power to destroy the written constitution under which it was created.[10] A provincial legislature also has constituent powers and the entire framework of government in the province (except for the office of lieutenant governor) can be altered by the passage of any ordinary statute. Five provincial legislatures in Canada have abolished one chamber in the legislature but it may be doubted if they could legally abolish the legislature altogether or abolish elections;[11] all of them have changed their original four-year term to five, and on four occasions the existing term has been extended as a war measure; the Legislative Assembly

7/*Supra*, pp. 28–9; *infra*, pp. 213–17.

8/W. R. Riddell, *The Canadian Constitution in Form and in Fact* (New York, 1923), pp. 15–16. The quotation is an over-statement; the acts of the imperial Parliament, for example, are not signed by a lieutenant governor appointed by another government, nor are they subject to disallowance by another government.

9/Some authorities have reservations on this point. See, for example, *Saumur* v. *City of Quebec*, [1953] 2 S.C.R. 299; *Switzman* v. *Elbling*, [1957] 7 D.L.R. (2nd) 337; *Murphy* v. *C.P.R.*, [1958] S.C.R. 626.

10/*Ottawa Valley Power Co.* v. *Hydro-Electric Power Commission*, [1937] O.R. 265.

11/See Eugene A. Forsey, "Extension of the Life of the Legislature," *Canadian Journal of Economics and Political Science*, XXVI, no. 4 (Nov. 1960), pp. 604–16. Dr Forsey points out that provincial legislatures can constitutionally extend their own lives indefinitely, subject only to the use of rarely used sections of the BNA Act.

of Alberta – to give an extreme example – enacted in 1917 that twelve of its members who had enlisted for overseas service were to be members of the next legislature without the necessity of running in an election.

There is, however, one important constitutional limitation on the delegation of legislative powers, clearly enunciated in 1951 by the Supreme Court,[12] which arises from the nature of the constitution itself, namely, that neither Dominion nor province can directly delegate its powers to the other. This is by no means a purely theoretical point. Both Dominion and provinces have time and again run into difficulties because the jurisdiction of the one alone was not complete enough to enable it to regulate adequately an entire operation.[13] The regulation of the marketing of certain agricultural products, for example, is under the province so far as it involves merely buying and selling within the provincial area, but when these transactions enter into the field of interprovincial or export trade they come under Dominion authority.[14] Provincial statutes, which have endeavoured to hand over to the Dominion the jurisdiction of those provinces on such matters so that one standard of grading and inspection could be set up and enforced by the Dominion, have been declared *ultra vires* by the Canadian courts. Other expedients are therefore being tried out in order to avoid the difficulty, and in several areas administrative delegation, rather than legal, has been successfully employed. In the meantime, successive Dominion-provincial conferences have discussed direct delegation, and it is possible that the British North America Act will some day be amended to permit it under certain circumstances. The "Fulton-Favreau Formula," discussed in a later chapter, included a delegation clause which was severely criticized by many authorities.

The distribution of powers between the Dominion government on the one hand and the provincial governments on the other, dominates the entire federal scheme. The British North America Act stated this distribution in terms of legislative powers; but this grant implies a corresponding allocation of powers between the Dominion and provincial executive authorities. Other parts of the act[15] carried over the existing statutory executive powers to the governor general and the lieutenant governors of Ontario and Quebec within their respective fields and provided for the continuance of the executive authority in Nova Scotia and New Brunswick. The executive received also a delegation of prerogative powers from the Crown in Britain to the governor general, and from the governor general to the lieutenant governors by means of the pre-

12/*Nova Scotia Delegation Reference*, [1951] s.c.r. 31. The courts have, none the less, sanctioned indirect delegation. See *P.E.I. Potato Marketing Board* v. *Willis Inc. and A.G. of Canada*, [1952] s.c.r. 392.

13/See J. A. Corry, "Difficulties of Divided Jurisdiction," *Rowell-Sirois Report*, Appendix no. 7.

14/The transactions are supposed to come under provincial jurisdiction as "property and civil rights" when taking place within the province, and under Dominion jurisdiction as "trade and commerce" when reaching outside provincial boundaries.

15/Sections 12, 64, 65.

rogative instruments.[16] In all cases where executive or administrative powers are in doubt the courts will act as arbiters in the same manner as in those cases which involve disputes over legislative jurisdiction. In the judicial sphere, the federal idea which is so characteristic of the legislature and the executive is less noticeable. There are both Dominion and provincial courts; but these stand in vertical series, the one above the other, composing virtually one homogeneous system. The plan is doubtless somewhat illogical as a federal arrangement, but it is simple, and it is little troubled by conflicts of judicial jurisdiction; its continued existence in its present form is a matter of choice, since the Dominion undoubtedly has the power to establish additional courts to deal with matters under federal jurisdiction, and has used it.

The distribution of legislative powers in Canada was based on the federal principle that matters of a general interest were to be given to the Dominion and those of a particular or local interest were to be given to the provinces; and although many disagreements might have arisen as to the exact location of this line of division, it seems to have caused little controversy in 1864–7. The original allocation of power was not made, however, on any *a priori* basis; it represented the greatest common measure of agreement that could be formulated among conflicting interests at the time, and the primary test it had to meet was the approval it could command from the federating colonies. John A. Macdonald's comment that they had "avoided all conflict of jurisdiction and authority" was apparently a fair statement of the view entertained by those who had drafted the Quebec Resolutions, although it later proved to be a vain hope. Finance – a special aspect of distribution – had produced much greater difficulties; but an acceptable scheme had been arranged at the Quebec Conference, and these terms had been somewhat modified at London to make them more palatable to Nova Scotia and New Brunswick.[17]

In spite of this fairly auspicious start, the distribution of powers, and particularly the financial arrangements and the allocation of financial authority, has rarely, if ever, had the cordial and united approval of the provinces. Nova Scotia was dissatisfied from the outset with the entire scheme of Confederation; the financial disputes, grievances, and settlements, which have involved every province in Canada, have been unending;[18] a number of provincial and Dominion–provincial conferences have been held to consider constitutional changes and more favourable financial terms;[19] the careers of many provincial premiers, such as Mowat, Mercier, Blair, Fielding, and Duplessis, have been built on the sure foundation of opposition to federal policies[20] and existing

16/*Infra*, pp. 147–8.   17/*Supra*, pp. 24–6; 33–5.   18/*Infra*, chap. VI.

19/See J. A. Maxwell, *Federal Subsidies to the Provincial Governments in Canada* (Cambridge, Mass, 1937), pp. 96–9, 108–12, 145–7; *Minutes of the Proceedings in Conference of the Representatives of the Provinces, 1887, 1902, 1906, 1910, 1913, 1918, 1926* (1926).

20/Sir Arthur Keith has gone a step further than this: "The true federal character of the constitution, despite its tendency to centralization, was mainly secured by the energy

relationships. Recent years have created additional conflicts within the federation which are closely related to the distribution of powers. To the differences in language, religion, law, and culture – all of which existed at Confederation – has been added a galling difference in the economic position of the provinces. This economic inequality has had a profound effect not only upon the ability of the less favoured provinces to discharge their constitutional functions adequately, but also on the standards of living and on the general regard which the people of one province have for the people of another.[21] While it is doubtless true that the combined centripetal forces in Canada are stronger than in 1867, there is certainly no reason whatever to suppose that these have yet overcome the opposing forces of suspicion and disruption, as the separatist movements of recent years, together with their root causes, have amply demonstrated.

The early advocates of provincial rights, even when they threatened secession, were able to make little impression on the written constitution; but they had a high nuisance value and were able as a result to wring financial concessions from the Dominion. This element, which was always dominant in Nova Scotia in these early years, gradually increased in strength in other parts of Canada as the centralizing impulse began to weaken,[22] and as provincial rights became more closely identified with Liberalism, the Conservative federal government not unnaturally became less conciliatory. In the 1880s, however, the provincial rights movement received from an unexpected quarter substantial reinforcements which began to undermine the constitutional citadel itself. In 1883 the Judicial Committee of the Privy Council[23] rendered the first of a long series of decisions which had the effect of greatly increasing the powers and importance of the provinces and giving Canada a more evenly balanced form of federalism than Macdonald and his supporters had ever intended.[24] This

of Sir Oliver Mowat on behalf of Ontario. It was he who secured the recognition of the provincial rights as representing the Crown to escheats; of the power of the legislatures to define their privileges; of the power of the Lieutenant-Governors to receive authority to pardon offenders under provincial law; of the declaration of the provincial title to the freehold of the lands occupied by the Indians ... " A. B. Keith, *Responsible Government in the Dominions* (2nd ed., Oxford, 1928), I, p. 589. See also C. R. W. Biggar, *Sir Oliver Mowat* (Toronto, 1905).

21/*Infra*, pp. 105–7.

22/J. A. Maxwell, "Aspects of Canadian Federalism," *Dalhousie Review*, Oct. 1936, pp. 277–8.

23/This court, usually referred to as the Judicial Committee, although sometimes called by the full name or even under the misleading term Privy Council, sits in London, is composed of British judges (aided at times by judges from other parts of the Commonwealth), and is still the final court of appeal for a few members of the Commonwealth. Canadian appeals now cannot go beyond the Supreme Court of Canada, and many newer members of the Commonwealth have joined their older colleague in having local courts serve as final courts of appeal. *Infra*, pp. 387–8.

24/There were, of course, also anti-centralists in the 1860s, whose views are widely quoted by anti-centralists today. See L. P. Pigeon, "The Meaning of Provincial Autonomy," in Meekison, *Canadian Federalism*, pp. 159–67; *Report of the Royal Commission of Inquiry on Constitutional Problems*, pp. 152–71.

judicial enlargement of provincial powers was well established by the turn of the century, and the years immediately following introduced yet another element which greatly enlarged the sphere of provincial activity. This was the growing conviction – common throughout the world – that governments should actively intervene to promote social and economic welfare; and these parvenus were under the Canadian constitution largely members of the provincial family. This new development, however welcome to the provincial governments in the abstract, proved a doubtful privilege in terms of costs; and all the provinces, and especially the poorer ones, found the financial burden becoming more and more insupportable. The depression of the thirties (with its load of unemployment relief) greatly accentuated this, and the lessons of the depression and the war brought new ideas of state control which reversed the developments of three-quarters of a century and placed increasing powers in the hands of the Dominion, though judicial decision itself has played a somewhat equivocal role in this trend. The post-war period, again, has seen a swing away from centralized control.

The succeeding pages will indicate in some measure the way in which the constitutional distribution of powers has developed since Confederation. It is a story which might well point the moral in a dissertation on the futility of long-term political planning; for the greater part of the development has been away from the avowed intentions of the founders. This chapter is primarily concerned with the constitutional grant of powers to the Dominion and provincial legislatures and the way in which certain of those grants have been interpreted by the courts. The next chapter is devoted to one special kind of grant, finance; but here the constitutional provisions have been secondary. For although the financial relationships of the Dominion and the provinces received extensive treatment in the written constitution, the financial adjustments have taken place largely on an extra-constitutional basis.

The distribution of power is presented in only its main outlines. It is necessarily oversimplified and it will thus suggest, rather than give in any detail, the complexity of the subject and some of the difficulties which have surrounded the working of the Canadian federal system.

POWERS OF THE DOMINION PARLIAMENT

It will be recalled that the intention in 1867 was to create a strongly centralized federation,[25] and to that end the Dominion was endowed with substantial authority. This grant of power appears for the most part in section 91 of the act, and it is formulated in a double statement: first, a comprehensive grant to "make laws for the peace, order, and good government of Canada" in relation

25/This assertion is based on the BNA Act itself, not the *obiter dicta* of statesmen of the 1860s.

to those matters not given to the provinces; secondly, a list of specific powers which are given in detail "for greater certainty, but not so as to restrict the generality" of the comprehensive grant. Despite the double statement there is thus one general sweeping grant of power with certain explicit powers being mentioned by way of example. It will nevertheless be more convenient to deal here with the specific illustrative powers and return later to the general statement, while noting in passing that the act introduces this dichotomy not as a double grant, but as a means of emphasis and clarification.

The list of twenty-nine (now thirty-one) specific powers which were supposed to indicate the kind of exclusive authority vested in the Dominion includes the following: amendment of certain sections of the British North America Act dealing solely with the federal government (added in 1949); public debt; regulation of trade and commerce; unemployment insurance (added in 1940); raising of money "by any mode or system of taxation"; borrowing money; postal services; penitentiaries; defence; navigation and shipping; fisheries; marriage and divorce; currency; banks and banking; bills of exchange; promissory notes; copyright; naturalization; and criminal law. Certain other sections of the act add to this list, notably a subsection of section 92, which gives the Dominion jurisdiction over steamship lines, railways, canals, telegraphs, and other works extending beyond the limits of a province, and also over such works, even although wholly within a province, "declared by the Parliament of Canada to be for the general advantage of Canada or for the advantage of two or more of the provinces."

POWERS OF THE PROVINCIAL LEGISLATURES

Section 92 lists (with a few exceptions given elsewhere in the act) the chief provincial powers – not by any comprehensive grant, as in section 91, but only as an exclusive power to make laws in relation to matters coming within sixteen enumerated classes of subjects. These include the following: the amendment of the provincial constitution (except in regard to the office of lieutenant governor); "direct taxation within the province in order to the raising of a revenue for provincial purposes"; borrowing money on the credit of the province; establishment and maintenance of provincial offices; provincial prisons; hospitals; asylums; municipal institutions; local licences, incorporation of companies with provincial objects; solemnization of marriage; local works (other than those given to the Dominion); property and civil rights; administration of justice in the province, including the constitution, maintenance, and organization of provincial courts; procedure in civil matters; and the imposition of punishments for enforcing provincial laws.

While a few of these topics might conceivably have been given to the Dominion Parliament, they were at least intended to cover essentially local matters which could best be dealt with by the provincial authority; one of them, it will be seen, turned out to have unsuspected depths. A number of the subjects are explicitly confined by the additions of the necessary words "in the province," and others bear limitations which present a significant contrast to the wider scope of Dominion authority.[26] Thus taxation is "direct taxation" only, and to be spent for provincial purposes; "local" works are expressly limited by certain other and more general works given to the Dominion; the incorporation of companies is confined to those "with provincial objects." Almost every clause indicates the intention of the founders of the constitution to endow the provinces with extremely modest functions within a restricted sphere, and this is further emphasized by the nature of the last subsection which contains a grant of local residual power in keeping with the others – "generally all matters of a merely local or private nature in the province."

CONCURRENT POWERS

Two powers, immigration and agriculture, are given to both Dominion and province by section 95 of the original act. Either or both legislatures may exercise jurisdiction in relation to these subjects, but if a conflict of legislation should result, the Dominion law is to prevail. These concurrent powers were written into the constitution with some misgiving;[27] but while in agriculture there has been an overlapping of administrative activity, the duplication has been small when compared to the volume of work performed. A persistent effort has been made in recent years to delimit the Dominion and provincial fields, and genuine co-ordination and co-operation have usually been obtained.

In 1951 section 94A was added to the British North America Act, thereby giving the Canadian Parliament authority to enact laws in relation to old age pensions. Inasmuch as this power was also possessed by the provincial legislatures, a third concurrent power was thereby created. In this particular case, however, the rule to be applied in the event of a conflict was reversed as compared to that for agriculture and immigration, for section 94A stated that Dominion legislation relating to old age pensions should not affect existing or future provincial legislation on that subject. Section 94A was amended in 1964.[28]

EDUCATION

Education is nominally and normally under the jurisdiction of the province, but under certain circumstances the Dominion is given a power of intervention.

26/See, for example, section 94 of the BNA Act.
27/Pope, *Confederation Documents*, pp. 80–1.
28/*Brit. Statutes*, 14–15 Geo. VI, c. 32; 12–13 Eliz. II, c. 73.

Section 93 of the British North America Act states that "in and for each province" the legislature shall have the exclusive power to make laws in relation to education, provided it does not prejudicially affect any right or privilege with respect to denominational schools which any class of persons had established by law in the province at the time of union, and subject to an appeal by the Protestant or Roman Catholic minority in any province to the Governor-in-Council from any act or decision of any provincial authority affecting such rights or privileges which may exist or to be later established in the province.[29] The Governor-General-in-Council, acting on its own initiative or in response to such an appeal, may order remedial measures, and the Canadian Parliament is empowered to enact legislation in accordance with these recommendations, or in any other way it may see fit, in order to execute the provisions of this section of the act.

The education clause in the agreement under which Newfoundland entered the federation gave substantially the same protection to sectarian rights in education as section 93 mentioned above, but differed in the sanction provided for their enforcement. No provision was made for an appeal to the Governor-General-in-Council or for the intervention of the Parliament of Canada, so that the only guardian of these sectarian rights in education therefore became the courts who will have to decide upon any alleged violation.[30] This has, in fact, been found for years past to be the most satisfactory method in the other provinces which were affected by section 93, and the participation of the Governor-General-in-Council and the Parliament of Canada has in practice become obsolete.

A MERE STATEMENT OF SUBJECT-MATTER IS NOT IN
ITSELF DECISIVE IN DETERMINING JURISDICTION

The distribution of power outlined above is not nearly as simple as the enumeration might suggest, and even without touching upon other complications (some of which will be discussed presently) it is well at this point to indicate a few difficulties.

(a) There is in some instances a seeming incompatibility between grants of power to the Dominion and to the province, for a number of the subsections in 91 and 92 apparently overlap. This overlap does not necessarily rule out the effective exercise of the stated powers by both authorities; for clearly no actual conflict was contemplated when the act was drafted, and it must be interpreted, if at all possible, in such a way that any clash is avoided. The most obvious illustration is in regard to taxation, the Dominion having power to raise money "by any mode or system of taxation," and the provinces being given authority

29/Special sections designed to protect minority rights in education appear in the acts creating Manitoba, Alberta, and Saskatchewan.
30/*Can. Statutes*, 13 Geo. vi, c. 1. Schedule, section 17.

to impose "direct taxation within the province in order to the raising of a revenue for provincial purposes." Thus both Dominion and province can impose direct taxes, even those of the same kind and levied on the same source. Both Dominion and province have imposed income taxes on the same income and succession duties on the same estate. Nevertheless the powers are deemed to be separate and to involve no actual conflict. "They are two independent powers springing from the same source which do not interfere with each other. The power granted to the Dominion is broad and inclusive of any and every sort of taxation, while the power of taxation given to the provinces is definitely limited in kind and area ... Each power is the necessary adjunct of mutually independent governments and the distinction is one of purpose, not of kind."[31]

It may be mentioned in passing that the courts have drawn the distinction between "direct" and other taxes on the apparent incidence of the tax; a direct tax being interpreted according to the words of John Stuart Mill as one which is "demanded from the very persons who it is intended or desired should pay it." Any modern economist will criticize the feasibility of making any useful distinction of this kind, and the courts have, indeed, stated that "it is the nature and general tendency of the tax and not its incidence in particular or special cases"[32] which must determine the category in which it is to be placed. Thus a provincial tax on a person who purchased fuel oil within the province at the time of its first sale after manufacture or importation into the province was held to be *ultra vires* because the tax would in all likelihood be passed on to someone else, and it was therefore considered to be indirect.[33] On the other hand, the courts have held that a provincial tax imposed on a consumer of fuel oil (in proportion to the amount of oil consumed) was a direct tax, because it would generally be borne by the person who actually paid it, and the tax was therefore declared to be *intra vires* the provincial legislature.[34]

Other clauses dealing with specific grants of power furnish further illustrations of apparent conflicts. Thus property and civil rights are given to the province; while banking, bills of exchange, promissory notes, patents, and copyrights, are given to the Dominion, although these would all normally be included in property and civil rights. "These sections of enumeration," said Edward Blake, "must be construed so as to avoid a conflict; and this is to be done by cutting out of whatever may be the larger, the more general, the wider, the vaguer enumeration of one section, so much as is comprised in some narrower, more definite, more precise enumeration in the other section. As, for example, in one section you find 'property and civil rights,' in the other 'bills

---

31/W. P. M. Kennedy and D. C. Wells, *The Law of the Taxing Power in Canada* (Toronto, 1931), p. 15.

32/*City of Halifax* v. *Fairbanks Estate*, [1928] A.C. 117, at p. 126.

33/*Attorney-General for British Columbia* v. *Canadian Pacific Railway Co.*, [1927] A.C. 934.

34/*Attorney-General for British Columbia* v. *Kingcome Navigation Co.*, [1934] A.C. 45. See Kennedy and Wells, *Taxing Power in Canada*, pp. 49–65.

and notes'; you excise from 'property and civil rights' so much as is comprised in 'bills and notes.' "[35] The same general principle of interpretation has been applied to other clauses with varying results. Thus the restricted meaning which has been attached to the Dominion's power over "the regulation of trade and commerce" has been derived in no small measure from a similar attempt to reconcile and interpret different but related parts of sections 91 and 92.[36]

(b) Legislation may be enacted by Dominion or province which may on the surface be within its legal powers, but which may have the actual effect of trespassing on the territory of the other. The courts look to "the pith and substance" of the statute and not to its superficial character, and they will not hesitate to declare *ultra vires* a law which in their opinion is only ostensibly and not in fact within the jurisdiction of the enacting body. Thus the Dominion cannot by purporting to enact a criminal law under its admitted powers in section 91 "appropriate to itself exclusively a field of jurisdiction in which, apart from such a procedure, it could exert no legal authority," and the courts have declared such attempts *ultra vires*.[37] Similarly, when Alberta levied a tax on the paid-up capital and on the reserve funds of the Canadian chartered banks doing business in the province, the Judicial Committee held that the true intent was not an effort to raise a revenue for provincial purposes, but to interfere with banking operations, which are placed by the British North America Act under the Dominion. The act was accordingly declared *ultra vires* the Alberta legislature.[38]

(c) A particular subject may not be wholly under the jurisdiction of either Dominion or province, but certain aspects of the same subject may be under the one while other aspects are under the other. "Subjects which in one aspect and for one purpose fall within section 92," the Judicial Committee of the Privy Council frequently stated, "may in another aspect and for another purpose fall within section 91." An outstanding illustration is liquor legislation, a subject not explicitly mentioned in the British North America Act. A decision in 1882[39] held that the Canada Temperance Act (which provided for local option) was *intra vires* the Dominion Parliament in that it was in relation to public order and safety; whereas in the following year an Ontario act, which provided for the licensing and local control of the sale of liquor by the provincial authority, was also upheld on the ground that it involved essentially police and municipal regulation of a local character.[40] Other kinds of liquor legislation have exhibited the same double characteristics. Similarly, a pro-

35/In *Canadian Pacific Railway Co.* v. *Corporation of Bonsecours*, quoted in A. H. F. Lefroy, *Canada's Federal System* (Toronto, 1913), pp. 113–14. See also *Citizens Insurance Co.* v. *Parsons*, 7 App. Cas. 96, at pp. 108–9, 112–13.

36/See *Toronto Electric Commissioners* v. *Snider*, [1925] A.C. 396; Senate of Canada, *Report on the British North America Act* (1939), Annex 1, pp. 78–109; Bora Laskin, *Canadian Constitutional Law* (3rd ed., Toronto, 1966), pp. 316–19.

37/*Attorney-General for Ontario* v. *Reciprocal Insurers*, [1924] A.C. 328, at p. 342.

38/*Attorney-General for Alberta* v. *Attorney-General for Canada*, [1938] A.C. 117.

39/*Russell* v. *the Queen* (1882), 7 App. Cas. 829.

40/*Hodge* v. *the Queen* (1883), 9 App. Cas. 117.

vincial statute which prohibited the sale of skim milk to a cheese or butter factory without declaring its deficiency at the time of sale was upheld as being essentially a regulation of private business,[41] while a Dominion statute which forbade the sale of all skim milk to a cheese or butter factory and make any such sale a crime was also upheld on the ground that it was aimed at the prevention of fraud.[42]

These aspects may not, indeed, remain constant, and legislation which would be *ultra vires* at one time may, through a change of circumstances, become legitimate, and the field of jurisdiction may change accordingly.

Their lordships do not doubt that some matters, in their origin local and provincial, might attain such dimensions as to affect the body politic of the Dominion, and to justify the Canadian Parliament in passing laws for their regulation or abolition in the interest of the Dominion. But great caution must be observed in distinguishing between that which is local and provincial, and therefore within the jurisdiction of the provincial legislatures, and that which has ceased to be merely local and provincial, and has become a matter of national concern, in such sense as to bring it within the jurisdiction of the Parliament of Canada. An Act restricting the right to carry weapons of offence, or their sale to young persons, within the province would be within the authority of the provincial legislature. But traffic in arms, or the possession of them under such circumstances as to raise a suspicion that they were to be used for seditious purposes, or against a foreign state, are matters which their lordships conceive might be competently dealt with by the Parliament of the Dominion.[43]

The splitting of jurisdiction over certain subject-matter, whether it flows from the application of the "aspect" principle or from a division resulting from specific enumerations in the act, gives results which, while not the same as those occurring under concurrent jurisdiction, nevertheless bear a superficial resemblance. Under the former the field of jurisdiction is really divided and not jointly shared; but the subject-matter being the same, the two authorities are forced into intimate and possibly conflicting relations with each other, and they have not the legal means available (as with concurrent powers) to establish unified control. Jurisdiction over the marketing of natural products, the investigation of labour disputes, and the regulation of insurance companies has thus in each instance been cut in twain, and jurisdiction over the fisheries is also divided although on somewhat different grounds.[44] The results, however, are uncertain and confusing.

Where both federal and provincial legislation exist in a field, the question of which is paramount is of course another question for the courts, and the doctrine of "paramountcy" has for long attracted the attention of constitu-

41/*Regina* v. *Wason* (1890), 17 Ont. A.R. 221.
42/*Regina* v. *Stone* (1893), 23 Ont. R. 46.
43/*Local Prohibition Case*, [1896] A.C. 348, at pp. 361–2.
44/Fisheries are under Dominion jurisdiction; but this is complicated by provincial ownership of non-tidal fisheries, and also by different arrangements having been made with different provinces regarding administration.

tional scholars. In recent years the Supreme Court appears to have moved in the direction of holding that unless a clear conflict between the two jurisdictions exists, both federal and provincial legislation can occupy the same field, with the court deciding each case on its merits, and not necessarily recognizing the federal power as paramount.[45]

RESIDUAL POWER OF THE DOMINION PARLIAMENT

A return may now be made to the Dominion powers under section 91 of the British North America Act. The opening clause states that the national Parliament shall "make laws for the peace, order, and good government of Canada, in relation to all matters not coming within the classes of subjects by this Act assigned exclusively to the legislatures of the provinces; and for greater certainty, but not so as to restrict the generality of the foregoing terms of this Section, it is hereby declared that (notwithstanding anything in this Act) the exclusive legislative authority of the Parliament of Canada extends to all matters coming within the classes of subjects next hereinafter enumerated." Then follow the thirty-one (originally twenty-nine) specific classes of subjects already noted.[46] The section concludes: "And any matter coming within any of the classes of subjects enumerated in this Section shall not be deemed to come within the class of matters of a local or private nature comprised in the enumeration of the classes of subjects by this Act assigned exclusively to the legislatures of the provinces."

This clause gave to the Dominion Parliament (as the Fathers of the Confederation certainly intended) the residual power; that is, explicit grants of power were made to the provincial legislatures and all the remainder was to go to the Dominion. The words "peace, order, and good government" were not intended to be taken in any literal sense; the phrase was simply one which was frequently used by the British Parliament when it wished to make a comprehensive grant of legislative power. Section 91 then proceeded to illustrate the general authority thus bestowed by specifying a number of these powers, and, to prevent possible misinterpretation, explicitly stated that these enumerated powers were inserted "for greater certainty, but not so as to restrict the generality of the foregoing terms of this Section." These illustrations were, in fact, unnecessary, for the entire distribution had been completed when the provinces had been allotted their powers and the Dominion had been given the remainder; but the London Resolutions, like the Quebec Resolutions, had contained a list of specific Dominion powers, and in order to comply with the resolutions and "for greater certainty" the enumeration was included.

45/See, for example, *Reference Re Section 92 (4) of the Vehicles Act, 1959 (Sask.),* C. 93, [1958] S.C.R. 608; *O'Grady* v. *Sparling,* [1960] S.C.R. 804; Laskin, *Canadian Constitutional Law,* pp. 104 ff.
46/See *supra,* pp. 82–3.

The federal powers are wholly residuary for the simple reason that the provincial powers are exclusive; and the twenty-nine "enumerations" in Section 91 cannot add to the residue; they cannot take away from it ... They have no meaning except as examples of the residuary power, which must be as exclusive as in the grant of legislative powers to the provinces. The enumerated examples of the residuary power cannot occupy any special place; they cannot be exalted at the expense of the residuary power, for that would "restrict the generality" of that power. It all looks reasonably simple, and Sir John A. Macdonald was perhaps justified as he looked at the scheme in hoping that "all conflict of jurisdiction" had been avoided.[47]

So much for the intention of those who planned the constitution and for the clear and – one would suppose – unambiguous terms in which those intentions were embodied in the text of the act. But, after a sound start, the Judicial Committee of the Privy Council succeeded through a long series of decisions in substantially frustrating this intention and supplying an interpretation of its own far removed from the text. "Seldom," wrote Professor Kennedy in 1943, "have statesmen more deliberately striven to write their purposes into law, and seldom have they more signally failed before the judicial technique of statutory interpretation."[48] The extent of the failure can be measured by two remarkably clear statements. Speaking during the Confederation debates on February 3, 1865, John A. Macdonald said: "We thereby ... make the Confederation one people and one government, instead of five peoples and five governments ... one united province, with the local governments and legislatures subordinate to the General Government and Legislature."[49] Speaking of the British North America Act in 1892, in rendering the decision in *Liquidators of the Maritime Bank of Canada* v. *Receiver General of New Brunswick*, Lord Watson said: "The object of the Act was neither to weld the provinces into one, nor to subordinate provincial government to a central authority."[50]

This extraordinary result was made possible by the presence, among the subjects of provincial jurisdiction in section 92, of one subject as vague and general in its connotation as "peace, order, and good government" in section 91, namely, "property and civil rights in the province." For if the assumption could be made that "property and civil rights" were not rigidly and necessarily confined to matters of purely provincial and local interest, and if it could also be assumed that when a topic fell under this general head it was clearly provincial unless the act positively asserted the contrary, then the constitutional stage was set for a new scene in which the lead could be taken from the Dominion and handed over to the province.

47/W. P. M. Kennedy, "The Interpretation of the British North America Act," *Cambridge Law Journal*, 1943, pp. 150–1. For a contrary view, see G. P. Browne, *The Judicial Committee and the British North America Act* (Toronto, 1967), especially pp. 36–58.
48/W. P. M. Kennedy, "The Workings of the British North America Acts, 1867–1931," *Juridical Review*, 1936, p. 60.
49/*Confederation Debates*, pp. 41–2.
50/[1892] A.C. 437.

For over twenty years after Confederation these parts of the British North America Act were interpreted in accord with the original intentions as indicated above. The leading case was *Russell* v. *the Queen* (1882) where a Dominion local option law was upheld on the ground that it was of general or national importance relating to public order and safety.[51] In considering the question whether such a law could properly be brought under provincial jurisdiction as one relating to property and civil rights, the Judicial Committee stated: "Few, if any, laws could be made by Parliament for the peace, order, and good government of Canada which did not *in some incidental way affect property and civil rights,* and it could not have been intended, when assuring to the provinces exclusive legislative authority on the subjects of property and civil rights, to exclude the Parliament from the exercise of this general power whenever any *such incidental interference* would result from it."[52] In short, the court admitted the potential inclusiveness of property and civil rights in that almost all legislation would be bound incidentally to touch on these matters; but it insisted that the decisive factor was the primary purpose of the law, and if the question was of nation-wide importance the Dominion could take jurisdiction under the peace, order, and good government clause. "The true nature and character of the legislation in the particular instance under discussion," said the Judicial Committee, "must always be determined in order to ascertain the class of subject to which it really belongs."

It is not possible here to trace the movement of the courts away from this position. The Judicial Committee later divided the Dominion grant of powers into two separate and distinct parts, general and enumerated; it followed this bisection with the astounding discovery that the general Dominion grant was not the governing one but was *"in supplement of* its enumerated powers";[53] and it then proceeded to relegate this general and now degraded power to a position of inferior strength and authority. The enumerated Dominion powers, which had begun as illustrations of Dominion authority, thus became a greater consequence than the general power which they were supposed to illustrate. The Judicial Committee held that while the legislative power of the Dominion under the enumerated heads of section 91 would override the provincial powers as enumerated in section 92, the enumerated powers of section 92 would normally override the general power of the Dominion to legislate for the peace, order, and good government of Canada. Once the primacy of the latter general power vanished, "interpretation of the legislative powers of the Dominion and the provinces settled down to a competition between the specific enumerated heads of Sections 91 and 92. In this competition, the provinces enjoyed an advantage because Section 92 contained two heads capable of a general and inclusive signification, *viz.,* 'property and civil rights in the province' and 'generally all

51/*Supra,* p. 87.
52/*Russell* v. *the Queen* (1882), 7 App. Cas. 829, at p. 839 (italics added).
53/*Local Prohibition Case,* [1896] A.C. 348, at p. 361.

matters of a merely local or private nature in the province,' while Section 91 contained only one such head, 'the regulation of trade and commerce' and it received a restricted interpretation."[54]

The peace, order, and good government clause thus found itself not only treated as an isolated and supplementary grant of Dominion authority, but deprived of most of its applicability by the indiscriminate inclusiveness of property and civil rights in section 92. Virtually no field of jurisdiction could be found which was not covered on the one hand by the enumerated clauses of 91, or, on the other, by the enumerations of 92, which included especially property and civil rights.[55] Residual power had thus slipped away from the Dominion and had reappeared in a somewhat altered guise in section 92; property and civil rights had become, indeed, the true residual clause.[56]

The Judicial Committee was nevertheless faced with the necessity, or at least the obligation, of placing some kind of meaning on "peace, order, and good government," and it decided that in these words lurked a comprehensive emergency power which the Dominion could invoke in time of dire necessity or grave national peril. On such rare occasions, therefore, this general clause came into its own, and at such times it was held to override any or all of the provincial powers which stand in the way of the national interest. It was under these circumstances that the Dominion was able to assume at its own discretion virtually unlimited powers during (and for a time after) the two world wars and in the war in Korea. The length of time that the emergency may exist and hence relevant Dominion legislation be upheld on emergency grounds, is uncertain; but the question is essentially a political one and the courts are therefore very loath to question the decision of the dominion Parliament on the length of the emergency period.[57] The federal statutes known as the War Measures Act[58] and the various Transitional Measures Acts and Emergency Powers Acts[59] have been used in the past to authorize the federal cabinet to take the necessary speedy action in time of real or apprehended war, invasion, insurrection, or national emergency, and, in doing so, to assume powers which would under normal conditions belong to the provincial legislatures.

Having enunciated the emergency doctrine, the Judicial Committee was still

---

54/*Rowell-Sirois Report*, I, p. 58.

55/A very small number of Dominion laws were upheld as coming under "peace, order, and good government" alone. See C. P. Plaxton, ed., *Canadian Constitutional Decisions of the Judicial Committee of the Privy Council, 1930–1939* (Ottawa, 1939), pp. xxxi–xxxiii.

56/A centralist analysis of this whole problem is found in Senate of Canada, *Report on the British North America Act* (1939), Report and Annex 1. A criticism of this is in Browne, *The Judicial Committee and the British North America Act*, especially pp. 58–71. See also W. R. Lederman, *The Courts and the Canadian Constitution* (Toronto, 1964); Peter H. Russell, *Leading Constitutional Decisions* (Toronto, 1965).

57/*Fort Frances Pulp and Paper Co.* v. *Manitoba Free Press*, [1923] A.C. 695.

58/*Rev. Stat. Can.* (1952), c. 288.

59/For example, *Can. Statutes*, 15 Geo. VI, c. 5.

confronted with the awkward decision of *Russell* v. *the Queen,* and its response to this challenge was as original as it was startling. The early decision, said the court, can now be supported only on the assumption that drunkenness in Canada had reached such alarming dimensions in the 1870s that nothing short of federal action would have been sufficient to cope with the evil and avert an impending national calamity.[60] But even so, the benign co-operation of the Judicial Committee could not always be relied on to rescue an unhappy nation from disaster, for an economic cataclysm, such as the world depression of the thirties, was apparently not considered to be grave enough to warrant the invocation of this emergency power. Thus a Dominion legislative programme of social and economic reform (the so-called "New Deal legislation" of the Bennett government, which was permanent legislation) was declared *ultra vires.*

But in 1946 a case before the Judicial Committee,[61] which was concerned with reviewing the validity of the legislation formerly upheld in *Russell* v. *the Queen,* served to disturb once again the interpretation which is to be placed upon "peace, order, and good government." The result of this decision was to cast a very grave doubt on the "emergency" doctrine as an adequate explanation of that clause (despite the committee's frequent past statements and applications of that doctrine) and also to suggest that the national importance of the subject-matter of legislation may be in itself sufficient to determine its aspect and its validity, notwithstanding the court's rejection of this principle in many earlier cases.[62] In the following year, 1947, the Judicial Committee reasserted the emergency doctrine.

It would be heartening to be able to conclude this summary of the vacillations of the Judicial Committee of the Privy Council with a round assertion that the abolition of appeals to the committee in 1949, and the subsequent elevation of the Supreme Court of Canada to the role of final arbiter over the British North

---

60/These words of Lord Haldane deserve, and doubtless will enjoy, immortality. "Their lordships think that the decision in *Russell* v. *the Queen* can only be supported today ... on the assumption of the Board [the Privy Council], apparently made at the time of deciding the case of *Russell* v. *the Queen,* that the evil of intemperance at that time amounted in Canada to one so great and so general that at least for the period it was a menace to the national life of Canada so serious and pressing that the National Parliament was called on to intervene to protect the nation from disaster. An epidemic of pestilence might conceivably have been regarded as analogous." *Toronto Electric Commissioners* v. *Snider,* [1925] A.C. 396, at p. 412. It should be noted that the statute which was supposed to stem the tide of national drunkenness provided only for *local* option.

61/*Attorney-General of Ontario* v. *Canada Temperance Federation,* [1946] 2 D.L.R. 1.

62/"The true test must be found in the real subject-matter of the legislation: if it is such that it goes beyond local or provincial concern or interests and must from its inherent nature be the concern of the Dominion as a whole ... then it will fall within the competence of the Dominion Parliament as a matter affecting the peace, order, and good government of Canada, though it may in another aspect touch upon matters specially reserved to the provincial legislatures." *Ibid.,* p. 5. But see *Co-operative Committee on Japanese Canadians* v. *Attorney-General for Canada,* [1947] A.C. 47, and *Canadian Federation of Agriculture* v. *Attorney-General for Quebec,* [1951] A.C. 179.

America Act, was followed by the emergence of a clear judicial doctrine. Such, however, has not been the case. The court began, indeed, by following the Judicial Committee, by a decision in 1950 which "was a straight application of the doctrine of implied emergency powers as extending to the aftermath of war."[63] The Supreme Court did not, in the succeeding decade, have many opportunities to display its talents in regard to interpreting a constitution. By 1960 its record was such that Mr. Justice MacDonald of the Supreme Court of Nova Scotia was able to say cautiously of a leading case (in which the court held *ultra vires* a provincial law because it dealt with a matter – aeronautics – which lay outside section 92 but within the residuary clause of section 91 as a matter of national importance) that: "This sphinx-like case holds out some hope for the future application of the doctrine of 'aspects' of the Residuary Clause so that Parliament may have overriding power to legislate in relation to the national aspects of matters otherwise within Provincial classes of subjects, and which though not affected with the urgency of emergency have nevertheless become 'matters of national concern.' "[64]

Two more recent cases[65] have seen further applications of the peace, order, and good government clause to uphold the Dominion powers, and the Supreme Court's era of interpretation thus includes four fairly consistent indications that the clause may be making a comeback; but given the court's record, four cases over twenty years cannot be taken as convincing evidence. On the one hand, the Supreme Court has before it a series of strict interpretations of the British North America Act through which provincial powers were steadily enlarged at the expense of the Dominion. "While the ship of state now sails on larger ventures and into foreign waters," Lord Atkin wrote of the Canadian constitution in 1937, in describing the "conservative" view that has resulted from these interpretations, "she still retains the water-tight compartments which are an essential part of her original structure."[66] On the other hand, the court also has before it more "liberal" interpretations of the act by the Judicial Committee, notably the decision of 1946 which questioned the emergency doctrine,[67] and its own four cases cited above. "The Act planted in Canada a living tree capable of growth and expansion within its natural limits," Lord Sankey wrote as early as 1930. "Their Lordships do not conceive it to be the duty of this Board – it is certainly not their desire – to cut down the provisions of the Act by a narrow and technical construction, but rather to give

---

63/Vincent C. MacDonald, *Legislative Power and the Supreme Court in the Fifties* (Toronto, 1960), p. 12. The case was *Wartime Leaseholds Reference*, [1950] S.C.R. 124.

64/*Ibid.*, p. 22. The case was *Johannesson* v. *West St. Paul*, [1952] 1 S.C.R. 292.

65/*Munro* v. *National Capital Commission*, [1966] S.C.R. 663; *Off-Shore Mineral Rights Reference*, [1962] S.C.R. 792.

66/*Attorney-General for Canada* v. *Attorney-General for Ontario*, [1937] A.C. 326, 354 (P.C.).

67/*Supra*, p. 93.

it a large and liberal interpretation."[68] As Professor Edward McWhinney has indicated, much depends on whether the Supreme Court of Canada chooses to regard the constitutional act as a ship or a tree.[69]

The broad consequence of the main trends in interpretation was, for a long time, a great increase in provincial powers at the expense of the Dominion: not that the powers of the Dominion have actually diminished, they have on the contrary increased; but the province has acquired most of the new territory which recent years have made available for government action and control.[70] The chief Dominion gains (to be taken up presently) have been aeronautics, broadcasting, and off-shore mineral rights; while the provincial gains have included the regulation of intraprovincial production, trade, and marketing; wages; hours of labour; unemployment insurance (later given to the Dominion by constitutional amendment); workmen's compensation; industrial disputes; trade union legislation; health regulations; and insurance legislation. (The one general exception to provincial jurisdiction over labour questions is the Dominion's power over industries which are themselves within Dominion jurisdiction.) The British North America Act thus lost elasticity at the very point where elasticity in recent years has been most needed. The powers of the Dominion (except in time of emergency) were largely confined to those which happened to be considered the most urgent in 1867; and this pattern of the distribution of governmental powers is clearly not suited to the present. Social and economic conditions have greatly altered in the intervening century, as have people's attitudes towards them, and matters which were at Confederation unmistakably local in their nature and other matters which were not considered to be of any concern to governments at all, have now become of first-rate importance, not alone to a particular locality, but to the nation as a whole. Such modern problems as those concerned with the regulation of competitive industry and the provision of various social services often cannot be adequately treated at the provincial level, nor is it generally desirable to have ten (or, if the Dominion is also involved, eleven) separate and perhaps conflicting policies striving to cope with questions which go far beyond the provincial boundaries. The British North America Act has thus frequently been found wanting in its ability to endow the proper government with adequate authority; and while it would be most unfair to place the entire blame for this deficiency upon the courts, it is they, rather than the draftsmen of 1867, who must assume the

68/*Edwards* v. *Attorney-General for Canada,* [1930] A.C. 124, 136 (P.C.).

69/See Edward McWhinney, *Judicial Review in the English-speaking World* (2nd ed., Toronto, 1961).

70/In 1938 Professor Frank R. Scott listed eleven additions to the powers of the Dominion and twenty-one additions to those of the provinces as a result of judicial interpretation since Confederation although not all are due to the particular conflict discussed above. "The Royal Commission on Dominion-Provincial Relations," *University of Toronto Quarterly,* Jan. 1938, p. 144.

chief burden of responsibility. Canadian legal scholarship finds at least some
reasons for optimism in recent decisions of the Supreme Court of Canada. Mr
Justice MacDonald wrote in 1960, in words that are still true:

The score or so of decisions in the last decade provide reasonable evidence of an
intention to adopt a policy of gradual adaptation of Privy Council decisions and
doctrines. I venture to think that the Court, in time, will prove itself to be as free
of that ghostly influence in fact as it is in law and that it will re-work its way through
the precedents of its predecessor in such a way as gradually to make the Constitution
as well adapted to the 20th Century, as it was to the conditions which gave it birth.[71]

THE TREATY POWER

There has been no uncertainty regarding the powers of the Dominion and the
provinces so far as the *negotiation* of treaties with foreign countries is concerned. This was originally the function of the Crown acting through the
British government, and with the growth of Dominion self-government it has
gradually come under the control of the government of Canada.[72] But the
location of the power to *implement the terms* of a treaty after it has been ratified has been uncertain, although a special section of the British North America
Act dealt expressly with the question. Section 132 reads: "The Parliament and
Government of Canada shall have all powers necessary or proper for per-
forming the obligations of Canada or of any province thereof, as part of the
British Empire, towards foreign countries arising under treaties between the
Empire and such foreign countries."

It will be noted that the section deals expressly with the treaty obligations of
Canada as part of the empire and not as a separate nation, and also that the
section could conceivably cause a serious disturbance in the distribution of
Dominion and provincial powers. There has always been the possibility that it
might allow the Dominion to negotiate treaties dealing with certain subjects
normally under provincial control (such, for example, as an international convention affecting conditions of labour) and thereby acquire the right to legislate
on such topics by virtue of its obligation to carry out the terms of these treaties.
Appeals to the Judicial Committee in the thirties resulted in the Dominion
acquiring in part by the treaty route complete jurisdiction over aeronautics[73]
and radio broadcasting.[74] The courts in these and subsequent decisions enunci-

71/MacDonald, *Legislative Power and the Supreme Court*, p. 27. A similar optimism
can be found in Laskin, *Canadian Constitutional Law;* Martha Fletcher, "Judicial
Review and the Division of Powers in Canada," in Meekison, *Canadian Federalism,*
p. 151; Strayer, *Judicial Review of Legislation in Canada*, p. 28.

72/*Supra*, pp. 44–7; 49–50.

73/*Aeronautics Case*, [1932] A.C. 54. This decision was confirmed by the Supreme
Court of Canada in *Johannesson* v. *West St. Paul*, [1952] 1 S.C.R. 292.

74/*Radio Case*, [1932] A.C. 304.

ated several general principles affecting the implementation of treaties, and from these the following principles emerge:

(*a*) Section 132 does not apply to all treaties to which Canada is a party, but only to those which she enters "as part of the British Empire," namely, those obligations arising as a result of action by the imperial government. With the growing emphasis on Canadian autonomy in all such matters, this group of treaties has now become obsolete.

(*b*) The implementation of treaties which fall in the other group – those to which Canada is a separate party by virtue of her new status as an international person – is not covered by any special section of the British North America Act, and must therefore depend upon the normal distribution of legislative power between the Dominion and the provinces. "There is no such thing as treaty legislation as such," said the Judicial Committee. "The distribution is based on classes of subjects: and as a treaty deals with a particular class of subjects so will the legislative power of performing it be ascertained."[75]

(*c*) The enlargement of the Dominion powers in the international field and the steady growth of provincial powers in the domestic field thus pull in opposite directions in the area of treaty performance. It is now quite possible for the Dominion to negotiate and ratify a treaty and yet be left in default by provincial refusal to carry out the terms of the agreement, although, had this same commitment been made by the British government, the Dominion would possess all the authority necessary for legislative enforcement.

(*d*) The implementation of treaties is thus determined in the first place by the type of treaty, and then, in most instances, by the devious process of unravelling sections 91 and 92 as discussed in the preceding pages.

The source of treaty-performing power in Canada now turns first upon the type of treaty, i.e., upon how and by whom it was brought about, etc. If it is of one type (Empire) the power resides in section 132; if of another (Canadian) the power resides (*a*) in section 92 or (*b*) in section 91, and in the latter case it may reside either in (i) the enumerated heads or (ii) (in case of national emergency) in the "peace, order and good government" clause. This is the judicial labyrinth through which Canadian diplomats and Canadian legislators must be able to see their ways if effective treaties are to be made.[76]

To these considerations must be added another that has become relevant in recent years: provincial claims notwithstanding, and despite the according of diplomatic status to Quebec officials by General de Gaulle, provinces have no constitutional power to enter into international agreements with foreign governments except as agents or delegates of the government of Canada.[77] The tech-

75/*Labour Conventions Case,* [1937] A.C. 326, at p. 351.
76/Vincent C. MacDonald, "The Canadian Constitution Seventy Years After," *Canadian Bar Review,* June 1937, p. 418. See also McWhinney, *Judicial Review,* p. 65, especially n. 12.
77/See Laskin, "The Provinces and International Agreements" and R. D. Delisle,

nical position is none the less somewhat misleading, for *de facto*, as Professor McWhinney has pointed out with corroborative evidence: "the provinces, in respect to subjects within their specific constitutional powers as defined in the *B.N.A. Act*, are fully competent to conclude, in their own authority, transnational agreements not having international law consequences."[78] Modern technology, through arousing the interest of the provinces in such matters as off-shore mineral rights and broadcasting by satellite for education purposes, thus threatens to effect yet more changes in the working of the distribution of powers.

Since this chapter has dealt exclusively with the distribution of powers under the British North America Act, and judicial review thereof, it is necessary to emphasize that the distribution of powers is not the sole topic of importance in cases of constitutional significance, and that there are other important judicial decisions besides those dealing with the distribution of powers.[79] Cases involving the regulation of trade, provincial powers in relation to municipal institutions, provincial taxation, and civil liberties, for example, do not always fall formally into the areas generally covered by the phrase "distribution of powers," and in some of these other fields the record of the courts is somewhat more consistent than in their interpretations of sections 91 and 92. The Supreme Court has upheld the rule of law on several occasions in recent years, the most notable example being in the case of *Roncarelli* v. *Duplessis*, in which the premier and attorney general of Quebec was assessed heavy damages for exceeding his powers in cancelling a tavern licence.[80]

"Treaty-Making Power in Canada," in Ontario Advisory Committee on Confederation, *Background Papers and Reports*, pp. 103–47.

78/Edward McWhinney, "The Constitutional Competence within Federal Systems for International Agreements," in *ibid.*, p. 156.

79/On this point see Peter H. Russell, "The Supreme Court's Interpretation of the Constitution since 1949," in Paul Fox, ed., *Politics: Canada* (Toronto, 1962).

80/*Roncarelli* v. *Duplessis*, [1959] S.C.R. 121.

6 Dominion-provincial financial relations

THE DISTRIBUTION OF FINANCIAL POWERS between the Dominion and the provinces has been one of the most troublesome of the many problems raised by Confederation and certainly has the longest history. Every province has been embroiled, some of them many times, in financial disputes with the Dominion, and only our shortest-lived cabinets at Ottawa have been able to escape the constantly recurring nightmare of provincial dissatisfaction and the apparently insatiable demands on the Dominion treasury. The nature of the demands has changed in recent years, as more of the provinces have shown a desire to stand on their own feet in matters of provincial jurisdiction (as Quebec always has); but the present cannot be understood without some knowledge of Canada's financial history.

At Confederation the Dominion secured the bulk of the provincial revenues, for customs and excise were relinquished by the provinces. Approximately 83 per cent of the provincial revenues of each of the three provinces came from these two sources; and even if municipal revenues were included, these two taxes accounted for 56 per cent of the total provincial and municipal revenues of the Province of Canada, 75 per cent of those of Nova Scotia, and 72 per cent of those of New Brunswick.[1] The provinces were thus left with only 17 per cent of their former provincial revenues with which to meet the demands of the future. These demands were, however to be greatly reduced by the burdens assumed by the Dominion, for the latter was to take over the provincial debts and the bulk of what were then considered to be both actually and potentially the most costly functions of government.

National security, national development, and the fostering of trade and commerce by appropriate regulation were regarded by the Fathers as the great functions of government. They were also the functions which they thought likely to expand in the future. When these had been transferred to the Federal Government the provinces were left with functions, the burden of which was not expected to grow. They

1/*Rowell-Sirois Report*, I, pp. 41, 45n.

would be required to support a civil government establishment; to maintain a number of local public works and to undertake the administration of justice. But the heaviest duties of civil government and the onerous burden of the great public works would be lifted from their shoulders. The support of education was to come within their sphere and their control over "generally all matters of a merely local or private nature in the province" and over "the establishment, maintenance and management of hospitals, asylums, charities and eleemosynary institutions in and for the province" implied responsibility for social welfare problems which got beyond the resources of charitable and municipal organization.[2]

But even this great diminution in the number and costliness of the provincial functions did not bring the expenditure of the provinces down to a level where it would not exceed the revenue. The two sources of income remaining were direct taxes and the odd fees, royalties, permits, and sales of small services which the province still retained. No one in the 1860s expected direct taxation to be used to any degree, so the main reliance was placed on the second miscellaneous group which was clearly insufficient. The gap was therefore filled by the Dominion agreeing to make a number of payments or subsidies to the provinces, and these contributions were embodied in sections 102–26 of the British North America Act. Those payments which might conceivably lead to further claims being made on the Dominion were optimistically declared to be "in full settlement of all future demands on Canada" – a statement which joined the group of non-operative clauses in the act shortly after Confederation. The original payments to the provincial governments fell into four classes:

PAYMENTS ON DEBT ALLOWANCES

Although the Dominion assumed the debt of each province at Confederation, this was by no means an act of pure generosity; for most of these debts had been incurred for railways or other property which passed under Dominion ownership or jurisdiction. In order to equalize the treatment among the provinces, so that the extravagant would not reap the same reward as the frugal, the device of the debt allowance was used. Each province was given a debt allowance in round numbers which was based on approximately $25 a head (according to the 1861 census) and this amount was applied as a credit in making a bookkeeping adjustment with the Dominion. Any province whose actual debt was less than its debt allowance received in perpetuity from the Dominion an annual payment of 5 per cent on this difference; any province which had a debt in excess of this allowance paid interest on the excess at the same rate. Under this arrangement New Brunswick broke even; Nova Scotia received a small annual payment from the Dominion; and Ontario and Quebec, having a common debt of $10,400,000 in excess of the allowance, were to pay to the Dominion 5 per cent a year on that sum.

2/*Ibid.*, p. 43.

Almost from the beginning these debt allowances were used as a method of obtaining an increase in the payments from the federal government. Nova Scotia in 1869 had her debt allowance raised, partly as an adjustment against assets taken over by the Dominion, but partly also to induce her to acquiesce in Confederation. Ontario and Quebec, being unable to agree on how their payments to the Dominion under the debt allowance arrangement were to be divided, were able in 1873 to have their allowance increased until it covered the original debt; and later they received back interest payments they had made in the meantime, together with a credit for interest on this interest. The other provinces thereupon had their allowances raised in the same proportion. New provinces were also given debt allowances on their entrance to the federation, and the amount of this allowance varied with the circumstances: Prince Edward Island, for example, received a debt allowance of $50 a head, while other new provinces, such as Manitoba, Alberta, and Saskatchewan, which had no debt whatever and which had no assets to transfer to the Dominion, nevertheless were given on entrance a generous debt allowance, and they thus received an annual payment of the difference between this amount and the amount of the non-existent debt. Finally the debt allowances were at times manipulated to increase payments to a province which had become involved in difficulties. Manitoba's allowance was increased in 1885, for example, by estimating her population at the fictitious figure of 125,000.[3] Debt allowances are still paid.

ANNUAL GRANTS TO SUPPORT PROVINCIAL GOVERNMENTS
AND LEGISLATURES

The four original provinces received grants ranging from $50,000 to $80,000 a year (in order of size) for the above purpose, and as new provinces entered the federation, they received similar grants. In 1907, when a general revision of the provincial subsidies took place, this grant was raised and made to vary with the population from $100,000 for provinces under 150,000 population, to $240,000 for those over 1,500,000.

PER CAPITA GRANTS

This grant was meant to be the major contribution of the Dominion government to provincial revenues. It was fixed at eighty cents a head on the population of each province as shown in the 1861 census. The grants to Nova Scotia and New Brunswick, however, could increase with population with a limit in each case of 400,000, after which the payment would remain fixed at the amount

3/Maxwell, *Federal Subsidies to the Provincial Governments in Canada*, pp. 26–8, 33–50, 51–63, 85, 120–1.

so ascertained. It was this eighty-cent grant that gave rise to the bitter anti-Confederation slogan in Nova Scotia, that the province had been "sold for the price of a sheep-skin."

The per capita grant has been manipulated on a number of occasions to render aid to needy provinces; but as it was difficult to raise the grant for one province without precipitating awkward demands from other directions, the Dominion fell back upon the ingenious and much safer method of inventing a population for some of the provinces where heavy prospective immigration furnished a convenient excuse. Thus Manitoba was assumed to have a population in 1870 of 17,000 (it was 12,200, of whom 1,600 were white settlers and the rest Indians and half-breeds); British Columbia in 1871 was credited with 60,000 (instead of 34,000, of whom 25,000 were Indians and Chinese); and in 1882 the Manitoba subsidy was changed and calculated on a population of 150,000, although the census a year before had returned only 64,800.[4] In 1907 the subsidies were revised for all the provinces. Each province was from this time forward to receive a subsidy which would vary with population: eighty cents a head up to a population of 2,500,000; sixty cents a head on any excess over that number.

SPECIAL GRANTS

These have been allotted ever since Confederation for a wide variety of causes: some were given to satisfy legitimate claims; some for convenient grievances; some simply in response to political pressure. New Brunswick received as part of the Confederation agreement $63,000 a year for ten years, for the excellent reason that she could not balance her budget without it. The "better terms" agitation in Nova Scotia resulted not only in the increase in her debt allowance, but also in an extra $82,698 a year for a ten-year period. British Columbia received on entrance to the union $100,000 a year in perpetuity, nominally as compensation for land taken for the transcontinental railway, actually in order to enable her to meet her expenditures. Saskatchewan and Alberta received special grants on entering the Dominion to compensate them for the Dominion retention of their natural resources. Although these resources were returned in 1930 and although the provinces were compensated for any loss they might have sustained, they nevertheless demanded, and the Dominion conceded, a continuance of the original special payments in lieu of the resources which had now been returned. The Maritime provinces, as a result of a long agitation for redress of grievances, received in 1932 additional subsidies totalling $2,225,000 a year, and in 1958 another $25,000,000 annually, increased to $35,000,000 in 1962. Newfoundland was included as a beneficiary of the latter grants, and

4/*Ibid.*, pp. 33–5, 39, 79–80.

that province has received additional sums designed to keep its public services and taxation levels comparable with those of the other three Atlantic provinces.

The subsidies have thus undergone almost continuous alteration, and they are under discussion again as part of the general constitutional debate of the contemporary period.[5] There have been over two dozen special and general revisions since Confederation, and the period since the Second World War has seen the most thorough and far-reaching changes of all. Yet the intention at Confederation was that the original financial arrangements would be permanent, and a number of the subsequent adjustments have been declared to be "final and unalterable." The world of Dominion-provincial finance has for much of its history an air of grotesque unreality, untrammelled by logic and the ordinary restrictions and meanings of words, and it furnishes a fitting accompaniment to the constitutional wonderland of sections 91 and 92 where the examples of peace, order, and good government succeeded in gobbling up the general rule which they were originally intended to illustrate. The history of the subsidies demonstrates not only that final and unalterable agreements can be and are subject to frequent revision, but that population figures can be invented when the actual ones prove unsuitable; that debt allowances can be made for debts which have never existed; that natural resources can be returned and enjoyed and at the same time compensated for on a basis of their original alienation; and that when a subsidy is increased in order to equalize the treatment among the provinces, further adjustments become immediately necessary in order to overcome the injustices which have been occasioned by the very act of equalization.

The clue to this extraordinary condition is not hard to find; and the subsidy problem and the virtual disappearance of "peace, order, and good government" as an effective Dominion power will be found to be closely connected with each other. It is clearly impossible to justify all of the arguments advanced and the expedients used to raise many of the provincial grants; but there has been under all this manoeuvring and pressing for greater and greater financial assistance a genuine need for money to replenish the provincial treasuries. Undoubtedly some of this deficiency was caused by provincial extravagance, but at bottom the revenues of most provinces have simply not been sufficient to meet the inescapable demands which have steadily mounted every year.

The original financial provisions for the provinces were based on the provincial functions of 1867, and these functions were expected to be comparatively modest and inexpensive. But circumstances over which the provinces had virtually no control operated to increase greatly, and at an accelerating rate, the quantity and intensity of provincial activity. Certain existing functions,

5/See Pierre Elliott Trudeau, *Federal-Provincial Grants and the Spending Power of Parliament* (Ottawa, 1969); E. J. Benson, *The Taxing Powers and the Constitution of Canada* (Ottawa, 1969).

notably education and highways, developed enormously and made demands on provincial revenues that were never contemplated in earlier days. Equally important was the tremendous expansion in the number of provincial duties which a changing economy and a new conception of the part which the state must play in that economy made necessary; and the province found itself undertaking measures of public health, mothers' allowances, old age pensions, unemployment relief, and the like, which were almost or quite unknown at the time of Confederation or for many years thereafter. Thus the expenditure of all the provinces for education and public welfare in 1874 was a trifling $4,000,000; by 1937, it had multiplied over sixty times and reached $250,000,000, and by the late 1960s the total had multiplied to two and a half billion.[6] It is probable that many of these newer duties might have become the concern of the Dominion under the "peace, order, and good government" provision; but the interpretation of the courts kept these matters in provincial hands and progressively increased the disparity between provincial revenue and expenditure. Provincial revenues have also none the less expanded, through judicial interpretations of "direct taxation," and income from natural resources.

The original financial provisions of the British North America Act thus broke down. Provincial powers have outstripped the provincial facilities to pay for their proper exercise, and this has naturally been felt most acutely in those provinces which are economically the weakest. It has been this effort to maintain solvency that has made the provincial pressure on the Dominion exchequer so severe, and has led to the adoption of a number of the above expedients to increase the provincial subsidies.

There has been, of course, another source of relief available in provincial taxation, and it has not been neglected. The provinces have long since abandoned their happy independence of direct taxes, and provincial ingenuity has been strained to the utmost, particularly in the poorer provinces, to find new sources of taxation. This shift in emphasis in provincial budgets is best appreciated by noting that in 1874 federal subsidies accounted for almost two-thirds of the total provincial revenues, but by 1937 these had dropped to less than one-tenth of the total and there they have remained.[7] The tax agreements which dominated Dominion-provincial financial relations after 1942 make comparisons with earlier periods difficult, but statutory subsidies to the provinces have continued to be a shrinking proportion of their total revenues, looming largest in the budgets of the less prosperous provinces.

6/Total expenditures of health, welfare, and social security of all governments – federal, provincial, and municipal – have shown an almost unbelievable increase. In 1871 these expenditures were around $1,000,000 a year; in 1913, $15,000,000; in 1958, $2,000,000,000; in 1964 (latest totals available), $3,698,958,000. See *Canada Year Book, 1968*, p. 1007.

7/*Rowell-Sirois Report*, I, p. 245. The proportion varied greatly in different provinces. In Prince Edward Island in 1937, for example, the subsidy was still 41 per cent of total revenue; in Ontario, 3 per cent. In 1965 the comparable figures were 46 per cent and 1.6 per cent. See *Canada Year Book, 1968*, pp. 1046–9.

For a number of the provinces a bad financial situation became a desperate one when the Dominion (with unlimited power to tax under the constitution) invaded a number of the most profitable taxing fields of the provincial governments. Thus during the First World War the Dominion introduced a personal income tax, which proved to be permanent, and during the Second World War it levied a succession duty, although this field was in many instances already doubly covered by rival provinces. These imposts, together with certain corporation taxes, sales taxes, and others imposed by the Dominion, are directly competitive with provincial taxes, and seriously limit the productivity of the latter. An extreme illustration was furnished by any resident of Alberta who might be so unfortunate as to have had in 1938 an income of $1,000,000; he would have been liable for 105 per cent of this amount in Dominion and provincial income taxes. One apparent solution of the problem would be for the Dominion to withdraw completely from the field of direct taxation and leave it entirely to the provinces; but even if this were possible (and few can be found who would voice so vain a hope) it would not meet the difficulty. Certain provinces, probably Ontario, Quebec, Alberta, and British Columbia, might in such an event have an adequate revenue; but the other provinces would find that this would do little more than effect a moderate improvement in their finances.

Another method of meeting the Dominion-provincial problem of finance has been the device of the grant-in-aid or conditional subsidy, now generally called "shared-cost programme." This is a grant from the Dominion to the provinces for some specific purpose, and it is conditional on each province which accepts it complying with certain standards of performance, and, as a rule, contributing a proportionate amount of money. Grants-in-aid have been made since 1912, and the scheme has been used for various purposes, such as technical and agricultural education, public health services, employment agencies, highways, old age pensions, and unemployment relief. Some of them were for limited periods only, others have been permanent. One purpose of the grant-in-aid is excellent: it is designed to help the needy provinces pay for certain desirable services; and it has undoubtedly succeeded in this endeavour. But it gives no help towards securing a balanced provincial budget and may leave a province financially worse off than before. Some grants-in-aid have increased provincial expenditures, sometimes on matters which were not the provinces' own top priorities: some have induced the poorer provinces to undertake admittedly praiseworthy and even necessary activities, but activities for which they could ill afford to pay under prevailing theories of taxation; while those grants which were of limited duration frequently left a province saddled with a venture which was beyond its means to retain. The provinces, in short, do not benefit financially from the grants-in-aid; they receive more and better services, but they pay out more of their income in the process, and few of them can always afford assistance on these terms. In more recent years, the shared-cost programmes have become so burdensome to the federal treasury (they grew from 50 to 900 million dollars in less than two decades after 1945) that the prime minister was moved to assert: "I might say in a general way that we indicated in 1966 and repeat now that it is our intention to get out of a lot of these areas of social services and let the provinces assume them. We will give them the tax room which goes along with these expenditures."[8]

Financial difficulties have arisen not alone from the inadequacy of provincial revenues to meet provincial functions as compared to those of the Dominion, but also from the alarming economic inequalities existing among the provinces themselves. The federation is composed of members with widely varying financial capacities for carrying on their equal constitutional functions, and hence while a redistribution of certain powers or a reassignment of taxing fields might solve one of the fundamental problems, that of Dominion and province, neither could solve the second – that caused by the unequal economic strength of the different provinces. Some provinces are wealthy and prosperous, others are relatively poor, while others stand midway between these two extremes. Personal income per person in 1967 varied from $1,424 in Newfoundland to $2,624 in Ontario, all, except the four Atlantic provinces and the northern regions, being over $2,000.[9] Such diversity has a corresponding effect upon provincial revenues, upon the ability of the provinces to perform their functions, upon the standards which they are able to maintain, and even upon the general health and well-being of the people.

The general situation in Nova Scotia is unhappily all too clear. It can, for example, be easily demonstrated that the per capita income in Nova Scotia averages only about 80% of the national average, and that, except at the depth of the depression (when the prairie provinces suffered most severely) per capita income in the Maritime Provinces has been consistently lower than the rest of Canada. Similarly, a comparison of gross production per capita will show that of Nova Scotia to be well under 65% to 70% of the Dominion average, and to have been for years past always less than one-half of that for the province of Ontario. This has inevitably lowered the standards of living and may, indeed, have affected the general health of the people. Statistics on the latter point are, however, inadequate and far from conclusive; but a higher rate of infant mortality than most provinces, a lower average height (although apparently a better physical condition) among those called up for service, and the occurrence of certain dietary deficiencies, suggest that low income and malnutrition have left their mark upon the population.[10]

Expenditure on education – to make a specific illustration – varies enormously from province to province. In 1964, for example, Newfoundland spent

8/*Can. H. of C. Debates*, Nov. 4, 1968, p. 2361; see also *ibid.*, Dec. 18, 1964, pp. 11336 ff; Trudeau, *Federal-Provincial Grants and the Spending Power of Parliament*.

9/Dominion Bureau of Statistics, *National Accounts, Income and Expenditure*, 1967, p. 36.

10/*Report of the Royal Commission on Provincial Development*, 1944 (Nova Scotia), no. 1, "Report of Transmission," pp. 54–5, 87–9. See also *The Economy of the Atlantic Provinces, 1940–1958* (Halifax and Fredericton, June 1960).

$166 per pupil in the elementary and secondary schools; Prince Edward Island spent $219; Nova Scotia, $259. Yet Ontario spent $410; Alberta, $423; and British Columbia, $411.[11] Expenditure per child in attendance was therefore almost three times greater in some provinces than in others. Median salaries for women teachers in elementary schools ranged in 1966 from $2,933 in Newfoundland, $2,797 in Prince Edward Island, and $3,200 in New Brunswick to $4,996 in Alberta and $5,416 in British Columbia.[12] No one suggests for a moment that these discrepancies are explained by a difference in provincial regard for the value of education; the coincidence of small provincial revenues and low educational appropriations is all too evident.

The situation has been rendered more acute by the conviction held in the less favoured provinces that their retarded or warped development is due in part to the operation of certain national policies, notably the protective tariff, that these have built up Central Canada at the expense of West and East, and that the Dominion – and also the provinces of Ontario and Quebec – has not been sufficiently aware of the duty which it owes to the provinces which have been impoverished in this process. The general argument was well stated by the late Norman McL. Rogers in words written long before the Second World War had given enormous impetus to the further industrialization of Central Canada:

It is urged that Nova Scotia is entitled to relief and compensation, not merely in pursuance of the assurances given on the occasion of its entrance into the Canadian federation, but also on the broad equitable ground that a federation defeats its primary purpose if through its constitutional arrangements or through policies instituted by the national government it accomplishes the gradual debilitation of one or more of the provincial communities of which it is composed.[13]

The Royal Commission on Dominion-Provincial Relations (the Rowell-Sirois Commission) was appointed by the Dominion government in 1937 to make the first objective assessment since 1867 of the economic and financial basis of Confederation, the distribution of federal and provincial powers, and the financial relations of these governments. Its report, one of the great state papers in Canadian history, was focused primarily on the two fundamental problems discussed above – the position of the provinces vis-à-vis the Dominion, and the inequality of resources in the different provinces. For the first, the commission recommended a transfer of certain functions and a shifting of taxing powers; for the second, it urged the payment from the Dominion treasury of special grants which would be based on the needs of each province and would be designed to equalize to some degree the economic and financial position of all the provinces. The commission thus sought not only to re-establish the

11/These statistics are based on total expenditures on education: that is from provincial grants, local taxation, fees, and other sources of income. *Canada Year Book, 1967*, pp. 352–3; 1968, p. 375.

12/*Ibid.*, 1968, p. 374.

13/*Royal Commission, Provincial Economic Inquiry*, 1934 (Nova Scotia), "A Submission on Domonion-Provincial Relations," p. 198.

general balance between provincial revenue and expenditure, but also to break away entirely from the old subsidy system. The latter, which had been formulated essentially on provincial equality (tinged with special treatments for an underlying but seldom avowed necessity), was to be replaced by a plan of Dominion contributions given solely on the principle of provincial need. These were "designed to make it possible for every province to provide for its people services of average Canadian standards and they will thus alleviate distress and shameful conditions which now weaken national unity and handicap many Canadians."[14] Each province would thus be able "without resort to heavier taxation than the Canadian average, to provide adequate social, educational, and developmental services."[15]

The detailed proposals need not be given here, but the essentials, which greatly influenced Dominion-provincial relations after 1940, were as follows. The provinces would relinquish the personal income tax, taxes on corporations and on corporate income, and succession duties; and they would also surrender all the old provincial subsidies. In return the Dominion would assume (with a few special adjustments) all the provincial debts and accept responsibility for all relief of the employable unemployed. The Dominion would also "respect the remaining revenue sources of the provinces," would pay to a province 10 per cent of the net revenue derived from mining and oil-producing companies within that province, and would pay to the more needy provinces a "national adjustment grant." The latter was determined in the first instance for each province (Ontario, Alberta, and British Columbia were to receive nothing) by its existing financial position, and this amount was to be permanent and irreducible. It could, however, be increased; and it was to be subject to review every five years by an independent commission which would advise whether any change should be made. Emergency grants, made for one year at a time, could also be given to any province which had suffered under exceptionally bad economic conditions.

The Rowell-Sirois report was presented in May 1940 and was considered at a Dominion-provincial conference in the following January; but opposition from several provinces caused it to be shelved. However, other forces were at work. In 1940 jurisdiction over unemployment insurance was passed over to the Dominion by constitutional amendment. The drastic federal war taxes imposed in 1941, as part of the comprehensive financial policy of the government compelled the provinces to enter into an agreement with the Dominion in the following year whereby for the war period they relinquished certain taxes (notably the personal income and corporation taxes) in return for guarantees and payments by the Dominion. A number of the Rowell-Sirois recommendations were thus carried out piecemeal. The Dominion began in this period to impose succession duties; by agreement it acquired complete though temporary

14/*Rowell-Sirois Report*, II, p. 125.
15/*Ibid.*, p. 86.

control of the income and corporation taxes; and it permanently annexed jurisdiction over unemployment insurance. In addition, in 1944, it passed legislation to establish a nation-wide system of family allowances. The stage was thus set for the post-war scene; and the Dominion, trained during the preceding years in the exercise of masterful leadership, was prepared to step into the leading role. The constitutional decision was referred to a series of Dominion-provincial conferences which met in 1945 and 1946.

The new factor in the situation which the depression and the war experience had brought into prominence was the enormous significance of national financial and allied policies as the instruments of economic and social welfare. It was generally admitted that if unemployment and depressions were to be held at least partly under control, aggressive and comprehensive measures in wide variety must be undertaken, and no power in Canada, save the Dominion, was in a position to cope adequately with the problems involved. A large national income, a high standard of living, and stability of employment were the paramount objectives, and the means to achieve these were many. They involved a large export trade (to be secured by such expedients as low costs of production, freer and reciprocal trade, export credits, sales promotion abroad, research, and anti-inflation controls); a sustained consumers' purchasing power (to be aided by unemployment insurance, health insurance, family allowances, old age pensions, floor prices, and war pensions); and widespread private investment, supplemented by public works (which would be affected in no small measure by taxation policies, industrial and other loans, and public works assistance). Over a very large part of the field the Dominion had exclusive jurisdiction; in other matters provincial action would be bound to be disjointed and in many respects ineffective. The problem thus resolved itself into an effort to find a solution which would enable the Dominion to assume responsibility or at least leadership in most of the above matters while strengthening the provinces (especially the weaker ones) financially, so that they could discharge their normal constitutional functions and deal with those measures of social welfare in which the Dominion had become so greatly concerned.

The first post-war Dominion-provincial conference held a number of meetings extending from August 1945 to May 1946. The Dominion laid before the provincial premiers a substantial number of proposals which were designed to widen the federal responsibilities, increase the Dominion's control over taxation, and merge to a large degree the provincial financial system with that of the Dominion. The proposals embodied a number of the Rowell-Sirois recommendations, but looked to more positive and aggressive federal action than the earlier suggestions. The most drastic part of the new scheme brought forward was that the old annual subsidies should be replaced by very much larger ones which would be calculated for each province on one of several alternative formulae. These would constitute the *minimum* payment to be made to each province and would each year be adjusted (above that minimum) to correspond to any increases in the national income. In return for this grant the Dominion would be given complete control of the personal tax, corporation taxes, and succession duties, or, to use a phrase which became popular, the Dominion would "rent" the use of these taxes by the payment of the new annual grant.[16] The Dominion, in turn, offered to accept wide responsibilities for old age pensions, unemployment assistance, health insurance, public works, and aid in the development of natural resources. These proposals, as reconstruction measures, were to be tried initially (and by agreement, not constitutional amendment) for a three-year period; but they clearly envisioned a continuation into the post-war period of the Dominion's domination of the financial field. The Dominion would give no pledge that it would guarantee the provinces control of the minor fields of direct taxation untouched by the proposals.

The proposals[17] rejected provincial need as a basis for federal grants (one of the fundamental principles of the Rowell-Sirois report) and put in its place a straight per capita subsidy. To be sure, provincial need was recognized incidentally by the new grant in that poorer provinces might receive more thereby than they would lose by conceding the taxing powers above named, so that a certain levelling off would be likely to occur. But there was no reason to suppose that the poorer provinces would not be returning, under any such arrangement, to the old intolerable situation of being unable to keep abreast of their opulent neighbours in some of the essential services, for by its very nature a per capita grant is unable to discriminate between recipients in different economic circumstances.

After prolonged discussions the Dominion-provincial conference of 1945–6 broke up without reaching an agreement. A month later the minister of Finance offered to conclude with individual provinces for a trial five-year period the same financial agreements which he had offered earlier to the provinces as a group. This offer was subject to the necessary reservation that unless all the provinces accepted (which was most unlikely) the Dominion would have to hold in abeyance certain of its other proposals, notably those dealing with social security. Months of negotiation with the provinces ensued with various formulae being offered as extra inducements, and eventually all the provinces except Ontario and Quebec accepted the Dominion's terms.[18] The first five-year rental agreements ran out in 1952, and with some changes were renewed to 1957. A fresh alternative was designed to meet the demands of Ontario and after a

16/There was a special provision whereby a province could continue to impose succession duties and make an adjustment with the Dominion government, and others which were designed to overcome the possible inequities which might arise between provinces which agreed to the proposals and those which remained aloof. *Can. H. of C. Debates*, June 27, 1946, p. 2910.

17/*Proposals of the Government of Canada*, Dominion-Provincial Conference on Reconstruction, 1945. Ontario produced counter-proposals of its own; but these met with little support. *Submissions by the Government of Ontario* (1945).

18/*Can. Statutes*, 11 Geo. VI, c. 58. See *Can. H. of C. Debates*, 1947, pp. 5276 ff.

brief hesitation the province agreed to it, leaving only Quebec outside the plan.[19]

The year before these agreements were due to expire the federal government drafted a totally new plan for 1957–62. The needs of the country had changed since 1952, and the necessity for economic stabilization through complete federal control of taxation had been supplanted by a growing recognition of the principle of fiscal need. At the same time it seemed desirable that fiscal need subsidies should be determined on an objective basis, rather than arrived at by individual bargaining between the provinces and the federal government. The new agreements, based on an act of Parliament passed in July 1956[20] were also designed to secure the benefits of the old tax rental agreements, while allowing the provinces greater freedom of choice in the use of their right of direct taxation.

The acceptance of these aims led to separate provision being made for three main purposes: equalization grants to meet the problem of fiscal need, stabilization grants to ensure provincial income against economic recession (both of which meant the abandonment of the straight per capita principle for grants), and tax rental and collection agreements to maintain simplicity in tax administration. In addition, the provinces were left in a position to decide for themselves to what extent they would use their rights in the fields of direct taxation and this choice would not have any effect on their stabilization or equalization grants.

The equalization grants were unconditional grants to the poorer provinces based on fiscal need. They were designed to enable the less affluent provinces to provide a moderate level of provincial services without the necessity of carrying an abnormal load of taxation; and computed on a set formula designed to bring the per capita yield of the three "standard taxes" up to the *per capita* yield of the same standard taxes in the two most wealthy provinces in each year. "Standard taxes" were those amounts that would be derived from a tax within a province equal to 10 per cent of the tax payable under the federal Income Tax Act, 50 per cent of the tax payable under the Dominion Succession Duty Act, and 9 per cent of the net taxable income of a corporation. These percentages were also referred to as the "standard tax rates."

Stabilization grants were included in the agreements only as insurance against economic decline. They guaranteed to a province that the revenue from the standard taxes (or the rental of these to the federal government) and the equalization payments would not decline more than 5 per cent below the average of the two preceding years.[21] A province was also guaranteed that under no circumstances would it be worse off under the new system than under the old.

19/*Can. Statutes,* I Eliz. II, c. 49. See *Can. H. of C. Debates,* 1952, pp. 3359 ff.
20/*Can. Statutes,* 4–5 Eliz. II, c. 29. See *Can. H. of C. Debates,* 1956, pp. 5986 ff.
21/Other provisions were made for the first years of the plan when such a comparison of yields was obviously impossible.

The third part of the new agreements provided an opportunity for the provinces to rent the exclusive use of their succession duties, income taxes, and corporation taxes to the federal government. If a province wished to rent one or more of these taxes to the federal government it had to enter into an agreement for the five-year duration of the plan. Any province doing so then received in payment the yield in that province of the standard rate of that tax that was rented, which, in most provinces, would (as has been pointed out) be augmented by equalization grants. No deduction was made for collection.

For those provinces which rented the exclusive use of a tax field to the federal government the full rates of federal tax applied; the province would collect no income tax, for example, but would receive from Ottawa 10 per cent of the income tax payable under the formula outlined above. If a province did not rent its taxes, a plan of "tax abatements" was provided, under which a citizen living in the province could deduct from his federal income tax an amount equal to the full standard tax rate. Other subsidiary arrangements were also provided.[22]

All the provinces except Quebec signed the 1957 tax-sharing agreements with the Dominion, though Ontario, as before, rented only personal income tax. The agreements were destined to be administered not by the government that created them, but by the new Conservative ministry which took office in 1957 and at once began to express its dissatisfaction with the agreements by adding to their terms. In 1958 the 10 per cent standard rate set for income tax was increased to 13 per cent, thus raising the payments to provinces which had signed agreements. In the same year new subsidies totalling $25,000,000 annually for four years were provided for the Atlantic provinces under the Atlantic Provinces Adjustment Grants Act, and in 1959 the Newfoundland Additional Grants Act gave that province another $36,500,000 spread over five years. In 1960 an alternative method of paying federal grants to universities was devised, involving a tax abatement of one per cent on corporation taxes within any province not renting corporate taxes to the Dominion.[23]

Concurrently with these changes, new series of Dominion-provincial conferences, supplemented by meetings of officials representing their various governments, were held in which, as the minister of Finance observed, the provinces "in their statements indicated to us quite a marked difference in approach to the problem than one might have inferred from the signing of those agreements."[24] Though the provincial proposals concerning the tax agreements

22/For example, the federal tax authorities were willing (for a set charge) to administer specified provincial tax laws, and collect provincial taxes. Special provision was also made for provincial corporation taxes (other than taxes on net income), and for provincial mining and logging taxes. These provisions were in effect previously, and with minor changes continued.

23/See Canada Year Book, 1961, pp. 1067–9.

24/Proceedings of the Dominion-Provincial Conference, 1957, p. 102. See also Proceedings of the Dominion-Provincial Conference, 1960.

varied, the poorer provinces in general wanted more money, and the wealthier, while prepared to take more money, also wanted greater freedom to levy their own direct taxes. Possibly alarmed by the magnitude of the sums involved in provincial demands, the Dominion came to the conclusion that it would have to abandon the tax-rental system, and announced its decision to the provinces in yet another conference in 1961. The prime minister said subsequently of the system:

It placed on the federal government the whole responsibility for levying the additional taxes to support large increases in provincial expenditures. The provincial governments assumed no responsibility for imposing the rented taxes on which they depended for revenues nor had they any freedom to amend the rates of these taxes in line with their current needs. Such a system was clearly destructive of provincial responsibility and initiative, and incompatible with the constitution which grants equal access to the federal and provincial governments in these fields of direct taxation.[25]

The Dominion government proposed to replace the tax agreements, upon their expiry in 1962, with a new *tax collection* scheme whose essentials are neatly summarized in a resolution which the minister of Finance moved in the House of Commons on July 11, 1961:

Resolved that it is expedient to introduce a measure to authorize tax collection agreements with the governments of the provinces and to provide that the minister may pay to a province, out of the consolidated revenue fund, in respect of any fiscal year in the period commencing on the 1st day of April, 1962 and ending on the 31st day of March, 1967,

(*a*) a tax equalization payment;

(*b*) a provincial revenue stabilization payment;

(*c*) additional annual grants of ten and a half million dollars to each of the provinces of Nova Scotia, New Brunswick and Newfoundland, and three and a half million dollars to the province of Prince Edward Island;

(*d*) a further additional annual grant of eight million dollars to the province of Newfoundland;

(*e*) where a province does not levy a succession duty, an amount equal to the standard estate tax applicable to the province for the fiscal year; and

(*f*) advance payments on account of amounts collected under a tax collection agreement that may be entered into with the province.

The main result of these proposals, when amended somewhat and enacted into law, was that the provinces were obliged to levy their own direct taxes in order to maintain an income comparable with that formerly obtained with the aid of tax-rental agreements. The Dominion acted (and still acts) as tax collector for provinces which wished it, provided that the provincial tax base was identical with that of the Dominion. The Dominion progressively reduced the federal personal income tax (by 16 per cent in the first year of the new arrangement, 17 per cent in the second, and so on) and the federal corporation tax by 9 per cent, to make room, in effect, for the provinces to move into these two tax fields.

25/*Can. H. of C. Debates*, July 11, 1961, p. 7910.

A taxpayer in a province which levied an income tax which was 16 per cent of the federal tax during the first year of the arrangement, and which agreed to let the Dominion collect its taxes, would thus fill out one form reporting his income, on which he would pay no increased tax, but the tax was distributed between two governments. If his province levied a tax higher than the federal abatement of 16 per cent, his total tax would of course be larger.

This basic scheme, with major modifications, still underlies federal-provincial financial relations for the period following 1967, and most of the current arrangements are for an indefinite term rather than the five-year contract which characterized earlier agreements. The agreements for 1962-7, after the inevitable conferences, were modified in 1964 to permit further federal withdrawals from the personal income tax field, so that by 1966 the federal abatement had reached 24 per cent, thus enlarging the tax room available to the provinces. The fiscal arrangements in the mid-sixties were changed also by a variety of adjustments concerning, among other topics, payments to the provinces for federal income tax collected from power utilities, alterations in the equalization formula, interest-free loans for university students, and the Canada Pension Plan.[26]

The core of the agreements after 1967 is to be found in the Federal-Provincial Fiscal Arrangements Act, 1967.[27] This statute provides for agreeing provinces: (a) a provincial revenue equalization payment based on a complex formula that takes into account all of the province's revenues, rather than a few selected "standard taxes"; (b) a provincial revenue stabilization payment which guarantees, in effect, that a province's net general revenue in any year will be at least 95 per cent of that of the preceding year; (c) post-secondary education adjustment payments, by which each agreeing province receives from the federal government either 50 per cent of the operating costs of post-secondary education, or an amount equalling the province's population in 1967 multiplied by $15, whichever is greater. The same statute provides for the continuation of the federal collection of provincial income taxes, on terms to be agreed on in each contract. The payments to be made under these general provisions for the first year are estimated in Table I; a summary of the total payments to other governments out of the federal treasury for selected years, which conveys some indication of the complexity of the subject, is shown in Table II.

To this chronicle of massive transfers of money between governments must be added a note on massive new administrative arrangements. The abandonment by the Dominion of the tax-rental agreements in 1962, and the adoption of tax-collection agreements, obliged the provinces, as was intended, to levy their own income taxes. The further adoption of "opting out" arrangements, referred to below, and the Dominion's announced decision to withdraw from

26/See *The National Finances* for relevant years for summaries of developments.
27/*Can. Statutes*, 14–15–16 Eliz. II, c. 89.

TABLE I

Estimated payments to the provinces under the federal-provincial Fiscal Arrangements Act, 1967, for fiscal year 1968–9 (all dollar figures except per capitas in thousands)

	Nfld.	PEI	NS	NB	Que.	Ont.	Man.	Sask.	Alta.	BC	Total
Estimated population April 1, 1968	505,000	110,000	760,000	624,000	5,923,000	7,283,000	969,000	959,000	1,520,000	2,002,000	20,665,000
Provincial revenues											
Individual Income tax 28 per cent[b]	12,942	2,571	28,231	20,056	342,699[a]	615,003	61,505[b]	54,224[b]	89,967	156,736	1,383,934
Corporation Income tax 10 per cent[c]	10,012[c]	1,089	11,381	8,916	182,279[ac]	295,869[ac]	26,684[ac]	19,242[c]	45,258	61,106	661,836
Estate tax (75 per cent of 3-year average)	667	292	5,884	1,716	39,473[a]	63,312[a]	4,003	3,370	7,076	12,050[a]	137,843
Estimated revenue from all sources	109,162	19,320	134,292	166,231	1,913,571	2,638,422	271,055	321,628	559,110	704,632	6,837,423
Equalization (for all revenue sources)											
Yields at national average rates	94,497	22,014	169,197	131,536	1,675,033	2,614,363	280,664	314,998	744,952	790,169	6,837,423
Per capita yield at national average rates	187.12	200.13	222.63	210.79	282.80	358.97	289.64	328.47	490.10	394.69	331.03
Deficiency from national average ($331.03)	143.91	130.90	108.40	120.24	48.23	—	41.39	2.56	—	—	—
Equalization amount from above	72,675	14,399	82,384	75,030	285,666	—	40,107	2,455	—	—	572,716
Guaranteed equalization[d]	48,763	13,835	57,638	54,128	—	—	—	18,391	—	—	192,805
Payments to provinces											
Equalization payment[d]	72,675	14,399	82,384	75,030	285,666	—	40,107	18,391	—	—	588,652
Individual income tax collected	12,942	2,571	28,231	20,056	—	615,003	61,505	54,224	89,967	156,736	1,041,235
Corporation income tax collected	10,012	1,089	11,381	8,916	—	—	26,684	19,242	45,258	61,106	183,688
Share of estate tax collected	667	292	5,884	1,716	13,158	21,104	4,003	3,370	7,076	—	57,270
Share of income tax on power utilities	851	150	1,438	77	1,527	3,575	626	25	6,548	383	15,200
Statutory subsidies	9,656	657	2,133	1,745	4,023	4,624	2,136	2,151	2,955	1,672	31,752
Total payments to provinces	106,803	19,153	131,451	107,540	304,374[e]	644,306	135,061	97,403	151,804	219,897	1,917,797
Value of Income tax abatements for post-secondary education included in above											
4 per cent of individual income tax	1,849	367	4,033	2,865	48,957	87,858	7,455	6,573	12,852	22,391	195,200
1 per cent of corporation income tax base	834	109	1,138	892	15,190	24,656	2,426	1,749	4,526	6,221	57,741

[a]Quebec collects its own personal and corporation income taxes and Ontario its own corporation income tax. Quebec and Ontario collect 50 per cent of their shares of estate taxes through their succession duties and BC collects its 75 per cent share through its succession duties. Amounts entered are value of federal abatements for income taxes and full 75 per cent abatement of estate taxes. [b]Individual income tax rate in Manitoba and Saskatchewan is 33 per cent. [c]The provincial corporation income tax rate is 12 per cent in Ontario and Quebec which collect their own corporation income tax, 12 per cent in Newfoundland, 11 per cent in Manitoba and Saskatchewan, and 10 per cent in the other five provinces. Amounts entered for Ontario and Quebec are value of federal abatement. [d]See text for bases of equalization payment. [e]Does not include value of extra abatements to Quebec for opting out of certain joint programmes.
SOURCE: Department of Finance; and The National Finances, 1968–69 (Toronto, 1968), p. 145.

TABLE II

Summary of federal contributions to the provinces, municipalities, and territories, fiscal years 1958-9, 1962-3, and 1966-7 to 1968-9 (million dollars)

	1958-9	1962-3	1966-7[a]	1967-8[ab]	1968-9[ab]
PAYMENTS TO PROVINCES					
Unconditional grants					
Tax rentals	248.7	23.5	—	—	—
Equalization and stabilization	166.1	158.6	335.4	547.6	588.7
Share of federal estate tax	— [c]	16.6	48.1	53.7	57.3
Atlantic provinces grants	33.0	43.0	43.0	—	—
Power utilities income tax	8.7	10.0	6.0	6.3	15.2
Statutory subsidies	20.6	23.5	23.6	31.7	31.8
Total unconditional grants	477.1	275.3	456.1	639.3	692.9
Conditional grants					
Recreation and culture	1.7	1.6	.6	1.2	—
Hospital insurance	54.7	335.8	569.9	672.6	—
Other health	45.9	50.3	59.8	88.2	—
Welfare	74.1	159.5	244.2	408.7	—
Education	8.1	207.5	245.8	207.9	—
Transportation	55.4	44.1	103.9	92.5	—
Agriculture	1.9	4.5	27.8	23.2	—
Other natural resources	5.3	11.6	34.3	17.5	—
Civil defence	1.0	3.8	5.3	4.8	—
Municipal winter works	.2	27.0	37.5	30.3	—
National centennial	—	—	18.6	10.5	—
Other	.1	.1	1.1	.8	—
Total conditional grants	248.4	845.9	1,348.8	1,558.2	—
Total payments to provinces	725.5	1,121.1	1,804.9	2,197.5	—
PAYMENTS TO MUNICIPALITIES					
Grants in lieu of property taxes	21.9	29.8	39.0	41.9	48.1
Other grants	8.3	17.7	70.4	45.0	55.7
Total payments to municipalities	30.2	47.5	109.4	86.9	103.8
PAYMENTS TO TERRITORIES					
Statutory subsidies and tax rentals	1.1	3.6	6.4	9.4	12.0
Other grants	.4	2.8	2.8	3.0	3.5
Total payments to territories	1.5	6.4	9.1	12.4	15.5
TOTAL FEDERAL PAYMENTS	757.2	1,175.0	1,923.4	2,296.8	—
Federal per capita grants to universities	25.5	37.0	98.6	—	—
Estimate value of federal "standard" tax abatements (income and estate taxes)	—	673.4	1,399.6	1,879.0	2,081.7

financial involvement in health and welfare plans under provincial jurisdiction, has inevitably created a necessity for new techniques of liaison and co-ordination among governments. The growth of federal-provincial branches of administration at both levels of government constitutes one side of this; the establishment of both *ad hoc* and continuing committees of officials and political figures another, of which there are in existence well over one hundred examples.[28] In Ottawa a Federal-Provincial Relations Secretariat has been established in the Privy Council Office, directly under the prime minister, and the Department of Finance has a Federal-Provincial Relations Division. It appears improbable that Canada has continued a practice, which concerned the Tremblay commission over a decade ago, of following a "halting and unaware federalism which carries with it all the inconveniences and none of the advantages of true federalism."[29]

If some of the foregoing comments on administrative developments appear to suggest that recent developments in Dominion-provincial financial arrangements have been in the direction of increasing centralization, it must be emphasized that the contrary is true. The tax collection agreements so clearly thrust powers, or at least the use of powers, back on the provinces that at their inception they were hailed by some as a return to the "tax jungle" of the thirties, a prophecy not yet fulfilled. But taken in connection with the "opting out" arrangements provided for in the Established Programs (Interim Arrangements) Act of 1965,[30] which permits provinces to withdraw from shared-cost programmes in return for more tax room, and the federal government's declared intention of opting out on its own, it is plain that the federation is currently going through another swing towards decentralization. The shared-cost programmes undoubtedly played an indispensable rôle in permitting the poorer provinces, especially, to obtain services which they could not otherwise have afforded, although, as noted above, the programmes had their weaknesses. Only Quebec has adopted the policy of opting out of virtually everything available, but the temper of the federation in the early 1970s is none the less one that requires all provinces to assume a larger responsibility for their own direct taxes, and the uses to which they are put. This raises grave questions about the Dominion's ability to use fiscal policy as a tool for the stimulation

28/On this general theme see Meekison, *Canadian Federalism*, especially pp. 271–334; *Federal-Provincial Tax Structure Committee* (Ottawa, 1966).

29/Quoted by A. R. Kear in Meekison, *Canadian Federalism*, p. 306.

30/*Can. Statutes*, 13–14 Eliz. II, c. 54, amended by *ibid.*, 14–15–16 Eliz. II, c. 89.

NOTES TO TABLE II

*a*Conditional grants include value of tax abatements to Quebec plus equalization and operating cost adjustments for those programmes from which Quebec has opted out. *b*Estimates only. *c*Included in rental payments.

SOURCES: DBS, *Financial Statistics of the Government of Canada, 1958 and 1962*; Department of Finance; Dominion Bureau of Statistics; Public Accounts; Budget Papers; Estimates; and *The National Finances, 1968–69* (Toronto, 1968), p. 148.

of full employment and economic growth, and it may well be, as an astute observer recently wrote, that while federal-provincial disengagement in specific programmes may resolve some problems, it may also lead to "a sharper confrontation in broader areas of economic significance, particularly in fiscal policy, tax administration, and general economic development."[31]

And to that it can be added that the entire structure of the taxation system in Canada is once more undergoing a comprehensive review.[32]

31/T. K. Shoyama, "The New Federal-Provincial Fiscal Arrangements," mimeo. (Ottawa, 1968), p. 23.

32/See Trudeau, *Federal-Provincial Grants and the Spending Power of Parliament*; Benson, *The Taxing Powers and the Constitution of Canada*.

7 The development of the constitution

CONSTITUTIONS ARE CONTINUALLY CHANGING and becoming adapted to new ideas, new problems, new national and international forces. "Constitutions," said Lord Brougham, "must grow if they are to be of any value; they have roots, they ripen, they endure. Those that are fashioned resemble painted sticks planted in the ground ... they strike no root, bear no fruit, swiftly decay, and ere long perish." But while change and growth are inevitable phenomena in constitutional life, these follow an uncertain and largely unpredictable course. Certain fundamental principles, however, are apt to remain stationary or to yield to pressures very reluctantly, and constitutions can therefore afford as a rule to be rigid in essentials provided they are so framed that in other respects they are free to conform to the changing needs of the contemporary world. Inasmuch as a constitution is not confined to one document or one group of principles but assumes many forms, these forms will all bear to a varying degree the marks of the development and will also to some extent influence the course which that development will follow.

The diversified character of the Canadian constitution has already been described in some detail, and these components will furnish the key to the manner in which the constitution has been growing since its establishment. There are chiefly five ways in which this has taken place, although these are not at all exclusive; they frequently overlap and may to some degree support one another. The five chief methods of development are: (1) formal amendment of the British North America Act; (2) legal amendment authorized by the British North America Act; (3) acts of Parliament and orders-in-council; (4) convention; (5) judicial decision.

FORMAL AMENDMENTS TO THE BRITISH NORTH AMERICA ACT

The formal constitution, the British North America Act, has several claims to distinction, but the most unique are surely these: first, no one knows exactly how many times it has been amended; secondly, there is still doubt as to what is the actual (as distinguished from the nominal) process of amendment. The chief reason for these peculiarities is that the act contains no amending clause; and the result of this neglect is that a substantial portion of the act is still amended by the passage of an ordinary act of the British Parliament. No one is certain why an amending clause was omitted; although it may be supposed that a British statute appeared to be the normal instrument through which another British statute might be changed. (The colonies had been accustomed to requesting and obtaining changes in statutes concerning their affairs.) Everyone knows, however, why the omission has continued: the people of Canada have so far (1970) been unable to decide what method of amendment they would like to have inserted in the act, and no action can be taken until they somehow contrive to make up their minds. The Parliament of the United Kingdom would undoubtedly be pleased to be relieved of the task; but in the meantime, Canada occupies a somewhat humiliating position; for after many years of insistence on her independent status, she is compelled to admit that she is dependent upon an outside legislative body for the exercise of one of the most basic powers of self-government.

The fact that part of the British North America Act is amended by an ordinary act of the British Parliament gives a clue to some of the haziness surrounding the past amendments; for it will be recalled that ordinary British statutes may also be part of the Canadian constitution[1] and yet be formally quite unrelated to the British North America Act. A fair number of these, indeed, were passed before 1867. Acts of the legally omnipotent British Parliament have by virtue of that omnipotence a far-reaching and overriding effect, and while for many years they have not had any force so far as Canada has been concerned unless they have been made applicable by "express words or necessary intendment."[2] there have been some of these passed, and the line between acts amending the constitutional act and others has frequently become blurred. There have been acts, for example, which have dealt with matters which were at the time of passage beyond Canadian legal competence. These have not actually changed any part of the British North America Act, and while they may have affected what one might call the potential constitutional powers of the Dominion, it is difficult to consider them as authentic amendments to the act itself.[3] Other British statutes dealing with questions of loan priorities, boundaries, etc., while having reference to Canadian matters, are of such trivial importance that they can qualify as amendments in name only. Altogether, at least seventy-five British statutes have been passed since 1867 which apply to Canada to a greater or less degree; but of this total less than

1/*Supra*, pp. 62–3.
2/Colonial Laws Validity Act, 1865.
3/The Colonial Laws Validity Act, 1865, quoted above, and the Merchant Shipping Act, 1894 (*supra*, pp. 50, 62) are examples.

one-quarter would be accepted by most authorities[4] as genuine amendments. Since 1931, however, the identification of an amendment passed by the British Parliament is simple, for no act of the British Parliament extends to a dominion "as part of the law of that Dominion unless it is expressly declared in that Act that the Dominion has requested, and consented to, the enactment thereof."[5]

While there is still some disagreement on the eligibility of those British statutes which should be described as *bona fide* amendments to the British North America Act, the following comprise most of them, and certainly all the important ones:[6]

(1) *1871.* An act to remove doubts as to the power of the Dominion to establish new provinces, to provide for the representation of those provinces, and to validate certain Dominion statutes regarding the government of Rupert's Land and of Manitoba. The act further stated that once the Dominion Parliament had set up a new province, it could not alter the act of creation except in regard to provincial boundary changes which could be made with the province's consent.

(2) *1875.* An act to remove doubts as to the privileges, immunities, and powers of the Dominion Parliament and its members.

(3) *1886.* An act to empower the Canadian Parliament to provide for the representation of territories in the House of Commons and the Senate, and to allow the Parliament to alter the representation of new provinces in the House of Commons and the Senate.

(4) *1889.* An act to determine the boundaries of Ontario.

(5) *1895.* An act to remove doubts as to the power of the Canadian Parliament to provide for a Deputy Speaker for the Senate and to validate a Canadian statute already enacted on the subject.

(6) *1907.* An act to substitute a new section for section 118 of the British North America Act. It thereby raised the per capita monetary grants to the provinces and also the grants for the support of the provincial governments and legislatures.

(7) *1915.* An act to alter the scheme of representation in the Senate and House of Commons. It provided as follows: (*a*) the number of senators was increased to ninety-six; (*b*) a new western senatorial division of twenty-four senators was created, each of the four western provinces being given six senators; (*c*) the members in the Senate might be increased under section 26 of the British North America Act by four or eight instead of three or six, representing equally the four senatorial divisions; (*d*) the senators to which Newfoundland would be entitled in the event of its admission to the federation was raised to six; (*e*) a province would always be entitled to as many members in the House of Commons as it had senators.

4/The best analysis of this whole question is given in P. Gérin-Lajoie. *Constitutional Amendment in Canada* (Toronto, 1950); and Guy Favreau, *The Amendment of the Constitution of Canada* (Ottawa, 1965).

5/Statute of Westminster, section 4. See Appendix.

6/Dr Gérin-Lajoie and Mr Favreau include the Statute of Westminster and Mr Favreau's list also includes the Rupert's Land Act, 1868, and the Statute Law Revision Acts of 1893, 1927, and 1950. All of these, with the possible exception of the Rupert's Land Act, can also be regarded as basic statutes outside the BNA Act itself, though legally they may also be amendments. The variations between the lists of Gérin-Lajoie and Favreau are themselves revealing indications of the difficulty of defining an amendment.

(8) *1916*. An act to extend the life of the existing House of Commons by one year.

(9) *1930*. An act to confirm the agreements which transferred to the Prairie provinces the natural resources which had been held by the Dominion since their admission to the federation.

(10) *1940*. An act to give the Dominion jurisdiction over unemployment insurance. Section 91 was amended by adding as subsection 2 (a) "unemployment insurance."

(11) *1943*. An act to postpone the constitutional redistribution of seats in the House of Commons until the first session of Parliament after the cessation of hostilities.

(12) *1946*. An act to redistribute the seats in the House of Commons. This involved an entirely new draft of section 51 of the British North America Act.

(13) *1949 (no. 1)*. An act to admit Newfoundland to the federation.

(14) *1949 (no. 2)*. An act to give the Parliament of Canada power to amend the British North America Act except as regards provincial matters and subjects, constitutional guarantees regarding education and the use of the English or French language, and the parliamentary annual session and five-year maximum term. In time of real or apprehended war, invasion or insurrection the five-year term may be extended by act of Parliament if the extension is not opposed by the votes of more than one-third of the members of the House of Commons.

(15) *1951*. An act to give to the Parliament of Canada the power to make laws in relation to old age pensions, though not so as to affect the operation of any existing or future law of a provincial legislature on this subject.

(16) *1960*. An act to retire judges of provincial superior courts at the age of seventy-five.

(17) *1964*. An act to extend and clarify the pension amendment of 1951.

To this list of British statutes must be added two Canadian acts passed under the authority of the second amendment of 1949:

(18) *1952*. An act to provide a new safeguard for the representation in the House of Commons of a province whose population is becoming a relatively smaller fraction of the Dominion's; and to give a second member to the territories.

(19) *1965*. An act to retire senators appointed after June 1, 1965, at the age of seventy-five.

It is immediately apparent that the British statutes include several amendments of questionable standing if the criterion of genuine change is applied or the somewhat irrelevant but important one of duration. Certainly it is true that the earlier amendments particularly are not all of the same constitutional significance. The total can be broken down into three groups:

(a) *Amendments passed to clarify the powers granted by the British North America Act*. Three of the above amendments (nos. 1, 2, and 5) are in declaratory form – "an act to remove doubts" – but there can be little hesitation in declining to place in this class the 1871 amendment and the 1875 amendment regarding parliamentary privileges (nos. 1 and 2) on the ground that, whatever their form, they did make substantial changes in the existing act. There is thus one amendment in this class: no. 5 (1895).

(b) *Amendments of only temporary duration.* Two amendments, both caused by war conditions, fall into this class: no. 8 (1916) and no. 11 (1943). The first was operative for about one year; the second for three.

(c) *Amendments which have made substantive changes in the act.* These, determined after a process of elimination, are the unimpeachable amendments to the British North America Act, and the list now includes both British and Canadian statutes. There may be, as indicated above, more amendments than these; there cannot very well be less. They are: nos. 1, 2, 3, 4, 6, 7, 9, 10, 12, 13, 14, 15, 16, 17, 18, and 19, dated respectively 1871, 1875, 1886, 1889, 1907, 1915, 1930, 1940, 1946, 1949 (nos. 1 and 2), 1951, 1960, 1964, 1952, and 1965.

It has already been intimated that a search for the body which is legally competent to amend the British North America Act will be short and decisive: though discussions whose purpose is to bring to Canada the whole amending process have been going on for years, and with increasing intensity, that authority is still unquestionably, for several fundamental parts of the act, the Parliament of the United Kingdom. But here once more there emerges the familiar contradiction between legal procedures and actual practice; for the British Parliament has become simply the agent which is used by the Canadian people for accomplishing this particular political end – the formal amendment of their constitution. Where, then, is the real decision made? On whose request does the British Parliament proceed to the legal formalities of amending the act?

The precedents have furnished one answer in two different forms. A precedent was established, even before Confederation, that constitutional changes in the colony would be made by Great Britain only on colonial initiative. This rapidly developed into a hard and fast rule, and no change has been made since 1867 except at the request of the Dominion. There have been two bodies, however, which have in the past presented the request on behalf of Canada. On two occasions in the last century, and again in 1965, the Canadian cabinet asked for an amendment,[7] although the Canadian Parliament placed itself on record as early as 1871 to the effect that "no changes in the provisions of the British North America Act should be sought for by the executive Government without the previous assent of the Parliament of this Dominion."[8] On all other occasions the Canadian Parliament has made the request, which has been set forth in a joint address passed by the Canadian House of Commons and the

7/In 1875 and 1895 (nos. 2 and 5), and in 1965. The 1875 request was defended in the House on the ground that it simply asked to have a disallowed bill of the Canadian Parliament enacted; the 1895 request sought to have validated a Canadian act of doubtful validity. The 1965 request, which was rendered abortive by the subsequent action of the Quebec legislature in abolishing its legislative council, was concerned solely with the powers of that provincial council, and the federal cabinet, while informing Parliament, did not ask Parliament for its assent, on the grounds that only the province was involved; opposition critics did not accept this reasoning. See *Can. H. of C. Debates,* June 16 and 30, 1965, pp. 2479 ff.

8/*Ibid.,* March 27, 1871, pp. 649–50.

Senate. Since 1940 the joint address has also been a simultaneous address considered concurrently by the two Houses and when (as in 1960) one House amends the address, the two must agree on a final form in order that one petition may proceed to London. The joint address has become by custom the accepted method of approaching the British Parliament.[9]

Even this does not furnish a complete answer; for the inquiry may be pushed a little further to ascertain whether the Canadian Parliament will itself take sole responsibility for the presentation of the request, or will act only after consultation with the Canadian provinces. The answer to this question is not yet clear: the part which the provinces may take is beclouded by precedents, and it has become a subject of political dispute. Early in the dispute a principle was discovered known as the "compact theory" of Confederation, according to which the original provinces (and other provinces also by subsequent inclusion) entered into a compact or treaty in 1867, with the alleged result that any alteration in the terms of that compact must involve consultation with all parties (namely, the provinces) and eventually the consent of all parties, before it can be made. The Dominion is therefore expected (according to the theory) to secure this unanimous approval before presenting its request to the British Parliament.

The theory, while plausible, is constructed on sheer invention. It has no legal foundation; it has no historical foundation;[10] and the precedents to support it are few. While five provinces, meeting in 1887 in an interprovincial conference, asserted the right to initiate amendments independently of the Dominion Parliament, there is no instance of the provinces being consulted about a constitutional amendment before that of 1907, even though two of these amendments affected provincial rights of representation.[11] The 1907 amendment (relating to provincial subsidies) was preceded by consultation with all the provinces, and an objection raised by British Columbia was the probable cause of a slight change of wording when the British Parliament passed the statute.[12] But this example of consultation, which occurred as a matter of political convenience, has not become a governing precedent; for of the thirteen subsequent

9/*Ibid.*, July 29, 1960, pp. 7193 ff. See Gérin-Lajoie, *Constitutional Amendment in Canada*, pp. 47–131; Favreau, *The Amendment of the Constitution of Canada*, pp. 8–16; *McGill Law Journal*, XII, no. 4 (1966–7), passim.

10/See N. McL. Rogers, "The Compact Theory of Confederation," *Proceedings, Canadian Political Science Association, 1931*, pp. 205–30.

11/A possible exception, which is not always listed as an amendment by authorities, is the Canada (Ontario Boundary) Act, 1889, to which Ontario gave assent, after having played an active role in its initiation. But under the British North America Act of 1871 Parliament was empowered to alter provincial limits with the consent of the provincial legislature, and the 1889 act concerns provincial consultation as a matter of right in a specific circumstance rather than as a practice in connection with constitutional amendment. See Gérin-Lajoie, *Constitutional Amendment in Canada*, pp. 62–71, for a sympathetic consideration of the provinces' position.

12/See Maxwell, *Federal Subsidies to the Provincial Governments in Canada*, pp. 108–17.

amendments, only four (1940, 1951, 1960, and 1964) received prior provincial consent,[13] although the compact theory was frequently raised and discussed during this period. The first two and the fourth of these amendments gave what had been exclusive provincial powers to the federal government, and the third concerned judges in provincial courts; all four thus furnished a special reason for consultation with the provinces. On one other important occasion, however, the compact theory had enough vitality to prevent the Canadian Parliament acquiring for itself the explicit power of direct amendment, for one sector of the Statute of Westminster (inserted as a result of provincial pressure on the Dominion)[14] provided that the British North America Act and its amendments were excepted from those British statutes which could be amended or repealed by Dominion legislation.

Other amendments have presented several interesting features regarding the procedure. The "unemployment insurance" amendment of 1940 was held up for some years awaiting the approval of Quebec, which was finally given and the desired unanimity thereby obtained. By this postponement, announced the Canadian prime minister, "we have avoided anything in the nature of coercion of any of the provinces. Moreover, we have avoided the raising of a very critical constitutional question, namely, whether or not in amending the British North America Act it is absolutely necessary to secure the consent of all the provinces, or whether the consent of a certain number of provinces would of itself be sufficient ... For the present at any rate we have escaped any pitfall in that direction."[15] This is a novel way of escaping a constitutional difficulty; for the raising of the compact theory was avoided by conceding all that it demanded, as well as creating another precedent to be stored up for future use. A few more escaped pitfalls of this kind and there is no doubt that the critical constitutional question would be most definitely settled. In 1960, interestingly enough, the Dominion cabinet, having obtained unanimous provincial support for its proposal to retire judges at seventy-five, declined to accept an opposition amendment to its resolution because it felt it would have had to go back to the provinces.[16]

On the 1943 amendment, which postponed the redistribution of seats in the Commons, Mackenzie King took an entirely different stand. On this occasion the provinces were not consulted, even though the legislature of Quebec passed a resolution of protest and the Quebec leader of the opposition, Duplessis,

13/A suggested amendment in 1936 (regarding provincial and Dominion-provincial finance), which was killed in the Senate, received the assent of all the provincial governments.

14/See Memorandum and Letter of G. Howard Ferguson, in R. MacG. Dawson, *Constitutional Issues in Canada, 1900–31* (Toronto, 1933), pp. 28–34.

15/*Can. H. of C. Debates*, June 25, 1940, pp. 1117–18. Mr Diefenbaker repeated this disclaimer in 1960; see *ibid.*, June 14, 1960, p. 4886.

16/*Ibid.*, July 29, 1960, p. 7201. The government did not feel obliged to go back to the provinces because the Senate amended the original resolution in the same terms as had been proposed by the opposition in the Commons.

asked King to forward the protest to the British prime minister together with Duplessis' request that the British Parliament should refuse to pass the desired amendment. King declined to do so for the following reasons:

(i) The matter did not concern the provincial legislature, but was a matter for the federal Parliament.
(ii) "The theory that the British North America Act is a pact between the provinces which cannot be amended in any particular without the prior consent of every province ... does not appear to be supported either in history or in law."
(iii) "Any such intervention by the Government or Parliament of Great Britain in the internal affairs of our country would be the negation of Canada's equality of status with the United Kingdom ... It is true that it is still legally necessary to ask the Parliament of Great Britain to amend the British North America Act. The situation, however, is acceptable only so long as such amendments are made automatically and without question on the request of the appropriate representatives of the Canadian people."[17]

The above indicates the answer to be given to another allied question, namely, the obligation laid on the British Parliament to carry out any request from the Canadian authorities. There have been four instances when the British Parliament did not take immediate action to implement such a request, and in each instance there were excellent reasons to justify a postponement, in which Canada apparently concurred. It may therefore be stated with confidence that formal action will be, as King intimated above, automatic and without question. "The seventy-year old practice of the Canadian constitution, the solemnly expressed conventions of Dominion status, and the usage of fellow-members of the British Commonwealth of Nations all combine to show that the sovereign British Parliament has now accepted a formal and technical role in relation to Canada similar to that long held by the Crown both in Britain and in Canada."[18]

All this did not mean that the provinces could be ignored in the amending process. But down to the last few years, when negotiations between the Dominion and the provinces on the amending process have proceeded on the assumption that if the process is to be brought to Canada the provinces must participate in at least some kinds of amendments, the provinces were not considered as having a formal role, and no compact or similar theory has restricted the conventional power of the Dominion Parliament to request the passage of amendments from the British Parliament, and the obligation laid on the latter to follow this request. No one would for a moment deny that the provinces have certain rights as well as powers under the British North America Act, and that at least matters which involve the exercise of provincial powers should not be arbitrarily changed by unilateral action of the Dominion Parliament. The provinces and the Dominion also have common interests in a variety of

17/Montreal *Gazette*, July 16, 1943.
18/H. McD. Clokie, "Basic Problems of the Canadian Constitution," *Canadian Journal of Economics and Political Science*, VIII, no. 1 (Feb., 1942), p. 24.

matters: for example, the status of Canada's two languages, and university education. But the recognition of constitutional rights – whether they be explicit or implied – did not give the provinces any comprehensive cast-iron protection such as that stated in the compact theory. The legal and conventional position as it existed for decades was accurately stated by Mr St Laurent, then minister of Justice, when the proposed 1946 amendment was before the House. In reply to a query whether section 133 (regarding the use of the English or French languages in Canada and Quebec, a situation subsequently changed by section 91 (1)) could be altered without provincial consent, he said:

Legally I say it can. The situation appears to me to be this. There are persons and nations who reach a high estate in the affairs of men, and the high estate they reach imposes upon them high obligations ... I feel – and I believe my fellow Canadians of my race and my religion can feel – that a better guarantee than anything that might be found in Section 133 is to be found in that respect, for those who have been formed under the principles of British freedom and British fair play, to protect what are our essential rights.

It is not the manner of those who have themselves had, and whose ancestors have had, the formation that comes from that long history which has brought us to this point in the civilization of mankind, to do things which the conscience of humanity at large would regard as dishonourable; and the conscience of humanity at large would frown upon an assemblage in this house that attempted to take from me and from those of my race the right to speak the language I learned in my infancy as one of the official languages in which the deliberations of this house may be carried on. So it is of everything else that is not within Section 92. If it is fair, if it is just, if it is proper according to the standards of human decency, it will be done; if it is unfair, if it is unjust, if it is improper, all members of this house will say, "It is not our manner to do such things."[19]

The essential difficulty in the situation arises from the endeavour to accomplish two desirable yet apparently contradictory things: (a) the written constitution should be kept rigid in order to give adequate protection to the minority, and this is best ensured by insisting that every province must agree to any change; (b) the written constitution should be kept elastic so that new conditions and demands can be readily met by constitutional changes adapted to the altered circumstances. The contradiction is partly superficial; for the parts of the constitution which are to be cherished and guarded are not all the same parts which must be adjusted to varying conditions. Thus one solution that has in the past appealed to many authorities lies in providing different methods of amendment for different kinds of constitutional provisions.

This was the remedy proposed at a Dominion-provincial conference in 1935 which gave consideration to this problem. The proposal distinguished four different kinds of clauses in the British North America Act, and each of these would have its appropriate process of amendment.[20]

19/*Can. H. of C. Debates*, June 18, 1946, pp. 2621–2. See, however, Gérin-Lajoie, *Constitutional Amendment in Canada*, pp. 155–84, 213–17.
20/*Canadian Annual Review, 1935–6*, p. 323.

(i) Clauses concerning the constitution of the House of Commons and the Senate would be amended by the Dominion Parliament.

(ii) Clauses relating to the Dominion and one or more, but not all, provinces would be amended by the Dominion House of Commons and Senate and the legislatures of the provinces concerned.

(iii) Clauses relating to matters of mutual concern to the Dominion and provinces would be amended by the Dominion House of Commons and Senate and the legislatures of two-thirds of the provinces, provided that the population of these provinces was at least 55 per cent of the population of Canada. (This would ensure that either Ontario or Quebec was included in the two-thirds majority.)

(iv) Clauses relating to provincial and minority rights would be amended by the Dominion House of Commons and Senate and the legislatures of all the provinces.

If the Senate should refuse to pass an amending bill sent from the House of Commons, and if the same bill should again be passed at the next session of the House, it would then go to a joint session of the two houses and final decision would rest with the latter body.

This proposal was finally dropped in 1936 because of the opposition of New Brunswick; and what was substantially the same suggestion came before a similar body in 1950. The scheme came to grief over the apportionment of clauses among the different amending authorities, which was, of course, the crux of the matter.[21] It had the advantage of recognizing that the amending process should be marked by some flexibility as among the various sections of the British North America Act but when, a decade later, the Dominion and the provinces again took up the problem, a general hardening of opinion in favour of rigidity was discernible.

In a lengthy series of conferences beginning late in 1960 and held almost annually thereafter, the eleven governments discussed the two fundamental issues at stake: how to transport to Canada the amendment of the act, and how to amend the act thereafter. The conferences encountered the inevitable and somewhat paradoxical dilemma: the parties agreed unanimously that the amending power should rest within Canada, but they were unable to agree unanimously on how to bring it to Canada, or how to amend the act once domiciled. There appears at first to have been almost unanimous agreement that the unanimous consent of the provinces was necessary for any amendment affecting the distribution of powers, with Saskatchewan alone vigorously opposing the entrenchment of all provincial powers.[22] The negotiations produced over time a draft amendment which became celebrated as the "Fulton-Favreau Formula" (named for two ministers of Justice) and sought to leap the double hurdle of bringing the act to Canada and providing for its amendment thereafter through a deceptively brief and simple set of proposals. In general, it provided for amendment of the act by Parliament with the unani-

21/Constitutional Conference of Federal and Provincial Governments, January 10–12, 1950, and September 25–8, 1950, *Proceedings*.

22/See *A Review of Saskatchewan's Position Regarding a Basis for the Amendment of our Constitution in Canada*, Department of the Attorney-General, Regina, 1962; B. L. Strayer, "Saskatchewan and the Amendment of the Canadian Constitution," *McGill Law Journal*, XII, no. 4 (1966–7), pp. 443–73.

mous consent of the provinces for four fundamental classes of subjects,[23] and in other subjects with the consent of all affected provinces when fewer than the entire ten were involved. Amendments to less firmly entrenched sections of the act, not referring to one or more of the provinces, could be made by Parliament if concurred in "by the legislatures of at least two-thirds of the provinces representing at least fifty per cent of the population of Canada."[24] The draft also provided for delegation of legislative authority between the Dominion and the provinces under carefully defined circumstances, a provision that had been the subject of much controversy in the conferences but on which substantial agreement in principle had been reached.[25]

These proposals, which were widely considered to be both reasonable and reasonably flexible, foundered on an ancient shoal. In so far as the distribution of powers was concerned, the proposals of the 1960s, unlike those of 1935 and 1950, accepted in fact, if not in form, the compact theory of Confederation which the Dominion had so often scouted in the past. The criticisms of the compact theory thus also apply to some of the main proposals of the Fulton-Favreau formula:

It would give a single province a power of veto over constitutional changes desired by the remaining ... provinces and by a vast majority of the Canadian electorate. It would mean that Canada would be taking a deliberate step towards greater rigidity in its constitutional arrangements when the whole trend of modern economic life is emphasizing the vital importance of flexibility in a rapidly changing world. It would arrest the growth and hamper the expression of the national idea in Canada ... It would provide the most remarkable illustration in history of a national community refusing to trust its own judgment in the determination of its domestic arrangements and its way of life.[26]

Saskatchewan's early view was stated unequivocally. "No single province," its spokesman argued, "should be able to thwart the reasonable demands of the Canadian people as a whole provided proper guarantees exist for minority rights and for the civil code in Quebec."[27] And when Saskatchewan changed its mind and began to favour the formula (after a change of government in 1964), it was Quebec which developed misgivings, and early in 1966 Premier Lesage announced that further consideration of the formula by Quebec would be indefinitely postponed.[28] The formula has since been considered dead, and subsequent federal-provincial conferences have concentrated on other matters. The ambitions which the formula sought to attain, however, remain very much alive.

23/The classes were: (a) the powers of the legislature of a province to make laws; (b) the rights or privileges granted or secured by the constitution of Canada to the legislature or government of a province; (c) the assets or property of a province; and (d) the use of the English or French language. See Favreau, *The Amendment of the Constitution of Canada*, pp. 110–15.
24/*Ibid.*, p. 111.   25/*Ibid.*, p. 113.
26/N. McL. Rogers, "The Constitutional Impasse," *Queen's Quarterly*, Winter 1934, p. 486.
27/*A Review of Saskatchewan's Position*, pp. 18–19.
28/*Can. H. of C. Debates*, Jan. 28, 1966 (Appendix), pp. 421–3.

The sections of the British North America Act suggest to a limited degree the kind of solution to the amendment problem which has been advanced above; for these sections art not all equally rigid. While the bulk of the act can still (1970) be amended only by the British Parliament, some parts can be altered by the Dominion Parliament, some by provincial legislatures, some by other authorities.

The British North America Act provided not only a form of government for the future, but also an immediate government for the new Dominion, and some of its terms had therefore to be of a temporary nature. The temporary clauses, designed to give the Dominion government its initial impetus, were therefore prefaced by the clause "until the Dominion Parliament otherwise provides," so that at any time they could be amended by an ordinary act. Thus the electoral districts for the House of Commons, the election law, the qualifications and disqualifications of members of the House of Commons, the franchise, the trial of controverted elections, and other matters, are provided for in the act (directly or by reference) subject to any later changes Parliament may desire.

There were also other provisions which the Dominion has altered but which, it is safe to assert, were not intended to be changed, namely, the sections dealing with financial grants to the provinces. Indeed, special precautions were taken to ensure the permanence of at least two of these grants by stating that they were to be "in full settlement of all future demands."[29] The first break in the financial provisions came in 1869 when the "better terms" for Nova Scotia were conceded, and although the validity of such legislation was questioned in the House, the Colonial Office stated that such grants were within the legal competence of the Canadian Parliament. Since then, the Dominion has availed itself many times of its inherent right to spend its revenue as it sees fit, and the financial provisions have proved in practice to have been the most flexible of all the clauses of the British North America Act.[30]

To these original clauses of the act empowering the Canadian Parliament to alter certain sections must now be added (as already noted) the provisions of the 1949 (no. 2) amendment.[31] This covers all matters which concern the federal government only, except for the annual meeting of Parliament and the five-year maximum term. It is phrased, however, as a *general* amending power, subject to the above "federal" exceptions (which, while important, are not

29/Section 118. See *supra*, pp. 100–1.
30/J. A. Maxwell, "A Flexible Portion of the British North America Act," *Canadian Bar Review*, March 1933, pp. 149–57. The family allowances, paid by the Dominion, have been justified by virtue of the same right of unrestricted largesse.
31/*Supra*, p. 122; Appendix.

likely to cause difficulties) and subject also to "provincial" powers and "minority" rights – both of which are very important indeed. The amendment states that the exclusive legislative authority of the Parliament of Canada should extend to all matters coming within the following classes of subjects:

The amendment from time to time of the Constitution of Canada, except as regards matters coming within the classes of subjects by this Act assigned exclusively to the Legislatures of the provinces, or as regards rights or privileges by this or any other Constitutional Act granted or secured to the Legislature or the Government of a province, or to any class of persons with respect to schools or as regards the use of the English or French language or as regards the requirements that there shall be a session of the Parliament of Canada at least one each year, and that no House of Commons shall continue for more than five years from the day of the return of the Writs for choosing the House; provided, however, that a House of Commons may in time of real or apprehended war, invasion or insurrection be continued by the Parliament of Canada if such continuation is not opposed by the votes of more than one-third of the members of such House.

Though only two amendments have so far (1970) been passed under this authority, it appeared to give a new flexibility to certain parts of the British North America Act and it is an interesting commentary on the Fulton-Favreau formula that it proposed to limit the substance of the British North America Act, 1949 (no. 2), as a concession to several of the provinces.

It will be recalled that the immediate purpose of the British North America Act was not confined to the launching of a new government for the Dominion alone; two other governments, those for Ontario and Quebec, had to be formed from the old Province of Canada. So another group of clauses began with the words "until the legislature of Quebec [or Ontario] otherwise provides," and these may be amended by an ordinary act of the provincial legislature in question.

Finally, there are changes in the provisions of the act which may be made by other authorities. The provinces may amend their own constitutions except as they concern the office of lieutenant governor. The lieutenant governors of Quebec and of Ontario can change the original composition of their respective Executive Councils and the designs on their Great Seals; the seats of the provincial governments are named in the act, subject to change by the provincial executives; and Ottawa is declared to be the capital of Canada "until the Queen otherwise directs."

ACTS OF PARLIAMENT AND ORDERS-IN-COUNCIL

The importance to the constitution of the acts of Parliament and orders-in-council, which deal with constitutional matters, has already been discussed.[32] These, being readily passed, form one of the most common methods of

32/*Supra*, pp. 63–4.

adapting the offices and functions of government to the current needs of the state, and many changes of this kind take place every year. The enormous output of orders-in-council dealing with "organic" material and the rapid proliferation of committees, controllers, directors, administrators, censors, custodians, registrars, commissioners, and other officials which occurred during the Second World War are examples of what a government can do by this method when it really sets its mind to it. Only a small proportion of changes effected in this way may properly be considered additions to the constitution; their number at any one time is not readily determined.

CONVENTION

The place of usage and conventional devices in Canadian government has also been described in some detail.[33] The fact that so large a part of the constitution is composed of these conventions makes it a virtual certainty that when changes occur many of them will also be conventional. There is, of course, nothing to prevent changes in existing conventions being brought about by some other means, such as legislation, and it is not uncommon to have them confirmed in this way. The passage of the Statute of Westminster, which was designed to place in legal form the conventional practices of the preceding years, is an excellent illustration. But the most natural way to alter one convention is by the gradual infiltration of another. A convention may involve action in a certain way or according to certain principles, or it may simply involve an abstention; but there must normally be a succession of incidents or, more rarely, one act which meets with such general acceptance that it thereby acquires a special authority. "Every act is a precedent," according to Sir Ivor Jennings, "but not every precedent creates a rule. It can hardly be contended that if once the House of Lords agrees with the House of Commons it is henceforth bound to agree with the lower House ... It is more important that there is a course of precedents ... Precedents create a rule because they have been recognized as creating a rule."[34]

While it is true that conventions will tend to change by the new supplanting the old, the discussion in earlier chapters will indicate that they will often occur as a mellowing influence on other more rigid parts of the constitution. The exceptional rigidity of the British North America Act, as attested by the small number of formal amendments, exerts a constant pressure to have the act altered in some other way, and convention is frequently at hand to work the miracle. Convention has, in fact, operated in three major constitutional fields: in those of pure custom, in those of legislation, and in those of the written constitution itself.

(a) *In fields which are not covered by legislation or by the written constitu-*

33/*Supra*, pp. 57–60; 64–8.
34/W. Ivor Jennings, *Cabinet Government* (3rd ed., Cambridge, 1950), p. 6.

tion. This is the realm of pure custom where Parliament and the written constitution have been content to allow precedents to build up and solidify. One tremendously important constitutional change, for example, has been the establishment of the convention that the cabinet must resign when the House of Commons withdraws its support, and from this another custom has grown, namely, that a government which has been clearly defeated in a general election will immediately resign without awaiting the verdict of the House. Another well-established usage in Canada is that after the popular defeat of a government, the governor general will normally choose the leader of the opposition as his new prime minister. The choice was for many years indirectly controlled by the opposition members in Parliament, who selected their leader; but this practice has been altered in the last few decades during which time the custom has become established of selecting the leader by a national convention composed of party representatives from all parts of the Dominion. The relations of Canada with Great Britain are filled with examples of one custom being built on and adding to a custom which has been previously established, and which, in turn, may be an outgrowth of an earlier practice. Within Parliament, as has been noted, English has been by custom the working language for most purposes and French the language of translation. Many of the important relationships between English- and French-speaking in Ottawa are similarly governed by convention.[35]

(*b*) *In fields covered by legislation.* Here the changes brought about by usage are rather infrequent, for the natural and speedy way to effect a change is by an amendment to the statute. In some instances, usage may work with the statute towards some constitutional end. The composition of the cabinet, for example, is not controlled directly by any law, but it is determined by custom; for custom ordains that virtually all the legally constituted departments shall have their ministers sitting in the cabinet. The office of postmaster general is thus created by statute, but it is only a convention that places the incumbent in the cabinet. A rare example of a convention that has almost completely nullified a statute is provided by the tenure of the civil servant. The act of Parliament states that the civil servant holds office at pleasure, yet for well over a century the tenure of the civil servant has in practice been one during good behaviour.[36]

(*c*) *In fields covered by the written constitution.* Here convention has virtually amended the British North America Act, sometimes changing the nominal operation of the act, on rarer occasions actually rendering the act completely obsolete. A number of illustrations have already been given,[37] but one which has been touched on above, may be somewhat elaborated.

35/See Ward, "The National Political Scene"; J. D. Hoffman and N. Ward, *Bilingualism and Biculturalism in the Canadian House of Commons,* report prepared for the Royal Commission on Bilingualism and Biculturalism (Ottawa, 1970).

36/R. MacG. Dawson, *The Civil Service of Canada* (Toronto, 1929), pp. 9–13, 178–9; *Can. Statutes,* 14–15–16 Eliz. ii, c. 71, 524.

37/*Supra,* pp. 57–60.

In 1867 the act gave the governor general the power (which, unlike some of the other powers, he was supposed to exercise himself) to reserve certain classes of bills (indicated in his Instructions) for the "signification of the Queen's Pleasure," that is, the assent of the British government. From 1867 to 1878 some twenty-one bills were so reserved. The result of the Blake correspondence[38] was a change in the governor's Instructions and the occasions for reservation became very rare, for any difficulties of this kind became a matter of discussion and adjustment between the British and Canadian governments. Thus those Canadian acts which involved matters of imperial concern and were now the only ones to be considered would frequently not come into effect until proclaimed, and such proclamation would not be made if no solution of the difficulty could be found.[39] The Imperial Conference of 1926 and the conference of 1929 went a step further and declared that any interference of the imperial government with the legislation of a dominion was no longer in accordance with constitutional practice, and the latter meeting proposed facilities for deleting the offending clause from the British North America Act. The clause, however, has now by convention become so completely inoperative that no one even bothers about its continued presence in the act.[40] Thus one practice built upon another has gradually rendered obsolete the legal power and procedure which is laid down in the British North America Act. The clause still remains in the act; but its shining letters have become dull and tarnished like some forgotten name-plate on a door long closed.

JUDICIAL DECISION

It becomes largely an act of supererogation to indicate after the preceding chapters the way in which the courts develop the constitution and particularly the way in which one decision and interpretation prepares the way for further interpretations in the future. The effect on development may be negative or positive, restrictive or broadening, depending on whether the court declares a particular statute *ultra vires* or upholds its validity and gives greater precision to its terms.

It is not proposed to discuss at length the arguments for and against the power of the courts to set aside laws which in their opinion run counter to the

38/*Supra*, pp. 42–7.
39/Keith, *Responsible Government in the Dominions*, II, p. 751.
40/The power of the British government to disallow a Canadian act (which was contained in section 56 of the BNA Act) came under the same declaration of the conferences of 1926 and 1929. It had, however, been effectively dropped at a much earlier date. The one Canadian act disallowed was in 1873, and it was clearly *ultra vires*. The power of the governor general to refuse his assent to a bill passed by the two Houses of Parliament has never been exercised since Confederation, and Sir John A. Macdonald repeatedly held that it was obsolete, as was the similar power of a lieutenant governor. (The lieutenant governor's power has none the less been used some thirty times, the last one in 1945.)

supreme written constitution;[41] but a few points may be raised. There are, of course, many countries where the courts do not exercise this power and where the legislature is able successfully to determine the scope of its own authority. But the situation under a federal form of government is unique in that the system inevitably results in a constant clash of governmental powers, and there is thus a never-failing demand for the services of an austere and impartial arbiter to decide questions of jurisdiction. This function the courts can perform more acceptably than any other agency yet devised, not alone because of the legal nature of the matters involved or the excellence of the work done, but also because of the confidence they are able to command. The security of the Canadian provinces, to make the argument more explicit, would vanish over-night if the Dominion Parliament were to be given the last word on the extent of its own powers, and, what is equally important, no province would be con-vinced that in arriving at any such decision its rights had been given fair and impartial consideration.

Judicial review has been frequently criticized on the ground that under it vital questions of public policy are determined in the courtroom and not on the floors of the legislature where such decisions should be taken. Undoubtedly this is to a degree true; but the force of the argument is in most instances derived from the experience in the United States, where "due process" and several other wide and ambiguous phrases in the constitution have lured the courts into a position where they have become in a very real and disturbing sense the rivals of the legislature. Such an opportunity is often lurking in the background where the courts have the power of review, but it can be kept under fair control by careful constitutional phraseology and by an acute sense on the part of the judiciary of its proper function as an interpreter of the constitution. It has been suggested,[42] for example, that the Judicial Committee may have been influenced by this latter consideration when it proceeded to emasculate the "peace, order, and good government" clause. If, it is argued, the clause was to be given the pre-eminence to which it was apparently entitled, one of two alternatives had to be faced. First, the national scope and character of all federal legislation would be decided by a simple declaration to that effect by the Dominion Parliament, in which event the provinces would obviously have little or no protection against any attempted inroads by the Dominion. In the alternative, the determination of this crucial question would be left to the courts, with the result that the latter would find themselves deciding questions which were not judicial but were essentially matters of expediency and public policy. It is therefore suggested that rather than face either of these alternatives, the Judicial Committee may have fallen back on the Dominion's enumerated powers as presenting a fairly definite statement of jurisdiction which the com-mittee felt could be judicially determined without deciding what were essen-tially legislative questions.

41/See McWhinney, *Judicial Review.*
42/*Rowell-Sirois Report,* I, pp. 56–8.

The judicial review of legislative powers is frequently attacked because it allows the courts to read into the constitution virtually anything they wish, and it is not unnaturally urged that such authority is highly undesirable in any judicial body. The flaw lies in the first part of the argument. While it is undoubtedly true that the courts by throwing their weight on one side or the other can shift the constitutional centre of gravity, the extent of the movement will depend in large measure upon the number of vague clauses and provisions which are available. If these are absent, the disputes which arise can generally be decided either way without any very serious impairment of the constitution; while at all times the great bulk of the provisions cannot be seriously attacked through court action.

Courts may modify, they cannot replace. They can revise earlier interpretations, as new arguments, new points of view are presented; they can shift the dividing line in marginal cases; but there are barriers they cannot pass, definite assignments of power they cannot reallocate. They can give a broadening construction of existing powers, but they cannot assign to one authority powers explicitly granted to another, or modify the provisions of the B.N.A. Acts regarding the organization of the executive and legislative branches of the Dominion.[43]

Finally, it is well to remember that the supreme power in the state is not the courts, but the constitution-amending authority. Any decision which is clearly contrary to the wishes of the people can be overcome by constitutional amendment; and while this may involve delay, even that is not always a disadvantage. The fundamental difficulty – if it is a difficulty – in this procedure will be that the outraged public may prove to be not very outraged after all, and perhaps, as a body, not even annoyed, and therefore constitutional amendment may not be readily obtainable. Criticize the Privy Council as one may, the fact remains that its enlargement of provincial rights in the decades before and after the turn of the century was not as shocking as many would like to believe, and it appears to have been in substantial accord with the general trend of opinion in Canada. Even today, despite complaints about judicial distortion of the constitution, there are doubts as to the degree of unanimity among the Canadian people on many of the measures which are being advanced to promote social and economic welfare and on the matter of the jurisdiction under which these measures should be placed. One thing is beyond dispute: the placing of unemployment insurance in section 91 in 1940 is the only clear example to suggest that the Canadian people genuinely desire to enlarge Dominion jurisdiction at provincial expense. The old age pension amendments of 1951 and 1964 enlarged the Dominion's powers, but were worded so as to establish that provincial jurisdiction was not to be affected; Dominion legislation is inoperative in any province which chooses to pass its own legislation.

The courts, when performing their normal function of interpreting a statute, have always relied on the text itself in their endeavour to ascertain the exact

43/O. D. Skelton, Evidence before the Special Committee on the British North America Act; see its *Report*, 1935, p. 28.

intentions of the legislature, even although at times the application of this principle might lead to results which the legislature had never contemplated. The task of the courts is to place a reasonable interpretation on the document which they have before them and not force into it any strained meaning which is not in accord with the wording of the individual clause taken in relation to the statute as a whole. Their duty "is to interpret, not to enact ... The question is, not what may be supposed to have been intended, but what has been said."[44]

This rule is by general consent an admirable guide for ordinary statutory interpretation; but it is much more doubtful if it should be carried over intact to a written constitution. The Supreme Court of the United States has not hesitated to relax its rules of construction when endeavouring to interpret the American constitution, and it has always been conscious of the fact that the constitution was not an ordinary law but one which should have unique character and flexibility adapted to the purpose it was to serve. "We must never forget" said Chief Justice Marshall in a famous case, "that it is a *constitution* we are expounding," and it was in a large measure this enlightened attitude which made John Marshall's contribution to the development of the American constitution so outstanding.[45] To quote an American authority:

The true method of interpretation is a resultant of these somewhat divergent forces – a combination of the precise, strict, verbal, narrow mode of the lawyer, and the broader, freer habit of the statesman. The one looks mainly at the letter, disregarding consequences, motives, reasons – *ita lex scripta est*; the other passes by the letter, and concerns itself with great principles, with considerations of a high expediency, with far-reaching national results ... The one [school] would cramp and dwarf the energies of a growing nation; the other would remove all the barriers which have been set up lest those energies should finally become self-destructive. Combine the two, and the essential ideas of a positive law, and of a political society as the subject of that law, are preserved; the safety and stability of the government are ensured; the national development may go on uninterrupted by arbitrary restraints, and unbroken by sudden shocks.[46]

The Judicial Committee of the Privy Council resolutely adhered to the narrow and less adaptable principle by insisting that the courts "must treat the provisions of the Act in question [the British North America Act] by the same methods of construction and exposition which they apply to other statutes."[47] It refused to admit, for example, that the Quebec and London

44/*Brophy* v. *Attorney-General for Manitoba* (1895), App. Cas. 202, at pp. 215–16.
45/See also the opinion of Chief Justice Marshall in *Dartmouth College* v. *Woodward* (1819), 4 Wheaton 518, at pp. 644–5; that of Justice Story in *Martin* v. *Hunter's Lessee* (1816), 1 Wheaton 304, at pp. 326–7; that of Justice Holmes in *Missouri* v. *Holland* (1920), 252 U.S. 416, at p. 433.
46/J. N. Pomeroy, *Introduction to the Constitutional Law of the United States*, edited by E. H. Bennett (Boston, 1886), p. 16.
47/*Bank of Toronto* v. *Lambe* (1887), 12 App. Cas. 575, at p. 579; see also p. 587.
A careful analysis of the Privy Council's course, from a particular point of view, is Browne, *The Judicial Committee and the British North America Act.*

Resolutions and material of a similar nature[48] could be accepted as giving any assistance in interpreting the terms or intent of the British North America Act. It also developed, as already indicated, its own ideas of federalism; but it made little or no endeavour to reconcile these with the known intentions of the founders or, in recent years, with the pressing demands of modern life. "The Act is to be expounded and given effect to according to the terms set out in it, finding the intention from its words, upholding it precisely as framed, ascertaining its true meaning within itself and clear of any qualifications which the Imperial Parliament has not expressed in it, and apart from any questions of expediency or of political exigency."[49]

Since the Supreme Court of Canada has taken over from the Privy Council the task of interpreting the British North America Act, it is relevant to add that on rare occasions the Privy Council momentarily discarded the rules and traditions of many years, and ventured into more uncharted seas:[50]

Their Lordships do not think it right to apply rigidly to Canada of to-day the decisions and the reasons therefor which commended themselves, probably rightly, to those who had to apply the law in different circumstances, in different centuries, to countries in different stages of development ... Their Lordships think that the appeal to Roman law and to early English decisions is not of itself a secure foundation on which to build the interpretation of the British North America Act of 1867 ... The British North America Act planted in Canada a living tree capable of growth and expansion within its natural limits. The object of the Act was to grant a constitution to Canada. "Like all written constitutions it has been subject to development through usage and convention": *Canadian Constitutional Studies*, Sir Robert Borden (1922), p. 55.

Their Lordships do not conceive it to be the duty of this Board – it is certainly not their desire – to cut down the provisions of the Act by a narrow and technical construction, but rather to give it a large and liberal interpretation so that the Dominion to a great extent, but within certain fixed limits, may be mistress in her own house, as the provinces to a great extent, but within certain fixed limits, are mistresses in theirs. "The Privy Council, indeed, has laid down that courts of law must treat the provisions of the British North America Act by the same methods of construction and exposition which they apply to other statutes. But there are statutes and statutes; and the strict construction deemed proper in the case, for example, of a penal or taxing statute or one passed to regulate the affairs of an English parish, would be often subversive of Parliament's real intent if applied to an Act passed to ensure the peace, order, and good government of a British colony": See Clement's *Canadian Constitution*, 3rd ed., p. 347.[51]

48/See Vincent C. MacDonald, "Constitutional Interpretation and Extrinsic Evidence," *Canadian Bar Review*, Feb. 1939, pp. 77–93.

49/W. P. M. Kennedy, "The British North America Act: Past and Future," *Canadian Bar Review*, June 1937, p. 393.

50/*Edwards* v. *Attorney-General for Canada*, [1930] A.C. 124. In one other decision five years later the committee edged cautiously in the same direction. *British Coal Corporation* v. *the King*, [1935] A.C. 500, at pp. 518–19. See also *supra*, pp. 89–96.

51/*Edwards* v. *Attorney-General for Canada*, [1930] A.C. 124, at pp. 134–7. Even here the court is careful (at p. 137) to point out that it is not considering the distribution of legislative powers under sections 91 and 92.

Too much should not be expected, however, from isolated precedents, and even contemporary writers held their enthusiasm well in hand when the foregoing decision was recorded. "For a nation," wrote Professor Kennedy in 1934, "whose constitution has been divorced by judicial decision from its origins and historical intentions, it is, perhaps, pardonable to clutch, respectfully, but not without hope, at any straws thrown to us in the whirlpool of judicial chaos."[52] The Privy Council, with the notable exception of the Canada Temperance Federation case of 1946, threw out few additional straws, and the course of the Supreme Court of Canada since 1949 has been, as already noted, too short and unsettled to establish with clarity what judicial review in the 1970s is likely to mean.[53] It appears to be leaning towards a broader view of what is involved in "peace, order, and good government."[54]

The extent to which any one method of constitutional development is used will depend upon a wide variety of circumstances, such as the rigidity or flexibility of the constitution, the popular regard or veneration for it, the affection for old institutions and tried procedures, the respect for law, the habits of the people, their love for political experiments, etc. Each method has its own peculiar qualities which help to determine its suitability for a given set of circumstances.

Formal amendment is, of course, the most obvious method of change; but it is usually difficult to bring about, the degree of difficulty being measured with some exactness by the formalities which must be followed in order to secure the amendment's adoption. Legal enactment by the legislature or some other body is admirable for many purposes: it is easily effected, and it is thus readily available when further adjustments are necessary. For the same reason, it lacks the stability and permanence of the text of the written constitution. Convention is the most quiet and unobtrusive of all methods, and is, perhaps, for that reason the most dangerous; for precedents are insidious things and creep in by the back door when the attention may be concentrated on the front. But usage is rarely stubborn, and it is essentially the child of compromise, concession, and expediency. Judicial interpretation is, like convention, a slow and gradual process of change. It, too, can make concessions, and if for a time a particular doctrine seems to have gone too far, distinctions can be drawn and exceptions found which will veer away from what promised to be embarrassing consequences. Court decision cannot repeal a law; nor, in fact, can convention, although the latter can often render an undesirable law completely innocuous. Judicial decision is likely to be responsive to public opinion, although only over a long period of time. Usage is extremely sensitive to such

52/*Round Table*, Sept. 1934, p. 812.
53/*Supra*, pp. 92–6.
54/*Supra*, pp. 93–5. See Laskin, *Canadian Constitutional Law*; W. R. Lederman, *The Courts and the Canadian Constitution* (Toronto, 1964); Peter H. Russell, *Leading Constitutional Decisions* (Toronto, 1965).

opinion and will make frequent adjustments to meet the needs and demands of the moment, trying and discarding expedients until a suitable one is found.

Although the above pages have indicated how all these methods are in constant use in Canada, yet the greater part of the development has occurred through convention and judicial interpretation. There are a number of reasons why these two have been especially favoured.

First, there has been a strong tendency since shortly after Confederation to leave formal amendment alone if it could be avoided. The possible raising of the issue of provincial consent; the difficulty of getting a general consensus of opinion; the overcoming of provincial prejudice and distrust; the disinclination in some quarters to tamper with the act at all; the ability to get around the act in other ways, such as, for example, the use of various administrative expedients between Dominion and provincial officials – all have discouraged the use of the amending process.

Secondly, the constitution being a federal one, disputes on jurisdiction are constantly occurring and recourse is had to the courts for settlement. Special facilities have, indeed, been created to enable puzzled governments to take their constitutional troubles to the courts in "reference" or hypothetical cases, so that uncertainties of jurisdiction can be cleared up without waiting for cases to arise in the ordinary course of events.[55] Paradoxically, the conservation of judicial interpretation of the British North America Act has also stimulated not only the Dominion and the provinces, but other influential elements in the Canadian polity, to seek various ingenious ways of by-passing the written constitution as interpreted.

Thirdly, an exceptionally large part of the constitution, notably the relations of the cabinet to the governor general and to the Parliament, is conventional, and this naturally tends to breed changes through usage.

Fourthly, the most important *constitutional* change in Canada since the First World War was the enormous advance in self-government in external affairs and the growing independence of Great Britain which was its necessary accompaniment. The powers involved were almost entirely prerogative powers and the Canadian participation rested primarily on usage. Thus the changes which took place not unnaturally occurred almost entirely through the gradual adoption and modification of practices and precedents of one kind or another – through a dispatch to the Dominions Office; through the adoption of a new form; through the refusal to follow a certain suggested policy; through an objection to a procedure; through a cabinet minute; through a resolution of the imperial conference; through informal discussions at cabinet and at lower levels; in short, through any of the multitude of decisions and statements and actions which make up conventional procedure.

55/Strayer, *Judicial Review of Legislation in Canada*, chap. 7. Of 197 cases involving the distribution of powers before the Privy Council and the Supreme Court from 1867 to 1966, 68 were reference cases.

Part III   THE EXECUTIVE

8 The monarchy and the governor general

EXECUTIVE POWER IN CANADA has always borne a strong resemblance to the executive power in Great Britain from which it is in large measure derived. The monarch, as head of the state, is represented in Canada by the governor general, and the general position of the latter corresponds today, more than ever before, to that of the sovereign. The governor has tended to follow the same path which had been marked out a few generations earlier by his august principal and he now shares substantially the same disabilities, with some additional ones of his own that come from *not* being the monarch. He is a legal survivor who has contrived to remain a political necessity – the once supreme chief whose powers have largely passed into other hands, yet who has nevertheless retained a substantial residue of his former ascendancy and importance. Authority has gradually been succeeded by influence; obvious and aggressive leadership has been replaced by the more subtle and intangible pressure of suggestion and persuasion. For the governor's influence on government is not negligible, although it rarely occurs through the exercise of his visible and more public functions. His talents find expression quietly and unobtrusively behind the scenes; and this is made possible and effective because the office itself carries an established tradition of integrity, unselfishness, and public service. This tradition as well as the atmosphere which surrounds the institution derive much of their potency from the influence which flows from the throne itself; for while Canadians in general do not look upon the monarchy with the same regard which is usually bestowed on it in Britain, there is undoubtedly an emanation of a milder sort which makes itself felt across the Atlantic. The historical monarchy, in short, strengthens not only the modern monarch but her representative as well; the prestige, the dignity, the antiquity, the past record of the monarchy are all transferred in some measure and help substantially to maintain the repute and vitality of the office of the governor general. The contemporary monarchy, thanks to modern communications and transportation systems which have made the Queen's voice and face so familiar, undoubtedly contributes to the same ends.

The general decline in the governor's position and especially the effects of the introduction of representative and responsible government have been traced in some detail in the preceding pages. His powers, originally autocratic but progressively diminishing with advances in self-government, were by the turn of this century beginning more and more to resemble those of the monarch, and the time was clearly not far distant when the identification would be virtually complete. Here and there, however, the governor had been able to withstand the encroachments of the cabinet, notably in 1896, when Lord Aberdeen had refused to agree to appointments made by a defeated government. Thirty years later another refusal occurred when Lord Byng declined to grant a dissolution which had been requested by the prime minister.

In this last dispute the governor general won but an empty victory, for the consequences were far-reaching and to the detriment of the long-run powers of his office. Not only did the prime minister, W. L. Mackenzie King, win the general election which almost immediately ensued; he was also free to interpret its results so as to support his own views, and a few months later went to the imperial conference in London, determined to prevent in the future any recurrence of what he considered to be an undue interference with the constitutional powers of the prime minister. The result was the formal statement by the conference,[1] that the governor general of a dominion was the representative of the Crown and not of any department of the British government, and that his position in relation to the administration of public affairs in the dominion was essentially the same as that of His Majesty the King in Great Britain. (This had, in fact, been the view taken by Lord Byng and Arthur Meighen throughout the Canadian crisis of 1926.)

The Imperial Conference of 1926 thus not only endeavoured to clarify the position of the governor general in relation to the government of a dominion, but it declared his complete divorce from the British government as well. This was a radical change, and directs attention to another important side of the governor's former activity. From earliest times he had been called upon to discharge a double task: he had been not only the head of the dominion (or colonial) government, but also the representative and mouthpiece of the British authorities, in that he was charged with the duty of guarding the wider interests of the empire from colonial interference and encroachment. The former task had affected his relations with his cabinet and the Canadian people, and necessitated (at least in later years) the utmost neutrality in Canadian politics; the latter might compel him to take a stand which, while reflecting the desires of his principles in Britain, would nevertheless exacerbate his relations in Canada. In very early days the British interests were carefully cherished; but as responsible government became more firmly rooted, local welfare tended to become the dominant consideration. This was partly owing to greater Canadian control over matters which had formerly been earmarked as of imperial concern and

1/*Supra*, p. 49.

also (another aspect of the same basic growth of Canadian nationhood) to a change of attitude and approach by the British government. Imperial considerations, in short, not only arose less frequently, but they became subjects for discussion and compromise rather than dictation and summary action. This general tendency was rapidly accelerated by the active Canadian participation in the First World War and the stimulating effects of the struggle on the growth of national sentiment.

The governor general's powers had thus by 1926 been assailed for almost sixty years by two forces moving in from opposite directions, yet both dominated by one common purpose – the desire of the Canadian people for more self-government. Canadians disliked an irresponsible official interfering in the political affairs of the Dominion and they were equally unwilling to permit their external affairs to remain outside their own control. The governor general as an active head of the local government and as the guardian of imperial interests, stood in the way of both these legitimate ambitions, although precedents had been steadily accumulating which made his old position more and more difficult to maintain. Thus by 1926 the besiegers had captured many of the outer works of the governor's citadel; and it needed only one or two imperial conferences and the Statute of Westminster to complete the conquest, or at least to capture so much of the main stronghold that one or two small bastions could be generously and safely left in the hands of the defender.

The British North America Act, as has been already indicated, is curiously silent on the subject of the executive power in Canada. While this reticence may be explained in part by the influence of custom and precedent in the colonial governments of the Confederation period and the anticipated continuance of that influence in the government of the new Dominion, it was also a logical consequence of the reliance placed on the common law as a vital interpreter of the unwritten portion of the constitution. The courts of England had been accustomed for centuries past to define the scope of executive authority,[2] and it was assumed in 1867 that the colonial and English courts would continue to perform the same useful function in the Dominion of Canada.

The central institution exercising general executive authority was the Crown. Writers on the British constitution have vied with one another in coining striking phrases to illustrate the unique character and position of the British Crown: it has been labelled by one scholar "a convenient working hypothesis," and by another "a convenient cover for ignorance." While the concept is undoubtedly elusive and difficult to confine within the terms of a simple definition, it may be described as that institution which is possessed of the sum total of executive rights and powers, exercised by the sovereign, by the individual or collective action of his or her ministers, or by subordinate officials. It is the supreme executive authority which may become manifest through a number of outlets.

2/For example, the powers of the executive regarding government in settled and conquered colonies, *supra*, pp. 4–5.

Its nature and its profound importance in English government are best indicated by the fact that the greater part of English constitutional development for centuries was concerned with the changing conception of the Crown and the shifting in the exercise of its powers. The long struggle in which Parliament tried to block and mitigate and direct the powers of the sovereign finally resulted in the former taking almost complete control, not, however, by checking the sovereign or openly seizing power, but indirectly and almost surreptitiously by gaining possession of and exercising his functions through the supplying of advice and the maintenance of the authority of the Crown. The monarch is now able to do virtually nothing without the authorization of his or her constitutional advisers, the cabinet, who are, of course, always accountable to Parliament. The constitutional monarch is like the man possessed of devils: the spirits have gained the upper hand, he no longer controls his own movements, and he cannot, therefore, in all fairness be held to account for his official acts and decisions. Queen Elizabeth II today can do no wrong, simply because her advisers lift the responsibility from her shoulders and transfer it to their own.

The personal king of history has thus been in large measure displaced by or transformed into the modern Crown, the formal institution; and while the powers of the old English kings have in one sense remained to a material degree unchanged, they have now (except for the reserve powers) become the powers of the Crown, not exercisable by the sovereign in person but through responsible officials speaking and acting in the monarch's name. The Crown is thus the institution apart from the incumbent of the moment: kings and queens may come and go, but constitutionally and legally the Crown goes on forever, relatively undisturbed by the impermanence of sovereigns.

The powers of the British Crown are very wide indeed and are derived from two sources – statute and common law. The powers springing from the former source are, of course, found in acts of Parliament; those derived from the common law are the survivors of the original powers possessed by the early English sovereigns before Parliament in the modern sense existed, and are generally described by the term "prerogative."[3] "Prerogative," says Dicey, "is the residue of discretionary or arbitrary authority which at any given time is legally left in the hands of the Crown."[4] The authority was originally extensive, and included the general powers vested in the monarch as supreme executive, law-giver, judge, and warrior; but succeeding centuries have seen these reduced and limited by various contractual agreements (such as Magna Carta), by statutes (such as the Bill of Rights), and by simple disuse. The remainder is clearly not nearly so extensive as the original powers, but there is still a very substantial "residue" which Parliament has permitted to remain under the control

3/These are the prerogative *powers*. "Prerogative" may also include certain *rights* and *attributes* of the Crown, such as escheat, perpetuity, etc.
4/Dicey, *Law of the Constitution*, p. 420.

of the Crown, although any of this can, of course, be abolished by Parliament whenever it desires to do so.

Prerogative powers have the same legal validity as those conferred on the Crown by statute, and while they are almost entirely exercisable on the responsibility of ministers, there is within this area a very small segment of independent authority. Statutory powers are fairly simple, obvious, explicit, and readily ascertained; but the prerogative, finding its origin in the misty past and interpreted by the courts only as the occasion has arisen, is comparatively uncertain and indefinite. Statutory powers are constantly being increased and have, in fact, been enormously extended in recent years. Prerogative powers, on the other hand, can shrink but clearly cannot be enlarged; for if a new executive power rests on valid precedent, it is no extension but merely a revival, and if it is given a new lease of life by act of Parliament it becomes a statutory power and not prerogative. Yet the prerogative is extremely important, and its significance may be readily appreciated by considering the part played in English government by the following, which are broadly prerogative powers, although they may to some degree have been affected by the enactment of statutes: the appointment and dismissal of public servants; the summoning, prorogation, and dissolution of Parliament; the creation of peers and conferring of titles of honour; the pardoning power; the power to do all acts of an international character, such as the declaration of war and neutrality, the conclusion of peace, the making or renouncing of treaties, and the establishment or termination of diplomatic relations.

Executive power in Canada is similarly vested in the Crown, which manifests itself in both Dominion and provincial governments, but in each instance the Crown naturally acts on the advice of a different cabinet. The powers of the Crown in Canada spring from the same double origin of statute and prerogative, although both are one step further removed from their respective sources.[5] The statutory powers come for the most part directly or indirectly from the British North America Act, the great majority being found in acts of the Canadian Parliament. The prerogative powers are delegated by the Queen on the advice of the Canadian cabinet to her representative, the governor general. The appointment of the latter and this delegation of power occur through what are known as the prerogative instruments – the Letters Patent, the Instructions, and the Commission;[6] although in addition to this specific passing-on of the prerogative powers there is also assumed to be a general implied devolution by both statute and prerogative which is coextensive with the Dominion's legislative power and is as great as may be necessary to enable the executive govern-

5/Provincial prerogative powers (but not statutory powers) are removed yet another step, for they are delegated by the prerogative instruments issued by the Governor-General-in-Council.
6/"The letters patent ... are not varied for each Governor, but made applicable to him by the commission which appoints him to the office defined in the letters patent and regulated by the instructions." Keith, *Responsible Government in the Dominions*, I, p. 81.

ment to be effectively conducted. Prerogatives which affect the Dominion may now be swept away by enactments of the Canadian Parliament, and prerogatives which have lapsed may on occasion be revived by executive authority if such revival is sustained by the courts.

A significant difference, however, between the use of the prerogative power in Canada and Great Britain is that substantial parts have not in practice been exercised by the governor general, but remain in effect with the Queen acting on the advice of the Canadian cabinet. Canadian prerogative powers (leaving those of the provincial governments out of consideration) are thus divided into those customarily performed by the Crown in Canada and those customarily performed by the Crown in England on Canadian advice – a dichotomy which is, however, not nearly so confusing as might appear at first glance. For the line had been drawn with fair clarity in the earlier days when the British government advised the Sovereign on certain matters which have now passed under complete Canadian control, and that earlier distinction has been perpetuated in somewhat altered form by substituting the Canadian for the British cabinet. That part of the prerogative which deals with the granting of honours and the conduct of foreign relations is in this special category; and hence if the Canadian government now wants to have honours bestowed,[7] or war declared, or plenipotentiaries appointed, or treaties ratified, or action of a similar kind taken, it advises the Queen and not the governor general to give the necessary authority. This distinction was until 1947 a legal one inasmuch as the Sovereign by the Letters Patent did not delegate to the governor general the part of the prerogative powers indicated above. But by new Letters Patent, effective on October 1, 1947, the King made a complete delegation of all powers to his representative the governor general, so that the latter, acting on the advice of the Canadian Privy Council, may now legally exercise *all* the prerogative powers so far as they affect Canada if and when the Canadian cabinet so desires. The distinction between these two sets of prerogative powers, however, is still maintained in practice even though it no longer exists in law, and there seems to be no desire on the part of the Canadian government to substitute the governor general for the Queen in such matters.

The press release of October 1, 1947, described the new Letters Patent and their use as follows:

By the introductory words of Clause 2 of the new Letters Patent the Governor-General is authorized to exercise, on the advice of Canadian Ministers, all of His Majesty's powers and authorities in respect of Canada. This does not limit the King's prerogatives. Nor does it necessitate any change in the present practice under which certain matters are submitted by the Canadian Government to the King personally. However, when the new Letters Patent come into force, it will be legally possible for the Governor General, on the advice of Canadian Ministers, to exercise any of the powers and authorities of the Crown in respect of Canada, with-

---

7/For obvious reasons these could not include peerages if they were to involve seats in the House of Lords.

out the necessity of a submission being made to His Majesty. (The new powers and authorities conferred by this general clause include, among others, Royal Full Powers for the signing of treaties, Ratifications of treaties and the issuance of Letters of Credence for Ambassadors.) There will be no legal necessity to alter existing practices. However, the Government of Canada will be in a position to determine, in any prerogative matter affecting Canada, whether the submission should go to His Majesty or to the Governor General.

The new Letters Patent revoke and supersede the existing Letters Patent and the existing Royal Instructions. The Royal Instructions have been incorporated in the new Letters Patent which have been issued under the Great Seal of Canada.

The Governor General is therefore not in quite the same position as the Sovereign in regard to the exercise of certain prerogative powers, although it would not be impossible to bring about an approximate equality in this respect. But such an effort would not begin to meet the demands of the Imperial Conference of 1926 and give the governor "in all essential respects the same position in relation to the administration of public affairs in the Dominion as is held by his Majesty the King in Great Britain." Such a task is beyond the competence of any imperial conference or any Parliament, for there are inherent fundamental differences of position and status that cannot be overcome, and these will frequently influence the functioning of the office and introduce factors which make any real parallel in some respects quite impossible.

The most obvious difference lies in the way in which the two positions are filled, for there can be nothing in Canada to match the hereditary element which is so vital a part of the British monarchy. The history of the choice of governors general in Canada presents one of the best examples of a constitutional development which has been brought about through changes in custom and procedure and entirely apart from statute and formal amendment. The old method of appointment was by the Sovereign on the advice of the colonial secretary with the approval, of course, of the British prime minister. After 1890 (following a protest from Queensland) the method was altered by consulting with the dominion government before the appointment was made, though this procedure, while common, was not invariably followed. In 1916 the Canadian prime minister was simply informed, without any preliminary consultation, that the Duke of Devonshire was to be the new governor; while on the other hand it is understood that on one occasion at least another dominion was sent a list of three or four names from which the cabinet was allowed to make its choice – a decided step in the direction of greater dominion participation.

The Imperial Conference of 1926 ushered in the modern period of appointment; for if the governor general "is not the representative or agent of His Majesty's Government in Great Britain or of any Department of that Government," the British cabinet obviously could not continue to make the choice. In short, the prime minister of Canada recommends the appointment to the Queen, and the latter acts on the advice so given, although it seems to be customary to ascertain Her Majesty's wishes in the matter by previous consultation, inasmuch as the governor is in a very real sense the Sovereign's representative. Yet another consultation occurred on at least one occasion in Canada: Bennett stated in 1936 that when Lord Tweedsmuir's name was being considered, he, as prime minister, first discussed the matter with Mackenzie King, the leader of the opposition, so that the governor's appointment was in effect non-partisan inasmuch as it carried the approval of the leaders of both major parties. This precedent, however, did not establish a practice, and the latest several governors were appointed without consultation with the leader of the opposition.[8]

Certain parts of the British North America Act relating to the governor's position have also been affected, yet no amendments to the act have been made to bring it into conformity with modern conditions. The governor has power (sections 55–7) to withhold his assent from a bill passed by the Canadian Parliament or to reserve a bill for the signification of the pleasure of the Queen in Great Britain. Both these powers, although still legally extant, have been rendered obsolete by disuse and the declarations of the imperial and other conferences from 1926 to 1930.[9] The explicit obligation imposed by the British North America Act to keep the British government informed of the acts passed by the Canadian Parliament (to permit of possible disallowance) was faithfully observed until 1942 when it was quietly discontinued.[10] This was followed in 1947 by the passage of an act amending the Canadian statute which had provided for transmission of copies of current acts to the governor general and to the British government.[11]

Past governors general have varied widely in quality. All have possessed the essential qualification of being what Queen Victoria called "proper persons," that is, of excellent social standing, although this has sometimes led to other more essential attributes being slurred over or ignored. It is difficult, for example, to avoid the feeling that the emphasis was somewhat misplaced when Queen Victoria approved the appointment of her son-in-law, the Marquess of Lorne, with the comment that the office would provide a "distinction for Lorne" and a "fine independent position for dear Louise."[12] When Lorne's term had expired the Queen suggested the appointment of her son, Prince Leopold, but the British government preferred Lord Lansdowne.[13] Other mem-

---

8/Bennett's consultation with King took place under unusual circumstances. See J. R. Mallory, "The Appointment of the Governor General," *Canadian Journal of Economics and Political Science*, XXVI, no. 1 (Feb. 1960), pp. 96–107. See also J. W. Pickersgill and D. F. Forster, eds., *The Mackenzie King Record, 1944–1945* (Toronto, 1968), II, pp. 435–6. I am indebted to Rt. Hon. J. G. Diefenbaker, Rt. Hon. Louis St Laurent, and Rt. Hon. L. B. Pearson for letters concerning recent appointments.

9/Imperial Conferences of 1926 and 1930; Conference on the Operation of Dominion Legislation and Merchant Shipping Legislation, 1929. *Supra,* pp. 48–50.

10/*Can. H. of C. Debates*, April 5, 1943, p. 1829.

11/*Can. Statutes*, 11 Geo. VI, c. 44.

12/*Letters of Queen Victoria* (London, 1907) (Second Series), II, p. 631.

13/*Ibid.*, III, p. 422.

bers of the royal family, however, have occupied the position and have served with moderate distinction. Sir Robert Borden, who was by no means an unfriendly critic, has recorded that the Duke of Connaught "laboured under the handicap of his position as a member of the Royal Family and he never fully realized the limitations of his position as Governor General," an estimate which can scarcely be regarded as strengthening the argument for such appointments.[14] Perhaps an adequate comment on another "proper person" who became governor was that supplied by a contemporary Canadian periodical which described the Duke of Devonshire as one who "does not overpower with his brilliance, nor is his intellect an amazingly bright one, but he has a pleasing manner."[15]

A small but important group, of dubious merit in earlier years, was composed of professional soldiers whose inelastic minds, and experience and outlook far removed from the complexities and compromises of politics, sometimes proved an inadequate equipment for the trying role of constitutional monarch. A hundred years ago appointments of this nature were much more common than later, although the complaint of Joseph Howe regarding governors whose minds had become disciplined through years of military service "into a contempt for civil business and fractious impatience of the opinions" of all of lower rank retains at least some of its force.[16] Lady Byng, for example, has recorded with an air of complacent virtue that both she and her husband "always shunned and detested politics,"[17] an attitude which, whatever its justification, provided a strange equipment for the tasks awaiting them at Rideau Hall. But the above types include the dull governors and the failures; there have happily been others whose capacity was undoubted, whose interests were comprehensive, and whose talents won recognition not in Canada alone but other countries as well; and since three of the last five governors have been generals and marshals who also served with distinction in Ottawa, the military governor has rehabilitated himself. He now joins Dufferin, Lansdowne, Grey, Tweedsmuir, and Massey as an able man in any company; and despite the prevalence of reigning Queens in Canada's history, no one has ever appointed a woman as governor general.

The term and tenure of the governor general furnish further illustrations

14/*Robert Laird Borden: His Memoirs* (Toronto, 1938), II, p. 604.
15/Hugh S. Eayrs, "The New Governor-General," *Canadian Magazine*, Feb. 1917, p. 312.
16/Letters to Lord John Russell, 1839, in Chisholm, *Speeches and Public Letters of Joseph Howe*, I, p. 235. "If then Governors are to be selected from the united services, it is evident that mere soldiers or sailors are not to be preferred. I do not say that men should be rejected because they have fought for their country: the highest qualities of the warrior and the statesman have often been combined. But if we are to have rulers snatched from the tented field or the quarter-deck, they should be men to whom the British Constitution does not appear a prurient excrescence, defacing the articles of war; men of enlarged minds, accustomed to affairs; studious of the history of their country and possessing great command of temper." Letters to Lord John Russell, 1846, in *Speeches and Public Letters of Joseph Howe*, I, p. 619.
17/Viscountess Byng, *Up the Stream of Time* (Toronto, 1945), p. 171.

of the impossibility of making his position simply a replica of that of the monarch in Great Britain. His term may be simply, if somewhat ambiguously, stated as being officially recognized as six years, customarily treated as five years, while on occasion it has been seven years. His office was formerly held at the pleasure of the British government, a tenure which made him virtually independent of any control by the Dominion although a petition for his recall would probably have been heeded by the Colonial Office. This situation has perforce changed since the imperial conferences of 1926 and 1930 declared his complete freedom from the British government. He may now be removed by the Queen acting on advice tendered by the Canadian cabinet.

The result is that the governor is placed, potentially at least, at the mercy of his own cabinet, a subordination which makes assertions of independent opinions unlikely and any strong line of conduct impossible, and is apt as well to undermine his influence and reputation for impartiality. For it must be assumed that this power of advising the Queen to remove a governor is not merely nominal but real, and that the Queen will act on advice so given. The period of full dominion status had hardly begun when there occurred one decisive precedent on the fate of a governor who happened to incur the enmity of his cabinet. Mr James McNeill, the governor general of the Irish Free State, was removed in this way in 1932 for the most trivial reasons and a successor was chosen who was more closely identified with the De Valera government. Such drastic action, it need scarcely be added, was quite at variance with the tradition of the independence and party neutrality of the King's representative: the removal under the particular circumstances violated one aspect of this tenure, the new and partisan appointment violated another. This unsavoury precedent stands, however, as a menace to the tenure of all future governors.

The British North America Act states that the governor general is to receive a salary of £10,000 a year "unless altered by the Parliament of Canada," although it may probably be assumed that the amount would not be reduced during a governor's term of office. One year after Confederation the Dominion Parliament passed legislation to cut the salary to £6,500, but the retiring governor, with a strong appreciation of trade union principles, reserved the bill for the signification of the pleasure of Her Majesty's government in Great Britain. The British government thereupon refused its assent, giving as a reason that the proposed reduction would place the office in the third salaried class among colonial governments and that the small return would make it very difficult to induce an outstanding person to accept the position. The proposed reduction was, in fact, too much for Lord Mayo and he refused to accept the post. He chose instead the governor generalship of India, in which office he was assassinated. The Canadian Parliament at a later date, indeed, found that it had to augment the salary with fairly generous amounts for living expenses. Today the salary is still £10,000, but at the old exchange rate; it is really $48,666, with an allowance of $72,000. Additional expenses, including the salary of the governor general's secretary and staff, are provided for separately by annual votes in Parliament. Since 1967 present and previous governors have been entitled to a pension equalling one-third of the governor's salary at the time he leaves office.[18]

The functions of the governor general are many and varied, but they may be divided into two broad categories depending upon the manner in which the governor participates in their discharge. The first comprises those functions which are, so far as he is concerned, purely nominal and are performed automatically and inescapably on the advice of his cabinet. These (which may spring from either prerogative or statute) need not be dealt with here, for they are more properly considered as functions of the cabinet, the governor's participation being that of giving his consent as a matter of routine to the advice tendered. If his duties were confined to procedures of this nature, the post could most certainly be regarded as superfluous and its continuance would be extravagant folly. There is, however, a second group of functions arising from both statutory and prerogative powers which, unlike some other powers of the same origin, has continued to be closely identified with the governor as a person and has not been brought under cabinet control. In these functions the governor as an individual takes an active part and their exercise will vary greatly with his special capacity and character. It is these which furnish the major justification for the simulacrum of kingship at Ottawa. The constitutional monarchy as it is known throughout the Commonwealth is far from being a useless survival which through inertia or kindness of heart has been allowed to linger on. It is no atrophied organ of the body politic, but an important part with useful and even vital duties to perform. Cabinet government, in short, presupposes some central, impartial figure at its head which at certain times and for certain purposes supplements and aids the other more active and partisan agencies of government.

In the first place, the governor general is charged with the duty of seeing that there is always a prime minister and a responsible cabinet in office. One of the merits of cabinet government is its ready adjustment to change and particularly the speed and ease with which a new administration can step into the shoes of its predecessor. On most occasions this change of rulers is a purely mechanical operation, for it may happen that only one person will be in a position where he can accept the prime ministership with the assurance of receiving the indispensable parliamentary support. At such times the task of the governor is extremely simple and calls for nothing but a formal request to the obvious person to take the responsibility of constituting a new cabinet. Thus if a prime minister resigns after his party's defeat in a general election, the leader of the opposition or of the major opposition party must be the automatic choice; or, if the vacancy can be anticipated or if time permits, the majority party will select its leader and thus again make the governor's choice

18/The governor's salary is now governed by the Governor General's Act, *Rev. Stat. Can.* (1952), c. 139. The pension provisions, created by 14–15–16 Eliz. II, c. 81, also protect widows.

merely a formal one. In 1920, for example, when the retirement of Sir Robert Borden was imminent, the cabinet and the government party members held prolonged conferences and even took a ballot to ascertain the views of all the party supporters. Although a difference of opinion developed between the rank and file and the cabinet, agreement on Meighen (the rank and file's choice) was eventually reached, and three days before Sir Robert Borden resigned the governor requested Meighen to form a new government.[19]

There are other times, however, when the choice is neither obvious nor simple. A sudden death or resignation or party dissension may cause the office of prime minister to fall unexpectedly vacant and someone must be charged with the duty of seeing that it is filled immediately and to the satisfaction of the Commons. It is the governor's task to take the initiative and pursue the matter unceasingly until a new prime minister is in office. This may involve consultation with those who the governor feels can give sage advice or it may necessitate preliminary negotiations with potential prime ministers to discover if they want the position, if they can form a cabinet, and if they are able to command the support of a majority in the House. In any event the responsibility for making the final choice rests with the governor, subject, of course, to the selection being sustained in the House of Commons. Thus Lord Aberdeen in 1894 called in Sir Frank Smith to advise informally on a successor to Sir John Thompson, and in 1896, after first sounding out Sir Donald Smith, he asked Sir Charles Tupper to succeed Sir Mackenzie Bowell. Except for 1926 when Lord Byng, in a sense, selected Meighen as his prime minister by refusing King a dissolution, the governor general has not since 1896 had to use his own judgment in this regard; but there is no reason whatever to assume that the power has vanished in the interval. There have been three occasions in recent years for the exercise of this power in Great Britain,[20] and the conscription crisis in Canda in 1944 might easily have resulted in the governor being compelled to choose a successor to Mackenzie King.[21]

A second duty of the governor general is to offer his services as a mediator and conciliator between the political party leaders when the occasion warrants.

19/See Roger Graham, *Arthur Meighen*, I, *The Door of Opportunity* (Toronto, 1960), pp. 287–302.

20/King George V in 1916 called a conference of Mr Asquith, Mr Lloyd George, Mr Bonar Law, Mr Balfour, and Mr Arthur Henderson to aid him in choosing a successor to Mr Asquith who would be reasonably sure of support in the Commons. In 1923 he exercised a genuine choice when he selected Mr Baldwin in preference to Lord Curzon as the successor to Mr Bonar Law. Queen Elizabeth II in 1957 took advice from Sir Winston Churchill and Lord Salisbury before choosing Mr Macmillan rather than Mr Butler to succeed Sir Anthony Eden.

21/An unusual example of this succession occurred in Australia in July 1945. On the death of the prime minister the governor general chose Mr Francis Forde as his successor. Within a few days, however, the Labour party caucus met and somewhat unexpectedly chose Mr J. B. Chifley as their new leader, an act which resulted in Mr Forde's immediate resignation and the governor general requesting Mr Chifley to assume office. See also R. MacG. Dawson, *The Conscription Crisis of 1944* (Toronto, 1962), and Pickersgill and Forster, *The Mackenzie King Record, 1944–1945*.

Intervention of this kind is usually of an emergency nature and will occur only in time of crisis. Thus the Duke of Devonshire in 1917 summoned Sir Robert Borden, Sir Wilfrid Laurier, and four others to a meeting at Government House to discuss the general political situation, involving coalition government, conscription, and the possible avoidance of a war election.[22] Governors have sometimes intervened in a different kind of quarrel, that between the Dominion and a province. Shortly after British Columbia's entrance into Confederation Lord Dufferin endeavoured to charm away the bitterness between that province and the Dominion,[23] and twenty years later Lord Aberdeen held a series of interviews with the premier and attorney general of Manitoba on the separate school issue. Efforts of this kind, however, rarely meet with more than a modicum of success, and there is always bound to be some doubt at what moment, if at all, intervention by the governor general should occur or whether matters should be allowed to take their normal though admittedly more troubled course. In short, the governor's mediation in the past has been of doubtful utility, and on a few occasions has been a downright irritant; there is nothing to suggest that it will be given encouragement in the future.

Governors general have also been expected at times to act as quasi-diplomatic agents, formerly under instruction from the British government, latterly from that of Canada. This activity has in practice been confined to the paying of official visits to the United States. In early days these trips frequently had a definite and avowed diplomatic purpose, but today they are, on the surface at least, nothing more than gestures of goodwill and friendliness to a great neighbour. But, as President Roosevelt pointed out, there was nothing to prevent him and Lord Tweedsmuir from sitting on the same sofa and soliloquizing aloud; and if one overheard what the other said, that was unavoidable. It is, indeed, probable that these social calls are still occasionally used to review unofficially and tentatively matters which are of common interest to the two nations, although their usefulness for purposes of diplomatic intercourse is very obviously restricted. Within Canada, diplomatic enterprise of another kind is now clearly involved in the governor generalship: the incumbent from now on will almost certainly have to be a bilingual Canadian, with the office alternating between those of English- and French-speaking descent.

The governor is also the social head of the country and has always been supposed to exercise a moral leadership as well. This is, of course, a direct inheritance from England and one which received far greater prominence in Victorian times when the Queen was a model of the social if not of all the constitutional properties.[24] Greater emphasis is laid today upon leadership in

22/A British parallel is found in the conference of party leaders called by the King in 1914 when the Home Rule controversy reached the most acute of its many acute stages.
23/Not always in a manner acceptable to the prime minister. See Thomson, *Alexander Mackenzie: Clear Grit*, pp. 264–8.
24/Even Victoria's leadership in society was occasionally questioned. Sir Charles Dilke once told of a peer "who had enumerated certain houses in which you must be at home if pretending to the exclusive social set. It was objected that the inmates of some among

various fields of worthy endeavour and music, art, social service, public health, youth movements, history, literature, education, the universities, the theatre, and all commendable phases of the national life come under the notice and patronage of the governor and his wife.[25] But in voicing his views on any of these matters he must go warily lest he should unwittingly trespass upon what some touchy person, political party, or organization considers to be a controversial issue on which officially and publicly he must have no opinion. A governor has been severely called to task for praising in the most general terms a distinguished Canadian statesman; others have been accused of trying to win converts for aiding imperial defence or for promoting imperial trade; Earl Grey was attacked for giving his views on such innocuous topics as co-operative societies and retail merchants' associations. "For nearly five years," said Earl Grey, "I have, quite conscious of my constitutional limitations, walked the tight-rope of platitudinous generalities and I am not aware of having made any serious slip." Distrust of the expressed opinions of the governors in office before 1926 was certainly due in some measure to their intimate relationship to the British government. Exceptional discretion in all public utterances is nevertheless an inescapable although somewhat galling consequence of a system under which the cabinet must assume responsibility for any words of the governor on a public question and where opposition parties lie in wait for unguarded words with which to belabour the responsible minister. The governor is perforce compelled to express himself as best he may in what Lord Tweedsmuir described as "Governor Generalities." "Once," said Lord Tweedsmuir in addressing the United States Senate, "I was like you: I was a free and independent politician. I could liberate my mind on any subject, anywhere, at any time, at any length I pleased. I had an official character, and, like you, I had also a private character ... Now, I am in the unfortunate position of having no private capacity, but only an official one."[26]

One side of the governor general's social activity is entertainment, and this is expected to include members of Parliament, the civil service, the diplomatic corps, and any person of distinction who may be within reach. Here, again, time has brought some changes, for even the most sociable of modern governors could not hope to rival the determination and thoroughness with which their Victorian predecessors flung themselves into the absorbing task of providing entertainment for their guests. Sir Harold Nicolson has recounted with mingled awe and delight the hospitable efforts of his relatives, the Dufferins:

---

these houses were persons whom the Queen would not receive. 'The Queen!' said ———— in a tone of pained surprise, 'the Queen was *never* in society!' " S. Gwynn and Gertrude M. Tuckwell, *Life of Sir Charles Dilke* (London, 1917), II, p. 554.

25/These well-meaning efforts are not always appreciated. "The Earl [of Aberdeen] himself was a sensible and inoffensive man, but his wife was the most aggressive busybody who ever presided over Rideau Hall." *Toronto Saturday Night*, Oct. 4, 1898.

26/Lord Tweedsmuir, *Canadian Occasions* (Toronto, 1942), pp. 59-60.

The record of their entertainments leaves one aghast. There were drawingrooms, picnics, receptions, "drums," dinners, balls, torchlight processions, garden parties, bazaars, regattas, and amateur theatricals. There were concerts also and carefully prepared *tableaux*, "The first part of the programme," Lady Dufferin records, consisted of vocal music by amateurs. Then Rosa d'Erina sang four songs capitally. Three very pretty *tableaux* closed the entertainment: The Death of Cleopatra; The Expulsion of Hagar; and a group of flower girls. Nelly being one of them ..."

It was not so much by the reckless expenditure of his personal fortune that he won the heart of the Dominion as by the zest with which he flung himself into Canadian interests and pastimes. Day after day he could be seen skating, sleighing, tobogganing, snow-shoeing, or in summer fishing at Tadoussac or sailing his cutter in and out of the shipping of the St. Lawrence. He became particularly adept at curling, spending hours in the little curling rink at Montreal, which to this day is plastered with photographs of his matches or of the competitions which he encouraged.[27]

Closely associated with the governor's social activity are his duties as the ceremonial head of the government. He must, of course, open Parliament, receive foreign diplomatic agents, and perform similar routine functions; but he must also go on tour throughout the Dominion once or twice a year and, in the course of his travels, lay cornerstones, listen to innumerable addresses from municipal authorities, attend exhibitions, open museums and hospitals, and generally carry out all the wearisome tasks which the monarch is expected to do in Britain.[28]

The cynic may well question the purpose that is served by many of these barnstorming performances throughout the Dominion; but there can be little doubt that even the most democratic countries desire this sort of thing, and the only real question to decide is what person is to spend his time at it. History records, for example, that President Coolidge ("Silent Cal") thought it necessary to deliver twenty-eight speeches to various bodies in the year 1925. He "addressed the Germans on March 12, the Norwegians on June 8, the Negroes on June 25, the Swedes on July 1, the Irish on July 21, the Latin-Americans on October 28, and the Italians on November 24. Among the groups to which he talked were automobile men, contractors, trust-company officers, investment bankers, newspaper editors, motion-picture magnates, marine engineers, mining engineers, mechanical engineers, and farmers."[29] On one occasion three hundred school children were brought to Washington and were allowed, as the culminating incident in a day crammed with wonders, to walk through one end of the president's office and see the chief executive at work. No doubt the

---

27/Harold Nicolson, *Helen's Tower* (London, 1937), pp. 155–6. See also J. T. Saywell, ed., *The Canadian Journal of Lady Aberdeen* (Toronto, 1960).

28/Certain of the ceremonial functions may occasionally lead to the governor general forgetting that in these he is primarily an ornament and not a responsible official. The Duke of Connaught, for example, was for a time impressed with the importance of his post as commander-in-chief of all the Canadian armed forces and Sir Robert Borden was forced to remind him that his command was supposed to remain as nominal as that of the King in England. *Robert Laird Borden: His Memoirs*, I, p. 461; II, p. 604.

29/C. M. Fuess, *Calvin Coolidge* (Boston, 1940), p. 370.

impression left on the children's minds was a vivid one and the enjoyment of
their day was greatly enhanced by what they saw in the White House, but it is
difficult to believe that Coolidge accomplished very much while three hundred
giggling school children shuffled across his office floor. These things, however,
would appear to be a necessary concomitant of democratic governments, and
nations of the Commonwealth are fortunate in that they have accidentally at
hand the means of satisfying these demands for display and for official performances. In short, the prime minister's time is usually much too valuable to be
frittered away in trivialities of this kind; and so long as there is a governor
available, he can do the job acceptably. Furthermore, he can do it in such a
manner as to suggest the monarchical tie to those Canadians of royalist bent,
without offending those of more republican tendencies; and also in such a
manner as to help make Canadians aware of their heritage, as recent governors, for example, have made well-publicized trips to the far north.

Another function of the governor general is that of adviser and consultant to
the cabinet and more especially to the prime minister. Walter Bagehot, in discussing the English monarchy, gave the classic definition of this function when
he wrote: "The sovereign has ... three rights – the right to be consulted, the
right to encourage, the right to warn. And a King of great sense and sagacity
would want no others."[30] Queen Victoria, the sovereign at the time Bagehot's
book was written, had her own peculiar ideas as to what this involved, and did
not hesitate to favour one party or one prime minister when it suited her
purposes to do so,[31] but it is generally believed that her successors have had a
greater regard for the niceties of the institution and have used these rights
carefully and conscientiously. The Canadian governor general is expected to
follow the same practice. Thus while on all but the most exceptional occasions
the governor must follow the advice of his cabinet, he is not supposed to be
blindly subservient to them: he must co-operate with them fully and in the last
resort follow their counsel; but he is free, indeed it is his duty, to give his own
opinions whenever he feels these opinions are worthy of consideration.

If [the governor] has tact and ability, there is open a wide field of influence. He is in
theory entitled to similar treatment by his Ministers to that received by the King;
he should be taken into their confidence in all weighty matters, and be informed as
early as possible of the outcome of deliberations in Cabinet on important issues.
He can point out objections, he can criticize, suggest, and obtain alterations even
in purely local policy ... But he can do so only by remaining behind the scenes and
avoiding any rumour that the Governor controls the progress of affairs ... If he
remains in one Government for a full term of office, he may easily come to acquire
much weight especially if Ministers are unaccustomed to office. But it must be
admitted that no Governor has anything resembling the prestige of the Crown,

30/Walter Bagehot, *The English Constitution* (London, 1872; 1908 printing), p. 143.
31/"The Queen interpreted the right to be consulted, the right to encourage and the
right to warn as the right to obstruct, the right to bully and the right to go behind her
Ministers' backs when their policies were displeasing to her." Kingsley Martin, "The
Evolution of Popular Monarchy," *Political Quarterly*, VII, 1936, p. 171.

and Ministers in the Dominions have never adopted towards their Governors the attitude that full trust and consideration are his due, and must be rendered as a matter of course.[32]

It is very evident that the usefulness of this function of the governor general and the extent to which it can be employed with profit will depend primarily upon the character, capacity, and temperament of both governor and prime minister and the confidence and good faith existing between them. Exceptional knowledge or the highest of motives is not in itself a sufficient guarantee of success. The governor must know when to interfere and when to abstain; and when he endeavours to give help and advice he must possess sufficient restraint, balance, and tact that he will persuade and not antagonize his cabinet. Lord Dufferin's attitude towards his chief advisers in Dominion negotiations with British Columbia, for example, has been described by Alexander Mackenzie's biographer as "treacherous."[33] Lord Byng insisted on one occasion on receiving a delegation of strikers in an industrial dispute, despite the fact that several of his ministers told him that such action was both irregular and improper,[34] and his stubbornness could scarcely have increased his influence with his constitutional advisers. The Duke of Connaught became much concerned in 1916 because the Canadian cabinet did not take certain steps which he considered desirable, and after lodging a number of unusually strong protests (which appear to have been singularly inappropriate) he added that he was remonstrating also because of his personal objections "as Governor-General and a Field-Marshall in His Majesty's Forces, against the undoubted danger both to Canada and the Empire, which apparently the Canadian Government did not appreciate or entertain." It would be painting the lily indeed to attempt to do more than quote verbatim a part of the reply of Sir Robert Borden:

I hope that my colleagues and I shall not be found wanting in respect or indeed in admiration for the wide military experience of Your Royal Highness and the high position which you hold as a Field-Marshal in His Majesty's Forces. It would appear to us that the matters under consideration do not call so much for the exercise of military skill or the application of military experience as the consideration of international law and the exercise of the common-place quality of common sense.[35]

Confidence between the governor and his prime minister is, however, rarely present to the same degree as in the similar situation in Great Britain, a lack which may be attributed to many things, such as the mediocre talents of certain governors, the old functions of the governor as imperial officer and the consequent distrust of his attitude when national and empire issues clashed, and the fear of a revival or perpetuation of certain of the governor's former

32/Keith, *Responsible Government in the Dominions,* I, p. 106.
33/Thomson, *Alexander Mackenzie: Clear Grit,* p. 268.
34/E. M. Macdonald, *Recollections, Personal and Political* (Toronto, n.d.), pp. 487–90.
35/*Robert Laird Borden: His Memoirs,* II, p. 603.

independent powers. Canadian cabinets, it seems, have not always kept the governor as well informed as they should of matters under consideration or even decisions made,[36] although a change in certain of the factors noted above may in the future bring the governor and his advisers more closely in touch with one another. Even the wisest governor can do little or nothing if he is not apprised of cabinet business, for (though Dufferin may have revived the practice sporadically in the 1870s) he has not since at least 1858 sat regularly in cabinet meetings, and thus has no way of acquiring knowledge except with the active assistance of the prime minister. Lord Dufferin's plea that while he had no desire "to fidget with the administration of the country or to interfere in any way with the free action and official responsibility of my Ministers"[37] he was nevertheless worried about his growing separation from the business of the cabinet, was an early indication of a difficulty which appears subsequently to have grown more acute. Thus the Imperial Conference of 1926, while providing for the new status of the governor, felt it necessary to add that "a Governor-General should be supplied with copies of all documents of importance and in general should be kept as fully informed as is His Majesty the King in Great Britain of Cabinet business and public affairs."

The extent to which the governor general is now used as a consultant by the Canadian cabinet and the influence which he exerts are both matters on which few can pronounce with certainty. The relations of the governor and the prime minister must in the nature of things remain generally unknown and the matters dealt with are even more deeply veiled by official secrecy. Only here and there are a few disclosures made, and these become public so long after the event that they often have little applicability to existing conditions. The following opinions, the first by Sir Wilfrid Laurier, the second by Sir Robert Borden, and the third by Rt. Hon. J. G. Diefenbaker, indicate the value attached to this function of the governor general by those who came in direct contact with him:

The Canadian Governor General long ago ceased to determine policy, but he is by no means, or need not be, the mere figure-head the public imagine. He has the privilege of advising his advisers, and if he is a man of sense and experience, his advice is often taken.[38]

It would be an absolute mistake to regard the Governor General [as the office was altered by the 1926 conference] as a mere figure-head, a mere rubber stamp. During nine years of Premiership I had the opportunity of realizing how helpful may be the advice and counsel of a Governor General in matters of delicacy and

---

36/See, for example, the protest of the Duke of Connaught in 1915 when Sir Robert Borden, while right on a technicality, was wrong on the general principle involved. *Ibid.*, I, pp. 528–30.

37/Pope, *Correspondence of Sir John Macdonald*, p. 203. Dufferin elsewhere urged his absolute right to express his opinions or feelings to the cabinet just as freely as his ministers. Duke of Argyll, *Passages from the Past* (London, 1907), II, pp. 416–17.

38/O. D. Skelton, *Life and Letters of Sir Wilfrid Laurier* (Toronto, 1921), II, p. 86n.

difficulty; in no case was consultation with regard to such matters ever withheld; and in many instances I obtained no little advantage and assistance therefrom.[39]

During the time when I was prime minister there were two governors general ... [and] they were fully consulted as the representative of the Queen has a right to be. He also has the duty to give an opinion to the Prime Minister with regard to those things he believes necessary for Canada.[40]

In recent years there has been a general disinclination for the prime minister to use the governor general in this way: the necessary information is not always forthcoming, and consultation on matters of state has sometimes almost disappeared. This may, of course, vary with the personal elements in the situation. Thus a veteran prime minister like Mackenzie King, while remaining on the friendliest terms with Lord Alexander, did not make a practice of consulting the famous soldier, presumably because he was confident that Alexander's advice on Canadian politics would be quite worthless. On the other hand, it is possible that a different prime minister and a seasoned governor general of outstanding ability might conceivably lead to the establishment of a different relationship where the opinions of the governor might not only be sought but also be given the most careful consideration.

Finally, the governor general has a reserve power in certain grave contingencies to act on his own initiative. The extent of this power is vague and the occasions on which it may be used are debatable and to some degree uncertain; but such a power most certainly exists, although its exercise must be regarded as justifiable only under the most exceptional circumstances. The broad rule, of course, still holds: the governor general will follow the advice given by his ministers, for they accept the responsibility and with it accept the praise or blame for the decision and its results. The advice given may be bad; it may be short-sighted; it may be foolish; it may be dangerous – these considerations may induce the governor to remonstrate with his ministers and try to win them over to his point of view; but if they persist, his only course is to shrug his shoulders and acquiesce. The decision is not his, but that of his government, and eventually the people and their representatives will deal with those who have proffered the advice. Should the governor set his will against that of his cabinet, his action at once tends to become a political issue and he, whether he likes it or not, finds himself a party leader in the opposition's interests.

At very rare intervals, however, the cabinet may pursue a policy which threatens to disrupt the proper and normal working of the constitution. This may sometimes be overcome by allowing matters to take their course or by the governor persuading his advisers to alter their policy and adopt a more seemly

39/"The Imperial Conference," *Journal of the Royal Institute of International Affairs,* July 1927, p. 204.
40/*Can. H. of C. Debates,* April 4, 1967, p. 14479. In the same passage Mr Diefenbaker paid tribute to the late Governor General Vanier.

procedure than the one proposed. Such courses of action, however, may not prove feasible, and it may then become the thankless duty of the governor to intervene and insist on certain steps being taken more in accordance with the constitutional proprieties, even although this may necessitate – as it usually will – the virtual dismissal of his advisers and a search for another prime minister and cabinet to take their place. If, for example, a prime minister were shown beyond any reasonable doubt to have accepted a bribe and he then refused to resign or to advise that Parliament be immediately summoned to deal with the matter, the governor would have an undoubted right to dismiss him from office. Or if a prime minister, having obtained a dissolution, was returned with a minority of members and promptly demanded another dissolution, the governor would have no real alternative but to refuse the advice and force the resignation of the cabinet.[41] Mackenzie King was hardly celebrated as a champion of the powers of the governor general, but in 1926 he explicitly upheld the right of a governor not merely to refuse a prime minister a dissolution under certain circumstances, but also to dismiss him. "I may say," he asserted of the latter possibility, "that as Leader of His Majesty's loyal Opposition I am prepared to take responsibility for the dismissal of the hon. gentleman opposite."[42]

No exact rules can be laid down for the exercise of these "reserve powers." Necessarily, they involve discretion (in both senses of the word); and threats to the constitution may be infinite in variety. There is even great divergence of informed opinion on certain recorded cases where governors acted on their own initiative. Two have arisen in Canada in the last seventy years. Lord Aberdeen, in 1896, refused to make appointments on the advice of a government which had just been defeated at the polls.[43] Lord Byng, in 1926, refused to grant a dissolution to a government which had had one only nine months before, which had been defeated in the House of Commons, and against which a motion of censure was under debate. He insisted that a second election so soon after the first would be justified only if no alternative government in the existing Parliament was possible. Since the official opposition had 116 seats to the government's 101, there seemed a reasonable chance that an alternative government was possible. Arthur Meighen, the leader of the opposition who accepted office and responsibility for Lord Byng's action, added that no government was entitled to a dissolution which would prevent the House of Commons from pronouncing judgment on its conduct. Both these cases resulted in long and lively controversies.[44]

41/See Jennings, *Cabinet Government*, pp. 295–340.
42/*Can. H. of C. Debates*, July 1, 1926, pp. 5254, 5261.
43/See John T. Saywell, "The Crown and the Politicians: The Canadian Succession Question, 1891–1896," *Canadian Historical Review*, XXXVII, no. 4 (Dec. 1956), pp. 309–37.
44/See Keith, *Responsible Government in the Dominions*, I, pp. 146–52, 173–4; Eugene A. Forsey, *The Royal Power of Dissolution of Parliament in the British Commonwealth* (Toronto, 1943, reprinted 1968); H. V. Evatt, *The King and His Dominion Governors*

While admittedly the occasions which will warrant the use of the reserve power of the governor are impossible to define, two conditions, it is submitted, ought to be present. The operation of the usual constitutional procedures (as directed by the cabinet) in the matter in question must be such that it would not simply involve some moderate delay or temporary inconvenience – it would have to perpetuate for some time a state of affairs which is plainly intolerable and a violation of the spirit and intent of the constitution. Further, there should also be no reasonable doubt whatever of the essential wisdom and justice of the governor's intervention; and if any such doubt is present, it constitutes *prima facie* evidence that he should hold his hand. For if the governor moves on his own responsibility, he must at once obtain other advisers and will thus sooner or later be compelled indirectly through his new cabinet to seek justification at the polls for the use of his emergency power. In short, he must be so sure of the inherent righteousness of his intervention and his popular vindication that he is willing to stake both his reputation and his office upon its general acceptance. If it be objected that the above two conditions are very seldom found and hence any assertion of the reserve power will be very extraordinary indeed, the argument is not weakened but confirmed; for the great justification of the retention of this prerogative is that it is an emergency device invoked to re-establish genuine democratic control at a time when the normal constitutional procedures have faltered and are in danger of being improperly and unscrupulously employed. The mere existence of this power will, in fact, tend to prevent the need for its exercise ever arising.

Neither the King nor the Governor has a blanket authority to use his reserve power to correct the mistakes of his advisers; and each will serve his country best by jealously keeping that power for only those rare emergencies when nothing else is adequate. Like the gold piece under the mattress, it serves not by continued use but through its potential power to cope with emergencies; the successful household is the one which never has occasion to resort to it, yet which derives a feeling of additional security and well-being by its mere presence and the knowledge that it can be used when disaster threatens.[45]

A review of these functions of the governor general will immediately reveal that a successful governor must possess certain qualities above all others: he must have ability of a somewhat unusual kind and he must also be able to

---

(London, 1936); Dawson, *Constitutional Issues in Canada*, pp. 72–91; H. Blair Neatby, *William Lyon Mackenzie King, 1924–1932* (Toronto, 1963); Roger Graham, ed., *The King-Byng Affair, 1926: A Question of Responsible Government* (Toronto, 1967). In two other notable disputes involving the governor general, the latter acted on the advice of his ministers, but his acceptance of it profoundly aggravated the opposition. See George Stewart, *Canada under the Administration of the Earl of Dufferin* (Toronto, 1878), chap. III; Joseph Collins, *Canada under the Administration of Lord Lorne* (Toronto, 1884), chap. II. The proposals of the government of Canada for the constitutional conferences of the late 1960s, it should be noted, explicitly retained the governor general's powers to choose a prime minister and to refuse a dissolution.

45/R. MacG. Dawson, in *Canadian Journal of Economics and Political Science*, X, no. 1 (Feb. 1944), p. 93.

maintain the most conscientious disinterestedness and impartiality towards Canadian political affairs. If he is to be allowed to choose a new prime minister, if he is to be of any service as a mediator between conflicting parties, if his advice is to carry weight in cabinet councils, if in emergencies he is to act as the guardian of the constitution, and, to a less degree, if he is to provide social and cultural leadership, his political opinions and prejudices must be above criticism and he must enjoy sufficient security to speak and act both honestly and fearlessly. Lord Dufferin's half humorous description of the governor and his necessary qualities has lost none of its force with the years:

If there is one obligation whose importance I appreciate more than another, as attaching to the functions of my office, it is the absolute and paramount duty of maintaining not merely an outward attitude of perfect impartiality towards the various parties into which the political world of Canada, as of the mother country, is divided, but still more of preserving that subtle and inward balance of sympathy, judgment and opinion ... I suppose I am the only person in the Dominion whose faith in the wisdom and in the infallibility of Parliament is never shaken. Each of you, gentlemen, only believes in Parliament so long as Parliament votes according to your wishes. I, gentlemen, believe in Parliament, no matter which way it votes ... As a reasonable being [the governor general] cannot help having convictions upon the merits of different policies. But these considerations are abstract, speculative, devoid of practical effect in his official relations. As the head of a constitutional state, as engaged in the administration of parliamentary government, he has no political friends – still less need he have political enemies; the possession of either, nay, even to be suspected of possessing either, destroys his usefulness.[46]

Recent constitutional changes, moreover, have made it far more difficult than before for the governor general to remain impartial and aloof, to discuss public matters frankly with the prime minister, and to give advice and to take action without fear of immediate consequences. The governor's dependence on the Dominion government has, since 1930, become complete; for he owes to it his appointment, his salary and allowances, and his tenure of office. The Imperial Conference of 1926, which ingenuously asserted the similarity of the positions of king and governor, took in fact the very steps which began to destroy much of that cherished similarity. The conference cut the governor loose from British control; but in so doing, it brought him under the control of the Dominion government, and the latter status was as unlike that of the British King as the former. For while it is true that the Sovereign holds office in Great Britain at the will of the British Parliament, it is no less true that the traditions and prestige of the office and his unique position in the history of Britain and in the affections of the people give him a bulwark of defence which is built deep into the national life. The governor will always be at a disadvantage in any comparison with his principal, for not only does his position by comparison lack tradition and prestige, but his term of office is temporary and his detachment and neutrality are by no means so firmly established. In-

46/Stewart, *Canada under the Administration of the Earl of Dufferin*, pp. 193–6.

deed, with the growing popularity of royal tours, so exhaustively covered by radio and television, a governor general may sometimes appear to be overshadowed even in his own country by his principal.

But although it is quite impossible to create any exact copy of the original institution in Canada, certain safeguards can be erected which will materially increase the prestige and security of the governor's position and enable him to be a more useful member of the government. Appointment on the advice of the Canadian government must be retained; but (as suggested above) this could be purged of any partisan implications by prior consultation with the other major party leaders. The precarious term and tenure of the governor as it exists today could be changed by giving him a fixed term of five years, tenable during good behaviour, with removal only by joint address of the two Houses of Parliament. The salary could be explicitly guaranteed for the governor's entire term. Such (or similar) measures would give him an independent position approximately equal to that enjoyed by the sovereign and they would enable him to act more effectively and usefully than under existing conditions.

These changes, however, would have little merit and might even prove dangerous if they were not reinforced by the selection of suitable men who would be both able and politically impartial at the time of their appointment. Such a demand, in former days, frequently raised a question which has since been answered, namely, the desirability of appointing a native Canadian. Mr Vincent Massey became the first Canadian governor general in 1952; he was succeeded in 1959 by Major General Georges Vanier; and in 1967 Rt. Hon. Roland Michener, a former Speaker of the House of Commons, assumed the office.

At the time of Mr Massey's appointment, grave doubts were expressed in many quarters, for although Mr Massey had a distinguished record of public service in many fields, he was also unmistakably identified with the political party whose leader selected him in 1952. An opposition newspaper then commented:

The new Governor-General for all his very high personal qualities, unfortunately cannot detach himself entirely from the fact that he was once a Cabinet member in a Liberal Government, or from the fact that he was once the president of the National Liberal Federation, or from the fact that he has held many appointments from the Liberal Government – such appointments as are rarely, if ever, made from among those outside the party fold.[47]

The misgivings implicit in the quotation, as the careers of Mr Massey and his successors have demonstrated, are no necessary part of Canadian appointments to Rideau Hall, any more than they are of the appointment of Canadians to the Supreme Court. Certainly (as the history of the office of lieutenant governor has amply shown[48]) there will always be dangers in partisan appoint-

47/Montreal *Gazette*, Feb. 29, 1952 (editorial).
48/See Saywell, *The Office of Lieutenant-Governor*.

ment, but these could be lessened, if not entirely removed, by the simple process of consulting the opposition. Far from being, as Sir Wilfrid Laurier once put it, "a laudable but misguided expression of national pride," the first three Canadian appointments have been resounding successes, so much so that there is no pressure whatever to return to selections from the United Kingdom or (as has often been suggested in the past) to appoint governors from other Commonwealth countries. In any event, should Canadian appointments become unsatisfactory, there is nothing to prevent the choice of future governors general from other countries, including the United Kingdom – a potential development which would no doubt be hailed as one more of the nebulous ties that bind Crown and Commonwealth together.

Whatever the nationality of the governor general, it remains true, as Professor MacKinnon recently wrote:

The monarchy therefore serves democracy. It keeps the ministers in second place as servants of the state – electable, responsible, accountable, criticizable, and defeatable – a position necessary to the operation of parliamentary government. The people and their parliament can control the head of government because he cannot identify himself with the state or confuse loyalty to himself with allegiance to the state and criticism with treason. He is discouraged from the common tendency of officials, whether elected or not, to regard and make themselves indispensable, to entrench themselves in expanding power structures, to resent accountability and criticism, and to scoff at the effects of prolonged tenure of office or advancing years. Moreover, such control avoids the charges of treason, executions, assassinations, revolutions, and miscellaneous other expensive upheavals which so often accompany attempts to control and change governments that take themselves too seriously.[49]

All that is so; and yet with an absentee monarch it remains difficult to maintain the *mystique* of the monarchy in Canada. In 1965 Prime Minister Pearson affirmed that it was his government's policy "to maintain the monarchy as a cherished, strong and important part of our constitution which has earned and will receive our loyalty and our respect."[50] His statement was prompted by the passage of a motion by a university group of his own party in favour of abolishing the Queen's position as head of state.

49/Frank MacKinnon, "The Crown in a Democracy," in *Dalhousie Review*, 49, no. 2 (Summer 1969), pp. 238–9.
50/*Can. H. of C. Debates*, Feb. 23, 1965, p. 11624.

9 The cabinet: position and personnel

THE MOST STRIKING FEATURE of the Canadian form of government is undoubtedly the superficial absurdity of the dual nature of the executive power. In the absence of the Queen, the governor general, as her representative, is the official head of the state; but the active and puissant head of the government of the state is the prime minister. Appointments are made, acts of Parliament are proclaimed, mails are carried, criminal prosecutions are instituted, war is declared, treaties are negotiated and ratified, in the name of the Queen or of the governor general, although the prime minister and the cabinet are in fact the ones who make the selections and decide the policies which lie behind all these activities. Pomp, ceremony, and the external symbols of power and high regard are lavished on the one executive, while the other (though supported of course by a majority in the House of Commons) must in contrast rest content with an occasional expression of popular confidence moderated at all times by systematic opposition and carping criticism.

This curious characteristic of Canadian government is a direct inheritance from England, where it appeared in the struggle between King and Parliament as a tentative method of curbing the royal power. Sir John Seeley said that England conquered half the world in successive fits of absence of mind; he might have added that this absent-mindedness also occurred in other matters, resulting in the development of a most successful form of democratic government. Cabinet government was the product of a series of historical accidents, experiments, and temporary expedients, so haphazard in its origin and development that no one could have planned it in advance, or, even if this had been possible, would have been so rash as to suggest that it could ever be made to work. There can be little cause for wonder that foreigners are frequently bewildered and exasperated by the curious mentality of a people who can remain satisfied with so preposterous and illogical an institution. "These miserable islanders do not know," exclaimed the father of Mirabeau, "and will probably not know till their wretched system has exploded, whether they are living under a Monarchy or a Republic, a Democracy or an Oligarchy."

If a political system can be said to have a centre of gravity, that centre of gravity in Canada is most certainly the cabinet, for the whole weight of the government is concentrated at that point. Abolish the cabinet or remove any part of its primary functions and the entire balance of the existing political structure would be destroyed. "A Cabinet," said Walter Bagehot, employing a different metaphor, "is a combining committee – a hyphen which joins, a buckle which fastens, the legislative part of the state to the executive part of the state." The cabinet links together the governor general and the Parliament. It is, for virtually all purposes, the real executive. It formulates and carries out all executive policies; it is responsible for the administration of all government departments; and it also prepares by far the greater part of the legislative programme and exercises almost exclusive control over all matters of finance. The curious paradox which marks the cabinet's relations with the governor general appears also in a modified form in its relations with Parliament. The cabinet is the servant of the governor, yet in practice it tells him what to do; it is also the servant of the House of Commons, yet it leads and directs the House and is in a real sense the master of that chamber.

The activities of the cabinet (as indicated elsewhere) receive scant attention in the written constitution or, in fact, in any statute. The British North America Act has a few provisions which mention the Privy Council, the chief of these stating that "there shall be a Council to aid and advise in the Government of Canada, to be styled the Queen's Privy Council for Canada; and the Persons who are to be Members of that Council shall be from Time to Time chosen and summoned by the Governor General and sworn in as Privy Councillors, and Members thereof may be from Time to Time removed by the Governor General" (section 11). Yet this Council is not the cabinet, although by custom the cabinet constitutes the active part of the Council. Acts of Parliament have created the government departments and individual ministerships, but again it is through custom that the ministers who occupy these positions are in the cabinet. Moreover the cabinet as a body is almost completely ignored by all the statutes, although in the past an occasional casual reference was to be found.[1] The prime minister and the cabinet undoubtedly exercise very extensive power, but this power is not explicitly given them by the law, and they exercise it formally through some other body in accordance with the custom of the constitution. The really vital things about the cabinet rest on the constitutional conventions. When should a cabinet resign? How does it obtain office? What are its powers? What is the relation between a prime minister and his cabinet, between one cabinet minister and the others? How many should there

1/For example, Can. Statutes, 21–22 Geo. v, c. 13 (repealed in 1958) stated that the minister of Justice or "such other member of the Government" as may be designated may be empowered to do certain things arising out of the act. Prior to 1931 the Senate and House of Commons Act contained a reference to "the administration." See Can. H. of C. Debates, June 1, 1967, pp. 827–34; here the House of Commons, led by the cabinet, chose not to define "Governor in Council" in realistic terms.

be in the cabinet? How is a prime minister chosen? One may search the British North America Act and the Canadian statute books in vain for answers to these questions.

The cabinet and the ministry have usually been treated in Canada as though they were the same body, and during a large part of Canadian history they have in fact been identical. But from time to time one or two members would appear in the ministry or the government who were not in the cabinet; and since the Second World War a fairly large penumbral group of parliamentary secretaries, attached to the cabinet yet not formally considered as part of either the cabinet or the ministry, has appeared. A maximum of sixteen parliamentary secretaries, appointed for one year each from among the members of Parliament and assigned to assist designated members of the cabinet, is allowed by the law governing their creation;[2] as of October 1969 there were sixteen secretaries serving sixteen separate ministers, and thirty ministers in the cabinet. The ministers must have seats in one or other House of Parliament by custom only, and custom also decides that the retirement of the cabinet will always involve the retirement of the other members as well. Whether a salaried parliamentarian employed as a member of the executive is in or out of the cabinet depends not on the political nature of his position, but on whether he has been invited by the prime minister to join the select circle of colleagues who meet together from time to time to decide matters of high policy. To this extent the line between a member who is within and one who is without the cabinet is potentially an arbitrary and variable one; but in practice the great bulk of the members of the cabinet are there *ex officio*. The headship of a government department, for example, is held to entitle its occupant to a seat in the cabinet, while, on the other hand, the occupants of certain offices are commonly left outside. One or two positions have followed no consistent rule.

Members of the executive are thus by no means alike in status; there are, indeed, five different types of position to be distinguished. The first of these is the prime minister. He differs from his colleagues in many ways, such as, for example, the manner in which he obtains and relinquishes his office. He is requested by the governor general to form a government, while he himself issues the invitation to all other members. Whenever the prime minister vacates his office, that act normally carries with it the resignation of all those who compose the government; but whenever any other member leaves, the tenure of the remainder is undisturbed.

The second group, comprising the great bulk of the personnel of the cabinet, is composed of cabinet ministers who are the political heads of the various departments, and are thus the immediate associates of the prime minister in the

2/*Can. Statutes*, 7–8 Eliz. II, c. 15. Before 1959, parliamentary secretaries were provided for by parliamentary appropriation. See *Can. H. of C. Debates*, May 12, 1959, p. 2362, for a statement in which the prime minister made clear that the secretaries are not junior ministers.

day to day business of departmental administration. This group in 1970 had twenty-five members and within it there was an informal hierarchy, as some portfolios are widely regarded as being senior to others.

A third small group, which has fluctuated in size, is made up of ministers without portfolio, who are in the cabinet, but who have no department to administer. Before 1969 the cabinet commonly, although not always,[3] included a minister without portfolio who was the government's spokesman in the Senate; in 1969 the position of government leader in the upper house was made a full portfolio with the accompanying salary. Apart from representation in and for the Senate, one or more individuals may for a wide variety of reasons be taken into the cabinet without being assigned a department. A minister, for example, may not have sufficient ability to warrant giving him a portfolio, yet his presence in the cabinet may provide desired provincial or sectional representation; he may be unusually able and experienced, but no longer capable of meeting the heavy demands of departmental work; he may be very competent, yet wish nothing more than to sit in the seats of the mighty and be available for special ministerial duties whenever needed.

The fourth type of position is that of the penumbral group whose members are recognized as being in the ministry, but not necessarily the cabinet. Before 1959 there was some doubt about whether the parliamentary assistants belonged in this group, but there was no doubt about a few other office holders. In the 1890s two political officers, known respectively as the controller of Customs and the controller of Inland Revenue, were in the ministry, but not in the cabinet; they then became members of the cabinet for a time, and later reverted to their early status for a few months until the offices were abolished, new ministries created, and the heads given places in the cabinet.[4] For over twenty years the solicitor general, an office created in 1892, remained consistently outside the cabinet; but he then embarked upon a series of entrances and exits that terminated only with the absorption of his office and functions by the attorney general. In 1945, however, the position was again made separate; and as its occupant has since been in the cabinet (and now with extended duties), the arrangement is presumably permanent.

The fifth group consists of the parliamentary assistants or secretaries, who are clearly executive officers, but since 1959 equally clearly not junior or quasi-ministers, and thus not in the ministry.

Another essential distinction which must be borne in mind has already been lightly touched upon: the distinction between the Privy Council and the cabinet. The Privy Council, as the British North America Act states, is composed

3/Mr Diefenbaker had no representative of the Senate in his cabinet for most of the period from 1957 to 1962. Ministers without portfolio have on occasion been called "member of the administration."

4/Parliamentary Guide, 1901; N. O. Coté, Political Appointments, 1896–1917 (Ottawa, 1917); Guide to Canadian Ministries since Confederation, July 1, 1867, January 1, 1957 (Public Archives of Canada, 1957).

of those chosen by the governor general, and they are, by custom, always recommended by the prime minister. All cabinet ministers must first be made members of the Privy Council, although it may contain other persons of distinction, such as a Prince of Wales, a British prime minister, and a Canadian high commissioner in London, all of whom have been members. In 1953 the chief justice of Canada, the Speakers of the House of Commons and the Senate, and the leader of the opposition were all made members of the Privy Council before they left for the Coronation where they formed a part of Canada's official delegation, and in 1967 the ten provincial premiers were admitted as part of the centennial celebrations. Those appointed to the Privy Council remain members for life, and hence will include not only ministers from the present cabinet, but also all surviving ministers of past cabinets as well. The Privy Council would therefore, if active, be a large[5] and politically cumbersome body with members continually at cross-purposes with one another; but it has saved itself from this embarrassment by the simple device of holding almost no meetings of the whole Council. The Privy Council as such none the less does meet: a meeting was called in 1947 to receive the formal announcement by the King of his consent to the marriage of Princess Elizabeth and the Queen herself chaired meetings in 1957 in Ottawa and in 1959 in Halifax. Quite apart from such ceremonial occasions, "routine meetings are considered to take place every time the Governor General participates by approving an Order in Council ... In this century the Council has met formally at least nine times, three times since 1945. On two of these occasions non-ministers attended, and at some of the meetings Government business was discussed."[6]

It remains true, none the less, that the truly operative part of the Privy Council is the cabinet; and the cabinet, lacking any legal status of its own, masquerades as the Privy Council when it desires to assume formal powers; it speaks and acts in the name of the entire Council. The Governor-in-Council is therefore the governor acting on the formal advice of ministers of the cabinet, and the instrument of such formal decisions becomes an order or a minute of Council. The cabinet, even when it acts informally, will consider itself to be functioning as the Council (and enforce, for example, the council's oath of secrecy upon its members) but, for the most part, in the conduct of its discussions and in its settlement of policies it is simply a group of the leading members of the majority party. The prime minister and cabinet as such thus exercise no formal powers; they decide rather how some regularly constituted authority

5/In recent years the Privy Council has had at least one hundred members, the dates of their appointments ranging from 1917 to the present. Many of them, as the official lists show, were never members of a Canadian cabinet. See, for example, *Canada Year Book, 1968*, p. 77.

6/Henry F. Davis, "Nature of the Privy Council," *Canadian Legal Studies*, 1, no. 5 (Dec. 1968), pp. 305-6. This quotation corrects errors made in previous editions of this book, and I am indebted to Mr Davis for drawing it to my attention. See also Forsey, "Meetings of the Queen's Privy Council for Canada."

– the Governor General, the Governor-in-Council, a particular minister – is to discharge functions with which that authority is legally entrusted and concerning which it will, as a matter of custom and convenience, accept direction from the prime minister and the cabinet. The governor is not president of the Council; orders and minutes of Council are ordinarily passed by the cabinet and then forwarded to the governor for his approval and signature.

The principle that the members of the cabinet must not only have seats in one of the Houses of Parliament[7] but that they are at all times responsible to the House of Commons lies at the very root of Canadian politics, and it was the acceptance of this convention, as indicated above, that a century ago transformed representative into responsible government. This implies that a fundamental agreement and sympathy exist between the cabinet and the House, and that this condition will always be maintained. Though for some years after Confederation practices were more flexible, if the House of Commons withdraws its confidence from the cabinet, one of two consequences must ensue: either the cabinet must be changed so that the Commons can obtain an executive which will give it the leadership it desires, or the Commons must itself be changed to provide the cabinet with the support which it must have if it is to remain in office.[8] One of two courses of action is thus ordinarily available following a cabinet's defeat: the resignation of the cabinet, or the dissolution of the House; the one gives the House a new cabinet, the other gives the cabinet a new House. The second alternative, of course, may not be decisive in the way expected. If the electorate chooses a House which will support the cabinet, harmony has once more been restored. If, on the other hand, the electorate elects a majority of members opposed to the prime minister who advised the dissolution, the result will be a continuance or even accentuation of the discord between the cabinet and the House, and the former must then resign to make room for a new administration in which the House will have confidence. The final appeal in resolving any dispute of this kind is thus a general election; for the House as a representative body derives its power from the people, and the cabinet justifies its right to office by the support it can command in the House of Commons.

7/A cabinet minister, even the prime minister, may for a brief period not have a seat in either house; but one must be obtained within a reasonable time. No one can define with certainty what is "a reasonable time." The extreme example was furnished by General A. G. L. McNaughton, who while minister of National Defence in 1944-5, was without a seat for over nine and a half months, although he made two unsuccessful attempts to obtain one.

8/A series of minority governments, Dr Forsey has suggested, could easily force a return to a looser view of what constitutes a defeat for a government, unless Canadians were ready to accept very frequent general elections. The defeat of the government on a major measure, but by a snap vote, on Feb. 19, 1968, and the subsequent affirmation of the House of Commons' confidence in it, is an interesting demonstration of his point. The events of 1968 suggest a third course to supplement the two above: the House, having defeated the government, may decide that it did not. See Eugene Forsey, "The Problem of 'Minority' Government in Canada," *Canadian Journal of Economics and Political Science*, xxx, no. 1 (Feb. 1964), pp. 1–11.

The House of Commons might conceivably change its mind from month to month or even from day to day as to the leadership it desired, and this vacillation would bring about continual changes in the cabinet or a never-ending succession of elections. The chief reason why this does not happen is found, of course, in the existence and operation of well-organized and stable groups which have proved to be a highly necessary adjunct to democratic government. Virtually all members of the House of Commons belong to political parties; each is elected as a member of a particular party, and each acknowledges the leadership of and gives consistent support to the head of his own party. Thus the prime minister, as the leader of one of these parties, is assured of the steady backing of a large part of the House, and as his party usually holds a majority of the seats, he and his cabinet can rely on their measures being passed and the measures offered by their opponents being defeated. If there should be more than two major parties in the House, then the stability of the government may be threatened and may at times depend on such uncertain factors as the goodwill and co-operation of a rival group; Canadian experience with cabinets whose own party is a minority of the House reveals that such Parliaments can either be short-lived (as in 1925-6, 1957-8, and 1962-3), or enjoy a normal span (as in 1921-5 and 1963-8). It is no accident that cabinet government is the child of a two-party system and that its greatest successes have occurred where that system has flourished. But even the existence of only two parties will give no positive assurance that the cabinet is immune from defeat, for the emergence of an unforeseen or challenging issue may shatter the solidity of the support on which it normally relies. If at any time a substantial number of the majority party members cease to remain in accord with their fellows or if their allegiance to their leader is seriously weakened, the resulting adverse vote or even, perhaps, the mere abstention from voting, may bring the prime minister and the cabinet down (as in 1873). The far-reaching consequences of such action or inaction, however, will in themselves operate as a powerful check on party members setting up their individual opinions against their leaders, for in order to attain what admittedly may be a minor good, they are forced to face the possibility of the defeat of a government with which they are generally in sympathy. "If the effect of voting against a measure of which he disapproves," wrote Lord Morley, "would be to overthrow a whole Ministry of which he strongly approves, then, unless some very vital principle indeed were involved, to give such a vote would be to prefer a small object to a great one, and would indicate a very queasy monkish sort of conscience."[9]

The normal Canadian cabinet is therefore composed entirely of members owing allegiance to the same political party. This homogeneity creates a much more efficient executive body, gives more consistent leadership, discourages internal dissension, and develops a stronger fighting organization to ward off the constant attacks of the opposition. "There is something more required to make a Strong Administration," wrote Joseph Howe over a hundred years ago,

9/*Studies in Literature* (London and New York, 1891), p. 338.

"than nine men treating each other courteously at a round table. There is the assurance of good faith – towards each other – of common sentiments, and kindly feelings, propagated through the friends of each, in Society, in the Legislature and in the Press, until a great Party is formed ... which secures a steady working majority to sustain their policy and carry their measures."[10]

Union or coalition with another party will take place only as a last resort to create or to maintain a majority in the House or because some issue of transcendent importance obliterates, for the time being at least, the normal party lines. Except for the Confederation coalition, Canada has had since 1867 only one experience of this kind,[11] when a Union government was formed during the First World War to enforce the terms of the Conscription Act of 1917. The coalition worked smoothly at first, and Sir Robert Borden repeatedly paid tribute to the sincere and cordial co-operation which he received from those Liberal ministers who had been his former opponents, although some of Sir Robert's party found the novel association most distasteful. But the war had scarcely been concluded when disintegration set in, and the Liberal supporters of the government began gradually to slip back to their former allegiance. In a few months' time the strain was increased when the Liberals held a national convention to choose a new leader, and a little later the illness of Sir Robert Borden forced his resignation as prime minister. The Unionists tried repeatedly to avert the collapse of the coalition; but to little avail.[12] The necessity for compromise and the spirit of conciliation had vanished.

The members of the Canadian cabinet acknowledge three separate and distinct responsibilities: a responsibility, through the governor general, to the monarch, which is now rarely invoked; a responsibility to the prime minister and to one another, which produces what is called the "solidarity" of the cabinet; and a responsibility, both individual and collective, to the House of Commons.

The responsibility to the governor general is, of course, the survival of the original responsibility which the royal advisers owed to their principal and which, in Canada, was owing in the early days to the colonial governors. Its essence is stated in the British North America Act (section 9): "The Executive Government and Authority of and over Canada is hereby declared to continue and be vested in the Queen." It is by virtue of this authority, the section authorizing the Privy Council,[13] and the prerogative instruments that the governor general requests the prime minister to form a government, that the members of the cabinet become the advisers of the Crown, that the governor is entitled to be taken into the full confidence of the cabinet (which, in fact, rarely occurs) and that the ministers act in the name of and for the Crown. It was this

10/Quoted by Chester Martin, *Empire and Commonwealth*, p. 209.
11/Coalition governments have not been uncommon in the provinces.
12/See Graham, *Arthur Meighen*, I, chap. IX; R. MacG. Dawson, *William Lyon Mackenzie King*, I, *1874–1923* (Toronto, 1958), chaps. X–XIII.
13/Section 11, *supra*, p. 168.

relationship which the minister of Finance had in mind in 1945 when he stated that "the authority of the Government is not delegated by the House of Commons; the authority of the Government is received from the Crown"[14] – a statement which horrified certain ultra-democrats in the House who had apparently been believing that they lived in a republic. The responsibility to the governor general is, it is true, largely inactive and is rarely invoked against the cabinet, because democratic controls have for the most part rendered it unnecessary. For over a hundred years the Canadian House of Commons (or its provincial predecessors) has taken upon itself the duty of ensuring that the cabinet follows virtuous paths, and this surveillance is normally quite sufficient and far preferable to scrutiny or punishment from any other source. But, as earlier pages have indicated,[15] there may be certain contingencies – rarer in their occurrence and threatening the normal operation of the constitution – which would make it desirable for the governor to intervene and invoke the latent responsibility to the head of the state. To that degree and only to that degree can the responsibility to the governor be invoked as an active or punitive measure. The fact remains that constitutionally the cabinet must have the confidence of the governor, just as it does the confidence of the Commons.

The members of the cabinet are responsible to one another, and particularly to the prime minister. It is an essential cabinet convention, dictated by convenience, the need for a united policy, and fear of the opposition, that all members must openly agree on all important public questions; and apparent contradictions among ministers must be explained away. Israel Tarte once said that the Laurier cabinet (of which he was a member) "fought like blazes" at their meetings, and there is no reason to doubt it; but on the platform and in Parliament that cabinet stood as one on any major issue. It follows that all members of a cabinet must consider the views of one another in making any important announcement or in taking a decision which might be considered as involving government policy; and this leads in practice to prior consultation and discussion in cabinet, or, at least, with the prime minister. This done, if the minister secures agreement on his proposal, the cabinet will support it to a man; failing such agreement, the dissenting member must acquiesce in the rejection of his ideas or tender his resignation. Tarte furnished an admirable occasion for the application of his principle of cabinet solidarity in 1902 when he persisted in advocating a higher tariff despite the declared government policy of not considering any tariff changes or revisions at that time. Sir Wilfrid Laurier, in commenting on his demand for Tarte's immediate resignation, stated:

The gentlemen who are assembled at the Council board are not expected to be any more unanimous in their views because they sit at Council, than would be expected from any other body of men. It is in human nature to differ. It is in human nature,

14/*Can. H. of C. Debates*, Nov. 12, 1945, p. 2020.
15/*Supra*, pp. 161–3.

even for the best of friends; even for men professing the same views politically to differ and to differ materially on some points. But the Council sits for the purpose of reconciling these differences – the Council sits for the purpose of examining the situation and, having examined it, then to come to a solution, which solution then becomes a law to all those who choose to remain in the Cabinet. It would be a mere redundancy for me to affirm that the necessity for solidarity between the members of the same administration is absolute; that the moment a policy has been determined upon, then it becomes the duty of every member of that administration to support it and to support it in its entirety.[16]

The members of the cabinet are above everything else responsible to the House of Commons, not as individuals alone, but collectively as well. This responsibility has been the key to the control of the executive power in Canada as in Britain; the powers of the Crown have remained for the most part intact or have even been increased, but the exercise of those powers has come under the cabinet and this body in turn under the general scrutiny of Parliament. This is the central fact of parliamentary democracy; for it is this practice which keeps the system both efficient and constantly amenable to popular control. The minister at the head of every department is responsible for everything that is done within that department; and inasmuch as he will expect praise or assume blame for all the acts of his subordinates, he must have the final word in any important decision that is taken. Only if the minister can clearly demonstrate his initial ignorance of the offending act and convince the House of the prompt and thorough manner in which he has attempted to remedy the abuse, can he hope to be absolved from at least opposition censure. R. L. Borden, when leader of the opposition, aptly described the ideal situation as follows:

A Minister of the Crown is responsible, under the system in Great Britain, for the minutest details of the administration in his department; he is politically responsible, but he does not know anything at all about them. When anything goes wrong in his department, he is responsible therefor to Parliament; and if he comes to Parliament and points out that he entrusted the duty to an official in the ordinary course and in good faith, that he had been selected for his capacity, and ability, and integrity, and the moment that man has gone wrong the Minister had investigated the matter to the full and punished that man either by degradation or dismissal, he has done his duty to the public. That is the way matters are dealt with in Great Britain, and it is in that way, it seems to me, that our affairs ought to be carried on in this country.[17]

It must be added that if a majority of the Commons supports a cabinet in a

16/Can. H. of C. Debates, March 18, 1903, pp. 132–3. For accounts of ministerial manoeuvring which involved two resignations and an abrupt change in a prime minister's policy, see Dawson, The Conscription Crisis of 1944; Pickersgill and Forster, The Mackenzie King Record, 1944–1945; Norman Ward, ed., A Party Politician: The Memoirs of Chubby Power (Toronto, 1966). Another ministerial crisis that resulted in the defeat of a government is chronicled in Can. H. of C. Debates, Feb. 4–5, 1963.
17/Ibid., May 15, 1909, p. 6723.

clear evasion of responsibility, as is not unknown, neither the opposition nor the electorate has an effective instrument to enforce responsibility before the next election.[18]

An allied element in cabinet solidarity is the custom that the entire cabinet will normally accept responsibility for the acts of any of its members, so that the censure of one will become the censure of all. The members of the cabinet therefore resign office simultaneously. It is not impossible, however, for the House to censure one member or to allow a cabinet to throw an offending minister to the wolves, and to accept such drastic action as offering sufficient amends for wrong-doing, provided, of course, the cabinet clearly does not countenance the objectionable act and that the purge is made with promptitude and without equivocation. Such charity cannot be expected as a matter of course, and it must depend both on the mitigating circumstances and on the way in which the House chooses to regard the whole incident.

Two negative comments on this relationship may be added. First, a government defeated at the polls is not obliged to resign until it meets defeat at the hands of the House, although there is a well-established body of precedents favouring immediate resignation under such circumstances. If the result of the election is such that there is any doubt of what the outcome will be when the House assembles, then the cabinet is justified in awaiting the verdict of the people's representatives. Thus when the 1925 election deprived the Liberal government of a majority of seats and gave a larger number (though not a majority) to the Conservatives, the former was entitled to stay in office until the House had cleared up the ambiguous situation. In 1957, none the less, another Liberal cabinet in an analogous situation resigned promptly after an election in which no party won a majority; and in 1962 a Conservative cabinet with minority support remained in office until two weeks after the election of April 8, 1963, when, again failing to get a majority, it resigned without meeting the House. Secondly, the cabinet is in no sense responsible to the Senate. One master is sufficient; and no Senate would dare to assert any control over any Canadian cabinet's tenure of office.[19]

This emphasis on the responsibility of the cabinet to the lower and not to the upper house, and the constant need for the administration to remain in the closest touch with the Commons – to answer questions, to introduce and guide bills, to explain estimates, etc. – have led to a marked diminution in the number of senators in the cabinet. For about forty years the custom was followed of having two or three (and on occasion four or five) members of the cabinet in the upper house, and every portfolio, save Finance, Railways and Canals, Customs, and secretary of state for the provinces, was held at some time or

18/See Eugene A. Forsey, "Mr. McGregor's Garden – Keep Out!" in *Public Affairs*, xv, no. 2 (Winter 1953), pp. 20–9.
19/But see R. B. Bennett's statement, *infra*, p. 401n.

other by a senator.[20] Indeed, two prime ministers, Sir John Abbott and Sir Mackenzie Bowell, directed their governments from the rarefied though somewhat enervating atmosphere of the Red Chamber. Sir Wilfrid Laurier was the first prime minister to have only one senator in his cabinet, after 1908, and Sir Robert Borden continued the practice on the formation of his first government in 1911, though he returned to two, and then three, in 1917 and 1918. Mackenzie King completed the process in 1921 by announcing that "except for very special reasons, Ministers of the Crown holding portfolios will hereafter be selected from Members of Parliament occupying seats in the House of Commons." (The rule that the only senator in the cabinet should be a minister without portfolio, who normally acted as the government leader in the Senate, suffered some major infractions.[21]) The practice has naturally diminished greatly the prestige and influence of the upper chamber with the result that that emaciated body, already weakened by years of undernourishment, has been brought perilously close to collapse. Several remedies have been suggested, and Senate reform remains a useful election plank; but no government of recent years showed convincing concern over the Senate's gradual debilitation until 1968, when Prime Minister Trudeau made a number of far-reaching proposals about the Senate as part of a general scheme of constitutional change.[22] Weak or strong, the Senate still furnishes a constant supply of sinecures for staunch government supporters. By a paradox, a cabinet that showed great concern for Senate reform, Mr Diefenbaker's, had no senator in it for five years after the election of 1957, except for a few months in 1957–8.

The most notable characteristic of the Canadian cabinet is the representative nature of its membership: the cabinet is in a unique degree the grand co-ordinating body for the divergent provincial, sectional, religious, racial, and other interests throughout the nation. Cabinets in other countries, as, for example, in Great Britain and the United States, frequently exhibit similar tendencies, but not over as wide a field or in compliance with the same rigid requirements. The inevitable consequence is that the choice of the prime minister is seriously restricted and he is often compelled to push merit to one side in making some of his selections. Cabinet positions will undoubtedly be avail-

20/N. McL. Rogers, "Evolution and Reform of the Canadian Cabinet," *Canadian Bar Review*, April 1933, pp. 232–4. Hon. E. N. Rhodes, appointed to the Senate while minister of Finance in 1935, never sat in the Senate as minister of Finance because of prorogation and dissolution.

21/Two minor cases occurred in 1925–6, and another in 1935, when existing ministers were appointed to the Senate and continued to retain their portfolios for some months thereafter. The important exceptions were Senator Robertson, who was minister of Labour in the Bennett cabinet; Senator Macdonald, who was made solicitor general in the St Laurent cabinet in 1954; and Senator McCutcheon who was made minister of Trade and Commerce in the Diefenbaker cabinet in 1963. On occasion the number of senators serving in the cabinet without portfolio has exceeded one, and has been as high as three, as in 1896 and 1935. The leader of the government in the Senate, as noted above, now holds a full portfolio.

22/Trudeau, *The Constitution and the People of Canada*, pp. 76–7.

able for the best four or five of the government's supporters; but the balance may be filled from the ranks of the party for reasons as varied as they are unconnected with parliamentary and administrative efficiency. One observer of ready sympathies, who witnessed at close quarters the formation of the Borden cabinet in 1911, has supplied the following bitter comment:

Those who have not witnessed the making of a Government have reason to be happier than those who have. It is a thoroughly unpleasant and discreditable business in which merit is disregarded, loyal service is without value, influence is the most important factor and geography and religion are important supplementary considerations.

The Borden Ministry was composed under standard conditions and was not, therefore, nearly as able, as honest, or as industrious an administrative aggregation as could have been had from the material available. Industrial and other magnates were present during the process of gestation, not, of course, in the public interest but in their own, which was quite a different thing. There were some broken hearts – in one instance, literally. In others, philosophy came to the rescue, but the pills were large and the swallowing was bitter ...[23]

The first requisite to be met is that every province must have, if at all possible, at least one representative in the cabinet. The cabinet, in short, is federalized, a turn of events which was shrewdly forecast by one of the critics of the Confederation proposals in 1865,[24] and accepted by Sir John A. Macdonald in forming his first ministry in 1867.[25] Despite the emergence of additional political and mathematical difficulties as the number of the provinces has increased, the practice has continued to flourish. The cabinet has, in fact, taken over the allotted role of the Senate as the protector of the rights of the provinces and it has done an incomparably better job. Any province today would relinquish all its senators without the slightest compunction or regret if by so doing it would be allowed to double its representation in the cabinet.

The importance of provincial representation, which is now a rigid convention of the constitution, has been well illustrated many times, but never better than in 1921 when King formed his first cabinet. The Province of Alberta had by a singular oversight neglected to return even one Liberal to Parliament, and none of the twelve United Farmers of Alberta would betray his party for a portfolio or help King and advance the provincial interest by resigning in

23/Paul Bilkey, *Persons, Papers and Things* (Toronto, 1940), pp. 140–2. The above account is confirmed by one member of the cabinet appointed at this time. W. S. Wallace, *Memoirs of the Rt. Hon. Sir George Foster* (Toronto, 1933), pp. 154–61. See Heath Macquarrie, "The Formation of Borden's First Cabinet," *Canadian Journal of Economics and Political Science*, XXIII, no. 1 (Feb. 1957), pp. 90–104.

24/*Confederation Debates*, 1865, p. 497. There have been major exceptions: Prince Edward Island has had no minister for over two-thirds of the period since it joined Confederation; Manitoba had no minister till 1892, British Columbia till 1888, Saskatchewan till 1917.

25/In order to give provincial and sectional representation two of the leading figures in Confederation, D'Arcy McGee and Charles Tupper, were left out of the first cabinet. N. McL. Rogers, "Federal Influences on the Canadian Cabinet," *Canadian Bar Review*, Feb. 1933, pp. 106–7. See also Ward, *The Public Purse*, p. 44.

favour of a Liberal. The new prime minister, however, was not easily discouraged, and after some inquiry and negotiation found a solution: he appointed to the cabinet Charles Stewart, a Liberal ex-premier of Alberta, and then opened up a seat for him in the Province of Quebec. In 1935, Alberta again caused some worry, for the province returned one Liberal, one Conservative, and fifteen Social Crediters; but after some hesitation, extending over three years, the sole Liberal was made a member of the cabinet without portfolio. Prince Edward Island, with only four members, has had the greatest difficulty in retaining its right to a representative in the cabinet, though the obligation has been repeatedly acknowledged by different prime ministers;[26] but in actual fact, the Island has had, since the turn of the century, a minister for barely fifteen years.

The convention that each province, if at all possible, must have at least one representative in the cabinet makes another convention almost mandatory, namely, that the two large provinces must each be given more than one representative. "Each of the Maritime Provinces having received representatives," Sir John A. Macdonald had explained as early as 1868, "the least that could be given to Quebec, with a due regard to population, was four, while the least that could be given to Ontario, the largest Province of the Confederation, was five."[27] The actual pattern followed by successive prime ministers in forming their cabinets has, of course, varied considerably with their individual judgments and prejudices and with their various strengths in the provinces, but the fundamental rule enunciated by Macdonald has never been abandoned. Thus Ontario's representation has varied from three to eleven ministers, but has never dropped as low as two. Quebec's has varied from two to ten, but never as low as one. Paradoxically, with the increase in the number of provinces, the need to keep the size of the cabinet within manageable limits has meant that the smaller provinces' minimum (if possible) of one has also tended to become their maximum, barring special circumstances. Special circumstances occur with considerable frequency (Nova Scotia, for example, had three ministers from 1940 to 1944, and Saskatchewan two after 1957) and make generalization difficult, but a smaller province cannot ordinarily count on more than one minister. To this must be added one further qualification: with the rise of the four western provinces, the number of ministers allocated to them has tended to grow too, and in recent years they have shared as many as seven and eight cabinet seats; more recently still, Quebec's share of seats has been growing.

Numbers alone do not tell the whole story. The peculiar position of Quebec has added another element, for Quebec's representation in the cabinet has to be divided between French- and English-speaking members, with the former outnumbering the latter; thus (although again there is no set rule), French-

26/Rogers, "Federal Influences on the Canadian Cabinet," pp. 114–15.
27/*Can. H. of C. Debates*, April 3, 1867–8, p. 450.

speaking Roman Catholics have generally held from three to six or more posts, with the English-speaking Protestants holding one or two and occasionally none. Ontario obviously cannot be outdone, so that province may commonly expect to have a more or less guaranteed minimum number of ministers that bears some relation to the total allocated to Quebec, although here as with Quebec, the total number of government supporters from the province in the House is an important factor. Within these two provinces divergent loyalties and interests have given this representation a local territorial basis as well. Thus the French-speaking constituencies in Quebec have tended to fall into two groups, one centring on Quebec, the other on Montreal, while the English-speaking constituencies (formerly most of the Eastern Townships) have formed another unit; each of the three will claim its own cabinet minister.[28] Ontario has not been so clearly divided; but both northern and western Ontario have claims which are usually recognized, and in the past Toronto has been known to complain because its special views have had no advocate in the cabinet councils, while Mr Pearson's cabinet was criticized for being top-heavy with urban members, reflecting the bias of his party's seats in the Commons.

Provincial representation has frequently been further elaborated in that a few portfolios, for prolonged periods, have been recognized as the special preserve of certain areas. The Department of the Interior was early headed by an Ontario member most of the time; but as western Canada developed, the portfolio drifted in the direction of the major interest. Agriculture (with one break occasioned by a shortage of personnel) has gone to the Prairie provinces for over four decades; Fisheries has generally gone to the Maritimes, or more rarely British Columbia, because of the coastal provinces' close association with this activity. The minister of Finance has always (with two exceptions) come from eastern Canada with a leaning in favour of the Maritime provinces for much of the department's history. For many years there was a tendency to give the French Canadians (usually from Quebec) either Public Works or the Post Office and to choose the minister of Justice from Quebec. In recent years, however, prime ministers have shown more flexibility in the allotment of portfolios.

The federal character of the cabinet is emphasized still further in the practice of ministers in discharging their conventional functions as provincial representatives. Each minister is constantly concerned with the widely scattered interests of his special province and he acts, and is supposed to act, as its spokesman, advocate, and (where necessary) dispenser of patronage and possibly electoral organizer.[29] In cabinet councils he will be expected to advise, not only on matters within his particular department, but also on any topic whenever it concerns his province; and his opinion, by virtue of superior knowledge of that locality, will merit exceptional consideration. An interesting

---

28/Rogers, "Federal Influences on the Canadian Cabinet," pp. 116–18.
29/A first-hand account of a minister's varied duties is in Ward, *A Party Politician*.

illustration occurred in 1947 when the Dominion government held up its proposal for Newfoundland's entry in the federation until there was a New Brunswick representative in the cabinet. Mr St Laurent (then minister for External Affairs) announced:

We look upon this as a very important decision to make ... We wish all members of our Government, representing all Provinces, to be in a position to decide what share all parts of the Dominion should bear ... The fact that we were so unfortunate as to lose through death the services of Fisheries Minister H. F. G. Bridges [from New Brunswick] has delayed matters. We regard the Maritime Provinces as particularly concerned in this matter, and for that reason we had Justice Minister Ilsley [of Nova Scotia], Senator Robinson of Prince Edward Island, and the late Mr. Bridges on the Cabinet committee. But no final decision will be attempted by an incomplete Cabinet.[30]

When the provincial government is controlled by the same political party as that in power in the Dominion, the province will commonly expect its special cabinet minister at Ottawa to use his good offices to promote the requests which the provincial government may make. Consultations and negotiations will proceed through the normal channels of the appropriate federal and provincial departments, but these will often be supplemented by the more informal proceedings through the province's representative in the cabinet. The latter may, indeed, show some resentment if the province ignores him and approaches another minister for intervention on behalf of the area which he feels to be peculiarly his own. Dominion appointments in a particular province (when not made by the Public Service Commission) are thus made on the formal recommendation of the minister in whose department the office lies, but he will as a rule first consult the minister representing the province concerned before making his recommendation. "While all members of the Cabinet," runs an order-in-council in 1904, "have an equal degree of responsibility in a constitutional sense, yet in the practical working out of responsible government in a country of such vast extent as Canada, it is found necessary to attach a special responsibility to each Minister for the public affairs of the province or district with which he has close political connexion, and with which his colleagues may not be so well acquainted."[31]

The possibilities of sectionalism in the cabinet have not been exhausted by giving special representation to provincial interests alone. Race and religion are also carefully considered, although they are to some degree taken into account in determining the provincial quota. The majority of French Canadians from Quebec are always Roman Catholic, the English Canadians usually Protestant. But almost invariably the cabinet will contain an Irish Roman Catholic, usually from outside Quebec, and the Acadian French or the French-

30/Montreal *Gazette*, Sept. 30, 1947. Senator Robinson was not a member of the cabinet, but was apparently invited to serve on this committee.
31/See Dawson, *Constitutional Issues in Canada*, pp. 112–13. See also pp. 111–16.

speaking from Ontario or the West may also be given a special representative. Some balance of Protestant denominations is at least considered when making cabinet appointments, although it is doubtful if people today are as conscious of these differences as when Alexander Mackenzie (prime minister, 1873–8) congratulated himself on the finely balanced Cabinet which he had called into existence. "I may, with feelings of pride," said he, "refer to the standing of the members of the Cabinet. No one will deny it has a large amount of ability ... In the matter of religious faith, there are five Catholics, three members of the Church of England, three Presbyterians, two Methodists, one Congregationalist, and one Baptist."[32]

A host of other conflicting interests and claims will need to be considered, weighed, and, if possible, reconciled, by assigning portfolios where they will afford the greatest satisfaction to a wide variety of people. Mr Diefenbaker prided himself on his sensitivity to groups not previously recognized, and his first cabinet included the first woman to serve as a minister, and the first Canadian of Ukrainian descent. The minister of Labour has when possible been associated in a theoretical or practical way with organized labour, though, in fact, such an association has existed for less than half the history of the department. The Orange Order, the Manufacturers' Association, the wheat co-operatives, the financial interests, and others have all in the past demanded consideration; and they cannot always be satisfied by appointments to the cabinet from among the members of the Commons; since 1867 over sixty ministers have been brought in from outside Parliament, many of them to give special representation to a particular interest, or to recognize the claims of a provincial premier or leader. The actual occupation of the members of the cabinet has never been a major issue, although it has been used for campaign material at elections. In 1940, for example, the Conservatives drew attention to the fact that of the sixteen members in a cabinet which was engaged in directing the war, eleven were lawyers, three school-teachers, one was a college professor, and one a financier and engineer. On an earlier occasion, in 1921, however, the biter had been the bitten; for the Conservative government had been criticized by the farmers for the same legal bias in its personnel.[33] Provincial premiers, especially if they have been active in winning the election for the government at Ottawa, may prefer claims to cabinet positions which must be met, although in recent years fewer premiers seem to have been attracted by federal ministerial status than used to be the case. Ex-cabinet ministers, if they are still in Parliament, constitute another group which can rarely be passed over, even when they have outlived their usefulness.

The roster of demands is thus a long one, and the pressure to increase the size of the cabinet in order to meet all these demands is tremendous. Few

32/W. Buckingham and G. W. Ross, *The Hon. Alexander Mackenzie: His Life and Times* (Toronto, 1892), p. 354.
33/*Grain Growers' Guide*, Oct. 5, 1921.

prime ministers can enjoy the undignified scramble which occurs after each successful election: the winners are many, but the prizes are pitifully few. The number of prizes has been appreciably increased in recent years by the growth in size of the cabinet, and by the institution of parliamentary assistantships and secretaryships, for these have opened up new possibilities in meeting demands for sectional representation. Mackenzie King had stated in 1935 that Prince Edward Island would receive a parliamentary secretary as its representative in the government, and when these new officers were created some years later the pledge was ultimately honoured. Although the remainder of the first assistantships bore few signs of having been made for sectional reasons, later crops have suggested that the old fundamental forces of geography and race were once more at work. If the early precedents of promoting parliamentary assistants to cabinet positions continue to be followed, the demand for regional representation among the assistants will be inevitable; for the surest way to gain a seat at the Council table will be by preferment from the junior ranks. But leaving this speculation aside, the temptation to turn the assistantships to a good advantage and produce the finer shades of sectional representation has in fact proven irresistible, and a modern roster of parliamentary assistants reads like a miniature cabinet. It is easy, of course, to decry the practice of forming a cabinet which is in large measure based on many varieties of sectional representation, and there is no doubt that it is never conducive to efficiency in its narrow ministerial sense. Excellent men are passed over and mediocrities take their places, and every cabinet within living memory has contained examples which prove only too well the validity of the argument; good men passed over all too frequently quit politics. But some consideration must be given to the divergent views and interests which are an inescapable condition of such a large and varied country, and ethnic, religious, and cultural differences add to the difficulty. A practice which selects cabinet ministers on grounds of religious beliefs may seem short-sighted, inefficient, and generally reprehensible; but from another and wider aspect, it is simply an acknowledgment of the fact that men's confidence in one another is based, in part at least, upon qualities of this kind, and that efficient government in its broadest sense is unobtainable if these human limitations are ruthlessly overridden and ignored. In short, a regrettable practice may have to be accepted because the alternative will be even worse. The real problem here is one of degree: the cabinet must be constructed with an eye to the representative character of its members, but these factors should rarely, if ever, be permitted to displace the highest qualities of mind and character which a cabinet must contain if it is to function effectively in the complex environment of modern times.

I trust there will come a time when considerations of race and religion will have less weight than they have to-day. But we must frankly recognize these conditions to-day, and we know that in the best interest of all Canada it is well that in making up a Cabinet you should have regard to these things, as we know them in the past. On reflection it will be seen that for the good government of Canada we must have a larger Cabinet than perhaps would be required by any other country of the same population.[34]

Conflicting interests which exist on such a comprehensive scale and are so clearly defined might well appear to be a shaky foundation on which to build cabinet unity and a common policy. But while these undoubtedly tend to make general agreement more difficult, the conditions of the cabinet's existence provide the opportunity and the compulsion which make compromise possible. Some of these centripetal forces have been already indicated. The most powerful of these is the membership in one political party which, while it does not necessarily imply unanimity on all things, nevertheless creates an atmosphere of friendliness, confidence, and forbearance in which agreement thrives. A long history of past struggles, shared antipathies, similar habits of thought, loyalty to the party leader, the desire to defeat the enemy at all costs and the allied determination to stay in office, all have the same general tendency and are reinforced by the conventional insistence on the solidarity of the cabinet in public and the joint responsibility of its members in Parliament. Two other characteristics of the cabinet also assist this unifying process – the secrecy of its deliberations and the pre-eminence of the prime minister.

The miracle of cabinet solidarity, as suggested above, is frequently no miracle at all, for the simple reason that it may have no existence save as a common bulwark against an aggressive enemy. The fiction can be successfully maintained primarily because no information on what is proposed or discussed or decided in the meetings of the cabinet can be released, even in confidence, until the moment arrives for the announcement or implementation of a decision. The deliberations of the cabinet, despite the growing importunities of journalists seeking scoops, are held in secrecy. All members are Privy Councillors and as such are bound under oath to "keep close and secret all such matters as shall be treated, debated and resolved on in Privy Council, without publishing or disclosing the same or any part thereof, by Word, Writing or any otherwise to any Person out of the same Council, but to such only as be of the Council." The consequences of this secrecy are far-reaching. Relying on this protection, cabinet members are free to voice their opinions without reserve on all subjects which come up for discussion; the motives which have influenced the cabinet in coming to its decision will not be disclosed; the dissentients can support the corporate policy without being themselves singled out for special attack or having their motives impugned; and the cabinet derives no inconsiderable strategic advantage in being able to reveal hitherto undisclosed proposals at the most opportune moment.

34/W. S. Fielding, in *Can. H. of C. Debates*, May 15, 1909, p. 6725. Sir John A. Macdonald used precisely the same argument when defending the large size of his first cabinet after Confederation.

Unless secrecy exists and is maintained in its most rigid form, the Cabinet system will never work satisfactorily, will tend, rather, to prove a source of weakness and distraction. It will breed hate and temper, dissolve agreements, and give rise to a sense of treachery where there should be confidence, and of restlessness where there should be security. The reason why secrecy should be preserved, not from fear of penal regulations, but in accordance with the strictest code of personal honour, is not far to seek. Men in a Cabinet must be loyal to one another, to their chief, and to the Committee as a whole, or they will be undone. By loyalty we do not mean that they are merely to refrain from backbiting or from undermining each other's position, or, again, from trying to better their own positions by pushing a colleague down. We mean something a good deal more elemental. When a matter has been decided upon in the Cabinet, then the men who opposed the course ultimately adopted must make their choice either of resigning or else of whole-heartedly adopting the will of the Cabinet as their own. If their choice is in favour of remaining in the Cabinet, then both in public and in private they must defend the action of the Government exactly as if their own private wishes had been accepted. The will of the whole must become the will of each.[35]

The informality or unbusinesslike conduct of cabinet affairs, which was, until the Second World War, another characteristic, was always justified as necessary in order to preserve this secrecy. Whether these habits were conducive to efficiency and to economy of time and effort may be left to the imagination, but secrecy was usually preserved, although unscrupulous or garrulous ministers were the source of occasional leakages. On the whole, serious lapses were rare, although they served to indicate how embarrassing such revelations could be when used as levers against a supposedly united government. The development of an elaborate secretariat for the cabinet since the late 1930s, and the subsequent admission to the cabinet's inner sanctum of a growing number of civil servants, has not in any way endangered cabinet secrecy.[36]

The oath thus obtains substantial reinforcement from the collective moral pressure of the cabinet and the constant need of the members for self-protection. In 1904, for example, R. L. Borden read to the House a confidential memorandum on the transcontinental railway prepared by the former minister of Railways, and used it with devastating effect against the government. Sir Wilfrid Laurier was most indignant, for the document had clearly been improperly obtained from the Privy Council Office. "This is a confidential memorandum," he protested, "presented by a member of the Privy Council to the Privy Council. No member of the Council gave out that report, for that would have been a violation of the oath of secrecy which every member takes

35/*Spectator*, London, April 29, 1916. Notwithstanding these general principles, it is worthy of note that Mr Trudeau, shortly after assuming office in 1968, found it necessary to remind his colleagues of the need for secrecy. His predecessor, even more remarkably, had felt obliged to supply ministers with a code of ethics. See Peter C. Newman, *The Distemper of our Times* (Toronto, 1968), p. 281.

36/See *infra*, chap. XI. Civil servants, it may be noted, are more to be trusted with confidential material than ministers. It is not without significance that the minister of Finance does not disclose his budget proposals to the cabinet until a few hours before their announcement to Parliament although a number of civil servants have had the information for weeks.

on joining the Council. My honourable friend said that Mr Blair [the ex-minister of Railways] did not publish it. But it is published. Who then published it, who then gave it away? How has it come into the hands of my honourable friend?"[37]

The rule of secrecy is customarily somewhat relaxed on those occasions when a minister's resignation makes it desirable that the reasons for his disagreement with his colleagues should be made known, and at such times the permission of the governor general (through the prime minister) is first obtained. In any event, if a debate develops on the minister's explanation, the general tenor of the discussions in council is almost inevitably revealed. In 1944, for example, the disclosures in regard to the essential facts preceding the resignation of J. L. Ralston were so complete that he was led to remark in the House that "in this debate and especially in the Prime Minister's speech the other night the doors of the Privy Council have been pretty well opened, and there is not very much that has taken place there, which one recollects, that has not been revealed to the House and to the public."[38]

The cabinet is also given unity and purpose by the pre-eminence of the prime minister and his leadership in its counsels, both of which have been growing in recent years. A common description of the position of the prime minister and his associates is to say that he is *primus inter pares* (or, more rarely, *inter stellas luna minores*); neither phrase does him justice. He cannot be first among his equals for the very excellent reason that he has no equals. The idea contains, however, some truth: it calls attention to one very important aspect of this relationship, namely, that the other ministers are the colleagues of their chief and not his obedient and unquestioning subordinates. Their position bears little resemblance to that of the members of the federal cabinet in the United States, whom the president may appoint or dismiss, instruct or forbid, consult or ignore, as he may see fit and without any great fear of the consequences. A prime minister who would try to issue orders to his ministers or would interfere persistently in their departmental work might find that before long he was out of office; for if at any time the ministers chose to rebel, their combined influence in the party and in the House could, and in all likelihood would, bring about his speedy downfall.[39] All members of the cabinet are responsible to the House; and while they gladly acknowledge the

37/*Can. H. of C. Debates*, April 15, 1904, p. 1306. Borden's reply was that he did not receive it "wrongfully," that it "was placed in my hands without any restrictions whatever as to the use which should be made of it" by one who had no connection with the government.

38/*Ibid.*, Nov. 29, 1944, p. 6659. See *ibid.*, Nov. 22, 1944, pp. 6505–10. By contrast, the resignation of Mr Dupuis in 1964 was followed by a notable lack of explanation. See John T. Saywell, ed., *Canadian Annual Review for 1965*, pp. 5–6.

39/The outstanding cabinet rebellion in Canadian history was that of seven members of the Bowell ministry in 1896, which had the result that the prime minister was compelled to agree to the terms dictated by the rebels. A smaller revolt in 1963 none the less played a part in the defeat of the Diefenbaker government in the House of Commons. *Can. H. of C. Debates*, Jan. 31–Feb. 5, 1963.

leadership of the prime minister, and will in fact usually bow to his decisions, they can never completely surrender their individual judgment or responsibility. Sir Winston Churchill once gave an illuminating description of the prime minister's dominating position in the realm of executive decision:

Power in a national crisis, when a man believes he knows what orders should be given, is a blessing. In any sphere of action there can be no comparison between the positions of number one and number two, three or four. The duties and the problems of all persons other than number one are quite different and in many ways more difficult. It is always a misfortune when number two or three has to initiate a dominant plan or policy. He has to consider not only the merits of the policy, but the mind of his chief; not only what to advise, but what it is proper for him in his station to advise; not only what to do, but how to get it agreed, and how to get it done. Moreover, number two or three will have to reckon with numbers four, five and six, or may be some bright outsider, number twenty. Ambition, not so much for vulgar ends, but for fame, glints in every mind. There are always several points of view which may be right, and many which are plausible. I was ruined for the time being in 1915 over the Dardanelles, and a supreme enterprise was cast away, through my trying to carry out a major and cardinal operation of war from a subordinate position. Men are ill-advised to try such ventures. This lesson had sunk into my nature.

At the top there are great simplifications. An accepted leader has only to be sure of what it is best to do, or at least to have made up his mind about it. The loyalties which centre upon number one are enormous. If he trips he must be sustained. If he makes mistakes, they must be covered. If he sleeps, he must not be wantonly disturbed. If he is no good he must be pole-axed. But this last extreme process cannot be carried out every day; and certainly not in the days just after he has been chosen.[40]

The powers of the prime minister are therefore potentially enormous; in Lord Oxford and Asquith's phrase, "the office is what its holder chooses to make it," and few holders show any marked desire to limit their commitments. "The powers of the Prime Minister," said Arthur Meighen, "are very great. The functions and duties of a Prime Minister in Parliament are not only important, they are supreme in their importance."[41] They spring from his position of primacy in the government reinforced by his leadership of the majority party, which usually owes its majority, indeed, to his leadership during the last election. The prime minister as such may possess virtually no legal authority; but operating through the governor general, the Privy Council, a minister, or sometimes as a minister in his own right, his powers are very great indeed. To these must be added the extensive legal authority of Parliament which in large measure he indirectly controls. He is the directing force in both cabinet and Parliament, and he thus presides over the one and guides the deliberations of the other. He determines the cabinet's agenda and is the major influence in helping it arrive at decisions; he leads the

40/W. S. Churchill, *Their Finest Hour* (London, 1949), p. 15.
41/See *Can. H. of C. Debates*, Jan. 8, 1926, pp. 15–16; H. R. G. Greaves, *The British Constitution*, pp. 108–17.

Commons, answers many of its questions, apportions (with its consent) its time, and submits the measures of his government for its approval. He must be consulted on important decisions by all cabinet ministers and he can if necessary advise the governor to dismiss a minister. He serves as the one great co-ordinator of executive policies. In addition to his normal duties, he has a special interest in and responsibility for foreign affairs. He is the link between governor general and cabinet, and is in a special sense an adviser to the former. He recommends all important appointments to the Council. He also has the responsibility for advising the governor when Parliament should be convened and when it should be dissolved – a power which adds greatly to his strength, not only in the House of Commons, but in the cabinet as well.[42] Increasingly he performs on his own initiative acts which were formerly considered to be the responsibility of the whole cabinet.

In many of these matters the prime minister is able to obtain substantial aid from the members of his cabinet, and this is particularly true when a decision touches upon their respective departments or the special interest or area which they individually represent and on which they speak with exceptional authority. The successful prime minister is he who can merge the many diverse talents and interests of his cabinet so that they form a united team, working in good spirit for the benefit of all. Party ties and association will not only create trust and confidence, they will also make it easier for the members of the cabinet to criticize freely and yet maintain their friendly relations intact. When the goodwill breaks down and the tension mounts, or when a dispute between ministers or departments develops, the prime minister is usually the diplomat who is able by resorting to persuasion, threats, appeals to party and personal loyalty, to bring about reconciliations and keep the cabinet together. King frequently reinforced his own leadership by the ingenious device of offering to abandon it.[43]

The degree to which the prime minister will use his colleagues to advise and assist him will depend on many factors, the chief of which are purely personal. The most obvious ones to be considered are their ability and loyalty. A fair proportion of the average cabinet are barely capable of performing their own departmental duties efficiently, and these are probably useless also as consultants in the wider field of general government policy. Others may not have the full confidence of the prime minister or the respect and unreserved approval of their colleagues. Thus there usually arises within the cabinet a small group of four or five ministers who, because of ability of various kinds, exceptional local or sectional confidence, personal qualities or character, will be highly regarded by the prime minister and will be con-

42/See, for example, P.C. 1639, July 19, 1920, in Dawson, *Constitutional Issues in Canada*, pp. 125–6. The books based on the diary of W. L. M. King convey a clear impression of how an astute prime minister employs all these tools.

43/See J. W. Pickersgill, *The Mackenzie King Record*, I, *1939–1944* (Toronto, 1960); Pickersgill and Forster, *The Mackenzie King Record, 1944–1945*.

sulted by him on all matters of importance. Occasionally the prime minister may have a special colleague whose intimacy makes him a friend and almost a partner in the office. Ernest Lapointe, for example, was for many years a great friend and counsellor to King, and there can be no doubt that King derived no small assistance, particularly in all matters involving French Canada, from his colleague; Mr St Laurent, a French-Canadian prime minister, similarly relied heavily on his redoubtable colleague from Ontario, C. D. Howe; Mr Diefenbaker appeared to have a special colleague in Howard Green; and Mr Pearson, for a time at least, in Walter Gordon. But these close relations are not common, and most prime ministers unbend only to the extent of recognizing an inner group of advisers. For the position of prime minister does not encourage intimacies and friendships. These are apt to create jealousies and antagonisms and may also expose him to exploitation by selfish interests, so that he finds his greatest protection lies in partial seclusion and a withdrawal from many normal human relationships. He may, indeed, have closer contacts with a selected group of civil servants and members of his personal staff than with some of his political associates.[44] In the words of a former member of the British Cabinet secretariat:

The change from being a Cabinet Minister to being a Prime Minister is far from being merely an exchange of chairs around a table; it is not only a change of position but of climate; the Prime Minister enters the stratosphere and becomes telescopically distant to his colleagues. There is no generosity at the top, Lloyd George declared, speaking from the cold isolation of the summit. On the other hand, to the public the Prime Minister now becomes microscopically near, no celestial being but a terrestrial insect whose every movement is watched, recorded, magnified, broadcast.[45]

The prime minister may also be compelled to preserve his aloofness for a more selfish reason, as Lloyd George indirectly suggested, namely, to defend his own position against an attack from within the cabinet. It is a rare prime minister who will be so sure of his invulnerability that he will be prepared to run the risk of developing the capacity and building up the reputation of other ministers to a point where they might become powerful enough to challenge his primacy. If such a threat should arise, the prime minister's powers and prestige in both party and government are usually so enormous that the would-be Crown Prince disappears from the political scene. There seems to be little doubt, for example, that Israel Tarte considered himself as a possible successor to Laurier, but his somewhat premature moves to build up a following to that end met with quick and decisive defeat.[46] Other incidents in Canadian history point the same moral. The leader of the pack, so long as he maintains his vigour, will tolerate no rival, and he possesses both the will and the means to enforce his suprem-

44/For a provocative story on this theme, see *Maclean's*, Oct. 1969.
45/Thomas Jones, "Prime Ministers and Cabinets," *Listener*, Oct. 13, 1938, pp. 788–9.
46/Skelton, *Life and Letters of Sir Wilfrid Laurier*, II, pp. 176–83.

acy. Thus King, when he had persuaded J. L. Ralston to enter his cabinet in 1939, jubilantly confided to his diary: "If I were designating tomorrow the man for Prime Minister, I would select Ralston without a moment's hesitation. Years ago, I felt the same way about him. He is the most unselfish man, I think, that I have met ..." Yet when tomorrow came, and it appeared that in fact Ralston might be an acceptable leader to conscriptionist forces in the Liberal party, King felt very differently: "The truth is he just wants to have his own way and is prepared to sacrifice me or the party to have it; justifying no doubt his conscience in that this is a war where men are being slain and that conscription is necessary for victory.[47]

The dominance of the prime minister in cabinet and Parliament inevitably accentuates his importance in the country as well, although some of the ministers will have a local or restricted prestige which may within a smaller sphere be the equal of his own. His position and person are so eagerly dramatized by press, platform, television, and radio that he has difficulty in securing his personal privacy; his merits are extolled and exaggerated by his friends; his faults are described and exaggerated by his enemies. The spotlight of each election campaign is fixed on him and on the leaders of the opposition parties, and their personalities and qualities and the images they present on television become even more decisive factors in the election than the issues themselves. Indeed, the issues will be in large measure formulated and selected by the leaders, and it is therefore the prime minister who will determine the emphasis which is to be given to the different policies of the government, although in this he must clearly respect the opinion of the party. Thus while Bennett did not hesitate on the eve of an election to announce a new and radical reform programme, a large section of his party did not approve of it, and were thus forced to choose between an acceptance of the platform or the repudiation of the prime minister – an unhappy dilemma which certainly did not improve the party's position in the election which followed. Election manifestoes are largely the work of respective party leaders and essentially personal pledges given by them to the electorate, and elections tend increasingly to resemble plebiscites or popularity contests between leaders. Mackenzie King on a number of occasions announced that, while he had accepted the party platform, he nevertheless regarded it as no more than a statement of policy of a very general kind which he would implement at his own discretion. Mr Diefenbaker campaigned in part in 1962, not on the basis of his adherence to his party's platform, but the promises he had himself made and kept.

The qualities of leadership which any prime minister worthy of the name is bound to possess and the opportunities for leadership which are an inescapable accompaniment of the office thus combine to exert a steady pressure

47/Pickersgill, *The Mackenzie King Record*, I, pp. 25–6 and 385. The upshot of this particular episode was that the erring minister resigned, while the prime minister adopted his policy and stayed in office. See *ibid.*, II, pp. 111–277.

towards autocratic methods and decisions. "Much of the authority of. the Cabinet," says Sir Sidney Low regarding the government of Great Britain, "has insensibly passed over to that of the Premier, as the powers of a Board of any kind tend to be concentrated in the Chairman, especially if his colleagues are much below him in ability and reputation."[48] The successful prime minister is he who can be both the unchallenged master of his administration and yet at the same time avoid the faults and dangers of absolutism. For he must always strive to have it both ways. Even a casual student of the lives of Macdonald, Laurier, Borden, and King cannot fail to be impressed with the rigorous authority that frequently marked their political relations; and when some cabinet discord or internal dispute gave an occasion for action, firm and even ruthless decision was the unfailing response. The development of autocratic characteristics in the prime minister is, however, always restrained by at least one major check – he must retain the confidence of his party, and the latter's chief and most reliable spokesmen are usually the cabinet. Thus the ministers, while generally acquiescent, may feel it necessary to oppose him if they believe that he has gone too far. They are bound to keep him in touch with fluctuations in public opinion; they are in close contact with the party supporters in Parliament and throughout the nation; their political lives, like his, are forfeit if wrong decisions are taken, and they dare not permit unwelcome proposals to pass unchallenged. There is, moreover, the potent sanction which always lies behind all their representations, protests, and expressions of opinion, that in the last resort they can not only criticize but dethrone him.

It is here that any parallel between the democratic ruler and his totalitarian counterpart breaks down. The prime minister may have enormous powers, but the basic conditions under which he governs compel him to wield his authority strictly on sufferance: he moves in an atmosphere of friendliness, tolerance, and suspended judgment in his own party, in one of constant criticism, suspicion, and outspoken condemnation elsewhere. His retention of office is thus continually under attack; he can never ignore incipient dissatisfaction and revolt among his own supporters, and he must soothe the ruffled feelings and anticipate the indignant outbreaks before they reach the acute stage. He can never lose sight of the paramount necessity of retaining the confidence of the House and, behind the House, of the electorate. No matter how lofty his position, he can always be defeated and displaced. The war for political supremacy is unending, and a victorious engagement today may be speedily followed by disastrous defeat tomorrow, as the confident Liberal party of 1956 discovered in 1957–8, or the Conservatives of 1958, with the largest majority in Canadian history, discovered in 1962–3. The most any prime minister can hope for is a temporary success, which will give him time and opportunity to consolidate his position and prepare his defences for the next encounter.

48/Sir Sidney Low, *The Governance of England* (2nd ed., London, 1918), p. 158.

10 The cabinet: functions

WHILE THE SUCCESS OF A PARTICULAR CABINET, as the preceding pages have suggested, may depend in no small measure upon the shrewdness with which the prime minister has given recognition in its personnel to certain elements in the national life, it is obvious that the adequacy of the cabinet's performance will be primarily determined by the individual and collective competence of the members. The position and experience of the prime minister – in the House, in the party, and in the country – are usually such as to enable him to choose his colleagues wisely and to give the proper weight to each of the many forces to be considered. He will normally have had parliamentary experience in opposition, probably as leader (Mr St Laurent and Mr Trudeau are the significant exceptions and it is no coincidence that both were Liberals, for that party in all its leadership conventions has passed over more experienced members to select less); and perhaps also as prime minister or other major cabinet officer; he will presumably enjoy the confidence of his party;[1] he has usually the prestige and authority which spring from a recent electoral victory; and he is almost certain to possess qualities of leadership, not the least of which will be the ability to judge the capacities of his fellow men and to gauge with some accuracy the strength of the rival political influences with which he is surrounded.

The prime minister is likely to find close at hand a reservoir of good and fair cabinet material composed of those party members who have been elected to the House of Commons; and he can, on occasion, go outside the House (to a provincial cabinet or, in a few instances, to the Dominion public service). Going outside Parliament is fairly common, and continues to provide a normal recruitment channel used more by some prime ministers than others; it has the disadvantage of casting some doubt on the quality of the

1/This is not a certainty. Sir Mackenzie Bowell did not have the confidence of his party in Parliament, nor did Sir Robert Borden or Mackenzie King enjoy the full confidence of their followers for years after being chosen.

party's representation in the House, and it necessarily involves the opening up of a seat by the resignation of a sitting member, or his appointment to the Senate or an office of emolument, and a subsequent election to secure the vacant seat for the new minister.

The prime minister is fortunately not compelled to seek cabinet members who are in any real sense of the term experts in the particular fields which they are appointed to supervise. For while the House may be able to furnish here and there an outstanding authority on a special subject or activity (and he would be worthless as an expert unless he were outstanding), the fates which preside over elections can scarcely be expected to produce on the government side of the House top-flight experts in agriculture, public health, naval affairs, mineralogy, fisheries, foreign politics, transportation, and in a dozen other fields as well. The president of the United States, if he wishes, may ransack the nation for specialized talent of any kind; but the choice of the Canadian prime minister is almost entirely restricted to the few score members of the majority party who have secured seats in the House of Commons. Some Canadians profess to be much alarmed by the situation and have on occasion produced solutions of terrifying ingenuousness. In the House of Commons itself a member once said:

In the present Cabinet – and I do not say this in any unkindly spirit – I do not see the representation I should like to see. In the Dominion we find industry, agriculture and labour. These three groups compose the major part of our population. In my view the labour portfolio should be administered by one who knows labour, and agriculture by one who knows agriculture. The portfolio of national revenue is not, in my opinion, a legal portfolio at all. It has been my view that that is a portfolio suited to a businessman, because the Minister would deal with industry, with tariffs, with regulations connected with customs duties, and matters which are connected solely with the industrial life of the country.

The Minister of Public Works – and again I say this in the most kindly spirit – should be someone who is a builder, or who knows something about building ... It is my belief that the men who should administer departments in the post-war [sic] should be men who have not been particularly trained in law or medicine, but men who have been trained in the hard way in the departments over which they would have to preside. I believe the people would have more confidence in the new departments if men with practical knowledge of the various subjects involved were chosen to head those departments.[2]

To place a member of Parliament who is a third- or fourth-rate specialist at the head of a modern department because he is supposedly an expert, and to give this pretender the control of those who are really masters in their fields, would not merely be useless, it could be disastrous. In the days that preceded civil service reform, when departmental work was simple and a civil servant was likely to be as politically minded as his minister, there might conceivably have been a case for specialist ministers, though even then their value would have been questionable. But nowadays, with the enormous com-

2/Karl Homuth, MP, *Can. H. of C. Debates*, July 17, 1944, p. 4941.

plexity of government, an amateur minister of first-rate capacity is in large measure dependable and safe because he knows he is technically ignorant, and he is therefore willing to seek and to take the best advice obtainable; the third- or fourth-rate specialist does not adequately comprehend the extent of his own ignorance and is continually setting up his judgment on technical matters against the opinion of his advisers. The latter interferes on the grounds of special knowledge, which he really lacks, whereas the former's interference is based on common sense and judgment, which he in all likelihood possesses in uncommon measure. But even a specialist who is first-class is likely to make a poor minister.[3] Practice has given this an unequivocal double confirmation. Not only has the use of the amateur minister been vindicated by long experience; the expert minister – the one who has presumably a profound technical knowledge of his department's work – has proved time and again to be a failure. The exception that proves the rule in Canadian history is Mr Pearson's undoubted success as secretary of state for External Affairs from 1948 to 1957, after twenty years' service within the department as an expert.

A minister will need to possess a somewhat specialized talent, though it will be of a quite different sort and will rarely be associated with the professional work of any particular department. It will be in part an ability to perform parliamentary duties acceptably and in part also – and the two are almost always found in conjunction – a skill in administration which will enable its possessor to oversee departmental activity on a large scale. Talent of this kind is infinitely more useful to a minister than any specialized technical efficiency; and years spent on the floor of Parliament seem to be exceptionally well designed to produce not only the parliamentary capacity, which is a natural consequence, but also the allied though more unexpected quality of administrative ability of a high order. (To such generalizations there will always of course be exceptions.)

The prime minister in his search for cabinet material will thus look for those general qualities of mind and character which enter into genuine administrative capacity and parliamentary leadership. Intelligence, integrity, and common sense head the list of requirements; and these may be supplemented by such useful attributes as energy, imagination, enthusiasm, courage, tolerance, a gift of expression, a desire for public service, a sense of proportion, and a willingness to pool individual ideas and desires to promote the common ends of the government. "In choosing Ministers of the Crown," said Mackenzie King, "I believe the best administration is to be achieved where regard is had first and foremost for the intelligence and integrity of the persons appointed. A man of ability, sound judgment and high attainments would to my mind fill much better any portfolio of government that might be allotted to him than could possibly be the case with others who

3/This is developed later at greater length, *infra*, pp. 202–4.

might seem to have qualifications on the grounds of calling or occupation, but who did not have the required attainments in other ways.[4] (This emphasis on amateurism in the cabinet is not intended to minimize the growing needs of modern government to mobilize vast amounts of knowledge for a multitude of purposes; but Canada has chosen not to concentrate the means for acquiring it directly in the cabinet or Parliament, which has virtually no research facilities, but in the bureaucracy or in such *ad hoc* creations as "task forces" or royal commissions, discussed below.)[5]

The prime minister will rarely exercise his power of selection without consulting with leading members of the party both inside and outside Parliament. Indeed, these preliminaries, accompanied as they may be by indirect and surreptitious influences, may be so involved and prolonged (as at the time of the formation of the Borden government in 1911) that they become almost a national scandal.[6] Consultation with members of Parliament is usually confined to the select few who are especially in the confidence of the prime minister; although it was alleged in one instance where the party leaders of the Dominion and a province were at loggerheads that the party members of Parliament from that province were asked to indicate their own choice as to who should receive a particular portfolio before the appointment was actually made.[7] The allotment of ministries may also be materially affected by the special preferences of those who are invited to join the cabinet, and the demands of an exceptionally able or influential member may cause a reshuffling of several offices in order to make compliance with them possible. Despite the above considerations, the selection of his colleagues always remains the unquestioned right of the prime minister, and this is no inconsiderable factor in securing the solidarity of the cabinet and cementing the loyalty of its members to their chief.

The cabinet has been called "the mainspring of all the mechanism of government" and as such, it makes itself effectively felt over far more than the narrow executive field. Its influence and power are in fact so great and so pervasive that any clear-cut division of authority between the executive and legislative branches of government cannot be maintained. Even in a country like the United States where the constitution attempts to preserve a sharp distinction between the two, the line of cleavage is being continually crossed, and the president is compelled by the exigencies of practical politics to exercise directly and indirectly very important legislative powers. In

4/*Can. H. of C. Debates*, July 17, 1944, p. 4941. See also *Ottawa Journal*, Aug. 5, 1944.
5/See J. E. Hodgetts, "Public Power and Ivory Power," in Trevor Lloyd and Jack McLeod, eds., *Agenda 1970: Proposals for a Creative Politics* (Toronto, 1968), pp. 256–80. On task forces see Fred Schindeler and C. Michael Lanphier, "Social Science Research and Participatory Democracy in Canada," *Canadian Public Administration*, XII, no. 4 (Winter 1969), pp. 481–98.
6/Bilkey, *Persons, Papers and Things*, pp. 140–2; Wallace, *Memoirs of Sir George Foster*, pp. 154–61; Macquarrie, "The Formation of Borden's First Cabinet."
7/Toronto *Globe and Mail*, Jan. 24, 1939.

Canada, where the cabinet sits in Parliament and must be responsible to it, the co-operation between the two naturally goes much further and begins to approach the point where the one becomes merged in the other. From this develops an inevitable tendency for the cabinet to push the House of Commons into the background and make the latter an approving and checking body which on only the rarest occasions will assert a genuine independence of its leader. Despite this intimate association, however, it will be clearer for purposes of exposition to divide the functions of the Canadian cabinet into two broad categories, executive and legislative. Both spring from what are legitimate executive functions; but while one is executive in the narrow sense, the other is particularly concerned with the contacts which the cabinet makes with the legislature and the part it takes in the work of legislation.

EXECUTIVE FUNCTIONS OF THE CABINET

(a) The outstanding duty of the cabinet is to furnish initiative and leadership: to provide the country and Parliament with a national policy and to devise means for coping with present emergencies and future needs. On minor matters this is the concern of only the department affected; but as the importance or scope of the issue increases, it becomes more and more a matter for the prime minister and the whole cabinet who, after much consideration and discussion, will decide what is known as "government policy." The process of deciding may admittedly be a long one, for as both Sir John A. Macdonald ("Old Tomorrow") and Mackenzie King demonstrated, leadership in a country as diverse as Canada, in the interests of national unity, can sometimes take the form of appearing to provide none at all. As King confided more than once to his diary, *preventing* something from happening can involve statesmanship of a high order.

All government measures with very few exceptions are the joint product of the cabinet and the public service. The initial inspiration or impulse will often originate with an individual minister or the cabinet, and a rash minister will sometimes make public commitments without consultation with his staff or even with his colleagues; but this is only a beginning. The proposal must be examined, criticized, appraised in the light of past experience, adapted, and recast many times before it is ready for trial or for incorporation in a government bill; and at all stages in this proving process the practical knowledge and information of the public servants are of inestimable value. On the other hand, the process may be reversed; for an enormous number of new and modified policies grow out of the administration of existing statutes and regulations. These policies will almost invariably originate with the public servants themselves who alone are in a position to draw upon the experience and wealth of data which have been built up through many years of administrative practice. Any significant change of this kind must receive, of course, the endorsement of the minister, who will usually approach the question from a different angle than his civil servants and will be especially conscious of the political implications of any new departure. Matters of greater scope or consequence will need to secure cabinet approval as well, and if they involve a statutory change or are of major importance, they will be submitted to Parliament.

The cabinet may sometimes feel the need for more information than it and its public servants possess, and it may take the initiative to secure assistance from other sources before making its decision on a new policy. It may seek advice from various party organizations (though Canadian parties are not noted for their research facilities), or it may consult with those economic or social groups which are likely to be most affected by any change. It may go further and obtain more formal assistance either by introducing a resolution into Parliament to appoint a select committee of members (a body discussed in a later chapter)[8] or by itself appointing a royal commission, under the Inquiries Act or some other statute, or a "task force."[9]

The royal commission is usually composed of one or more members (three is a common number) whose special qualifications will not only equip them for the investigation but will also tend to create public confidence in their work. Their special qualifications may consist of exceptional proficiency in a narrow field or, on the other hand, a judicial detachment and freedom from bias, a wide experience, or a familiarity with matters allied to that under investigation. Not infrequently both the expert and the enlightened amateur will be represented; the chief requirement being that the talents of the commissioners should be those which in each case are most likely to throw some light on the problems involved.

But while it is true that a cabinet will pick a royal commission for the ability of its members, few if any commissions are chosen on that ground alone. A cabinet is always careful to see that the dice are not loaded against it, and the surest way to take care of that eventuality is to load them slightly in its own favour. In other words, a cabinet will never choose a commission which is likely to prove antagonistic; and it will try, if possible, to secure commissioners who, although they will not be partisan, are nevertheless in general sympathy with the government's policies. Thus although

8/Chap. XVIII.
9/There are many types of commissions of inquiry, not all of which are designated royal commissions, and the total number created since Confederation is now approximately 1,300. See Keith Callard, *Commissions of Inquiry in Canada, 1867–1949* (Privy Council Office, 1950); Hodgetts, "Public Power and Ivory Power"; John C. Courtney, "In Defence of Royal Commissions," *Canadian Public Administration*, XII, no. 2 (Summer 1969), pp. 198–212; Schindeler and Lanphier, "Social Science Research and Participatory Democracy in Canada."

the commission, since it is responsible to neither Parliament nor the cabinet, will have perfect freedom to conduct its investigaton as it pleases, the cabinet gives the minimum number of hostages to fortune and it can usually count on a mild prejudice in its own favour.

If the commission should submit a report with which the cabinet agrees, no problem is likely to arise; but difficulties may occur if the commission's report proves to be distasteful. In theory, the cabinet is free to accept or reject the findings of a commission as it wishes, for the latter has made an independent non-political investigation which the cabinet could obviously not control and for which it can take little, if any, responsibility. But this freedom of the cabinet is to some extent imaginary, for it cannot ignore the commission's moral authority, derived from its qualifications, its freedom from control, and its lack of ulterior purposes, which greatly enhances the difficulty of the government's disregarding recommendations which have so disinterested an origin. Moreover, as the government itself decided on the inquiry and appointed the commission, it is rarely able to suggest either that the whole matter be dropped or that the report of the commission is in any way unfair; the situation is, of course, different when the government that receives a commission's report is not the same one that appointed it.

It is common for a royal commission to help create a public opinion favourable to a particular project; or its establishment may help the cabinet shelve a matter which is controversial or which threatens to become a cause of embarrassment. In the latter case a valuable respite is thereby ensured;[10] the commission may actually produce an acceptable solution; and the postponement may conceivably lead to a cooling-off in popular interest and enthusiasm. The responsibility is, for the moment, shifted to other shoulders; although as soon as the report is presented, the cabinet is forced to pick up the responsibility once again and determine its course. Whether this course involves action or inaction will turn upon the report itself, the desires of the cabinet, the political situation, and – by no means least – upon whether the opposition will allow the government to follow its own choice. In recent years new investigatory bodies called "task forces," *ad hoc* committees usually composed partly of public servants and partly of outsiders, and lacking the formal constitution of royal commissions, have examined a number of matters, commonly as a precursor to a change of policy.

The initiation of cabinet policies is undoubtedly related in a democracy to

10/Sir Alan Herbert, whose wit never obscured his shrewd appreciation of political realities, described the creation of a royal commission thus:
    "The necessity for action was clear to everyone,
    But the view was very general that nothing could be done,
    And the Government courageously decided that the Crown
    Should appoint a score of gentlemen to track the trouble down –
      Which always takes a long, long time."
         – Sir Alan P. Herbert, *Mild and Bitter* (London, 1936), p. 254.

trends in public opinion, but the connection is never constant and cannot be readily defined by any clear principles. Certainly the cabinet does not produce a succession of new ideas which it then tries to persuade the nation to accept; nor, on the other hand, does the cabinet wait until popular clamour is unmistakable before advocating a particular measure. The process tends to be something between the two, an interplay of forces among the many pressure groups and interests throughout the country with the political parties and their leaders and representatives in Parliament playing the most important parts. "A Government," wrote Sir Ivor Jennings, "must perpetually look over its shoulder to see whether it is being followed. If it is not, it must alter direction ... A Government, even with an enormous majority, cannot neglect the feeling of the House. The temperature of the party is, in large measure, the temperature of the electorate."[11] The federal composition of the Canadian cabinet is at least partially vindicated in the performance of this function, for the members can speak for many of the conflicting views and can endeavour with some chance of success to work out a policy which is likely to command fairly general acceptance. A cabinet will inevitably be forced to compromise on many issues; but its position is usually so strong and dominant in both party and Parliament that it will be able to secure the adoption of the measures on which it has finally secured agreement.

But occasions will arise when the cabinet may outstrip public opinion to its own grave danger, and it may be compelled to make substantial concessions or even withdraw proposals entirely in order to save face. Thus in 1963, in an unprecedented move, Mr Gordon, as minister of Finance, withdrew a large portion of his first budget;[12] and in 1945 the King government dropped certain projected changes in the tariff because they had proved to be exceptionally unpopular. A most unusual case occurred in 1906 when the pressure of public opinion induced the Laurier government to introduce a bill to repeal an act which granted pensions to cabinet ministers, although the same government had secured the passage of that act only a year before. On the other hand, there are also those rare times when the cabinet may deliberately take an unpopular stand because of its conviction that such a policy is the only one possible under the circumstances. The King government's conscription policy during the latter part of the Second World War is in this category. An important consideration in making such a decision is often the fact that the information and expert advice at the cabinet's disposal are not equally available to anyone else and cannot for one reason or another be readily made available. An unyielding attitude by a government on a complex question raises a presumption that it may well be right,[13] for underneath

11/*Cabinet Government*, pp. 364–5.
12/See Saywell, *Canadian Annual Review for 1963*, pp. 195–204.
13/An exceptionally good illustration of such a position occurred in Great Britain in 1942 when Winston Churchill announced the stand which his government was prepared to take in response to the popular agitation for the opening of a second European front

its decision is almost certainly the conviction that time and a wider knowledge will vindicate the wisdom of its policy. "But there are times," one of Canada's most experienced politicians wrote, "when unpopularity will be found necessary in the interests of the country, and risks must be taken."[14]

(b) Each member of the cabinet is individually charged with the responsibility of exercising a general supervision over the work of his particular department. These broad departmental divisions will change somewhat in number and character in accordance with the fluctuating demands and needs of the nation, and any unusual event like a war will see very marked alterations made in response to the exceptional conditions. A number of minor activities may be grouped for reasons of convenience under one political head, and it is thus not uncommon to find a minister in charge of two or more departments or divisions. The following were the portfolios in Canada in 1970, the nature of their activities being broadly indicated by the titles: external affairs; finance; justice; state; agriculture; industry, trade and commerce; post office and communications; national health and welfare; veterans affairs; national defence; labour; fisheries and forestry; transport; energy, mines and resources; national revenue; public works; manpower and immigration; Indian affairs and northern development; solicitor general; treasury board; regional economic expansion; consumer and corporate affairs; supply and services; presidency of Privy Council; and leader of the government in the Senate.

Each minister in the Commons serves as the spokesman for his department there: he answers questions concerning all phases of its many activities; he pilots the estimates for proposed departmental expenditures through the House; he defends it and its civil servants against attack and criticism. He also introduces into Parliament any bills which the government is putting forward which affect the work and plans of the department; and such measures include in the mass by far the greater part of the government's legislative programme. The two critical tests to which most acts of Parliament are daily subjected are their administrative practicability and the extent to which they meet the need for which they were designed, and acts of

---

at that time: "No amount of pressure by public opinion or from any other quarter would make me, as the person chiefly responsible, consent to an operation which our military advisers had convinced me would lead to a great disaster. I should think it extremely dishonourable and indeed an act of treason to the nation to allow any uninstructed pressure however well meant, or sentimental feelings however honourable, to drive me into such reckless or wanton courses. Again and again, with the full assent of my colleagues in the War Cabinet, I have instructed the Chiefs of the Staff that in endeavouring to solve their problems they should disregard public clamour, and they know that His Majesty's Government, resting securely upon this steady House of Commons, is quite strong enough to stand like a bulkhead between the military authorities and the well-meant impulses which stir so many breasts." (*Brit. H. of C. Debates*, Nov. 11, 1942, p. 26.)
14/Ward, *A Party Politician*, p. 404.

Parliament are being continually amended and recast as their shortcomings under these two tests become apparent. The task of the minister, however, is not only to secure the desired amendments and thus obtain a better legal framework within which departmental administration can function, but also to familiarize the members of the House with the problems involved and convince them that the proposed changes are both desirable and necessary to achieve the ends which the House has in mind.

(c) While the minister, as stated above, is almost always technically ignorant of the special activity of his department, he need not and should not for that reason be nothing more than a useless ornament at the top of the administrative pyramid. (French-Canadian ministers, it should be noted, have on occasion had to overcome the additional handicap of being a French-speaking executive marooned at the top of a predominantly English-speaking department which was, furthermore, established in accordance with English and American concepts of organization.) It is true that the civil servants under him know infinitely more about the inner workings of the department and the minutiae of the varied tasks on which they are engaged than he can ever hope to know himself; but his own contribution, although made along quite different lines, is no less valuable. While the civil servant must supply the technical knowledge, the minister on his part will add much to the drive and vigour in the department and will endeavour to keep the aims and efforts of his assistants in proper focus. The civil servants are apt to be too much concerned about their immediate task and their own official convenience; their expert knowledge acts as a screen obscuring their view of other departments, interfering with other contacts and relationships, and cutting them off from public opinion; the bias of their profession may distort their outlook and make them distrust new and unfamiliar ideas; precedents and well-worn methods may become inviolable, and the road to the goal may be regarded as of equal consequence with the goal itself, or even greater consequence.

The amateur minister, if intelligent, enters this oppressive atmosphere like a fresh breeze from the sea. He possesses few predilections, and those he has are of an entirely different kind from those of his subordinates, a fact which makes him far more useful to the department than if he were simply one more expert among many. He can ask an infinite number of questions and can demand exact and exhaustive answers; he can, when he desires, bluntly refuse to follow a suggested policy; he can shake up the lethargic and transfer the bunglers to a place where they can do little harm. "I am certainly not one of those," declared Winston Churchill, "who need to be prodded. In fact, if anything, I am a prod";[15] and it was this faculty which helped to keep Churchill's department, whatever it might happen to be, both alert and efficient. The minister introduces a different point of view into the department; he poses

15/*Brit. H. of C. Debates*, Nov. 11, 1942, p. 23.

problems for solution; when future departmental plans are being formulated, he is the one who can gauge the views of the public and can insist that all sides of a question be carefully considered before final action is taken.

But the minister is in the nature of things bound to act throughout in constant consultation with his expert civil servants, and his own ideas, whether valuable or useless, are necessarily tempered by the advice he will receive; his highest-ranking advisers, he may find, will have policies of their own. His reforming zeal is certain to suffer many defeats, and properly so, for the departmental methods and policies which he may criticize will frequently prove to be right. But the mere fact that the civil servant knows that his proposals must be able to satisfy a curious and perhaps sceptical minister, bound by no professional prejudices, has in itself a wholesome effect and tends to produce wiser proposals. The minister can never afford to forget that he will be expected to defend and justify his department's policies before Parliament and the country, and yet at the same time he realizes that those policies must be technically and administratively sound if they are to meet the need which has called them into being. Success in administration, said Walter Bagehot, "depends on a due mixture of special and non-special minds – of minds which attend to the means, and of minds which attend to the end."

Inasmuch as the minister is politically responsible for everything done in his department, he is given supreme authority, and he therefore has the power to overrule any of his civil servants at any time. They, for their part, give the best advice they can; and if the minister persists in disregarding it – as he has a perfect right to do – they must then acquiesce, and bend all their energies to the problem of making the best of what they are convinced is a mistaken policy. The minister has the privilege of overruling his civil servants even although it involves the making of blunders, and the minister also has the privilege of defending those blunders in Parliament and suffering, if need be, for them.[16]

16/The following is, therefore, quite incomprehensible on any sound theory of the relationship between minister and civil servant (or military adviser). (Italics have been added.)

"*Mr. Harkness:* Why was the original plan [of discharging the armed forces] abandoned in favour of the present? ...

"*Mr. Abbott* (Minister of National Defence) : I can only answer that the present system was worked out and decided upon by competent officers whose names I have mentioned, men in the field in whose judgment I have confidence and in whose judgment I am sure my predecessor had confidence ...

"*Mr. Ross* (Souris): The whole system is most unsatisfactory, and the fact that the Minister says that the Chief of Staff organized all this, and that the Government is satisfied with it, is not good enough for the people of this country at the present time.

"*Mr. Abbott: I could fire the Chief of Staff, I suppose.*

"*Mr. Ross:* Some better explanation is required, because the Government are responsible for the acts of the Chief of Staff.

"*Mr. Abbott: But the Government must either accept the advice of its senior military officers or replace them ... All these men are, I think, doing a difficult task extremely well, and as long as I have confidence in them I must accept their advice as to what is*

The necessity of maintaining democratic control and the necessity of securing technical efficiency are thus two principles which are quite capable of being reconciled: the one is a complement and corrective of the other; the two combine to produce the administrative paradox that the best person to wield final authority is one whose major interest has been largely outside the specialized field with which his particular department is primarily concerned.

This is not to suggest that the average run of Canadian ministers will measure up to all the opportunities which await them in their departments. They will not. Too many find it much easier to swing with the tide; to accept methods and procedures with little or no question; to refuse to take the trouble of trying to grasp the real functions and aims of their departments; to be led off by some things they can readily understand and neglect those which are difficult or bothersome and hence demand genuine concentrated effort; to become absorbed, like their civil servants, in some of the trifling questions which are immediately in front of them while they ignore the more remote and intangible problems which can be postponed for a month, six months, or five years. Even some of the best ministers may have trouble in extricating themselves from the morass of detailed administration; for Canadian tradition and practice – maintained in no small measure by the ministers themselves – have done little to set the cabinet free from such impediments and restraints.[17] And if the prime minister's post is soon to be vacated, even some of the best ministers may find themselves distracted by their own personal ambitions – as they may, indeed, on other occasions.

(d) The cabinet is not only a planning and executing body; it is also a co-ordinator. When two or more departments are involved in a particular piece of work they may create *ad hoc* or permanent committees at suitable levels to eliminate overlapping, friction, and wasted effort; but the only body which can do this on a grand scale is the cabinet. It represents all the departments and it is in touch with all government business, and it has the further enormous advantage of possessing the power of final decision. Moreover, if legislation should prove necessary to supplement the cabinet's wishes, it is in a position to turn to Parliament and secure the legislation desired. For many decades after Confederation the cabinet was an impressively ineffective co-ordinator, for it was so loaded with detail that it hardly had the time to give adequate attention to co-ordination. Since (and largely as a result of) the Second World War, the cabinet's internal organization has improved vastly, and with that its capacity to co-ordinate governmental activities. At the same time the rise of the Depart-

the best method. I may query them as to particular points, but so far as my own limited knowledge of these matters is concerned I have not been able to see that the plan which they have worked out and which they recommend to me is an unsound plan, and until I am convinced it is I intend to support it."
                                                     – Can. H. of C. Debates, Oct. 29, 1945, pp. 1591–2.
17/Infra, pp. 224–32.

ment of Finance, and then the emergence of the president of the Treasury Board and the minister of Supply and Services as separate portfolios but still as centralizing influences, have contributed to the same end.[18]

(*e*) Finally, the cabinet performs collectively a wide variety of explicit executive acts, usually in the name of the Governor-in-Council and on the immediate initiative of the prime minister. A number of the more important of these acts are listed below:

(i) The making of appointments, which may range from comparatively minor positions to ambassadors, high commissioners, privy councillors, judges, senators, etc. A very large number of appointments to the civil service are, however, made by the Public Service Commission.[19]

(ii) The removal or dismissal of public officials. Some hold office at pleasure and may thus be removed with few formalities. Others, like the civil servants, may hold office legally at pleasure, but in practice during good behaviour, and the removal is then "for cause," usually after an inquiry. Others, like the County Court judges, enjoy a legal tenure during good behaviour and can be removed only after a formal investigation. A limited number, such as the judges of the Supreme Court and the auditor general, can be removed by the Governor-in-Council only after a joint address asking for removal has been passed by both Houses of Parliament. In these last cases, the function of the Governor-in-Council is almost if not entirely automatic.[20]

(iii) The summoning, prorogation, and dissolution of Parliament. The summoning of Parliament is simply its convocation whenever a meeting is deemed to be necessary; it must meet "once at least in every year." Prorogation is the act of terminating a parliamentary session. Dissolution terminates a Parliament, and a general election must then be held to select a new House of Commons. The summoning and dissolution of Parliament now is done on the advice of the prime minister.

(iv) The participation in international affairs by the appointment of plenipotentiaries, the issuing of instructions to those plenipotentiaries, the ratification of international agreement and treaties, etc. Parliament may be consulted and even asked to approve international agreements and treaties, but this is largely a matter of convenience and political strategy; the actual ratification is purely an executive act. Some agreements and treaties (such as a commercial treaty to alter the tariff) will, of course, need later legislative action to carry their terms into effect.

(v) The power of clemency, that is, the issuing of a reprieve or pardon to offenders against the laws of the Dominion, notably, of course, for criminal

18/See chap. x; W. E. D. Halliday, "The Executive of the Government of Canada," *Canadian Public Administration*, Dec. 1959, pp. 229–41; Ward, *The Public Purse*, especially chaps. x–xiv.
19/*Infra*, pp. 249–55.
20/*Infra*, pp. 400–2.

offences. This may be applied to individuals or, a more unusual example, to a group, such as the general amnesty given to offenders under the Military Service Act after the First World War.

(vi) The decision of certain matters relating to the provinces. Two of the most important, the disallowance of provincial legislation and the decision on reserved provincial bills, are discussed later in this chapter. The cabinet appoints the lieutenant governor in each province, gives him general instructions and from time to time supplementary instructions, and may remove him if he proves unsatisfactory.[21] It also may hear appeals from sectarian minorities in the provinces on educational matters, and may make recommendations thereon.[22]

(vii) The hearing of appeals from decisions of the Canadian Transport Commission on transportation rates by railway, air, and water, and allied matters. The power to sit on appeals or decisions from other executive bodies can be expanded or contracted by statute, and the use of the power may vary considerably over a period of time.

LEGISLATIVE FUNCTIONS OF THE CABINET

The legislative functions of the cabinet necessarily involve the close relations which exist between the cabinet and parliament and particularly between the cabinet and the House of Commons. Only one side of this relationship will be considered here, namely, the influence of the cabinet on the House; the other side, the ways in which the House questions, attacks, and criticizes the cabinet, will be discussed in a later chapter.[23]

It has already been pointed out that the influence which the cabinet wields over the House of Commons and which enables it to get its own way in almost every instance is firmly embedded in the party system and the conditions under which the cabinet is placed in power. Its supporters in the House are elected as party members and as followers of the leader who has become the prime minister; their associations with the party have probably been both long and intimate, and they naturally have a genuine sympathy with the government's measures; they must respect the pledges they have given, and they will be very reluctant to disappoint the expectations of their constituents by erratic or vacillating behaviour. They are thus willing and anxious to expedite the proposals which the cabinet places before them. This co-operative attitude can usually be relied upon, although it may be sensibly weakened at times by the emergence of some disturbing factor which asserts a temporary ascendancy

21/Two lieutenant governors have been removed: one in Quebec in 1879; one in British Columbia in 1900. See Saywell, *The Office of Lieutenant-Governor*, pp. 233–56.
22/*Supra*, pp. 84–5.
23/Chap. XIX.

over the party influences and may spring from the dissatisfaction of individual members, the special interests of certain constituencies, the activities of pressure groups of different kinds, provincial agitation or jealousy, and so forth. The cabinet, however, is usually able to deal with any incipient revolt among its supporters in Parliament; for it has constantly at its disposal a number of instruments for this purpose. These are not weapons which are ruthlessly used to bludgeon the unfortunate nonconformist into submission, but rather softening or moderating influences which soothe the uneasy and make rebellion not only difficult but also profitless and short-sighted.

The first of these aids to unfaltering and unruffled party support is the parliamentary caucus. The members in Parliament from each party meet together in strict privacy at intervals during the session (and occasionally at other times) to discuss and decide policies and parliamentary strategy. The general scope of an opposition party caucus is usually restricted, for it can do little more than criticize the majority party, and its chief concern will almost certainly be the determination of its attitude to government proposals and the way in which its members may best combat them. The government caucus, on the other hand, has a wider responsibility flowing from that which the cabinet must bear in all matters of legislation; and while practices undoubtedly vary with different prime ministers and cabinets, members will discuss (or at least endorse) the government's proposals with the assurance that their decisions will become operative and that they will be held accountable for them. The stand taken by the government caucus is thus of paramount importance to its members, and their attention will be directed to the task of improving the terms of the cabinet's proposals, ensuring that they will be such as to secure approval in the country, and expediting their passage in the House. The government therefore finds the caucus an extremely useful laboratory in which it can test its measures by inviting friendly criticisms and suggestions.

A parliamentary caucus [said Mr Mackenzie King] is nothing more than a gathering of a certain number of members of Parliament. In the case of a Government caucus it is the bringing together of the majority of members in the House of Commons supporting the Government. It is the means whereby a Government can ascertain through its following what the views and opinions of the public as represented by their various constituencies may be. It is not a means of over-riding Parliament. It is a means of discovering the will of the people through their representatives in a manner which cannot be done under the formal procedure which is required in this chamber ... A Government has to be careful in the matter of the legislation it brings into Parliament, to be sure that it is in accord with the public will. How can that best be ascertained? Wait until the legislation is brought down in Parliament and put on the table; or by a conference with the Government's own following, if there is any doubt one way or the other in regard to any phases of the legislation? After all, what a Government has to keep before it, if it is to be worthy of the name of a Government, is, first of all, the support it will receive in the country for the measures it introduces; secondly, the support it will receive in Parliament ... [The caucus] is simply coming into closer consultation with the people's representatives in a manner that permits of the greatest freedom of expression on their part.[24]

The cabinet, however, derives an additional benefit from the caucus, for it will use it to ensure the support of all the government party members in the House. It is true that the member who attends these meetings is allowed and expected to express his views without restraint, that he is given an opportunity to present his case to a sympathetic audience, and that he may thereby be able to secure substantial modifications in the government's programme. But he pays well for these facilities. In return for them (and they are from his point of view extremely valuable) he tacitly agrees to accept the decision of the caucus as final and to relinquish his right, except under very unusual circumstances, to object to or vote against these government measures when they come before the House. The cabinet thus obtains a triple advantage: it is enabled to try out its measures on a representative body before it finally submits them to the House; it is insured against overt rebellion; and it obtains additional security from the fact that the opinions of its supporters have not been dangerously suppressed but have been allowed to find frank and vigorous expression in the caucus to the general profit and satisfaction of all concerned. It should be added that a cabinet long in office tends to take the caucus increasingly for granted, and shows a growing inclination less to consult the caucus than to inform it.

Members of one party from Quebec, the Prairie provinces, or some other province or provinces will frequently hold a separate caucus of their own. It is usually very informal, and is called to discuss some matter which is of common and special concern to the members from that area. The purpose is, of course, to get agreement and then exert a greater pressure on the other members of the party and on the cabinet. In 1916 an unusual instance occurred when all the Liberals in Parliament met in provincial caucuses to determine their attitude on the question of bilingualism in Ontario schools.[25] Provincial caucuses formerly met to discuss the decennial redistribution of seats in the Commons.

Members of Parliament are also induced to follow a moderate rather than an extreme course on matters of cabinet policy by the knowledge that the government (through the power of the prime minister to advise the governor general to dissolve the House) can bring the Parliament to an abrupt close. How a prime minister will use this power of course varies with the individual, and the state of party finance and organization; but the power is always there. Few members, though most of them enjoy campaigning, wish to face the labour, cost, and worry of a general election, involving, as it must, the possi-

24/*Can. H. of C. Debates*, Feb. 12, 1923, p. 219. Eugene Forsey, citing Arthur Meighen as his authority, recalls that after the First World War the Unionist caucus vetoed a governmental proposal to give Sir Arthur Currie $250,000.

25/Skelton, *Life and Letters of Sir Wilfrid Laurier*, II, p. 484. For modern members' attitudes towards caucuses see Hoffman and Ward, *Bilingualism and Biculturalism in the House of Commons*, chap. 6.

bility of personal defeat; a mere hint of such a step will have a marked effect on any government supporter who shows signs of restiveness or excessive independence, and even the members of the opposition, which usually has more to gain by an election than the government, can be made to observe the parliamentary courtesies with a better grace if they are reminded of the ominous possibilities which may lie ahead.

Patronage has lost some of its usefulness in recent years as an oiler of the wheels of government, for the reform of the civil service has removed from ministerial control a large number of appointments which were at one time passed out through government supporters in the House, and members now have far less influence over the letting of contracts than their predecessors had. The threat that party irregularity will mean a removal of patronage has therefore been deprived of much of its former influence although it is still a factor to be considered. It can be reinforced by the withdrawal of the kindly influence of the cabinet in other ways. The knowledge that a member is in doubtful standing with the government and the refusal of the central party organization to make contributions to his campaign from the central party fund (assuming it has money to dispense, which is not always the case) will rarely enhance a member's prestige in his constituency, although the government's influence is rarely strong enough to deprive him of his nomination for the next election. It should be remembered, moreover, that the really choice positions in the gift of the cabinet are still filled by patronage and these may be of direct and very personal concern to the members of Parliament. The young member with ambition can with little effort see himself as a cabinet minister, and he knows that two of the indispensable prerequisites are party loyalty and dependability. An older member, whose chances for a portfolio have almost certainly vanished, can still look forward to a possible position on a permanent board or commission, a judgeship, or, most coveted of all by those in whom ambition has languished, a senatorship.[26] A series of votes against the party and the consequent displeasure of the prime minister would bring hopes such as these to a sad and premature end, except in those rare instances where a member is promoted or otherwise disposed of to silence him.

In this environment and with these influences working steadily in its favour, the cabinet succeeds in exercising legislative powers of the first magnitude.

(a) The basic legislative power of the cabinet is the general control which it is able to exercise over the House of Commons at all times; for it is through this control that the other powers become effective. The prime minister, assisted by the cabinet, leads and directs the House in virtually everything it attempts to do. He writes the speech from the throne for the governor general to deliver

26/The Bennett government, for example, appointed no less than seventeen Conservative members of Parliament to choice positions in the few weeks before the general election in 1935: ten to the Senate; three to the Bench; two to be deputy heads of departments; one to the Civil Service Commission; and one to be chairman of the Board of Railway Commissioners. For appointments to the Senate, see *infra*, pp. 283-7.

to Parliament indicating the chief measures to be considered during the session. The House will choose his nominee for its Speaker, though it may now be established that the leader of the opposition will concur, after consultation, in the choice. The prime minister and the cabinet will determine the daily order of business and the time to be devoted to different matters,[27] and the rules of the House are designed to facilitate the legislative work of the cabinet. This programme is, of course, always subject to interruptions by the opposition, which may avail itself of those opportunities for inquiry and criticism which are also provided by the rules,[28] although there is a tacit understanding that government affairs must have first claim on the time of Parliament and enjoy a general preference; the rules do provide, none the less, that the opposition members can move a motion on any matter within parliamentary jurisdiction on certain days each session. The underlying control of the cabinet is perhaps best exemplified by its power to take a stand on any question and enforce that stand upon its party followers. It may announce that it will treat the vote on even a trivial matter as a vote of confidence, and the members of the majority party will be compelled to fall in line and give their support. The cabinet will also interpret the vote of the House and will determine the significance to be attached to it. It may thus decide to regard a vote as decisive and consider that it is no longer required to carry on the government, or it may accept a defeat on certain points as of little consequence (as was not uncommon in the years following Confederation) and challenge its opponents, if dissatisfied, to move a straight vote of want of confidence. The nature of this relationship between cabinet and House is more fully examined in subsequent chapters.[29]

(b) The cabinet dominates all legislation.[30] Public bills (which deal with matters of a public or general nature) may be introduced by any member; if he is of the ministry or a parliamentary assistant, they are known as "government" bills. The great bulk of pending legislation falls in the category of government bills, which emanate from the cabinet, enjoy its explicit support, and take up on the average at least four-fifths of the time of the House.

The public bills which are fostered by private members (members of either house who are neither members of the ministry nor parliamentary assistants) do not often reach the statute books, though a patient member who annually brings up a pet project may live to see its merits finally recognized by the

27/See infra, pp. 351–6.
28/See infra, pp. 365 ff.
29/Chaps. XVIII, XIX.
30/The following unofficial summary gives the different kinds of bills and their subdivisions:
   I. Private bills
  II. Public bills
      (A) Public bills sponsored by a member
      (B) Government bills
          (1) Non-financial bills
          (2) Financial bills
              (a) Bills to spend money, or supply
              (b) Bills to raise money, or ways and means, i.e., loans, taxes, etc.

government. The time for the consideration of public bills of this type is limited; most of them will fail to be heard at all, or at best will be debated for a short time and then talked out without coming to a vote. The cabinet may give one of these bills or resolutions a mild support or even on rare occasions formally adopt a private member's measure as its own and expedite its passage. But the general practice is for the cabinet to remain indifferent or opposed to the public bills which it has not fathered; it is usually indifferent too to private bills, those quite different measures which deal with the much more restricted interests of individuals and corporations.

The public bills fostered by the cabinet are, on the other hand, its chief concern. They represent the cabinet's legislative plans for the future and may vary from proposals of first-rate importance to those for the simplification of departmental procedures, from the most comprehensive reforms to those which are intimately related to and which arise out of the day by day administration in the departments. Because these proposals spring from the one source, there is a presumption that they will form a part of a fairly consistent programme, and because they are drafted by those who are charged with the executive and administrative functions of the government, there is also a virtual certainty that these measures will be realistic and administratively practicable.

The cabinet is extremely sensitive about the general excellence of its own measures; and while it may at times consider and even accept suggested amendments, the overwhelming tendency is to refuse to make any important revisions in the bill as originally introduced.[31] Any concessions to the opposition or any acceptance of substantial help from that quarter may be interpreted as a sign of weakness or incompetence on which the opposition will not fail to capitalize at the earliest opportunity. "Love me, love my dog" is the rule, for the cabinet assumes that if the House desires its leadership, the House will be prepared to embrace its programme. Hence the great corollary of cabinet government: that the defeat of a government measure will normally bring about the defeat of the government itself. The only general exception now is the occasional snap vote which may defeat a government measure but does not accurately represent the opinion of the House. Any uncertainty on this score can be speedily resolved by an explicit vote of confidence. If the House should (apart from a snap vote) decide to reject a government bill or to amend it in a way unacceptable to the cabinet then "Her Majesty's Government will consider that it is relieved of the duty of carrying on any longer the government" of the country, or, as an alternative, the prime minister will ask the governor general for a dissolution. The effect of this firm stand on any hesitant government supporters in the House is clear, and in all but the most unusual circumstances the government measures will be passed intact.

(c) The cabinet controls all financial legislation. Financial bills are simply

31/An unusual exception was the Official Languages Act passed in 1969. Although overwhelmingly supported by opposition parties in the House, the original draft was amended to meet opposition from outside.

a special variety of public bills, distinguished by their subject-matter, their exceptional importance, and by their annual recurrence. They may deal with the spending of money (supply), or with the raising of money (taxation or ways and means); and the cabinet has the sole responsibility for preparing and submitting to Parliament the estimates for departmental needs and the scheme for meeting these expenditures which is presented in the form of the budget.

The British North America Act requires that any measure for the spending of public funds can be considered by the House of Commons (where it must also originate) only after it has been first recommended by a message from the governor general, and by constitutional usage such a message can be transmitted to the House only through a cabinet minister. Custom and the standing orders of the House have established a companion principle that any proposal for the imposition of a tax must also be made by a member of the cabinet.[32] These two rules have been further reinforced by the practice, implied in the standing orders, that no amendment to increase taxes or appropriations can be made except upon the motion of a minister, although any member may move to have any tax or appropriation reduced or struck out.[33] All the above principles have been derived from long English practice,[34] and collectively they place the cabinet in a position where its responsibility in all financial matters is complete and ineluctable.

The cabinet must therefore introduce and sponsor all measures to spend or to raise money; and as any proposed amendment which would endeavour to diminish a tax or an expenditure contrary to the cabinet's wishes would almost certainly be treated as a vote of lack of confidence,[35] its control over finance is not likely to be seriously threatened. Admittedly this places enormous powers in the hands of a very small group, although these will be exercised under constant scrutiny and criticism. The system has, however, undoubted advantages. The cabinet is in the best position to judge the purposes to which public money should be directed as well as the productivity and incidence of possible measures of taxation, and the fact that those who spend the funds are likewise charged with the task of devising ways and means to raise them places a wholesome restraint on extravagance.

(d) The cabinet, acting as the Governor-in-Council, enacts subordinate legislation under the authority (and only under the authority) delegated to it by acts of the Canadian Parliament. Its legislative output may be known as minutes or orders-in-council, the distinction being largely one of form and

32/Arthur Beauchesne, ed., *Rules and Forms of the House of Commons of Canada* (Ottawa, 1943), pp. 156-7, 163-9, 181-3. The new rules adopted in 1969 do not require that the imposition of a tax must be made by a minister, but the principle is implied, as under the old rules.

33/*Ibid.*, pp. 179, 182-3.

34/They were not always practised, however, in Canada. See *supra*, pp. 13-16.

35/Governments were a little more casual for a few years after Confederation (see Ward, *The Public Purse*, pp. 49-50) and again on Feb. 19, 1968. See *supra*, pp. 172n.

apparently of little consequence,[36] and it must also give formal approval to the minutes of the Treasury Board.[37] The subject-matter of this legislation may range from questions of purely departmental routine to those of first-rate importance with far-reaching consequences, from the approval of a contract or the amendment of a minor regulation to the establishment of a nation-wide system of price control in time of war.

The number of these orders and minutes is very large: even in ordinary times they reach five or six thousand a year, while in time of war they naturally increase greatly with the additional cabinet responsibilities and the need for immediate executive decision and action.[38] Thus from August 25, 1939, to September 2, 1945, the Governor-in-Council disposed of 92,350 items of business,[39] a tremendous total, although not so impressive as it appears at first glance. A very large part of these orders and minutes were concerned with routine matters, and not more than 4 or 5 per cent of the total represented action which was legislative in any real sense of the term.[40] Even so, the numbers give a very good idea of the cabinet's enormously important function in supplementing the legislative activity of Parliament. The extent to which the Canadian cabinet has been endowed with legislative power and the justification for this delegation will be discussed further in another chapter.[41]

(e) Finally, the cabinet wields a negative legislative authority in the provincial field. Any act of any provincial legislature may be disallowed and rendered void by an order-in-council, passed on the recommendation of the minister of Justice, provided such action takes place within one year after the

36/"The difference between the order and minute is one of form rather than substance and is not clearly or consistently maintained. Normally, the order is employed for the exercise of explicit statutory authority for the making by the Governor-in-Council of orders or regulations; the minute covers a much wider field in which the Governor-in-Council gives approval to ministerial action." A. D. P. Heeney, "Cabinet Government in Canada," *Canadian Journal of Economics and Political Science*, XII, no. 3 (Aug. 1946), p. 285.

37/"Treasury Board minutes deal almost entirely with appointments, resignations, and other personnel matters in the civil service; with payments to firms and persons for services rendered; with remissions of taxes, and the like." L. S. St Laurent, *Can. H. of C. Debates*, Oct. 2, 1945, p. 681. See *infra*, pp. 359–60.

38/A large part of this increase will be authorized by special emergency legislation, notably the War Measures Act.

39/Heeney, "Cabinet Government in Canada" (p. 286), gives the following breakdown:

Orders-in-Council and minutes of Council	56,202
Proceedings of Treasury Board	36,148
	92,350

40/The same authority (*ibid.*) classifies the orders and minutes as follows:

Approval of contracts for supplies requiring approval of the Governor-in-Council	45 per cent
Other administrative acts — changes in establishments, appointments, refunds, etc.	50–51 per cent
Acts of a legislative character	4–5 per cent

41/*Infra*, chap. XIV.

receipt of such act by the Dominion government. The Governor-in-Council may also be called upon to give or refuse its consent to any provincial bill which the lieutenant governor of the province has not signed but has "reserved" for its consideration.[42] Intervention through disallowance or reservation is, of course, exceptional, although legally there are no limitations whatever on the frequency with which either device may be exercised. This will depend primarily upon the good sense and self-restraint of the Dominion cabinet (or the lieutenant governor), and to some degree upon the good sense and self-restraint of the provincial legislatures as well. Out of the thousands of acts passed by provincial legislatures since Confederation only 112 have been disallowed, although in a number of other instances provinces were induced to modify the law in order to escape disallowance. At least seventy provincial bills have been reserved; and of these, fourteen were eventually approved by the Dominion and thus became law.[43] Disallowance and reservation have not in practice, therefore, constituted very serious limitations on provincial powers, and the validity of this statement is strengthened by the modern tendency to use these expedients even more sparingly than in former years. The reaction to the revival of the power of reservation by the lieutenant governor of Saskatchewan in 1961 confirms this conclusion.[44]

Disallowance and the treatment of reserved bills have followed an irregular and inconsistent course, although some general tendencies can be traced. The few pages following will discuss in main outlines disallowance only; but the same trends are not unnaturally discerned in the Dominion government's handling of reserved bills, for this is simply another manifestation of what is essentially the same characteristic, the attitude of the Dominion cabinet to provincial legislation.[45]

The first period extends from Confederation to the defeat of the Conservative government in 1896. Disallowances were for the first twenty years very common.[46] The free use of the power was justified on many grounds: the provincial acts were considered objectionable because they were *ultra vires*, or prejudicial to private rights, or discriminatory and unjust, or contrary to "sound principles of legislation." Disallowance was therefore used, as in all

42/BNA Act, 1867, sections 56, 90.

43/See E. A. Forsey, "Disallowance of Provincial Acts, Reservation of Provincial Bills, and Refusal of Assent by Lieutenant-Governors since 1867," *Canadian Journal of Economics and Political Science*, IV, no. 1 (Feb. 1938), pp. 47–59. See also *Dominion-Provincial Legislation, 1867–1895*; *Provincial Legislation, 1896–1920*; La Forest, *Disallowance and Reservation of Provincial Legislation*.

44/J. R. Mallory, "The Lieutenant-Governor's Discretionary Powers," *Canadian Journal of Economics and Political Science*, XXVII, no. 4 (Nov. 1961), pp. 518–21.

45/La Forest, *Disallowance and Reservation of Provincial Legislation*; James McL. Hendry, *Memorandum on the Office of Lieutenant-Governor of a Province* (Ottawa: Dept. of Justice, 1955); Eugene A. Forsey, "Canada and Alberta: The Revival of Dominion Control over the Provinces," *Politica*, June 1939, pp. 95–123.

46/From 1867 to 1887 the Dominion disallowed fifty-nine provincial acts; from 1867 to 1896, sixty-six.

likelihood the founders of the federation had intended it to be used, as a means of keeping the provincial legislatures in order and (in the absence of any Canadian equivalent of explicit constitutional restraints such as those in the American constitution) as a check on unjust and oppressive legislation.

The provinces, as might be expected, objected vigorously to this assertion of Dominion power over what they considered to be solely their own business, and towards the end of this period their protests received indirect legal aid by judicial decisions, which took a decided turn in the direction of augmenting the power and general importance of the provinces.[47] The most emphatic statement of provincial claims came from a representative conference of five provinces in 1887 which unanimously passed a resolution deploring the Dominion's "arbitrary control over legislation of the Provinces within their own sphere" and demanding that they should be placed in respect of disallowance in precisely the same position as the Dominion, that is, with disallowance vested in the British government. While no formal change followed this protest, the remaining nine years of Conservative rule at Ottawa saw a very sharp drop in the number of provincial acts disallowed.

The next period (1896–1920) coincided with the increasing emphasis on provincial autonomy and the general enlargement of provincial powers which have already been mentioned as beginning in earlier years. This quarter-century was thus naturally characterized by a growing belief that disallowance was an intrusion on provincial powers. If a provincial law was deemed to lie within provincial jurisdiction, then any mere injustice or any violation of private rights which might ensue was no longer considered to be the concern of the Dominion government. The remedy, if there was a remedy, rested with the people of the province; they could ignore the whole matter or take whatever measures they thought fit. The disappearance of the idea that the Dominion was to keep paternal watch over provincial legislation inevitably caused a marked reduction in disallowance for reasons of this nature; and the total disallowances in this period would, indeed, have been small had British Columbia not embarked upon a statutory campaign to place various restraints upon the activities of aliens living in that province. Inasmuch as this legislation raised questions which threatened to cause both empire and international complications of a serious character, the Dominion felt bound to interfere and disallow the offending statutes on grounds of public policy. The total disallowances for the twenty-four years were thirty; but of these nineteen were attributable to the above efforts of British Columbia.

The third period, which includes the years from 1921 to the present (1970), shows a partial recession at times from the extreme laissez-faire attitude of the earlier period tempered with a continued reluctance to interfere with provincial business. Only sixteen provincial acts have been disallowed in this period, and these have been irregularly spaced. For twelve years (1925–37), the

47/*Supra*, pp. 81–2; 90–6.

power was not used in a single instance, although there was no reasonable doubt[48] that it was merely in abeyance. Once again, however, the legislative activity of one province virtually forced the Dominion to take action. Alberta, in an endeavour to put some of her government's peculiar monetary theories into operation and to institute a wholesale system of debt relief, embarked upon a series of legislative measures which trespassed on the powers of the federal Parliament, and the Governor-in-Council promptly disallowed them. Of the sixteen disallowed provincial acts mentioned, twelve originated in Alberta and eleven dealt directly or indirectly with the above subjects. No provincial act has been disallowed since 1943.

In this modern period, although the disallowances have been comparatively few, the reasons advanced for disallowance or a refusal to disallow have been, perhaps, even more uncertain and inconsistent than in earlier years – no inconsiderable achievement. Thus while one disallowance at the beginning of the period rested in part on the gross unfairness of the provincial statute, a later minister of Justice affirmed that he favoured leaving such acts to the judgment of the people in the province concerned. While there has been an increasing tendency to leave *ultra vires* legislation to the judgment of the courts, illegality is nevertheless still recognized as an important contributory factor in determining if disallowance should occur. The activity of the Governor-in-Council in disallowing Alberta legislation furnishes, moreover, a disturbing contrast to its refusal to disallow the ill-visaged "padlock law" in Quebec, on which action could have been taken under any one of a host of past rules which have been invoked in recent years.[49] The truth is that no one in the Dominion knows with any approach to certainty what action to expect on disallowance from the Governor-in-Council. Guesses may be ventured on the fate awaiting a particular statute; but if the guesses are to be at all accurate, they must be based not so much on a weighing of constitutional principles as on a shrewd appraisal of the ideas and opinions and prejudices of the minister of Justice (and the cabinet), which, in turn, will almost certainly be affected by the political situation at that particular time, and the size of the province concerned.[50]

What is most necessary is not the abolition of the power of disallowance

48/The premier of Alberta nevertheless alleged the power was obsolete, a question which was referred by the Dominion government to the Supreme Court in 1938 and which was answered by a judgment declaring the power to be unimpaired. *Disallowance and Reservation Case*, [1938] S.C.R. 71.
49/For example, a "clear and palpable attempt to invade the field of the Dominion"; "unusual"; "without parallel"; "arbitrary powers"; "leaves no adequate remedy in the courts"; "opposed to principles of right and justice," etc. See Forsey, "Canada and Alberta," pp. 95–123.
50/Of the 112 disallowances since 1867, 6 have been of Quebec statutes, and 10 of Ontario; other provinces' totals are: British Columbia, 43; Alberta, 12; Saskatchewan, 3; Manitoba, 28; New Brunswick, 1; Nova Scotia, 9; Newfoundland and Prince Edward Island, none.

(and it is noteworthy that the federal government's comprehensive proposals for constitutional reform in 1968 did not recommend its abolition), but a clear consistent enunciation of the occasions which will justify its use. That these occasions should be rare and exceptional, there can be little doubt. The old idea of the Confederation period that the Dominion should be the mentor of the provinces and save them from error and excesses of all kinds has become obsolete: generally speaking, the provinces should have the privilege of making their own mistakes as they see fit. Questions of *ultra vires* are as a rule better settled by the courts; although there would seem to be little if any objection to the Dominion in exceptional cases of this kind threatening disallowance unless the province would consent to an immediate court reference to determine jurisdiction.[51] Three classes of cases, however, would seem to justify disallowance, although it should be assumed that all these would first be discussed with the province before final action was taken. First, those provincial acts which interfere seriously with Dominion legislation or Dominion policy. Secondly, those provincial acts which destroy rights of citizens living in other provinces. The normal protection against unjust legislation is that the people affected have a political remedy which they may use against their government and thus, perhaps, secure redress; but in this instance the people concerned are residents of other provinces and have no way of protecting themselves against the abuses of the offending legislature. Thirdly, those provincial acts which affect fundamental rights of Canadian citizens. These rights should be the same in all provinces of Canada and should be unassailable by provincial statutes. If they should at any time be given special enunciation in the British North America Act, the courts would see to their enforcement, and in such an event the need for any additional protection by disallowance would become unnecessary. The Bill of Rights passed by Parliament in 1960 is a federal statute only, and leaves untouched all those aspects of rights under provincial jurisdiction. Current federal proposals include a comprehensive bill of rights entrenched in the constitution.[52]

51/This alternative was in effect offered by the Dominion to Alberta in 1937, when the former stated it was "considering" the disallowance of three acts. Alberta refused to hold up the legislation pending a court decision, and the acts were accordingly disallowed.

52/*A Canadian Charter of Human Rights* (Ottawa, 1968). See Scott, *Civil Liberties and Canadian Federalism*; Schmeiser, *Civil Liberties in Canada*; Tarnopolsky, *The Canadian Bill of Rights*; Donald V. Smiley, "The Case against the Canadian Charter of Human Rights," *Canadian Journal of Political Science*, II, no. 3 (Sept. 1969), pp. 277–91.

11 The cabinet: organization

THE GROWING COMPLEXITY OF SOCIETY, coupled with the rapid technological change of recent years, has inevitably been reflected in the strategy and methods employed by the government of Canada in approaching its tasks. Ten years ago the cabinet had twenty-three ministers; as this is written it has thirty, many of them holding wholly new portfolios. A medical Research Council under the minister of National Health and Welfare, a Science Council attached to the Privy Council Office, and an Atlantic Development Council to advise the new minister of Regional Economic Expansion were all created in the period from 1966 to 1969 inclusive.[1] In the same period, the staff attached to the Prime Minister's Office and the Privy Council has grown enormously, and the financial administration of the government has been substantially reorganized, partly in the direction of decentralization by giving individual departments greater autonomy in the spending of public money and the management of their staffs, partly in the direction of centralization through the assignment of new duties particularly to the Treasury Board (whose president now holds a portfolio) and the minister of Supply and Services, who is also receiver general and the wielder of powers formerly assigned to the comptroller of the Treasury in the Department of Finance.[2]

Many of these alterations had their immediate origin in the massive report of the Royal Commission on Government Organization, which was created by one government, but whose recommendations had to be dealt with by two others.[3] The commission, by the nature of its own assignment, had to direct its

1/The major relevant legislation is *Can. Statutes*, 14–15 Eliz. II, c. 25; 17–18 Eliz. II, c. 27 and 28. The debates on these bills in 1966 and 1969 are unusually revealing of both ministers' and members' attitudes towards fundamental problems of government organization.

2/The most recent authoritative statements on the duties and organization of the government of Canada are to be found in the *Canada Year Book*, an annual publication, and *Organization of the Government of Canada* (Ottawa), a compendium kept up to date as occasion requires.

3/*Report of the Royal Commission on Government Organization* (5 vols., Ottawa,

attention to, among other things, the assignment of tasks to ministers and departments, and in that problem had to consider that the great scope and variety of the cabinet's functions place an enormous load on many ministers. "The upper limit of the burdens which can be borne by a minister," in the opinion of the commission, "although indefinite, is nonetheless absolute, rooted as it is in human capacity and endurance – themselves not limitless qualities."[4] The way in which business is transacted, the organization of the cabinet, and the expedients used to reduce effort and to make it more enlightened and effective are therefore matters of first-rate consequence. Yet for many decades after 1867 the Canadian cabinet contrived to worry along and to conduct its affairs under conditions which made careful deliberation difficult and quick informed decision well-nigh impossible. Nor, indeed, did the ministers appear to be much concerned about these difficulties, although in almost any other walk of life efforts would most certainly have been made to bring about comprehensive reforms. Whether ministers were simply reluctant to abandon old practices, or broad political benefits (such as that gained from the representative character of the cabinet) were deemed more important than efficiency, or successive cabinets were so conscious of their vulnerability that they saw little purpose in introducing reforms which might awaken additional criticism, it is difficult to say; but the fact remains that little or nothing was done in the direction of improvement until external circumstances forced a change. This was true both of the cabinet's internal organization, and of the way in which the forces of the cabinet were deployed to meet external problems.

Cabinets are potentially, of course, among the most elastic bodies conceivable. Their organization is quite informal; they make their own rules and precedents and determine their procedures; they are not hedged about by restrictive laws, or, if any law should stand in the way, the way to its amendment lies in their own hands. In practice they are compelled to make frequent adjustments; for the march of events, the interplay of different personalities, the emergence of new issues and problems, all bring necessary concessions and modifications of various kinds. But in spite of these minor diversions the Canadian cabinet until the Second World War proved to be a most conservative body in matters concerning the transactions of its own business. Thus the First World War came and went leaving no permanent imprint on Canadian cabinet organization or methods of conducting business, although a couple of years before and immediately after the war two excellent reports on this topic had been submitted, both of them advocating substantial changes.[5] Successful British experience, which is frequently followed by Canadian political institutions

---

1962 and 1963). The commission was created in 1960, and the auditor general, in his annual reports, has assumed the task of following up its recommendations.

4/*Ibid.*, v., p. 43.

5/*Report of Sir George Murray on the Public Service of Canada* (1912); *Report of the Special Committee on Machinery of Government*, Senate of Canada (1919).

without hesitation or, indeed, adequate discrimination, was in matters of cabinet organization consistently ignored, although certain lessons to be derived
from this source were clear and unmistakable. The Second World War, however, proved to be by far the most powerful stimulant to cabinet practices ever
administered in Canadian history, and a number of extensive reforms were
introduced in order to cope with the intensified demands. The conversion was
belated, but none the less real for all that.

The most serious handicap of the Canadian cabinet as an executive body
has long been its excessive size. "You cannot run a war with a Sanhedrin"
was Lloyd George's succinct way of stating the same difficulty during the First
World War in Great Britain, although the problem at that time was obviously
accentuated by emergency conditions. But whether the time be war or peace,
a cabinet is not a debating society; it exists not so much to air views as to make
decisions; and while the latter will undoubtedly involve the former, the difficulty of obtaining executive action increases in almost geometric proportion
with every increase in the numbers of those who participate. In a crowded and
varied gathering, hesitation and indecision flourish; too many proposals must
be carried over to await the time when general approval will be forthcoming;
the task of the prime minister, who must drive and direct and persuade the
team, becomes well-nigh insupportable. "With a larger number of people,"
to quote Lloyd George once more, "it meant so many men, so many minds;
so many minds, so many tongues; so many tongues, so much confusion; so
much confusion, so much delay."[6] There has been, in fact, general agreement
that an ideal cabinet would comprise about ten or twelve members, a number
which would allow the body to retain some of its representative character, yet
would not seriously weaken it for executive work.[7]

The discouraging feature of this problem in Canada is the strength of the
forces which are constantly endeavouring to keep the cabinet large or to make
it even larger. If the representative federal principle which has been described
in an earlier chapter is to be scrupulously observed, the theoretical *minimum*
number in the cabinet would be one English-speaking and three French-speaking members from Quebec, four from Ontario, at least one from each of the
remaining eight provinces – a total of sixteen, so that the problem gets out of
hand almost before it can be considered at all.[8] The Canadian cabinet was held
at from thirteen to sixteen until well into this century, but it has in recent years
ballooned to thirty, with the end, according to Prime Minister Trudeau, not
yet in sight.

Indirect attempts were made to reduce the size of the executive during the
two world wars by the use of a powerful committee which would in fact, if not

6/D. Lloyd George, *War Memoirs* (London, 1933–36), III, p. 1060.
7/Report of the Machinery of Government Committee (Great Britain), *Parliamentary
Papers* (1918), Cd. 9230, pp. 5, 16; *Report of the Special Committee on Machinery of
Government*, Senate of Canada (1919), pp. 12–14.
8/For qualifications on this generalization, see *supra*, pp. 178–85.

in name, take over the cabinet's chief function of making major decisions on war problems. In the first war the cabinet was divided into two large groups of ten members each with the prime minister as a common chairman. One was known as the War Committee and was composed of those ministers whose work was primarily concerned with war activities; the other was called the Reconstruction and Development Committee and included for the most part the remaining ministers. This represented a deliberate effort to clear the cabinet meetings of many of the routine and detailed problems which made such enormous inroads on the time and attention of its members; and the topics assigned to the committees covered the whole sweep of administrative activity.[9] The results of this experiment apparently did not come up to expectations, but it undoubtedly served to lighten materially the load carried by the whole cabinet and to increase to a moderate degree the effectiveness of those most concerned with the prosecution of the war.

In the Second World War the paramount authority was wielded by a small committee of the cabinet known as the War Committee, presided over by the prime minister and comprising from a minimum of six to a more frequent maximum of ten senior and leading cabinet members. It exercised a general comprehensive supervision over the war activity of the government. It initiated, approved, and co-ordinated all major projects; and although it reported to the full cabinet of eighteen or twenty members and although the fiction of its being no more than a committee was carefully maintained, there seems little doubt that to all intents and purposes it displaced the parent body. "While the War Committee like other Cabinet Committees was never an executive body but was, in fact as in form, purely advisory in character, its prestige was such that its decisions were for practical purposes the decisions of the Government. The sanction for its acts was in the authority of its members not in any formal delegation of authority. The complete Ministry continued to meet as in peacetime and, upon important matters of government policy, reports were commonly made to the full Cabinet."[10]

The return to peace, however, brought the activities of the War Committee to a speedy end, and re-established the primacy of the whole cabinet. "Major questions of policy reverted to the Cabinet as a whole, and a new series of standing Cabinet committees was developed";[11] but none of these bodies could pretend to occupy the dominant position formerly held by the War Committee. With the passage of the Financial Administration Act of 1951, however, the Treasury Board, a committee of the Privy Council chaired by the minister of Finance and including five other ministers, emerged as a kind of War Committee empowered to deal with almost everything except war, and in the Gov-

9/R. MacG. Dawson, "Canadian and Imperial War Cabinets," in Chester Martin, ed., *Canada in Peace and War* (London, 1941), pp. 196–9.
10/Heeney, "Cabinet Government in Canada," p. 289.
11/*Ibid.*, p. 290. See also W. E. D. Halliday, "The Executive of the Government of Canada," in *Canadian Public Administration*, Dec. 1959, pp. 229–41.

ernment Organization Act of 1966 the Board was newly constituted as a central management agency for government functions; it still includes the minister of Finance and four other ministers, but is presided over by a chairman with his own portfolio. While the cabinet of course must retain final responsibility, the Treasury Board is charged with (among other things) "general administrative policy in the public service"; "financial management, including estimates, expenditures, accounts, charges for services, rentals, licences, leases, revenues from the disposition of property, and procedures by which departments manage, record and account for revenues received or receivable from any source whatever"; and "personnel management in the public service." Under these statutory powers "a very large number of matters which formerly required submission to the Governor-in-Council are now dealt with finally by the Treasury Board or by the Minister of the department concerned. A number of other matters are by custom and according to statutory requirements dealt with first by the Board and finally by the Governor-in-Council."[12] The president of the new board, which is declared in statutory terms to be the same as the old board, is charged with exercising and performing "such of the powers, duties or functions of the Board as the Board may, with the approval of the Governor in Council, determine"; he is potentially, in short, a ministerial star of the first magnitude.

But the Treasury Board alone cannot solve all the problems of cabinet organization, and three additional methods of aiding the cabinet, all of which have been tried with varying degrees of success, must be commented on: reducing the size of the cabinet, a device apparently now obsolete; using more minor or quasi-ministerial posts to supplement the cabinet; and using more committees, with adequate secretarial assistance.

At various times piecemeal attempts have been made to reduce the size of the cabinet, but they have been of little permanent avail; for no sooner do the numbers fall off than the needs of government force the creation of new departments and with them, as a rule, new ministers. Mackenzie King, whose hand in cabinet adjustment became more skilful with each year's experience, made a heroic effort in 1935–6 to lessen the number of ministers and to rationalize the allotment of departmental work. He cut down the ministers without portfolio to one; he assigned the functions of the solicitor general to the minister of Justice and attorney general; and he placed the Department of Railways and Canals, the Department of Marine, and the civil aviation branch (from National Defence) under a new minister of Transport, with the result that the cabinet was reduced to sixteen members, where it remained for some years. But the outbreak of war brought about a rapid increase in portfolios, and the theoretical minimum of sixteen is not possible as long as all ministers must be in the cabinet, a practice accepted unquestioningly by the Royal Commission on

12/Halliday, "The Executive of the Government of Canada," p. 235.

Government Organization.[13] A prime minister is fortunate if he is able over a period of years to hold his own against this political hydra which tends to grow portfolios faster than they can be eliminated. Needs are continually changing and the demands for new departments are plausible and difficult to resist, reductions will almost invariably lead to criticism and dissatisfaction, and the abolition of one portfolio may even accentuate the pressure for a new one to replace the old. The only time which holds fair promise of successful effort is the honeymoon period immediately after an election. "From experience," advised King with a somewhat rueful humour, "I can tell my right honourable friend [Mr Bennett] that he will find it much easier to make his consolidations in the first year than he will thereafter, provided he is in office any length of time. If he does not contemplate being in office any length of time, he will find avoiding consolidations a much simpler matter."[14] Mr Diefenbaker's cabinet honeymoon was a short one indeed, and one unprecedentedly productive of progeny: he soon headed a cabinet which, though without a representative from the Senate, none the less had twenty-four members, while both his successors outbid him.

At times it has appeared that the most hopeful way of reducing the cabinet is via the somewhat paradoxical route of enlarging the ministry; that is, by clearly distinguishing between those who are primarily responsible for questions of major policy and the other members of the government who do not need to have seats in the cabinet.[15] At present, no distinction is drawn between cabinet and ministry in Canada: the two consist of exactly the same individuals.[16] The obvious obstacle to the plan is its doubtful political acceptability when subjected to the federal and representative tests, although it can offer inducements along the same lines which might make it palatable. For while the cabinet itself would admittedly be composed of only the leading members and those who hold the key positions, the total number of members in the government would almost certainly be larger than at present, and they would thus more than fill out any gaps left by the cabinet in provincial and sectional representation. The members who would belong to the ministry but who would not be in the small cabinet group would doubtless be (as in Great Britain) of two kinds, ministers of a lower grade than those in the cabinet, and the parliamentary secretaries. The Royal Commission on Government Organization, as noted, said nothing about reducing the size of the cabinet, but did suggest that ministerial burdens could with profit be redistributed.

13/*Report of the Royal Commission on Government Organization*, v, p. 46.
14/*Can. H. of C. Debates*, April 23, 1931, p. 939.
15/This was proposed by the *Report of the Special Committee on Machinery of Government* (1919), pp. 8–9. The British ministry commonly has thirty or more ministers not in the cabinet.
16/See *Organization of the Government of Canada*, Jan. 1969, p. 1–&82–1, for a list of "Committee of the Privy Council, the Canadian Ministry." Each Wednesday's edition of the daily reports of *Can. H. of C. Debates* contains an up-to-date list of cabinet members.

The greater use of members of the House as parliamentary secretaries or assistants to certain ministers would do much to relieve the work of their seniors, and it would incidentally also make it easier to reduce the number of those in the cabinet proper. The British Parliament has been using parliamentary under-secretaries (as they are called in Great Britain) on a liberal scale[17] for many years, and it has been repeatedly recommended that Canada adopt them.[18] Only recently, however, have they been used in Canada in any appreciable number, and only in 1959 was the parliamentary secretary made a statutory creation. The burdens which the First World War imposed upon the cabinet led to the temporary creation of three parliamentary under-secretaryships, but they did not long survive the war. Mackenzie King, on becoming prime minister for the first time in 1921, announced that early attention would be given to the desirability of creating a number of honorary under-secretaryships, and he confirmed this by appointing, as his own assistant, an under-secretary for external affairs. Although he suggested to his colleagues that they should follow his example, they failed to respond; because (so it was rumoured) they did not relish the presence in their departments of any other political officers who might conceivably weaken their position and dim a prestige which already gave off a flickering and uncertain light. In 1935 King announced that paid parliamentary under-secretaries for the more important departments would be authorized at the first session of Parliament; but the matter was again dropped. The Second World War provided the necessary pressure, and in 1943 ten parliamentary assistants (as they were then called) were mentioned in the estimates, seven of whom were actually appointed. For a while this number diminished, but it then began to pick up once again and by 1957 had reached twelve. In 1959 Parliament passed an act to permit a maximum of sixteen parliamentary secretaries at any one time, each incumbent having a maximum term of twelve months, and ceasing to hold office "when he ceases to be a member of the House of Commons,"[19] that is, a general election vacates all the secretaryships. The parliamentary secretary differs from a minister in two other respects: he is now, according to Prime Minister Diefenbaker, in no sense a junior minister;[20] and since he is not a minister, he is not bound by the doctrine of collective responsibility.

The theoretical case that can be made out for a broader use of parliamentary

17/In 1969 the British ministry included thirty-three parliamentary under-secretaries or those who performed similar functions, as well as an almost equal number of ministers who were not in the cabinet, and thus ranked below those who were.
18/*Report of Sir George Murray on the Public Service of Canada*, p. 10; *Report of the Special Committee on Machinery of Government*, pp. 11–12.
19/*Can. Statutes*, 7–8 Eliz. II, c. 15. In 1967 a bill proposed by R. A. Bell, then in opposition, would have restored the name of parliamentary assistant, and made the incumbents subject to appointment during pleasure. The government appeared to accept its principles, but no legislation followed. See *Can. H. of C. Debates*, April 7, 1967, pp. 14685 ff.
20/*Can. H. of C. Debates*, 1959, p. 2362.

secretaries is overwhelming. They could make possible, through a greater consolidation of departments, a desirable reduction in the number of members in the cabinet; they would allow the prime minister to give more equitable and wider representation to various provinces; they furnish the finest training for young promising members who aspire to cabinet positions. Mackenzie King once outlined in some detail the many ways in which the secretary can discharge his primary function of lightening the load of his minister.

Other duties of assistants to Ministers would be to assist the Minister in Parliament, to answer questions – not all questions – and also to take part in departmental debates so that the house may be given fuller information in regard to some matters than it otherwise would. To assist in the explanation of the estimates. I can conceive of occasions when an assistant to the Minister might relieve the Minister entirely of a large part of the explanation of the estimates. To appear before House committees on behalf of the Minister, participate in interdepartmental committees on behalf of the Minister, to keep the House itself informed more promptly on matters which may arise in the course of debates; to assist in the planning of some of the post-war work of the Government which will have to be done under the direction of the Minister ... Also to receive deputations – the Ministers are beset with deputations – they cannot possibly see many of them. An assistant to the Minister could see them and I should hope be able to be of real assistance in seeing that their representations were carefully considered ... Then there is the matter of a link with members of Parliament ... An assistant to the Minister will be mixing with members generally and will be able to bring to the Minister many matters that otherwise could not possibly be brought to his attention ... Then there is deputizing for the Minister on different occasions, fulfilling specific duties. The duties will vary between one department and another, one Minister may wish his assistant to perform certain duties and another other duties. Then there is the signing on behalf of the Minister of many documents that otherwise would require his signature. There is the supervision of officials in some branches where an assistant minister can be of great help. The assistant to the Minister can be of great help in regard to outside engagements as well as engagements inside the House. Almost any service that will help relieve the Minister of a burden and give the House of Commons and the public more information with regard to public business is the kind of position which the parliamentary assistant to the Minister will be expected to fill.[21]

Not only is the catalogue of advantages thus a long one, but the need for some assistance of this general kind is demonstrably present. To this may be added the unquestioned success of British experience, and the testimony of Canadian prime ministers who have put the experiment to the test.[22] The very terms in which the parliamentary secretary attained a statutory basis in 1959, however, suggest that there are still some misgivings in high places about the office and the uses to which it should be put. Undoubtedly, some ministers use their secretaries freely; others sparingly, as if wary of enhancing the importance

21/*Ibid.*, April 20, 1943, pp. 2366–7.
22/For example, Sir Robert Borden, *ibid.*, Aug. 7, 1917, p. 4205; Mackenzie King, *ibid.*, March 27, 1944, p. 1852. Mr Bell (*ibid.*, April 7, 1967, pp. 14685–91) made interesting observations on his own experiences as a secretary, and included statistics on the number of secretaries attaining cabinet rank.

of possible rivals. All secretaries have in practice acted for their principals in the House; some have had fairly extensive departmental duties to perform, others have had none. On occasion, some attend meetings of interdepartmental and other committees either as the representatives of their ministers or on behalf of their departments. Yet recent developments suggest that it is not only the intention of the government *not* to use the secretary to make the cabinet smaller; it is also intended to widen rather than narrow the gap between minister and parliamentary secretary. The latter still occupies a parliamentary no man's land where he is no longer an ordinary member of the House nor is he in the ministry. The invariable British practice is that the under-secretaries form part of the ministry, and this circumstance naturally adds to the prestige and enhances the desirability of the position. The Canadian refusal to make a similar concession is but another sign of the reluctance to accept the new office wholly, and thus make the most of its possibilities.

Another common difficulty which is closely related to the size of the cabinet has been the congestion of cabinet business. While this is not in one way as serious a problem in Canada as in some other countries because the provinces assume a substantial portion of the work of government, the volume tends nevertheless to be unduly large because of the amount of detail which the cabinet has attempted to handle directly. This has sprung partly from a political and administrative immaturity and a consequent reluctance to delegate power and responsibility to others, and partly from the representative nature of the cabinet and the expectation that each section or interest will have an opportunity to participate in every decision which will be likely to affect it. Sir George Murray commented on this in 1912 at some length:

Nothing has impressed me so much in the course of my inquiry as the almost intolerable burden which the present system of transacting business imposes on Ministers themselves. They both have too much to do and do too much.

Speaking broadly, it may be said that every act of the Executive Government, or of any member of it, requires the sanction of the Governor-in-Council which, under present practice, is identical with the Cabinet ...

Almost every decision of a Minister, even of the most trivial importance, is thus – at least in theory – brought before his colleagues for the purpose of obtaining their collective approval, which is necessary for its validity.[23]

This summary remained substantially accurate for thirty years after it was written, and even now it has not lost all its force. Such a prolonged delay in accomplishing some measure of reform scarcely seems to substantiate the existence of an "almost intolerable burden"; but Murray would doubtless have replied that the question was qualitative as well as quantitative, that there was probably a deterioration in the nature of the work done, that time and effort were not available for major questions simply because they had been expended on trivialities. The changes of the past few years, however, have gone far to

23/*Report of Sir George Murray on the Public Service of Canada*, sections 5, 6, 8.

meet many of Murray's criticisms, and Mr Trudeau, the latest prime minister to cope with cabinet organization, early in his administration announced plans to delegate actual decision-making to cabinet committees.[24]

The cabinet, like any other organization of appreciable size, has for a long time been in the habit of using committees and sub-committees as a device to accelerate business, although the whole body has retained general powers of control. The Second World War, for example, brought about an unprecedented proliferation of cabinet committees devoted to a wide range of activities. In December 1939 ten committees of the cabinet (including the War Committee, mentioned above) were created in order "to co-ordinate the work of the Government, to prevent duplication of effort, and to promote efficiency."[25] The ministers could in this way make a much more effective disposal of their talents: a number of committees were able to sit simultaneously; special problems were assigned to those best qualified to deal with them, either directly or through their departments; and the committees could make decisions which would be accepted in the main by the entire cabinet without prolonged discussion. Some of these committees proved to be of little merit and gradually became obsolete; others served usefully for a time and then handed over their work to a more suitable authority; others made themselves quite invaluable. On the whole, they succeeded in their main object of distributing a substantial part of the cabinet's work so that the War Committee with its more select personnel was better able to devote its energies to the outstanding and urgent problems of the war.

While the return to peace was followed by some retrenchment in the delegation of power to committees, the post-war use of committees, both standing and *ad hoc*, has remained high. The many committees naturally vary from time to time, but they can be conveniently classified under four general headings.[26]

(*a*) Committees of the Privy Council. These rest on both statutory and customary bases, and have executive authority. By far the most important is the cabinet itself, and from within it is drawn another major body, the Treasury Board, already referred to. There is also a special Committee of Council, referred to below.

(*b*) Committees of the cabinet. With one exception these have no legal powers and are established by the cabinet to provide information and possibly advice, and, as of 1968, to make some decisions. Their number, size, and purpose vary with individual cabinets: Mr Pearson's gov-

24/Office of the Prime Minister, Press Release, April 30, 1968.
25/W. L. Mackenzie King, *Can. H. of C. Debates*, July 8, 1940, p. 1396. The leading cabinet committees appointed in 1939 (Dec. 5, 8, 1939, P.C. 4017½, 4068½) were as follows: war committee, war finance and supply, food production and marketing, shipping and transportation, price control and labour, internal security, fuel and power, legislation, public information, and demobilization.
26/This follows closely the arrangement in Halliday, "The Executive of the Government of Canada," pp. 240–1.

ernment at one time had ten standing committees, of which the prime minister chaired three, and twelve special committees, of which he also chaired three; all of these fed material into the cabinet, which made all the final decisions. Mr Trudeau, on assuming office, created four major standing committees (on external policy and defence; economic policy and programmes; communications, works and urban affairs; and social policy) and four main co-ordinating committees (on priorities and planning; legislation and planning for the parliamentary programme; federal-provincial relations; and the Treasury Board); all of these were intended to relieve the full cabinet of part of its work load, leaving it free to deal with broad matters of policy.[27] The Trudeau cabinet was barely a year and a half old before two new standing committees (on science and technology, and culture and information) had been added, and that on communications, works and urban affairs dropped, while special committees on public service, security and intelligence, and labour relations had been created. Of all these committees it can still be said, as was said of some of their predecessors:

Their life [that of cabinet committees] is governed, their survival determined by the operation of laws as inexorable as those of the physical universe. Created to provide a means for concentrating ministerial attention upon problems which, at the time, require special treatment, they tend to diminish in activity and influence as the need diminishes and ultimately to disappear. In some instances their functions are taken over by the development of new organs. Their authority, effectiveness, and longevity are inevitably affected by the prestige and initiative of the Ministers who compose them but their active continuance is in the end determined by whether or not they serve necessary purposes.[28]

(c) Interdepartmental committees. These are committees of public servants operating below the ministerial level, but reporting to a cabinet committee or the cabinet itself. They largely replace the older and haphazard practice (never widespread except in war), of having civil servants occasionally attend cabinet meetings because of their special qualifications, and are ordinarily set up by the cabinet, the Treasury Board, or the minister(s) concerned. Some are short-lived, but others have met over many years.

(d) Advisory committees. These are used to bring the talents of people outside the public service into play, and include not only federal civil servants but representatives of provincial departments and major interest groups such as the professions, organized labour, business, and so on. They are usually created by statute or order-in-council, and cover a variety of topics from unemployment insurance to maternal and child care.

Another instance of the devolution of authority is concerned with the method

---

27/See Newman, The Distemper of Our Times, pp. 490–7; Office of the Prime Minister, Press Release, April 30, 1968. I am also indebted to Mr P. M. Pitfield of the Privy Council Office for letters dated June 2 and Oct. 29, 1969.
28/Heeney, "Cabinet Government in Canada," p. 288.

used to pass routine orders and minutes of Council. Formerly all these (as indicated in the above extract from the Murray report[29]) were approved by the full council, a proceeding which did little good and involved an enormous waste of time. The present practice, which has developed from a procedure instituted during the war, is for a special committee of Council to review and dispose of formal business which raises no policy implications, while reserving the exceptional material for the consideration of the cabinet. The result is that almost all minutes and orders are passed today by this special committee and do not come before all the ministers in council. To these must be added the large number of formal decisions made by the Treasury Board[30] and expressed as Treasury Board Minutes.[31] These changes embody one of the suggestions made by Sir George Murray to lessen the amount of business submitted to the full cabinet; but another and accompanying recommendation, that there should be a sweeping devolution of authority on many minor matters to individual ministers and to deputy ministers has only recently begun to be carried out. As a direct result of the report of the Royal Commission on Government Organization, there has been an extensive devolution of both signing and decision-making authority in administrative matters, including the filling of vacant positions in establishments constituted as approved by the Treasury Board. Decisions having political implications (and in a country as large and diverse as Canada almost anything can have political implications) must of course be considered by the cabinet, and there is no democratic way of lightening the burden on ministers in that regard.

Finally, the transaction of cabinet business was until the Second World War very loosely organized. The pre-war methods, if not chaotic, were incredibly haphazard, and any self-respecting board of directors would have discarded them in five minutes. No formal agenda were prepared for cabinet meetings; no minutes of its deliberations were kept, although the prime minister might make a few scanty notes; no secretary attended its sessions; and even the time of meeting (and to a lesser degree the place) was uncertain. If the decisions were to be carried out in orders or minutes of Council, they appeared, of course, in that form; but otherwise they were unrecorded. Most of these peculiarities were defended on the ground that they were necessary to preserve the secrecy and desirable informality of the proceedings, but there can be little question that these excessive precautions must have seriously hampered the effectiveness with which cabinet business was conducted.

The British cabinet had laboured under the same handicaps, but these went by the board during the First World War and never returned. But neither the

29/*Supra*, p. 226.
30/*Infra*, pp. 359–60.
31/See J. R. Mallory, "Delegated Legislation in Canada," *Canadian Journal of Economics and Political Science*, XIX, no. 4 (Nov. 1953), pp. 467–71; A. A. Sterns, "The Treasury Board," A. M. Willms and W. D. K. Kernaghan, eds., *Public Administration in Canada* (Toronto, 1968), pp. 196–203.

British experience, nor the report of the Senate Committee on Machinery of Government, nor the extravagant clumsiness of its own business was sufficient to change the easy-going anachronistic methods of the Canadian cabinet. Nothing short of a second world cataclysm could accomplish so formidable a task; and although the price would seem to have been somewhat excessive, this reform can be placed as an item on the credit side of the national ledger.

"The great increase in the work of the Cabinet and particularly since the outbreak of war," stated an order-in-council in March 1940, "has rendered it necessary to make provision for the performance of additional duties of a secretarial nature relating principally to the collection and putting into shape of agenda of Cabinet meetings, the providing of information and material necessary for the deliberations of the Cabinet and the drawing up of records of the results."[32] This was begun by appointing the clerk of the Privy Council to a new position as secretary to the cabinet, although his additional functions were first discharged primarily for the benefit of the War Committee. In 1945, following the disappearance of the War Committee, the cabinet adopted the same methods which had been successfully tried out in the smaller body.

The present usage therefore presents an impressive contrast to the old. Agenda are now prepared under the direction of the prime minister for the regular meetings of the cabinet, and these, accompanied by relevant documents, are circulated in advance to all members. Ministers who have questions to bring up are required to submit explanatory documents so that their colleagues can be in a position to inform themselves before the discussion takes place. The conclusions reached at the meeting, together with a terse summary of the essential points, are noted by the secretary, and the Privy Council Office (divided in 1969 into "plans" and "operations" sections, each headed by a deputy secretary to the cabinet) informs and reminds the appropriate ministers of the cabinet decisions. The same staff will also provide secretarial help for cabinet committees; and it will act as a link between these committees, any of the special inter-departmental committees which may be attached to them, and the cabinet itself. As a result of these comparatively simple expedients, discussion in the cabinet can be materially shortened, uncertainties and ambiguities are lessened, decisions are brought more sharply into focus, and urgent questions can be more readily given priority when occasion demands.

The volume of work arising from these activities has necessitated a substantial growth in staff, and apart from the Privy Council Office and the prime minister's Office as branches of the public service, the president of the Privy Council now holds a portfolio which, after frequent temporary separations in the past, now seems likely to remain separate from the prime minister. The

---

32/March 25, 1940, P.C. 1121. The wording of this order is clearly borrowed from the Report of the Machinery of Government Committee (Great Britain), p. 6. See also, *Can. H. of C. Debates*, Feb. 10, 1947, pp. 246–7.

prime minister's Office itself now has a larger staff than the Privy Council Office usually had until well into the Second World War.

The chief purpose beneath most of these changes is not merely to relieve the cabinet of an excessive amount of work, although that is far from negligible; it is primarily to allow the ministers, as individuals and as a group, to substitute one kind of work for another, to pass over routine and minor affairs to subordinates and to be thereby released for other tasks which are far more vital. "The business of a Minister," to quote Sir George Murray again, "is not to administer but to direct policy"; and while the members of the Canadian cabinet would no doubt have accepted this maxim in theory, they were a long while before they made any serious attempt to adopt it in practice. In 1936 the minister of Finance (Mr Dunning) spoke in the House as follows:

The reference I made was to the functions of government as at present constituted, and the ever-increasing weight of responsibility which rests upon the Governor-General-in-Council – meaning the Government of the day – and a responsibility which I do not hesitate for a moment to say is fully up to the physical and nervous capacity of any man occupying a position in any government under these conditions. The constant multiplication of functions is due to a change which has come about in the conception of government functions. They have been constantly widening for the last twenty years, and indeed I am one who thinks one of the problems we shall have to face in the not distant future is the problem of adjustment, and an adjustment which will in some manner be consistent with our system of responsible government. It will have to be an adjustment of the load in a way which will ensure that members of Governments will at least have time to think about the things they are supposed to deal with.[33]

The Second World War forced this issue, and conditions which were up to then extremely onerous immediately threatened to become insupportable. The ministers, whether they liked it or not (and there is every reason to suppose that a number of them were reluctant to change), had no real choice but to revise many of their customary procedures and abandon some of their cherished functions – to public servants on the one hand, and to some of their colleagues on the other. Whether this delegation and revision of methods have as yet gone far enough, it is difficult to say; for the criterion is not, as stated above, the demands which are being made on a minister's attention, but the nature of the work to which that attention is devoted. It is a notorious fact that most ministers rarely have time to study the documents and memoranda which are submitted to them on which their decisions must be formulated, nor are they free to explore thoroughly even the essential circumstances surrounding the problems which are demanding consideration. The alternatives under such

33/*Can. H. of C. Debates*, June 9, 1936, p. 3575. "A Prime Minister must inform himself on important public questions. If his vision is to be clear, and his judgment sound, he should have some time to read, and to think. A nation, which is wise, will ensure this opportunity to its leaders." W. L. Mackenzie King, in a radio address, Jan. 23, 1939.

conditions are that either the policy slips too easily and completely into the hands of the public servants, or the minister gets into the habit of making snap judgments based on an insufficient appreciation of the issues involved. Neither alternative is consonant with a government which tries to secure efficiency and at the same time endeavours to maintain democratic control. If the members of the cabinet – and each individual minister – are properly to perform their functions they must somehow contrive to discuss in their main outlines the problems which arise, to obtain the best advice their public servants can offer, to find time for study and reflection, and, having done these things to the best of their ability, they can then make their decisions. Even so, the decisions will, no doubt, frequently be wrong; but they will at least be based on as much wisdom as a group of fallible men can reasonably hope to achieve in a complex and unpredictable world.

Part IV THE ADMINISTRATION

12 The public service

THE PUBLIC SERVICE OF CANADA was in the 1960s profoundly affected by two extraneous developments: the appointment of the Royal Commission on Government Organization in 1960, and the final acceptance of collective bargaining for public servants in the Public Service Staff Relations Act assented to in 1967. Few commissions have had so immediate an impact on any area of government as has the Glassco commission (popularly identified by the name of its chairman), and none on the federal administration: by the end of 1968 the government had accepted over two hundred of the commission's two hundred and ninety-four recommendations, and rejected only twenty-six "as having been overtaken by events or as impracticable," while the rest were still under active consideration.[1] Collective bargaining not only transferred rates of pay and allied matters outside the direct jurisdiction of the cabinet, but also necessitated the creation of new institutions to provide for certification of unions, and conciliation and arbitration, and new bodies to negotiate with public servants on behalf of the government of Canada; it also prepared the way for the first strikes by federal employees.

None of these changes, all of which helped produce a massive reorganization of the executive and the public service of Canada, altered the fundamental fact that executive and public service in Canada have always in one respect discharged a common function, the enforcement, application, and development of the national policies. But the distinction between the two is never in any doubt: the executive is a political body; the public service is non-political, and consists of the growing number of employees of the state who work in either a department of government, or a Crown corporation or other agency engaged in administering some particular law or laws.

Each department has a minister in undisputed command of it: he possesses not only the authority bestowed on him by law, but also the moral authority derived from his position as a government representative in a popularly elected

1/*Can. H. of C. Debates*, Nov. 18, 1968, p. 2833.

Parliament. The departmental public servant is always nominally the subordinate; and even on those not infrequent occasions when he may take the initiative and to a limited degree determine policy, he does so within the bounds assigned by his superior and always subject to possible intervention. The minister's omnipotence, however, is limited in duration; for his tenure of office is subject to all the uncertainties and caprices of politics, or more explicitly, to the continued confidence reposed in him by the prime minister, by the Commons, and by his constituents. Most public servants today, whether employed in a department or a Crown agency, enjoy a permanent position, little affected by the frequent changes of their political superiors, and they are thereby able to achieve the continuity, the experience, and the specialized knowledge which must form the framework about which good administration is built. The characteristic marks of the minister are a seat in Parliament, an uncertain tenure of office, and the opportunity to exercise complete power within his own department.[2] The non-departmental agencies, which are discussed below, are largely free from direct ministerial control, and most of them were, in fact, established partly to by-pass the political direction inherent in having a minister as head.

It is obvious that the opportunity to exercise control becomes more and more unreal as functions become more varied and complex and as the number under the minister's direction increases. A carefully planned organization can do much to overcome these handicaps, yet even with the most efficient methods, the subordinates at some level under the minister will inevitably acquire more power. The constant assertion of the principle of ministerial responsibility will cover to some degree the actual delegation of authority which has taken place, but this cannot conceal the fact that no minister (or his deputy) can hope to make even the major decisions for the five or ten or twenty thousand employees who may be nominally under him. Yet there is much to be said for the retention of the idea of continuous responsibility; for, harsh though it may be, it undoubtedly helps to prevent the slovenliness and inefficiency which would be

---

2/The absence of this distinction caused considerable difficulty in Canada at the time of the introduction of responsible government, for it necessitated two vital steps as preliminaries to the introduction of the new system, namely, the creation of explicit heads of the government departments (which were formerly lacking) and the insistence that these and no other office-holders should occupy seats in the legislature. Only when this was done could the major change be made effective: that the department heads in the legislature would relinquish office whenever this body withdrew its support.

"Those public servants, who held their offices permanently, must upon that very ground be regarded as subordinate, and ought not to be members of either house of the Legislature, by which they would necessarily be more or less mixed up in party struggles; and, on the other hand, those who are to have the general direction of affairs exercise that function by virtue of their responsibility to the Legislature, which implies their being removable from office, and also that they should be members either of the Assembly or of the Legislative Council." Earl Grey (colonial secretary) to Sir John Harvey (governor of Nova Scotia), March 31, 1847, *Brit. H. of C. Papers* (621) xlii, 1847–8, p. 79.

bound to occur if every minister or deputy or other official could plead ignorance and impotence whenever anything went wrong.

The public service is, of course, by far the most numerous part of the Canadian government, although the exact numbers cannot be stated with assurance. They vary somewhat from year to year, especially in times of emergency, and there is always the problem of knowing what groups should be counted. The "Public Service," as defined in the Public Service Employment Act of 1967, includes the employees in nearly sixty departments, commissions, and boards; in the same year, the total number of federal employees was 398,928, of which 162,736 were in crown companies, and the total payroll was approaching the two billion dollar mark.[3]

The totals are impressive and give some idea of the great numbers needed to run the modern Canadian government. The public service reaches into all kinds of human activities, and a cross-section of the personnel would show that almost every occupation in the Dominion is represented. The problems presented by so large and varied a host are many, although they may for the most part be placed within two chief categories: first, those concerned with the organization or general framework of governmental activity, discussed in this chapter; second, those which are essentially concerned with matters of personnel, discussed in the next.

The primary division of administrative activity in the Canadian government (as in most governments) rests in the main on *function*, that is, the work of the departments and agencies is apportioned according to its general purpose, and similar functions are grouped together under one direction. The Departments of Justice, Agriculture, Fisheries and Forestry, Finance, and many others are thus largely if not entirely devoted to the primary ends indicated. Several others embrace not identical but allied functions. National Defence thus covers the armed forces; the Department of Transport includes the different but related fields of railways, canals, marine, and aviation. The various corporations and agencies discharge functions clearly suggested by their names: Canadian National Railways; National Museums of Canada; Unemployment Insurance Commission; Canadian Broadcasting Corporation; Crown Assets Disposal Corporation, and the like.[4]

Other principles of grouping are also found, although these are of comparatively minor significance. One of these is *work process,* the gathering together of similar activities which would otherwise be scattered through a number of departments because of their association with the major purposes to which those departments are devoted. The government of Canada thus gathers most of its

3/*Can. Statutes,* 14–15–16 Eliz. II, c. 71 and 72; Public Service Commission, *Annual Report,* 1967, Appendix B, p. 36; *Canada Year Book, 1968,* p. 157.
4/A full list of departments and agencies, and a brief description of each, can be found in *Organization of the Government of Canada.* See also *Canada Year Book, 1968,* pp. 127–62.

printing under one agency, the Canadian Government Printing Bureau, in the Department of Supply and Services, while the Queen's Printer, as a publisher, is scheduled to move to a new institution called Information Canada. The Department of Supply and Services is a comprehensive purchasing agent, providing both goods and services. Another service agency of vital importance in a bilingual state is the Translation Bureau in the secretary of state's department.

Clientele may furnish a third basis for combination. Here the major concern is with a group of people who for some reason are singled out for special attention and can be given that attention more effectively by segregation. The Departments of Veterans Affairs, and Manpower and Immigration, and Indian Affairs and Northern Development are all based on this principle; so is the Unemployment Insurance Commission.

Territory is a fourth possible principle which may be used for organizing departmental work. Any organization as it spreads downwards may tend to arrange some of its activities along geographical lines, and even a highly centralized department may have a field staff distributed on a geographical basis. Under a thorough application of the territorial principle the area becomes the essential basis for the appointment of work. A decentralized service is found in the twenty-six research stations and thirteen experimental farms of the Department of Agriculture, in which the locality becomes the chief justification for the establishment of the local experimental farm; the locality will even determine the kind and variety of work in which the enterprise will engage and thus the qualifications of its personnel. The government of the Northwest Territories under the Department of Indian Affairs and Northern Development is an example of an administration set up on a purely territorial basis.

Each of these schemes of organization has its own advantages and limitations and the choice made will depend on a balancing of factors.[5] Problems of organization in departments on the one hand, and Crown corporations and agencies on the other, are not always the same, although the same principles apply in practice. The next several paragraphs, for brevity, concern primarily the organization of departments.

The legal work of all departments could conceivably be done, and perhaps done better, by the Department of Justice, and all medical work could be assigned to a common medical service; but the delay and general inconvenience which such a plan would entail would make it in many instances administratively undesirable. In practice, much of the legal work is concentrated in the Department of Justice and the solicitor general's department, while the medical staff is more widely diffused. Principles of organization are thus not mutually exclusive, and a department may find it advantageous to utilize more than one to secure the best results. Stenographers, for example, are often formed within

5/See Schuyler C. Wallace, *Federal Departmentalization* (New York, 1941), pp. 91–146.

any department into a common pool to which any branch may send appropriate work or from which any branch may draw additional help when needed. Consistency in such matters has no inherent merit; the major test must always be the suitability of the particular organization to the work which it is called upon to perform.

Departmental functions and organization are, moreover, always in a state of flux. A new demand begets a gradual increase in activity, this leads to an enlarged staff, and this in turn to a further accretion of extra functions and officials, which are not always tied in easily or logically with those of the remainder of the department. When this phenomenon has occurred in five or ten or twelve different places and over a number of years, the operations invariably suffer and become progressively more complex and cumbersome. The only effective remedy is to break up the existing organization and to regroup the positions so as to make them more amenable to control, thereby bringing their activities into closer co-ordination with others related to them. Thus on one unusual occasion when four departments were consolidated into one, the aim was to remedy the following conditions:

In the four departments there are at the present time three deputy ministers and one deputy superintendent-general, three assistant deputy ministers and one assistant deputy superintendent-general, four legal advisers, two editorial staffs, three publicity staffs, four translation staffs, two architects' offices, four sets of secretarial and stenographic and other staffs, purchasing agents, four officers engaged in accounting for revenue and expenditure, three photographic establishments, three departments in which land business is carried on and four in which surveying is carried on; doctors are employed by two departments; welfare of natives is a concern of two departments; maps are prepared in two departments. At the present time there are eighteen branches all told in these four departments. Under the proposed legislation the number of branches will be limited to eight. Another direction in which considerable economy should be effected is in the housing of these various departments. We hope before very long, it will become possible to bring the various units together into a single building where staffs will be more immediately under the supervision of those who are at the head of the different branches and of the department as a whole. At the present time the four departments are housd in twenty-four buildings throughout Ottawa.[6]

While the elimination of overlapping functions and the establishment of new relationships and greater co-ordination would seem to be an obvious remedy for conditions such as those described above, such reforms are rarely welcomed in any department. There is an ineradicable tendency not only for every department to expand, but for its officials to resist any change which threatens to reduce its personnel and hence diminish its power and importance. Reasons can always be produced to justify the existing arrangements, some undoubtedly genuine, others far less cogent. "There never was a department that you tried

6/*Can. H. of C. Debates*, June 2, 1936, pp. 3308–9. See *ibid.*, June 9, 1936, pp. 3533–40.

to cut down," stated R. B. Bennett after his experience as prime minister, "that was not different from any other. They are all different; they always will be."[7] The initiative is therefore most likely to come from someone who is not too closely identified with the department itself; and the Canadian practice from 1918 to 1962 was to give the major responsibility in such matters to the organization branch of the Civil Service Commission; but after 1962 the commission had only an advisory role and its successor, the Public Service Commission, has been relieved of the advisory role.[8] The latest shake-up began with the Royal Commission on Government Organization.

The organization of all Canadian departments assumes a hierarchical or pyramidal form. At the apex stands the minister (with or without a parliamentary secretary) and immediately under him is the deputy minister, the public servant who is the head of the departmental organization and who remains undisturbed in office when a reshuffling of the cabinet or a change in government causes the minister to make way for his successor. Under the deputy is a small group of permanent officials who are in charge of the main activities of the department; each of these in turn has the supervision of another small group who are in charge of their respective sub-divisions; and the work and oversight of these is similarly and progressively divided and relayed until the most humble member of the department is affected. The chain of responsibility works always upward to the immediate superior, and through him to his superior, until the minister is finally reached with all the reins of control theoretically in his hands. Instructions and orders flow from the supreme head down through subordinates until they culminate in action at the appropriate level.

This "line" organization (as it is generally called) is usually augmented by another group of officials known as "staff," a term also borrowed from the structure of army control. The deputy minister has working with him a small group largely concerned with general planning, the provision of common services, and the securing of necessary co-ordination among the different parts. These officials (unlike their "line" colleagues) rarely give orders: they make recommendations and provide information and advice, and their relations are directly with those for whose primary benefit this special form of staff organization has been created.

The chart on page 242 gives in bold outline the organization of a fairly simple department, the Department of Insurance, of interest because, although the department was founded in 1924, its head has never held a separate portfolio: the minister responsible is the minister of Finance.[9] The following is a brief account of the services performed by that department and the officials who supervise them. In November 1969 it had no deputy minister and was

7/*Ibid.*, Feb. 11, 1937, p. 803.
8/See *Can. Statutes*, 9–10 Eliz. II, c. 57, s. 6; 14–15–16 Eliz. II, c. 71.
9/See *Organization of the Government of Canada*, pp. 3 In 1–3.

responsible for nine related statutes; it was, and is, a small department, but one of considerable importance.

(1) The Actuarial Branch checks actuarial valuations of policy liabilities of registered life insurance companies, compiles reports relating to insurance companies, and supervises employee pension plans and actuarial services for other departments.

(2) The Administrative Branch is responsible for, among other things, personnel administrations, the collection of premium taxes under part I of the Excise Tax Act, accounting, and the estimates of the department.

(3) The Examination Branch conducts examinations of companies at their head offices or chief agencies in Canada, verifies their annual statements, etc.

(4) The Registration and Deposit Branch is responsible for the registration of companies, the maintenance of deposits by registered companies, the valuation of securities, and the compilation of statistics relating to trust and similar companies, including co-operative credit societies.

Since all departments discharge different functions, no one of them can be considered as typical of all the others. As of November 1969 there were twenty-nine departments, exclusive of the prime minister's, a few of them being combined under a single minister. In addition, as has already been indicated, an increasingly important segment of the public service is non-departmental and is conducted by a group of separate boards or commissions, each created for a particular purpose. The exact number of these bodies is not readily ascertained, since definitions of them vary, but there are currently over thirty which are more or less independent, not counting a variety of similar bodies assigned specifically to the jurisdiction of particular departments.[10] The departmental and non-departmental organizations of the government of Canada were officially classified for the first time in the Financial Administration Act, 1951:[11]

In Schedules A, B, C and D of the Act will be found a list of government departments proper (Schedule A); "departmental corporations" (Schedule B); "agency corporations" (Schedule C) and "proprietary corporations" (Schedule D). This classification is based on two factors; the extent of financial independence and the general nature of the activity. The departmental corporations have administrative, supervisory or regulatory functions, closely akin to an ordinary department and are financed by appropriations. Agency corporations undertake trading, service and procurement operations and are usually given controlled "revolving funds." Finally, proprietary corporations manage lending, financial, commercial or industrial operations, and are normally expected to finance themselves from the sale of goods and services.[12]

10/See *ibid.*, and J. E. Hodgetts and D. C. Corbett, eds., *Canadian Public Administration* (Toronto, 1960), esp. pp. 184–245; A. M. Willms, "Crown Agencies," in Willms and Kernaghan, *Public Administration in Canada*, pp. 159–66.

11/*Can. Statutes*, 15–16 Geo. VI, c. 12 (2nd session, 1951).

12/J. E. Hodgetts, "The Public Corporation in Canada," in Hodgetts and Corbett, *Canadian Public Administration*, pp. 187–8.

DEPARTMENT OF INSURANCE

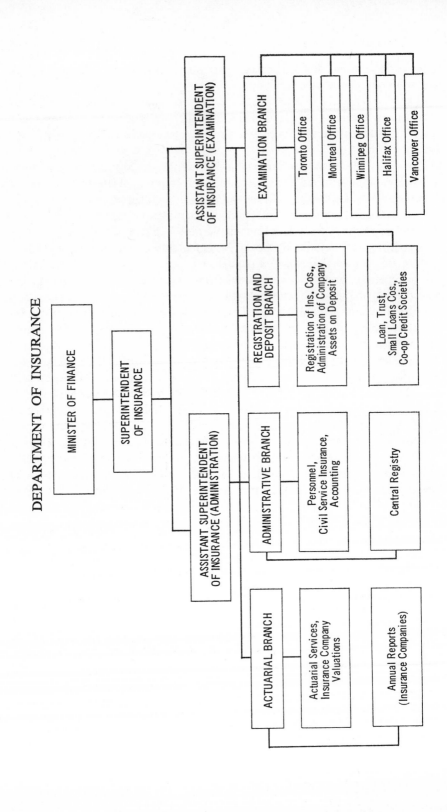

MINISTER OF FINANCE

SUPERINTENDENT OF INSURANCE

ASSISTANT SUPERINTENDENT OF INSURANCE (ADMINISTRATION)

ASSISTANT SUPERINTENDENT OF INSURANCE (EXAMINATION)

ACTUARIAL BRANCH

Actuarial Services, Insurance Company Valuations

Annual Reports (Insurance Companies)

ADMINISTRATIVE BRANCH

Personnel, Civil Service Insurance, Accounting

Central Registry

REGISTRATION AND DEPOSIT BRANCH

Registration of Ins. Cos., Administration of Company Assets on Deposit

Loan, Trust, Small Loans Cos., Co-op Credit Societies

EXAMINATION BRANCH

Toronto Office

Montreal Office

Winnipeg Office

Halifax Office

Vancouver Office

The several types of non-departmental enterprises can be classified further into several categories. Professor Hodgetts, in an illuminating study, has divided them into (1) credit and financial agencies (such as the Bank of Canada, and Central Mortgage and Housing Corporation); (2) commodity trading and procurement agencies (such as Canadian Wheat Board and Defence Construction Limited); (3) producing and business agencies (such as Canadian National Railways, Polymer Corporation, and Atomic Energy of Canada, Limited); and (4) management and research agencies (such as National Battlefields Commission, Dominion Coal Board, and St Lawrence Seaway Authority).[13]

Another useful and similar classification divides these enterprises according to function, but in a different manner. One group of agencies, for example, is largely *advisory*, and the members of these bodies tend for the most part to be on a part-time basis. The National Research Council, for example, is composed of prominent scientists in many fields of endeavour who meet several times a year and place their exceptional knowledge at the disposal of the president of the council, who is a full-time director of the general research activities of the Canadian government carried out under the National Research Council; the Canada Council is similarly organized, and discharges a somewhat similar function for the stimulation of the humanities and social sciences. The Fisheries Research Board, the Tariff Board, and the old Commission of Conservation discharge, or discharged, the same kind of functions in other fields.

Secondly, there are the commissions whose primary functions are those of *regulation*, or *supervision*, or *administration*, or any combination of these.[14] Thus while the Canadian Pension Commission has the fairly straightforward task of applying a particular statute to cases which come before it for settlement, the Canadian Transport Commission (formerly known as the Board of Transport Commissioners) discharges duties which include the settlement of rates, and of disputes on rates and on alleged discrimination, the regulation and inspection of certain railway operations, the investigation of accidents, and many matters concerning not only railways but also telephones, telegraphs, aeroplanes, and inland water carriers. The Public Service Commission has the task of conducting tests for admission to the public service, certifying promotions, and in general ensuring that the merit principle is applied in the making of appointments; the Board of Grain Commissioners applies the terms of the Canada Grain Act to the varied operations of the grain trade; and the Unemployment Insurance Commission administers the Unemployment Insurance Act.

Thirdly, there are the boards which are primarily *operating* bodies, those which conduct some special activity of the government of essentially the same

13/*Ibid.*, pp. 188–9.
14/See *ibid.*, and John Willis, ed., *Canadian Boards at Work* (Toronto, 1941).

character as a private business. The Bank of Canada, the Canadian National Railways, and the Canadian Broadcasting Corporation are all examples of this kind of government enterprise; and to these might be added most of the thirty-one Crown companies which were set up during the Second World War, and the Crown companies which still survive.[15] Each of these is placed under a board created for the purpose which bears a decided resemblance to the board of directors of a private corporation.[16]

The justification for creating all these special boards is the nature of the work which they perform, which is supposed to demand a somewhat greater independence and initiative than the usual department activities which are kept more closely under ministerial control. But the work of these boards will, as has been seen, vary enormously; and hence their composition, the tenure of members and the method of removal; their relationship to the minister to whom they are attached nominally or in a real sense, and their relationship to Parliament, will be modified to suit the particular conditions. Thus in some instances, such as the Public Service Commission or the Canadian Radio-Television Commission, there is great need for removing the operations from any suspicion of political interference, and the situation resembles in some degree that of the judiciary. These particular commissions must therefore be assured of a substantial measure of independence. In other cases, there may be simply a desire to keep the work of the board on a different plane from that of general government administration; or again, there may be a need for freeing its activity from some of the restrictions, formalities, and rules which inescapably hedge about and hamper a government department. Occasionally the desire for more permanence, consistency, and continuity will be considered sufficiently important to justify this particular form of administration. In all these cases a moderate degree of freedom will suffice. The Crown company formation was adopted for a number of reasons – to induce business men to aid in government operations under conditions with which they were familiar, to allow them more freedom, to give greater flexibility, or to aid in preserving secrecy; and although they were usually conceded a wide scope, they were nevertheless kept directly under the minister. In general, all these bodies are viewed differently by Parliament than are the ordinary departments with a minister at the head; some (especially those affecting affairs in many constituencies, such as the Canadian National Railways and the Canadian

15/The Crown companies were, in fact, widely different in function and might be divided into administrative and supervisory, manufacturing, and merchandising companies, but all used the corporate structure and more properly come under the third general category. See speech of C. D. Howe, *Can. H. of C. Debates*, May 14, 1946, pp. 1509–18.

16/See J. A. Corry, "The Fusion of Government and Business," *Canadian Journal of Economics and Political Science*, II, no. 3 (Aug. 1936), pp. 301–16; and J. W. Dafoe, "Public Utilities and Administrative Boards," *ibid.*, pp. 317–30.

Broadcasting Corporation) have received a great deal of parliamentary attention, and others have been all but ignored.[17] It is relevant to add that the Royal Commission on Government Organization, after careful study, reported: "Although the Crown corporation is widely considered to be the principal alternative to departmental organization, your Commissioners are of the opinion that whatever meaning the term 'Crown corporation' may have had originally, it has none today."[18]

The absence of ministerial control and the degree of independence of any board are best gauged and most effectively guaranteed by the security of tenure which the office-holders enjoy and the ease or difficulty of their removal. Here, as might be expected, the practice is widely different for members of different boards. At one extreme are those who have a long term (commonly ten years), hold office during good behaviour, and can be removed, like the judiciary, only after passage of a joint address of both Houses of Parliament. An intermediate status is that enjoyed by those with a three- to ten-year term, tenable during good behaviour, and removable by the Governor-in-Council "for cause," that is, for some adequate reason which seriously impairs efficiency. At the other extreme are those who hold office at pleasure for a short term and can be removed at any time by the Governor-in-Council or minister. The whole question of tenure was raised but not settled in 1961 when the government sought legislation to remove Mr James Coyne, the governor of the Bank of Canada, who was nearing the end of a seven-year term and who had refused to resign at the government's request, by the simple device of declaring his office "to have become vacant." The House of Commons passed the bill but the Senate rejected it; and in due course the governor resigned anyway. The dispute raised many issues, but one clear result of it was that confidence in the "independence" of the Bank of Canada (and by implication of other independent agencies) was severely shaken.[19]

It is therefore well to bear in mind that the precise legal status of the members of these bodies may not give an entirely accurate picture; it indicates what are essentially their defences against attack. Much will depend on the spirit in which the relations between a particular board and the government are conducted. There may, for example, be a tacit understanding (as seems to have been the practice in many Crown companies) that despite the precarious position of the directors, they are to use their own judgment in all matters save those that impinge on government policy, occasions which may prove to be rare in some activities and common in others. On the other hand, a hostile cabinet could do much (and has, indeed, at different times in the past

17/See Ward, *The Public Purse*, especially pp. 214–16; Lloyd D. Musolf, *Public Ownership and Accountability: The Canadian Experience* (Cambridge, Mass., 1959).
18/*Report of the Royal Commission on Government Organization*, v, p. 68.
19/See John T. Saywell, *Canadian Annual Review for 1961*, especially pp. 193–207, and 290–1.

tried to do much) to thwart and embarrass the work of a body like the former Civil Service Commission, despite the legal entrenchments which have protected the members of the latter body against overt attack. The bill which sought to remove Mr Coyne from the Bank of Canada was widely characterized at the time as a "Bill of Attainder"; yet Mr Coyne's successor, echoing in part Mr Coyne himself, averred that the government, not the bank, had the ultimate "responsibility for the monetary policy to be followed," and said further that if the governor of the bank could not agree with the government, "his duty would be to resign."[20]

Thus it should be noted that the conditions under which the members of a board work will determine not their freedom from interference alone but also the political responsibility of the cabinet for the board's actions. If the members hold office at pleasure and are not protected by some conventional practice from interference, then the cabinet will not only interfere on occasion, but it will quite properly be held accountable for whatever the board may do. If, on the other hand, the tenure of the members of a board has been made secure through legal means, or convention, or both, the cabinet has no right of interference and no power of removal except for extreme inefficiency or wrongdoing, there is more assurance that the board will be able to perform its duties with no outside molestation, political or otherwise. It must also follow that if the cabinet cannot direct or remove, it cannot be held responsible, except in a situation so grave that unusual procedures must be invoked. But if the cabinet *is* responsible, it also follows that the independence of a board's members is subject to restrictions.

It is thus not yet clear whether the expedient of detaching these boards from ministerial control places them in a position similar to that of the judiciary. Presumably, the higher the legal and conventional barriers against interference are raised, the closer the parallel with the judiciary becomes. An assurance for the efficient performance of a board's duties and a protection against ordinary abuses must then be sought (as with the judiciary), not in threats and punishments, but through more intangible influences, such as integrity of character, professional pride, tradition, and similar factors. The weight of political responsibility is, in effect, lifted, and a moral responsibility – a responsibility to the public official's own conscience – is called in to take its place.[21] Where the public official is not fully independent, it is not his conscience, but the cabinet's, which is the governing factor.

Ultimately, of course, the final sanction for all actions concerning both departmental and non-departmental organizations must come overtly or tacitly from Parliament, which could if it wished withdraw its confidence from a ministry for its attitude towards (say) the tenure of office of a high public official; or censure the official himself. Parliament is familiar with the depart-

20/*Ibid.*, pp. 207 and 291.
21/For judicial independence and its implications, see *infra*, pp. 395–410.

ments, and (though their course is erratic) has several traditional methods of examining their affairs. Parliament has barely begun, however, to work out devices for the debating of annual reports from non-departmental enterprises, the asking of questions about their affairs, or the scrutiny of their financial activities. The result is that while some segments of the public service are annually discussed in Parliament, others remain virtually outside the parliamentary purview. Many of these same agencies are also outside the purview of the Public Service Commission.

13 The public service: personnel

WHILE NO ONE WILL QUESTION the value of a plan of governmental organization which is well adapted to the task in hand, this is a quality of secondary consequence compared to the quality of the officials who compose the service. A perfect organization badly staffed will at best achieve mediocrity; but a very able staff poorly organized will usually contrive to circumvent many of the obstacles and turn in at worst a fairly adequate performance. "The men of Massachusetts," said Bagehot, "could work any constitution," although it may be assumed that even the men of Massachusetts could do better work under some constitutions than under others. It is the most elementary and axiomatic of statements that good government depends in large measure upon good administration; and this demands that the most persistent and intelligent effort should be directed not only to the external framework of organization but also to the much more difficult and intricate questions of personnel. The selection of good public servants and their training after entrance; the gradation of the service; the system of promotion and the rewards offered to stimulate effort; the maintenance of morale; the methods used to secure initiative and turn it to the best advantage; the need for consistency, for fairness, for operating efficiency – each of these presents its own difficulties in any large-scale organization, and the government service, lacking some of the more spectacular rewards of private business, tends to present many of these difficulties in an accentuated form. Many of these problems are further complicated in Canada by the existence of two main language groups and two cultures: the public service, based almost exclusively on English-Canadian concepts and dominated by English-Canadian personnel, has in some ways resembled an impregnable mountain range to French Canadians, who have complained endlessly about the small proportion of their compatriots on the public payroll, especially in its upper reaches.[1]

1/See Ward, "The National Political Scene," pp. 260–76; "The well-paid are English," *Globe and Mail*, Feb. 18, 1969. Several of the reports and research studies of the Royal Commission on Bilingualism and Biculturalism contain relevant material.

The problems of staffing a public service no longer turn solely on the negative consideration of avoiding poor appointments, as was the assumption underlying Canadian legislation until recent years. The positive problems of obtaining and keeping highly skilled people from every imaginable profession and trade are now equally important, and sometimes more difficult to solve. Further, Canadian experience has shown that legislation that is both rigid enough to provide all the necessary protections against political patronage and nepotism and flexible enough to provide institutions and regulations that allow for rapid adaptation to change, and the utmost use of available resources, is not easy to devise. One result of trying to adapt a law aimed primarily at eliminating patronage to modern governmental organization can be illustrated by a single statistic: a member of the former Civil Service Commission testified in 1959 that "the commission is at the moment responsible for little more than one-third of the public service (if you include in 'public service' the Canadian National Railways)."[2] The exemptions had accumulated over the years (despite the fact that the Civil Service Act of 1918 clearly contemplated a single unified service) and resulted from the interpretation given a particular provision of the act and from other statutes, particularly those creating public corporations and similar agencies. The Civil Service Commission reviewed these exemptions in 1958, was highly critical of them and the problems they create in manning and maintaining the public service, and recommended that with a few stated exceptions all public employees should be brought under the Civil Service Act; the government rejected the recommendation then, but the Public Service Commission established in 1967 has a considerably wider jurisdiction.[3] None the less, it is necessary to remember throughout the following discussion that the "public service" proper is still only a part of the total of public employees, and that a large number belong to a "second 'outside service' ... which applies varying standards in personnel administration."[4]

ENTRANCE

Although exceptionally competent men have always been as useful in public administration as elsewhere, they have not always been as indispensable as they are today; for the driving necessity to recruit first- and not third-rate ability for the civil service has been in large measure the outcome of the last sixty years. Andrew Jackson's idea that "the duties of all public officers are, or at least admit of being made, so plain and simple that men of intelligence may readily qualify themselves for their performance" was not in his time conspicuously wide of the mark; and for many years thereafter honesty, ordinary ability, and

2/House of Commons, Standing Committee on Estimates, *Minutes of Proceedings and Evidence*, May 19, 1959, p. 304.
3/*Can. Statutes*, 14–15–16 Eliz. II, c. 71 and 72.
4/*Personnel Administration in the Public Service*, p. 136.

a fair amount of common sense were the only essential attributes of a civil servant. The same general condition obtained in Canada before and after Confederation, and it lent itself admirably to the necessities of current party politics. For while most Canadian public men readily accepted the negative implications of the above principle, they (like Jackson's followers) showed much less eagerness in trying to obtain the very rudimentary qualifications which a complete application of the principle required.

In the early years of the Dominion all appointments to the public service were made on the recommendation of cabinet ministers, members of Parliament, and the defeated candidates who belonged to the party in power, which meant that with very few exceptions these positions were given out as patronage to the friends of the majority party. "We must support our supporters," said one of the early leaders; and there were many politicians who did not hesitate to advance also the convenient corollary that if the rewards were scanty, party opponents should be thrown out of office in order to create the vacancies for deserving workers. But while this filling of positions by party patronage was very common, dismissals for party reasons never received quite as general or as fervid an endorsement. A victorious government, it is true, was not above dismissing a generous number of officials, but the ministers were usually somewhat apologetic about the matter and alleged (in most instances with a good deal of truth) that those affected had forfeited their rights by being active participants in the elections. The most unfortunate circumstance, and one which naturally tended to perpetuate the system, was that the appointment which followed such a dismissal was almost invariably made in recognition of party services. The new civil servant thus felt that he was expected to give support to the government in power, although eventually, when his party suffered defeat, this was bound to prove his undoing. It was then his turn to be dismissed, and the unhappy cycle began once more.

It soon became evident, however, that in Canada, as in the United States, this system offered no assurance that the official would possess even the modest qualifications which at that time were necessary for the proper performance of his work. Some able men were undoubtedly appointed; but these could scarcely compensate for the large number of notorious incompetents who were being constantly foisted on the public service. The wielders of patronage were exceptionally anxious to apportion rewards; but they were also exceptionally careless about the suitability of the recipient, apart from the irrelevant quality of his party helpfulness. The effect on the service was as unfortunate as it was inevitable. To quote from the report of a royal commission in 1880:

To this baneful influence [patronage], we believe, may be traced nearly all that demands change. It is responsible for admission to the service of those who are too old to be efficient; of those whose impaired health and enfeebled constitutions forbid the hope that they can ever become useful public servants; of those whose personal habits are an equally fatal objection; of those whose lack of education should disqualify them; and of those whose mental qualities are of an order that has made it impossible for them to succeed in private business. It is responsible too for the appointment of those who desire to lead an easy and, what they deem, a genteel life.[5]

Great Britain had begun to root out patronage from its service as early as 1870 by compelling candidates to demonstrate their fitness for the vacant positions by means of open competitive examinations.[6] Canada, in response to an agitation carried on by a number of reformers led by George Elliot Casey, MP, and enlightened by the investigations of a committee of the House of Commons (1877) and a royal commission (1880), took the first cautious step towards improvement in 1882.[7] The Civil Service Act of that year provided that candidates who were to be appointed to a large number of positions in Ottawa would first be compelled to pass examinations set by a board created for that purpose. This was at best a timid and half-hearted measure which did not try to come to grips with the real problem. The examination was not competitive, and the minister was therefore still free to appoint anyone he chose, subject to the trifling restriction that the candidate was required to pass a very elementary test. Sub-normal and illiterate candidates were shut out; but almost anyone else could squeeze through and, if he had the necessary political influence, he could slip into the appointment as before.

The service was therefore still forced to depend for its quality upon the conscience of influential party members; and the same desire to reward deserving supporters, aided, it may be, by the comfortable belief that almost anyone could fill the positions adequately, proved to be the dominant influence in making most appointments. "The distribution of patronage," wrote Sir Wilfrid Laurier's biographer in a revealing sentence, "was the most important single function of the government."[8] Once again, effect followed cause with embarrassing precision, and the government of Canada reaped the sickly crop which it had persistently sown. In 1907, after a disillusioning experience of twenty-five years with the new act, a royal commission reported that "the public service ... not only at Ottawa but elsewhere throughout the Dominion has fallen back during the last fifteen years."[9]

The opening decade of the present century, however, brought a growing appreciation by the government and by the public of the need for greater efficiency in the civil service. Government functions were rapidly multiplying in scope and in complexity and were demanding in increasing numbers intelligent and highly skilled officials, who would have the native ability and training to

5/*Canadian Sessional Papers*, 1880–1, no. 113, p. 16.
6/The first reform was not introduced in the United States until 1883.
7/For this and other parts of the history of the Canadian civil service, see Dawson, *The Civil Service of Canada*, and for a discussion of many modern problems, Taylor Cole, *The Canadian Bureaucracy* (Durham, NC, 1949); Hodgetts and Corbett, *Canadian Public Administration*; Keith B. Callard, *Advanced Administrative Training in the Public Service* (Toronto, 1958); Willms and Kernaghan, *Public Administration in Canada*.
8/Skelton, *Life and Letters of Sir Wilfrid Laurier*, II, p. 270.
9/*Canadian Sessional Papers*, 1907–8, no. 29a, p. 15.

perform the difficult tasks with which they were confronted. A service which formerly had been admittedly inefficient could no longer hope to blunder along and cover up its deficiencies; for under the new demands which had arisen, gross inadequacy or lack of knowledge was little short of disastrous and would bring open and palpable discredit on the entire government. Even the public, which had long remained quiescent on the subject of civil service reform, began vaguely to comprehend the great value of efficient administration and appreciate the wasteful results of patronage; and this – and an imminent election – at last brought legislative action.

A new Civil Service Act was passed in 1908.[10] It created a Civil Service Commission, which was to set examinations for entrance to a large number of positions in the so-called "inside" service at Ottawa. These examinations were not only open to all who chose to apply but, unlike their predecessors, they were competitive, that is, the candidate who had proved his merit by coming at the top of the list, secured the appointment. In order that the commission might not be influenced by party politics and, in particular, might be made quite independent of the cabinet, its members were given a tenure during good behaviour,[11] subject to removal only by the governor general on an address passed by the Senate and House of Commons.

These changes constituted the first genuine measure of civil service reform in Canada. The act was, of course, limited in its extent, for it did not cover all the officials at Ottawa or any of those elsewhere in the Dominion, a fact which was convincingly demonstrated in a short time. In the three years following the defeat of the Laurier government in 1911 some 11,000 civil servants resigned or were removed from office, the reason assigned in most cases being that the official had been guilty of political partisanship. While the system of making appointments through the commission could not guarantee political neutrality, this neutrality was definitely encouraged, and very few officials who had been so appointed got into trouble because of party activity.

The widest advance was made in 1918, when the entire service, with trifling exceptions, was placed under the Civil Service Commission, and the latter was given the power to base virtually all appointments upon open competitive tests which it administered. Certain parts of the service were, as already noted, later withdrawn from the commission's jurisdiction, some of them because they were genuinely unsuited to this method of recruitment, others because of various pressures which developed, some sinister and some otherwise, to give the system a little more flexibility. The inefficiency of the commission itself during part of this period did not help the cause of reform; appointments, which had to be preceded by advertisement and examination, were bound to be slow and the delay was frequently irritating; and many civil servants and politicians were not at heart in sympathy with so drastic a change. The net result was a steady reduction in the scope of the merit system as administered by the commission;

10/*Can. Statutes*, 7–8 Edw. VII, c. 15.
11/Life tenure was changed in 1918 to a ten-year term.

and although the latter repeatedly called the attention of Parliament to this shrinkage, the protests had up to the outbreak of the Second World War no apparent effect.

After both world wars a special influence helped undermine the potential quality of appointments, namely, a flood of ex-service men and women, who were (and still are in all competitions for positions open to persons outside the public service) given a preference over other candidates, if they are able to meet the minimum qualifications of the tests applied.[12] Thus from 1946 to 1952 out of 160,028 males appointed, 98,547 or 61.5 per cent were veterans.[13] Although in the early years many of these were extremely capable, a substantial proportion might not have qualified on ability alone, and the standards of entrance were thereby weakened. The fact that the number of veterans has diminished gives a misleading impression that this weakness is transitory. The tendency is for the quality of these candidates to deteriorate every year; for those veterans who have failed to make good in other walks of life turn as a last resort to the civil service where the law comes to their rescue and gives them an advantage over their competitors. The Civil Service Commission recommended in 1958 that the preference given to veterans be reduced to a single bonus of 5 per cent of attainable marks on any one examination, but the government rejected the recommendation;[14] current legislation continues a broad veterans' preference in entrances to the public service.

Canada has thus still a dual system rather than one based completely on merit. A part of the service is appointed on merit as ascertained by competitive examination, and even within that part the law permits a member of a minister's personal staff, under defined circumstances, to establish claims "without competition ... in priority to all other persons, to a position in the Public Service for which in the opinion of the Commission he is qualified."[15] Another part of the service is chosen on various grounds, such as the particular theories of administration being applied by the exempt portions of the public service; competition with the preference for veterans; or simply as recommended by cabinet ministers, by members of Parliament, and, most indefensible of all, by defeated candidates of the majority party, who, in the circumstances, cannot have a vestige of responsibility.[16] At its worst, a system such as this can resemble the description given in 1939 by an interested member of Parliament:

The chief handicap imposed on the Commission has been imposed by the hon. members of this House who are determined to force political patronage upon the civil

---

12/This preference for veterans goes back to the First World War. It is currently defined in *Can. Statutes*, 14–15–16 *Eliz.* II, c. 71, ss. 16–17.

13/Civil Service Commission, *Reports*, 1946–52.

14/*Personnel Administration in the Public Service*, pp. 19–20; *Can. H. of C. Debates*, March 7, 1961, p. 2760.

15/*Can. Statutes*, 14–15–16 Eliz. II, c. 71, s. 37.

16/"*Mr. Nicholson*: Is it customary for the Post Office Department to write to defeated government candidates in connection with recommending suitable postmasters? *Mr. Mulock* (Postmaster-General) : Yes, where revenue of the office is under $3,000." *Can. H. of C. Debates*, Nov. 27, 1940, p. 453.

service. One of the most astounding revelations made before that Committee was that which showed the growth of political patronage in connection with appointments to the civil service under the present administration.[17] We were presented with long lists containing thousands of positions which had been exempted from the provisions of the Civil Service Act, first by statute, again by the estimates, and again by orders-in-council. This has had a demoralizing result within the civil service, since we have attempted to merge two systems, a merit system under the Civil Service Commission, and a political patronage system, with all the conflict and confusion thus involved ...

The Civil Service Commission has made an honest attempt to establish the principle that appointments to the civil service of Canada should be available to every citizen of the Dominion, and that appointments should be secured by open competitive examination. There is no proper system of qualification, there is no suggestion of competition, when appointments are secretly made on the recommendation of a sitting member, a defeated candidate, or a political committee.[18]

Both the Civil Service Act of 1961 and the Public Service Employment Act of 1967 continued the double standard in public employment. Both followed extensive study, the first by the Civil Service Commission and a House of Commons committee, the second by the Royal Commission on Government Organization and a joint committee of the House and Senate. Both emphasized the merit principle, and the act of 1967 attempted to meet at least some of the reservations expressed by the Glassco commission about the elaborately careful application of the merit principle as it was then employed: "The merit system, in many of its current practices, frustrates the attainment of the principle; in its name many absurd procedures are tolerated; the system has become an end in itself ..." On the same page, the commission noted that "many Crown corporations and agencies have taken advantage of their autonomy to avoid patronage with as much success as where the Civil Service Commission is in control"; and the commission proposed that departments and agencies should be empowered to recruit their own personnel above a stated level.[19] The act of 1967 did not go nearly so far. Its objectives, as stated by Mr. E. J. Benson, who presented the bill to the Commons, were:

First, to preserve and extend the merit system of appointment and promotion under the control of an independent commission responsible only to parliament; second, to provide the commission with a flexible framework of law with which to operate, one well suited to the task of staffing a modern public service with qualified personnel; and third, to relieve the commission of any responsibility for the regulation of classification, pay and conditions of employment, or for the control of personnel policy, and to remove from the law any detailed provisions relating to these matters,

---

17/This blame was, in fact, properly to be apportioned between "the present administration" and the one which preceded it.

18/C. G. MacNeil, *Can. H. of C. Debates*, Feb. 21, 1939, pp. 1160–1.

19/*Report of the Royal Commission on Government Organization*, I, pp. 261–5. It is to be noted that the commission drew a distinction between the merit principle and the particular application it was then receiving. The commission's strictures on the former system do not necessarily apply today.

in order to make possible a genuine system of collective bargaining and provide in Treasury Board a focal point of central managerial authority.[20]

It is noteworthy that by 1966 the government no longer felt it necessary to assert that a primary objective of civil service reform was bilingualism, as had been done in 1961.[21] But still in 1967, as before, large sections of the public service were left outside the legal definition of "Public Service"; while, paradoxically, within its area of jurisdiction the Public Service Commission "retains exclusive jurisdiction in the recruitment, selection, promotion and transfer of employees in agencies which are subject to the Public Service Employment Act."[22] The commission may delegate these powers to departments, and extensive delegation is planned and begun: Public Service Commission offices in a number of centres have been closed, for example, and the hiring of clerical and allied workers has been delegated to branches of federal departments and agencies, working generally through Canada Manpower centres. Such delegation is permissive, and the commission retains final authority and can recall its own delegation.[23]

Undoubtedly one of the chief reasons for retaining the commission's final authority in its new role after 1967 was that the great majority of the members of Parliament give at least an open approval to the merit system and identify it with a commission with extensive powers; but they are not above using the little jobs as useful rewards for humble workers, and the occasional big job as a safe refuge for themselves when the skies become dark and threatening. Certainly the merit system, augmented by direct and indirect influences which have flowed from it, has brought about an enormous improvement since its adoption over fifty years ago. The public servants no longer feel that their positions rest on the shaky foundation of party patronage; they take a genuine pride in their profession; the standards of ability and performance have been immeasurably raised; and the service is attracting into its ranks some although not nearly enough of the best material in Canada. A major fault of the old merit system, as will be explained further below, was (in the words of an able critic) that it did not facilitate "the planned development of administrative talent."[24]

TENURE AND REMOVAL

Tenure in the civil service has always been at pleasure, but this has by long-established custom become tenure during good behaviour; an incompetent em-

20/*Can. H. of C. Debates*, May 31, 1966, pp. 5802–3.
21/The government's policy on bilingualism in the public service was enunciated in the House of Commons on April 6, 1966. See *ibid.*, April 6, 1966, pp. 3915–23.
22/R. H. Dowdell, "Personnel Administration in the Federal Public Service," in Willms and Kernaghan, *Public Administration in Canada*, p. 371.
23/*Can. Statutes*, 14–15–16 Eliz. II, c. 71, s. 6.
24/Callard, *Advanced Administrative Training in the Public Service*, Introduction (unpaged).

ployee, subject to an appeal, can now be released on a recommendation from his deputy minister to the Public Service Commission. Political activity has until recently been considered to be misbehaviour (particularly when it has favoured the wrong party) but the act of 1966 permits public servants to attend political meetings and contribute money to a candidate or party, and also to obtain leave of absence (without pay) to contest a candidacy or an election. Political activity is, none the less, still generally forbidden, and the great bulk of the public servants in recent years have carefully preserved their political neutrality and, with it, their security. But as is almost inevitable, dismissals have tended to follow those appointments made under the most flagrant conditions of patronage, notably in such minor positions as the small rural post offices. Thus from 1922 to 1938, for example, 2,385 postmasters were dismissed, an average of almost 150 a year, and in the great majority of cases political partisanship was the reason given. For the general election of 1968, with the new legislation in force, seventeen public servants requested permission to seek nomination as a candidate, sixteen received it, eight were actually nominated, and three were elected.[25] Prior to 1961, a civil servant dismissed for alleged political partisanship could defend himself under the terms of an order-in-council that was in force for many years.The Civil Service Act of 1961, and the Public Service Employment Act of 1967, both provided for statutory appeals or inquiries on the receipt of complaints from candidates about the political activity of public servants.

GRADATION

The elimination or, more accurately, the curbing of patronage has been the major move in the improvement of the administration, for little genuine progress could be expected as long as considerations other than merit were steadily undermining the quality of the public servants. But while this was an essential step it was only a preliminary one; as has been suggested above, the acquisition and subsequent encouragement of an efficient personnel demand positive as well as negative measures. Thus the precise nature of the examination which is given and the use to which this examination may be put are allied matters of first-rate consequence. The test should be more than a barrier to keep patronage out and to ward off the importunities of job hunters. It should endeavour to do more than select the best candidates from a list of mediocre applicants; it should also induce those with the best natural capacity and training to present themselves as candidates. Such a problem raises in turn two others no less vital: the way in which the personnel in each department are graded, and the system of promotion which is used to reward the deserving.

25/R. MacG. Dawson, "The Canadian Civil Service," *Canadian Journal of Economics and Political Science,* II, no. 3 (Aug. 1936), p. 290; *Can. H. of C. Debates,* March 11, 1938, pp. 1272–4; W. D. K. Kernaghan, ed., *Bureaucracy in Canadian Government* (Toronto, 1969), p. 103.

The plan of gradation or the relationship which the different positions and officials bear to one another will affect the place which the public servant occupies in his department, the position in which he starts at entrance, and the avenues of promotion which lie before him. In the early years the Canadian service had little organization of a formal kind; this was succeeded at the opening of the century by a tentative attempt (although with little conviction behind it) to copy in a small way the English scheme of gradation; and this in turn was supplanted in 1919 by a plan which derived its inspiration from the United States, a move which was accompanied by some conviction but little comprehension of the real issues involved.[26]

The outstanding characteristic of the English plan (which is itself under review) is that it has frankly acknowledged the necessity of bringing in new recruits for the administrative and clerical service at two chief levels – the lower group to be drawn from the high schools, the higher from university graduates. The keys to the plan are especial care taken in selecting members of the higher group and the effort made to provide them with subsequent training. The examinations which admit candidates to the upper level are extremely difficult and are set on a wide variety of academic subjects, so that the most brilliant of university graduates will not only be induced to compete but will be able to compete effectively in the fields they know best. The selection is thus made on evidence of exceptional natural ability rather than on that of exceptional knowledge relating to the positions which the candidates expect to fill; the theory being that if the examination does its part and secures men of genuine talents, they should have little difficulty in later acquiring the administrative skill and specialized qualifications which their departmental duties will require.[27] Indeed, their early careers in the service are planned in such a way that they will receive the best possible training to fit them for those future responsibilities. They are spared the drudgery of routine work and the consequent deadening of their powers of initiative, and they are so placed, encouraged, and instructed that they are soon able to provide a pool from which the higher administrative posts can be filled. It is quite possible, however, to rise by promotion from a lower horizontal or clerical group to the one above; but this is reserved for those who have been able to show capacity of a higher order.

The Canadian service, as stated before, was not entirely oblivious of the English system. On several occasions after 1900 it endeavoured to secure more widely educated recruits by admitting university graduates to a slightly preferred clerical grade; but the idea made little progress. The difference between the preferred and other grades was small, the examinations were never really difficult, little was done to give the new recruits work which would provide

26/Dawson, *The Civil Service of Canada*, pp. 154–65.
27/There are, of course, many positions where high technical or professional qualifications are essential. These are also recruited in Great Britain at a high level, but on the basis of the candidates' specialized knowledge and not their broad academic qualifications.

the proper training and advancement, and neither the extent of the scheme nor the time during which it was used was sufficient to provide a fair trial.

In 1919 Parliament, without any clear conception of the principles at stake, scrapped the existing plan of gradation, and introduced a new act, a new theory of gradation, and a new classification of positions. Any idea of admissions at two general levels was discarded, and its place was taken by a plan which, in theory at least, recruited all the staff through the lowest offices at the bottom and promoted them, step by step, to the top. Admission to any position – administrative, clerical, manual, technical, or professional – was to be through special competitive examinations or tests for each particular office. Though the Civil Service Act of 1961 permitted appointments from within the civil service without competition under some circumstances, the office-boy-to-president organization envisaged in 1919 remained the basis of the Canadian public service, and its influence is still felt.

None the less, under the Public Service Employment Act of 1967, which was influenced by the introduction of collective bargaining at least as much as by the Royal Commission on Government Organization, an extensive reappraisal of manpower utilization has been undertaken, which cannot yet be assessed. The service is now divided "into six broad occupational categories which are further divided into groups of occupationally similar jobs. For each major occupation or group of occupations, there is a program of development, recruitment, selection and placement."[28] It is too early to determine what degree of rigidity, if any, will be added to this approach by the demands of collective bargaining; but it is not irrelevant to note that the demands of collective bargaining have been known to introduce many kinds of rigidities into job classifications in other contexts. Whether or not this will be true of Canada's revised public service remains to be seen. Perhaps one should recall a critical description of the old civil service system by an able observer in 1958; it suggests that the new system, whatever it does, is unlikely to rival the old in some respects at least:

(i) Each job is classified and its appropriate skills and experience are set out in great and often unreasonable detail. Recruitment is then designed to fill that job.
(ii) Advancement is expected to take place when a job with higher status becomes vacant and the individual is promoted to it. This is the merit system in which each man is free to progress according to his own achievements and desires. It assumes that a group of eager and suitable applicants will normally be available to compete for any vacancy, and it overlooks the possibility that a good civil servant may be trapped in a job where his experience does not help qualify him for advancement.[29]

The former Civil Service Commission was from 1919 entrusted with the general oversight of the classification, a work which involved continuous super-

28/*Canada Year Book, 1968*, p. 155.
29/Callard, *Advanced Administrative Training in the Public Service*, Introduction (unpaged).

vision, rearrangement of positions, additions and subtractions, alterations in salary schedules, and so on. Originally there were 1,729 standard categories, which by 1939 had increased to about 2,400, and by 1946 to about 3,700; by 1960, as a result of rigorous redefining, the total was back down to 1,800, but it worked its way back to 2,100 by 1965. As a result of the changes of 1967, the Treasury Board was made responsible for the general management of the public service, including classification of positions, and to prevent collective bargaining from becoming chaotic a massive simplificaton of the classification system was effected (seven hundred basic classes, for example, being reduced to about seventy). The change was long overdue: the old system, contained in a *Schedule*, was a bewildering document for the uninitiated, for each variation in a position's function or place in the hierarchy had tended to create a new position under a new name. At one time there were seventeen classes of lighthouse keepers; and the variety of clerks was almost incalculable: clerks, grade one; clerks, grade two; clerks, grade three; clerks, grade four; principal clerks, head clerks, chief clerks, etc. The effect of this on the public service was once described by a royal commission:

It is our considered opinion that certain of the fundamental difficulties and weaknesses of the civil service today are due to the persistent attempt to work within the confines of this rigid and complex system of classification ...
At the gateway to the service recruitment is conducted by rating applicants on the basis of some specialized knowledge or some particular experience rather than on the basis of general intelligence and capacity. This practice has undoubtedly contributed to the failure to obtain sufficient recruits to supply the ranks out of which administrators of high calibre may be drawn. In particular it has militated against the recruitment of young men and women of capacity from those parts of the country where the educational system is not directed towards specialized types of training.
Inside the service, the classification system, through lack of flexibility, has hindered the adequate development and best utilization of high grade personnel ... The career of a Canadian civil servant is bestrewn with a vast number of closely spaced blocks. The result is that many persons of ability and promise are lost in blind alleys or emerge from them too late in life ...
The truth is, that the Canadian civil service as presently organized and managed does not provide its own leadership ... There are not enough men of high quality and training in senior and intermediate administrative positions.[30]

The abused classification was not entirely without merit. Classification is itself "an essential ingredient of a sound merit system"[31] on the Canadian model. Its principle of special tests for each individual position, speaking generally, has been quite proper and useful when applied to those people who require some special aptitude or training, such as stenographers, chemists,

30/Report on Administrative Classifications in the Public Service (1946), pp. 13–15. See also Callard, *Advanced Administrative Training in the Public Service.*
31/*Personnel Administration in the Public Service*, p. 12.

accountants, librarians, statisticians, and very many others. It has also been reasonably successful in equalizing similar positions throughout the service, in stopping patronage in those offices under its control, and in checking indiscriminate promotions and increases in salary. But the price paid for some of these advantages has been high, and many of them could have been obtained through other methods which would have neither the same rigidities nor the same limitations. In the main, the influence of the detailed classification was to restrict and hamper and not to invigorate and enrich; it concentrated on the problem of how to block undesirable influences, while paying insufficient attention to the encouragement of those desirable qualities in the civil servant which are no less essential to his efficiency. The assignment to the Treasury Board of "personnel management in the public service, including the determination of terms and conditions of employment of persons employed therein," coupled with the major changes introduced by the Public Service Employment Act and the Public Service Staff Relations Act of 1967, is expected to eliminate many of the problems of the old *Classification Schedule*.

PROMOTION

The Board of Examiners created in 1882 began the practice of setting promotion examinations to serve as a minimum requirement for promotions made by the minister. Its successor, the Civil Service Commission, always had a part in weighing and testing promotion qualifications; and the Public Service Commission today may impose such tests as it deems proper and, acting on these other data, make the promotions. Whether or not this is a proper function to be vested in the commission, when personnel management is the statutory responsibility of the Treasury Board, is at least arguable, but it is justified on the ground that promotions, like entrance requirements, must be protected against political influences and favouritism. Such a danger, however, is largely imaginary under a reformed service; if sinister influences cannot secure appointments, they will have little reason to try to affect the subsequent careers of those who have obtained their positions by independent means. Moreover, the qualities which should determine promotions are not always examinable and can best be gauged by those who are in daily contact with the work of the staff. Nevertheless, the commission can play a useful part. It can guard against favouritism and assure that all candidates will be considered; enforce standards and encourage transfers from one department to another; administer a system of appeals, which is designed not only to check injustice but also to demonstrate to the staff that every care is being taken to give the promotion to the candidate who deserves it. If the commission's powers of delegation are widely and successfully used, vesting promotion in the commission may in the event involve transferring the use of the relevant powers to the individual departments and agencies.

STAFF RELATIONS

The former Civil Service Commission for several years showed a growing interest in staff relations, and two major developments stemmed from this. The rôle of the departmental personnel officer, which began in the immediate post-war period, evolved to the place where he became more or less standard equipment in the departments. And the commission paid increasing attention to the civil servants' own organizations, such as the Civil Service Federation and the Civil Service Association of Canada (amalgamated in 1966 into the Public Service Alliance of Canada), and the Professional Institute of the Public Service of Canada. The logical outcome of these developments, spurred on by repeated requests from staff associations, and the undeniable fact that many employees in the public service (such as in the Canadian National Railways) were already members of certified unions, was collective bargaining. The Civil Service Act of 1961 provided for consultation with staff associations; the Public Service Staff Relations Act of 1966 established full collective bargaining.[32]

Under the legislation, the Treasury Board is designated as the government's agent for purposes of negotiation, and a Public Service Staff Relations Board, with a chairman and vice-chairman removable only upon an address of the Senate and House of Commons, has comprehensive powers to determine bargaining units of employees, certify their bargaining agents, and generally facilitate negotiations between the government and its employees. A Public Service Arbitration Tribunal, and Conciliation Boards, to perform the usual acts of such bodies when appropriate, are provided for, and a grievance procedure is established. The right of public employees to strike is explicitly recognized, though the largest unions have in fact elected to forego the right to strike in favour of arbitration. The early years of the Public Service Staff Relations Act were remarkably similar to those of other labour legislation: complaints of tardy and reluctant negotiation were heard, and both legal and wildcat strikes were enjoyed.

TREASURY CONTROL

An interesting development of recent years has been the growing intervention of the Treasury Board[33] in matters affecting the civil service proper, and other parts of the public service too. The cabinet has, of course, always exercised the power given it by the public service acts of formally approving certain of the decisions and regulations of the commission; but for many years this remained almost entirely nominal control. About 1932, however, as a result of

32/*Can. Statutes*, 14–15–16 Eliz. II, c. 72.
33/*Supra*, pp. 221–2.

the depression, the cabinet (through the Treasury Board) began to intervene in order to effect a reduction in the size and cost of the service; and the advent of the war gave the board a further opportunity to issue a number of directives which in effect imposed additional limitations on the Civil Service Commission's authority. A substantial degree of Treasury control was thus read into a statute and applied to an organization, both of which were originally designed for quite different circumstances, and this unanticipated and unnatural practice for years led to much confusion and dissatisfaction with the administration of the service.

The distribution of authority between the former commission and the Treasury Board was, indeed, far from clear. The Financial Administration Act of 1951 unequivocally listed among the Treasury Board's responsibilities "establishments, the terms and conditions of employment of persons in the public service, and general administrative policy in the public service."[34] The Civil Service Commission, under the Civil Service Acts of 1918 and 1961, had complete control over appointments and promotions in all parts of the service under its jurisdiction. Prior to 1962, however, the commission, before effecting any changes in departmental organization, had first to submit its proposals to the Governor-in-Council (in effect, the Treasury Board) and the latter was then free to take whatever action it chose. In 1962 the commission's powers in departmental organization were reduced to a purely advisory rôle, the primary initiative being given to individual deputy heads of departments, and final authority to the Governor-in-Council. The respective rôles of commission and Treasury Board were thereby considerably clarified. the commission provided the manpower for establishments devised on executive authority. Similarly with the pay of civil servants, the commission made recommendations on remuneration and the Governor-in-Council, "after the Commission [had] had an opportunity of considering the matter and after considering any recommendations made by the Commission," established the rates.

The considerable powers of the Treasury Board over the public service were clarified beyond any doubt in amendments made to the Financial Administration Act in 1966-7:

5. The Treasury Board may act for the Queen's Privy Council for Canada on all matters relating to
(a) general administrative policy in the public service;
(b) the organization of the public service or any portion thereof, and the determination and control of establishments therein;
(c) financial management, including estimates, expenditures, financial commitments, accounts, charges for services, rentals, licences, leases, revenues from the disposition of property, and procedures by which departments manage, record and account for revenues received or receivable from any source whatever;
(d) the review of annual and longer term expenditure plans and programs of the

---

34/*Rev. Stat. Can.*, 1952, c. 116, s. 5 (1).

various departments of Government, and the determination of priorities with respect thereto;

(e) personnel management in the public service, including the determination of terms and conditions of employment of persons employed therein; and

(f) such other matters as may be referred to it by the Governor in Council.

The Treasury Board is also authorized to exercise major powers of the Governor-in-Council under several statutes.

Many other considerations enter directly and indirectly into the creation and maintenance of an efficient civil service, but these can be only suggested here. The salary paid, superannuation, the security of the office, the general amenities of the service, the causes of removal, and similar matters will often materially affect the quality of an official's work and may prove decisive in inducing a good man to leave or remain in government employment. Inevitably comparisons will be made with similar positions in the business and professional world. In many respects the service will suffer by such comparison: it cannot, for example, offer salaries which will equal those available elsewhere for top executives. But in other ways it can more than hold its own, for the scale of operations is large and they are usually of such a nature as to appeal to those with imagination and ambition. The conviction that the public servants are doing the big things in the nation which really matter, that their influence on the formation of the national policies is far from inconsiderable, that they have an intimate knowledge of what really happens in government circles to a degree that no one else in the country can hope to rival – these are the kind of intangible and elusive influences which exercise a subtle appeal over the minds and emotions of men and will materially affect an official's interest, his enthusiasm, and his devotion to his work. Mention has been made above of the extremely useful function of the minister in stirring up the mind of the public servant and in giving him a more accurate sense of proportion. Yet the chief reliance for these things should not be placed on the minister, but on the official himself; and this leads back once again to the fundamental requirements already discussed. Efficient administration depends on the recruitment of public servants of first-rate ability and the creation of an environment which will demand their utmost in initiative, resourcefulness, and conscientious devotion to the welfare of the state.

14 Administrative powers

IT IS SAFE TO ASSERT that a book on Canadian government written thirty or so years ago would not have contained a chapter on administrative powers. Such powers existed, of course, at that time, but they presented no serious problem. Acts of Parliament gave powers in varying degrees to ministers of the Crown, and through them to public servants, and occasionally administrative powers were conferred on members of a specially constituted board; but except for the last expedient (which was conceded to be exceptional) the statutes defined very specifically the powers of the administration. The rule of law[1] was based on the firm belief that official discretions were uncertain and by their very nature uncontrollable and evil; "wherever there is discretion," said Dicey, "there is room for arbitrariness,"[2] and arbitrariness was to be abhorred by a free people. Thus a legal system which cherished freedom would suppress official discretions by being sufficiently explicit in its grants of power that no discretionary acts and decisions of any consequence remained. The rules laid down by the law would be applied by the courts, and the actions of the officials would thereby be kept in careful conformity with the clearly indicated intentions of Parliament. Abuse of administrative powers was therefore carefully prevented by the courts, and their proper exercise was also ensured by the responsibility of ministers to Parliament for all acts of their civil servants. Here and there, as indicated above, occasional boards had been created to perform some special function, and these had been given a fairly independent position and had been granted discretionary powers within a specified area; but resort to this unusual device simply emphasized the exceptional nature of their functions and set them apart from the ordinary administrative officials.

Some mention has already been made of the tremendous changes which have taken place in comparatively recent times in the comprehensive interests and functions of government. The negative laissez-faire state has been more

1/*Supra*, pp. 73–4.
2/*The Law of the Constitution*, p. 184.

and more transformed into the positive state which is continually recognizing a greater and greater responsibility for the welfare of its citizens. The government is becoming yearly more assertive and its activities more widespread; it has long since ceased to regard as its sole or even its chief function the enunciation of general rules of conduct and the assigning of punishments for their breach, and it is quite prepared to direct and drive people into righteousness; it has taken the position that it will not only punish deviations from its rules, but it will endeavour in many areas of social life to prevent such deviations taking place on any significant scale. The extreme application of this principle occurred during the Second World War and the succeeding period of emergency,[3] when virtually every activity of the citizen came to a greater or less degree under the direction of the state; and there is little or no reason to believe that government participation in the life of the citizen will ever return to the level it was in 1939. The chief uncertainty for the future is the point at which this participation will stop.

The outstanding manifestations of this vigorous government activity (leaving aside those directly concerned with the war) have occurred in the economic and social fields. The constant trend has been and continues to be from merely police functions, controlling external conditions of public order, to what are often known as "service functions" – the promotion by positive measures of such things as public health, housing, continuity of employment, higher standards of living, conservation, price stability, etc. In these latter fields it is frequently not restraint, but active compliance with positive commands which is being sought. The role of the public servant undergoes a change in quality and becomes both more difficult and more challenging, with corresponding demands on his ability and resourcefulness. He is bound to enter to a far greater degree into the very lives of the people: he issues orders and regulations; he decides disputes; he refuses one application, and accepts the next. He must be prepared not only to discharge narrow administrative functions but to provide constructive and far-reaching solutions as well; he must plan and help initiate (through his minister, if he is in an ordinary department, and on his own whether he is or not) policies which he has developed out of his own experience and observation.[4] While his success will in large measure be derived from his specialized skill and his familiarity with his work, it will also rest upon a breadth as well as a depth of knowledge, a grasp of the main purposes of his endeavour, and an appreciation of their social implications. Much of this work will force the higher officials to rely upon their own discretion and to substitute a careful and to a substantial degree an independent judgment on the circum-

3/According to one observer, judicial interpretation of the National Emergency Transitional Powers Act of 1945 gave the Dominion government greater authority than the War Measures Act. See D. A. MacGibbon, "The Nolan Case," in Hodgetts and Corbett, *Canadian Public Administration*, p. 501.
4/Sir Josiah Stamp, "The Administrator and a Planned Society," *Public Administration*, Jan. 1938, pp. 4–11.

stances of particular cases for the older conscientious adherence to rigid and invariable rules and forms. Initiative and a willingness to make important decisions have not been unknown qualities in civil servants in the past; but the whole tendency today is to multiply the number of occasions when these become necessary. The mere volume of decisions alone makes it impossible to consult political superiors on many matters, and when to this is added a prerequisite of intimate knowledge and experience, a minister's participation, if any, tends to be largely confined to the settlement of questions of policy and those of outstanding importance. And as already noted in preceding chapters, a large portion of the public service is in any event outside direct ministerial control. Public corporations are subject to "at least four types of ministerial control ... appointment and dismissal of members of corporate boards, issuance of ministerial directives, approval or veto of certain corporate actions, and – largely as a supplement to the other powers – requiring information."[5] Not all public corporations are subject to all four of these controls, and all four together are not a substitute for the kind of jurisdiction which a minister exercises over his department; nevertheless, it is the opinion of a discerning critic that Canadian public corporations "do not possess sufficient autonomy to endanger a system of ministerial responsibility."[6]

The preceding pages have discussed the effect which the sheer weight and complexity of state activity have had on the public service, and they have indicated how these have added to its stature as an important part of the working government. This, however, is but one side of a comprehensive shifting of power which has been occasioned by the same fundamental factors; for some of these gains in executive and administrative control have been made at the expense of Parliament and some at the expense of the judiciary. Parliament discovered that it could not take over all the additional burdens which fell to its lot under this new conception of state activity, and the judiciary was also unable to bring its functions into perfect harmony with the new demands which were made upon it. Parliament had neither the time nor the special knowledge to enact adequate legislation on many of these complex topics, nor, indeed, could such legislation always be drafted in sufficient detail or be made flexible enough to cover the widely varying conditions which it encountered. The courts, for their part, if given extensive powers of deciding disputes arising out of this type of legislation, would not only be inundated with cases, but they would also lack the specialized knowledge which is necessary to do the work acceptably, and there would be little assurance that they would approach their task with that sympathy and understanding which is an indispensable part of proper administration in some of these newer fields. The few examples which follow will illustrate in greater detail the nature of these difficulties. Parliament has thus been compelled to abandon any desire it might have had to state

5/Musolf, *Public Ownership and Accountability*, pp. 42–3.
6/*Ibid.*, p. 68.

detailed statutory plans in precise language. It has outlined its purposes in sweeping terms and provided for their elaboration and application through the appropriate department or board, and in many cases has given only a very limited power of supervision to the courts.[7] The powers thus delegated by statute to the administration are of two broad types:

(1) powers to enact subordinate legislation by order-in-council or departmental regulation;

(2) powers to render judicial or quasi-judicial decisions in disputes arising on administrative questions with little or no opportunity of appeal to the courts.

In both types, unlike in the proceedings of Parliament and the courts, "administrative secrecy" can quickly become a problem.[8]

DELEGATED LEGISLATIVE POWERS

An earlier chapter has indicated[9] how the Canadian Parliament has delegated to the cabinet what is in effect the power to enact subsidiary legislation within the limits of the enabling statutes, and this legislative power may also be given to an individual department or to a board or commission. Delegations of both kinds are extremely common. As early as 1933, for example, at least one-half of the 225 public acts of the dominion in force gave power to the executive to legislate by order-in-council or departmental regulation,[10] and the tendency has been for this proportion to increase rather than diminish. Many statutes do no more than permit the addition of technical details, although in many cases this is covered by a vague phrase authorizing such regulations "as may be deemed necessary for giving full effect to the provisions of this Act." Other statutes, however, go much further than mere amplification. Some give the executive the power to vary the provisions or extend the scope of the act in an important respect; some purport to give the Governor-in-Council power to declare the true meaning of the act in case of doubt; while the Relief Act of 1931 gave the Governor-in-Council a blanket power "to make all such orders and regulations as may be deemed necessary or desirable for relieving distress,

7/See John Willis, "The Administrator as Judge: The Citizen's Right to an Impartial Tribunal," in Hodgetts and Corbett, *Canadian Public Administration*, pp. 514–24; Willms and Kernaghan, *Public Administration in Canada*, chap. 10, "Administrative Responsibility."
8/See Donald C. Rowat, "The Problems of Administrative Secrecy," in Willms and Kernaghan, *Public Administration in Canada*, pp. 455–66.
9/*Supra*, pp. 212–13.
10/J. A. Corry, "Administrative Law in Canada," *Proceedings, Canadian Political Science Association, 1933*, p. 196. In Ontario in 1937 no less than 271 out of 399 acts made provision for supplementary legislation by various authorities. J. Finkelman, "The Making, Approval, and Publication of Delegated Legislation in Ontario," in Willis, *Canadian Boards at Work*, p. 172.

providing employment and, within the competence of Parliament, maintaining peace, order and good government throughout Canada."[11] The Immigration Act of 1952 gave the Governor-in-Council power to prohibit or limit the admission of persons to Canada by reason of (among other things), "peculiar customs, habit, modes of life or methods of holding property," and "probable inability to become readily assimilated or to assume the duties and responsibilities of Canadian citizenship within a reasonable time after their admission."[12]

The most extreme example of such a delegation of subsidiary legislative power was furnished during and after the Second World War. The War Measures Act[13] gave authority to the Governor-in-Council to take such orders and regulations as it "may deem necessary or advisable for the security, defence, peace, order and welfare of Canada" so long as the war emergency should continue – a grant of power so sweeping that it conveyed to the Governor-in-Council most of the enormous war-time emergency powers made available to the Dominion Parliament under the "peace, order, and good government" clause of the British North America Act. With this went the authority to redelegate powers, including the power of delegation itself:

Parliament may entrust to the Governor-in-Council the power to delegate to an administrative body the power to delegate to a controller the power to issue a directive having the force of law. Laws may now emerge typewritten on letterheads signed by John Smith, of which only a carbon copy is kept on file. This is adaptation with a vengeance. Let it no longer be said that totalitarian regimes can act more expeditiously and efficiently than democracies. And though there are dangers in this situation let it not be said either that this is no different from totalitarianism. All such powers stem from Parliament, in whose jurisdiction the control ultimately rests. What Parliament gave, Parliament can take away. We have retained our ultimate parliamentary control over the administration; what we have not done is to develop administrative tribunals and a body of administrative law adequate to control the exercise of the new state powers.[14]

The clear justification for so comprehensive a delegation was of course the national safety, but the degree to which this would be warranted in the period following the cessation of hostilities is naturally much more debatable. In December 1945 Parliament passed the National Emergency Transitional Powers Act,[15] which declared that a condition of emergency still existed (and hence the residual power of the Dominion Parliament was, in its opinion, still dominant over the provincial powers stated in section 92 of the British North America Act); that very substantial powers were therefore by this act delegated anew to the Governor-in-Council; and that all existing orders and regulations

11/Corry, "Administrative Law in Canada," pp. 196–7, 202; *Can. Statutes*, 21–22 Geo. v, c. 58, s. 4.

12/*Can. Statutes*, 1 Eliz. II, c. 42, s. 61(g).

13/*Rev. Stat. Can.* (1952), c. 288.

14/F. R. Scott, "Constitutional Adaptations to Changing Functions of Government," *Canadian Journal of Economics and Political Science*, XI, no. 3 (Aug. 1945), p. 334.

15/*Can. Statutes*, 9–10 Geo. VI, c. 25.

under the War Measures Act could, at the order of the Governor-in-Council, be continued in full force. In a few months' time it was discovered that one of these orders-in-council, which had been passed secretly on October 6, 1945 (and was continued under the powers given by the Emergency Transitional Powers Act), gave the minister of Justice authority to issue an order to interrogate and detain "in such place and under such conditions as he may from time to time determine" any person who might in his opinion be likely to communicate secret information to an agent of a foreign power or act in any manner prejudicial to the public safety. This furnished the authority for the arrest, interrogation, and detention of suspects (approximately half of whom were subsequently acquitted in the courts) which characterized the spy investigation of 1946. The arbitrary character of this piece of subsidiary legislation and the degree to which it abrogated some of the most cherished rights of the citizen afford the best illustration of how extreme was the authority which had been delegated by Parliament to the government and how grave are the dangers implicit in such a wholesale delegation. The emergency powers legislation of the post-war period was not permitted to expire until 1954.

While few will question the basic necessity for frequent delegations by Parliament of subsidiary legislative power, certain precautions should be taken in order to provide substantial protection against the worst of the dangers which may arise in practice. The most obvious safeguard is for Parliament to avoid the delegation of vague comprehensive legislative powers for an uncertain period. In times of national danger, grants of this sweeping nature are admittedly necessary, but they should be most jealously reserved for such extraordinary occasions. The methods used in Canada in the spy investigation in 1946 were unfortunate, but the incident had at least a most wholesome effect, for Parliament weighed out the next delegations for the transitional period with grudging suspicion. No delegation of legislative powers should be made unless it is clearly necessary for the purpose contemplated, and, when made, it should specify in careful detail the extent of the delegation.[16] Again, special provision should be made for parliamentary scrutiny of subordinate legislation, either by having it tabled in the House or by making parliamentary approval necessary for its permanent validity. Finally, it is highly desirable that the departments concerned should be compelled to publish their rules and orders and make them readily available to the public within a reasonable time. A long step was taken to realize two of these objects by the passage of the Regulations Act of 1950,[17] which made compulsory the publication and tabling of all instruments made under the delegated legislative powers.[18] But the opportunities for making parliamentary review and criticism effective, once the tabling has taken

16/Corry, "Administrative Law in Canada," pp. 196–8.
17/*Can. Statutes*, 14 Geo. VI, c. 50.
18/Exceptions of certain categories may be made by the Governor-in-Council, but if so, such categories must be published and tabled. See L. S. St Laurent, *Can. H. of C. Debates*, May 31, June 12, 1950, pp. 3039–40, 3497–501.

place, are not yet adequate, and depend in large measure on the co-operation of the government.[19]

DELEGATED JUDICIAL AND QUASI-JUDICIAL POWERS

Acts of Parliament may also delegate to the executive or other authority nominated by the executive, powers which either are purely judicial in their nature or at least bear a strong resemblance to these and are for that reason known as quasi-judicial. The distinction between the two is not at first glance apparent. In a formal dispute at which contesting parties present their cases, facts will be ascertained through the examination of evidence and questions of law determined by the submission of legal arguments. If the decision which follows is rendered on the facts in accordance with the law, it is said to be a judicial one. If, however, the presiding officer, having ascertained the facts, is not legally obliged to give a decision solely in accordance with the law, the decision is quasi-judicial. The distinction rests therefore upon the absence or presence of a discretionary power, whether the official making the decision is bound to follow an explicit route mapped out by the law once the facts are ascertained or whether he is free to give weight to other factors, such as considerations of public policy. Both judicial and quasi-judicial powers may be delegated to a minister, to a public servant, or to an independent body such as a board or commission.[20]

The power which is delegated to an administrative body such as the Canadian Pension Commission is almost, if not entirely, a judicial one. The commission has the final determination of the pension rights of war veterans, and these are determined by the applicability of the statute and the rules of the commission to the ascertained disabilities of the applicants. Similarly a part of the work of the Canadian Transport Commission is judicial; for it will hear disputes between a railway and its customers (for example) and decide on the facts in accordance with rules laid down by Parliament. Certain of its decisions will, however, lean heavily towards the quasi-judicial, such as, for example, rulings concerning discrimination by the railways in favour of one shipper as against others, for while some of these matters may be statutory, many others are not

19/J. R. Mallory, "Delegated Legislation in Canada," *Canadian Journal of Economics and Political Science,* XIX, no. 4 (Nov. 1953), pp. 463–7. Parliamentary review of Crown corporations is discussed in Musolf, *Public Ownership and Accountability,* pp. 102–45; Ward, *The Public Purse,* pp. 214–16. See also John E. Kersell, *Parliamentary Supervision of Delegated Legislation* (London, 1960); Willms and Kernaghan, *Public Administration in Canada.*

20/See Report of Committee on Ministers' Powers (Great Britain), *Parliamentary Papers* (1932), Cmd. 4060, pp. 73–5. Some writers, however, have insisted that the line between judicial and quasi-judicial powers is so blurred that the distinction becomes quite meaningless. See Jennings, *The Law and the Constitution,* pp. 263–84. According to this conception, there are judicial powers and legislative powers – and there's an end on't.

so defined or are defined in such vague terms that they really rest on general principles gradually worked out by the experience of the commission. To this may be added the interesting but somewhat confusing statement that some of the commission's functions may even be considered legislative, for when it issues orders on particular cases it is in effect legislating by a series of special enactments.[21] This is most clearly seen in its decisions on rates; for these have not only a temporary effect, but become rules which are to be observed for the future. The truth is that a number of these administrative bodies exercise functions which cannot be entirely confined in one category, and what may appear at first glance to be a fairly simple power will be found on analysis to fall within two or more classifications.

The more common delegation is the delegation of quasi-judicial functions which involve the exercise of official discretion. This allows the administration of a statute to be tied in effectively with its interpretation, and gives a flexibility and quick adaptability to the administration which most certainly could not be achieved without some such device – a very real need when dealing with such things as dumping duties, fair market values, and variable tariffs, which occurred in the 1930s, or with the enormous number of possible methods of evading the high taxes which became a serious administrative problem during the Second World War. Similarly, in all statutes dealing with social and economic regulation the clear impossibility of providing for all eventualities by rigid enactment or regulation inevitably places large discretionary powers in the hands of the officials in charge. The war experience with its host of economic and industrial controls is an excellent illustration of the absolute necessity of multiform official discretions in a complex regimented society.

The advantages of this delegation of discretionary powers have already been anticipated in part. The statutes and regulations thereby acquire a valuable and even, as suggested above, an indispensable flexibility without which they would involve too great a tax on even the admitted versatility of the judiciary. The proceedings (and this is particularly true for those through which many of the social service payments are determined) cannot be allowed to become expensive nor should a settlement be allowed to be unduly delayed, and both these goals are achieved more surely through administrative rather than judicial channels.

In the majority of these delegations of discretionary powers, the decision of the administrative officials (and, through them, of the minister, if there is one responsible) is final; that is, there is no appeal allowed to the courts. Such an appeal would, indeed, largely vitiate the whole purpose of the delegation, which is designed to substitute for judicial rigidity of interpretation the flexibility of an administrative discretionary determination. It would also largely destroy the merits of the device as indicated in the last paragraph. Where the questions decided are, however, judicial in nature and involve pure questions of law an

21/Corry and Hodgetts, *Democratic Government and Politics*, pp. 529–31.

appeal to the courts may well be permitted; and in those cases involving the exercise of discretionary powers where the decision turns on a question of public policy, an administrative appeal court may be used to provide greater consistency and give reassuring evidence of impartiality.

There are, of course, serious risks involved in this erection of barriers between the citizen and the courts of justice, and few can contemplate with equanimity any substantial interference with so fundamental a constitutional principle as the rule of law. For while discretionary power does not necessarily result in arbitrary power in the sinister sense (the officials being subject to a number of very potent restraints of various kinds[22]), it does introduce the possibility of ill-controlled authority; it will always raise a strong suspicion of abuse; and on many occasions the inability of the injured party to appeal to the courts cannot fail to convert suspicions into apparent certainties. The mere willingness of a cabinet minister to accept political responsibility for administrative decisions is in the vast majority of cases not nearly as real or as effective a safeguard as that which a review of the courts would provide.

The prevention of appeals from administrative decisions to the courts, however, does not mean that the courts are completely excluded from all scrutiny of the dispute. The exact nature of the power of the official who has acted in the matter is, as suggested above, a proper subject for judicial review; and no official (minister or public servant) can wield any more or any different power than has been conferred on him by statute, nor can he exercise powers not conferred on him. In short, the courts always stand ready to name the bounds of delegated power and to see that those bounds are at all times respected; and they also possess a general authority to review administrative procedure to ensure that it is fair and does not violate the canons of "natural justice."[23] "Generally speaking," one authority has noted, "while the courts will not review the substance of the deciding authorities' decision, they will review the process whereby the decision is arrived at."[24]

Extreme illustrations of this grant of discretionary powers were provided by the terms of the Canadian Income War Tax Act and the Excess Profits Tax Act, 1940, which are not yet too old to serve as salutary examples. These statutes, in a praiseworthy endeavour to prevent tax evasion on a large scale and particularly the manipulation of accounts and expenditures by business concerns, gave to the minister of National Revenue enormous latitude in the interpretation of the law, in the making of regulations, and in the allowance or disallowance of certain expenditures as tax deductions. Charges for business repairs, for depreciation, for replacement of machinery, for advertising, for salaries, could be disallowed for taxation purposes by the minister (which, in practice, meant the public servant) if they did not comply with a certain stand-

22/See Willis, *Canadian Boards at Work*, pp. 65–72.
23/See Report of Committee on Ministers' Powers, pp. 75–80.
24/Willis, "The Administrator as Judge," p. 522. See H. J. Lawford, "Appeals against Administrative Decisions: The Function of Judicial Review," in Willms and Kernaghan, *Public Administration in Canada*, pp. 424–30.

ard – only too frequently a vague or even unascertainable standard – set up by the department. Ninety-five sections of the Income War Tax Act gave the minister discretionary power; twenty-eight sections of the Excess Profits Tax Act gave him other discretions. These were phrased in many ways: by references to "the opinion of the Minister"; to cases where the minister "has power to determine"; to others where a matter is "in the Minister's discretion," and so forth.[25]

The most disturbing aspect of the exercise of these wide discretionary powers was naturally the inability of those most seriously affected to take the decisions to court on appeal. No appeal lies to the court against the exercise of the minister's discretion if legally used; "the Court has no right to examine into or criticize the reasons that led the Minister to his opinion or question their adequacy or sufficiency; it is not for the Court to lay down the considerations that should govern the Minister's discretionary determination; Parliament requires the Minister's opinion, not that of the Court ... It is the Minister's reason, not that of the Court, that Parliament relies upon, and 'no other tribunal can substitute its standard of sufficient reason or its opinion or belief for his.' "[26]

The court may, however, have a right under the statute to intervene and examine the grounds on which the discretionary decision was *based* in order to satisfy itself as to their adequacy. Thus the minister, while he is the only judge of the wisdom or propriety of his decision, does not exercise a purely arbitrary power, but a discretionary one; and underlying the exercise of that discretion is the assumption that the minister possesses sufficient material on which a judgment can be intelligently formed. To quote from an important decision of the Privy Council:

The section makes the Minister the sole judge of the fact of reasonableness or normalcy and the Court is not at liberty to substitute its own opinion for his. But the power given to the Minister is not an arbitrary one to be exercised according to his fancy. To quote the language of Lord Halsbury in *Sharp* v. *Wakefield* (1891) A. C. 173 at page 179 he must act "according to the rules of reason and justice, not according to private opinion; according to law and not humour. It is to be not arbitrary, vague and fanciful, but legal and regular" ... The Court is ... always entitled to examine the facts which are shown by evidence to have been before the Minister when he made his determination. If these facts are in the opinion of the Court insufficient in law to support it the determination cannot stand ... The Court is not at liberty to overrule [the determination] merely because it would itself on those facts have come to a different conclusion ... As in the case of any other judge of fact there must be material sufficient in law to support his decision.[27]

25/See *Proceedings of the Special Committee on the Income War Tax Act and the Excess Profits Tax Act*, 1940, Senate of Canada (1945, 1946).

26/Mr Justice Thorson in *Pure Spring Co.* v. *Minister of National Revenue*, [1946] Ex. C.R. 471, at pp. 502–3.

27/*Minister of National Revenue* v. *Wrights' Canadian Ropes*, C.T.C. (1947), 1, at pp. 14–15. The Privy Council held that the minister had not shown possession of the necessary material on which a decision such as that given by him could have been reasonably formed, and the decision (an assessment for taxation) was therefore set aside by the court.

In 1946 a Special Committee of the Senate recommended the establishment of an independent Board of Tax Appeals which would be empowered to hear appeals in law or fact from the exercise of administrative or ministerial discretionary powers, the levying of assessments, or the imposition of penalties. Parliament, however, did not accept this recommendation in its entirety. It set up an Income Tax Appeal Board which has power to review the decisions of income tax officials in law and fact; but the board has no authority to receive appeals regarding the use of their discretionary powers, which was the most serious charge laid against the system.[28] The statute provides, however, for a second board which may advise the minister on the use of "specified" discretionary powers; but its opinion is to be purely advisory and therefore need not be followed. This second board was never set up, chiefly because later amendments to the Income Tax Act eliminated so many of the ministerial discretions that the need for such a body in large measure disappeared.

The remedy for the dangers and abuses of delegated judicial and quasi-judicial powers, as for those of delegated legislative powers, is to be sought not in abolition, but rather in the exercise of discrimination in the manner and extent of the delegation and in the erection of proper safeguards against the more common evils. Some discretionary authority is exercised by every public servant, a very great deal of discretionary authority is exercised by an increasing number, and the primary endeavour should be to keep this delegation in strict accordance with the nature of the work which is to be performed. The powers, if given on any considerable scale, should be parcelled out to officials with fastidious care, and the operation of the laws which make the grant should be kept continually under the jealous eye of Parliament. A delegation of power under one statute and to one department will not in itself justify a similar delegation to another, and the onus of proof as to its necessity should rest heavily upon the shoulders of those who ask for it.

Such discrimination would naturally start with a separation (whenever this is feasible) between judicial and quasi-judicial functions, the former being exercised by the courts of law or by an independent tribunal.[29] There is some reason to suppose that further distinctions or gradations of function would also be possible, and that delegation to individual departmental officials might be superseded to a greater degree by delegation to independent bodies or even departmental boards. The changes mentioned above in regard to Canadian tax appeals constituted a practical application of this principle. Other safeguards which should always be maintained, whether the powers being exercised are judicial or quasi-judicial, are that all procedures should be kept as simple, direct, and inexpensive as possible; that decisions, when given, should be communicated to the interested parties with reasoned statements attached; that such parties

28/The board since 1958 has been called Tax Appeal Board. See Willis, "The Administrator as Judge," pp. 517–18; Can. Statutes, 10 Geo. VI, c. 55 and 7 Eliz. II, c. 32.
29/See Report of Committee on Ministers' Powers, pp. 92–109.

should always have access to the version of the facts on which the administrator has made his decision; and that intelligible summaries of decided cases should be published at frequent intervals for the guidance of the general public.

In the last resort, however, abuse of power – in administration, as in all other fields of government – cannot be controlled by formalized checks and barriers alone; these must be supported and constantly reinforced by other means, the chief of which is a House of Commons which is sharply and intelligently critical of administrative procedures. Moreover, the surest guarantee of obtaining such a House is found in the vigilance of an alert public, fully aware of the constitutional rights of the citizen and jealous of any government which needlessly sacrifices those rights to its own administrative convenience. "I do not think we need to fear the overweening ambition of the Ottawa official," said Professor Corry some years ago, "nearly as much as our own general indifference. The fact that there was no protest outside Parliament against the wide terms of the Relief Act of 1931 is rather astounding ... We cannot escape the growth of administrative discretion in the world in which we live, but it may be open to doubt whether we have the energy and public spirit necessary for its effective control."[30] The Canadian House of Commons has given credence to Professor Corry's doubts by being extremely slow to invent methods of ensuring that Parliament exercised an adequate scrutiny of administrative powers. In 1968 the House created a special committee "to report on procedures for the review by this House of instruments made in virtue of any statute of the Parliament of Canada," and by late 1969 the committee had progressed to the place where it was empowered to establish subcommittees and retain counsel and assistant counsel.[31] The House has not so far become convinced of the need for an ombudsman, although several provinces have created that office, and the need seems obvious enough.[32]

30/Corry, "Administrative Law in Canada," p. 207.
31/*Votes and Proceedings of the House of Commons of Canada*, Sept. 30, 1968; Feb. 14 and 17, 1969. The debates in the House of Commons for Sept. 24, 25, and 30, 1968, on the motion to establish the committee, contain numerous examples of the type of delegated legislation that has disturbed members.
32/See Donald C. Rowat and Henry Llambias, "The Ombudsman in Canada," in Willms and Kernaghan, *Public Administration in Canada*, pp. 430–7. For another view, see *Royal Commission Inquiry into Civil Rights* (Toronto 1968–9), II, no. 4, pp. 1340–90.

Part V THE LEGISLATURE

15 The senate

CANADA IS SLOWLY DEVELOPING some institutions of government which, if they cannot yet be placed in the vestigial class, are in danger of attaining that questionable distinction. The governor general, as already indicated, is still a useful part of the government; but there can be little doubt that a succession of mediocrities in the position accompanied by a continued unwillingness of the cabinet to make use of it (the two possibilities being closely bound together) would certanly cause the office to deteriorate to such a degree that its continuance would be difficult to justify. The Senate – the upper house of the legislature – is all too clearly being undermined by forces which threaten to lead to eventual obscurity and obsolescence. Some years ago its end as an effective branch of government seemed imminent; it had, through the acts of others and its own lack of assertiveness, become so sluggish and inert that it seemed capable of performing only the most nominal functions.

Recently, however, there have appeared sporadic periods of industry, and after the general election of 1968 a vigorous new leader of the government in the Senate, Mr Paul Martin, attempted to do what new appointees to the Senate have attempted to do before: revive it.[1] It would now seem possible to hope that the patient may be emerging from the long coma and might, if given the proper stimulants, become a useful, even though not an extremely active, member of political society.

The Canadian Parliament is composed of the Sovereign, the Senate, and the House of Commons, and the consent of all three is necessary for the passage of legislation. The governor, as the representative of the Queen, can (saving the reserve powers) be ruled out as an effective separate party; for in such matters he follows the advice of his cabinet, and the latter will approve of whatever action has been taken by the Commons with which it must have remained in complete accord. The Senate, however, is in theory an independent

1/See *Can. Senate Debates*, Sept. 18, 1968, pp. 3–11; Trudeau, *The Constitution and the People of Canada*.

legislative body, although in practice the degree to which it will act independently will depend in some measure upon certain legal restrictions on the exercise of its powers, the distribution of party strength in the houses, and the extent to which it feels it can count on popular support against the expressed wishes of the House of Commons.

The circumstances which gave rise to the creation of the Senate in 1867 have been already outlined,[2] but its place and the functions it was expected to perform in the new government need fuller explanation. The Senate, although endowed with comprehensive legal powers which were almost the equal of those of the Commons, was, of course, intended to be the minor legislative partner. This intention was placed beyond any possibility of doubt by three constitutional arrangements: two were stated in explicit form; the other, while no less clearly understood, rested on the established practices of the past. The British North America Act provided the explicit statements. Only the House of Commons was to be based on popular election; and while that alone gave the Commons the upper hand, the act added a further clause that the same body should also have the sole power to originate all bills for the raising or spending of money, a grant of power which clinched the matter. The third guarantee of the supremacy of the Commons was unwritten, but equally vital, namely, the constitutional understanding that the cabinet was to be held responsible to the lower and not to the upper house. Once these three fundamental propositions were enunciated, the general position of the two houses was permanently settled, although there was still room for development and adjustment within the areas and functions thus allocated.

Although the role of the Senate was thus intended to be a minor one, it was nevertheless expected to take upon itself certain particular duties which might be neglected by the Commons. (The Senate, indeed, received far greater attention during the Confederation debates of 1865 than the Commons.) In the first place, the Senate was to protect the interests of the provinces, for although the small provinces were not given the same number of senators as the two large ones, they had nevertheless a much greater representation proportionally than in the lower house. Quebec, while conceding representation by population in the Commons, was given the explicit assurance of special protection in the Senate. "The very essence of our compact," said George Brown, "is that the union shall be federal and not legislative. Our Lower Canada friends have agreed to give us representation by population in the Lower House, on the express condition that they shall have equality in the Upper House. On no other condition could we have advanced a step."[3]

To maintain this condition intact, it was not sufficient merely to equate representation in the Senate from the major provincial areas; certain other requirements had to be met. The senators from each area had to be definitely

2/*Supra*, pp. 25–30.
3/*Confederation Debates*, 1865, p. 88.

limited in number, or, if any increase whatever were allowed, the sectional balance had to be maintained. Further, members should not be elected; for this might easily lend itself in the future to an agitation to place this chamber, like the Commons, on a more strictly representative basis which would, in turn, push it back on population. It was clearly recognized at the time, however, that the maintenance of local and sectional interests would not depend entirely upon the Senate; for these interests would have other vigorous and powerful defenders in the federal cabinet and in the House of Commons.[4]

Secondly, the Senate was intended to act as a revising and restraining body to deal with possible errors or impulses of the Commons. On this point the opinion of Sir John A. Macdonald may be taken as typical:

There would be no use of an Upper House if it did not exercise, when it thought proper, the right of opposing or amending or postponing the legislation of the Lower House. It would be of no value whatever were it a mere chamber for registering the decrees of the Lower House. It must be an independent House, having a free action of its own, for it is only valuable as being a regulating body, calmly considering the legislation initiated by the popular branch, and preventing any hasty or ill-considered legislation which may come from that body, but it will never set itself in opposition against the deliberate and understood wishes of the people.[5]

Thirdly, the Senate was to represent property and conservatism. This was to a limited degree implied in the preceding function of the restraining power of the upper house, but it was also explicitly stated on a number of occasions.[6]

CONSTITUTIONAL PROVISIONS

The major provisions whereby these aims were to be achieved are contained in the British North America Act, 1867, and the 1915 amendment.[7] They are as follows:

The Senate originally consisted of 72 members: 24 from Ontario; 24 from Quebec; 24 equally apportioned between Nova Scotia and New Brunswick, although 4 of these were to be assigned to Prince Edward Island if the Island entered the union. (This adjustment took place in 1873.) As the western provinces came into the federation, they were given 2 or 3 or 4 senators depending upon the circumstances;[8] and in 1915 all of western Canada was made a fourth senatorial area represented also by 24 senators, 6 from each of

4/See R. A. MacKay, *The Unreformed Senate of Canada* (rev. and reprinted, Toronto, 1963), pp. 36–50. This excellent study has been freely used throughout the greater part of this chapter. See F. A. Kunz, *The Modern Senate of Canada* (Toronto, 1965), and Eugene Forsey's review of it in *Canadian Forum*, XLV (March 1966), p. 285.
5/*Confederation Debates*, 1865, p. 36.
6/MacKay, *The Unreformed Senate*, p. 47–8, 136–42.
7/*Supra*, pp. 77–8.
8/See ss. 21–36, 147 of the BNA Act.

the four western provinces, thus making a total of 96. This number became 102 when the entrance of Newfoundland added 6 more.[9] The maximum membership can, however, be slightly increased on the recommendation of the governor general – the intention of this provision being to give some elasticity to the Senate in the event of a deadlock developing between the two houses. Only four or eight additional senators (three or six before 1915) can be added in this way – one or two from each of the four senatorial areas, and the rules governing their appointment are rather complex; since they have never been used, no controversy has arisen. But the number of senators cannot at any time exceed one hundred and ten, with the normal complement set at one hundred and two.[10]

Senators are appointed by the Governor-General-in-Council, and they originally held office for life; since 1965, new appointees retire at seventy-five.[11] They represent their respective provinces, but each senator from Quebec represents also one of twenty-four senatorial districts in that province. All senators must be residents of the provinces they represent.

A senator may belong to either sex;[12] he must be at least thirty years of age and a British subject; he must own real property within the province he represents[13] to a net value of $4,000, and be worth at least $4,000 over and above all debts and liabilities. (It should be noted that in 1867 this was a very large property qualification.)

A senator can vacate his seat by resigning, or failing to attend the Senate for two consecutive sessions; by ceasing to be a citizen; by being adjudged bankrupt or insolvent; by being attainted of treason or convicted of "felony or of any infamous crime"; or by being no longer qualified in respect of property or residence, though he may reside in Ottawa if he holds an office under the Dominion government which requires his presence there.

The Speaker of the Senate is appointed by the Governor-General-in-Council; he is in fact the choice of the prime minister.[14]

It would be idle to deny that the Senate has not fulfilled the hopes of its founders; and it is well also to remember that the hopes of its founders were not excessively high. Professor MacKay has rightly called attention to the fact that today many Canadians expect the Senate to have some of the prestige and glamour of the House of Lords on the one hand, and some of the power and

9/Provision had been originally made that in the event of Newfoundland joining the federation, she was to be given 4 senators; and this was raised to 6 by the 1915 amendment.

10/See *A Consolidation of the British North America Acts, 1867 to 1967*, ss. 26–8.

11/Senators appointed before the establishment of the retirement age had the option of remaining for life, or retiring on a pension. All senators retiring at seventy-five will henceforth receive a pension. See BNA Act, 1965.

12/*Edwards* v. *Attorney General for Canada*, [1930] A.C. 124.

13/BNA Act, 1867, s. 23.

14/The privileges of the Senate as a body and of its members as individuals are given with those of the House of Commons, chap. XVII.

importance of the United States Senate on the other;[15] whereas the original plans were drafted on much more modest lines. But even the sober expectations of the fathers had little chance of ever being realized, for the dice were plainly loaded against the Senate from the start; and later developments have served but to increase the initial difficulties. The senators themselves seem to have done little to counteract these handicaps; they have for the most part accepted their fate, and on the whole have turned in what must be considered an undistinguished performance.

APPOINTMENT

The first great handicap which was placed on the Senate at Confederation was the system under which its members were appointed. The founders of the Dominion accepted as inevitable the fact that if the cabinet appointed the senators, it would be for party reasons; but even they could scarcely have expected party gratitude to become so dominant a motive.[16] Senatorships have been invariably regarded as the choicest plums in the patronage basket, and they have been used without compunction as rewards for faithful party service. Few prime ministers have appointed opponents to the Senate, and fewer have appointed Independents.[17] Every prime minister admits that the system is unsatisfactory except to promote narrow party interests; but every prime minister continues to make appointments for the same reason. Sir Wilfrid Laurier described his recurring dilemma as follows:

When it comes to the appointment of senators, it is a difficult matter. With all the good will I have, if I were to advise His Excellency to take a man from the Opposition side, I do not know that my action would be well received. My hon. friend ... would hardly expect me to submit to His Excellency the name of a man who represented us to be everything that was bad, who had nothing good to say of us, who declared that we were corrupt and wicked and guilty of all the sins in the calendar. That would be, I think, more than Christian charity could be expected to endure ... Even if I were to offer to His Excellency the name of one of the lukewarm Conservatives, who is not very strong on one side or the other, perhaps gentlemen on the other side would be the very first to find fault with such an appointment. Therefore on the whole I believe these appointments have to be made as all of them are made ... Sir John Macdonald in his day ... appointed one gentleman from the Liberal side; but this gentleman was a personal friend of his and one who on a particular occasion had stood by him in very trying circumstances. I am sorry to say that I have not yet found in the ranks of the Conservative party a man of such independent views as John Macdonald was in the ranks of the Liberal

15/MacKay, The Unreformed Senate, pp. 50–2.
16/Original appointments to the Senate in 1867 represented all political groups.
17/See John N. Turner, "The Senate of Canada – Political Conundrum," in Robert M. Clark, ed., Canadian Issues: Essays in Honour of Henry F. Angus (Toronto, 1961), pp. 69–70. The opponents appointed were close personal friends of the prime minister who appointed them.

party. With all the diligence with which I have scanned the other side, I have not been able to find such a man.[18]

On certain occasions appointments for party reasons may well be considered imperative. Generally speaking, a party which once retains office in the Dominion government stays there for many years; and thus when its rival at last steps into power, the new government is confronted with a Senate which is almost entirely filled with its opponents.[19] At such a time a prime minister has no real alternative; for he is virtually forced to fill all Senate vacancies with his own supporters in order to redress the balance. Unfortunately, by the time this state of equilibrium is reached, appointment for party services has apparently become such a habit that it cannot be shaken off; and the scene is then rapidly set for a new government which, when it is in turn confronted with a hostile Senate, must begin the congenial task of redressing the balance anew. And in this merry-go-round the "third parties," however significant a minority they may be in the country, can never expect to have a single representative in the Senate.

Even a casual examination of the personnel of the Senate will show how party services have been the controlling factor in appointments, although faithful personal support or generous financial contributions, unaccompanied by more overt party activity, are not readily ascertained from the records. In 1969 a total Senate membership of ninety-three had the following antecedents.[20] No less than thirty-one senators had been former members of the House of Commons, nine of whom had been cabinet ministers; seventeen others had seen service in provincial legislatures, five of whom had been in provincial cabinets;[21] ten others had been unsuccessful candidates, and several more had held high party office (as had a number of those included in the above categories). Thus over 70 per cent had been active in party circles, ranging from federal cabinet ministers and provincial premiers down to party office holders and defeated candidates.

It is a favourite device for an astute prime minister to keep his supporters eager, active, and toiling unceasingly for the party until the election is near at hand, and then, having wrung them dry, to reward the most faithful by translation to a higher and more restful sphere of usefulness. Thus few appointments to the Senate will be made in the year or two before a general election is

18/*Can. H. of C. Debates*, Jan. 20, 1908, pp. 1573–4.
19/The founders of the federation, naturally influenced by the rapidly changing cabinets of that period, did not expect this stability or, of course, this result which has appeared as a by-product. The limitation on total membership, said Macdonald, "will prevent the Upper House from being swamped from time to time by the Ministry of the day" (*Confederation Debates*, 1865, p. 36). It is true that swamping has become a deliberate and not a precipitate process, but once accomplished, it lasts for a long period by virtue of the very defences which were erected against it.
20/*Parliamentary Guide*, 1969.
21/A number of the ex-members of Parliament had of course also seen service in provincial legislatures.

anticipated; and then within a few weeks of that event the vacancies will be rapidly filled. Thus from July 20 to October 14, 1935 (the day of the election), seventeen Conservative senators were appointed (ten of them being members of Parliament fleeing from the impending storm); and in the two months preceding the 1945 election, eighteen Liberals (eleven of them from the Commons) were made senators.[22] The Liberal government in 1957, somewhat over-confident about winning the general election of that year, ironically left sixteen vacancies to be filled by its grateful successors.

This system is clearly not likely to produce an upper chamber of first-rate material, eager to work, independent in outlook, and calm and dispassionate in its approach to public questions. The Senate will contain a fair number of party supporters whose past contributions have been so inconspicuous as to be generally unknown. It will also contain a sprinkling of defeated candidates, who, while they may have been able to create a party obligation, have certainly no claim to public recognition. Recently, for example, one person ran in four elections and was defeated in all of them. A grateful government granted what an unappreciative electorate had denied, and the perpetual candidate triumphantly entered the legislative halls as a senator. The most important group, however, will be a large number of senators with distinguished records; but the great bulk of these enter the chamber only when their active political life is over. They are tired of politics, or they have reached the age of retirement and are willing to accept a pension *via* the Senate. Their whole lives rise up to make it difficult to adopt an attitude of political neutrality; and the fact that they are still associating with their old colleagues and are only a few feet away from the thickest of the fight, makes party detachment and independence little more than a fanciful aspiration which has lost contact with the facts of life.

It is, of course, easy to overstress this partisan aspect of the Senate's personnel; but the system tends to crack the very foundation of the Senate's efficiency. There is no doubt that many of these appointments are well made and that many of those appointed are a credit to the Senate; there is no doubt that the system is most useful as an instrument of party discipline and service; but there is equally no doubt that the chief purpose underlying these appointments is not the public good, but party patronage and advantage, and that this is reflected in the general low regard in which the Senate is popularly held:

The Senate ... has become the refuge and reward of old party servants, each party filling up the vacancies of death with its friends and rarely on a basis of ability ...

22/In the twenty years from 1925 to 1945, sixty-seven appointments to the Senate were made in the two or three months before elections (covering in all a combined period of ten months), whereas all other senatorial appointments (over a combined period of nineteen years) totalled only fifty-five; the first being at the *rate* of over eighty appointments a year, the second at the *rate* of less than three. In 1955 a bill to ensure the filling of Senate vacancies within six months was introduced in the upper house, but failed to pass second reading. *Can. Senate Debates*, March 29 and May 11, 1955, pp. 361 and 447–57.

As the Senate criticizes but does not seriously interfere, the Canadian people generally regard it with amusement, tolerance, or contempt, and while Governments have frequently promised to reform it, nothing is done. The genial old gentlemen who populate the snug red-velvet chamber ... live on, undisturbed, meeting for a few weeks in the year, bumbling and grumbling at the Government, making a few good speeches, and drawing an annual indemnity ... for less work than any other citizens of Canada.[23]

The appointments to the Senate are frequently used to give not only provincial representation, but also representation to economic, racial, and religious groups in the provinces. Organized labour and other economic interests have been given special, although very uneven, representation. The Roman Catholic minority in Ontario and the Protestant minority in Quebec have both been overrepresented in the Senate on the theory that they do not obtain an adequate number of seats in the House. "Similarly," writes Professor MacKay, "senators have been appointed as the avowed representatives of the French in Ontario, of the Germans in Ontario, of the French in Western Canada, of the Acadians of the Maritime provinces, and more recently of the Ukrainians, the Icelanders, the Indians, and the Jews."[24] And of course the scramble for recognition on special grounds was greatly increased when the question of sex was introduced. In 1930 Mrs Cairine Wilson was made a senator avowedly as the representative of the women of Canada. The natural consequence was not long delayed, and the demand was made that the women of each province should have their own senators; but at the end of 1969 there were only five ladies in the Senate, from five provinces.

The system of appointment has, however, a special advantage in that it allows the prime minister a welcome latitude in changing and reorganizing his cabinet. A very troublesome problem which is rarely absent from the mind of a prime minister is how to get rid of dead wood in his cabinet, men who have served their country faithfully, but whose best days are over and who may or may not still have a modest contribution to make to public life. "The first essential for a Prime Minister is to be a good butcher," said Mr Asquith, and then added, "there are several who must be pole-axed now."[25] The honest and fitting solution would be to give them a generous pension; but that has been possible only since 1952. A worse plan, but one which has been quietly followed for years, is to place the minister in the Senate pasture for the rest of his days.

These appointments have yet another use in facilitating cabinet adjustments. It is sometimes necessary, in order to give sectional representation in the cabinet or for some other reason, to appoint as minister a person who is not in Parliament, and hence a seat in the House must be found for him without delay.

23/Bruce Hutchison, The Unknown Country (Toronto, 1943), p. 82.
24/MacKay, The Unreformed Senate, p. 149.
25/Winston S. Churchill, Great Contemporaries (London, 1937), p. 141.

A member of the Commons, who represents what is considered to be a safe constituency for the government, may be induced to resign so that the minister may be elected to fill the vacancy; and in a few months or a year the obliging member's sacrifice is rewarded by his appointment to the first available senatorship from his province.

TERM

The second great handicap imposed on the Senate at Confederation was the life term. The original purpose was, of course, to render the senators independent and comparatively free to decide questions on their inherent merits, without being unduly influenced by the pull of party motives and the fear of electoral defeat. Such advantages as these, however, were rendered nugatory by the partisan antecedents of the senators combined with the depressing consequences which flowed from so secure and so prolonged a tenure.

In the first place, the life term inevitably led to a large number of senators remaining in the chamber long after they had passed the age of genuine usefulness.[26] There were undoubted exceptions; but in the Senate, as in virtually all other positions, the rare meritorious case should not be allowed to establish the standard for the remainder. The great bulk of the over-age senators could not perform their duties with the same effectiveness as younger men. The House of Commons can clearly furnish no parallel; for the process of election furnishes an automatic check and an automatic method of retirement which can discriminate between cases with merciless efficiency. Canada has had on at least two occasions the singular distinction of possessing the oldest legislator in the world: Senator Wark, who died in 1905 in his 102nd year, and Senator Dessaulles, who died in 1930 in his 103rd year. The obituary of the latter bears unconscious but eloquent testimony on the point under discussion as well as on the one which follows:

Senator Dessaulles, dead at St. Hyacinthe, who held a seat in the Senate of Canada since 1907, had a remarkable record. So far as is recalled by those around the Senate since he was there, he never once participated in any debate or gave expres-

---

26/See MacKay, The Unreformed Senate, p. 177. In 1945, 1953, 1961, and 1969 (Parliamentary Guide, 1946, 1953, 1961, and 1969) the age distribution of senators whose age was known was as follows:

	1945	1953	1961	1969
30 to 40	1	0	0	1
41 to 50	3	0	2	14
51 to 60	22	7	14	14
61 to 70	37	37	30	30
71 to 80	23	35	32	20
Over 80	9	4	16	10
	95	83	94	89

sion to an opinion; but he followed the discussions closely and was there when the division bells rang. He was a kindly old man, held by all parties in venerable respect because of his great age.[27]

The life term (and probably now the high retirement age) also had an unfortunate effect on the age of appointment, for no one goes to the Senate with an eye to a future career, but always with the sense of opening up the last chapter. Even the House of Lords has a steady infusion of younger men, and some of them, of course, are very young indeed. In the 1969 Senate twenty-eight out of ninety senators for whom dates were available had been over sixty years of age at the time of their appointment.[28] The Senate has thus so far been a shelter for those whose active life is almost over and who are primarily concerned with a pleasant, secure, and not very strenuous old age. "A senatorship isn't a job," says Mr Grattan O'Leary, who has had ample opportunity to observe the institution and its members, "it's a title. Also it's a blessing, a stroke of good fate; something like drawing a royal straight flush in the biggest pot of the evening, or winning the Calcutta Sweep. That's why we think it wrong to think of a senatorship as a job; and wrong to think of the Senate as a place where people are supposed to work. Pensions aren't given for work."[29] Mr O'Leary was subsequently appointed to the Senate.

The assurance of a secure existence, which is quite unrelated to performance, and the constant association with others similarly situated have a deplorable, but in no way surprising, psychological effect which militates against initiative and intensive effort. There will be those who may be largely unaffected, whose zeal for public service and whose habits of mind and training will have become so ingrained that they will toil unselfishly, unremittingly, and with conspicuous competence for years; but these will be exceptional. For while the Senate may supply the opportunities, it does not supply at all adequately the incentives for work: political ambition is dead;[30] the needs of the future are guaranteed; the salary, while not munificent, is ample. There is generally a sense of futility in

27/*Ottawa Citizen*, April 21, 1930. Senator Dessaulles actually made at least two speeches: one, on his entry, to deny that his appointment came from a corrupt bargain; the other to thank his colleagues for his portrait, on his hundredth birthday.

28/Ages of senators at time of appointment (*Parliamentary Guide*, 1946, 1953, 1961, 1969):

	1946	1953	1961	1969
30 to 40	3	1	0	4
41 to 50	16	12	16	23
51 to 60	43	33	35	35
61 to 70	31	32	35	25
Over 70	2	5	7	3
	95	83	93	90

29/*Ottawa Journal* (editorial); quoted in *Financial Post*, Feb. 28, 1942.

30/"I have to-day signed my warrant of political death ... How colourless the Senate – the entering gate to coming extinction." Entry in the diary of Sir George Foster on his appointment to the Senate. Wallace, *Memoirs of Sir George Foster*, p. 207.

the red chamber: few people listen to the speeches; the usual drama and excitement of politics are lacking; no vital issues hang on the Senate's votes; there are no reputations to be made; there are no fresh, aggressive, stimulating young minds to satisfy. Occasionally a senator takes an opportune moment to remind his fellows of the achievements in extreme old age of the Shaws who wrote plays, the Churchills who wrote books, and the Connie Macks who operated baseball teams – an exercise as revealing as it is touching.

It is not merely improbable, but inconceivable, that setting the senators' retirement age at seventy-five, with a pension beyond that, will by itself materially change the Senate.

GENERAL POSITION

A third handicap is the vulnerability of the Senate's fundamental position in the government of the nation. This is not because the Senate is not the co-equal of the Commons or because it is not a popularly elected body; it is rather because it rests on no political foundation, and it therefore can look nowhere for support or justification save in the essential rectitude or excellence of its own acts which is rarely sufficiently impressive to carry much weight. A recent analyst concluded in 1961: "The Senate, in terms of current facts, no longer plays a useful part in the government of Canada."[31] By the late 1960s this had become so obvious that the Senate was being included in comprehensive proposals for constitutional reform.[32]

CABINET MINISTERS IN THE SENATE

To its original handicaps, which have been laid on the Senate since its creation, others have been added. There has been a tendency, for example, for successive prime ministers to ignore its potentialities and give it an insufficient amount of work, which has been reflected in a diminished prestige. Again, senators have frequently been left out of party caucuses, not in order to encourage or maintain their independence of the party or of the Commons, but apparently because they were not wanted. But by far the most crippling blow which has been dealt the Senate since Confederation is the modern practice of keeping the number of senators in the cabinet low. The first government after Confederation for a time contained five members of the upper house; but the number varied greatly in succeeding years and on the whole tended to diminish, although in the nineties two prime ministers (Abbott and Bowell) were also senators. Sir Robert Borden introduced the custom of having no ministers in

31/Turner, "The Senate of Canada," p. 79.
32/Trudeau, *The Constitution and the People of Canada*, pp. 28–34 and 76–8.

the Senate who were heads of government departments, and since 1921 this has become an accepted practice, though one occasionally broken.[33] After 1957 the cabinet included no representative from the Senate for five years, though the rôle of the government leader in the Senate was continued; the leader of the government in the Senate now holds a full portfolio in his own right. The primary reason given for the contemporary convention is that spending departments must have a minister in the House to defend departmental estimates, so that democratic control requires all these ministers to be in the representative body.

To a legislative chamber whose position was none too secure and whose prestige was already badly battered, this decision was little short of catastrophic. For the cabinet, which was already disposed to ignore the Senate, now possesses the best of all possible excuses for doing so. A minister will always wish to introduce his own measures into Parliament – "to bring his own child," as Senator Dandurand said, "to the baptismal font" – and even if the government leader who sits in the Senate is also a minister, there will be few government bills introduced there. As a partial remedy for this condition the Senate in 1947 amended its rules so that it was able to give permission to a cabinet minister from the Commons to appear in the Senate chamber and speak on a measure which had originated there. The experiment has not proved successful; for although ministers on rare occasions have availed themselves of the privilege, the action has gained little favour with either the Senate or the government, and the rule has lain dormant for several years.

The absence of ministers has yet another weakening influence on the effective participation of the chamber in the business of government. Information cannot readily be obtained through day to day inquiries or in the course of debate or other proceedings, and when finally secured after irritating delays it has become stale and uninteresting. A government leader with the best of intentions and the most extraordinary industry cannot be expected to have available at a few hours' notice all the relevant factual material which may be demanded by his inquiring fellow members. Though much has been done to improve the Senate's communications with the rest of the government, even today the government leader cannot always know the views and intentions of the cabinet on many matters which arise. He is, indeed, frequently embarrassed by his inability to speak for the government with any assurance, and an amendment proposed in the Senate may have to be held over until the leader consults with the appropriate minister in order to ascertain whether it will be acceptable. While some senators apparently believe that the old days may return and departments will once more be represented in the upper house, the realists have long since conceded that any such reversal is most unlikely.[34]

33/*Supra*, pp. 177–8. Borden himself had department heads who were senators in his Union government.
34/See opinions of Senators Arthur Meighen and Sir Allen Aylesworth, *Can. Senate Debates*, March 8, 14, 1934, pp. 141, 162.

LEGISLATIVE ACTIVITY

In view of these original and acquired weaknesses, any very impressive performance from the Senate could scarcely be expected. Its legislative functions have, by most accounts, been discharged with moderate but not conspicuous success. The legal prohibition on the introduction of money bills in the Senate[35] and the tendency of ministers to introduce all their own measures in the Commons have usually deprived the Senate of any major part in the initiation of government bills. Strenuous efforts by the government leader to secure a share for the Senate have usually proved unavailing, but recent years have seen an extraordinary change. In twenty-two years (1924–45) only 36 government bills were introduced in the Senate; but in the next eight years (1946–53) this number jumped to 138, and in the following decade another 78 bills began in the Senate. Part of the explanation for these figures is that in the immediate post-war period Parliament was overhauling and consolidating the bulk of the Canadian statutes, and the cabinet (supported by a majority of both Houses) allowed the Senate to participate in this arduous labour. The results were excellent and were praised unreservedly by both government and opposition in the Commons.[36] But when in 1957 the new Conservative government faced a Liberal majority in the Senate, the number of government bills introduced in the upper House not unnaturally dropped off until the Senate had earned the government's confidence, when the number rose markedly. Then the Senate shook the government's confidence in 1961 by rejecting a bill the cabinet was particularly interested in, and the legislative business of the Senate dropped sharply until the return of another Liberal government with a majority in both Houses. Clearly the Senate's rôle is affected by the confidence which the government has in the upper House.

A further limitation was indicated years ago by Arthur Meighen when he deplored the fact that only one cabinet minister was available (and from 1957 to 1962 there was none) to carry the burden of direction and responsible leadership:

His duties with respect to any measure which he introduces are very much greater [than with other government legislation]. He may have considerable work to do in amending it, perhaps in recasting it entirely. He has to attend meetings of the committee which considers it and, if necessary, hears witnesses. He has to spend hours upon it; in some instances very many hours and days and weeks ... In the senate he will never succeed in getting his legislation passed until he does make himself thoroughly conversant with it. At the present time the committee work, as all honourable members know, is undoubtedly the most useful work that the Senate does.[37]

35/For comment on the Senate's rôle in parliamentary control of finance, see Ward, *The Public Purse*, pp. 8–10; E. A. Driedger, "Money Bills and the Senate," *Ottawa Law Review*, vol. 3:25 (Fall 1968) pp. 25–46.
36/*Can. H. of C. Debates*, Nov. 22, 1949, pp. 2061–3.
37/*Can. Senate Debates*, March 8, 1934, p. 141.

292 THE GOVERNMENT OF CANADA

One result of the reluctance to introduce government measures in the Senate is that there is a lull in its activity in the early days of the session while it is awaiting bills from the other house. The Senate copes with the problem by taking a holiday; and it is thus not at all uncommon for the chamber to adjourn for long periods immediately after the passage of the address in reply to the speech from the throne,[38] and frequently later in the session. Thus in 1968-9 the Senate sat on ninety-four days, the Commons on over twice that number. In the same session there were five days when the Senate debates covered less than *six* pages of Hansard; eleven days when they covered less than *eleven* pages; thirty-five days when they covered *fifteen* pages or less; and fifty-nine days when the Hansard report *exceeded fifteen* pages. An ordinary day in the House of Commons will fill *sixty or more* pages of the same size. While the value of the contributions made by the members of the Canadian Parliament can scarcely be measured by the convenient method of totalling pages of debate, partly because so much work is done in committees, it is difficult to believe that the senators have achieved so remarkable a brevity without losing much of the content in the prodigious effort of concentration. A perusal of their remarks amply confirms the accuracy of this observation.

The senators are able, however, to participate with some effectiveness in the legislative work by the consideration of measures after they have passed the Commons, and, if they so desire, by proposing amendments or rejecting the entire bill. Detailed examination of these measures is rarely given in Committee of the Whole, but rather in one of the Senate's standing committees. These committees often hold meetings at which interested citizens may present their views; and at other times members of the cabinet will appear before a committee for the purpose of giving information and explaining a particular proposal. In addition to the joint committees on which senators sit in association with members of the House of Commons, there are sixteen standing committees of the Senate. These often function on days or weeks when the upper house is not in session, and thus for some senators, at least, the frequent adjournments and brief sittings do not always bring relief from parliamentary labours. The committee which formerly passed on divorce cases was kept so busy that the work was often given to two, and sometimes to three, committees; and even with this help they were compelled to sit five days a week. After 1963-4, following an extended debate that lasted several years, an officer of the Senate who was also a judge of the Exchequer Court took evidence in divorce cases and made recommendations to the Senate, which was thus relieved of one of its most onerous duties. Until 1968, divorce was then granted by a resolution of the Senate, and in 1968 the entire burden was shifted to the courts.[39]

A number of Senate committees are normally inactive, and some go for

38/This is done over the protests of some members of the Senate. *Ibid.*, Oct. 31, 1945, pp. 170-3.
39/*Can. Statutes*, 12 Eliz. II, c. 10; 16 Eliz. II, c. 24.

years without meeting. It was suggested in 1945 by the government leader that these committees were too numerous, that a few were too large, and that some members were on too many of them; and a special committee was accordingly set up to investigate the matter. Its report (which was adopted by the Senate) retained all the committees; contemplated no reductions in their size; and proposed to increase the membership of thirteen of the committees and the total assignments from 340 to 539, so that on an average every senator would be able to be a member of more than five committees.[40] The committee system was being re-examined in 1969–70.

There can be no doubt that the Senate was in the past useful in revising bills which were sometimes sent from the Commons badly drafted, hastily assembled, and, in some instances, almost unworkable. However, for some years it has been the rule that "all government measures must be approved by the Department of Justice," and public bills are now subjected to a formal procedure which minimizes the possibility of poor or hasty drafting, without of course entirely eliminating it.[41] The need for the Senate as a ground crew for a high-flying Commons has therefore been profoundly modified, and senators, while they have more leisure and fewer distractions than their colleagues in the Commons, also have fewer opportunities than they formerly had to display the fruits of their wisdom in the repairing of legislation.

In any event, adequate consideration of bills is often made difficult if not impossible by their late arrival from the Commons, and they appear before the upper house in the dying days of the session. "It is little less than a travesty," exclaimed Meighen, "that this chamber, prepared for work, ready to serve the people of this country, should be compelled to wait more or less idly for weeks, perhaps months, while discussions, which are no doubt necessary under any democratic system, are proceeding in the other chamber, and that a plethora of legislation should be thrown at us in the latter part of each session, when we have no opportunity to do what we ought to do in the way of reviewing it, and all that the other House expects of us is that we shall pass it without thought, without amendment, and without delay."[42] It is now a normal practice, indeed, for the Senate to be notified of the imminent visit of the governor general's deputy for the giving of royal assent to sundry bills, and then to receive some of the actual bills, "to which the Senate is clearly expected to give all three readings within an hour or two, or else keep the Governor General's deputy waiting."[43] It is indicative of the weak position of the Senate that although this irritating procedure is a regular occurrence, the chamber has only once or twice had the moral courage to try to stop the practice by making the Commons wait while the tardy bills receive careful and deliberate consideration.

It is generally supposed that if the Senate and the House of Commons are

40/*Can. Senate Debates*, Nov. 19, Dec. 5, 7, 1945, pp. 265–9, 374–5, 384–7.
41/See Elmer A. Driedger, *The Composition of Legislation* (Ottawa, 1957), especially pp. xviii–xxii.
42/*Can. Senate Debates*, March 8, 1934, p. 140.
43/Ward, *The Public Purse*, p. 9.

controlled by opposite parties (which will occur after a change in a long-established government) the Senate will be much more disposed both to amend and to reject bills coming from the lower house. Professor MacKay's report on the experience of almost sixty years is instructive, and subsequent research has confirmed his conclusions.[44] He found that there was little or no justification for the charge that the senators *amended* legislation from partisan motives; but it was true that they were very much more eager to *reject* public bills[45] when the majority belonged to a different party than the cabinet and hence also differed from the majority in the Commons. It was not that the power of rejection was used capriciously, but that the senators were much more likely to disagree and were not at all adverse to setting their opinion against that of the Commons when they belonged to opposite sides. This finding is confirmed by an examination of the thirty years which followed the first edition of Professor MacKay's study. When during that period the majority party in the Senate was not the same as the majority party in the House, its amendment of government bills showed little increase as compared to those times when the majorities in both Houses belonged to the same party; but the rejections of government bills under the former condition were greater than when the Houses were politically in agreement. Since the early 1940s, the Senate has rejected very few government bills under any circumstances.[46] The basic cause, when rejection did occur, was the system of partisan selection. Party appointments to the Senate produce, naturally enough, party senators; and their independence, their calm judgment, their impartiality (which Sir John A. Macdonald emphasized at length) tend to vanish when subjected to strain. Over six decades ago Senator Perley summarized the situation in terms which still have validity:

It is generally accepted that this Senate is as partisan as the House of Commons. I am willing to stake my reputation before the country upon that assertion. The Senate is not independent. Why would it be? The moment you say that a senator should be independent and should not vote against the Government, you virtually say that he must be a man without gratitude ... It is a characteristic of most men to be grateful. It is a noble trait in the mind of any man, and when a Government takes a man from the cold shades where the people have left him and puts him in the Senate, it is a commendable trait in that man's character to feel that he must support the Government. He must be a partisan, and he is a partisan; the evidence shows it clearly.[47]

It should be added that even a partisan action of the Senate's is not necessarily solely partisan: the Senate's rejection in 1961 of the bill which would have vacated the office of governor of the Bank of Canada was certainly partisan, but it also permitted the governor to be heard in his own defence after the

44/MacKay, *The Unreformed Senate*, pp. 87–112, 199; Turner, "The Senate of Canada"; Kunz, *The Modern Senate of Canada*.
45/The rejection of *private* bills showed no significant difference.
46/See Kunz, *The Modern Senate of Canada*, p. 378.
47/*Can. Senate Debates*, June 20, 1906, p. 823.

Commons had decided that he would not be summoned to appear before a committee in that house.[48]

The Senate has never taken the position that its power of rejection and amendment are absolute and independent of public opinion; but it has ventured to oppose the Commons on the ground that a measure was not only inadvisable but that the lower house had no popular mandate for this particular proposal. If the will of the people is clearly expressed, the Senate, even although it disagrees with the wisdom of the bill, will acquiesce in the popular decision. The number of instances which give credence to this doctrine is small; but in 1926, for example, the Senate rejected the Old Age Pensions Bill, but passed the same bill a year later, largely because an election had intervened, the bill had been an election issue, and the government which had initiated it had been returned to office.

It may be noted here that the deadlock clause in the British North America Act[49] has never been used by a cabinet to overcome opposition in the Senate. In part this may be explained by the fact that when a government is most likely to need it – on its accession to office – the possible increase in senators is so small that it would be inadequate to redress the balance; but the power has also remained dormant because the Senate, while repeatedly defeating a new Government's measures, could rarely be accused of sheer perverse obstructiveness and intransigence. On three occasions the use of the deadlock clause was considered. Alexander Mackenzie applied in 1873 for permission to appoint additional senators, but the British government properly refused to agree, pointing out that the clause was designed to be used only in the event of a serious collision between the two Houses and then only when the creation of senators would furnish an adequate remedy. Sir Wilfrid Laurier made a tentative inquiry some years after he had become prime minister, but he received no encouragement on apparently the same general grounds; and Sir Robert Borden discussed the possibility on several occasions from 1912 to 1914. Any limitation on the use of this power today would depend largely on the self-restraint of the Canadian cabinet,[50] for no British government would be invited to give even its opinion on the subject.

The power of the Senate to amend a money bill is a matter of dispute between the two houses. The British North America Act is silent on the point; but the House of Commons, taking its precedent from the British Parliament, has always contended that the Senate has no such power, and it has committed

---

48/See Saywell, *Canadian Annual Review for 1961*, pp. 16–19.
49/*Supra*, pp. 281–3.
50/See Eugene A. Forsey, "Appointment of Extra Senators under Section 26 of the British North America Act," *Canadian Journal of Economics and Political Science*, XII, no. 2 (May 1946), pp. 159–67; Eugene A. Forsey, "Alexander Mackenzie's Memoranda on the Appointment of Extra Senators, 1873–4," *Canadian Historical Review*, XXVII, no. 2 (June 1946), pp. 189–94. Dr Forsey suggests that if the cabinet tried to take undue advantage of this section the governor general might invoke his reserve power against his advisers.

its opinion to writing in the formal rules of the House of Commons. "All aids and supplies granted to Her Majesty by the Parliament of Canada are the sole gift of the House of Commons, and all bills for granting such aids and supplies ought to begin with the House, as it is the undoubted right of the House to direct, limit, and appoint in all such bills, the ends, purposes, considerations, conditions, limitations and qualifications of such grants, which are not alterable by the Senate."[51]

The Senate has indignantly rejected what it alleges is an addition to the constitution. It has insisted that in view of the explicit reference in the British North America Act to the origination of money bills in the Commons, the omission of the act to mention the amendment of money bills is conclusive evidence that no restriction on the Senate's power in this regard was ever intended. It adds, further, that if the Senate is to perform its expected function as the guardian of provincial rights, it must have the power to interfere in legislation of this kind. The Senate does not contend, of course, that it could increase votes of expenditure or revenue without the usual motion of a minister.[52]

The theoretical argument is interesting; but not nearly so important as the practice. The Senate has in fact repeatedly amended money bills and by this term is meant not only ordinary bills which have contained money clauses,[53] but also bills dealing exclusively with financial matters, notably a number of income tax bills. At such times, it has not been at all uncommon for the lower house to acquiesce in the Senate's amendments, while adding the futile clause that the incident was not to be considered as a precedent.[54] While the Senate would not openly reject a simon-pure money bill, the power to amend in a manner which is unacceptable to the Commons may be construed as a virtual power of rejection. Apart from its handling of specific money bills, the Senate's rôle in the broader field of parliamentary control of finance is negligible.[55]

No mention has yet been made of the field of legislation where the Senate does its most useful work, namely, the consideration of private bills. The nature of these bills and the procedure used tend to make the committee stage by far

51/*Standing Orders of the House of Commons*, No. 63. This goes back to the earliest rules of the House in 1867, and originated in a resolution passed by the English House of Commons in 1678. Canadian Appropriation Bills are presented to the governor general in the name of the House of Commons alone.

52/See report on this matter in *Can. Senate Journals*, 1918, pp. 193–203; Ward, *The Public Purse*, pp. 8–10; Driedger, "Money Bills and the Senate."

53/What constitutes a money bill is often a matter of some dispute, and different definitions have been advanced to suit the convenience of the moment.

54/The following motion was passed on the initiative of the minister of National Revenue in concurring in Senate amendments to the Income War Tax Act: "That this house concur in the said amendments, and while doing so it does not think it advisable at this period of the session to insist on its privileges in respect thereto, but that the waiver of the said privileges in this case be not however drawn into a precedent, that the clerk do carry back the bill to the Senate and acquaint their honours that this house has agreed to their amendments." *Can. H. of C. Debates*, June 1, 1939, p. 4846.

55/See Ward, *The Public Purse*; Driedger, "Money Bills and the Senate"; Kunz, *The Modern Senate*, pp. 257–61.

the most important, and by general admission the Senate's committee work is its most effective endeavour.

Private bills are different from public bills in purpose and widely different in procedure.[56] The object of a private bill is "to alter the law relating to some particular locality or to confer rights on, or relieve from liability, some particular person or body of persons."[57] Bills for the incorporation of a company, or for authorizing the extension of a line of railway, or (until 1964) for divorcing specified persons, are examples of private bills. The procedure followed in passing private bills is partly legislative and partly judicial in character; but (except for divorce bills from 1964 to 1968) they go through the usual three readings as do other bills. The private bill originates in a petition. The promoter of the bill presents a petition asking for its passage, fees must be paid, plans and maps (if necessary) must be submitted to indicate the changes proposed, and notices of intention must be advertised. These and other formalities are all checked by the Committee on Standing Orders and, if satisfactory, the bill is read the first and second time in the same way as a public bill. It is then referred to a standing committee of the Senate; and this body will hold hearings at which counter-petitions may be presented, counsel from both sides heard, and something very similar to a judicial inquiry will take place. The committee then reports to the Senate, and the Senate acts on the report, with or without further discussion. The tendency is for the Senate to accept its recommendations. If accepted, the bill is read a third time, and sent to the Commons.

Private bills may be introduced first into either house; but all divorce bills (which formed one category)[58] originated in the Senate down to 1968; divorce no longer requires an act of Parliament. It has been suggested that the Senate should be given a monopoly of originating all private bills, although members in the lower house have been reluctant to lose this opportunity for demonstrating their usefulness to their constituents. As one way of diverting the flow of private bills, the fee for those which originate in the Commons was raised in 1934 to $500, and additional charges have been added, while the fee for those originating in the Senate remained at $200.[59] The obvious advantage to be gained from any device which will give the Senate a preference in dealing first with these bills is that private bills (which under the standing orders must always be presented early in the session) can be conveniently considered by the Senate in the long interval when it is awaiting the public bills which are to be sent up by the Commons. The differential charge has served its purpose, and in practice all private bills now originate in the Senate, although the rules of the houses still allow them to originate in either chamber.

56/For public bills, see *supra*, p. 210; *infra*, pp. 356–64.
57/Beauchesne, *Rules and Forms of the House of Commons of Canada*, p. 280.
58/See J. Murray Beck, "The Canadian Parliament and Divorce," *Canadian Journal of Economics and Political Science*, XXIII, no. 3 (Aug. 1957), pp. 297–312.
59/See *Can. Senate Debates*, March 8, 14, 1934, pp. 141–2, 162; *Can. H. of C. Debates*, June 30, 1934, pp. 4509–10; House of Commons, Standing Orders, Jan. 1969, chap. XVIII.

INVESTIGATIONS

Aside from the Senate exercising a revising power of moderate value and its useful participation in the passage of private bills, it has also been successful in conducting investigations at various times into current political or social problems. One special committee of the Senate, for example, held an inquiry into the operation of the Income War Tax Act and the Excess Profits Tax Act[60] and it did a thoroughly competent piece of work; in 1969 a Senate committee chaired by Senator Keith Davey began a comprehensive study of the mass media, while others examined poverty, science policy – and the Senate. Such inquiries would appear to be a most fruitful field for Senate endeavour; for every year produces situations which are badly in need of some such scrutiny and drastic overhauling, and the Senate has the leisure, ability, and freedom (if not a very constant desire) to investigate them. The debates of the Senate abound with the sad plaints of senators who feel that their exceptional talents[61] are being neglected, but this yearning for strenuous public service is not very convincing. For while the activities of the Senate may be blocked in certain directions, they are quite untrammelled in others, and yet the average yearly performance is far from impressive. The failure to utilize at all fully its inquisitorial powers is a case in point. The Senate's highest recommendation will consist not in the unconvincing eulogies of its own members, but in the efficient performance of those duties which lie at hand.

THE PROTECTION OF RIGHTS

Some mention may be made of the extent to which the Senate has succeeded in protecting property, provincial, and minority rights. Minorities as well as provinces (as has been stated above) are often given special representation in its membership, and it is also true that an inventory of senatorial wealth would yield far more per capita than one taken in the House of Commons. The late Mr Woodsworth once enumerated at some length the directorships held by certain senators,[62] and the list is still both long and impressive.[63] The antecedents and present condition of the senators are, in short, such as to make them usually aware of the need for preserving many of the rights mentioned.

60/*Supra,* pp. 272–5.

61/*Senator Aseltine:* The Senate is one of the most democratic bodies in the world ... Anyone is at liberty to appear before our Senate committees, and anyone who does so receives a most sympathetic hearing ... It is very seldom that we decide an issue on straight party lines. Moreover, the members of the Senate represent the best brains in the country." *Can. Senate Debates,* Feb. 5, 1943, p. 48.

62/*Can. H. of C. Debates,* March 9, 1927, pp. 1039–42.

63/Forty senators were listed in 1945 as directors in Canadian companies; in 1961, thirty-six; in 1969, twenty-four. The apparent decline may reflect nothing more than a growing desire on the part of senators not to reveal all their interests.

What the Senate has actually done in these matters is not easily discovered. Professor MacKay, however, surveyed the ground with some care, and reached certain conclusions.[64] The Senate, he found, has no consistent record as an upholder of the interests of the provinces, and the party lines have usually proved stronger than those of the section or province affected. Quebec, in fact, is probably the only province which looks with any confidence to the Senate to protect its position against encroachment or abuse; for much surer lines of defence are found in the federalized cabinet, in threats of party secession, in the stalwart fighters elected to the House of Commons, and, over the long haul, the trend of judicial decisions in constitutional cases. In the maintenance of the rights of other minorities, the Senate has proved to be of moderate but not exceptional service, although its alertness in private bill legislation has been of considerable help in protecting individual property rights and public interests against the attacks of predatory corporations. Its attitude towards measures of social reform has not been particularly cordial, although here, as in the questions just mentioned, party lines and policies make bold generalizations difficult, if not impossible. Thus although the Senate originally defeated the Old Age Pensions Bill, the most important factor in that vote was that the Senate was controlled by the Conservatives, the House of Commons by the Liberals, and the one party was not at all reluctant to use this opportunity to embarrass the other.[65]

INDEMNITY

The indemnity of the senators is determined by statute. In 1970 it was $12,000, with a tax-free allowance of $3,000; the allowance of MP s is $6,000.[66] The generous treatment given senators is frequently criticized for, as Mr George Drew, when leader of the opposition, pointed out in 1954, the arguments adduced to justify an increase in the indemnities of the Commons were not applicable to the senators:

They are not elected, so they have no election expenses – that is, no local election expenses. They have no necessity for that measure of contact with their constituents which is referred to by the Prime Minister as an essential consideration in keeping themselves informed, nor have they as lengthy a stay in Ottawa, nor are these stays broken by the legitimate and proper demands on members of the House of Commons to address various meetings and maintain these contacts that are essentially a proper part of our political system.[67]

64/MacKay, *The Unreformed Senate*, pp. 112–28.
65/The bill was defeated in the Senate by 45 votes (all Conservative, but three) against 21 (all Liberals, but one). After the election of 1926 the Senate passed a second pension bill, acknowledging that the government now had a mandate.
66/The salary is subject to the same deductions for absences as is the salary of the member of Parliament. *Infra*, pp. 334–7.
67/*Can. H. of C. Debates*, Feb. 1, 1954, p. 1642.

When it is remembered that the senators perform a relatively small portion of the parliamentary work and that their indemnity is paid until the age of seventy-five there would seem to be no reason whatever to pay them virtually the same amount as that paid to members of Parliament. The Senate now costs the people of Canada well over $1,000,000 in indemnities alone.[68] The Speaker of the Senate receives a total of $28,000, including his indemnity and allowances; the government leader, $32,000; the opposition leader, $21,000.[69]

REFORM

The Senate has been by no means a useless body; but there are certainly the gravest doubts whether its cost of operation yields anything like a commensurate return unless it is looked upon simply as a pension scheme for retired commoners. Nor is the fact without significance that the position of the Senate in the scheme of government is never mentioned without the question of abolition or reform being at once raised, for virtually no one has any desire to maintain it in its present unsatisfactory condition. The only admirers are the senators themselves, and even they have been known in their franker moments to consider the possibility of improvement.

Politically, Senate abolition or reform tends to become an issue which is supported by the opposition or government chiefly on those occasions when the other party gains control, and it ceases to be an issue when the party balance in the Senate swings the other way. The CCF party and its successor, the New Democratic party, have demanded abolition, and will doubtless continue to do so as long as the Senate is filled with supporters of other parties. The Conservatives during their long stay in the wilderness before 1911 loudly demanded reform, but after a year or two in office these cries died down and gradually disappeared. The Liberals in 1924 called for changes in the Senate; the House of Commons in 1925 declared by a vote of 120 to 32 that the Senate as constituted was not of the greatest advantage to Canada, and a Dominion-provincial conference in 1927 (summoned by a Liberal government), while not in favour of abolition, considered a wide range of reform measures. But as Conservative senators died and Liberal ascendancy in the Senate mounted, Liberal enthusiasm for reform – other than by Liberal appointments – rapidly vanished. Some measure of the Liberal attitude in 1957 may be suggested by

68/The total annual cost of the Senate is impossible to determine, because the public works it uses are shared with the Commons. A speech of the late Senator Murphy, which senators frequently quote, stated that the Senate had saved the country at least $103,000,000, this estimate resting on the extraordinary assumption that because certain grants had been rejected by the Senate this represented a "saving" to the nation. One can admire, for example, the courage if not the logic of the statement that Canada saved $35,000,000 by not contributing three battleships to the British navy in 1913. *Can. Senate Debates*, March 1, 1934, pp. 105–11.

69/See *Canada Year Book, 1968*, pp. 88–9, and *Can. Statutes*, 17–18 Eliz. II, c. 28, s. 97.

noting that in that year the opposition held only five senatorships out of a possible 102, and the Liberal government, partly out of embarrassment, and certain it was about to be re-elected anyway, refrained from filling a large number of vacancies before the election of 1957. The new Conservative ministers once more emerged as champions of reform, but by 1962 the sole result had been the proposal for a statutory retirement age for senators, and it was their successors who proceeded with that.

This is not the place to discuss the problem of second chambers in general or that of Canada in particular; but some indication of the possibilities may be given. For one thing, the attitude of the provinces makes the continuance of the Senate a virtual necessity.[70] For although the Senate is admittedly of little use in preserving provincial rights, it does furnish some additional security for Quebec, and it provides the Maritimes wth a pool of patronage which is a most important factor in sustaining amicable party relations in that small area. Ontario and the West are not nearly so convinced of the Senate's indispensability, but even there it receives a scattered support. Thus political demands as well as other more abstract reasons for maintaining a second chamber combine to rule out abolition.

Some measure of reform, however, should not be impossible. The prime difficulty is that the Senate can be improved in so many ways that the multitude of alternatives smothers any particular measure of reform which may be advanced. A few of these may be mentioned as illustrations, most of them having being put forward at the Dominion-provincial conference of 1927:[71] (a) the senators should be elected, directly by the people, or indirectly by some other body; (b) they should be partly elected, partly appointed; (c) there should be a fixed and limited term of office; (d) senators should be retired at a definite age, a reform finally consummated in 1965; (e) the powers of the Senate should be limited like those of the House of Lords, so that it could exercise only a suspensive veto over ordinary legislation and have no control over money bills. Less elaborate proposals which have been put forward would involve a permission for ministers to introduce bills and speak in either house, although they would vote only in the house in which they held their seats; or would utilize the parliamentary secretaries by placing a number of them in the Senate, or, if ministers were re-admitted to the Senate, by placing their secretaries in the Commons.

Most recently the Trudeau government, moved by the belief "that the Senate

70/It has been suggested that genuine reform of the Senate "would require an amendment of the B.N.A. Act which is constitutionally beyond the scope of the federal government alone." (See Turner, "The Senate of Canada," p. 80.) The wording of the BNA Act, 1949, no. 2, does not support this suggestion, and in any event it is Parliament, not the federal government, which under s. 91(1) can do what it likes with the Senate.

71/See, for these and other proposals, Dawson, *Constitutional Issues*, pp. 265–83; Mackay, *The Unreformed Senate*, chap. 11; Kunz, *The Modern Senate of Canada*, chap. 13.

should be reorganized to provide for the expression in it, in a more direct and formal manner than at present, of the interests of the provinces," has made tentative but specific proposals which include: provincial selection of some (perhaps half) of the senators from each province; a fixed term, probably six years, for senators; and new exclusive powers for the Senate, including the approval of cabinet nominations for judges of the Supreme Court, ambassadors, and unidentified "heads of cultural agencies." All these proposals (and more) are part of a comprehensive scheme of constitutional reform under intensive study in 1969–70,[72] and if Canadian history is any guide, their fate may not be settled for years, or even decades.

Without embarking on any discussion of a subject which has been endlessly debated (except for some of those proposals in the paragraph immediately above) it may be suggested that while many features or powers of the Senate might conceivably be altered, any scheme of reform would have to accept certain conditions as unchangeable: the unquestioned supremacy of the House of Commons; the existing distribution of provincial seats in the Senate, or something like it; the maintenance of the Senate's function of revision and, possibly, of rejection of legislation, although the more extreme use of these might be substantially curbed.

If the Senate is not to be considered as a rival of the House of Commons – and, as just stated, it must never be that – one of the most attractive alternatives, popular election, is almost certainly ruled out, unless one could somehow invent an electoral system that provided no power base for the victors. If it is desirable to emphasize more decidedly than today the provincial element in the Senate, some real improvement *could* possibly be achieved by allowing the provincial legislature to elect or the provincial government to nominate part or all of that province's senators, though it is not easy to think of reasons why provincial choices would be better than (or even as good as) Dominion, or how responsible government could work in a Parliament containing members for whose appointment nobody at the federal level was responsible. None the less, it is a serious fault that under the present system, a minority party, even though it may control the provincial legislature and elect a majority of the members of Parliament from that province, may not be able to secure even one representative in the Upper House.[73] There is also much to be said for giving the Senate some kind of suspensive veto like that exercised by the British House of Lords. "It may be doubted," writes Professor J. A. Corry, "whether any reform is of such immediacy that a year or two spent in broadening consent

72/Trudeau, *The Constitution and the People of Canada*, pp. 28–34 and 76–8.
73/Alberta has had since 1921 a United Farmer or Social Credit government in office and until 1958 consistently elected a majority of members from one or other of these parties to the House of Commons; but the senators from Alberta during this period have all been Liberals or Conservatives. A similar picture exists for Saskatchewan, where the CCF was in power provincially from 1944 to 1964, and in British Columbia, where the Social Credit party has been in power since 1952.

to it through the slow erosion of opposition is not well spent. For democracy is as much a matter of gaining the consent of minorities as it is of giving effect to the will of the majority."[74] But the most needed reform probably arises from the deadening effects of the long term. Incentive, interest, and vitality must be brought into the Senate, and the inflow of younger and more active members increased. For it is these qualities, rather than increased powers and challenging divisions, which will enable the Senate to discharge its functions adequately. There is every reason for the Senate to remain a secondary partner in the Canadian Parliament. There is no reason for it to remain the comparatively unimportant and ineffective body it has become; if it remains so, it must be emphasized, it will be by the Senate's own choice.

74/Corry and Hodgetts, *Democratic Government and Politics*, p. 188.

16 The House of Commons: representation

THE HOUSE OF COMMONS is the great democratic agency in the government of Canada; the "grand inquest of the nation"; the organized medium through which the public will finds expression and exercises its ultimate political power. It forms the indispensable part of the legislature; and it is the body to which at all times the executive must turn for justification and approval.

The fundamental importance of the House of Commons is thus derived from its essential representative character, the fact that it can speak, as no other body in the democracy can pretend to speak, for the people. It presents in condensed form the different interests, language groups, religions, classes, and occupations, whose ideas and wishes it embodies (sometimes with approximate exactness, sometimes not). It serves as the people's forum and the highest political tribunal; it is, to use Mill's phrase, "the nation's committee of grievances and its congress of opinions." One of its greatest merits is derived from the fact that it is not a selection of the ablest or most brilliant men in the country, but rather a sampling of the best of an average run that can survive the electoral system, an assembly of diverse types and varied experience, the members of which are genuinely and actively concerned with the promotion of the national welfare as they see it. No cabinet which keeps in constant touch with this body can be very far removed from fluctuations in public opinion, for the House is always acting as an interpreter and forcing this opinion on the attention of its leaders; conversely, a cabinet which grows out of touch with the Commons is courting disaster. Thus while a government will be frequently embarrassed by the need for satisfying the many demands which the House will put forward, it will also derive no inconsiderable benefit from these encounters. For the House gives guidance, encouragement, advice, and support to a government as well as disparagement and criticism; and the presentation and interchange of views, making possible a more exact appreciation of the nature of the popular response to government policies, enable the cabinet to proceed with far more assurance and certainty to the work which lies before it. Mackenzie King was by no means a convincing champion of Parliament; but he declared in the gloomy days of 1940:

I can say frankly to hon. members that it is a source of comfort rather than the opposite to have Parliament in session at a time such as this. I say that quite sincerely. There is comfort in the sense of knowing that where the situation is as serious as it is, the body of the people's representatives are here and can express freely their views, as can the Government its views and what it is doing, in a manner which it is not possible to do through the press ... I would not wish a long period to elapse, with the country and the world in the state in which it now is, without having an opportunity of consulting with members of Parliament and having them fully informed with respect to what the Government is doing.[1]

The companion function of the Commons and one which can scarcely be separated from the first is that of educating and leading public opinion on many questions. The House is much more than a mere mouthpiece to repeat and advertise the views of the constituencies. It will, of course, do that to a large extent, but it will also discuss many questions on which the voters have as yet no certain convictions or on which they may need further information and guidance. The House will talk, argue, investigate, oppose, decide, and frequently postpone action on many matters, and in doing these things it arouses interest and helps to create a more enlightened opinion throughout the country. The process in Canada is in no way different from that in Britain as described by Professor Ivor Jennings:

So the discussion radiates from Westminster in waves of ever-decreasing elasticity. Arguments are transmuted, prevented, simplified, perhaps distorted. A "common opinion" develops, and creates new waves which find their way back to Westminster. They set going new arguments in the smoke-room and more formally in the House. In their turn these arguments produce new rays which go back to the ordinary people. In this way there is a constant interchange between Parliament and people which does produce a constant assimilation of opinion ... The purpose of Parliament is to keep them [the cabinet] in touch with public opinion, and to keep public opinion in touch with the problems of government.[2]

With society growing so rapidly in complexity, Canadian governments have of late years become increasingly concerned about their communications with the public, both in receiving information, and in disseminating news about governmental activities, and new institutions to supplement the Commons' traditional rôle are undoubtedly in the making.[3]

The House of Commons, under the unremitting guidance of the cabinet and with the co-operation of the Senate, also sets its formal seal of approval upon

---

1/*Can. H. of C. Debates*, June 20, 1940, p. 972. See speech of Sir Winston Churchill, *Brit. H. of C. Debates*, Jan. 22, 1941, p. 257.

2/Sir Ivor Jennings, *Parliamentary Reform* (London, 1934), pp. 18–19.

3/Prime Minister Trudeau, for example, established regional desks in his office to facilitate and expedite communication on a territorial basis, and they were not entirely welcomed by MP s who felt they were in danger of being by-passed. See also *Report of Task Force on Government Information* (Ottawa, 1969).

legislation and matters of state policy. Here the Senate, as indicated in the previous chapter, takes a decidedly subordinate part, and it is not at all likely to set itself in serious opposition to the Commons, particularly if the latter's popular mandate is assured. These decisions of the legislative chambers will assume various forms: (1) statutes; (2) the imposition of taxes and the authorization of expenditures (which are only a special kind of statute); (3) resolutions, such as those requesting the British Parliament to amend the British North America Act, or those calling upon the Governor-in-Council to remove a judge or public official; and (4) formal declarations of state policy, which the executive will certainly carry into effect, such as those dealing with treaties, the declaration of war, etc.

The House of Commons will almost invariably give its consent to all the measures which the cabinet has submitted, although not necessarily on the cabinet's preconceived notions of what is a reasonable timetable; for in the process it exercises what is easily one of its major functions: criticism. Here, as in virtually all the activities of the House, the nature of the participation of the individual members depends on their party affiliations; and although their share is largely indirect and often inconspicuous, the influence they exert on government measures is far from small. If they belong to the majority party, they make themselves felt in the privacy of the government caucus where, separately or in association with other members, they may carry enough weight to bring about substantial modifications in the cabinet's proposals. If they belong to an opposition party they can vent their criticism on the government's measures when these come before the House, and they may sometimes be able at this time to secure concessions. But the full impact of the opposition will be more far-reaching and significant than this. For normally the cabinet will already have done its utmost to forestall opposition criticism by drafting proposals in the most innocuous terms possible, knowing full well the criticism which would follow if the measure were to appear in another form or without being substantially toned down from the original draft. A further possibility is that the criticism of the opposition may not pay dividends until the next general election, although in the meantime it will serve as invaluable material to use against the government not only on the floor of the House, but in the press and in the country generally. In short, the cabinet is always aware of the danger of allowing its opponents any base from which they can launch their attacks, and the surest defence is for it to endeavour to present its measures in such a form that they will be able to withstand any assault from the enemy.[4]

A vital aspect of the critical function of the House of Commons is its power of general supervision. This takes many forms and will be discussed later at some length.[5] The House asks the ministers interminable questions; it conducts

4/For a more extensive development of this point, see chap. XIX.
5/Infra, pp. 365 ff.

investigations into the administration of the departments; it draws out the activities of the government into the light of publicity; it scrutinizes the financial statements and proposed taxes and expenditures; it checks to a limited degree departmental orders and orders-in-council; it listens to ministerial statements on government policy; it receives petitions for redress of grievances. Many of these matters are related, of course, to cabinet functions, and the responsibility of the cabinet to the House of Commons is always both present and active.[6] As a last resort the House of Commons can withdraw its confidence from the cabinet, and thus obtain a new government or force a dissolution; this has happened to four of the nineteen administrations since Confederation.[7]

Finally, the House of Commons is a selective body. It does not actually pick the cabinet, although the fact that the cabinet, chosen by the prime minister, must always be able to retain the support of a majority of the House may be considered as giving the chamber a negative power of choice. It is somewhat more correct to say that the House selects the prime minister, although here the party convention (and, in unusual circumstances, the governor general) has, as a rule, more initial authority in the matter. Once again, however, the Commons must give its seal of approval after the choice has been made. But the House selects ministers indirectly in yet another way. It provides the rigorous environment in which ministerial talent must prove its worth and establish its right to office. The prospective ministers often (although not always) serve an arduous apprenticeship in the House; and while many cease to be serious contenders long before their party comes to power or vacancies occur in the cabinet, the few able survivors have had ample opportunity to develop their capacity before they are called upon to assume office. There is, in the words of Professor Laski, "no alternative method that in any degree approaches it."[8] The result is that a cabinet will usually take office with a fair percentage of able ministers; for while many of them may have had little or no previous training in such positions, the majority have had a preparation which has been proved by experience to be a most effective substitute.

REPRESENTATION

Representation in the Canadian House of Commons is federal in nature, based on population, and apportioned by provinces. This representation is checked after each decennial census, and, when necessary, it is adjusted among the

6/*Supra*, pp. 175–7.
7/In 1873 (an unusual case since Macdonald actually resigned in anticipation of defeat); 1926 (King); 1926 (Meighen); 1963 (Diefenbaker). Two of the defeated prime ministers made successful comebacks.
8/H. J. Laski, *A Grammar of Politics* (4th ed., London, 1938), p. 300.

provinces in accordance with shifts in population.[9] When new provinces were admitted to the Dominion after 1867, they were given seats in the House,[10] and the number of their members was thenceforth determined in the same manner as that of the other provinces.[11] The territories were granted representation in 1887;[12] but after Alberta and Saskatchewan became provinces, the territorial representation dropped to one until 1952, when a second was added.

The scheme which was adopted in 1867[13] and which remained in effect until 1946 was simple in its main outlines, and was designed to provide elasticity without allowing the size of the House to become unduly large. Quebec was given 65 members (the same number she had had in the pre-1867 assembly), and this number remained fixed. Representation from other provinces was to vary as their populations varied with that of Quebec. In other words, a quota of representation was obtained after each census by dividing the population of Quebec by 65, and this quota was then divided into the population of each province to determine the number of its representatives. The total number of members in the House as well as those from each province (except Quebec) might thus vary from decade to decade.

Although the general rule was simple, a number of exceptions introduced in 1867 and in subsequent years made the scheme rather complex and eventually led to its abandonment in 1946. These exceptions were as follows:

(a) The population of Quebec was not the population of modern Quebec, but was that of Quebec within the boundaries existing before the extension of the province in 1912. A population of even moderate size within this additional area would obviously have affected detrimentally the representation of all the other provinces. Until recently its population has been very small and hence could have had little effect on the quota.

(b) After the quota had been divided into the population of a province, any remainder which was more than one-half of the quota entitled the province to an additional member.

(c) A province was guaranteed, as its minimum representation in the House of Commons, the same number of members as it had senators. This special rule was stated in the 1915 amendment to the British North America Act,[14]

9/This has always been observed except after the census of 1941, when war conditions made postponement desirable. See 1943 amendment to the BNA Act, *supra*, pp. 122–3.

10/Under the 1871 amendment, *supra*, p. 121.

11/There were minor exceptions. British Columbia was given on its admission six members, and this number could be *increased* under the terms of the BNA Act, but apparently not decreased. Alberta and Saskatchewan had a special adjustment of representation shortly after entrance, although it was based on the principles in the BNA Act.

12/Under the 1886 amendment, *supra*, p. 121.

13/*Supra*, pp. 30–1. A full exposition of the system is given in Norman Ward, *The Canadian House of Commons: Representation* (Toronto, 1950), pp. 19–58; "The Redistribution of 1952," *Canadian Journal of Economics and Political Science*, XIX, no. 3 (Aug. 1953), pp. 341–60; and "A Century of Constituencies," *Canadian Public Administration*, X, no. 1, 1967, pp. 105–22.

14/*Supra*, p. 121.

and was inserted primarily to save the representation of Prince Edward Island and to some degree that of the other Maritime provinces. The number of members from all these provinces had for years past been steadily declining. In 1882 Prince Edward Island had 6 members, New Brunswick, 16, Nova Scotia, 21; but by 1914 these had dropped to 3, 11, and 14 respectively. The 1915 amendment thus guaranteed these provinces a minimum of 4, 10, and 10.

(d) The British North America Act provided that if the population of a province did not keep pace with that of Quebec but was nevertheless able to maintain approximately the same rate of increase as that of the Dominion as a whole, it would not lose any members on a redistribution. The key calculation was as follows: the proportion which the population of a province bore to that of the Dominion was ascertained for both the census ten years earlier and the current one, and if the latter proportion was not more than one-twentieth less than the former, no reduction in the representation of that province would be made under the general rule.

This exception would have been quite unobjectionable if its application had given to the particular province concerned the actual number of seats to which it had been entitled under the operation of the general rule ten years before. But it did far more than this. It allowed the province to retain its existing representation unimpaired, even although that number might have been saved for it ten years ago by an earlier operation of the same one-twentieth clause. Thus a discrepancy between representation and population could be perpetuated from decade to decade and might become gradually worse if the population continued to decline in relation to Quebec and yet kept step with the general increase in Canada.

Unfortunately, this proved to be no mere arithmetical possibility. Further, the clause did not come to the rescue of one of the weaker provinces (a contingency which might have been borne with equanimity) but saved Ontario, the largest province of all and the one which presumably needed no special concessions to maintain its voice and influence in Parliament. In 1914 Ontario had been given 82 members in the Commons. In 1924 she was entitled to 81; but the one-twentieth clause came to her aid, and she kept 82. In 1933 she would have received, under the general rule, 78; the exception allowed her to keep 82. Under the census of 1941, she would normally have fallen back to 74; but once again the one-twentieth clause would have permitted her to retain 82, the number established thirty years earlier. And this might have gone on indefinitely, each decade bringing about a greater and greater disparity between population and representation. Quebec with a mounting population thus saw her representation tied down to a fixed 65; while Ontario, whose population was not increasing at as fast a rate, nevertheless kept its artificial number of 82 intact. Quebec, not unnaturally, began to demand "rep. by pop."; the whirligig of time had indeed brought in its revenges.[15]

15/*Supra*, p. 122.

If the original plan of redistribution (with its amendments) had been applied
to the results of the 1941 census, the following exceptions to the general rule
would have resulted:

PEI	instead of	2 seats would have had	4(1915 amendment)
New Brunswick	" "	9 " " " "	10(1915 amendment)
Ontario	" "	74 " " " "	82(1-20th clause)
Nova Scotia	" "	11 " " " "	12(1-20th clause)
Alberta	" "	16 " " " "	17(1-20th clause)

When a rule governs four provinces and the exceptions govern five, the time for
formulating a better rule would seem to have arrived.

The result was the passage of the 1946 amendment to the British North
America Act, further amended in 1952, which substituted an entirely new
section on the redistribution of seats.[16] Under this arrangement the total number of members is supposed to be a constant and not a variable; and Quebec
is not tied down to a definite number, but is treated exactly the same as any
other province. The guarantee of a minimum number of seats for each province under the 1915 amendment is retained as before.

But although the one-twentieth clause had been repealed the practical need
for some clause of this kind remained, and only a few years' experience showed
that provinces which found themselves out of step with population changes
elsewhere in the Dominion would not submit quietly to a drastic reduction in
representation. Parliament therefore amended the British North America Act
in 1952 and made two changes in the system which had been accepted only
six years before. The first was that after a decennial census no province's representation should be reduced more than 15 per cent below the representation
to which it was entitled at the last redistribution. The second change was that
there should be no reduction in the representation of a province as a result of
which that province would have a smaller number of members than that of any
other province which according to the most recent census did not have a larger
population.[17] The second change was clearly intended to remedy an embarrassment which might arise from the operation of the first; but it also had
another effect; it raised the minimum of each of the four western provinces, so
long as their populations exceed New Brunswick's, to ten (the New Brunswick
minimum under the 1915 amendment). That is, so long as any province can
retain a population larger than that of New Brunswick (or Nova Scotia, for that
matter) its minimum number of representatives is ten by virtue of the combined operation of the 1915 and 1952 amendments.

The present system is applied as follows:[18]

(1) The total number of members in the House of Commons is set at 263;
but, as will be seen, this may be slightly increased by the operation of rules
below.

16/*Supra*, p. 122.
17/*Can. H. of C. Debates*, April 9, 1952, pp. 1419–22.
18/See Ward, "The Redistribution of 1952."

(2) The territories receive two seats, one for the Yukon and the other for the Northwest Territories.

(3) Each province's share is calculated by dividing the total population of the provinces by 261, and the quota thus obtained is divided into the population of each province.

(4) If this operation does not fill all 261 seats (and it is unlikely that it will do so) the remaining seats are awarded to the provinces having the largest remainders after rule (3) has been applied.

(5) If, after this has been done, any province has fewer members than senators, it is forthwith given the same number of members as it has senators. The calculations of rules (3) and (4) must then be done again, excluding the province or provinces affected by rule (5).

(6) No province shall have its representation reduced by more than 15 per cent below the representation to which such province was entitled at the last redistribution.

(7) No province shall have its representation reduced if by such a reduction it would have fewer members than any other province with a smaller population.

(8) Any extra seats which may result from the prohibition of rules (6) and (7) are added to the total of 263 and are not included in the divisor used in rules (3), (4), and (5).

It is evident that substantial alterations in the boundaries of constituencies

TABLE III

Changes in representation in the House of Commons as a result of recent censuses

	1921	1931	1941	1951	1961
Prince Edward Island	4	4	4	4	4
Nova Scotia	14	12	13	12	11
New Brunswick	11	10	10	10	10
Newfoundland			7	7	7
Quebec	65	65	73	75	74
Ontario	82	82	83	85	88
Manitoba	17	17	16	14	13
Saskatchewan	21	21	20	17	13
Alberta	16	17	17	17	19
British Columbia	14	16	18	22	23
Yukon Territory	1	1	1	1	1
Northwest Territories				1	1
Totals	245	245	262	265	264

SOURCE: *Canada Year Book, 1968*, pp. 82–92. It will be noted that Prince Edward Island and New Brunswick are now both at their minimum representation, and Nova Scotia, which in the redistribution on the 1961 census was saved a seat by clause (6) above, will reach its minimum after the census of 1971, thus becoming the third province protected by special rather than general rules.

within a province will often be necessary in order to allow for these changes in provincial representation, and that similar alterations are, in any event, often desirable in order that the constituencies may be adjusted to the shifting population within the province. Redistricting for both purposes is carried out simultaneously, and is completely under the control of Parliament.

The early method of dealing with redistribution was for the government to introduce into the House a bill which gave the constitutional allotment of seats and outlined in detail the altered boundaries of the newly drawn constituencies. The bill was then put through Parliament like any other government measure. This does not appear at first glance to be very objectionable; but it was accompanied in practice by abuse of the government's power. The cabinet in 1872, 1882, and 1892 used the opportunity to draw the constituency lines so that they greatly favoured its own party. This was especially flagrant in 1882 when forty-six constituencies in Ontario were gerrymandered, although in this instance popular indignation was so aroused that it is possible the act may have actually recoiled on its creators.[19]

The system was altered by Sir Wilfrid Laurier at the redistribution in 1903, when the detailed determination of constituency boundaries was referred by the House to a select committee on which both political parties were represented. The size and procedure of the committee varied considerably over the years, but essentially the same plan was followed on all subsequent occasions until the 1960s. It was fairer to the opposition, for while a majority of the committee members always came from the government side, every party had an opportunity to voice its views and influence the final decision. The result was that a gerrymander on a comprehensive scale disappeared, although it could (and did) occur in a small way and sometimes gave rise to wrangling and accusations of sharp practice. "Undoubtedly," said Bennett, when prime minister in 1933, "where two courses were open, our friends chose the course that was more helpful to them ... just as in 1924 the course chosen was the one more favourable to the party then in power."[20] It is improbable that coincidence alone in 1947 was responsible for the fact that "the three seats most adversely affected in the entire country had ... been held by three leading members of the Progressive Conservative party."[21]

Since before Confederation proposals have been advanced to overcome this kind of difficulty by giving the power of redistricting to some impartial body. Thus Mackenzie King in 1933 suggested a commission of six judges from different provinces (three to be nominated by the government, three by the opposition);[22] C. G. Power disclosed in 1947[23] that the government had had a bill prepared in 1940 to set up a commission composed of a superior court judge

19/R. MacG. Dawson, "The Gerrymander of 1882," *Canadian Journal of Economics and Political Science*, I, no. 2 (May 1935), pp. 197–221.
20/*Can. H. of C. Debates*, May 23, 1933, p. 5342.
21/Ward, "The Redistribution of 1952," p. 354.
22/*Can. H. of C. Debates*, May 25, 1933, pp. 5468–9.
23/*Ibid.*, Feb. 21, 1947, pp. 698–9.

as chairman assisted by two commissioners appointed from each province in turn as its constituencies came under consideration; annually from 1958 to 1962 Mr Douglas Fisher introduced a bill to provide for an independent commission; and finally in 1962 the prime minister produced a government bill for an "electoral boundaries commission" which survived first reading but was not proceeded with because of the dissolution of Parliament.[24]

The short-lived Parliament elected in 1962 was too preoccupied to carry the plan further, but that elected in 1963 shortly gave its attention to redistribution, and after a protracted debate that broke out sporadically for most of a year, settled on a wholly new method for drawing constituency boundaries, under a set of rules that was also new.[25] In essence, the new legislation created a new public office, the representation commissioner, and ten *ad hoc* boundary commissions, one for each province, which were empowered to have the final word (whatever objections might be received from the public or the House of Commons) on the maps they drew. Each commission had four members: a chairman, chosen by the chief justice of each province from among the members of his court; two members chosen by the Speaker of the House of Commons "from among such persons resident in that province as he deems suitable"; and the representation commissioner. Each commission published its map, held hearings to receive representations about it from the public, considered any proposed changes, and then sent the map, as amended, to the Speaker. Any ten MP s could then object to, and precipitate a debate about, any maps, after which the map, with a copy of the objections and the record of the debate, was returned to the relevant commission. The commission considered the objections, accepting or rejecting them as it saw fit, and drew its final map, which then became law.

The commissions did not have a free hand in drawing the maps. A variety of principles, and of notions masquerading as principals, had been employed in redistributions by the House of Commons after 1867, the most durable being that which resulted in urban constituencies being more populous than rural. The acceptance of that, combined with the rapid urbanization of the population in most provinces, had by the census of 1961 produced some startling anomalies: seats within Toronto ranged from 53,000 to 88,000, and those outside the immediate city from 29,000 to 267,000; the smallest in Canada was Iles-de-la-Madeleine at 12,479. The statutory rules enacted in 1964 put an end to most of these discrepancies:

In preparing its report each commission for a province shall be governed by the following rules:
(a) the division of the province into electoral districts and the description of the boundaries thereof shall proceed on the basis that the population of each electoral

---

24/*Ibid.*, April 9 and 17, 1962, pp. 2645–52 and 3040–9.
25/See Ward, "A Century of Constituencies"; T. H. Qualter, "Representation by Population: A Comparative Study," *Canadian Journal of Economics and Political Science*, XXXIII, no. 2 (May 1967), pp. 246–68.

district in the province as a result thereof shall correspond as nearly as may be to the electoral quota for the province ...

(c) the commission may depart from the strict application of rules (a) and (b) in any case where
  (i) special geographic considerations, including in particular the sparsity, density or relative rate of growth of population of various regions of the province, the accessibility of such regions or the size or shape thereof, appear to the commission to render such a departure necessary or desirable,
or
  (ii) Any special community or diversity of interest of the inhabitants of various regions of the province appears to the commission to render such a departure necessary or desirable,
but in no case ... shall the population of any electoral district in the province as a result thereof depart from the electoral quota for that province to a greater extent than twenty-five per cent more or twenty-five per cent less.[26]

These rules eliminated wide variations within each province, but, because of the operation of the law for sharing seats, not those among the provinces. Thus the seats in Prince Edward Island could vary 25 per cent above or below 26,157, those in New Brunswick 59,794, those in Nova Scotia 67,001, while in the rest of the provinces the provincial average was, in round figures, 70,500; the two far northern seats have populations of 14,628 and 22,998.

REPRESENTATIVE CHARACTER OF THE HOUSE

All members of the House of Commons are elected from single-member constituencies. Two constituencies – Halifax (city and county) and Queens (PEI) – had two members until the redistribution of 1965–6, when they were eliminated.[27] Upwards of nine hundred candidates, and as many as five or more parties, seek seats in each general election; commonly over half of those elected have only minority support.

This discrepancy between popular support and individual representation may easily be reproduced on a larger scale throughout the nation, as a sample of actual results for parties forming governments can show.[28]

1930: The Conservatives polled 49 per cent, and elected 56 per cent of the House.
1935: The Liberals polled 47 per cent, and elected 73 per cent of the House.
1940: The Liberals polled 54 per cent, and elected 75 per cent of the House.

26/Can. Statutes, 13–14 Eliz. II, c. 31, s. 13. The commissions in general concentrated on the 25 per cent tolerance the law allowed them, while objecting MP s wanted wider use, and different use, of other departures from "strict application" of the rules.
27/At one time (1872–92) no less than ten constituencies returned two members each; but they gradually dwindled to the two mentioned above. See Norman Ward, "Voting in Canadian Two-Member Constituencies," in John C. Courtney, ed., Voting in Canada (Toronto, 1967) pp. 125–9.
28/These percentages will vary somewhat according to the classification given to Liberal-Progressives, Progressives, Independent Liberals, etc.

1945: The Liberals polled 39 per cent, and elected 48.5 per cent of the House.
1957: The Conservatives polled 39 per cent, and elected 42 per cent of the House.
1958: The Conservatives polled 53 per cent, and elected 78.5 per cent of the House.
1962: The Conservatives polled 37 per cent, and elected 44 per cent of the House.
1963: The Liberals polled 42 per cent, and elected 49 per cent of the House.
1965: The Liberals polled 40 per cent, and elected 49 per cent of the House.
1968: The Liberals polled 45 per cent, and elected 59 per cent of the House.

In one of these instances (1957) the party polling the most votes did not receive the largest number of seats, and in 1962 there was virtually a tie in the popular vote polled by Liberals and Conservatives, but the Conservatives received 116 seats to the Liberals' 99; in the same election the New Democratic party considerably outdrew Social Credit, but won only 19 seats to Social Credit's 30; the NDP, indeed, invariably polls a percentage of votes at least twice its percentage of seats in the Commons. In all other instances above, the party polling the most votes (and often the *two* parties receiving the most votes) received more, and sometimes far more, than a rightful proportion of representatives. These jumbled results may be due in part to the inequality in the size of the constituencies before 1966; in part to a mixture of sweeping victories by one party and closely won elections by another; and in part to the parties' varying regional strengths; but the major cause was the election of candidates on pluralities (and not actual majorities) in three-, four-, and five-cornered contests. A slight shift in popular favour can cause a major shift in representation, with no assurance that the winner will have a majority of the popular votes. The sensitivity of the single-member system when combined with several political parties has been demonstrated many times; a typical conclusion follows:

What happened [in 1930] was that out of every 100 voters two left the Liberal party for the Conservative party and one left the independent parties for the Conservative party. Forty-six out of every 100 voters had been Conservatives in 1926; 49 out of every 100 voters were Conservatives in 1930. From 1926 to 1930 Canada was ruled by a government which had been elected by 48.6 per cent of the voters; from 1930 to 1935 she has been ruled by a government elected by 49.2 per cent of the voters. A net change in party allegiance of one voter out of every thirty caused the landslide of 1930.[29]

Nothing has yet been done to solve the problem of representation which is raised by this condition. There is a natural reluctance to adopt any system of

29/Escott Reid, "Democracy and Political Leadership in Canada," *University of Toronto Quarterly*, July 1935, p. 540. For illuminating recent studies on the workings of the electoral system see Alan C. Cairns, "The Electoral System and the Party System in Canada 1921–1965," *Canadian Journal of Political Science*, I, no. 1 (March 1968), pp. 55–80; Duff Spafford, "Some Characteristics of the Electoral System in Canada," and "An Estimate of the Relationship between Votes and Seats in Federal General Elections, 1921–65" (unpublished manuscripts kindly loaned me by the author). Professor Spafford, after detailed statistical analyses, concluded that for the two older parties "the random component in the operation of the electoral system – the element of 'gamble' to which systems like the Canadian are supposed to be subject – is relatively minor."

proportional representation which might give further encouragement to the multiplication of political parties, and even the alternative vote in single-member constituencies is under suspicion as likely to exert some pressure in the same direction. The alternative vote was mentioned in the speech from the throne in 1924, and a bill to authorize it was actually introduced by the government in 1924 and 1925; but on neither occasion did it go beyond the second reading. A special committee of the Commons reported in 1936 and 1937 against both the alternative vote and proportional representation,[30] and though the voting system is a perennial favourite in Parliament, it remains unaffected by debate.

The membership of the House of Commons shows in some ways a remarkable stability, regardless of electoral turnovers. Most members, for example, enter Parliament between the ages of 35 and 50, and there is a general tendency to elect fewer young men and more men who are over 40. Provincial differences in this respect, however, are marked. There is not even a rough correspondence of the age composition of the House to that of the total adult population. "The new members (and indeed the whole House of Commons) do not represent adequately the younger age-groups; they grossly over-represent the middle age-groups; and approximately represent only the older ones."[31] The House of Commons has aged since 1867, for the median age in 1945 was about five years older than that in the five Parliaments following Confederation; it now fluctuates between forty-five and fifty.

The turnover of members from one Parliament to another (as measured by the new ones elected at general and by-elections) is very large: it has rarely dropped below 40 per cent, and on at least five occasions since Confederation more than one-half the members of the House have had no previous experience.[32] The low turnovers of the elections of 1962, 1963, and 1965 are not characteristic of the general trend so far. High turnover has also been associated with relatively short tenures by all members. In general terms each House of Commons will show approximately the following composition:

No previous experience	35 to 55 per cent
One to five years' experience	20 to 35 per cent
Five to ten years' experience	10 to 20 per cent
Over ten years' experience	8 to 10 per cent[33]

While a House with a fairly constant membership is not to be desired, transient membership is most unfortunate. Too much time must be spent by new members in acquiring familiarity with their work; too large a proportion of mem-

30/*Can. H. of C. Journals*, June 11, 1936, pp. 446–8; *Can. H. of C. Debates*, April 6, 1937, pp. 2638–40.
31/Ward, *The Canadian House of Commons*, pp. 118–21. Later research has not seriously altered any of these generalizations. See Hoffman and Ward, *Bilingualism and Biculturalism in the House of Commons*.
32/Ward, *The Canadian House of Commons*, pp. 115–18.
33/*Ibid.*, p. 137.

bers will be forced through ignorance to give automatic acquiescence to the proposals of their leaders; valuable experience and knowledge melt away just when they are beginning to yield the maximum return.

It will be recalled, however, that one of the greatest merits of the House of Commons is not its expert or specialized character, but rather that it furnishes a wide assortment of men of different types and with varied backgrounds. Almost all major occupations are found in the House, with a heavy emphasis on middle class professions and callings and on those with a great deal of formal education; but there is little or no correlation between the occupations of the members and the number or importance of these occupations in the country. This should not be unduly emphasized, for it is not desirable that the members should look upon themselves as the exclusive representatives of any special economic or social group. Yet this occupational distribution of members cannot be ignored. The fact that approximately one-third of the total number are lawyers, and that agriculture, business, manufacturing, finance and insurance, and teaching come next in about that order[34] will have its effect on the House and will influence the general approach of the members to many public questions;[35] the House rarely contains a carpenter, a truck driver, or a railway porter or indeed anybody from the non-professional wage-earning segments of society. It is difficult to believe that a distribution which corresponded more closely with the occupational census of the nation would not furnish a more useful Parliament for most purposes.[36] But the electoral system, as twenty-eight consecutive elections have proven, is highly selective, however open it is theoretically to all qualified citizens. The dominant single factor in this selectivity is almost certainly money.[37]

REPRESENTATIVE AND DELEGATE THEORIES

One vital aspect of representation is the attitude of the member and his constituency to one another, a relationship which is usually set out in terms of the conflicting delegate and representative theories. According to the former theory, the member is the mouthpiece of his constituency, the necessary human agent through which the voters continually register their will. According to the latter, the member is chosen to represent the nation as well as the local area,

34/*Ibid.*, pp. 131–6. The bias of the House in occupational matters has not materially changed in recent elections. For a general examination of élites in Canada, see John Porter, *The Vertical Mosaic* (Toronto, 1965).

35/Note, for example, the protest of one member of Parliament in 1941 concerning the composition of a proposed committee which included fifteen lawyers and only nine from other occupations, a personnel which he contended would be likely to impede seriously the work of the committee. *Can. H. of C. Debates*, March 5, 1941, pp. 1263–4.

36/See J. F. S. Ross, *Parliamentary Representation* (2nd ed., London, 1948), pp. 58–77.

37/See *Report of Committee on Election Expenses* (Ottawa, 1966), and its accompanying volume, *Studies in Canadian Party Finances*.

and he is expected to use his talents and make his decisions largely by the exercise of his own personal judgment. So far as any generalization on such a matter is possible, the bulk of the Canadian constituencies and of the members who sit for them favour the representative rather than the delegate idea, although in most instances a substantial dependence on the constituency is apparent. One of the clearest statements of this representative position was given some years ago by Mr C. G. Power in the House of Commons:

A better-class candidate is a man who has some respect for his conscience and for his duty, and proposes to come here and do it. A member of Parliament, when he is elected by his constituency ... is elected, not to be the mouthpiece or delegate of any group or class in his constituency, but to represent in this House the whole people of Canada. He comes here to give his best judgment upon the questions which are put before him – not to give a decision based upon instructions he may have received from people thousands of miles away who know nothing of the question under discussion ... If it be democratic to allow a small group of ward heelers ... to control the decisions which a member may make in the House of Commons in the performance of his duty, I do not believe in that kind of democracy.[38]

The delegate theory, however, is not without its defenders in Canada; for it has obtained support from some of the minor parties, which have followed it both by instructing their members and through the use or attempted use of the recall. Thus the United Farmers applied a recall procedure within that party about 1920 by compelling their candidates to agree to abide by it before they received the party nomination; and Alberta had a Recall Act on the statute book, although it was repealed in 1937. In the federal field the use of the recall and the allied restrictions on a member's freedom were prohibited some years ago. The Canada Elections Act now makes it illegal for any candidate for election to the House of Commons to sign any document which would require him "to follow any course of action that will prevent him from exercising freedom of action in Parliament if elected, or to resign as such member if called upon to do so by any person, persons, or association of persons."[39]

The relationship, however, rarely offers a clear-cut choice between these two alternatives of representation and delegation, and there are almost as many variations as there are members and constituencies. For a member is bound by many obligations, pledges, and loyalties; and any decision will incline one way or another in accordance with the relative strength of the many complex forces which are operating at that time and on that issue. One of these determinants is made up of the pledges which he has given to his constituents. Another is composed of the promises which his party has made and to which he, as the party's representative, is indirectly committed. His character, his knowledge, his experience, his loyalty to his party and its leaders, his own convictions on the

38/*Can. H. of C. Debates*, Feb. 24, 1939, pp. 1307–8.
39/*Can. Statutes*, 8–9 Eliz. II, c. 39, s. 105.

matter, these and similar factors may all enter into his decision and determine to what degree he will abide by his own judgment and that of others whom he esteems or in whom he has confidence. Other very important forces, of course, are the desires and opinions of his constituency, of his party executive, of the local newspapers, of the lukewarm opponents he may be trying to conciliate, and so on. To what extent will the constituency feel aggrieved if its expressed wishes are courteously but unmistakably ignored? How will this effect his re-nomination? His re-election? What likelihood is there that after a time the interest in this particular matter will die down; or that his constituency will realize that his position in Parliament gives him a better opportunity to form a more careful and accurate judgment, and that his opinion is, after all, apt to be right? A situation with so many possibilities can rarely be reduced to the two simple alternatives of a member making his own decision or allowing his constituency to make it for him.

The ideal relationship is one where, as Macaulay said, the electors choose cautiously and confide liberally; then, after the term has expired, they will review the conduct of the member and pronounce on his stewardship as a whole. The indispensable ingredients are tolerance, compromise, and mutual respect. The member must be conscientious, yet not stubborn; tactful, yet firm; he will give way when possible, and he will refuse to make concessions when he feels it unwise or against his deep convictions. The constituency will hold its representative to his pledges; it will at all times place its views before him and urge their acceptance; yet it should be willing to recognize the sincerity of his opinions, his honesty, his actual inability on some occasions to comply with all its wishes. It would, of course, be absurd to pretend that Canadian members and their constituencies move always or even customarily on this high plane; but there is no doubt that some allowance is continually made for differences of opinion, that explicit instructions to members are rarely issued, and that compromises and mutual understanding between a member and his constituency are common. An interesting case arose in 1942 when the Liberal government insisted on a plebiscite in order to secure release from an explicit anti-conscription pledge which the party had given at the election two years before. The plebiscite (which gave the desired release) did not, however, settle all problems, for some members found themselves in accord with the general verdict but in disagreement with the vote in their own constituencies. Mr Power was in this group; and he proceeded to put his theory of representation to the proof by voting on what he conceived to be national lines and against the clearly expressed wishes of his constituents.[40] At the next election Mr Power was returned with over ten thousand majority, although in the interval he had re-established the accord with his own constituents by resigning from the cabinet on the conscription issue.

40/See *Can. H. of C. Debates*, June 26, 1942, pp. 3723–4.

THE FRANCHISE

The franchise in Canada has had a chequered history.[41] In the first fifty years of the federation when political animosities were bitter and political standards were often low, it was not uncommon for the rival parties to try to gain an advantage by the manipulation of the franchise, and this effort was materially aided by party disagreements on the use of the provincial franchise in Dominion elections. Inasmuch as such changes were necessarily made by statute, these became the boundary lines which have marked off the different periods from one another.

(a) *First period:* provincial franchise (1867–85). The British North America Act (section 41) provided that all electoral matters in the first Dominion election were to be governed by existing provincial laws and would remain so for the future until they were changed by the Canadian Parliament. The reason for this provision was stated by Macdonald in the Confederation debates in 1865:

Insuperable difficulties would have presented themselves if we had attempted to settle now the qualification for the elective franchise. We have different laws in each of the colonies fixing the qualification of electors for their own local legislatures; and we therefore adopted a similar clause to that which is contained in the Canada Union Act of 1841, viz., that all the laws which affected the qualification of members and of voters, which affected the appointment and conduct of returning officers and the proceedings at elections, as well as the trial of controverted elections in the separate provinces, should obtain in the first election to the Confederate Parliament, so that every man who has now a vote in his own province should continue to have a vote in choosing a representative to the first Federal Parliament. And it was left to the Parliament of the Confederation, as one of their first duties, to consider and to settle by an act of their own the qualification for the elective franchise, which would apply to the whole Confederation.[42]

Five Dominion elections were held under the provincial franchises. For although Macdonald (as indicated above) believed that the Dominion should determine the qualifications of all those who voted in its elections, he was unable to persuade all his followers; and the Liberals stood firmly for provincial control which they considered to be more in accord with the idea of federalism. Several circumstances eventually brought a change. Some provincial governments had begun to disfranchise employees of the Dominion; and as these were appointed by patronage, and as Conservative governments had been in power at Ottawa for most of the time since Confederation, the great majority of those affected by these provincial laws were Conservatives. It not unnaturally irked a Conservative cabinet to see the most reliable of party supporters (including many on the payroll of the government-owned Inter-

---

41/Ward, *The Canadian House of Commons,* pp. 211–32. The pre-Confederation story is in Garner, *The Franchise and Politics in British North America.*
42/*Confederation Debates,* 1865, p. 39.

colonial Railway) deprived of an opportunity for showing their gratitude to the party which had given them their positions; indeed, there was something to be said for a perverted form of patronage which would give the Liberals all the government jobs in order to accomplish their disfranchisement. But the Conservatives preferred a more straightforward approach and therefore launched an attack on the franchise itself. Another factor was that a number of the provinces were abandoning the early property qualifications for the suffrage, and were thereby transplanting these electoral practices into Dominion politics. Macdonald and the Conservative party generally had little sympathy with such advanced ideas of democracy and wished to retain a property qualification. Finally, a Dominion franchise would necessitate Dominion election lists, and these in turn would involve widespread patronage in their preparation and frequent revision, an advantage which was not overlooked by the Dominion cabinet. Taken together, the arguments for a Dominion franchise were considered to be not only cogent, but conclusive.

(b) Second period: Dominion franchise (1885-98). The Electoral Franchise Act was enacted in 1885,[43] after some of the stormiest scenes in Canada's parliamentary history. It set up uniform qualifications for voting in a Dominion election, which were based on a low property test; its original draft extended the franchise to widows and spinsters with the property qualification, but the clause was defeated in committee and dropped. The Liberals opposed the bill vehemently on theoretical grounds and also because of the cost, the party jobbery, and the manipulation which it encouraged. It proved in practice to be very expensive. The Liberal opposition continued unabated for years afterwards, and at their national convention in 1893 they promised repeal if returned to power. In 1898 the new Liberal government repealed the Franchise Act.

(c) Third period: provincial franchise (1898-1917). The act of 1898[44] eliminated the separate Dominion franchise and returned to those of the different provinces. It provided, however, that no person could be disqualified from voting at a Dominion election because he was an employee of either the Dominion or a provincial government. When the Conservative government came to power in 1911, it made no move to change the existing law, which remained intact until the passage of two special measures brought about by the First World War.

(d) Fourth period: combined Dominion-provincial franchise (1917-20). For a few years the franchise was both fish and fowl: it used the old provincial franchises with additions and subtractions made by the Military Voters Act and the War Time Elections Act of 1917. The general purposes of these acts were plain and unmistakable: they were to give the vote to those who would support the government, to take it away from those who would oppose it, and to

43/Can. Statutes, 48-49 Vict., c. 40.
44/Ibid., 61 Vict., c. 14.

create a floating military vote, a large part of which would almost certainly be given to government candidates. The Military Voters Act[45] thus enfranchised all Canadian men and women on active service, and made it possible for a substantial part of the military vote to be cast in such constituencies as might be suggested to the voters at the time the poll was held. The War Time Elections Act[46] denied the vote to conscientious objectors, enfranchised the wives, widows, and other female relatives of men overseas, and disfranchised both those of enemy alien birth and those of European birth speaking an enemy alien language who were naturalized after 1902. A year later, the election being over, the vote was extended to all women who were otherwise qualified.[47]

(e) *Fifth period:* Dominion franchise (1920 to the present). In 1920[48] Parliament passed a new act which straightened out the confusion created during the previous years and once more set up a Dominion franchise for all Dominion elections. Since then all parties have accepted the general principle, and there is no reason to suppose that there will be any attempt to revert to the provincial basis. The provinces still, of course, control the franchise for provincial elections.

Canada has today full adult suffrage. Generally speaking, every man and woman may vote if he or she is qualified as to age, is a Canadian citizen, or other British subject who has been ordinarily resident in Canada for twelve months preceding the election and has been ordinarily resident in the electoral district at the date of issuing the writ authorizing the election. Certain persons are, however, disqualified for special reasons, these being the chief and assistant chief electoral officer; the returning officer in each district (except for a deciding vote in case of a tie); every judge appointed by the Governor-in-Council; lunatics; inmates in penal institutions; anyone who is found guilty of corrupt or illegal practices at elections; and persons in several other categories. Canadian Indians, who had been excluded from the franchise since shortly after Confederation, were made eligible as voters in 1960. In May 1970 the government introduced legislation to lower the voting age to eighteen.

ELECTIONS

General supervision over the Dominion elections is vested in the chief electoral officer, an independent official (created in 1920) who is given special protection in the Canada Elections Act.[49] He is chosen by a resolution of the House of Commons, holds office during good behaviour, may be removed

45/*Ibid.*, 7–8 Geo. v, c. 34
46/*Ibid.*, 7–8 Geo. v, c. 39. A full account of the origin and history of these acts is in Graham, *Arthur Meighen*, I, chaps. 6–8. See also Ward, *The Canadian House of Commons*, pp. 226–30.
47/*Ibid.*, 8–9 Geo. v, c. 20.
48/*Ibid.*, 10–11 Geo. v, c. 46.
49/8–9 Eliz II, c. 39. This 1960 consolidation and amendment of the Canada Elections

only for cause in the same manner as a judge of the Supreme Court of Canada (that is, by the Governor-in-Council acting on a joint address passed by both Houses of Parliament), and is entitled to all the benefits of the Public Service Superannuation Act. The chief electoral officer issues the writs for the elections to returning officers in each constituency (although the date for the election is fixed by the Governor-in-Council) and after the election these officers return the writs to the chief electoral officer together with all necessary reports and documents covering the elections in the constituencies.

The nomination of candidates for seats in the House of Commons is usually a dual process. The prospective candidate will, as a rule, secure in the first instance a nomination from one of the political parties, and this (or any other form of declaration constituting candidacy) will, if there is a vacancy in his electoral district, at once make him legally responsible under the Elections Act for his conduct as a candidate.[50] The second step which must be taken is largely a formality, but it is quite indispensable if the candidate wishes to have his name appear on the ballot paper and receive any votes on the day of the election. Any twenty-five qualified voters may formally nominate a candidate by signing a nomination paper giving the name, address, and occupation of the candidate in sufficient detail to identify him. This nominating paper must be accompanied by (a) the candidate's consent in writing or, if the candidate is absent, a statement to that effect on the nominating paper; and (b) a deposit of $200. The deposit is intended to discourage irresponsible or flippant candidacies, and will be returned if the person nominated is elected or if he polls at least half the number of votes cast in favour of the successful candidate. If only one candidate is nominated, he is declared elected by acclamation. If a candidate should die after the close of nominations (which is one or two weeks before election day) and before the closing of the polls, another nomination day and election day is set. The names of candidates are placed on the ballot in alphabetical order and the address and occupation of each are added to ensure identification, but the name of their political parties or any similar designations is omitted (except on lists of candidates printed especially for members of the armed forces). In some parts of Canada the identification of candidates is a continuing problem, for it is not unknown for a party faced with a strong opponent to find another man with the same name and to nominate him too, in order to split the strong candidate's vote.[51]

In the early days of the federation the nomination of candidates for the

Act was examined carefully by a House committee and in 1969–70 the electoral system was again subjected to a careful study. See House of Commons, Standing Committee on Privileges and Elections, *Minutes of Proceedings and Evidence,* 1959 and 1960, and 1969–70.

50/See *General Election Instructions for Returning Officers* (Queen's Printer, 1964), p. 151; *infra,* chap. XXII.

51/See *Can. H. of C. Debates,* July 12, 1960, pp. 6130–1. The Committee on Election Expenses made several recommendations concerning identification. See *Report of Committee on Election Expenses,* chap. 4.

House of Commons was made in public, voting was open and oral, and the elections were not all held on the same day, but extended over many weeks.[52] Open voting encouraged bribery and intimidation, and the same practice combined with a lengthy election period allowed the results in one part of the province or Dominion to influence subsequent voting. Plural voting, an offshoot of the property franchise and made possible largely by the prolonged poll, was also permitted in some provinces and hence was used in Dominion elections. All these electoral practices were closely related to the nature of political organization at the time. An act of 1874,[53] however, made many changes. It abolished public nominations, instituted voting by secret ballot, and provided (with some exceptions which were made necessary by geographical conditions) for elections to be held on one and the same day. Some small remnants of plural voting persisted in federal elections until as late as 1920, when with the return to the dominion franchise "one man, one vote" became the invariable rule.[54]

CONTROVERTED ELECTIONS

Closely associated with these matters is the decision of controverted election cases.[55] These involve irregularities or corrupt or illegal practices at elections, and they may result in the election being declared void and the successful candidate losing his seat. Election disputes of this kind had given a great deal of trouble before Confederation, and they continued to do so in the years which followed. Like the other early election procedures, they came under the existing provincial laws, and these provisions were by no means uniform. Thus the laws of two provinces gave disputes of this kind to a general committee of the House; in other provinces cases arising from elections went to select committees of the House; while in Manitoba and British Columbia these cases were tried by judges of the superior courts.[56] The system was not only clumsy, it was often grossly inefficient; for the disputes which went to the legislative committees were rarely, if ever, decided on any but partisan grounds. The practice of having the House hear these cases had been originally copied from Great Britain and constituted one of the privileges of Parliament; but when the British Parliament in 1868 handed them over to the courts, Canada began to consider a similar solution. Parliament passed the necessary legislation five

52/Thus in 1867, elections ran from Aug. 7 to Sept. 20; and in 1872, from July 20 to Oct. 12. See Sir Richard Cartwright, *Reminiscences* (Toronto, 1912), pp. 29–1; Ward, *The Canadian House of Commons*, chap. VII.
53/*Can. Statutes*, 37 Vict., c. 9.
54/*Ibid.*, 10–11 Geo. V, c. 46, s. 57; *Can. H. of C. Debates*, April 13, 1920, pp. 1158–9.
55/Campaign funds and election expenses are discussed in chap. XXIII.
56/See R. MacG. Dawson, *The Principle of Official Independence* (London, 1922), pp. 51–4.

years later in 1873,[57] and this has formed the basis of the existing law. Briefly, controverted election cases are now heard by two superior court judges (without a jury) from the province where the election has been held, and they report their findings to the Speaker of the House of Commons. An appeal from the court's decision on both law and fact lies to the Supreme Court of Canada.[58] Controverted election cases were extremely common for many decades after Confederation, but are now rare.

BY-ELECTIONS

Finally, representation in the House of Commons involves not only its periodic renewal at the general election, but also occasional appeals through by-elections, those contests which are held from time to time to fill vacancies which occur through death, acceptance of office,[59] resignation, or some other cause. By-elections are a useful adjunct to parliamentary government.[60] Though there is often room for disagreement about what their results really mean, they provide an opportunity for both cabinet and opposition to test their policies in sample constituencies; they furnish an instrument through which the people can give encouragement or warning to those in power; and the intensive discussion of public questions in the constituency is widely reported and has a marked educative effect throughout the entire nation. The by-election also introduces an element of flexibility into Parliament: the membership does not remain frozen into a shape determined some years before, but becomes to some degree adjusted to changing opinions and circumstances. "The essential test of an electoral system is not its static efficiency, but its dynamic efficiency ... What we require of the House of Commons is that it should be not a snapshot of the electorate at a particular moment, but a moving picture. By all means let the picture be as accurate as possible, but it is infinitely more important that it should move ... It will always be more important that the representative chamber should be sensitive than that it should be a mathematically accurate reflection of the electorate at a given moment."[61]

The by-election is no straw vote based on a cold uninformed opinion; it is a genuine contest conducted on well-prepared ground and under substantially the same conditions as a general election. A comparatively obscure constituency may thus suddenly find itself the centre of national interest and disputa-

57/*Can. Statutes*, 36 Vict., c. 28. Provincial legislatures later followed suit, and all have given their own controverted election cases to the courts. See Ward, *The Canadian House of Commons*, chap. XIV.

58/*Rev. Stat. Can.* (1952), c. 87.

59/This is a special way of vacating a seat which is more fully discussed later. *Infra*, pp. 329–31.

60/See Howard A. Scarrow, "By-Elections and Public Opinion in Canada," *Public Opinion Quarterly*, XXIX (Spring 1961), pp. 79–91.

61/*New Statesman*, March 11, 1922, p. 638.

tion, and every voter in the area is made to feel that momentous issues hang on his considered judgment. Opposition leaders pour into the district; the voters are overwhelmed by literature, canvassers, broadcasts, and public meetings; and even weary cabinet ministers will find time to participate and lend the government candidate a helping hand. For the issue is not simply a matter of winning or losing a seat: it is to a greater degree the increase or decrease in the size of the party vote which was polled in the last contest in that district and hence each party has a goal in view which may be quite within its reach. Victory is good, but in terms of comparative figures it may actually be disaster; defeat is a discouragement, but it may, in fact, indicate a growing ascendancy and a promise of later triumphs.

The consequences of a by-election or series of by-elections may be far-reaching. The votes will scarcely have been counted before calculators and interpreters will be wrestling with the results, newspapers will carry weighty editorials on the significance of the contest, and party councils will review their programmes with either complacency or consternation. For there is not the slightest doubt that the political leaders watch and weigh the by-election results with exceptional care, and several lost seats or a dwindling in popular majorities will do more to bring a government or party to its senses than all the attacks of its opponents in the Commons. In 1934, for example, six by-elections were held: the Liberals retained three seats, took two from the Conservatives, and reduced the Conservative majority in the sixth by 4,569 votes.[62] Five out of these six elections preceded by slightly more than three months Bennett's "New Deal" addresses, and it is difficult to escape the conclusion that this programme and the willingness of many of his party to accept so radical a departure were greatly influenced by the succession of electoral reverses which had just occurred.[63] In 1942 the defeat of Arthur Meighen, the newly chosen Conservative leader, in a by-election in a strong Conservative constituency[64] shook the Conservative party to its foundations, and most certainly lost Meighen the leadership. In 1945 the defeat of General McNaughton, the new Liberal minister of Defence, in a by-election was a clear sign of the dissatisfaction in English-speaking Canada with the Liberal conscription policy and, but for the favourable progress of the war, would in all likelihood have had serious political repercussions. When a cabinet does not have a majority in the House from among its own party supporters, as was the case in seven of the eleven years before the election of 1968, a single by-election can be crucial.

But the efficacy of the by-election depends in large measure upon its haphazard occurrence; and the more controlled the timing and the choice of locale, the less likely is it to serve its purpose. A contest held under conditions which

62/In all six districts the Liberals improved their 1930 standing by 23,133 votes, or an average of 3,855 votes for each district.
63/See Can. H. of C. Debates, Feb. 20, 1939, p. 1131.
64/South York turned a Conservative majority of 4,456 into a CCF majority of 2,482.

suit one side and not the other is always unsatisfactory, but it is an unavoidable concomitant of a general election. At a by-election it is equally undesirable, but not at all unavoidable. The time for calling the general election must be left within the power of the government to control; that for the by-election is better left to circumstance, although it is reasonable to suppose that a government ought not to be free to leave a constituency unrepresented indefinitely. As it is, the government has substantial leeway in the calling of a by-election, for it has six months from formal notification of a vacancy in the House of Commons in which to name a date, and can name any date it wishes; thus in the spring of 1962 the government announced autumn dates for some by-elections, and the writs were superseded by the calling of the general election on June 18. Until recently there were no restrictions at all on the government's control of by-elections, and it was free to call some and ignore others. For example, seven vacancies occurred in the House in 1934–5 following the disastrous series of by-elections noted above, but the government refused to take any risks and the vacancies remained until the end of the Parliament.[65] In 1947 a by-election was held in Montreal, while one in Halifax was put off for many months, the cabinet evidently thinking it could carry the one riding and not the other. The old system of requiring new cabinet ministers who accepted portfolios to seek re-election[66] had this genuine merit: it materially increased the number of by-elections, and they were invariably elections which could not be postponed. From this point of view, at least, the abolition of the practice was decidedly short-sighted.

65/See Can. H. of C. Debates, Feb. 14, 1939, pp. 902–3.
66/Infra, pp. 329–31.

17 The House of Commons: personnel

The qualifications of members of the House of Commons (unlike those of the senators) are not given in the British North America Act, but are determined by statute. Those of the members in the early Canadian House were fixed by the provincial laws which governed the respective provincial legislatures until the Dominion Parliament set up its own requirements. The present statutory qualifications are simple: the members must be Canadian citizens or other British subjects, qualified electors, and at least twenty-one years of age. Property qualifications disappeared in 1874 at the same time the ballot was introduced[1]

There are, however, certain positions or circumstances which will disqualify a person from being a candidate for or sitting as a member of the House of Commons. The following are ineligible: (1) those convicted of corrupt or illegal electoral practices (they cannot sit for a period of seven or five years respectively after conviction); (2) government contractors; (3) certain public officers, such as sheriff, County Crown Attorney, etc.; (4) members of a provincial legislature[2] or a territorial council; senators;[3] (6) persons holding offices of profit or emolument under the Crown, with the exception of cabinet ministers, parliamentary secretaries, members of the armed services on active service, and members of the militia.[4] While the House cannot on its own motion

1/*Can Statutes*, 37 Vict., c. 9, s. 20.
2/These were not always barred, although Nova Scotia and New Brunswick from the beginning prohibited the members of their legislatures from sitting in either Dominion house. The Canadian Parliament imposed a conditional prohibition in 1872 (35 Vict., c. 15) and a complete prohibition in the following year (36 Vict., c. 2) on members of a provincial legislature either running as candidates for or sitting in the House of Commons. It was possible for a member of the Quebec Legislative Council (abolished in 1968) to be at the same time a senator. See Ward, *The Canadian House of Commons*, pp. 65–9.
3/BNA Act, s. 39.
4/The grounds of ineligibility given above are not complete. See *Can. Statutes*, 8–9

(that is, without resorting to legislation) add to these disqualifications of candidates, it can by simple resolution expel a member or refuse to admit him. Louis Riel, for example, was in effect twice expelled,[5] Thomas McGreevy was expelled in 1891 for his part in certain scandals,[6] and in 1947 the House passed a resolution that Fred Rose "having been adjudged guilty of an indictable offence and sentenced to six years' imprisonment and not having served the punishment to which he was adjudged, has become and continues to be incapable of sitting or voting in this House, and it is ordered that Mr. Speaker do issue his warrant to the Chief Electoral Officer to make out a new writ for the election of a new member."[7]

Offices of profit or emolument under the Crown

The general rule that no person can hold an office of profit or emolument under the Crown and remain a member of the House of Commons was originally formulated in England to guard against members being brought under sinister executive control, an abuse which dates back to the efforts of Tudor and Stuart sovereigns to acquire parliamentary support through a careful if not too scrupulous use of the power of appointment.[8] If applied without exception, it would clearly exclude from the House not only judges, civil servants, and other officials (which is desired) but also any cabinet minister who received a salary – an absurd and impossible restriction under the British system of cabinet government.[9] Following the English precedent, the Canadian statute[10] for many years declared that if a member of the House accepted a portfolio (that is, a position in the cabinet and the headship of a department) he could regain his seat if, as minister, he was *then* elected to the House. In short, the constituency had to give its approval to the member *while holding the office of a salaried minister*. Thus if the members of a cabinet who were already in office were returned at a general election, they would not have to be re-elected; if, however, as a result of a general election the government

---

Eliz. II, c. 39, ss. 20, 80. An unusual aspect of disqualification came up in 1966 when it appeared that about forty MP s might have forfeited their seats by accepting fees from the CBC for appearing on broadcasts. See *Can. H. of C. Debates*, Dec. 14, 1966, pp. 1111–20.

5/Technically, Riel was expelled only the first time. The second time the House merely approved a motion that he "appears" to have "been adjudged an outlaw for felony," which disqualified him. See *Can. H. of C. Journals*, 1875, pp. 122–5. The House on this occasion rejected a motion to expel Riel.

6/Sir J. G. Bourinot, *Parliamentary Procedure and Practice in the Dominion of Canada*, ed. T. B. Flint (3rd ed., Toronto, 1903), pp. 255–61.

7/*Can. H. of C. Debates*, Jan. 30, 1947, p. 2.

8/Rectified in England by the Act of Settlement (1700), s. 3.

9/This curious situation actually arose in Prince Edward Island in 1859–63, when the law excluded from the legislature all office-holders in receipt of salaries. During this period the cabinet consisted entirely of ministers without portfolio and hence unpaid. Forsey, *The Royal Power of Dissolution of Parliament*, p. 222; Frank MacKinnon, *The Government of Prince Edward Island* (Toronto, 1951), pp. 97–8.

10/*Rev. Stat. Can.* (1927), c. 147, s. 13.

changed, or if at any other time one or more new ministers took office, the extra elections would become necessary. Special provisions were made to permit a mere exchange of portfolios taking place within the cabinet without the necessity of an additional election.[11]

This curious arrangement, although based on conditions which had long ceased to carry any weight, had one great merit: it caused from time to time a number of by-elections at which the record of the government was brought into special prominence, inasmuch as the immediate issue was the election or rejection of a cabinet minister. But certain other features were not so easily defended.[12] It was, for example, quite meaningless to have a general election and overthrow a government, to swear in a new cabinet immediately, and then to have the new ministers – fresh from an election a few weeks before – return to their constituencies and submit to further elections. These by-elections were, indeed, so superfluous that in almost every instance the ministers were returned by acclamation.

Another awkward situation arose when a cabinet was changed in the middle of the parliamentary session. On the new cabinet assuming office, some fifteen or twenty seats would become immediately vacant; there would be no cabinet to meet the House; and usually the most feasible alternative was to adjourn the House for some weeks until the by-elections could be held and the ministers had had an opportunity to regain their seats. If the new government's majority was uncertain (and, under the circumstances, it was almost bound to be so) its majority might easily have vanished after (or conceivably even before) the fifteen or twenty vacant seats had been filled. It was to avoid these delays and embarrassments that Meighen, when he accepted office in 1926,[13] formed his ministry. This was composed of Meighen, who had by the operation of the law automatically vacated his seat on becoming prime minister, and several others, who were made ministers without portfolio and acting ministers of the several departments; as such they received no salary and could therefore retain their

11/The notorious "double shuffle" of 1858 arose from a clause in the statute dealing with such a contingency. The statute at that time stated that a minister who resigned and within a month accepted *another* portfolio did not thereby vacate his seat. The Macdonald-Cartier government resigned in 1858, and after a few days came back into office. In order to avoid by-elections, most of the ministers took "offices which they had no intention of occupying permanently." The next day "they all changed back to their proper portfolios once more." D. G. Creighton, *John A. Macdonald: The Young Politician* (Toronto, 1952), p. 269.

12/See *Can. H. of C. Debates*, May 8, 1931, pp. 1407–14.

13/Mackenzie King's government, already defeated on a sub-amendment, had been in imminent danger of being defeated again by a vote pending in the House, and he had advised the governor general to dissolve. The latter refused, stating that as Arthur Meighen had the largest single party in the House and as an election had been held only eight months earlier, Meighen should be given an opportunity to form a government. King thereupon resigned and Lord Byng sent for Meighen. Meighen, although head of the largest party in the House, had no majority and was thus forced to depend on Progressive support.

seats. This kind of cabinet was legal, but (although known in Australia and New Zealand) quite new to the government of Canada. Its position was questioned by King, and enough Progressive support was detached to bring about its defeat in the House three days after it had taken office.[14]

The law was completely changed in 1931.[15] Today any member of the House of Commons may become a minister and the head of a department without such action in any way affecting his seat, and the parliamentary secretaries are allowed the same privilege under the statute regulating their appointment.[16] The general rule which makes a person who holds an office of profit or emolument under the Crown ineligible to sit in the House of Commons is still unimpaired.[17]

Residence

There is no residence qualification for members of the House of Commons, either in the British North America Act or in any statute. Nor can there be said to be any customary qualification, although undoubtedly there is a marked tendency for constituencies to prefer residents as members. But cases are not uncommon (particularly in Quebec, and in large cities) where members do not live in their constituencies and they occasionally represent constituencies in other provinces. The latter is most apt to occur when a seat must be found for a party leader or a cabinet minister who has been defeated or who is entering the House for the first time. The absence of any residence requirement gives a useful element of elasticity; for defeat does not necessarily mean exclusion from Parliament nor is an able member kept out simply because he happens to live in a district which is politically opposed to him.

LIFE OF PARLIAMENT

The maximum period for which a member of Parliament may serve is five years, which runs from the day on which writs are returned; but the minimum may be for almost any shorter period, depending on the time when Parliament is dissolved. During the First World War Parliament was extended to six years by a special amendment to the British North America Act;[18] the shortest Parliament, in 1957–8, was technically less than six months, while that of 1925–6

14/*Supra*, pp. 162–3.
15/*Can. Statutes*, 21–22 Geo. v, c. 52.
16/*Ibid.*, 7–8 Eliz. II, c. 15, s. 6.
17/See *ibid.*, 12 Eliz. II, c. 14, s. 3. This statute adds two new classes of salaried MP s: the leaders of recognized parties, apart from the government and opposition parties, with twelve or more members in the House; and the chief whips of the government and opposition parties. All of these since 1963 receive an extra allowance of $4,000, but without violating the independence of Parliament.
18/*Supra*, p. 122.

was slightly more.[19] The maximum may now be extended "in time of real or apprehended war, invasion or insurrection ... by the Parliament of Canada if such continuation is not opposed by the votes of more than one-third of the members" of the House of Commons.[20]

Despite the frequency of elections for a decade after 1957, the usual Parliament lasts about four years. It is, indeed, a tradition of Canadian political life that no prime minister will allow a Parliament to run for the full five years if it can possibly be avoided. This is based on experience as well as on other practical considerations. Three times Parliament has run its five years:[21] on two occasions (1896, 1935) the government was then beaten, and on the third (1945) it had a narrow escape. Moreover, a cabinet which puts off the election to the last possible moment is sure to be faced with the embarrassing accusation on the hustings that it had postponed the day of reckoning because it was afraid to face the people. It also runs the risk of failure in getting its measures through Parliament; for on such occasions time is a powerful ally of the opposition, which may be able to filibuster government proposals until the life of the House runs out. Thus the Liberals in 1896 prevented the remedial bill on Manitoba schools being passed by resorting to systematic obstruction.

But the weightiest objection to a five-year Parliament from the cabinet's point of view is that it thereby loses control of the political situation; the calendar and the accident of circumstances become the real masters. As long as there is an alternative time for an election, the prime minister is able to a material degree to pick his own issues and seize the most favourable moment for the contest. This is a tremendous advantage which no astute leader will ever relinquish unless, as occasionally happens, the present and immediate future appear so discouraging that nothing can be lost by postponing the election as long as possible. In all three instances of the five-year periods mentioned above, the risks incurred were apparently preferable to the difficulties which an earlier election might have precipitated; Mackenzie King, in 1945, was particularly desirous of avoiding a wartime election.

The uncertain length of each Parliament has one conspicuous merit, namely, that while it cannot guarantee that there will be a genuine issue to be decided at the election, it most certainly increases greatly the likelihood of such a fortunate synchronism. The combination may come about through skilful manoeuvring by the prime minister, or because the political situation forces an election, or because both factors work together to produce the same result. Canadian history supplies several excellent illustrations. The Pacific Scandal in 1873–4, the proposed reciprocity agreement in 1911, the Byng-King dispute in 1926, and the internal conflict over defence policy within the Conservative cabinet

---

19/That is, measured from the return of writs to the dissolution of Parliament.
20/BNA (no. 2) Act, 1949.
21/This omits the abnormal six-year term, 1911–17. In 1935 the Parliament elected in 1930 was two days short of a full five years.

in 1963 were all issues which were submitted to the people for a definitive verdict well before the five-year period had elapsed. In all four instances the election was called to settle a controversy; there was a real issue to be decided, and the government made an appeal to the electorate for support, in three instances after a real or anticipated defeat in the Commons. On other occasions which might be mentioned, the prime minister was better able to control the time and the issues, but this direction was made possible in a large measure because the issues were neither so vital nor so insistent.

There is clearly an appreciable risk involved in lodging this power of dissolution with the prime minister, and, as stated above, the Byng-King dispute centred about the propriety of the prime minister making his demand for a dissolution. But even when the circumstances surrounding the demand are more normal than they were in 1926, there is always the temptation for a prime minister to use his power to promote party ends; for few in such a position are able to distinguish at all clearly the exact place where the party prospects end and the public good begins. There is, however, fairly general agreement on two points: first the governor general should in the vast majority of cases allow the prime minister to exercise the power of dissolution without interference; second, the power is a weapon which has become extremely important to a prime minister in enabling him to keep his party and Parliament under control. The weakness of cabinets in pre-war France has been ascribed in no small measure to the lack of such a power.

Finally, while the uncertain life of each Parliament and the sudden election may at times have a disturbing effect on the economic and political life of the nation, it is very questionable indeed whether this is more injurious than the elaborate preparations which precede an election which is known and planned for long in advance. In any event, there can be little doubt that the psychological effects of uncertainty are both stimulating and wholesome in a democracy. The elements of speculation, hesitation, and suspense, the momentous decision, the dramatic appeal of the government for vindication at the hands of the electorate, the frequent emergence of a genuinely controversial issue, are all calculated to attract attention, to stir up interest, to induce discussion, to make people realize their importance as active and indispensable participants in the democratic process. Routine elections which can be anticipated far ahead and which are likely to owe their chief interest to the fact that so many months have passed since the last contest, appear, by comparison, somewhat stodgy and uninspiring affairs; they are also, because of the long campaigns that precede fixed election dates, very expensive for candidates and parties.

Parliament must hold at least one session a year, though there is no requirement as to its length;[22] and as this is one of the entrenched provisions of the British North America (no. 2) Act, 1949, it cannot be altered merely by a statute of the Canadian Parliament. Extra sessions may, of course, be held, and

22/BNA Act, s. 20. The first session of 1940 lasted only a few hours.

this has occurred in emergencies and sometimes following a change of government or a general election. Parliament, as stated before, is summoned by the governor general on the advice of the prime minister.

RESIGNATION

A member of the House of Commons, unlike his fellow member in Great Britain, is allowed to resign.[23] Even so, the act of resignation may be attended with certain complications. If the member's election is under dispute or if the time during which it may be questioned has not yet expired, his resignation is forbidden.[24] There may be in the minds of some an implied restriction that resignations are not to be made except for serious reasons. "A member," said Mackenzie King (though completely mistaken), "is elected to serve during the life of a Parliament. Unless there are grave reasons compelling him to return to private life, or he receives some appointment under the Crown, he is, I believe, in duty bound to keep the mandate he has received from his constituents."[25] When the member has actually decided to resign, he has more than one alternative as to the method he shall adopt. He may simply give notice from his place in the House of his intention to resign; or he may send a written declaration of his intention, attested by two witnesses, to the Speaker of the House. If the member is himself the Speaker or if there is no Speaker at the time, he may make the same written declaration and send it to any two members of the House,[26] provided enough time has elapsed since his election to comply with the law concerning controverted elections.

For many years a member might run and be elected from more than one constituency in the same election, but he was then compelled to make his choice and resign from the seat he had decided to abandon. Prominent party leaders could thus make sure of a seat and perhaps help to carry a constituency which was considered doubtful. This practice was forbidden in 1919.[27]

INDEMNITY

Members of the House of Commons and the Senate are not paid a salary, but rather what they are pleased to call an indemnity. This subtle distinction seems

23/This was explicitly stated in 1868, *Can. Statutes*, 31 Vict., c. 25, s. 7.
24/*Rev. Stat. Can.* (1952), c. 143, s. 9.
25/*Can. H. of C. Debates*, April 1, 1946, p. 473. See Eugene A. Forsey, "Mr. King and Parliamentary Government," *Canadian Journal of Economics and Political Science*, XVII, no. 4 (Nov. 1951), pp. 451–67.
26/*Rev. Stat. Can.* (1952), c. 143, ss. 6, 7.
27/*Can. Statutes*, 10 Geo. V, c. 18. See Ward, *The Canadian House of Commons*, pp. 80–2.

to rest on the assumption that members have their own occupations and that they are worth far more to the nation than what they receive in their capacity as members. The payment is thus merely a compensation for losses which they have sustained in sacrificing their time, energies, and talents in the public service. In the early years when the demands on the members were not nearly as numerous as they are today, there was doubtless much to be said for such an interpretation; but at present the parliamentary sessions tend to increase in length, and membership in the House has become a full-time occupation. It might seem to be more in accord with facts to regard the remuneration as a simple unpretentious homespun salary; in law it remains an indemnity.

The members of the first Assembly in Canada in 1758 were paid nothing; and those of the first Dominion Parliament received $600. The amount has since been raised on several occasions, the last being in 1963. The members now receive $12,000 a year plus a tax-exempt allowance of $6,000.[28] Before 1954 remuneration was based on the session, and might therefore be paid twice in the one year. But increased pressure of work, the longer period in Ottawa, the greater need for two sessions, and the growing impossibility of the member's finding time for other employment, made an increased annual remuneration imperative.

The attendance of members in the House and the Senate is encouraged to a small degree by a number of provisions which purport to penalize absences, but both the interpretation and the enforcement of these are so lax that they have little effect. A member is allowed twenty-one days' unexcused absences, and for every day missed over that number, $60 is deducted from his total payment.[29] This is not always so formidable a penalty as it appears, for the law has often been rendered nugatory by the action of Parliament. "Over the years," said one prime minister, "there have been many occasions – I think almost every year since I have been here – when in the supplementary estimates there was a special vote to enable payment to be made to members who, for one reason or another, had exceeded the number of absences provided for in the statute."[30]

There are further provisions to allow relief in the event of illness and other contingencies, and other provisions authorize the payment of travelling and telecommunications expenses, and moving expenses to and from Ottawa, the amount of these, in general, being prescribed by the House. Since 1952 members of the House who have served in more than two Parliaments (that is, about nine or ten years as a rule) and have made certain payments to the fund, are eligible for a pension provided they are not drawing a salary from the government in another capacity, and widows are also provided for.[31]

28/Can. Statutes, 12 Eliz. II, c. 14.
29/Ibid.
30/Can. H. of C. Debates, Feb. 2, 1954, p. 1717.
31/Can. Statutes, 1 Eliz. II, c. 45, amended by 12 Eliz. II, c. 14. On March 5, 1970, the government moved to reduce to six years the qualifying period for a member's

Cabinet ministers with portfolios receive the sessional indemnity of $12,000, plus the $6,000 allowance, plus an automobile allowance of $2,000, plus $15,000 a year – a total of $35,000. The prime minister receives (the first three items being the same) $45,000. The salary of the Speaker of the House of Commons (including his salary as a member) is $29,000, plus an automobile allowance of $1,000 and a residence allowance of $3,000.[32]

Canada has accepted since 1905 the principle that if it is a good investment to pay cabinet ministers to carry on the business of the country, it is equally sound to pay a leader of the opposition to criticize the government and even to try to prevent it from doing what the people of Canada desire. The logic may be a little obscure, but the arrangement is none the less satisfactory for that. The leader of the opposition is accordingly paid the same salary (including the automobile allowance) as a cabinet minister. The leaders of other parties with twelve or more members, as noted above, receive an extra $4,000.

The determination of how much a member of the House of Commons should be paid (leaving to one side the more imponderable senatorial services) is by no means easy or simple. One may state with some assurance, however, that the prevailing amount, whatever it may be at any one time, is not excessive, large as it may appear to a layman, but almost certainly not enough, considering the heavy demands made upon a member's purse. Two extremes, of course, must always be avoided. The indemnity must not be so low that desirable candidates will refuse to run because they cannot make ends meet. It must not be so low that the member finds himself compelled to secure an additional income to maintain his position, which income must be derived either from his own private resources, or from outside interests or organizations, or from other activities in which he may be forced to engage and which may seriously interfere with his work as a member. In short, the ordinary needs and moderate comforts of life cannot be ignored without suffering thereby a serious loss of efficiency. On the other hand, the indemnity must not be so high that it will attract the kind of candidate who sees in politics a remunerative opening which will pay more than any other within his reach or capacity. To demand a certain pecuniary sacrifice is not unreasonable, for politics has many other compensations of an intangible but none the less attractive and piquant nature. "There are," said Lord Haldane, "many kinds of glory. The glory of a popular preacher is very great, but he does not demand a large salary. The glory of a successful politician may be very great, and often he is as poor as a rat, but he does not mind. He has much more. He can dine with millionaires each night if he pleases."[33] Lord Haldane must have been significantly fortunate in his million-

---

pension, and to raise the maximum pension from $9,000 annually to $13,500. Twenty-five years' service was to be required for the maximum pension.

32/Ministers without portfolio receive $7,500 instead of the $15,000 paid to department heads. For a full statement of indemnities, allowances, and pensions, see *Canada Year Book, 1968*, pp. 88–90.

33/Report of the Coal Industry Commission (Great Britain), II, *Parliamentary Papers* (1919), Cmd. 360, p. 1090.

aires to draw such a curious picture of perfect felicity, and his sense of creature comforts is also a little out of perspective, but his underlying emphasis on the importance of factors other than money can scarcely be open to serious question.

In recent years some members have complained increasingly of the difficulty of making ends meet on their parliamentary indemnities; the legitimate costs of travelling on political business, of maintaining two domiciles (one in Ottawa and one at home), and of campaigning, have all been rising, but the indemnity has not. There would appear to be a strong argument for giving members substantially larger expense accounts, if not larger indemnities, but no government of recent years (down at least to 1970) has felt prepared to counter its own anti-inflationary policies by raising the pay of members. The problem of adequate indemnities remains a hardy perennial.

PARLIAMENTARY PRIVILEGE

The English Parliament has for many centuries enjoyed certain special privileges and powers for the protection of the houses and of their members against interference and for the more effective discharge of their duties.[34] These gradually developed during the years as the need for them arose, particularly as part of the parliamentary defences against the powers and the meddling of the Crown during the Tudor and Stuart periods. Occasionally, however, these privileges took a different turn and offered a serious challenge to the liberties of the subject. Privileges formed in themselves a special body of law and became known collectively as the *lex et consuetudo Parliamenti*. It had no statutory basis whatever; indeed, it sprang originally from the authority of Parliament as a court, and not as a legislative body: Parliament merely asserted a rather vague and elastic but dogmatic control over matters which affected its members and the conduct of its business. This special law was for long outside the common law and a rival to it; but the two eventually effected a partial reconciliation, and privilege is now regarded as a part, albeit a separate and independent part, of the common law. But while privilege is thus beyond the jurisdiction of the ordinary courts, the exact relationship between the authority of the courts and Parliament on some aspects of these matters is still under dispute. For if Parliament is conceded complete power and its decisions on such questions are subject to no judicial review, there is little, if anything, to stop arbitrary action and gradual encroachment on the main body of the law.

34/"Parliamentary privilege is the sum of the peculiar rights enjoyed by each House collectively as a constituent part of the High Court of Parliament, and by members of each House individually, without which they could not discharge their functions, and which exceed those possessed by other bodies or individuals. Thus privilege, though part of the law of the land, is to a certain extent an exemption from the ordinary law." Sir T. Erskine May, *A Treatise on the Law, Privileges, Proceedings and Usage of Parliament*, ed. Sir Gilbert Champion (14th ed., London, 1943), p. 41.

Thus while the courts will concede that the Houses have the power to enforce their privileges without interference, they will not admit that this implies complete control over the existence and the extent of the privileges themselves.[35]

Substantially the same customary privileges which had become recognized in England were asserted by the legislatures in the English overseas colonies,[36] and among these claimants were, although at a much later date, the Canadian provinces. Thus the Legislative Assembly of Nova Scotia in its first session in 1758 disciplined a citizen who had uttered threatening language against one of its members, and in 1759 the Speaker asked the governor (following the British precedent) for an assurance that the "usual privileges" would be granted.[37] The general practice was for the legislatures in all the colonies to assert and exercise their assumed privileges, and for the English government and the courts to question the validity of many of the pretensions.[38] A series of court decisions during the last hundred years, however, has clarified the situation, and there now seems to be little uncertainty as to the position of parliamentary privilege in Canada, though it is not at all clear that members fully understand it.[39]

The *lex et consuetudo Parliamenti* as known in England, unlike the major part of the common law, has not been transplanted to Canada. The creation of legislative bodies overseas did not endow those bodies with the privileges and powers of the English Parliament, which, as stated above, were primarily judicial in origin. Such creation did imply, however, that these legislatures would need to exercise certain very moderate privileges which were necessary for the maintenance of order and discipline during the performance of their duties. But these were to be protective and not punitive powers, for the latter were again considered to be characteristic of a court rather than of a legislative body.

The above restrictions on the privileges of the colonial legislatures apply, however, to their innate powers alone – their ability to assert successfully privileges and powers which rest only on tradition and on inheritance. This is quite apart from their ability to define privileges and to assume powers by *statute*, which ability is limited only by the general jurisdiction of the legislative body. The Canadian provincial legislatures (some of which, it must be remembered, antedate that of the Dominion by about one hundred years) thus enjoy a moderate disciplinary power, derived from their status as legislative bodies, and

35/*Ibid.*, pp. 148–75.
36/See Mary P. Clarke, *Parliamentary Privilege in the American Colonies* (London, 1943).
37/*Ibid.*, p. 91n.
38/*Ibid.*, pp. 235–61. See Murdoch, *Epitome of the Laws of Nova Scotia*, I, 65.
39/See W. F. Dawson, "Parliamentary Privilege in the Canadian House of Commons," *Canadian Journal of Economics and Political Science*, XXV, no. 4 (Nov. 1959), pp. 462–70; and *Procedure in the Canadian House of Commons* (Toronto, 1962). There are many cases on this subject, for example, *Kielley v. Carson*, 4 Moo. P.C. 63; *Doyle v. Falconer*, 4 Moo. P.C. (N.S.) 203; *Barton v. Taylor*, 11 App. Cas. 197; *Fielding v. Thomas*, [1896] A.C. 600.

also an authority to confer wide privileges and powers on themselves by the enactment of legislation to that effect. All the provinces of Canada have passed such laws.[40]

The inherent privileges of the Dominion Parliament were of the same moderate proportions as those allowed to other colonial legislative bodies. The British North America Act, however, made explicit provision for the immediate addition of statutory powers and privileges on a substantial scale. Section 18 read as follows: "The privileges, immunities, and powers to be held, enjoyed, and exercised by the Senate and by the House of Commons and by the members thereof respectively shall be such as are from time to time defined by Act of the Parliament of Canada, but so that the same shall never exceed those at the passing of this Act held, enjoyed and exercised by the Commons House of Parliament of the United Kingdom of Great Britain and Ireland and by the members thereof."

In 1868 the Canadian Parliament enacted a law which gave to each of the houses, in almost the identical words used above, the powers, immunities, and privileges enjoyed by the British House of Commons at the time of passing the British North America Act, "so far as the same are consistent with and not repugnant to the said Act."[41] A further section stated that these were part of the general and public law of Canada and "it shall not be necessary to plead the same, but the same shall in all Courts in Canada and by and before all judges be taken notice of judicially." The act also protected the publication of any proceedings against civil or criminal suit if these were published under the order or authority of the Senate or House of Commons.

This was followed in the same year by an act professing to give to the Senate or to any select committee on private bills of the Senate or of the House the power to examine witnesses on oath.[42] In 1873 the power to examine witnesses on oath was extended to any committee of either house.[43] This latter act was disallowed by the British government on the ground that it was *ultra vires*, in that it tried to give powers to the Canadian houses which were not possessed in 1867 by the British House of Commons. The earlier act had been, in fact, *ultra vires* also, although it had been allowed to stand. The sequel came in 1875 with an amendment to the British North America Act, which repealed the original section 18 and substituted another to the effect that the privileges, immunities, and powers of the Canadian Parliament and its members were never to exceed those enjoyed from time to time by the British House of Com-

40/In the early years of the federation, the Dominion government disallowed some provincial acts of Ontario, Quebec, and Manitoba, which sought to establish privileges of the legislatures of these provinces, on the ground that they were *ultra vires*. Other such acts were allowed to stand. Nova Scotia, whose laws on the question antedated Confederation, could not be subjected, for example, to these attentions.

41/*Can. Statutes*, 31 Vict., c. 23, s. 1. The last clause (in quotation marks) creates a limitation which may not have been implied in the BNA Act.

42/*Ibid.*, 31 Vict., c. 24.

43/*Ibid.*, 36 Vict., c. 1.

mons.[44] Another section confirmed the earlier Canadian act of 1868 noted above. Inasmuch as the British House of Commons in 1871 had given to its committees the power to examine witnesses on oath,[45] the Canadian Parliament was able in 1876 legally to endow its committees with the same power.[46]

The privileges, immunities, and powers of the Houses of the Parliament of Canada are thus potentially those of the British House of Commons, although their primary base is statutory and not established custom and inherent right. They can, of course, be increased beyond those of the British House by constitutional amendment, which under the British North America Act of 1949 (No. 2) would presumably be an ordinary act of Parliament.

The privileges, immunities, and powers of the Canadian Parliament fall into two chief categories: (a) those of individual members of either house; (b) those of the Senate or of the House of Commons as a body.[47] They are virtually but not quite the same for each house,[48] and the discussion which follows will, for the sake of convenience, deal only with the privileges (including "immunities and power") of the Commons.

Privileges of the individual member
Some of these are designed to enable the member to attend to his parliamentary duties without interference. He cannot be arrested or imprisoned under civil process while Parliament is in session or within a reasonable time going to and returning from the session.[49] This gives him no protection against arrest in any criminal action or for any indictable offence,[50] although, if he should be arrested, that fact must be at once reported to the Speaker. A "reasonable time" in England has traditionally been considered to be forty days, which, with existing transport facilities, would appear more than adequate. A member does not have to serve on a jury during the session; nor at such times can he be compelled to attend court as a witness although, if necessary, the House will give its permission for him to absent himself for such a purpose.

Other privileges are meant to encourage the member to speak and act freely without fear of undesirable consequences. The most vital of these by far is his

44/*Supra*, p. 121, Appendix.
45/*Brit. Statutes*, 34–35 Vict., c. 83.
46/*Can. Statutes*, 39 Vict., c. 7.
47/See Bourinot, *Parliamentary Procedure and Practice*, pp. 143–73; Beauchesne, *Rules and Forms of the House of Commons of Canada*, pp. 79–86.
48/The privilege of the Commons to settle controverted election cases, for example, could clearly not be a privilege of the Senate.
49/None the less, Mr Grégoire was arrested on Feb. 12, 1965, in connection with a relatively minor traffic infraction, and the Standing Committee on Privileges and Elections found that "the privilege of freedom of arrest of a Member has not been infringed in the present case." See its fourth report, March 19, 1965 (*Can. H. of C. Journals*, 1964–5, pp. 1141–2).
50/See statement on the occasion of the arrest of Fred Rose, MP. *Can. H. of C. Debates*, March 15, 1946, pp. 4–8.

right of freedom of speech, that is, an immunity from any legal prosecution for anything he says or does in his work as a member in the House or on its committees. The assumption is that occasional abuses of this privilege will be more than compensated for by the gain in complete frankness in discussion. A few restrictions do, in fact, exist, but these promote more orderly debate and the proper and seemly conduct of government. Members cannot be assaulted, or insulted, or threatened in the House or going to or from the House.[51] To offer a bribe to a member – or for a member to accept a bribe – is a breach of privilege and regarded as a "high crime and misdemeanour." These privileges may also be extended to any who attend the House under its orders (such as, for example, a witness before the House or a committee of the House) and the House's own officers on occasion.[52]

Collective privileges of the House

These privileges concern the House as a corporate body, and their breach is usually designated by the word "contempt," a term used in much the same sense as the more familiar "contempt of court" applied to judicial proceedings. Contempt is an invasion of the rights of the legislature as a whole, disobedience to its orders, or disorderly conduct before or within it.[53]

The fundamental collective privilege of this nature is the maintenance of order and discipline in the House; for clearly the legislature could not function if it had no authority to compel obedience from its members. The mildest exercise of this power is when the Speaker calls a member to order, and this will occur a number of times before the Speaker moves on to sterner measures. If necessary, he will then threaten to "name" the offender, that is, to call him by name instead of using the name of his constituency. If this threat fails, the member is named. The abashed member is thereupon led from the chamber by the Sergeant-at-Arms and the House decides what disciplinary measures shall be taken, the initiative being with the senior minister present. The House may suspend the offender for the sitting, or for a much longer time, or may even expel him.[54]

The House of Commons has always had the power to regulate its own internal concerns, including the right to decide whether a person elected should be allowed to take his seat. The power of expulsion is closely associated with

51/For an alleged threat against a member, see *ibid.*, Feb. 1, 1939, p. 519.
52/See Dawson, "Parliamentary Privilege in the Canadian House of Commons." For the latest case of alleged bribery, which was found to be unsubstantiated, see the second report of the Standing Committee on Privileges and Elections (*Can. H. of C. Journals*, 1964–5, pp. 425–6).
53/See R. Luce, *Legislative Assemblies* (Boston, 1924), pp. 499–518.
54/Liguori Lacombe, MP, was suspended in 1942; Donald Fleming, MP, in 1956; and Frank Howard, MP, in 1961. See *Can. H. of C. Debates*, March 24, 1942, pp. 1605–7; *Can. H. of C. Journals*, 1956, pp. 627–34; 1960–1, p. 238. For an earlier case, see Bilkey, *Persons, Papers and Things*, pp. 146–7.

this refusal to admit; and in either contingency the rejected person may run again as a candidate and he again elected – and conceivably be again refused admittance. The House had formerly the privilege to try all controverted election cases, but this right (as already noted) has been passed over to the judiciary in order to secure a more impartial and expeditious trial.[55]

Another kind of contempt proceeds from outside the House, and may consist of scandalous or libellous reflections on the proceedings, or on the members in their capacity as members. Inasmuch as attacks of this kind on a member may be construed as attacks on the privileges of the House as a body, the line between personal and collective privilege is here not very clear. Members are, indeed, inclined to overwork this privilege by raising a wide variety of petty questions as alleged infractions,[56] although, on balance, these protests do little harm and frequently enliven the proceedings and start the House on its day's work in a more cheerful frame of mind.

Breaches of privilege committed by persons outside the House may be followed up by summoning them to appear before the Bar to explain or to justify their action.[57] If guilty they may be punished by a public reprimand, delivered by the Speaker, or they may be imprisoned, although they cannot be kept in custody after the House has prorogued. There is nothing, however, to prevent the House at its next session from re-committing the offender to gaol for further punishment.

55/*Supra*, pp. 324–5.
56/See Dawson, "Parliamentary Privilege in the Canadian House of Commons."
57/Ward, "Called to the Bar of the House of Commons," *Canadian Bar Review*, May 1957.

18 The House of Commons: procedure

THE ORGANIZATION OF THE House of Commons, like that of the cabinet and the public service, was for most of the 1960s under close scrutiny, with the same object in mind: the adaptation of an essential institution to changing conditions. The House of Commons is of course unique in that it must not only be efficient, but efficient in ways that give ample recognition to the rights of minorities to be heard; and that, paradoxically, frequently means that the House of Commons has to have built into it machinery that facilitates the *delaying* of making decisions. In the decade of the 1960s, furthermore, there was an unprecedented number of general elections, three of which produced no majority for a single party; three prime ministers; and a considerable turnover of both House and cabinet personnel. None of this was conducive to continuing attention to the procedure of the House, or to the unbroken serenity of members' tempers as they considered alterations in it. The House sat under provisional and transitional rules for much of the decade, finally settling on a new list of Standing Orders in December 1968 to which, in July 1969, was added a highly controversial new provision for a form of closure which itself had to be forced through under closure.[1] The cabinet's view of all these changes, reflecting the normal ministerial attitude towards the more expeditious passage into law of any government's wishes, was expressed by the president of the Privy Council: "In 1968 and 1969, the House took giant steps to move forward from its colonial origins and to bring itself into step not only with the Mother of Parliaments, but, what is more important, with the needs of our country as it enters upon its second century."[2] Mr Stanley Knowles, one of the ablest parliamentarians to grace the House of Commons, reflected an equally typical opposition attitude when he said with specific reference to the latest rule of

1/See *Can. H. of C. Debates*, June 20 to July 24, 1969; Canadian House of Commons, Standing Orders, Jan. 1969; Donald Page, "Streamlining the Procedures of the Canadian House of Commons, 1963–1966," *Canadian Journal of Economics and Political Science*, XXXIII, no. 1 (Feb. 1967), pp. 27–49.
2/Donald S. Macdonald, Press Release, Sept. 5, 1969.

July 1969: "This is not free speech. This is not parliamentary democracy. Indeed, it is not participatory democracy, nor is it the involvement the Liberals prate about."[3]

It is noteworthy that a cabinet minister, commenting on a change in the rules of the Canadian House of Commons, should refer to the Mother of Parliaments. The similarity between British and Canadian political institutions and the tendency of the latter to cherish inherited traditions and precedents are nowhere so vividly illustrated as in the conduct of legislative business. Though the temper of Canadian politics is distinctively North American, from the first meeting of a newly elected Parliament to the moment of its dissolution an enormous number of British practices are followed as scrupulously in Canada as in the Mother of Parliaments itself. It has always been so;[4] and the general principle is still observed that whenever a matter of legislative practice or procedure is not covered by the Canadian rules, the usages and customs of the British House will be followed so far as they are applicable.[5] The original justification was, of course, that these were part of the great political inheritance which no Canadian, whether of British or French extraction, wished to forego, and to this must now be added an uninterrupted Canadian custom reaching back over two hundred years to the first Nova Scotia Assembly in 1758. The most colourful of these venerable customs are those which appear as part of the opening procedure of a new Parliament.

OPENING OF PARLIAMENT

The members of a newly elected House of Commons come together when summoned by the Governor-General-in-Council, and they at once sign the roll and take the oath administered by the Clerk of the House. After a short lull in the proceedings, three sharp knocks are heard on the door of the Commons chamber, and it is opened to admit an official of the Senate, the Gentleman Usher of the Black Rod. He walks up the centre of the chamber and announces in English and French that the deputy of the governor general[6] desires the presence of the Commons in the Senate chamber. The members of the Commons then proceed as requested to the other house, where the Speaker of the Senate makes the following announcement:

3/New Democratic party, Press Release, June 20, 1969.
4/Note the immediate assertion by the first Assembly of Nova Scotia of the right to exercise and enjoy the privileges of the House of Commons.
5/Canadian House of Commons, Standing Order no. 1. There are, as will be seen later, important differences as well between Canadian and British practices. Beauchesne, *Rules and Forms of the House of Commons of Canada*, pp. 1–5.
6/There are two deputies of the governor general, namely, the chief justice and the senior puisne judge of the Supreme Court. On the first occasion on which either one of them attends the Senate after his appointment, the commission granting his powers is read by the Clerk of the Senate in the presence of both Houses.

I have it in command to let you know that His Excellency the Governor-General does not see fit to declare the causes of his summoning the present Parliament of Canada until a Speaker of the House of Commons shall have been chosen, according to law; but this afternoon, at the hour of three o'clock, His Excellency will declare the causes of his calling Parliament.[7].

The members of the House thereupon retire to their own chamber to elect a Speaker. This does not take place every session, but only for each newly elected Parliament or, of course, at other times if it should become necessary to fill a vacancy. The House, which is as yet unorganized, is presided over by the Clerk, who points to the proposer and seconder of the candidate for the speakership.[8] In early times in the provinces it was not uncommon for more than one candidate to be nominated, but this has never happened in the House of Commons. Any member of the Commons may, of course, speak on the nomination, and almost invariably[9] the leaders of the various parties express their approval. The designated member having been declared elected, the mover and seconder conduct him to the speaker's chair. He thereupon thanks the House, and (following a very old English tradition) speaks modestly of his own qualifications. Mr Lamoureux, on his second election to the speakership, said in part on September 12, 1968:

I therefore thank you, Mr. Prime Minister, and I thank you, hon. members, for the great honour that you have just bestowed upon me.

I am deeply touched, of course, by the much too flattering remarks of the Prime Minister (Mr. Trudeau) and I am also grateful to the Leader of the Opposition (Mr. Stanfield) who, in much too gracious terms, was kind enough to support the Prime Minister's motion. The remarks made by the Prime Minister and the Leader of the Opposition as well as those made by the hon. members for York South and Témiscamingue (Messrs. Lewis and Caouette) are for me today a source of comfort and encouragement and will be a source of strength, if need be, in difficult moments.

In the discharge of the high office devolved upon me, I shall do my utmost to deserve the confidence placed in me today by all members of this house.

These remarks being concluded, the mace is then placed on the table before the Speaker. The mace is the symbol of the Speaker's authority, and accompanies him on all formal occasions. It leaves and enters the House with him, being carried before him by the Sergeant-at-Arms, and it reposes in his chambers between sittings and sessions of Parliament. When he leaves the chair, it is placed on the rests at the end of or "under" the table.

In Great Britain the Speaker is repeatedly re-elected irrespective of party

7/For example, *Can. Senate Debates*, Sept. 12, 1968, p. 2.

8/The proposer was conventionally the prime minister, and the seconder usually a cabinet minister, although in 1953, 1957, and 1958 the leader of the opposition seconded the motion. The latter practice was revived in 1968 when Mr Lamoureux was re-elected speaker.

9/In 1936 R. B. Bennett, leader of the opposition, disapproved strongly of the candidate nominated. *Can. H. of C. Debates*, Feb. 6, 1936, pp. 6–10.

changes or his own party affiliation; but in Canada, until 1968, a new Speaker was normally chosen for each Parliament,[10] and he did not come from any but the government party.[11] A potential exception occurred in 1957, when Prime Minister Diefenbaker offered the nomination to the post to Mr Stanley Knowles, the parliamentarian of the CCF party, and now the NDP; Mr Knowles declined the offer. Another exception to traditional practices, which is expected to become the rule, occurred in 1968 when Mr Speaker Lamoureux, by agreement, was unopposed by the official opposition for re-election in his constituency (although he was opposed by an NDP candidate who did not have his party's approval to do so) and subsequently re-elected as Speaker in the expectation that he would continue to be re-elected to the position for as long as he chose. The new practice has yet to survive a change of government; the old practice had one advantage, in that it enabled Parliament to alternate more frequently the Speakers from English and French Canada, a custom which has been regularly observed in recent years. It is still the rule that the Deputy Speaker must possess a "full and practical knowledge" of the language which is not of the Speaker.[12] The duties of the Speaker as well as the nature of the rules he enforces were well stated by R. B. Bennett:

The duties of a Speaker are very onerous ... The Speaker of our House first of all has to preside over our deliberations. He must protect the person of the members from insult. He must maintain decorum ... In addition to that he must put every question to the House that has to be considered by its members; any motion or resolution must be read by him ... His second duty is to see that the conduct of debate is maintained in accordance with the rules and practices of this House ... He must have a knowledge of the written rules, that is the standing orders and rules of the House of Commons, which are embodied in the little volume which I hold in my hand. That, as we lawyers might say, is the *lex scripta*, the written law governing the House of Commons in the conduct of debate. But there is a great body of law which is not written ... a great body of precedent which has to do with the conduct of debate. There is that accumulation which has come down, as Sir Wilfrid Laurier said, during all the ages to which we must pay regard and respect ... The Speaker is the guardian of the powers, the dignities, the liberties and the privileges of this House of Commons.[13]

The Speaker sits on a dais at one of the narrow ends of the rectangular Commons chamber. The members of the government party sit on the long side to the Speaker's right and face across the chamber where the opposition parties occupy the other long side to the left of the speaker. When the government supporters are very numerous, they fill not only the entire right side but

10/One Speaker, Rodolphe Lemieux, held the office for three Parliaments, and under two governments. Cockburn, Rhodes, and Michener also were re-elected to the speakership. See James H. Aitchison, "The Speakership of the Canadian House of Commons," in Clark, *Canadian Issues*, pp. 23–56.

11/Sir Wilfrid Laurier stated that he had approached Sir John A. Macdonald with the suggestion that the Canadian House should follow the English practice of permanency, but Sir John did not favour it. *Can. H. of C. Debates*, Jan. 20, 1909, p. 2.

12/This last provision is contained in the House Standing Order no. 53(2).

13/*Can. H. of C. Debates*, Feb. 6, 1936, pp. 3–4.

spread over to the far left as well. The prime minister occupies a desk one-third of the way down the chamber from the Speaker; he is flanked by the cabinet ministers, and the leader of the opposition is directly opposite, supported by his chief assistants. Other opposition parties form their own small groups around their respective leaders. Slightly in front of the Speaker on the central floor which divides the right side from the left is the table of the House holding the mace. The chair of the Clerk of the House (occupied by the chairman of committees when the House is in committee) is at the head of the table, and at the right of the Clerk is the Clerk Assistant. In almost the exact middle of the House are the small tables for the reporters of the debates; and, finally, near the entrance or "bar" of the House, sits the Sergeant-at-Arms. On the members' desks stand the microphones used in the remarkably efficient simultaneous translation system, by which speeches made in one official language can be heard almost concurrently in the other. Galleries occupy all four sides of the chamber, and the simultaneous translation system is available in them too.

The House breaks up after the Speaker has made his speech from the chair, and it reassembles shortly before the time appointed by the governor general. Again the Gentleman Usher of the Black Rod knocks, enters, and walks up the centre of the chamber. On this occasion, however, he bows profoundly three times as he progresses, and his message announces that the governor general (and not his deputy) desires the attendance of the House in the Senate. He backs out gracefully, bowing three times as he does so. Once again the members of the House go to the Senate chamber. But now, being organized, they go in more orderly fashion, preceded by the Sergeant-at-Arms (bearing the mace), the Speaker, and a small retinue. This time the governor general is present, usually in full regalia and surrounded by the utmost that Ottawa can offer in ceremonial splendour. The Speaker immediately announces his election to the governor general, and claims on behalf of the members of the House "all their undoubted rights and privileges, especially that they may have freedom of speech in their debates, access to Your Excellency's person at all reasonable times, and that their proceedings may receive from Your Excellency the most favourable consideration." These the governor, through the Speaker of the Senate, graciously confirms, to the enormous relief of all concerned. The time-honoured demand for the privileges of the House is taken almost verbatim from the English Parliament,[14] but it is there preceded by a request for the royal confirmation of the choice of the Speaker-elect. An early refusal of Lord Dalhousie in Lower Canada to confirm the choice of Louis Papineau as Speaker, led to that province dropping this request a few years later in 1841.[15] It has never been used in the Dominion Parliament.

The governor general then reads the speech from the throne. This is a

14/Sir W. R. Anson, *The Law and Custom of the Constitution* (4th ed., Oxford, 1935), I, pp. 67–8.
15/Bourinot, *Parliamentary Procedure and Practice*, pp. 184–6. Some provinces have the lieutenant governor approve the choice of Speaker, others do not.

statement, drafted by the prime minister and approved by the cabinet, which reviews concisely the state of the nation and recites in fairly general terms the programme which the cabinet proposes to submit to Parliament in the coming session. The reading being concluded, the Commons return to their chamber at the other end of the building.

The Speaker then informs the House that he has attended the governor and has there made the usual claims on its behalf for the customary privileges, which His Excellency "was pleased to confirm." At this point the prime minister moves for leave to introduce Bill No. 1, "respecting the administration of oaths of office." The motion is agreed to, and the bill is read the first time. This bill does not exist except by title, and the same phantom bill is introduced at the opening of every session at Ottawa as at Westminster.[16] It signifies the immemorial right of the House of Commons to attend first to its own business before considering the affairs of the Crown. The Senate also has its *pro forma* Bill No. 1, "a bill relating to railways," which enjoys the same fleeting honour. The independence of the House being thus vindicated, the Speaker announces that when he attended the governor in the Senate, the governor had read the speech from the throne, and adds that "to prevent mistakes" he has obtained a copy. The speech is then presented to the House by the Speaker, and a decision is made on the time when it will be further considered. The next move is usually the appointment of a striking committee of government and opposition members (which under the new rules has seven members)[17] to draw up the membership of the standing committees of the House for the duration of that Parliament. A few incidental pieces of business bring this sitting to a close.

At the next sitting the House begins to settle down to work. Consideration of the speech from the throne is normally the first order. An address in reply will be moved and seconded by two private members on the government side; it will be debated for not more than eight days and carried on a party vote. The committee which was to draw up the membership of the standing committees makes its report within ten sitting days and it is accepted by the House.

COMMITTEES OF THE HOUSE

The *standing committees* are distinguished by the fact that they are appointed in advance, for the consideration of whatever the House may refer to them.

16/The Canadian provinces follow the same practice. As a formal precedent this goes back in England to 1603. *Ibid.*, p. 187n. Only twice, in 1926 and 1950, was Bill No. 1 a real bill instead of the usual *pro forma* document, and the House then proceeded to consider other business before the address; in the short one-day session of Jan. 25, 1940, there was no Bill No. 1.

17/These were formerly two ministers, a government whip, and whips from two opposition parties; the committee established for the Parliament elected in 1968 consisted

Their number and the titles they bear are governed by the standing orders of the House and change little from year to year. There are at present (1970) eighteen of them and two joint standing committees, that is, committees with a combined Senate and Commons membership. The names suggest the subject-matter with which each of them is concerned – public accounts, broadcasting, films and assistance to the arts; finance, trade and economic affairs; justice and legal affairs; veterans affairs, etc. – and the same is true of the two joint committees, on the library and on printing. (There is a third joint committee on the restaurant which is not recognized by the rules, but set up regularly anyway.) The maximum number of members on a committee varies from twelve (procedure and organization) to thirty (agriculture; external affairs and national defence), and the rest have twenty;[18] a quorum is a majority of the members. Members serve on more than one committee; they are placed on those which deal with the topics in which they (and their constituencies) are interested; and the same members (with occasional variations to meet changing conditions) serve throughout a Parliament. Since several committees may meet concurrently, members often find it difficult to discharge their duties in two or more places simultaneously. The government members are in the majority on every committee when the government has a majority in the House, as all parties are represented in approximately the same proportion as their relative membership in the House; the chairman of each committee (except for that on public accounts) is invariably a government supporter.

Before 1968 the standing committees were sometimes supervisory, as the joint committee on the library still is; but the bulk of them were legislative and to some degree investigatory. They inquired into and studied any matters referred to them, they sent for persons, papers, and records, and they made reports to the House; but they were strictly limited by the terms of reference under which they were instructed. Beginning in the 1950s a disposition to refer estimates to committees culminated in the creation of a special and then a standing committee on estimates; committees receiving estimates used them as justification for inquiring into virtually all aspects of departmental activities.[19] Since the adoption of new rules in 1968, the work and scope of the standing committees have been enlarged and systematized to a degree unprecedented in Canadian parliamentary history. All governmental estimates for expenditure now go to a standing committee, the main ones, by House rule, on or before March 1 of "the then expiring fiscal year." Except for tax bills, all bills (except those based on supply or ways and means motions), unless the House orders otherwise are now referred to a standing committee. All committees can receive evidence, but make no decisions, without a quorum; all can sit during periods when the House is adjourned; all can delegate powers

of two Liberals (one of whom was a minister), two Progressive Conservatives, and one representative each from the New Democratic party and the Ralliement des Créditistes.

18/Until the adoption of new rules in 1968, most committees had from thirty-five to sixty members, and years ago some committees had well over one hundred.

19/See Ward, *The Public Purse*, especially chap. XIV.

to sub-committees; and some now have limited research assistance. It is too early to assess the workings of the new committee system, but it is a fair statement that most of the committees have found plenty to do; certainly the new system holds out greater promise than the old. Under the former system, it was not uncommon for important committees to go for years without meeting.[20]

The *special committees* of the House down to relatively recent times were often more useful bodies, for they were called into existence by special needs, and there was adequate work mapped out for them to do. The distinguishing marks of these committees are their *ad hoc* nature and narrowness of field, for they are usually appointed to consider or investigate a particular topic, petition, or bill. Some of these committees may be set up from session to session, and they may, says Beauchesne, be "turned into Standing Committees by instructions enlarging the original order of reference."[21] Thus the Special Committee on Estimates created in 1955 became a standing committee in 1958; on the other hand, the Committee on Railways, Air Lines and Shipping was designated "sessional" from 1924 to the 1960s.

With the enlarged scope of the standing committees, there may be less work in the future for special committees, although the heavy work load that appears to be a certainty for at least some of the standing committees could easily result in a continuing need for special committees. Certainly the special committee will remain the parliamentary prototype of the executive's royal commission. It differs from the commission not only in its method of appointment, but also, of course, in personnel, for its members are all in Parliament and are obviously working only part-time. They rarely possess the *expertise* which often characterizes the members of a commission; indeed, it is not infrequent to find that one of the main tasks of the committee is the education of its own members.[22] The result is that the commission will probably be used for wider investigations or those calling for more specialized qualities, while the select committee is preferred for the study of a specific situation which has been brought to the attention of Parliament. This is, however, only a tendency; and no hard and fast line of distinction is observed in actual practice.[23] There is not the slightest doubt that investigations by special committees have often been of substantial help to the cabinet and to Parliament in the drafting of new legislation and the modification of existing statutes.

The House and the Senate may decide to appoint a *joint committee* made up

20/See C. E. S. Franks, "The Committee System of the Canadian House of Commons," a paper presented to the annual meeting of the Canadian Political Science Association, 1969. For commentary on the old system, see the fourth edition of this book.

21/Beauchesne, *Rules and Forms of the House of Commons of Canada*, p. 199.

22/The Select Committee on the Civil Service in 1938 is an excellent example; so are contemporary committees on such matters as foreign and defence policy.

23/A select committee (on price spreads) in 1934 was continued after prorogation by being transformed into a royal commission.

of members from both chambers, a device which has obvious advantages in preventing waste of time and duplication of effort. Despite an occasional outbreak of these bodies, they have been used rather infrequently. In 1945 a joint committee was appointed to choose a design for a Canadian flag; in 1946 and 1947 another of these committees was set up to examine and consider the Indian Act and to report on a number of specific problems relating to Indian administration; in 1947 yet another was set up to examine and consider human rights and freedoms; in 1950 there was a joint committee on old age security; and in 1966 another on the public service.

A committee of an entirely different kind is the *Committee of the Whole House*, that is, the entire House of Commons acting as a committee and not in its ordinary capacity. The membership is, of course, identical with that of the House, but certain procedural practices are different. The presiding officer of the Committee of the Whole is not the Speaker, but the chairman of committees, who is the Deputy Speaker; and, as a result, when the House is in committee the mace is not on but under the table. Members in committee may speak any number of times on a measure, although the discussion must be strictly relevant to the particular item which is being considered. The discussion in committee is apt to become more informal: the speeches are short and to the point; and although under the rules all members must address the chairman, this is relaxed in actual practice and the members commonly address one another, ask questions, and receive direct answers.

The Committee of the Whole was altered drastically by the rules adopted in 1968, and almost all its former functions as Committee of Supply[24] and Committee of Ways and Means have either been assigned to standing committees or resumed by the House itself. The Committee of the Whole, like any committee, can deal with any matter referred to it, and thus can be used for any purpose the House wishes; undoubtedly one of its main functions will continue to be the considerations of bills based on supply motions (that is, proposals for expenditure) and ways and means motions (that is, proposals for raising money).[25] The entire committee system is of course directly related to the size of the government's majority, since all committees reflect the government's strength; the committee system is thus considerably modified during the life of a minority government.

RULES OF THE HOUSE

The advantage which the government has on all committees is fairly typical of the general favours which it enjoys in all parliamentary activity, the extent

24/The history of the Committee of Supply is recounted in Ward, *The Public Purse*, especially chaps. XIII and XIV.
25/Beauchesne, *Rules and Forms of the House of Commons of Canada*, p. 159.

of these favours being determined in large measure by the rules which Parliament follows in transacting its business. The rules hold the balance between the rights of the private members and the rights of the cabinet, but the balance tends to lean consistently to one side and help the cabinet get its measures passed and its supplies voted, for whatever else happens the government of Canada must go on. Members of all parties accept this gesture to majority rule as inevitable, although their stoicism naturally will not prevent them from protesting and disputing over any optional privileges and interpretations which the rules may allow. There is thus a constant pressure from the government side to dispose of government business and an opposing pressure by the private members to slow it up or to shelve it temporarily for their own favourite projects. Somewhere between the two a fairly amicable compromise is usually found. It must, however, be realized that government measures may and usually do furnish private members on both sides of the House with a wider opportunity for discussion than the bills and resolutions of private members, which are often more restricted in both scope and appeal.

The rules of the House set aside fixed periods for the special use of the government and private members respectively. For many years six Mondays and two Thursdays were set aside early in the session for private members' business, but in 1960–1 the House began to experiment with alternative methods of allowing time for private members, while simultaneously permitting the government to use Mondays and Thursdays for public business. In the session of 1960–1 the House eliminated the allocated days for MP.s and substituted the equivalent in time (a total of forty one-hour periods) at the rate of one hour on each of the first three days of each week; this change was effected on a provisional basis only, and became permanent in the rules adopted in 1968; private members now have in general one hour on each day except Wednesday, up to a maximum of forty on Mondays and Tuesdays, but with no fixed total for Thursdays and Fridays.[26] Government's demands for parliamentary time are never wanting, for the government's business is both extensive and urgent. Though the incident which called forth the following statement by one prime minister could not now happen, because of changes in rules, the point of the quotation is revelatory of a continuing parliamentary problem:

A good deal has been said on this motion with respect to the rights of private members. Odd as it may seem, I think something ought to be said as to the rights of the Government ... In the first place, may I point out that it is over a month since this Parliament assembled. In that time the Government has not been able, until to-day, to bring forward a single Government measure. That has not been the fault of the Government, but has been due to the fact that the entire time has

---

26/Standing Orders no. 15(4–6). For a history of the rules see W. F. Dawson, *Procedure in the Canadian House of Commons*; Page, "Streamlining the Procedures of the Canadian House of Commons."

been occupied by private members speaking in the debate on the Address in reply to the Speech from the Throne and on the motions with respect to the Bren gun contract ... Getting on with Supply is one of the major obligations of a Government. At the end of the session there is an outcry if the Government have a great deal of Supply left ... We have not had opportunity thus far to get into Supply at all.[27]

The business of Parliament – and of the government – is also greatly expedited by the rules of debate.[28] Only certain specific motions are debatable; speeches (though the practice is much abused) cannot be read; members cannot speak twice on the same question: these and other rules of a similar kind eliminate much needless discussion. In 1927 the House introduced a drastic curtailment, whereby no one was allowed to speak for more than forty minutes except "the Prime Minister and the Leader of the Opposition, or a Minister moving a Government Order and the member speaking in reply immediately after such Minister, or a member making a motion of 'No Confidence' in the Government and a Minister replying thereto"; in 1955 the forty minutes was reduced to thirty, and in 1968 the time limit, depending on what was before the House, was variously fixed at ten, twenty, thirty, and forty minutes. While such limits favour the cabinet and may cause occasional hardship, there can be little doubt that most speakers can make their contributions adequately in the time allowed.

A further limitation which greatly strengthens the command of the cabinet over the time of the House is the closure, a device used to terminate excessive debate or systematic obstruction. It was originally introduced at Ottawa in 1913 in order to bring the Borden Naval Bill to a vote, after a continuous session of the House (except for Sundays) of about two weeks. The closure rule, which has not been changed substantively for many years, is applied as follows. Any minister, who has given notice at a previous sitting of the House of his intention, may move that the consideration of a matter on which debate is to be resumed, or on which discussion in committee is proceeding, shall not be further postponed or that the debate in the House shall not be further adjourned. This motion is not debatable and must be voted on forthwith. If the motion is passed, the discussion or debate on the main question may be resumed; but speeches are henceforth limited to twenty minutes, and a vote must be taken at or before one o'clock the following morning.

A second and more specialized form of limiting debate was proposed by the committee on Procedure and Organization in 1968, and supported by the government, but was so strongly opposed by the parties in opposition that it was temporarily dropped, and came back to the House in June 1969. The proposal was, in essence:

27/W. L. Mackenzie King, *Can. H. of C. Debates*, Feb. 14, 1939, pp. 915–16. Debate on the Address is now limited.
28/See Beauchesne, *Rules and Forms of the House of Commons in Canada*, pp. 87–115; Standing Orders nos. 28–37.

(a) If the representatives of all parties agreed "to allot a specified number of days or hours to the proceedings at one or more stages of any public bill," a minister could announce the agreement and move forthwith that the agreed allocation of time be put into effect. His motion would not be debatable.

(b) If a majority of the representatives of the parties in the House reached a similar accord (including, if agreed upon, the combining in one motion of a time allocation covering the last two stages of a bill, that is, the report on the bill from a committee, plus third reading), a minister could again announce the agreement; his motion in these circumstances could be debated for not more than two hours, during which no member could speak more than once or for longer than ten minutes.

(c) If no agreement could be reached under either (a) or (b) above, a minister could announce this fact and then, having given notice, in effect propose, on a motion, a time allocation for the consideration of any public bill. The time allotted for any one stage of a bill was to be at least one sitting day, and again one motion could allocate time for the last two stages. The minister's motion for a time allocation could again be debated for not more than two hours, with no member having more than ten minutes.

The parties in opposition were prepared to accept proposals (a) and (b), but dug in their heels over (c), and finally on July 22, 1969, the government gave notice of closure to pass the new rules; they passed on July 24, 1969, "the first time," Mr Stanley Knowles observed, that "closure has been used to invoke further closure."[29] A government backed by a majority thus now has the power to allot, if it wishes, a maximum of four days to even the most complex bill.

The value of the closure lies not so much in its actual use (which has in fact been rare, though usually crucial) as in its presence in the rules of the House and the knowledge that the government may invoke it when ever necessary. Curiously enough, there are times when the opposition may desire to have the closure applied in order to give the party a point of attack. Thus in 1932 when the Liberals wished to call attention to the extreme provisions of the Relief Bill, they obstructed its passage in order to force the government to apply the closure and thus demonstrate still further the autocratic tendencies of which the opposition was so loudly complaining. In the elections of 1957 and 1958, as a result of the controversial use of closure by the Liberal government in 1956,[30] the Progressive Conservative party campaigned successfully on a platform which included abolition of the closure rule. The controversy over the rules for time allocations in 1969 suggests that an occasion could easily arise in which the opposition parties would try to force a cabinet to invoke the last of them.

29/Can. H. of C. Debates, July 22, 1969, p. 11472; see also New Democratic party Press Release, June 20, 1969. The new rules are Standing Orders nos. 75 A, B, C.
30/See Hugh G. Thorburn, "Parliament and Policy Making: The Case of the Trans-Canada Gas Pipeline," Canadian Journal of Economics and Political Science, XXIII, no. 4 (Nov. 1957), pp. 516–31; Eugene Forsey, "Constitutional Aspects of the Canadian Pipe Line Debate," Public Law, Spring 1957, pp. 9–27.

The regularity and certainty of the party vote on both sides are to a large degree maintained, as stated in an earlier chapter, through the caucus; and they are ensured on the floor of the House by the activity of party members called "whippers-in" or, more commonly, "whips." These are constantly checking on their colleagues, summoning them to caucus, discussing their grievances with them, arranging for their order of speaking,[31] and making certain that they are always on hand when a division (or vote) is called. The last endeavour is made very much easier by the device known as "pairing." This is simply an agreement between individual members of opposing parties that for a specified period neither will vote in a party division, either member or both thus being able to be absent without weakening his party's voting strength. Personal pairs are arranged between members themselves; official pairs through the party whips. The prime minister and the leader of the opposition have a sessional pair, which lasts for the entire session and becomes operative whenever one is absent from a vote on a party question.[32] Pairing may, of course, become too convenient and members absent themselves for weekends and holidays, leaving those members from the distant provinces to carry the legislative burden; members obliged to stay in Ottawa often refer disparagingly to their week-ending colleagues from central Canada as the "Tuesday-Thursday boys."[33] The use of pairing varies a good deal (in 1969–70, for example, it seemed to be on the decline), and will depend in large measure on party convenience. In 1947, for example, the Liberal majority was so small that the two chief opposition parties thought they might embarrass the government by constantly threatening defeat, and an order was issued forbidding the pairing of members save for exceptional reasons; and pairing was not practised in the Parliament elected in 1968. Pairs are not recognized by the rules of the House; and a member who through inadvertence breaks a pair and tries to correct it after the vote has been recorded is not allowed to do so. The Meighen government was defeated on July 1, 1926, by a vote cast under such circumstances.

Official hostilities between the parties rarely overlook the parliamentary courtesies, not merely on the floor of the House, but also "behind the Speaker's

31/The Speaker is usually given a list of speakers by the whips, and he endeavours to hear them alternately pro and con. According to the rules he gives the floor to the member who happens to "catch his eye"; but the process of selection is not nearly as casual as this would seem to suggest.

32/R. B. Bennett stated the terms of his pair with W. L. Mackenzie King thus: "Our pairs [were] to be in force on all matters introduced by the Government or for which the Government assumes responsibility, also in connection with all matters introduced by the Official Opposition or by any member on its behalf, and to apply also when the Speaker is in the chair as well as in Committee of the Whole House on such matters." *Can. H. of C. Debates*, Feb. 22, 1932, p. 385.

33/In one division on May 24, 1946, 124 members were paired. The absence of Toronto and Montreal members (and others as conveniently situated) over the weekends has even led to a custom that few divisions are called during Mondays and Fridays. *Ibid.*, Feb. 21, 1944, p. 679; see also pp. 676–91.

chair," when the leaders, and particularly the whips, endeavour to work out arrangements for the conduct of business which will meet the convenience of all parties. The struggle is, indeed, often carried on more in the spirit of a game than a war; and the onlooker, after hearing a vigorous assault on a minister early in the afternoon, may be surprised to witness a little later the attacker and the attacked walking together out of the chamber on the best of terms.

THE PASSAGE OF BILLS

The basic procedure in the passage of public bills[34] is that they should receive three readings in the House, three in the Senate, and then go to the governor general for his formal signature. If the bill originates in the senate, the order of passage in the two houses is, of course, reversed. If one house amends the bill passed by the other, it is returned to have these amendments considered and approved; and if these are not accepted, the house which originated the bill will state the reasons for rejection. Communication between the houses is by message; but if no agreement occurs through this medium, a conference will be held between representatives of each house to discuss and, if possible, to reconcile differences.[35] If agreement is not reached, the measure is, of course, lost.

The introduction of a bill [36] in the Commons must be preceded by forty-eight hours' notice, which appears on the *Notice Paper* of the House.[37] When the appropriate time arrives, the member must then move for leave to introduce the bill, giving the bill's title and perhaps a "succinct explanation" in a few sentences of its general purpose. Leave is almost invariably granted;[38] and the bill is read the first time without any debate or amendment being permitted. There may be a vote; but the first reading tends to be nothing more than a formality which serves to bring the bill into the swirl of the House's activity.

Until 1968, a bill which involved a charge upon the people, that is, a bill which necessitated the expenditure of public funds or the imposition of a tax had to be considered first as a resolution in the Committee of the Whole House, and debate on the resolution was often lengthy. In 1964 the House limited such debates to one day each, and in 1968 abolished the resolution stage altogether, thus saving as much as ten or fifteen days out of each session.

The second reading of a bill is normally its most important stage, and it presents the opportunity for full and lengthy discussion. The debate on the sec-

34/The distinction between government bills, public bills and private bills has been already made, and the passage of private bills has been described, *supra*, pp. 210–12; 296–7.
35/Beauchesne, *Rules and Forms of the House of Commons in Canada*, p. 73.
36/All possible alternatives and variations in the legislative process are not attempted here; but the main outlines are stated and are, except for these possible additions, correct.
37/The *Votes and Proceedings* are the daily minutes of the proceedings of the House. One section is reserved for notices of motions to be made later in the House.
38/It was refused in 1932. *Can. H. of C. Debates*, Feb. 22, 1932, pp. 380–5.

ond reading, however, is confined to the principle of the proposal and any attempt to discuss details or to deal with the clauses seriatim will be ruled out of order. The bill cannot be amended on second reading, but it may be defeated; the conventional way of accomplishing a defeat is to move an amendment that the bill be read "this day six months" or after "any other term beyond the probable duration of the session."[39]

If the House gives a bill a second reading, it has thereby expressed its approval of the general aim of the bill. The next logical question to be answered is whether the measure as proposed will best carry out this purpose. The following stage must therefore be devoted to a discussion of the detailed provisions. To accomplish this, the bill now goes to one of the standing committees, although it may be sent to a special or a joint committee if the House so orders. The committee goes through the bill clause by clause, possibly calling witnesses or otherwise collecting relevant information, and then reports it back to the House, with or without amendments. A lapse of forty-eight hours then occurs (unless the House takes action to shorten it) and the House then considers the bill as reported from the committee, accepting or rejecting the bill as it came from the committee and amending it at the report stage if it wishes, and the bill is finally given third reading. Third reading is by no means a formality, although the rules adopted in 1968 assume that all amendments which the House desires will have been made in committee or at the report stage, that is, after the bill has returned from a committee. The only debatable point is whether the bill should or should not be read a third time. Occasionally, the opposition will make at this stage a last desperate effort to encompass the defeat of a government measure or at least to establish its own position beyond any possible doubt. But a bill which has progressed thus far is not likely to be defeated as it comes into the last stretch.

The apparent simplicity of the procedure described above (and for financial legislation it is a little more complex, as the committee to which bills based on supply and ways and means motions are sent is the committee of the whole House) should not lead one to assume that every bill has an easy passage through the House. Highly controversial debates can occur both in the Commons chamber and in the committee room; bills do get withdrawn by cabinets in the face of opposition criticism; the parliamentary timetable is often such that bills die on the order paper (twelve government bills expired in the 1968-9 session); and once through the House of Commons a bill has to survive passage through the Senate. If the Senate makes any amendments, as noted, the bill has to come back to the Commons for consideration. The actual passage of any bill can be traced in detail with the aid of the two houses' respective *Journals*, which are in effect official diaries; a comparison of any bill's voyage through the House of Commons before 1968, with that of one passed after, will show that the new rules of the House have enormously simplified procedure.

39/Beauchesne, *Rules and Forms of the House of Commons in Canada*, p. 228.

FINANCE

Some attention has already been given to the authoritative position occupied by the cabinet in financial legislation. It is now necessary to develop this point a little further, and to indicate in greater detail the way in which such legislation is drafted and presented by the executive and considered and passed by the House of Commons. Some years ago in presenting a review of Canadian financial administration[40] the deputy minister of Finance outlined the essential features of the system. These may be briefly stated as follows.

(1) A budget system, that is, a systematic statement and consideration once a year of the financial standing of the government, so that cabinet, Parliament, and nation may know what the current position is and what it is likely to be in the future. (Occasionally, for special reasons, there have been two budgets in one year.)

(2) The acceptance by the cabinet of the responsibility of preparing this statement, of formulating estimates of future expenditure, and of devising expedients for raising funds to meet these expenditures – all of which it submits to Parliament.

(3) The acceptance by Parliament, and especially the House of Commons, of the responsibility of receiving these statements and plans, of scrutinizing them, of satisfying itself of their essential correctness and suitability, and of approving them.

(4) The acceptance by both cabinet and Parliament of the doctrine that approval by the latter in no way diminishes the responsibility of the former, either for the proposals as originally submitted or for any modification in these proposals which may be made after discussion.

(5) A combination of rigid control over major appropriation items with a degree of flexibility in matters of "supporting details," and power to abstain from making any authorized expenditure if the cabinet should consider such abstention desirable.

(6) As an aid to the foregoing and as an insurance that the wishes of both cabinet and Parliament will and can be carried out, there must be adequate administrative machinery. This involves not only proper accounting, reporting, and auditing facilities, but also the presentation of material in such a form that a body of laymen, such as the House of Commons, can deal with it intelligently. The House of Commons has its own auditor, the auditor general, and its own auditing machinery, primarily the Standing Committee on Public Accounts.

While a government – contrary to general belief – does not reverse the practice of the frugal individual and spend its money without worrying about its

40/W. C. Clark, "Financial Administration of the Government of Canada," *Canadian Journal of Economics and Political Science*, IV, no. 3 (Aug. 1938), pp. 391–419. See also Ward, *The Public Purse*, for a detailed account of parliamentary handling of financial matters to 1961; H. R. Balls, "Financial Administration in Canada," in Kernaghan, *Bureaucracy in Canadian Government*, pp. 57–64.

income, there is always an element of this happy inversion in its practice. Some months before the meeting of Parliament, the Treasury Board notifies all departments that the "estimates" or planned expenditures for the coming fiscal year should be prepared and submitted. An informal intimation of the general attitude which the cabinet is likely to adopt on projected expenditure will have reached the departments through their ministers, so that the amount of cloth from which the coats are to be cut will be vaguely, but none the less surely, known in advance.

The departmental officials at various levels accordingly make their plans for the future and draw up a draft of the expenditures involved,[41] which, it need scarcely be said, are always apt to be in excess of those which are absolutely necessary. These projects are laid before the deputy minister, who scans them carefully, interviews and questions the directors and chiefs of the various departmental activities, sends some items back for reconsideration, cuts other estimates out of hand, and finally passes on a revised proposal to the minister. The minister, although he has already made his wishes generally known through his deputy, may have further suggestions to offer and may insist on certain alterations being incorporated. The estimates then go to the staff of the Treasury Board (whose officials may have already greatly influenced the plans which result in the estimates), and from there to the Board itself.

The Treasury Board has already been described, and it will be recalled that it exercises very extensive authority in all financial matters, which it derives from the Financial Administration Act and other statutes.[42] In the consideration of estimates, its great merits are its small size, the ability and prominence of its members, and the presence of the ministers who are primarily responsible for financial matters and charged especially with the unhappy duty of raising the revenue to meet all contemplated expenditures. The Treasury Board is thus by the nature of its personnel and position implacably opposed to extravagance, and it has ample opportunity at this time to develop its peculiar talents. The ensuing struggle is best told in the words of one minister of Finance:

The staff of the Treasury Board ... go at those estimates and try to have them reduced. They are successful to a considerable extent in having them reduced. But various departments demur, and some go even farther than that and vigorously and violently protest against the proposed cuts. The matter is then taken up by myself with the various Ministers and by the Treasury Board with the various Ministers, and after a considerable amount of argument the estimates are still further reduced until they reach the form in which they appear before the House of Commons ...

We talk about putting a watch on expenditures, but how much assistance do we get in this House in watching expenditures? Nine-tenths of the speeches in this House are asking for bigger and better expenditures. That was the case all through

41/Any vote of money which is unexpended at the end of the fiscal year, lapses, and, if it is to be spent, must reappear in the new estimates and be re-voted in the new Appropriation Act.
42/*Supra*, pp. 221–2; Balls, "Financial Administration in Canada."

the last Parliament. While this session did not start out in that way, it finally got that way. If the Government is making large expenditures, it is not because the Ministers are trying to make those expenditures, it is because of public and parliamentary demands for those expenditures. That is why the expenditures are being made. At times I feel as though I am against the whole world when I try to keep a lot of these expenditures down. We just do the best we can, that is all, and keep them down.[43]

After this troubled passage through the Treasury Board, the estimates are approved by the cabinet (where a disappointed minister may make a last stand for a larger appropriation), and are recommended to the governor general for his approval, which is given as a matter of course. They are then transmitted (with the recommendation of the governor general) to the House of Commons early in the parliamentary sessions, and are at once referred to the relevant standing committees.

The estimates are not presented simply as enormous blocks of funds assigned to each department, for this would make it impossible for Parliament either to understand the expenditures or to exercise oversight of any consequence. Even a moderately effective control must be based on an intelligent appreciation of the exact purposes for which the money is to be spent, and this involves breaking down the proposals into a large number of comparatively small items. But, on the other hand, Parliament must not make its statutory provisions too rigid, for it would thereby greatly embarrass the administration in its task of applying the funds effectively to the need which is to be met. A combination of rigidity and flexibility is desired, and this is ingeniously achieved by stating and passing the appropriations in a double form. The main estimates are grouped under hundreds of items, and the Appropriation Act will be passed under these headings which cannot be changed. But behind most of the appropriation headings are "supporting details," and these designate the much smaller amounts assigned to the individual projects and are not entirely mandatory.

This second section of the estimates gives information to Parliament which is essential to the carrying out of its functions of scrutiny and criticism, but it does not form part of the Supply Bill or the Appropriation Act. Were these details enacted as part of the fund-granting statute, the hands of the executive would be too closely tied. A degree of flexibility is necessary if the administration of government services is to be carried out smoothly and efficiently. This flexibility, plus the necessary degree of control, are provided by giving the Treasury Board power to vary the details showing the objects of expenditure on which the vote is to be spent. No such variation, however, can be made by a department without the specific approval of the Treasury Board.[44]

The main estimates for each incoming fiscal year must now by House rule be referred to standing committees by March 1, and the committees, after

43/J. L. Ilsley, *Can. H. of C. Debates*, Dec. 18, 1945, pp. 3734–5. With the changes described *supra*, chap. x, the minister would now be the president of the Treasury Board rather than the minister of Finance.

44/Clark, "Financial Administration of the Government of Canada," p. 398. See also *Can. H. of C. Debates*, Feb. 3, 1938, pp. 148–9.

examining them item by item, must report back by May 31, thus having three months for the completion of their study. This practice, begun in 1968 after a good deal of serious criticism of traditional financial procedures by successive committees, does not prevent the House as a whole from considering supply. The new rules provide for the setting aside in each session of twenty-five days (five on or before December 10, seven more by March 26, and thirteen more by June 30) on which only members in opposition can present motions, on "any matter within the jurisdiction of the Parliament of Canada," thus preserving the ancient privilege of "grievances before supply." A maximum of six of these opposition motions, two in each period for which "allotted days" are provided, may be "no-confidence motions against the government." To facilitate the work of all members, but especially those in opposition, the estimates are presented in a form which shows comparative data for the previous year, thus permitting members to assess increases and decreases in the expenditure proposals. The final legislation becomes an Appropriation Act.[45]

Three other kinds of supply may be mentioned in addition to the one just discussed, which is known as the *main estimates. Supplementary estimates* (which are also referred to committees) are made necessary because of the impossibility of providing in the main estimates for all the contingencies which have occurred since their original preparation. The supplementary estimates are therefore introduced late in the session. They add to the main estimates both unexpected and increased items, and also those which could have been foreseen but have been only recently decided upon. There are also *final supplementary estimates* which are commonly introduced just before the close of the fiscal year. These are to provide for additional items and money already spent which have not been covered up to that time. It is clear that the greater the use which is made of these devices, the less appreciation Parliament can have of the true financial situation when the main estimates are being considered, and this ignorance must inevitably be accompanied by some relinquishing of effective control. The situation has been made much worse by the fact that the supplementary estimates are usually passed hurriedly on the verge of prorogation and they thus receive the most perfunctory examination; it is too early to assess the new financial procedures adopted in 1968, but before that it was not uncommon for the House to vote almost without consideration supplementaries for larger sums than used to occupy the House for an entire session of Parliament. Certainly under the old procedures the supplementaries formed ideal vehicles for "pork barrel" expenditures.[46]

Interim supply, a device formerly used to give a government a "down pay-

---

45/The Appropriation Bill is presented to the governor general in the name of the House of Commons only, and his assent is given in a special phrase (following English precedent), namely: "In Her Majesty's name, His Excellency the Governor General thanks her loyal subjects, accepts their benevolence, and assents to this bill." To ordinary bills the assent is given in these words: "In Her Majesty's name, His Excellency the Governor General doth assent to these Bills."
46/*Infra*, pp. 476–8.

ment" on its annual income because the passage of the main estimates might have been too dilatory to keep up with its need for money, has been considerably altered under the new rules. Since all main estimates have to be voted on by the end of June, it appears probable that interim supply, if needed, will be required only once, for the second quarter of each year. Any time taken to debate interim supply is deducted from the twenty-five days allocated for supply.[47]

Emergency and unforeseeable expenditure which has not been provided for by Parliament may be made by a governor general's warrant, a special authority issued under an order-in-council. It cannot be issued if Parliament is in session, and its use is severely restricted by other statutory provisions. Prior to 1958 it was customary for expenditure made under governor general's warrants to be included in the next supplementary estimates, so that Parliament was still able to review the expenditure *ex post facto*; since 1958 the practice has been required by statute.[48] Warrants have been used on occasion to finance virtually the whole of ordinary governmental expenditures for short periods.

The other side of the financial situation is, of course, revenue; and this is considered in the presentation of the budget – the balance of the contemplated expenditures with a corresponding income (derived from current revenue or loans) so that a financial equilibrium is obtained. "A notice of a Ways and Means motion may be laid upon the Table of the House at any time during a sitting by a Minister of the Crown, but such a motion may not be proposed in the same sitting ... When such an order is designated for the purpose of enabling a Minister of the Crown to make a budget presentation, a motion 'That this House approves in general the budgetary policy of the Government' shall be proposed." Thus Standing Order no. 60, replacing the ancient formula "that Mr. Speaker do now leave the chair for the House to go into Committee of Ways and Means," provides for one of the Commons' annual festivals, the budget debate, to which six days are now allocated. The main topics in the minister's opening speech have become fairly well standardized and embrace the following:[49]

(1) A review of the economic and financial conditions during the past year and the effects of government policies on these conditions.

(2) A review of the financial operations of the government during the past fiscal year (or, it may be, the year which is almost concluded). This presents the current situation and lays the necessary foundation for what is to come.

(3) A tentative weighing of the existing and, to some degree, known elements of the situation – the probable revenue to be derived from taxation at

---

47/For an example of the old practices, see *Can. H. of C. Debates*, March 29, 1946, pp. 386–90. On both supplementary estimates and interim supply see Ward, *The Public Purse*, especially chaps. XIII and XIV.

48/*Can. Statutes*, 7 Eliz. II, c. 31. On governor general's warrants see Ward, *The Public Purse*, especially chaps. XIII and XIV.

49/Clark, "Financial Administration of the Government of Canada," pp. 417–18.

present levels, and the almost certain expenditure as indicated in the estimates already presented and by the financial demands arising from existing statutory grants. These estimates, being outside limits on expenditure, may not represent accurately what the expenditure will actually be; and hence the minister will give some indication whether he believes the estimates already brought down to Parliament give an accurate indication of the total amount which will be needed.

(4) The adjustment which the above tentative computation has made desirable, in the government's opinion. If a surplus is indicated, the minister will probably either change the taxes in certain respects or reduce or abandon some of them. If a deficit is indicated, the minister may close the gap by tax adjustments, tax increases, new taxes, or capital borrowings, depending partly on how the government may be attempting to influence the business cycle. The government may, of course, choose the budget to announce any drastic changes, such as a departure in tariff policy, which are likely to have important financial consequences.

The above motion, which forms the occasion for the presentation of the budget, is debatable and subject to amendments, and it usually receives both. This is one of the most important debates of the year and it will naturally stress in particular the economic difficulties and outlook for the future. The motion is eventually carried, or the government will either have to resign or seek a dissolution. Legislation based on the budget proposals can of course also be debated under the usual rules for processing bills, so that the members have a minimum of two opportunities for discussing the governmental proposals.

The elaborate and complicated system of authorizing, auditing, and checking which forms a very essential part of the financial administration as it affects the receipt and, particularly, the disbursement of the public funds cannot be discussed here in detail.[50] The primary responsibility for the system is vested in the cabinet acting through the Treasury Board and the Department of Supply and Services. All expenditures are pre-audited before being made, to ensure that Parliament has actually voted the money for the proposed expenditure and that the money has not already been spent; this function, formerly vested in the comptroller of the Treasury, is now vested in Supply and Services, but the actual pre-auditing is being decentralized to the individual departments, which now enjoy far greater autonomy than they did before the report of the Royal Commission on Government Organization.

The expenditures are also post-audited by the auditor general, whose office was established in 1878. He is an official of Parliament – not of the cabinet – and he holds office during good behaviour, subject to removal only by the Governor-in-Council after the passage of a joint address by both Houses of

50/See *ibid.*, pp. 403–17; H. R. Balls, "The Development of Government Expenditure Control: The Issue and Audit Phases," *Canadian Journal of Economics and Political Science*, x, no. 4 (Nov. 1944), pp. 464–75; Ward, *The Public Purse.*

Parliament. His function is to check on all receipts and payments of the Consolidated Revenue Fund, to ensure that money has been or is to be paid for the purposes intended, and generally to investigate every aspect of the public service as it affects finance. His decisions can also be overruled by the Treasury Board, but these cases must be submitted to the consideration of Parliament in his annual report. In this report he is further bound to call attention to any irregularity, any exceptional procedure, any special payments by warrant, any refund of a tax or similar payment under statutory authority, or any matter which he feels he should bring to the attention of Parliament; and Parliament may, of course, take what it considers to be appropriate action.

Parliamentary consideration of the auditor general's report, primarily through the Standing Committee on Public Accounts, has had an exceedingly erratic history, though in recent years it has become increasingly systematic. In 1958, following British practice, a member of the opposition was elected chairman of the Public Accounts Committee, and shortly thereafter the committee undertook to follow up its own comments and criticisms to see what executive action had been taken on them. The committee's work and authority was shaken by the long period of minority government from 1962 to 1968, and it is clear that the House of Commons is still falling short of a comprehensive and effective scrutiny of financial affairs.[51]

The House of Commons, notwithstanding, has enormously improved its ordering of its own internal workings in the past decade. A "permanent" speakership has been established, although of course its continuance cannot be guaranteed. A serious investigatory body chaired by a member of the opposition, the Standing Committtee on Public Accounts, is now an accepted part of parliamentary procedure. The House no longer wastes time appealing Mr Speaker's rulings. The formless and commonly rambling debates on financial resolutions, before the relevant legislation had even been introduced, have been abolished. The House has divested itself of a major task which formerly showed it at its least edifying: the drawing of constituency boundaries. All estimates, instead of dawdling through the whole House, in Committee of Supply, with a large remainder usually being rammed through at breakneck speed in the dying days of each session, are now studied in detail by standing committees. Bills which in former times also limped through Committee of the Whole, now go to small committees too. The House has taken long strides towards setting itself an annual schedule which, according to its own rules, it must meet. No House, of course, is better than its members; but the members of recent years have given the House much thought, and the House of Commons has grown in stature.

51/Ward, *The Public Purse*, especially chaps. III to XII.

19 The House of Commons and the cabinet

THE ACCOUNT WHICH HAS BEEN GIVEN in several of the earlier chapters has shown the close connection between the Canadian cabinet and the majority of the House of Commons – a connection so intimate that it becomes virtual identification. Parliament is summoned and dissolved on the advice of the prime minister, who will no doubt often (though not always) exercise his powers after consulting members of his cabinet. The cabinet wields extensive authority over all legislation and exclusive authority over the initiation of all financial legislation; the cabinet controls the time, regulates the business, and apportions the energies of the House almost from hour to hour during every day of its meeting. There is virtually nothing which the House does or discusses in which the cabinet has not some interest, and in most of these matters it exercises a paramount control. The functions of Parliament would seem to have degenerated until all that it does is to pass on the measures which the cabinet chooses to offer within the time which the cabinet chooses to allow; to raise and spend the money which the cabinet desires without the opportunity of increasing either revenue or expenditure; to fall in constantly behind the majority, which in turn automatically falls in behind the cabinet. Responsible government would appear to have suffered a strange and alarming inversion: the cabinet is no longer responsible to the Commons; the Commons seems instead to have become responsible to the cabinet.

That there is a substantial measure of truth in this, no one can deny. The cabinet does dominate Parliament, and it is largely because of this masterful leadership that Parliament is able to make its expenditure of time and energy produce results which are moderately satisfactory. A House of two or three hundred members which wanders where it pleases will undoubtedly be able to do a lot of wandering, but it will not accomplish much more; and if it is to perform its functions as a useful part of the government, it must be willing to place some limits on its freedom and submit to direction. It does not thereby become of necessity subservient to the cabinet nor is the cabinet on that account unable to derive from the House much counsel and guidance. To regard the rare defeats of the cabinet by the House as a reliable indication of the efficacy of parliamentary control is to judge the efficacy of parental control by the number of times the child is punished. The House of Commons does control the cabinet – rarely by defeating it, often by criticizing it, still more often by the cabinet anticipating criticism before subjecting itself and its acts to the House, and always by the latent capacity of the House to revolt against its leaders.

This criticism may occur (as indicated elsewhere) in the secrecy of the government caucus; but the launching of open criticism and attack is primarily the responsibility of the opposition. It wages perpetual war on the government, finding out its faults, picking its policies and proposals apart, offering substitutes and amendments, and lying in wait for any sign of weakness or dissension. The preceding chapter has suggested that the rules of the House, while fair, tend to favour the cabinet and to give it a general right of way for its business; but there are also many rules which are designed to aid the other side and give the minority an opportunity to voice their opinions and register their protests. Some of these provisions have already been touched upon, notably the elaborate formalities in the legislative process which offer facilities at every turn for discussion and attack, and the rules for "Business of Supply" which give priority to opposition motions. It remains now to glance at those opportunities which are especially appropriate for this purpose and which allow the opposition – and, indeed, any private member – to vent its criticism, woo its public, and test its strength in the divisions.[1]

THE DEBATE ON THE ADDRESS IN REPLY TO
THE SPEECH FROM THE THRONE

This opportunity for general debate, lasting eight sitting days at most, is presented as soon as Parliament settles down to the work of the session. The leaders of the opposition parties direct the attack on the government's policies, past, present, and future, through the device of moving amendments to the main motion; such amendments were not moved before 1893 but are now the normal practice, and the rules specify the timing for the disposition of sub-amendments and amendments. The prime minister then defends the government's policies at length. After the big guns have spoken, those of smaller bore are free to be heard. The great merit of the debate on the address from the point of view of the private member is that the field of argument is

1/A formal division is a standing vote, the "yeas" being counted first, and then the "nays." Each member stands to be identified and have his vote recorded, and then sits down. Prior to a division, bells ring for several minutes (under the new rules, not more than fifteen) to summon members from all over Parliament Hill; when the bells stop, the doors of the chamber are closed.

virtually unlimited, and it is therefore possible to talk about anything under the sun and yet be in order.[2] Under such benign auspices even the dullest member can, and often does, fill up his thirty minutes with ease. Some idea of the diversity of subject-matter allowed may be gathered from a speech of the leader of the opposition (R. B. Hanson) on the address in November, 1940. Setting what may still be a record, he spoke on: the summoning of Parliament at that time; responsible government in Canada; the Canadian attitude to the war; the possible invasion of Britain; the manufacture of aeroplanes; the Canadian war effort in general; a speech made by General Crerar; the training of troops; Canada's external relations; finance; soldiers' hutments; wasted potato bags; the Montreal railway terminals; imports from the United States; the Rowell-Sirois report. Mr Hanson then added:

I did intend to say something about the St. Lawrence Waterway, but I do not think I should trespass much longer on the time of the House. The Prime Minister today tabled the correspondence, and I have not had opportunity to look at it. I shall therefore reserve what I have to say on that matter. I had also intended to say something about leadership in Canada, but also reserve my remarks on that subject until a later date. I cannot, however, refrain from saying something about the position of truck transportation in the province of Prince Edward Island ...[3]

The extent to which members take advantage of this field day formerly varied from year to year, and the tendency was for a large number to use it as a convenient sounding-board for the benefit if not the edification of their constituencies. Beginning in 1955 the debate was limited to ten and then eight days, and it is likely that the available time length will always be used. The great objection is not loss of time, but the utter pointlessness of many of these outpourings; the speeches lack both direction and force, and they splash ineffectively against the rocks of national indifference. The full measure of their worth is to be found in the fact that frequently nowadays they are not even prepared by the members who speak, but by hired hacks.

QUESTIONS ADDRESSED TO MINISTERS

Members of the House are given an opportunity to address both oral and written questions to cabinet ministers concerning various phases of public affairs.[4] A member can have up to three questions daily marked for an oral reply, and unmarked questions are answered on papers handed to the Clerk of the House and then printed in the debates. (In practice, "oral" replies are

2/This was not always so, but the rule has been greatly relaxed.
3/*Can. H. of C. Debates*, Nov. 12, 1940, p. 33.
4/See Harry W. Walker, "Question Time in Parliament," *Queen's Quarterly*, LIX (Spring 1952), pp. 64–71.

commonly typewritten too.) If the information required is lengthy or is apt to be delayed, it is passed as an order for return and is tabled in due course.

For many years the rules provided only for written questions, although in practice the Speaker permitted oral questions, theoretically those confined to matters of some urgency. The rules now permit an oral question period of up to forty minutes daily (again for matters of urgency), and any member not satisfied with a response to any question can give notice "that he intends to raise the subject-matter of his question on the adjournment of the House." These adjournment debates, held between ten and ten-thirty p.m. three days a week (and popularly referred to as "the late show") are often lively affairs.

The question must consist of an inquiry reduced to its simplest form. It must contain no argument or opinion, must not be provocative, and must be brief and to the point. The answers given must be equally concise and limited to the minimum explanation that is necessary to convey the information. The following are sample questions: the first, the most common, of the factual type;[5] the second, a written question converted into a motion for return, which illustrates those which are sometimes not answered because it is not advisable to do so;[6] the third, an oral question, asked on the orders of the day, which is given an evasive answer.[7]

FERTILIZER IMPORTS

Question No. 2,076 – MR. GLEAVE

1. How much fertilizer was imported into Canada from October 1968 to April 15, 1969 (a) tonnage (b) price at port of entry?

2. How much fertilizer was exported from Canada during the same period?

3. Was the Shell Oil Company the supplier of all or part of the supplies?

HON. JEAN-LUC PEPIN (MINISTER OF INDUSTRY, TRADE AND COMMERCE) In so far as the Dominion Bureau of Statistics is concerned: 1. The amount of fertilizer imported into Canada for the period October 1, 1968 to March 31, 1969 (latest statistics available) was (a) 124,867 tons; (b) valued at $5,684,153*.

*The value is the "Fair Market Value" at customs port of entry.

2. The value of fertilizers exported from Canada for the period October 1, 1968 to March 31, 1969 (latest statistics available) was $91,125,076. Quantities are not available.

In so far as the Department of Industry, Trade and Commerce is concerned: 3. Shell Canada Ltd. did not supply any fertilizer that was exported during that period.

TEXTILES STUDY

Motion No. 188 – MR. GILBERT

That an Order of the House do issue for a copy of the study on textiles as reported in the Annual Report of the Department of Industry, April 1, 1967-March 31, 1968, on pages 51-52.

MR. YVES FOREST (PARLIAMENTARY SECRETARY TO PRESIDENT OF THE PRIVY

5/*Can. H. of C. Debates,* June 11, 1969, p. 9980.
6/*Ibid.,* p. 9992.
7/*Ibid.,* June 10, 1969, p. 9929.

COUNCIL) Mr. Speaker, the Minister of Industry, Trade and Commerce cannot accept this motion as the study in question is confidential to the industries and cannot be released. The Minister of Industry, Trade and Commerce would ask that the member withdraw his motion.

MR. JOHN GILBERT (BROADVIEW) Mr. Speaker, I should like to have permission to have this matter transferred for debate.

MR. SPEAKER Is it agreed that it shall be transferred for debate pursuant to Standing Order 48?

SOME HON. MEMBERS: Agreed.

    SALMON – INQUIRY AS TO FISHING BAN IN INTERNATIONAL WATERS

MR. LLOYD R. CROUSE (SOUTH SHORE) Mr. Speaker, I should like to direct a question to the Minister of Fisheries. Since the international fishing authorities at Warsaw have recommended a ban on salmon fishing in the Northwest Atlantic can the minister say when he expects Canada to ratify the ban on Atlantic salmon fishing in international waters?

HON. JACK DAVIS (MINISTER OF FISHERIES AND FORESTRY) I would certainly want Canada to support this recommendation.

The purposes behind the interrogation are varied. It may be a simple inquiry for information; it may represent a covert attack on a minister; it may be a search for material to use in a later debate; it may be an attempt to win favour in a constituency; it may be an endeavour to call public attention to a grievance; or it may be a scheme to induce the government to commit itself to a policy, or force it to take a stand. The Canadian question period has improved greatly in recent years, and it is undoubtedly valuable, especially since dissatisfied questioners have been able to transfer their inquiries to the debates on adjournment motions. The whole process draws the acts of government out into full publicity and threatens at all times to submit the most obscure happenings to a sudden and unexpected scrutiny. It is one of the most formidable devices which the opposition has at its disposal.

The question, invaluable though it is, is clearly open to abuse unless it is surrounded with substantial safeguards. The minister is thus permitted to decline to answer any question and cannot be compelled to furnish a reason for doing so, although a blunt refusal would place him in a vulnerable political position. A common reason for silence is that an answer would not be in the public interest, and this is deemed adequate if the question demands confidential or secret information, which might occur in the course of a war, or with privileged correspondence, etc. Inquiries involving future government policy are also considered to be improper, as are trivial or hypothetical questions, those which seek information which is readily obtainable by members through other channels, and many others.

The most frequent abuse of the question privilege in the Canadian House of Commons is the demand for information which is of doubtful value, and to secure which involves a tremendous amount of labour. The government will usually take exception to such questions on the ground of expense, and they will be dropped from the order paper. The following is an example of one of these, with the prime minister's comments attached.

Mr. Mackenzie King: On today's list there is question No. 48, relating to civil servants. The question reads:

1. How many civil servants entered the various departments of the government under the provisions of the Civil Service Act, since 1920?
2. What was their place of residence when they entered the service?
3. How many are bilingual in each department?

That means a search from one end of Canada to the other for the information which is requested. I question whether the reply, while it may be possible to have it compiled, if it is to be accurate, can be made available within several years. That kind of question does not facilitate the business of the House nor does it keep down the expenses of government.[8]

The most recent innovation in the Commons' question period began in 1968 when Prime Minister Trudeau began the practice of platooning his ministers so that not all needed to be present for all question periods. The scheme was intended to be part of the general reform of Parliament and the executive that was being undertaken, and in the words of the government House leader:

At Ottawa, until last year, Ministers were expected to appear five times a week, to answer questions of which they had almost never received notice. For each Minister, this usually meant one hour of preparation each day and in excess of another hour of questions, or, to be more accurate, waiting for questions. During the 1960's, usually fewer than a dozen Ministers were asked questions each day. This meant that on the average, more than half the Cabinet – indeed, often two-thirds of the Cabinet – devoted up to two hours a day for questions that never came. In the last session and in the present session, we have altered this routine by reducing each Minister's appearance in the House of Commons to three times a week. While there still is no notice of questions, there is now a more predictable timetable for Ministers. Since this system was initiated, the average number of Ministers asked questions each day has remained virtually the same, that is, eight or nine each day. However, the number of Ministers required to attend the House for Question Period has been reduced by one-third. In other words, while formerly 60 per cent of the Cabinet had to waste its time preparing for Question Period when they did not receive questions, the new system has reduced this figure to 30 per cent. Needless to say, this has given Members of the Cabinet invaluable additional time to administer the affairs of their Departments and to carry on their other important functions as Ministers.[9]

Reasonable though these words sound, opposition members found it difficult to adjust themselves to the planned absence of ministers from the House, especially since the plans (initially at least) were not worked out perfectly; repeated attempts to compel ministers to attend in strict accordance with the rule which requires every member "to attend the service of the House" unless he has leave of absence; to have the planned absences investigated by a committee; and variously to get more ministers on hand more often; marked the

8/*Can. H. of C. Debates*, Feb. 1, 1937, p. 423.
9/President of the Privy Council, Press Release, Nov. 4, 1969.

opening years of the "roster" system.[10] "Anybody who has been in government," George Hees asserted roundly on one such occasion, "will recognize that for a minister to be in the house every day is the best thing in the world for him."[11]

A MOTION OF ADJOURNMENT TO DISCUSS "A SPECIFIC AND IMPORTANT MATTER REQUIRING URGENT CONSIDERATION"

This device enables the private member to break into the routine proceedings of the House and precipitate a discussion on an urgent current matter which he believes should be brought to the attention of the government and Parliament. The member (who must give the Speaker notice of the urgent matter prior to the opening of the sitting) asks leave to move the adjournment of the House and presents without argument the statement he has already given the Speaker. The Speaker decides, without any debate, whether or not the matter is a proper one, and is enjoined by the rules to consider "the extent to which it concerns the administrative responsibilities of the government or could come within the scope of ministerial action and he also shall have regard to the probability of the matter being brought before the House within reasonable time by other means." If the Speaker decides that the question is urgent, he asks whether the member has the leave of the House. If the member obtains leave, or at least twenty support his motion, the member may proceed; and if less than twenty but more than five support it, the question of leave is at once referred to the House for a decision. The House does not, of course, actually adjourn, and it is customary at the end of the discussion for the member to withdraw his motion. The motion is simply the means to enable the matter to be brought before the House. A member will probably succeed in doing more than force a discussion, for the cabinet can scarcely abstain from offering some comment on the issue which has been raised. A minister is therefore apt to attempt a defence or at least make a statement which will involve an enunciation of government policy.

There are a number of restrictions on the use of this motion for adjournment. The most controversial is that concerning the question of urgency. This is taken to mean that the matter is so pressing that the public interest will suffer if attention is not at once directed to it. The Speaker is the sole judge of the question of urgency, and there is no appeal from his decision on the point. The matter to be discussed cannot be one which has already been before the House that session, and it must deal with a subject which is within

10/See, for example, Can. H. of C. Debates, Oct. 4, 1968, pp. 800–10; Oct. 15, 1968, p. 1133; June 5, 1969, p. 9813.
11/Ibid., Oct. 11, 1968, p. 1095. Standing Order no. 5 begins: "Every member is bound to attend the service of the House ... "

the competence and responsibility of the Dominion government.[12] With all these restrictions on it, the device is one not often successfully exploited by members; the important point is that it is there.

OTHER ADJOURNMENT MOTIONS

Three days a week (Monday, Tuesday, and Thursday) any member who has given the Speaker proper notice can bring up at the ten p.m. adjournment virtually anything he has on his mind. He has seven minutes in which to make his point, and a minister or a parliamentary secretary may reply for three minutes. The total time allotted to these adjournment debates is thirty minutes, so that at least three members, on three occasions each week, have an opportunity to speak.

The adjournment device, first experimented with provisionally in the 1960s and now part of the Commons' standing orders, is regularly used by members to take up questions to which they have earlier received what they consider unsatisfactory answers, and to raise matters that need public attention. The members make excellent use of the time available, and the adjournment debates not only provide them with free time not formerly at their disposal, but also take a good deal of pressure off other proceedings of the House. The subjects aired after ten o'clock are so varied that it would be impossible to select representative examples.

ALLOTTED DAYS

Mention has already been made[13] of the new practices by which twenty-five days, spread over three defined periods in the parliamentary year, are set aside as periods in which motions by opposition members take priority over government motions; two such opposition motions in each of the three periods may be motions of want of confidence in the government. Prior to the adoption of the new rules in 1968, the chief similar opportunities available to members were motions (now abolished) to go into Committee of Supply or Committee of Ways and Means. Both these motions, but particularly the former, provided ample scope for the discussion of almost any conceivable subject for, as Mr M. J. Coldwell, an experienced MP who led the CCF party for many years, once said: "There is one place and one place only in this Parliament where private members are supreme, namely, in Supply when discussing the estimates. This is His Majesty's purse, and the age-old right of members of Parliament is to decide to what extent His Majesty's purse shall be filled.

12/Standing Order no. 26.
13/*Supra*, chap. XVIII.

This is what we are doing now, and I certainly wish to protest against any precedent being established that would curtail the right of this Parliament to discuss any matters in connection with the administration of the minister's department ..."[14]

The abolition of the Committee of Supply has not abrogated Parliament's ancient rights. The sending of all estimates to standing committees, instead of through a Committee of Supply, is expected to enhance the members' opportunities for scrutinizing expenditures; and of course all committees must report back to the House, where their reports can be discussed. All financial legislation, as distinct from the estimates, must still pass the whole House. The allotted days actually enlarge, rather than restrict, the opportunities for opposition members to criticize the government and air grievances. How effectively the new procedures will work naturally depends on the House of Commons, but there is nothing in the procedures themselves to suggest that the House has not strengthened itself in its relations with the cabinet.

BILLS AND RESOLUTIONS INTRODUCED BY PRIVATE MEMBERS

This is one of the simplest and most obvious ways for an ordinary member of the House to influence and to attack the government. The private member, as has been mentioned before, will have great difficulty in securing the necessary time on the parliamentary calendar for the consideration of his proposals, but hours are always found for some of them, and a debate develops. The subject is likely to be a special hobby or interest of the member (such as Senate reform, public ownership, federal aid to education) and its introduction gives the House an opportunity to express its views and perhaps vote on the question. It provides an opening for an attack on the government if the member wishes to use it for that purpose, for if the suggested change is desirable and if nothing is being done about it, some degree of blame can be attributed to the cabinet for its inaction. The normal government attitude is one of official indifference with no restrictions being placed on how its supporters speak or vote. If the government should wish to suppress such a measure, arrangements can be made to have it talked out (that is, debated to the full amount of time available, thus leaving no time for a vote), voted down, or passed and then dropped. The limited hours for private members' motions are always a reliable ally fighting on the side of the government. Occasionally a private member's bill, if after being brought up session after session a considerable body of support for it results, will be adopted by the government; or the government may accept the principle of the proposal in legislation of its own.

14/*Ibid.*, June 12, 1941, p. 3922. For the use of the Committee of Supply made by members, see Ward, *The Public Purse*, especially chaps. xi *and* xiv.

THE BUDGET

The budget furnishes the private member's second main sporting event of the session. Economic issues are so pervasive and the remedies for all economic ills so well known and so clearly comprehended that everyone will have his own contribution to make to the budget debate. Virtually all these contributions can be considered to be relevant. Almost all of them will involve some part of the government record as well as its proposals. The necessary practice of keeping all budget provisions a close secret until the minister of Finance presents his statement to the House makes preliminary consultation in caucus impossible, and occasionally the cabinet may be moved to make some modification in the original recommendations. In 1963 an interesting budget debate developed when opposition members discovered that the minister of Finance, Mr Walter Gordon, had consulted three non-departmental experts in the preparation of his proposals, and were able to score some solid points about the violation of secrecy. Since Mr Gordon's budget also included plans which turned out to be highly unsatisfactory to influential elements in the community, and were subsequently withdrawn, the 1963 budget debate was probably the most unusual in Canada's history.[15] With the development of third parties interested particularly in employing the state's resources for the support of welfare policies, and in monetary reform, the budget debate has tended to become increasingly important. It is now limited by the rules to six days.

A MOTION OF WANT OF CONFIDENCE IN THE GOVERNMENT

This is the most direct method of launching an attack on the cabinet, but it is usually brought in as an amendment to another motion or by an immediate attack on a government measure which inferentially becomes an issue of "no confidence." There are times when a cabinet may itself take the initiative and demand a vote of confidence from the House. Thus in January 1926, when no party had a majority, the Liberal government before the speech from the throne was considered, asked for a vote of the House to confirm its right to office. With rare exceptions, where the challenge to the cabinet has the formal support of an opposition party the prime minister will endeavour to facilitate debate and speed the taking of the verdict which his opponents profess to desire. A defeat on a clear confidence vote is of course a decisive defeat for the government.

It is clear that the private members, and particularly those private members

15/Can. H. of C. Debates, June 13–24, July 8 et seq., 1963, passim; see also Saywell, Canadian Annual Review for 1963, pp. 53–8 and 195–204.

of the opposition parties, have many occasions through the session when they may impress their views on Parliament and bring them to the attention of the country; and the re-writing of the rules in 1968-9, even if it did give the government an additional device for closure, also gave the opposition members new guarantees for their rights, and gave House committees new scope and direction. Prior to 1968 the rules had been almost stationary for decades, and what changes had been effected were partial and provisional; most of them appeared to be based on the assumption that the purpose of change was not to improve parliamentary surveillance of the executive, but merely to save the House's time by speeding the cabinet's proposals on their way.[16] Whether that can also be said of the new rules will depend on the use made of the current procedures by the members.

These are some of the formal conditions under which the political war is fought, and while there is little doubt that many changes in detail might still be made with profit, there is general agreement that the essentials cannot be changed suddenly – as the years preceding the rules of 1968 testify. The Committee on Procedure and Organization is a standing committee, and if the activities of its forerunners of the 1960s provide any criterion, it may be a very busy one. Yet the rules and the recognition of the rights of the majority and minority rest on something much more substantial than the mere votes of the House which have set up the former and maintain the integrity of the latter. The Committee on the Revision of the Standing Orders of the House of Commons declared in 1944: "Two fundamental principles govern the procedure of the House. They are, that the Government shall, so long as it can maintain a majority, be able to secure such legal powers as it considers necessary for administration, and that minorities, however small, shall be able to criticize that administration ... These rights cannot be alienated even if the House, in maintaining them, may protract sessions and lay itself open to severe criticism."[17]

The basic condition under which the House operates is thus a genuine spirit of tolerance and fair play, and an unwillingness to take undue advantage of the power which political fortune has temporarily placed in the hands of the majority. Indeed, time and again a party leader will be found to forego the momentary advantage and maintain a principle which strengthens the position of his adversary. A cabinet minister will frequently intervene, for example, on behalf of an opponent if he believes the ruling of the Speaker to be wrong or to have given insufficient weight to interparty arrangements which may have been agreed upon.[18] The leader of the opposition will prove

16/See Dawson, *Procedure in the Canadian House of Commons.*
17/*Ibid.*, March 7, 1944, p. 1239.
18/*Ibid.*, June 12, 1941, pp. 3921–2; *ibid.*, Feb. 19, March 28, 1947, pp. 580–1, 1832–5.

an even more zealous defender of the minority privileges, for his position – and interests – make him their especial guardian. In the words of R. B. Bennett:

I occupy a position in which I am placed by statute, and one of my duties is to do exactly what I am doing, to try to safeguard the liberties of Parliament from encroachment by the Government of the day. That is my duty. That is one of the difficulties of the position which I occupy, and I will discharge that duty whether it be on behalf of a member of the Opposition or of any other party when there is tyrannical exercise of power on the part of the Government by reason of a great majority, enabling the administration to destroy the liberties of this Parliament, which have been secured in the manner we all know. When that happens it is my unfortunate duty to protest against such an encroachment upon the liberties of members of the House, and I propose to do it so long as I am here.[19]

Intervention on the part of a cabinet minister may not all be undiluted sportsmanship blended with a love of minority rights. No government can be quite unmindful of the fact that in protecting the minority today, it is protecting itself tomorrow; and this sober reflection is likely to introduce a kindly note into its relations with other parties. Moreover, no government wishes to affront the basic political tolerance in the electorate, which would resent, and probably actively resent, anything which it considered flagrant interference with freedom of speech and criticism – a truism dramatically illustrated in 1956-7. Finally, the members of the minority always have their own defences, and a wise cabinet will know that it can often persuade far more successfully than it can drive. "Is it the Government's fault," asked Mr J. L. Ilsley, "that so much discussion goes on, that it takes so many days to get through a particular item? I tried just before the Easter recess to crowd the House a little. I will not do it again. If the Government starts to crowd the House, the House crowds the Government. That always happens. The moment we indicate to the House that we want to get ahead, we simply precipitate speeches about the right of the House of Commons to discuss matters and to discuss them thoroughly."[20] Inexperienced ministers, needless to say, are more likely to run afoul of the House in this regard than are the seasoned veterans.

While the rules and customs of the House will protect the rights of the rival forces, they can win no engagements for them. All contestants must therefore be conditioned and disciplined and equipped for service. Here the parliamentary organization of the parties plays a very useful part. Some mention has already been made[21] of the control which the government is able to exercise over its members; and the government has the tremendous advantage also of having leaders who are in actual authority and not merely at the head of party councils. To a useful prestige they can add the practical virtue of being

19/*Ibid.*, May 30, 1938, p. 3339; see also Stanley Knowles, *The Role of the Opposition in Parliament* (Toronto, 1957).
20/*Ibid.*, May 26, 1942, p. 2774.
21/*Supra*, pp. 207-8.

in a position where they can dispense favours and consolidate power. Ministerial leaders have also great ability at their disposal. They can draw freely on the talents of their public servants, who will supply them with ideas, prepare and execute their programmes, and furnish the debating material necessary for their vindication. For it is virtually impossible to draw any distinction between ministers as ministers and ministers as party leaders, between the government's proposals and the party's proposals. While the non-parliamentary sections of all political parties are becoming increasingly vocal, a cogent argument in the past for allowing the policy-forming functions of the non-parliamentary section of the party to fall into desuetude during the party's tenure of office was always the comparative inefficiency of that section when contrasted with the well-informed and well-schooled ministerial group.

An opposition party is rarely so generously provided with leaders and never so well equipped with assistance as the government. All members can, of course, employ the recently expanded reference services of the Library of Parliament. In 1968 the Trudeau government initiated the practice of setting aside annually a sum for the opposition parties' research purposes (at the start, $125,000 for the official opposition and $35,000 each for the New Democratic party and the Ralliement des Créditistes), and the parties began at once to make good use of the windfall. But the amounts are still small, and in no way affect the general lack of facilities provided for House committees.

Any opposition group can always enhance its effectiveness by a carefully planned scheme of organization. The Conservatives in the 1950s, for example, formed themselves into groups on separate fields, each under a leader especially responsible for his particular topic – reconstruction, finance and taxation, agriculture, trade and commerce, Dominion-provincial affairs, etc. Each group held meetings for discussion (some every week during the session), and current problems were turned over to the appropriate group for special study. These meetings did not affect the usual meetings of caucus, which determined the broad lines of attack which the party pursued in the House of Commons. These groups helped develop a number of the leaders who became ministers in 1957.

The House meets, and in march the Opposition, and sit there ready to attack Ministers and their measures; never, if possible, to make a concession, by word or vote, to official shrewdness or skill. For the time being they are Her Majesty's loyal sappers and miners, not to be very particular if only they can hack and hew their way to the treasury benches. They are waiters upon Providence – all animated with the most exalted, never-say-die, patriotism. If they only had a bandage on their brow inscribed "organized fault-finders," and a symbolical grid-iron, to be transferable, like the seals of office, the equipment would be complete. Broiling is a part of their special functions; and woe to the Minister when a chief with the spirit of an untamed Indian is at the head of his foes. For party aims, he is understood to be clothed with forked-lightning invectives; and in debate, wonder not, if he substitutes epithets for arguments and deals more with the motives than the logic of Ministers. In brief, he and his lieutenants must be quick to detect the joints in the armour of those in power; and, above everything, they are bound to cultivate the most wakeful and morbid suspiciousness.[22]

That is as applicable to Canadian government today as it was when it was written four years after Confederation; and although this hypersensitivity to error and "wakeful and morbid suspiciousness" have their absurd side, they nevertheless lie at the base of responsibility and good government. For the cabinet remains efficient primarily because the searchlight of publicity never ceases to play upon it; and the opposition directs the beams of the searchlight. The final objective of the opposition is a majority of seats in the House of Commons; and while this can rarely be obtained by the direct alienation of government supporters, it can most certainly occur as the result of the next general election. A shifting of a small number of popular votes from one side to the other may under Canadian conditions[23] bring about a change in government, and the eyes of the opposition are ever searching for material which will win over this detachable vote. The criticism, the amendments to motions, the divisions in the House, the long debates, the theatrical denunciations, the meticulous examination of the estimates, and scores of other manœuvres have this as their ultimate goal; and no expedient or weapon is so insignificant that it can be neglected in the unceasing engagement for prestige, for reputation, and eventually for power.

The government, for its part, must retain its existing majority and, whenever possible, extend it. While it has always the advantage of holding office and directing affairs, it also has the responsibility of exercising the initiative and of finding the remedies for the many ills that beset the country. The first essential is that it must get its measures and estimates through Parliament; and thus while it must give the opposition ample opportunity for criticism, it must also be continually pressing Parliament for action. "The Prime Minister is obliged," said Mackenzie King, "to keep constantly in mind two vital objectives: the one, to seek to provide opportunity for the fullest and frankest discussion of matters of public interest: the other, to see that sufficient time is provided for the full and proper discussion of the important business of government. It is a difficult and delicate task to hold the balance between the urgent demands of the government upon the time of Parliament, and a proper regard for the privileges, so essential to the sound functioning of a free community of the private members of Parliament."[24] From this flows the paradox that a government wants little verbal backing from its own supporters; what it needs is "brute votes," and while some parliamentary defenders are necessary to uphold its course on the floors of the House, every speaker over that

22/W. G. Moncrieff, *Party and Government by Party* (Toronto, 1871), pp. 58–9. For an insider's account of organization in the House, see Ward, *A Party Politician,* especially pp. 261–310.
23/*Supra,* pp. 314–15.
24/Radio broadcast, Jan. 23, 1939.

minimum simply impedes the passage of government measures.[25] Government backbenchers, indeed, frequently complain of having too little to do, and in 1969 Prime Minister Trudeau went to the unusual length of having a three-day conference with his parliamentary supporters, whose main purposes included improving relations between back and front benches, and enlarging the ordinary members' participation in policy formation and legislation. The proceedings involved a special session for the members' wives, who reportedly advised the prime minister fully and frankly of the domestic problems accompanying election to Parliament.[26] Late in 1969 the Liberal caucus established a formal system of committees for regular consultation with cabinet members.

The cabinet must avoid even the appearance of defeat or of weakness. This is the chief reason behind its stiff and unyielding attitude to many excellent suggestions coming from the opposition side. A few of these the cabinet may be able to accept with dignity and a creditable display of open-mindedness; but let this become frequent, and the electorate will naturally conclude that the simpler solution would be to place in power the party which is so fertile in valuable ideas rather than acquire them in this circuitous fashion. The same need explains the indirect influence of criticism which has already been discussed.[27] Criticism by the opposition casts its shadow before: it invades the cabinet meeting and the government caucus; it is most influential before it is formally voiced. How will the opposition attack this project? Will it be easier to defend next year than this? What will the farmers think of it? How will it affect the government vote in Ontario, or Quebec? What will be the attitude of the leading opposition newspapers? These will be anticipated as far as possible when the measure is being drafted, and the cabinet will then defend it ardently and refuse to accept any amendment of any consequence. If a serious flaw in the proposal is later discovered, the safest way of escape is to abandon it as unobtrusively as the circumstances (and the opposition) will allow.

Parliament concentrates and dramatizes the struggle for political power by bringing the political parties into immediate and continual conflict. Arguments are marshalled on one side and on the other, criticism and counter-proposals are made in full publicity, and the reputation of one side mounts as that of another falls away. Elections do not catch the voter by surprise and quite unprepared for the ballot. The ground has been worked over beforehand; the prestige of the government is frequently established or destroyed long before

25/"The most obvious duty (I do not say the only duty) of any individual member of a parliamentary majority is, speaking generally, to assist Government business, to defend Government action, and in particular to be found in the Government lobby when the House divides. He may further these ends by his eloquence. He may do so even more effectually perhaps by his silence." A. J. Balfour, *Chapters of Autobiography*, ed. E. Dugdale (London, 1930), p. 134.
26/See "Wives Complain to Trudeau," *Winnipeg Free Press*, June 21, 1969.
27/*Supra*, pp. 365-6.

polling day; and even new issues find their place in an environment which is by no means unfamiliar. Moreover, there is always an alternative government, if one is needed, near at hand; one which will pick up the work of its predecessor, make a few alterations here, develop certain things there, adapt old institutions to new ideas, and gradually press on a bit further the tentative experiment in human relations which is the business of government.

In government, as in most other spheres of life, man is journeying through a strange world. He is being pushed by forces which often he little appreciates or understands. At best, he is largely ignorant of much that will result, especially in the long run, from measures which he sponsors. Government is empirical. The statesman needs to be ready and quick to learn.

But no man is a ready critic of his own measures or quick to see their faults. It is eminently desirable, therefore, that in public affairs there should be an active body of critics, sharp to detect errors and persistent in pressing them home. Yet not captious, but responsible critics, who know that in due time they may have to stand by their criticisms and take their place in the dock.

There must also be readiness to embark on new measures so as to adjust government to changed conditions, ideas and aspirations. At the same time, every new measure is an experiment to be closely watched in its operation and results, and there should be no delay in pointing out mistakes.

These requirements are largely met by the party system ... It can easily be abused, and often is, and it may seem crude to the theorist. But given the right conditions, it has proved in practice a remarkably successful instrument for the journey through the uncharted seas of government.[28]

28/Sir Gwilym Gibbon, "The Party System in Government," *Public Administration,* Jan. 1937, p. 19.

Part VI THE JUDICIARY

20 The judiciary

THE FUNCTION OF THE JUDICIARY is primarily the settlement of disputes which are brought before the courts for that purpose. But in the course of performing this function, the judge does more than simply impose a punishment or deliver a judgment. He must interpret the laws and give them clarity and fuller meaning. He stands as guardian to see that the rule of law[1] is maintained: to ensure that no one will be punished except for a breach of the law, and to nullify the acts of any government or government official which are not legally authorized. The citizen therefore looks to the courts for the protection of his rights not only against his fellow-citizen, but also against his government and its agent; and, as an earlier chapter has shown,[2] abuses of official discretionary power find their most determined opponent in the courts of law. The judiciary will also act as interpreter of the written constitution, and in Canada this involves the power to set aside as *ultra vires* any laws which run contrary to the supreme law. Inasmuch as Canada is a federation, the courts are in a position where they must determine and maintain the respective fields of jurisdiction of the federal and provincial governments.[3] The judiciary therefore performs political and constitutional functions of the greatest consequence by applying legal criteria to the actions of government.

The laws which the courts enforce may be written or unwritten. The written law is the statutory law, which is stated in fairly explicit form and is being continually augmented by further legislative action. A number of these statutes may be collected and arranged in the form of an exceptionally comprehensive statute or code, such as the criminal code of Canada, which summarizes the Canadian criminal law. But no matter how carefully such a code may be drafted, it will need to be interpreted and applied to the facts as disclosed to the court; and in the process there will appear a parasitic growth of case law which clarifies and elaborates the written text.

1/*Supra*, pp. 73–4.
2/Chap. XIV.
3/*Supra*, pp. 69–71; 134–40.

The unwritten law is chiefly the common law, the established custom which has been enforced and developed by centuries of judicial decision in England and later throughout many parts of the civilized, and particularly the English-speaking, world. Decision has followed decision, precedent has been built on precedent, the courts in each case following (or distinguishing between) the decisions of other courts of equal or higher rank.[4] From these decisions principles have been derived and a system of law developed, which in turn has continued to grow in the same piecemeal but effective fashion.

At one stage in its early development, the English common law became rigid and formal, and its rigorous application often involved a denial of justice. Disappointed suitors petitioned the King for relief, and the King referred their petitions to one of his high officials, the chancellor, asking him to do what equity required. In the course of time, there arose a separate body of principles known as the doctrines of equity, and a separate Court of Chancery for applying them. This court developed its own distinctive procedure and some ingenious remedies of its own for enforcing rights and duties. So for several hundred years, English law was a dual system with separate courts of common law and equity operating side by side, the effect of which was to modify the application of the strict law by equity.

Today the duality of courts has disappeared, both in Britain and Canada, but the rules of common law and the doctrines of equity still remain distinct and separate. The superior courts of the provinces administer both law and equity, although one judge will sometimes be designated as the judge in equity. These courts now give, as a matter of course, what formerly used to be got by petition to the Court of Chancery. In effect, equity has become a part of the common law system, enriching it with a special procedure for certain kinds of cases, a wider range of remedies, and a modified application of certain of the strict rules of the common law.

Earlier pages have indicated the importance of the common law in Canadian colonial governments and in the government of today.[5] It still furnishes the great bulk of the Canadian civil law, although the statutory law has made substantial alterations in many fields. In Quebec, however, the civil law is different from that in the rest of Canada, for it is a French importation, based not on the common law of England but on the Roman law.[6] Thus matters concerning personal, family, and property relations are governed in Quebec by another and very different set of legal principles embodied in the civil code, although the law concerning commercial relations has been materially

4/This is known as the doctrine of *stare decisis*. It is characteristic of the common law (and equity); and is not obligatory, for example, in the civil law in Quebec.
5/*Supra*, pp. 4–5; 60–2; 145–8.
6/This goes back, of course, to the period of French rule; and it was preserved by the Quebec Act, 1774. *Supra*, pp. 6–7; 60–1; BNA Act, section 92, sub-section 13. See Louis S. St Laurent, Presidential Address, *Proceedings, Canadian Bar Association,* 1932, pp. 22–35.

modified by the influence of the common law.[7] It should be borne in mind, however, that very substantial portions of what would normally be within this general category of "property and civil rights" are uniform throughout the Dominion inasmuch as they are under the jurisdiction of the federal Parliament, namely, laws in relation to bills of exchange and promissory notes, banks and banking, navigation and shipping, patents and copyrights, bankruptcy and insolvency, and, in part, insurance, railways, and joint stock companies.[8] Inasmuch as the criminal law is under the jurisdiction of the federal Parliament,[9] it also is uniform throughout the Dominion. It is now, as stated above, in codified form, but its provisions have been almost entirely derived from the common law.[10]

The opening sentence of this chapter – that the function of the judiciary is primarily the settlement of disputes – needs some amplification. The court will normally come into action only after a wrong has been committed; while theories of the functions of the court are changing, its traditional task is to inflict punishment or ensure redress for infractions of the law rather than to intervene in order to prevent an infraction from taking place. In some classes of cases, however, the law provides (in equity) for such prior intervention if the court can be convinced that the commission of a legal wrong is contemplated and that compensation therefor would be difficult or impossible to assess. A court may also act in an administrative or supervisory capacity as, for example, when it assumes direction (usually through a person whom it appoints) over the estate of a deceased person or over the property of a bankrupt.

The courts may also be required to decide questions which have not come up in the ordinary course of litigation, but which have been specially formulated for the purpose and are referred to them for an opinion.[11] Laws of both the Dominion Parliament and most of the provincial legislatures authorize their respective governments to refer questions involving, among other things, the interpretation of the British North America Act or the constitutionality of Dominion or provincial legislation to the Supreme Court of Canada (or to the Supreme Court in the province) for a legal opinion. Parties will usually be heard on both sides (for provincial governments will wish to be represented on a case referred by the Dominion cabinet, and vice versa) and a judgment will be given by the court, which is subject to the same appeal as

7/Both common and civil law have influenced the development of each other in many directions. T. Rinfret, "Reciprocal Influences of the French and English Laws," *Canadian Bar Review*, Feb. 1926, pp. 78–81.
8/BNA Act, section 91.
9/*Ibid.*
10/There is a so-called provincial "criminal law" consisting of offences created by the provinces for the enforcement of provincial legislation. *Ibid.*, section 92, sub-section 15.
11/The Supreme Court of the United States has refused to decide cases of this nature on the ground that they were not disputes which could be judicially recognized.

cases which have arisen in the usual manner. The advantage of this method of obtaining a judicial interpretation of the British North America Act in advance of legislation or the application of legislation is obvious, and it is being used with increasing frequency. There is, however, some danger that controversial questions which threaten to cause embarrassment to a government may be passed over to the courts in order to shed, at least temporarily, responsibility for action, and the courts may thereby become involved in political disputes. "No one who has experience of judicial duties can doubt," said Earl Loreburn, "that if an Act of this kind were abused, manifold evils might follow, including undeserved suspicion of the course of justice and much embarrassment and anxiety to the judges themselves."[12]

THE SYSTEM OF COURTS

The Canadian system of courts, while presenting a number of characteristics derived from the federal nature of the Dominion, is far from following the American idea of what a court system under a federation involves. In the United States the federal and state courts are almost entirely separate from one another. There is a vertical line of cleavage between the two, with the federal courts and their field of jurisdiction on one side and the state courts and their field on the other, the nature of the controversy or the nature of the parties determining whether the action should be brought in the state or federal courts. Federal and state courts thus form their own hierarchies with final jurisdiction being vested in the Supreme Court of the United States or in the Supreme Court of Appeal in the state as the case may be. In certain circumstances a dispute may be transferred from one to the other. Thus if a case in a state court were found to involve the interpretation of the United States constitution or a federal statute it could be removed to a federal court for the settlement of that issue. Removals for these and other reasons, while not at all rare, are nevertheless far from being the rule; and a case will normally finish in the system in which it originated. The arrangement is necessarily complex, and can scarcely be considered to be very satisfactory.

The British North America Act establishes a plan of federal and provincial courts where the dividing line is horizontal rather than vertical. (In a separate category is Parliament, which is itself a court for certain purposes.[13]) Parliament is empowered to create a general court of appeal and may establish "any additional courts for the better administration of the laws of Canada."[14] The provincial legislature has jurisdiction over "the administration of justice

12/*Attorney-General for Ontario* v. *Attorney-General for Canada,* [1912] A.C. 571, at p. 583. See Strayer, *Judicial Review of Legislation in Canada,* especially chap. 7.
13/Ward, "Called to the Bar of the House of Commons," *Canadian Bar Review,* May 1957.
14/Section 101.

in the province, including the constitution, maintenance, and organization of provincial courts, both of civil and criminal jurisdiction, and including procedure in civil matters in those courts."[15] Procedure in criminal matters is, however, under the Dominion; and it also has control of the appointment, the remuneration, and, if necessary, the removal of the judges of both Dominion and provincial courts (with a few minor exceptions).[16] Complexities, such as they are, occur not in matters of jurisdiction over cases (as in the United States) but in the administration of the courts and the enforcement of Dominion laws by provincial authorities. For example, some parts of the criminal law are not always uniformly enforced across the Dominion because the initiative on enforcement rests largely with provincial attorneys general who must set provincial courts in motion. The great bulk of cases will originate in one of the provincial courts, and may then go on appeal to the Supreme Court of Canada. One Dominion court, the Exchequer Court of Canada, does not form a part of this symmetrical arrangement. It has been given specialized jurisdiction, and to that extent is not unlike a federal court on the American model.

Until 1949, any description of the Canadian system of courts would have had to include the Judicial Committee of the Privy Council in London, for that body was the court of final appeal for Canada in all but criminal cases. In view of its historical significance, and the fact that its decisions are still copiously quoted in Canada, it is still relevant to the Canadian judiciary. It consists of British privy councillors who hold or have held high judicial office, notably the lord chancellors, and the law lords of the House of Lords. There have also been an indefinite number of distinguished judges from the dominions and India made British privy councillors, such as the chief justice or a judge of the Supreme Court of Canada, or even a judge of a superior court in a Canadian province, but the attendance of these members was both irregular and rare. The Judicial Committee, as the name would suggest, is different from an ordinary court in that it gives no judgments, but rather reports its opinion to Her Majesty, and this advice is then acted upon by an order-in-council. The advice is given by the body as a whole, and the committee therefore records no dissenting opinions.

The abolition of the appeal to the Judicial Committee was canvassed for many years in Canada, and definite action was attempted on several occasions. Opinion in Canada, however, was for long divided, and there were legal difficulties in bringing about a change. For the appeal rested not only on statute, but also on the prerogative; and until the passing of the Statute of Westminster in 1931 a Dominion or provincial enactment to abrogate it would have been *ultra vires*. Thus the abolition of criminal appeals in 1888 was declared *ultra vires* in 1926;[17] but when the Statute of Westminster re-

15/Section 92, sub-section 1.
16/Sections 96–100.   17/*Nadan* v. *the King*, [1926] A.C. 482.

moved the limitations on the competence of Canadian legislatures, these appeals were abolished two years later.[18] A move for the Dominion to deal in the same way with the appeals in civil cases was questioned on the ground that part of the power might be vested in the provinces, but in 1947 the Judicial Committee held that the Dominion had jurisdiction.[19]

The arguments for and against appeals to the Judicial Committee need not be dwelt upon here,[20] although it may be noted that the voices raised in favour of their continuance tended to grow fainter as the years passed. It became more and more obvious that the risk of an occasional prejudice was far preferable to an objectivity which was founded on an Olympian remoteness from the scene of action; that the Judicial Committee knew little about the nature and problems of Canadian federalism; that it varied widely in the quality and continuity of its personnel;[21] and that the mental agility which its members were forced to display in order to cope with varied problems from all over the empire often inspired more wonder than confidence. For many people, however, the great arguments for abolition were linked with national pride and the dislike which most Canadians had for the idea of going outside the Dominion for a final verdict on legal disputes, particularly when they were likely to be of such profound constitutional significance for the future. Quebec was disposed for many years to support appeals because of the apparent protection they gave her against an intolerant majority in the other provinces;[22] but that phase gradually disappeared under the influence of strong nationalist sentiment. In 1949 a Canadian statute cut off all appeals to the Judicial Committee and made the Supreme Court of Canada the court of last resort for all cases which were begun after that time.

The plan of the Canadian courts is described below. The citizenship courts,

18/*British Coal Corporation* v. *the King*, [1935] A.C. 500.
19/*Attorney-General of Ontario* v. *Attorney-General of Canada*, [1947] 1 D.L.R. 801.
20/John S. Ewart and George H. Sedgewick, "Judicial Appeals to the Privy Council," *Queen's Quarterly*, Summer 1930, pp. 456–94.
21/"*Mr C. H. Cahan:* Not a single member of the Board [in 1937] was appointed to the Privy Council prior to 1928, and not a single member, who in 1932 heard the appeal in re The Regulation and Control of Radio Communication in Canada, sat as a member of the Committee which recently heard the appeals in respect of certain acts of Parliament enacted during the session of 1935. Two of the members of the Judicial Committee who heard and decided the recent appeals had practically no experience whatever in Canadian constitutional matters." *Can. H. of C. Debates*, April 5, 1937, p. 2574.
22/The success of the Judicial Committee as a defender of minority rights is, to put it mildly, open to question. F. R. Scott, "The Privy Council and Minority Rights," *Queen's Quarterly*, Autumn 1930, pp. 668–78. On the general subject of the "policies" followed by judges see S. R. Peck, "The Supreme Court of Canada, 1958–66: A Search for Policy through Scalogram Analysis," *Canadian Bar Review*, Dec. 1967, pp. 666–725; Stephen R. Mitchell, "The Supreme Court of Canada since the Abolition of Appeals to the Judicial Committee of the Privy Council: A Quantitative Analysis," a paper presented to the Canadian Political Science Association, June 7, 1967. See also Peter H. Russell, "The Jurisdiction of the Supreme Court of Canada: Present Policies and a Programme for Reform," *Osgoode Hall Law Journal*, 6 (1968), pp. 1–38.

which operate outside the regular judicial system (although the Citizenship Appeal Court, which hears appeals from applicants who have been rejected by a citizenship court, consists of one or more judges of the Exchequer Court) are not included.[23] The courts of Saskatchewan[24] have been used as an illustration of the provincial courts.

1 The Supreme Court of Canada (a Dominion court in every respect)
  (a) The Exchequer Court of Canada (a Dominion court in every respect, but not a fully integrated part of the system).
2 The Court of Appeal for Saskatchewan (a provincial court, with Dominion appointment of judges).
3 The Court of Queen's Bench for Saskatchewan (the same).
4 The District Court for Saskatchewan (the same).
5 Minor provincial courts (provincial courts solely)
    (i) Surrogate courts
    (ii) Provincial magistrates' courts
    (iii) Justices of the peace
    (iv) Other courts.

1 *The Supreme Court of Canada*

The Supreme Court of Canada was established in 1875, under the express authority of the British North America Act,[25] to exercise appellate civil and criminal jurisdiction for the Dominion.[26] The desire of some of its sponsors was to make it a court of final appeal and abolish the appeals to the Judicial Committee, but the doubtful legality of such a step and the opposition in both Canada and Great Britain resulted in the act cutting off only the statutory right of appeal and leaving the prerogative right unimpaired.

The court today entertains appeals from the provincial courts when substantial sums of money are involved, when questions of constitutional interpretation arise, when the validity of Dominion and provincial statutes is in dispute, and on various other matters. The conditions under which appeals are allowed from provincial courts are determined by the Canadian Parliament, and a provincial legislature has no power to define or restrict these conditions. The Supreme Court also hears appeals from the Exchequer Court and the Canadian Radio-Television Commission, and sits on a variety of matters under jurisdiction conferred on it by several statutes, dealing with such disparate subjects as aeronautics, controverted elections, bankruptcy, and immigration appeals. It gives advisory opinions to the Dominion government (as stated earlier in the chapter) on the interpretation of the British North

23/For a description of the citizenship courts and their work, see *Canada Year Book, 1968*, pp. 242–8.
24/The judicial systems of other provinces are described in a number of documents: for example, *Canada Year Book*; *The Canada Legal Directory*.
25/Section 101.
26/*Can. Statutes*, 38 Vict., c. 11. See Frank MacKinnon, "The Establishment of the Supreme Court of Canada," *Canadian Historical Review*, XXVII, no. 3 (Sept. 1946), pp. 258–74.

America Act, on the constitutionality of Dominion and provincial legislation, and on similar matters referred to it by the Governor-in-Council. Under certain conditions it will also hear appeals on like questions which have been referred to the provincial courts by the provincial governments.[27] The utility and prestige of the Supreme Court as an appellate tribunal was formerly weakened by the fact that appeals could be taken directly from the Supreme Courts of the provinces to the Judicial Committee of the Privy Council, and the abolition of appeals in 1949 has had such a wholesome effect on the character and standing of the Supreme Court of Canada that its reform has become a lively issue.

The Supreme Court was originally composed of a chief justice and five judges, the number of judges being raised to six in 1927 and eight in 1949. It has had from the beginning a representative federal character. The act always provided that at least two (and now three) of the judges should come from Quebec, a reasonable provision in view of the special character of the Quebec civil law. But when the original bill was before the Commons this proposal furnished the excuse for a member from British Columbia to demand a special representative from that province because, said he, "the judges of the other provinces know little about the management of Indian lands or of mining affairs."[28] The act, however, made no guarantee to any province except Quebec; but the practice of giving sectional representation on the court has been firmly established by custom for very many years. Ernest Lapointe, minister of Justice, made the following admission in 1927.

While geographical conditions should not be considered in the appointment of judges, because the best possible men should be appointed to the Supreme Court of Canada, there is one exception, namely, that two judges will always be members of the Bench or bar of Quebec, familiar with the civil law and procedure of that province. Apart from that there is no geographical condition mentioned in the Act. I must say, however, that since the creation of the Court such considerations have been taken into account in making appointments; there is one judge usually supposed to be a member of the bar or Bench of one of the Maritime Provinces, two come from Quebec, two have usually been appointed from Ontario, and one judge is usually appointed from the Bench of British Columbia. The prairie provinces were not then developed as they are to-day, and up to the present there has not been a judge from either the bar or the Bench of any of those provinces.[29]

The fulfilment of prairie ambitions, however, was not long deferred. Parliament in the same year increased the numbers of the Supreme Court by one;

27/*Rev. Stat. Can.* (1952), c. 259, s. 37.
28/*Can. H. of C. Debates,* March 30, 1875, p. 974. A more modern version of this same demand appeared in 1949 (*ibid.,* Oct. 11, 1949, p. 662) and in 1963 a member referred casually to "the Ontario vacancy on the Supreme Court of Canada" (*ibid.,* May 28, 1963, p. 354). See W. R. Lederman, "Thoughts on Reform of the Supreme Court of Canada," *Alberta Law Review,* VIII, no. 1 (1970), pp. 1–17.
29/*Can. H. of C. Debates,* March 10, 1927, p. 1079.

and the first appointment to the new judgeship came from the province of Saskatchewan.

The judges are appointed by the governor general on the advice of the cabinet and hold office during good behaviour, with compulsory retirement at seventy-five. They may be removed by the Governor-General-in-Council following a joint address by both Houses of Parliament.[30] The chief justice receives $40,000 a year, the other members of the court $35,000.

1(a)   The Exchequer Court of Canada*

This was originally closely associated with the Supreme Court of Canada, each being composed of the same members: the Exchequer Court was a court of first instance, the Supreme Court heard nothing except appeals. The two were separated in 1887. The Exchequer Court now consists of the president and six other judges, appointed by the Governor-in-Council. They hold office during good behaviour (with compulsory retirement at seventy-five) and may be removed by the usual joint address procedure.[31] The president is paid $32,000, the other members $28,000 each.

The court has original jurisdiction concurrent with the provincial courts in cases involving the revenues of the Crown (which implies an extensive jurisdiction in matters of review of taxation) and exclusive jurisdiction over suits brought against the Crown in federal affairs. The court deals with claims against the Crown for property taken for any public purpose or injuriously affected by the construction of any public work, and claims against the Crown arising out of any death or injury to person or property resulting from the negligence of any officer or servant of the Crown while acting within the scope of his duties or his employment upon any public work, etc. It hears cases which concern patents of invention, copyrights, trade marks, and industrial designs. It also has jurisdiction over certain classes of railway cases, when the railway is not wholly within one province or is otherwise subject to the authority of the Parliament of Canada. In most cases which involve any substantial amount, an appeal lies to the Supreme Court of Canada. As noted in the chapter on the Senate, from 1964 to 1968 a judge of the Exchequer Court acted as divorce commissioner.

If the legislature of a province has passed an act giving the necessary authority, the Exchequer Court has jurisdiction over controversies between the Dominion and that province or between that province and any other

30/*Rev. Stat. Can.* (1952), c. 259, s. 9.
31/*Ibid.*, c. 98, s. 9.

On March 2, 1970, Hon. John Turner, Minister of Justice, obtained first reading for a bill whose terms included a complete reorganization of the Exchequer Court, dividing it into two divisions with new duties, and increasing the number of judges. The section which follows should therefore be supplemented by reference to the latest legislation.

province or provinces which have passed similar acts. Such cases may be appealed to the Supreme Court of Canada.

The Exchequer Court also acts as a Court of Admiralty exercising a general jurisdiction in admiralty cases,[32] and in this capacity the court has original jurisdiction as well as jurisdiction in appeal. In practice, however, most of the cases are tried in the local Admiralty Court, although cases of special importance may be transferred and tried as of first instance at Ottawa. The Governor-in-Council may from time to time appoint a superior or County Court judge (or any barrister of not less than ten years' standing) to be a district judge in admiralty for a special Admiralty District, who will exercise admiralty jurisdiction within that district, subject to appeal to the Exchequer Court and the Supreme Court of Canada. Canada is divided into Admiralty Districts for this purpose.

2 The Court of Appeal for Saskatchewan

The Court of Appeal for Saskatchewan is composed of the chief justice of Saskatchewan and four other judges. All are appointed by the Governor-General-in-Council. It has general appellate jurisdiction in civil and criminal cases.[33]

The chief justice of Saskatchewan and the other judges of appeal are *ex officio* judges of the Court of Queen's Bench and for all purposes have all the powers, rights, privileges, and immunities of judges of the Court of Queen's Bench. They are eligible to preside over trials of criminal and civil cases and to sit in chambers as judges of the Court of Queen's Bench. The chief justice receives $30,000 and the others $26,000 each.

3 Court of Queen's Bench for Saskatchewan

The Court of Queen's Bench for Saskatchewan consists of the chief justice and six other judges.[34] However, the court may, subject to the Queen's Bench Act and to any Rules of Court, be held before the chief justice or before any one or more of the judges of the court. The judges of the court are *ex officio* justices of the peace and coroners for the province. They receive the same salaries as do the judges of the Court of Appeal.

The Court of Queen's Bench is a superior court of record of original jurisdiction, both civil and criminal, and may hear certain appeals. Every judge of the court has jurisdiction throughout Saskatchewan, and can exercise all the powers of the court except in those types of cases that are usually heard by the court as a whole.

The court's jurisdiction covers a variety of civil and criminal proceedings. Any party to an action may demand a jury (although he will not necessarily

32/*Ibid.*, c. 1.
33/*Rev. Stat. Sask.* (1965), c. 72.
34/*Ibid.*, c. 73.

get one) if the amount of money involved in a dispute exceeds $5,000, or if the action concerns any of several criminal types of proceedings, regardless of the amount claimed. An appeal lies from a judge of this court to the Court of Appeal. The judges of the District Court for Saskatchewan, described below, are *ex officio* local masters of the Queen's Bench.

The Court of Appeal and the Court of Queen's Bench (like the major courts in the other provinces) are, as already indicated, under both Dominion and provincial control. The province constitutes, organizes, and maintains the courts, and determines the procedure in civil matters, while the Dominion appoints, pays, and if necessary removes the judges. This is open to obvious objections; for the province may provide for more judges than are necessary and expect the Dominion to foot the bill. The system, however, seems to work smoothly; although there have been occasions when the Dominion has refused to make appointments because it considered the number was excessive.[35] The general position of the Dominion government on these questions was stated by the minister of Justice in 1946: "The provincial authorities ... are the ones who determine what courts they will have and how many judges constitute the Bench of each court. Of course we have something to say in the matter. We do not admit that they can provide for any number of judges, a number that would be out of all proportion to the number required to handle the judicial business. But we try to meet the desires of the provincial authorities in providing sufficient judges for the courts which they organize as being the ones required for their local needs."[36]

4 The District Court for Saskatchewan

The court consists of eighteen judges, and the court may be held before any one of the judges of the court.[37] There is only one judicial district: the whole province. Except as otherwise determined by the Lieutenant-Governor-in-Council, there are nineteen judicial centres in various cities and towns throughout the province at which proceedings may be taken. District Court judges, like county court judges elsewhere, receive $10,500. The lieutenant governor may at any time by proclamation increase or decrease the number of judges of the court, a decrease to take effect when a vacancy occurs.

The jurisdiction of the District Court extends, in general, to cases where the amount of money involved does not exceed $5,000. In addition, every District Court judge is *ex officio* a coroner, justice of the peace, and provincial magistrate, and exercises the same civil and criminal jurisdiction as is con-

---

35/Thus in 1928 Saskatchewan had twenty-three judicial districts but only eighteen district judges. *Can. H. of C. Debates*, March 19, 1928, p. 1490. In 1960 Quebec requested six new judges to help deal with a backlog of cases, and received only four (*ibid.*, June 6, 1961, pp. 5933–7). In the same debate, members of Parliament from other provinces also spoke of needing more judges.
36/*Ibid.*, July 23, 1946, p. 3732.
37/*Rev. Stat. Sask.* (1965), c. 74.

ferred on magistrates. An appeal lies to the District Court from most of the province's minor courts, and in turn, in most cases, an appeal lies from the District Court to the higher courts.

5 Minor provincial courts

These courts are entirely under provincial control as to organization and maintenance, and appointment, remuneration and tenure of judges.

(a) *The Surrogate Court for Saskatchewan.* The Surrogate Court Act designates the judges of the District Court to be judges of the Surrogate Court. The court therefore consists of the same number of judges as there are in the District Court for Saskatchewan from time to time, and the court may be held before any one of the judges of the court. The court has jurisdiction in testamentary matters, in relation to the granting or revoking of probate wills, etc.; that is, the area of its jurisdiction is, in general, the estates of deceased persons,[38] and the interpretation of wills. An appeal lies too from the Surrogate Court to the province's highest courts, provided the amount of money involved exceeds $200.

(b) *Provincial magistrates.* Most prosecutions for offences under Saskatchewan statutes are held before judges sitting in magistrate's courts;[39] these judges (who were formerly designated as "magistrates") are appointed by the Lieutenant-Governor-in-Council and hold office during pleasure. They have jurisdiction throughout Saskatchewan. When a judge of a magistrate's court is dismissed, he has a right of appeal, which includes an inquiry by one or more judges of the Court of Queen's Bench.

A judge's jurisdiction is extensive, for he possesses all the power that a magistrate may have under any Dominion act (including part of the criminal code), as well as that conferred on him by provincial legislation; in any given period a judge of a magistrate's court may hear a great variety of cases. Each judge is also a justice of the peace.

(c) *Justices of the peace.* The Lieutenant-Governor-in-Council appoints justices of the peace, who have jurisdiction throughout the province.[40] Their duties include hearings on charges under municipal by-laws, or other laws in force in Saskatchewan, both provincial and federal.

(d) *Other provincial courts.* There are some other provincial courts, such as juvenile courts and family courts, with jurisdiction over special classes of cases.

In addition there is provision made in the Small Claims Enforcement Act, 1959, whereby any person having a claim which does not exceed the sum of $200 may apply to a judge of a magistrate's court to have the matter adjudicated. An appeal lies to a judge of the District Court and then, under some circumstances, to the Court of Appeal.

38/*Ibid.,* c. 75.
39/*Ibid.,* c. 110.   40/*Ibid.,* c. 112.

Legislative provision is also made for the appointment of coroners and arbitrators.

THE POSITION OF THE JUDICIARY

The unique functions which the judiciary[41] perform in the government make it imperative that judges should be given a different position from that of the great majority of government officials.[42] They are not representative agents who, like the members of the legislature and the executive, are expected to reflect some interest or opinion and are chosen to carry out desired measures. The judge who would try to voice the opinion of the public, of the government, of a province, of the Canadian Pacific Railway, or of the United Steelworkers would obviously lose all value as a judge, for the whole weight and value of a decision depend on the very absence of influences of this kind. His opinion is not to be founded on what people want, but rather on what is the law, and the decision emerges from these principles when applied to the facts before him.

It is, of course, true that judges cannot remain completely unaffected by their environment and cannot and should not be indifferent to the effects of their decisions on the social and political needs of the nation. There will always be some interplay among the habits of mind of the judge, the society in which he lives, and the decisions which he renders. The judge should be constantly aware of the quiet and insidious pressures to which he is subjected so that he will be able to make suitable allowance for them. It is, moreover, possible to keep within fairly definite limits the opportunities which are given to the courts to invade other than purely judicial fields; for the laws can be so phrased that the situations where the judge is forced to make what are essentially political decisions – where judgment begins to slip over into policy – will be comparatively rare.[43] The problem, in short, will not be a grave one if Parliament (or, if necessary, the constitution-amending power) will assert its rightful authority to make all the major political decisions, a function which can quite properly involve not only the original enactment of a law or a constitution, but also any subsequent amendment if an undesired interpretation has been given by the courts.

The rendering of an honest unbiased opinion, based on the law and the

41/The words "judiciary" and "judge" are used hereafter as applying to members of the county or district and higher courts and not to members of the minor provincial courts.

42/There are a few other officials who for one reason or another must be given similar if not identical treatment and protection. The auditor general, the representation commissioner, the official languages commissioner, the chief electoral officer, and some of the boards and commissions which perform special functions are the closest examples. *Supra*, pp. 243–7.

43/*Supra*, pp. 134–9.

facts, is far from simple: it is one of the most difficult tasks which can be imposed on fallible men. It demands wisdom as well as knowledge, conscience as well as insight, a sense of balance and proportion, and if not an absolute freedom from bias and prejudice, at least the ability to detect and discount such failings, so that they do not becloud the fairness of the judgment. It is evident that the ordinary political environment is unable to provide the proper incentives which will call forth these qualities nor will it permit these qualities to be exercised without a large measure of interference which will deprive them of the greater part of their value. The judiciary, in short, must be given a special sphere, clearly separated from that of the legislature and executive.[44] They must, to accomplish this separation, be given privileges which are not vouchsafed to other branches of the government; and they must be protected against political, economic, or other influences which would disturb that de-tachment and impartiality which are indispensable prerequisites for the proper performance of their function. It is these unusual factors which create the condition known as the "independence" of the judiciary.

The removal of responsibility

Judicial independence, as will be seen later, has a positive side, but its most striking characteristics are negative. It involves the removal of most of the punitive influences which surround ordinary officials, particularly for the enforcement of political responsibility, which usually imply the power of a superior to remonstrate, reprimand, and even remove from office. The judge is placed on a firm base of his own, undisturbed by outside forces, present or apprehended. He is given assurance that his office is secure, that his means of livelihood are not imperilled, and that he may give decisions which are dis-pleasing to the government, to the public, or to anyone else without fear of consequences. "It is a strange doctrine," said Sir Wilfrid Laurier, "to preach that the judges are responsible to Parliament. Where is that responsibility? I have always understood that the judges were responsible only to their own conscience, and Parliament has no power over them. True, they can be removed, but only on an address of both Houses of Parliament. That law has been adopted to make them absolutely independent of Parliament, and they are only responsible to Parliament in extreme cases of malfeasance."[45]

To this political irresponsibility is added a civil and criminal irresponsibility as well. Under the common law a judge is not liable to civil or criminal action for acts committed within his jurisdiction while performing his judicial duties. He may act corruptly, maliciously, and oppressively, and the injured party has no remedy against him. "This provision of the law is not for the protection or benefit of a malicious or corrupt judge, but for the benefit of the public, whose interest is that the judges should be at liberty to exercise their functions

44/*Supra*, pp. 74–5.
45/*Can. H. of C. Debates*, Sept. 15, 1903, p. 11313.

with independence and without fear of consequences. How could a judge so exercise his office if he were in daily and hourly fear of an action being brought against him, and of having the question submitted to a jury whether a matter on which he had commented judicially was or was not relevant to the case before him?"[46]

Tenure

The foundation of judicial independence is security of tenure; for it is this which sets the judiciary free from the ordinary bonds of political responsibility. All the Canadian judges hold office during good behaviour. But this legal tenure is made even stronger by the practice of giving "good behaviour" an interpretation which for all supreme and superior court judges excludes removal on virtually any ground except deliberate wrong-doing.[47] A judge may be stupid, and make scores of wrong decisions; he may be indolent, and neglect his work; he may be, at least to a degree, biased and unfair, yet there is every likelihood that he will be retained in office. The government would certainly not punish him for stupidity, for over that he has no control. Nor is it at all likely that the government would take any action against him for the above, and many other, faults for which he is definitely to be blamed. While his conduct may be shocking and the administration of justice may suffer, the lesser evil is to leave him alone; for an attack and a removal for any but the most flagrant and scandalous offences would have a detrimental effect on the work, security, and peace of mind of all the other members of the judiciary. W. S. Fielding, when minister of Finance, expressed this position in quite explicit terms. "This responsibility of judges to Parliament," said he, "is very largely a dream, because we know that practically there is no responsibility. There are judges who are neglecting their duties, there are judges who are too old, there are judges who are ill, and there are judges who are not performing their duties, and every man in this Parliament knows it."[48]

In recent years, however, while this general principle has been in no way seriously infringed, Parliament has taken a much sterner view of one kind of judicial laxity and inefficiency, namely, that which comes as a result of old age and infirmity. The tenure of members of the Supreme Court and Exchequer Courts of Canada and of the County and District Courts rests on ordinary statute, and was set at seventy-five many years ago; that of members of provincial superior courts is guaranteed by the British North America Act, and in 1960 a constitutional amendment which caused some controversy retired those judges at seventy-five also.[49]

The argument against compulsory retirement at a definite age, and one

46/*Scott* v. *Stansfield*, 3 Excheq. Rep., 220, at p. 223.
47/The County or District Court judge may be removed for less serious offences, *infra*, pp. 400–2.
48/*Can. H. of C. Debates*, Sept. 15, 1903, p. 11316.
49/Saywell, *Canadian Annual Review for 1960*, p. 16.

which has been urged with exceptional vehemence on behalf of the judiciary, is that under any such scheme many of the old judges who remain fully competent to carry out their duties are forced out of office with the inefficient ones. This was adequately answered years ago by Chief Justice Taft when discussing the same problem in the United States:

There is no doubt that there are judges at seventy who have ripe judgments, active minds, and much physical vigour, and that they are able to perform their judicial duties in a very satisfactory way. Yet in a majority of cases when men come to be seventy, they have lost vigour, their minds are not as active, their senses not as acute, and their willingness to undertake great labour is not so great as in younger men, and as we ought to have in judges who are to perform the enormous task which falls to the lot of Supreme Court Justices. In the public interest, therefore, it is better that we lose the services of the exceptions who are good judges after they are seventy and avoid the presence on the Bench of men who are not able to keep up with the work, or to perform it satisfactorily. The duty of a Supreme Court Judge is more than merely taking in the point at issue between the parties, and deciding it. It frequently involves a heavy task in reading records and writing opinions. It thus is a substantial drain upon one's energy. When most men reach seventy, they are loath thoroughly to investigate cases where such work involves real physical endurance.[50]

The retirement in 1961 (when the constitutional amendment became effective) of provincial superior court judges at seventy-five applied to judges on the bench, and thirteen incumbents, ranging in age up to eighty-four, were summarily retired on March 1. Undoubtedly some of them were judges of considerable distinction, and their removal from the active list was not unaccompanied by grumbling.[51] Yet in the past the persistence with which some judges held fast to their positions when their usefulness was largely spent was frequently shocking, and Canadian courts before 1961 were commonly burdened with a large number of old judges.[52] R. B. Bennett, who was a lawyer, reviewed the situation just after his service as prime minister:

There is not much doubt that starting at one end of Canada and travelling to the other one may find large numbers of men endeavouring to discharge judicial functions who are physically unable to bear the strain of work and continuous effort necessary in the discharge of those duties. One makes that statement with great hesitancy, but it is a fact ... If all judges in Ontario were physically fit to discharge their judicial duties there would be no necessity of increasing the number by two [as proposed in the bill being considered]. I believe that is so obvious that it needs only to be mentioned ...
    This is the principle which I submit should govern Parliament in dealing with matters of this kind. First, if a man holds himself out as being qualified by

---

50/W. H. Taft, *Popular Government* (New Haven, 1913), pp. 159–60.
51/See "Amendment Forces 13 Eminent Judges to Retire on March 1," *Saskatoon Star-Phoenix*, Jan. 30, 1961.
52/In 1946, for example, the provincial superior courts contained six judges in their eighties, and thirty-one in their seventies. See *Can. H. of C. Debates,* April 17, 1946.

training to occupy any position requiring the services of an expert – whether it be judge, doctor, dentist or engineer; it matters not – unless he has the proper qualifications he should not be appointed to the position, whatever it may be. Second, when he ceases to possess those qualifications he should no longer continue in office. Is there any possibility of getting away from the second proposition? We endeavour to have some regard, in a small way, for the first one. But the second, which is a corollary of the first, has been the very foundation of the impartial administration of justice, namely that when men hold themselves out as being sufficiently trained in the law to enable them to undertake judicial duties, and when by reason of impairment of physical or mental capacity they are no longer able to give concentrated attention for periods extending over seven, eight, or nine hours a day, obviously they are no longer qualified for the positions they hold. It is an implied condition of the contract they make with the state that they will be able to discharge those duties and give the services indicated, and when they have reached the stage where they can no longer do so, it seems to me they should be content to retire.[53]

Parliament has developed other weapons besides the fairly high retirement age to cope with inefficient judges. In the first place, if the judge resigns after at least fifteen years in office or because of some permanent handicap which may disable him for judicial work, he may be given a pension up to two-thirds of his salary at the time of his resignation. If, however, the judge does not avail himself of this opportunity and if the minister of Justice reports that the judge has become incapacitated by reason of age or infirmity, the Governor-in-Council may stop his salary, provided, however, that the above report has been preceded by an investigation by one or more judges of equal or higher rank, appointed by the Governor-in-Council, and that the judge in question has been notified and given an opportunity to state his case.[54]

This stoppage of salary has been generally considered to be an excessively drastic measure, and for years no minister of Justice had the courage to apply it, a reluctance which may have been accentuated by the possibility of his being accused of trying to create vacancies for the government to fill. The major objection is, of course, that the decision to investigate and the decision to cut off the salary must always be taken by the cabinet, and these violate the sound principle that the executive should never give any cause for suspicion that it is exercising the slightest pressure on the judiciary. There is the further danger that such an investigation into the capacity of a judge to perform his duties is almost certain to disturb public confidence in the courts, and the final injury might therefore be worse than the situation it was designed to remedy. In 1936 Ernest Lapointe, then the minister of Justice, said that in the fourteen years in which the provision had been on the statute book it had never been applied,[55] but that if the Dominion or a provincial bar association should ask him to move in a case of this kind, he would feel bound to do so.

53/*Ibid.*, June 3, 1936, pp. 3360–1.
54/*Rev. Stat. Can.* (1952), c. 159.
55/*Can. H. of C. Debates*, June 15, 1936, pp. 3705–6.

In recent years, however, the provision has been used on several occasions. The minister of Justice has received complaints; he has made discreet inquiries; he has written the judge indicating that an investigation would have to be authorized; and in all cases up to 1946 he received the resignation of the judge;[56] since then there have been some cases where "discreet inquiries" did not lead to resignations.

Removal

The almost impregnable position of the federal and superior court judges is best seen in the difficulty of removal, that is, the forcible ousting of these judges from their positions when they are in full possession of their faculties and quite capable of doing a normal day's work. "Good behaviour," as suggested above, is given a most generous interpretation, and bribery, gross partiality, and criminal proclivities are probably the only offences which would lead to certain removal; one recent case, as will be seen, raised a fourth and somewhat unusual possibility. What is probably the best enunciation of the conditions which would justify removal was given by Edward Blake, a former minister of Justice, in 1883:

I am not one of those who at all object to this great, this highest court of all, this grand inquest inquiring by proper means into the conduct of the judges. I believe that to be our highest, our most important and also our most delicate function ... I have no quarrel with the statement of the hon. First Minister, in part, when he declared that a judge's conduct ought not to be attacked, at any rate, with view to an inquiry such as this, unless the charge against him be one of serious impropriety – a charge ... which, if true, would warrant his dismissal from office ... We could not complain of a judge because he erred in his judgment, or misconstrued the law, or misapplied the facts ... There is a constant error of judgment, because judges, like other men, are fallible, and it is [not] an error in judgment that should form the subject even of an observation here ... What was the cause, then, which could properly bring this judge's action under our consideration? It was a charge of partiality, of malfeasance in office – not that the judge erred, for all may err in judgment, but that he degraded his office, betrayed his trust, wilfully and knowingly did a wrong thing, perverted justice and judgment – that is the nature of a charge which could alone make it proper to have been brought here. Of that there is no allegation in the notice of motion.[57]

The process of removal for federal and superior court judges is a joint address of both Houses of Parliament, followed by actual removal by the Governor-in-Council. But this is hedged about with a great many formalities. Charges must be made by responsible parties and a petition submitted to Parliament praying for the judge's removal; the charges in the petition must be both explicit and of such a serious nature that, if substantiated, they would justify removal; a committee must be created to investigate the charges; the

56/*Ibid.*, Feb. 2, 1943, pp. 72–3; Aug. 2, 1946, p. 4270.
57/*Ibid.*, April 9, 1883, p. 522. On Canadian cases before 1966 see Eugene Forsey, "Removal of Superior Court Judges," *Canadian Commentator,* Feb. 1966.

committee must report unfavourably, and the House adopt its report; the address must then be passed by both houses;[58] and finally, although this would doubtless follow as a matter of course, the Governor-in-Council must remove.[59] Each of these steps adds enormously to the difficulty of making the process effective; so much so, that it is not far from the truth to say that these higher judges are virtually irremovable.[60] As a matter of record, while one or more of these stages have been reached in several cases, no federal or superior court judge has been removed since Confederation.

The closest that any judge since Confederation has come to actual removal was in 1966–7, when Mr Justice Léo Landreville of the Supreme Court of Ontario was subjected first to an inquiry by the provincial bar association, and then another by a royal commission consisting of Mr Ivan C. Rand, himself a former justice of the Supreme Court of Canada. The Rand report was referred to a joint committee of the Senate and the House of Commons which, after nineteen meetings, at eleven of which Mr Landreville testified on his own behalf, found "that Mr Justice Landreville has proven himself unfit for the proper exercise of his judicial functions and, with great regret, recommends the expediency of presenting an address to His Excellency for the removal of Mr Justice Landreville from the Supreme Court of Ontario."[61] Mr Landreville unsuccessfully petitioned to be heard at the bar of the House of Commons, and Parliament had begun to prepare for a joint address (starting it in the Senate) when the justice resigned. This at once raised the question of whether, if at all, he was entitled to a pension, and it was the official view that for that a special act of Parliament would be required. The most unusual aspect of the Landreville case was that, as the royal commission reported, "no question is raised of misbehaviour in the discharge of judicial duty"; rather, the allegations against the judge went back to transactions that occurred before he was ever appointed to the bench.

The defences of the County and District Court judges are not nearly as strong as those of the higher members in the hierarchy. In the first place, the reasons which will justify removal are not only malfeasance (the unwritten reason for the removal of higher court judges) but also "misbehaviour [a

58/One of the most astonishing statements ever made in the House was that made in 1933 by R. B. Bennett, when prime minister, in discussing the attitude his government would take if it decided on the necessity of removing a trustee of the proposed Railway Board who was to be subject to removal by the joint address procedure. Bennett said that the government would first remove the member, and then seek the joint address — an extraordinary inversion which it seems impossible to justify — and he then added the even more incomprehensible statement that if the address, initiated by the government, failed to pass the Senate, his government would unhesitatingly resign. *Ibid.*, May 4, 1933, pp. 4585–96.

59/See Dawson, *The Principle of Official Independence*, pp. 35–9.

60/There are older methods which might still be applicable for the removal of some judges, but these are considered to be obsolete. *Ibid.*, pp. 39–40.

61/*Can. H. of C. Journals*, March 17, 1967, pp. 1546–7; see also *Report of Commission of Inquiry re the Hon. L. A. Landreville* (Ottawa, 1969).

much wider term] or ... incapacity or inability to perform his duties properly by reason of age or infirmity."[62] Misbehaviour will thus justify removal; incapacity or disability gives the Governor-in-Council a choice of either removal or stopping the salary,[63] the crux of the matter being whether the judge will be removed, or allowed to resign and hence save his pension. Secondly, the removal of a County or District Court judge can be accomplished by the passage of a simple order-in-council after an investigation by a commission of inquiry instituted by the Governor-in-Council and conducted by a judge of a higher court appointed for that purpose. Such an inquiry will not be ordered unless the minister of Justice receives complaints from responsible parties or organizations (such as the bar association) in the province; and the judge is, of course, given every opportunity to defend himself against any charges.[64]

These provisions, while they give these judges very substantial protection, nevertheless make the process of removal an expedient which is undoubtedly workable. Two judges have actually been removed in modern times (the latest in 1933),[65] and others in the more distant past forestalled certain removal by resignation.

Salary

Salary is another factor determining the independence of the judge. The first condition is that it should be certain and not subject to the changing opinions of Parliament. Judicial salaries in Canada are therefore fixed by statute and do not appear in the annual parliamentary vote, and they are given special security by being made a charge on the Consolidated Revenue Fund. When the salaries of public officials were cut down during the depression those of the judiciary were not reduced, although a special income tax of 10 per cent was levied on judicial salaries, in order to maintain the principle – if not the income – intact. It is for the same reason, of course, that the provision for bringing about retirement by cutting off salaries, which has been discussed above, is viewed with alarm in some quarters; and the device will be justified only if the threat contained in the act continues to be used with exceptional caution.

The lowest limit of the judge's salary should clearly be sufficient to enable him to live in moderate comfort with financial security. In practice, however, the salary will have to be set at a much higher figure than this, for it must be large enough to induce many of the best lawyers to accept positions on the Bench. A good lawyer may not insist on an enormous salary, but he will

62/*Rev. Stat. Can.* (1952), c. 159, s. 32.
63/The County Court judges are subject to the same treatment for the results of age or infirmity as the others. *Supra*, pp. 397–400.
64/*Can. H. of C. Debates*, Oct. 17, 1932, pp. 255–6.
65/*Canadian Annual Review, 1933*, pp. 109–10.

demand one which will enable him to live on approximately the same scale as that to which he has become accustomed.[66] While it is true that the highest paid lawyer will not necessarily make the best judge, there can be no doubt that the correlation between legal and judicial ability is high, and that if the state wants the best material, it must be prepared to pay for it. In entering this competition, however, the government has a valuable item to throw into the balance in the prestige and security that go with the judicial appointment, and many lawyers are prepared to make a genuine sacrifice in exchange for the more intangible rewards of a judgeship.

There have been occasions in Canada, however, when the remuneration has been so low that the government has experienced difficulty in securing first-class judges, for the best talent would not accept appointment. Under such conditions the quality of the courts rapidly deteriorates, and this is soon reflected in the administration of justice. One of the openly avowed purposes of the salary increases in 1946 was to raise the standard of the judiciary through an improvement in the financial circumstances of the judges.

APPOINTMENT AND PROMOTION

The quality of the judge is the most critical of all the factors concerned in the proper exercise of his powers. The conditions under which he works after his appointment should allow full scope and opportunity for the display of his talents; but the great prerequisite for usefulness, the character of the judge, has been formed in earlier years and must be weighed and tested before he takes his seat on the Bench.

The appointment is made by order-in-council, and is the especial concern of the prime minister[67] and the minister of Justice. Party affiliations play a varying part; but they are not often entirely absent from an appointment, and at times actually prevent the choice falling on those with the more desirable qualities. Many potentially able judges have undoubtedly been effectively disqualified for appointment to the Bench because they belonged to the wrong party, and it must be realized that for lawyers who support parties other than the Liberal and Conservative, the disqualification is all but absolute. "There has been too much political patronage concerned in appointments to the Bench," said Bennett. "The result has been that the test whether a man is entitled to a seat on the Bench has seemed to be whether he has run an election and lost it. Very often that has been so. If he has run an election and

66/See Evidence, *Special Committee of the House of Commons on Judges' Salaries,* 1928, pp. 101–18.
67/In a formal statement in an order-in-council (July 19, 1920) on the functions of the prime minister, the recommendation to council of the appointment of chief justices of all courts is given as a special prerogative of the prime minister. See Dawson, *Constitutional Issues in Canada,* p. 125.

won it, peradventure he should not look for a seat on the Bench because he can better serve his country in some other capacity."[68]

It would, however, be quite erroneous to conclude that merit has been disregarded in making judicial appointments. "I have always laid down with respect to the judiciary," wrote Sir John Macdonald, "the principle that no amount of political pressure shall induce me to appoint an incompetent or unworthy judge,"[69] and while neither Sir John nor his successors have been as careful as this statement would suggest, judicial appointments have been kept on a high level. The law societies and bar associations take an active interest in the matter, and recommendations and representations from them are usually welcomed at Ottawa. Indeed, each major party includes enough lawyers actively interested in politics to ensure a constant supply of excellent material, although even so, the selection is not invariably confined to the supporters of the party in power. "Quite frankly," said Mr L. S. St Laurent, then minister of Justice, "I have been rather proud of the comments I have received about most of the appointments to the High Courts in the several provinces that it has been my privilege to recommend ... A number of excellent judges have been appointed who, I am told, were not at any time members of the party of this administration."[70] Mr Trudeau, while minister of Justice, said that "it has been my practice since becoming minister to consult with the president [of the Canadian Bar Association], and through him with the members of [the judicial nominations] committee of the Canadian Bar Association, before appointing any judge"; his successor, Mr Turner, made a similar statement in 1968.[71] In both instances, of course, the appointing power remained unmistakably with the government.

The idea of sectional representation on the Bench which appears in so clear a form in the Supreme Court of Canada, is evident to some degree in other courts. There is apparently a deliberate effort made to avoid choosing too many judges from the larger centres of population, so that a provincial superior court will give some representation to the different areas in the province. The practice of considering the religious beliefs of the judges in many appointments has been followed for years, but not consistently, and rarely with open acknowledgement.[72] While this may be readily attacked as narrow-minded prejudice, it may be based on other things than the mere political desire to cater to public opinion through a sectarian spoils system. For it is vital to maintain public confidence in the judiciary; and if that should

68/*Can. H. of C. Debates,* May 17, 1932, p. 2999.

69/Pope, *Correspondence of Sir John Macdonald,* p. 85. See Lederman, "Thoughts on the Reform of the Supreme Court of Canada."

70/*Can. H. of C. Debates,* March 24, 1944, p. 1848. A number of these, however, were promotions and not original appointments.

71/*Can. H. of C. Debates,* Nov. 30, 1967, pp. 4895–6; Oct. 16, 1968, p. 1220.

72/Dawson, *The Principle of Official Independence,* pp. 32–3; *Saturday Night,* Sept. 12, 1942 (editorial).

depend in some measure on a moderate regard for what may well be considered a purblind parochialism, some gesture in this direction is only wise. No one can deny that a Quebec Bench filled with Protestants or an Ontario Bench filled with Roman Catholics would, irrespective of the ability of the judges, discredit the administration of justice in that province.

While a system of promotion is usually most desirable within any organization, promotion from one judicial position to another is to be regarded with misgiving. If the executive is to exercise no control and no suggestion of control over the judiciary, any major promotions become impossible, for they may always raise the question of the executive paying its debts to its friends. To object to the elevation of a judge to the chief justiceship on the same court or even, perhaps, from one branch to another in the same court would doubtless be carrying this fastidiousness to extremes, but promotions involving greater rewards are most certainly inadvisable.[73] Even greater objections may be taken to the movement, which has not been entirely unknown in Canada, from politics to the Bench and back to politics again; for whatever effect such versatility may have on politics, its effect on the judiciary is wholly harmful.

EXTRA-JUDICIAL DUTIES

The employment of judges in extra-judicial work, and especially their employment on boards and royal commissions of different kinds, has been under attack for many years. The judges profess to dislike it, the legal profession opposes it, and the government always expresses great regret at each fresh assignment; but the practice shows not the slightest sign of abatement. One judge of the Appeal Court of Saskatchewan had in 1946 never sat on the court of which he was a member although he had been appointed eight years before; he was engaged in discharging various duties, chiefly diplomatic, for the government. Another Saskatchewan judge, shortly after his appointment to the Bench, was in 1961 made chairman of a royal commission on health, the investigation of which was expected to take up to two years; before the commission reported, the judge was appointed to the Supreme Court. Again in 1946 the minister of Justice admitted that "there are at present about fifteen judges who are doing some work that is outside the performance of their ordinary duties."[74] In September 1937 the chief justice of Quebec, in deploring the large number of cases which remained unheard, said:

I am fully confident that had we during the past year not been deprived of the assistance of so many members of the Bench the result would have been different ... For two years and more Mr. Justice Loranger, one of our most energetic and active workers, has, under a Commission from the Government, been seeking by

73/*Can. H. of C. Debates,* July 26, 1946, pp. 3910, 3914–15.
74/*Ibid.,* June 21, 1946, p. 2708.

application of a statute, to bring relief to our actual or imaginary long-suffering agricultural class ... What I have said of Mr. Justice Loranger is true, in full measure, of Mr. Justice Archambault. The paternal instincts of our Government induced it to create a Commission of which our brother, Joseph Archambault, is the head to inquire into and report upon the conditions prevailing in our jails and penitentiaries. The work has occupied his full time for over two years. When it will end is, to say the least, uncertain.[75]

Twenty-four years later Quebec members of Parliament were still complaining of the "tremendous backlog of cases" in some Quebec courts, and for that reason they welcomed the appointment of two more judges for the province's superior court.[76] Mr R. A. Bell, who from the opposition benches made a number of attempts to put statutory restrictions on what he called "moon-lighting by judges," commonly received a sympathetic hearing in the House, but made little genuine headway before his defeat in the general election of 1968.[77] In 1966 the government had gone part way to meet his goal by instructing County Court judges to divest themselves of further involvement as conciliators and arbitrators in labour-management disputes,[78] but no legislation barring judges from such activities has been enacted.

There would seem to be little purpose in taking elaborate care to separate the judge from politics and to render him quite independent of the executive, and then placing him in a position as a royal commissioner where his impartiality may be attacked and his findings – no matter how correct and judicial they may be – are liable to be interpreted as favouring one political party at the expense of the other. For many of the inquiries or boards place the judge in a position where he cannot escape controversy: he may be making decisions which at least touch on policy; he may be considering, or conciliating, or deciding disputes on labour questions and thus running the risk of becoming known as a "company man" or a "union man"; he may be investigating and interrogating by very questionable procedures persons suspected of treasonable activities; he may be conducting inquiries on definitely political matters such as the Hong Kong or Bren gun charges, or the allegations concerning one Gerda Munsinger. It has been proved time and again that in many of these cases the judge loses in dignity and in reputation, and his future usefulness is appreciably lessened thereby. Moreover, if the judge remains away from his regular duties for long periods, he is apt to lose his sense of balance and detachment; and he finds that the task of getting back to normal and of adjusting his outlook and habits of mind to purely judicial work is by no means easy.

The situation is made more difficult by the fact that these commissions and boards often carry with them a substantial addition to the judge's salary. The

75/Montreal *Gazette,* Sept. 9, 1937. The chief justice was himself on an international judicial commission.
76/*Can. H. of C. Debates,* June 6, 1961, pp. 5933–37.
77/See, for example, *ibid.,* Feb. 24, 1967, pp. 13442–54; Oct. 21, 1966, pp. 8992–8.
78/*Globe and Mail,* Sept. 20, 1966.

rule in the Judges Act is that he is not allowed to receive any extra remuneration,[79] but that he may receive a living allowance; and this is frequently on such a generous scale that it cannot fail to make a very welcome contribution to his income. Two judges on a Royal Commission on Coal received in living allowances in a little over two years $15,212.50 and $18,400.00 respectively, and, with other personal expenses added, the totals came to $17,349.94 and $24,351.69.[80] Another judge, it was alleged, received in an eight-year period more than $40,000 in addition to his salary because of services given on royal commissions.[81] The minister of Justice in 1963, Mr Lionel Chevrier, asserted that "if we are to go into these extracurricular activities ... we will find that there are police magistrates in certain parts of the country who are getting far more than judges," adding a common type of Canadian reassurance: "But police magistrates do not come under the jurisdiction of this parliament."[82] To assert that these things have no effect on a judge's independence may or may not be true; but even if that sinister factor were completely absent, the popular suspicion that such influences are present is in itself a most serious matter. One cogent speech in the Commons by a distinguished lawyer did not exaggerate the difficulties necessarily associated with the practice:

To the extent that these tasks [the work on commissions] are paid for, they are subversive of the principle of independence which is the bed-rock of our whole judicial system. If a judge is to receive remuneration in excess of his statutory compensation, which has been horribly inadequate for generations, he is beholden to the body paying him, be it the political party in power or be it a labour union or employer who commands his services ...

It is impolitic for a practising barrister to say anything which might be construed as criticism of the Bench. It is most unfortunate that stern necessity imposes on me the duty of pointing out the dangers to the greatest of our institutions inherent in this practice. I do not accuse the Government in power of being the sole offender, but circumstances have made it the most frequent and the most recent offender. Whenever it has had a difficult problem to solve, whenever it is confronted with a perplexity, it has pulled members of the Bench down into the dust of the political arena in quest of a solution acceptable because of the high authority and so far unimpeached integrity of the Bench.

I say with sorrow that the reputation for impartiality, dignity and honour enjoyed by the Bench has been exposed to criticism by this practice. All who believe in the law, who depend upon its fearless administration, and admit that the people at large must have complete faith in the integrity of the judiciary, must oppose the continuance of this practice.[83]

The objection to judges doing additional work is plainly not founded on any suggestion that this work is badly done; quite the contrary. It is, indeed, so well done that the government continually asserts that the great justification

79/*Rev. Stat. Can.* (1952), c. 159, s. 37.
80/*Can. H. of C. Debates*, Feb. 17, 1947, p. 468.
81/*Ibid.*, June 21, 1946, p. 2731.
82/*Ibid.*, July 29, 1963, p. 2773.
83/J. T. Hackett, MP, *ibid.*, p. 2709. On the use of judges on royal commissions see John C. Courtney, "In Defence of Royal Commissions," *Canadian Public Administration,* XII, no. 2 (Summer 1969), pp. 201–8.

for the practice is that no one else can fill the gap and no one else can command the same public confidence. There is probably a good deal of truth in both these arguments, although neither will lessen the bad effects on the judiciary itself. Some investigations are of such a nature that it is certain that no one but a judge could conduct them acceptably; but those in this class are certainly not as numerous as the past utilization of the judiciary might suggest. Even a minister of Justice has stated that there may be other groups of people in the country who are in a position to take some of these positions, "gentlemen now in universities and in other walks of life, who are sufficiently known to their fellow citizens to have their situation in life give that guarantee, which is necessary when one of these important public duties has to be fulfilled, that it is being fulfilled by the best men available for the purpose."[84]

Another possibility was suggested by the minister of Justice when introducing a bill in 1946 to enlarge the Exchequer Court.[85] He suggested that one purpose in adding to the numbers on the court was to create there a pool of judges who would be available to serve on royal commissions and thus avoid interrupting the work of the provincial courts. This comes very close to establishing a permanent office of royal commissioner,[86] who could conduct inquiries single-handed and who could also preside over larger commissions, who would develop a specialized talent and technique in elucidating evidence and information, and who could be relied upon to bring to an inquiry that detachment and impartiality which is necessary to secure the confidence of the nation in the work of a commission. A year or two of experiment might easily result in one of the Exchequer judges ceasing to exercise any judicial duties whatever and devoting his full time to investigations of a public nature.

JUDICIAL INDEPENDENCE

The above review will have indicated how unique are the functions of the judge and how completely the Canadian government has accepted the principle of division of powers as applied to the judiciary. It may be well, in conclusion, to go over this general ground and recapitulate what has been said and implied in some of the preceding pages. The fundamental decisions in a democracy arise from a constant interchange of desires and commands; tentative advances and retreats; experiments and consolidations; the adoption of one policy, the rejection of another, the haphazard and almost unconscious acceptance of a third; compromises without number – all forming a part of the extremely complex process of determining and applying public policy.

84/*Can. H. of C. Debates*, Aug. 2, 1946, p. 4277.
85/*Ibid.*, July 5, 1946, p. 3178.
86/For a development of this suggestion, see Dawson, *The Principle of Official Independence*, p. 182.

This works fairly successfully under a system of rewards and punishments, or, as it is called, political responsibility, whereby public officials of many kinds make their decisions (whether these be based on interpretations of public opinion, or on orders received, or on their judgment of what is fitting and best under the existing circumstances) in the full knowledge that in the event of these decisions being wrong – or, in some instances, merely unpopular – they must take the blame, or, in the event of their being right – or popular – they may take the credit. The responsibility which flows from people to Parliament to cabinet to administration and resulting action is thus both a stream of command – albeit somewhat uncertain and wandering, and sometimes showing little perceptible motion – and also a means whereby honesty and efficiency and devotion to public duty can be appraised and suitably recognized.

But the judicial function, as already indicated, does not involve this giving of commands, this carrying-out of plans, or this restless search for policies: on the contrary, any vestige of these things would destroy the value of the appraisements and judgments which the judiciary is called upon to make and which form the primary reason for its existence. Rewards and punishments likewise become not merely inappropriate, but dangerous; for they at once introduce the possibility that the judge may give his decisions not solely from his determination of the law, but influenced to some degree by the effects of these decisions on his own personal career and fortune. The problem of the judiciary thus becomes one of how to obtain the most conscientious performance of the judicial functions without involving intimidation or fear and without offering the hope of gain and preferment.

The solution has been found in judicial "independence." The judge must be made independent of most of the restraints, checks, and punishments which are usually called into play against other public officials. He is thus protected against the operation of some of the most potent weapons which a democracy has at its command: he receives almost complete protection against criticism; he is given civil and criminal immunity for acts committed in the discharge of his duties; he cannot be removed from office for any ordinary offence, but only for misbehaviour of a flagrant kind; and he can never be removed simply because his decisions happen to be disliked by the cabinet, the Parliament, or the people. Such independence is unquestionably dangerous, and if this freedom and power were indiscriminately granted the results would certainly prove to be disastrous. The desired protection is found by picking with especial care the men who are to be entrusted with these responsibilities, and then paradoxically heaping more privileges upon them to stimulate their sense of moral responsibility, which is called in as a substitute for the political responsibility which has been removed. The judge is placed in a position where he has nothing to lose by doing what is right and little to gain by doing what is wrong; and there is therefore every reason to hope that his best efforts will be devoted to the conscientious performance of his duty.

The judge will thus usually begin with the twin assets of character and ability, and these become the foundation on which the indirect appeals are based. He is paid a substantial salary, which not only removes some of the obvious temptations, but frees him from financial distractions. The importance of his office is continually stressed; his own rectitude and sense of fairness are invariably assumed; the dignity of the court and the respect accorded his office are rarely, if ever, challenged; his social position is always assured. These efforts to accentuate the eminence of the office are made infinitely more effective by the fortunate regard which the legal profession has for the judiciary and its ingrained habit of regarding a seat on the Bench as the crown of a legal career. Thus some of the very men who build up the tradition may be induced to accept judgeships a few years later, influenced to a material degree by the tradition which they themselves have helped to create. Not the least important result of this prestige is its effect on the public, who have come to accept it – and with some justification – at its face value, and who see in judicial independence a greater promise of justice than could be obtained through the application of ordinary political sanctions.

The judiciary, like so many aspects of the Canadian constitution in the 1970s, became involved in comprehensive proposals for reform. The Dominion suggested in 1969 "a general Court of Appeal for Canada to be known as the Supreme Court of Canada," nominations for which "could be placed before the Senate for approval prior to appointment." The proposed court would have its three members from Quebec designated to hear appeals from the province; and the whole court, it was suggested, should be specifically authorized "to depart from a previous decision when it appears right to do so."[87] These proposals, like so many proposals concerning the Canadian constitution, encountered considerable opposition, and rapid progress towards comprehensive revision seemed, as of June 1970, improbable.

87/Trudeau, *The Constitution and the People of Canada*, pp. 38–45, 82–7.

Part VII POLITICAL PARTIES

21 Political parties

POLITICAL PARTIES, as the preceding pages will bear witness, cannot be isolated from any account of Canadian government and then be brought in later as a perfunctory postscript to the main theme. For parties lie beneath the discussion of almost all governmental activities like the postulates underlying a book of Euclid; they provide the fundamental assumptions which are essential to the validity of the argument. But while parties and party considerations can be found to be involved, in one way or another, in much of the preceding discussion of constitutional, legislative, administrative and judicial activities, they have also a life of their own which deserves explicit attention. The following chapters therefore deal with parties as such, and their rôles as part of the political machinery in Canada.

The preceding paragraph, general though it is, none the less contains most of the generalizations about parties about which observers in Canada can still be said to be in agreement, for as the knowledge of parties has grown in recent years, so too has discussion not only about what parties do, but what they actually are. As will be seen, parties have always been indispensable as suppliers of candidates, issues, and manpower for high office; and as such they have had to be mobilizers of large armies of voluntary workers, paid and unpaid, raisers of vast sums, both from members and non-members, and spenders of those same funds. It is beginning to be seen that the very methods which parties use in performing their functions, and the nature of the support they thereby attract or repel, have profound implications for the parties' rôles in Canadian society. Fund-raising, for example, can have significant centralizing tendencies; and fund-spending, particularly through the modern use of advertising agencies and the mass media, can play a part in breaking old allegiances and introducing new instabilities into party support. With the new instabilities comes a natural questioning of the parties' traditional rôles as brokers between competing groups, and as unifiers of dissident elements in a diverse population.

One analyst, writing with specific reference to the general election of 1962, was able to refer to "the lack of any significant class basis for Canadian politics"; while another, after a meticulous study of a single by-election two years later, suggested that "social class is now the most important influence on the vote in Waterloo South."¹ Two others, in general agreement about "the weakness of social class factors," concluded that "of all the factors dividing Canadians in their political outlook and behaviour, religion is uppermost in importance," with the Roman Catholic voter generally being associated with the Liberal party;² but again a specific study of one constituency associated the chief Protestant denominations with Liberal support, while a majority of the Roman Catholics questioned had voted Conservative.³ John Meisel has written: "The most distinctive feature of the party system is not that it has four or five members but that among its chief tasks is that of promoting a sense of national community. This is the key to an understanding of Canadian parties and elections."⁴ Professor Cairns, arguing that parties are in part the product, as well as the manipulators, of the electoral system, challenges the view "that the party system has been an important nationalizing agency with respect to the sectional cleavages widely held to constitute the most significant and enduring lines of division in the Canadian polity."⁵ Several scholars including Messrs Cairns, Horowitz, Porter, and Wilson,⁶ have variously urged that the division into a left-right dichotomy is, or ought to be, the basis for a viable political system in Canada; while Professor Denis Smith has written: "The familiar distinction between Right and Left does not apply in Canada."⁷

All these points of view (and there are others) about Canadian political parties clearly make generalization difficult, if not dangerous, and it must be emphasized that these chapters themselves accept points of view at variance with some of those expressed above. Yet it must be emphasized that all these points of view, including those to follow, assume the existence of parties in

1/See Robert R. Alford in John Meisel, ed., *Papers on the 1962 Election* (Toronto, 1964), p. 209; John Wilson, "Politics and Social Class in Canada: The Case of Waterloo South," *Canadian Journal of Political Science*, I, no. 3 (Sept. 1968), p. 301.

2/F. C. Engelmann and M. A. Schwartz, *Political Parties and the Canadian Social Structure* (Toronto, 1967), p. 58; see also Alford, in Meisel, *Papers on the 1962 Election*.

3/George Perlin, "St. John's West," in Meisel, *Papers on the 1962 Election*, p. 10. See also Grace M. Anderson, "Voting Behaviour and the Ethnic-Religious Variable: A Study of a Federal Election in Hamilton, Ontario," *Canadian Journal of Economics and Political Science*, XXXII, no. 1 (Feb. 1966), pp. 27–37; J. A. Laponce, *People vs Politics* (Toronto, 1969).

4/*Papers on the 1962 Election*, pp. 287–8.

5/Alan C. Cairns, "The Electoral System and the Party System in Canada, 1921–1965," *Canadian Journal of Political Science*, I, no. 1 (March 1968), p. 55. See also Porter, *The Vertical Mosaic*, especially chap. XII.

6/See Cairns, "The Electoral System"; Porter, *The Vertical Mosaic*; Wilson, "Politics and Social Class in Canada"; and Gad Horowitz, "Toward the Democratic Class Struggle," Lloyd and McLeod, *Agenda 1970*, pp. 241–55.

7/"Prairie Revolt, Federalism and the Party System," in Hugh G. Thorburn, ed., *Party Politics in Canada* (2nd ed., Toronto, 1967), p. 191.

the plural, for it is obvious that democratic government as it is understood and practised in Canada cannot function without the aid of more than one party; the communist and fascist idea of a single party and the rigid suppression of all dissenters has clearly no place in a democracy. Admittedly there are occasions when the actions of parties are reprehensible; but these must be accepted as necessary concomitants of self-government. They eventually work themselves out (at least they have so far), and the nation presumably emerges sadder and wiser from the experience.

The merits and general usefulness of political parties need not be elaborated here. In all democracies they keep the public both informed and aroused by giving forceful expression to opinion and criticism on all subjects of general interest. They enable those who are concerned with these matters (whether they are actuated by selfish motives or otherwise) to organize for the more effectual propagation of their views and the more ready implementation of these views through practical political expedients. The parties are the outstanding agents for bringing about co-operation and compromise between conflicting groups and interests of all kinds in the nation; for as a rule it is only by a merging of forces that these can hope to become powerful enough to secure office. In Canada, indeed, the rôle of the national parties as a unifying agent in bringing together in amity some of the most powerful dissident forces in the country, despite contemporary argument to the contrary, could hardly be overestimated. Further, the parties, pragmatically pursuing their own interests, sort out issues for special attention, and narrow down potentially long lists of candidates to modest proportions, thereby simplifying the task of the voter so that he is enabled to form a fairly clear and relatively simple decision on a few major questions and a few leading people. The party (or parties) in opposition supplies an alternative government which is willing, and even eager, to assume power the moment it begins to slip from the hands of the party which has been in the majority. Moreover, this new government comes into office with its leaders virtually chosen and its programme largely prepared in advance, and the transition can thus be made with little uncertainty and with a minimum of friction. It is true that the party system also tends to bring with it many faults – a reliance on funds from sometimes questionable sources, an excessive selfishness, a distorted perspective, and favouritism, to name but four – and while it would be dangerous to idealize the party system, there can be no reasonable doubt that its merits decidedly outweigh its drawbacks. It is often overlooked that many of the faults of political parties are the faults of all large human associations; and that a party can become corrupt only with the active co-operation of large numbers of people, some of whom on occasion profess a disdain for politics.

It has long been held that the party system, and particularly the party system under cabinet government, will find the best conditions for its operation where there are only two parties, or, at least, two parties sufficiently large to provide as a rule a clear majority in the legislature. Canadian experience at the national level provides at least three important reasons for being sceptical of the traditional theory. The first is that Canada has in fact had a multi-party system since at least the election of 1921; the second is that the administration of the Canadian state was unquestionably a good deal more corrupt and less efficient under the old two-party system than it has become since; the third is that Canada had several years of minority government between 1957 and 1968, and they were very lively and interesting indeed, as well as productive.

It is true, none the less, that only two parties have ever attained power at Ottawa, and Canada has escaped some of the worst potential consequences of a multi-party system. If a legislature, for example, is under the shifting control of a number of parties, constantly seeking different alignments which will ensure a more permanent or more profitable majority, legislative programmes tend to remain in a constant state of flux, executive leadership becomes hesitant, and short-term views unavoidably supplant more permanent policies. Under a two-party system the responsibility of the opposition can become more definite and inescapable, and the conflict of interests and the assertion of local views are less likely to be either so divisive or so intransigent.

But whatever the theoretical justification of the two-party system, every Canadian general election since 1921 has been contested by from three to seven parties, and each House of Commons in the same period has included representatives from at least three, and sometimes six parties. Not all these groups qualify as major parties, of course, but it would be quite inaccurate to consider only the Liberals and Conservatives as major, and all the rest as minor. Some of the "minor" groups, such as the Progressives of the 1920s and the Co-operative Commonwealth Federation after 1935, have had a great impact on the policies of the other parties; others, such as Social Credit after 1935, have had a less discernible impact on policy, but have nevertheless been remarkably successful in retaining power in provincial legislatures, and in dominating provincial blocs of members elected to the House of Commons.

There is one genuine criterion by which one can classify the Liberals and Conservatives together, and apart from all the others, and that is age. Both the parties just named have pre-Confederation antecedents, and all the others are of much more recent origin. In the discussion which follows, it must be remembered that the primary classification of the parties is, for convenience, based on "older" and "younger," and not "major" and "minor."

THE ORIGINS OF THE OLDER POLITICAL PARTIES

The origin of the Conservative party can be fixed definitely at 1854, when a number of separate groups in the Province of Canada were brought together in a temporary coalition (which turned out to be permanent) under the contradictory but accurate title of Liberal-Conservative. It was composed of extreme Tories, who a few years before had fought against responsible government, and moderate Liberals from Upper Canada, together with French-Canadian moderates (or *bleus* as they soon were called) under the leadership of Cartier and some English-speaking members from Lower Canada. The coalition soon fell under the influence of John A. Macdonald, who was able by his own personality and later by the strong urge of the Confederation movement to weld the members, augmented by small groups from the other provinces, into a genuine political party.[8] So successful was this endeavour that the party was able to retain office, with but one five-year interval, until 1896.

The rôle and outlook of Macdonald and the Liberal-Conservative party have been compared not unjustly to those of Alexander Hamilton and the Federalists in the history of the United States. Each party was the party of centralization; each believed in identifying itself with the propertied, commercial, and industrial interests; each used these interests to advance nationalist as against local causes, and received in return the powerful support which they could give. The centralizing influences of Macdonald and the Liberal-Conservative party did not stop at Confederation; they found expression in the "national policy" of a protective tariff, in the construction of the transcontinental railway, and in many other secondary policies which bore in the same general direction.

This was the work of a generation, and it was to a remarkable degree the work of one man. But Macdonald's bold schemes never allowed him to forget the details of politics; indeed, his wider schemes often appeared to be little more than the means of attaining his more immediate political ends. He possessed an exceptionally shrewd political sense of both timing and tactics, and was far from fastidious in the instruments and expedients which he used in gaining his victories. His greatest talent was a genius for conciliation, aided by a warm personality. He was able to gain the support of Brown, his bitter enemy, for the Confederation project; he was able to induce Howe to accept defeat and join his cabinet; he was able to retain the backing of the English tories, French moderates, Orangemen, and Roman Catholics.[9] This trait was of inestimable value in the formative period of the Liberal-Conservative party;

8/See Escott Reid, "The Rise of National Parties in Canada," *Proceedings, Canadian Political Science Association, 1932*, pp. 187–200; F. H. Underhill, "The Development of National Political Parties in Canada," *Canadian Historical Review*, XVI, no. 4 (Dec. 1935), pp. 367–87; Bernard Ostry, "Conservatives, Liberals, and Labour in the 1870's," *ibid.*, XLI, no. 2 (June 1960), pp. 93–127, and "Conservatives, Liberals, and Labour in the 1880's," *Canadian Journal of Economics and Political Science,* XXVII, no. 2 (May 1961), pp. 141–61; Donald Creighton, *John A. Macdonald,* I (Toronto, 1952), especially chaps. VIII–IX; J. H. S. Reid, Kenneth McNaught, and Harry S. Crowe, *A Source-Book of Canadian History* (Toronto, 1959), especially Part IX; Engelmann and Schwartz, *Political Parties and the Canadian Social Structure,* especially chaps. 2–7; *Report of the Committee on Election Expenses* (both vols.).

9/See Creighton, *Sir John A. Macdonald.*

and later years were to show that leadership in any Canadian party, if it was to have any permanence, must continue to depend to an enormous degree on an ability to use conciliation and compromise.

The origin of the Liberal party is not so easily traced. Its ancestry undoubtedly goes back to the early reformers who fought for responsible government, but after Confederation the separate elements in the provinces were slow in coming together and forming a genuinely national body. Many of the Liberals had opposed Confederation, and this continuing lukewarmness, encouraged by the rival centralizing tendencies of the Conservatives, helped to make them the defenders of the rights of the provinces, a stand which in itself did not promote national party unity. If the Conservatives can be said to have had an earlier model in the Federalist party in the United States, the Liberals (or Clear Grits as they were called in Upper Canada) had their counterpart in Jefferson and the Anti-Federalists or States Rights party. Moreover, this resemblance went further than a mere belief in decentralized government, for both were based on a frontier agrarian democracy with distinct radical tendencies. The Clear Grits were indeed definitely influenced by the successors to the Jeffersonians, the Jacksonian Democrats. They were opposed to wealth and privilege in any form, and they favoured soft money, universal suffrage, frequent elections, and various other "republican" measures well known south of the border. Another group which was included in or affiliated with the Liberals was the *rouge party* from Quebec. It was anticlerical and had aroused the opposition of the Roman Catholic Church, and after Confederation it gradually declined in size and importance. To these two elements were joined some reformers, secessionists, and independents from New Brunswick and Nova Scotia.[10]

The first Liberal government came into power after the Pacific Scandal had broken over the head of Macdonald in 1873. This government was supported by the above groups which acknowledged also a separate allegiance to their own leaders: but Alexander Mackenzie, the prime minister, was no Macdonald, and after almost five years the party left office still a party in name only. The unimaginative leadership of Mackenzie, the troubled genius of his chief lieutenant, Edward Blake, the administration's support of practical policies rather than those with popular appeal, its misfortune in holding office during an economic depression, its excess (at least at the Dominion level) of political rectitude and stern principles, and its disbelief in patronage and lavish public expenditures, all combined to accomplish its defeat, and send the disunited Liberals into the wilderness for almost two decades.[11]

It was Laurier, who became Liberal leader in 1887, who made a genuine

10/Reid, "The Rise of National Parties in Canada," pp. 193–4. See also J. M. S. Careless, *Brown of the Globe,* two vols. (Toronto, 1959 and 1963); Thomson, *Alexander Mackenzie: Clear Grit.*
11/See Thomson, *Alexander Mackenzie: Clear Grit.*

national party from the local and personal sections which gave him their support. He approached his task with deep misgivings, but with the conviction which was to be his guiding political principle all his life, that the overwhelming need was the co-operation of the French- and English-speaking in Canada, and his first public address after he became leader was an appeal for national unity. The immediate party problem was to carry the local party successes in the provinces over into the federal field. For although the Liberals lost the general election of 1891, they were at that time in control in every province with the possible exception of British Columbia. In 1893 the Liberals held the first national party convention in Canada with the obvious intention (as indicated in the introductory remarks of Oliver Mowat) of consolidating the party's position, bringing the different elements together, and making the national leader better known to the party workers all over the Dominion. Laurier's first cabinet in 1896, which included three provincial premiers, was a clear demonstration of the same purpose.

"Laurier," states Professor Underhill, "had a more difficult and subtle role to play [than Macdonald], because he led a party in which the radical agrarian Grit tradition in Ontario and the radical anti-clerical *rouge* tradition in Quebec were still strong. Under Laurier the old party of Brown and Mackenzie and Dorion had to combine Jeffersonian professions with Hamiltonian practices."[12] Laurier managed to discourage the extreme *rouge* tendencies, to establish better relations with the Roman Catholic Church, and to capture a large part of the moderate element in Quebec, while he appealed to Ontario through the consideration which he showed for provincial rights and the imperial preferential tariff which his government introduced in 1897. Even in the 1893 platform the party had noticeably retreated from the extreme free trade position which it had earlier advocated; and when it took office it tacitly accepted the necessity for maintaining the industries which had grown up under the protective system – a tendency towards maintaining the status quo which became even more marked in the early years of the century. The imperial preference was an ideal compromise as a party straddle. It was a move towards freer trade; it had a certain retaliatory aspect against the high American tariff; it retained many of the Canadian protective features intact; and it was a reassuring gesture to those imperialists who had suspicions regarding the empire loyalty of a French-Canadian prime minister.

If the Liberals had been unlucky in the time of their accession to power in 1873, they were amply compensated in 1896; for they caught the tide at the flood and rode into a period of prosperity unmatched up to that time in Canadian history. The enormous influx of immigrants, the railway expansion, the opening and settlement of western Canada, the creation of two new provinces, the expansion of internal and external trade, the continuing growth of

12/Underhill, "The Development of National Political Parties in Canada," pp. 384–5. See Joseph Schull, *Laurier* (Toronto, 1965).

Canadian autonomy – these were counted as Liberal achievements, and the winning of three more general elections was their reward. The fifteen years in office not only gave the party strength, they enabled it to acquire a character and tradition which were to prove very useful reserves in the years ahead. Although it is true that the tides were favourable and the winds fair, the success of the party voyage was nevertheless due in large measure to the capacity of the captain; for Laurier, like Macdonald, brought to his task a broad tolerance, and a vision tempered with a skill in practical affairs which have had few equals in Canadian history.

THE ORIGINS OF THE THIRD PARTIES

This is not the place to recount in detail the full history of the Liberal and Conservative parties, much of which, indeed, is as yet unwritten.[13] Paradoxically, the origins and histories of some of the parties which have been established since Confederation have received considerable attention, and a small but excellent literature about them is now in print. All these parties, in one way or another, have reflected dissatisfaction with the older parties, and have been handicapped by the fact that when the dissatisfaction is soundly based and the new party threatens to become really successful, one or both of the older parties moves towards the appropriation of the new party's programme, and sometimes its key personnel. The younger parties have thus been catalysts in the chemistry of politics, but have hardly ever been able to keep far enough ahead of their would-be swallowers to establish themselves as major threats in their own right; not one of them has convincingly succeeded in permanently absorbing any significant part of one of the older national parties.

Only once, in 1921, has a third party won more than 20 per cent of the vote in a general election. The Progressive party then enjoyed a brief but unique success, for in 1921 it became the second largest party in the House of Commons, following which it showed what was perhaps a prophetic grasp of its own future by declining to serve as the official opposition.[14] There had been several farmers' political movements in Canada since the days of the Clear Grits, and this one, like the others, arose from the same basic conviction that the interests of the farmers were being grossly neglected. The general dislocations of the war and the fact that western Canada (normally Liberal) had shaken off its old party allegiance over the conscription issue greatly

13/See John R. Williams, *The Conservative Party of Canada, 1920-1949* (Durham, NC, 1956); J. W. Pickersgill, *The Liberal Party* (Toronto, 1962); J. L. Granatstein, *The Politics of Survival: The Conservative Party of Canada, 1939-1945* (Toronto, 1967); Heath Macquarrie, *The Conservative Party* (Toronto, 1965).

14/See W. L. Morton, *The Progressive Party in Canada* (Toronto, 1950); Denis Smith, "Prairie Revolt, Federalism and the Party System."

TABLE IV

Party standings in the House of Commons after each general election, 1921–68

Party	Liberal*	Conservative*	Progressive	Labour*	UFA	Lib-Prog.	Social Credit*	CCF*	Re-const.	UFO-Lab.	Unity	Bloc-Pop.	Lab-Prog.	NDP	Créditiste	Ind.
1921	117	50	64	3												1
1925	101	116	24	2												2
1926	116	91	13	3	11	9										2
1930	88	137	2	3	10	3										2
1935	176	40				2	17	7	1	1						1
1940	181	40				3	10	8								1
1945	127	68					13	29			2					5
1949	193	41					10	13				2				5
1953	172	51					15	23					1			3
1957	107	112					19	25								2
1958	49	208						8								
1962	100	116					30							19		
1963	129	95					24							17		
1965	131	97					5							21	9	2
1968	155	72												22	14	1

*Counts Independent Liberal and Liberal-Labour as Liberal, Independent Conservative as Conservative, Independent Labour as Labour, Independent CCF as CCF, and Independent Social Credit as Social Credit. The Ralliement des Créditistes split away from Social Credit. The various changes of name enjoyed by the Conservative party during the period are ignored.

lessened the difficulty of making a change; but the chief force of the movement was a distrust of the older parties, as such, and of the eastern commercial and industrial interests which supported them, the belief that no substantial reduction in the tariff could be expected from the other parties, and the desire to place on the statute book certain ideas and tenets of the new movement. The farmers' group (many of them refused to call it a party) therefore proposed the immediate abolition of the tariff on many raw materials, on all foodstuffs, and on certain machinery, together with substantial all-round reductions; reciprocity with the United States; increases in the imperial preference; direct graduated taxation on personal and corporation income and on large estates; assisted land settlement for veterans; public ownership of coal mines and all public utilities; and numerous political reforms, such as abolition of patronage, Senate reform, proportional representation, and the initiative, referendum, and recall.

The movement made its first great advance in Ontario in the provincial election of 1919, which resulted in the formation of a Farmer-Labour government. Two years later the United Farmers of Alberta obtained power as a result of an election in that province. In the Dominion general election in the same year the farmers – or Progressives – carried sixty-four seats in the House of Commons, all but four members coming from Ontario and the prairies. Although the Liberals did not have quite a majority in the House, they could count on the support of enough friendly Progressives to give them a moderate degree of security. The Farmer-Labour government in Ontario lasted only a few years; the Progressives in the Dominion House lasted a little longer but gradually petered out; while the UFA, both in Alberta and at Ottawa, showed much more vitality but eventually fell before the onslaught of the Social Credit movement.

The appeal of the Progressives was too much to particular groups and special areas, and they were never able to organize adequately on national lines. Many members, indeed, held impractical ideas about government by co-operative groups and not by parties, which they professed to hold in contempt; and their parliamentary tactics and lack of party responsibility did not make for general confidence. Much of the energy of the movement, moreover, was devoted to economic ends, and the wheat pools, or co-operative organizations for the marketing of wheat, were the result.

One important reason for their failure as a party was probably the unremitting efforts of the Liberals to absorb them, both by direct attack and by infiltration. The movement drew up its platform in November 1918 and so impressed were the Liberals with its excellence that nine months later a substantial part appeared in the Liberal platform. Progressives, the Liberals kept insisting in the following years, had been Liberals originally and still were nothing more than a special section of the old party. Mackenzie King missed no occasion to invite the wanderers to return, and the Liberal legislative programme bore such tangible signs of affection as reductions in the general tariff, increases in the imperial preference, lowered sales taxes, and other desired changes. "I have year in and year out," said King in August 1927, "sought to bind as one party these men and women with similar ideas. That has been the whole aim of my leadership." The defences of the Progressives crumbled. In the election of 1925 they elected only twenty-four members; and in the election of the next year they split into three groups, the UFA, the independent Progressives, and the Liberal-Progressives. This virtually eliminated them as an important element in Canadian politics. The UFA kept on for some years as a sectional group; but the bulk of the remainder linked up with the Liberals, and their leader accepted a portfolio in the Liberal government.

The Social Credit party, carrying on with at least some of the same personnel, succeeded the UFA in its native province and at Ottawa – a clear case of a party being hoist with its own petard. For where the UFA had capitalized on the discontent following the First World War, the Social Crediters capitalized on the discontent which arose during the depression; where the former had promised to relieve the Alberta farmers through free trade and co-operation, the latter produced fancy monetary schemes towards the same end. "The contest of the 1930's between the Social Credit government and the bankers was only one in the long series between east and west, city and country, banker and farmer, hard money and soft money, which had been going on ever since those early days when absences of hard cash forced resort to mooseskins, merchants' I.O.U.'s, or pieces of leather with holes in them."[15] More recently, the monetary ideas have been given a back seat, though the party apparently continued to believe in dark plots among the leaders of world finance and until recently often combined the announcement of this discovery with anti-semitic propaganda. Social Credit – despite a record tainted with authoritarianism – has become an ardent upholder of free enterprise and individual liberty.

For many years the Social Credit party made little progress outside Alberta, though a Quebec version, the Union des Electeurs, appeared in the 1940s. In 1952 a Social Credit government took office in British Columbia, and in 1962, after having been eliminated from the House of Commons in the election of 1958, Social Credit returned thirty members of Parliament, twenty-six of them from Quebec. Thereafter the Quebec wing assumed the ascendancy, soon emerging as a new entity known as Le Ralliement des Créditistes, while the English-speaking wing once more disappeared from the House of Commons; in 1968 two of its former members won seats as, respectively,

---

15/A. R. M. Lower, *Colony to Nation* (Toronto, 1946), p. 517. Admirable studies of the Social Credit party can be found in: John A. Irving, *The Social Credit Movement in Alberta* (Toronto, 1959); C. B. Macpherson, *Democracy in Alberta* (Toronto, 1953); J. R. Mallory, *Social Credit and the Federal Power in Canada* (Toronto, 1954).

424   THE GOVERNMENT OF CANADA

a Progressive Conservative (its one-time leader) and a Liberal, who shortly after appeared in Mr Trudeau's cabinet. Whatever else can be said of Social Credit, the history of its supporters is unmatched in Canadian history.[16]

While Quebec, except for 1958, has been predominantly Liberal since before the turn of the century, it is nevertheless a natural breeding-ground for minor parties which appear for a while and then vanish, or become sublimated and reappear in a somewhat different form.[17] All of them are strongly pro–French-Canadian and (with the possible exception of Mr Caouette's Crédit-istes) nationalist. An outstanding example was the Nationalist party in the early years of this century, which elected a group of members to the House in 1911, joined in a most unnatural alliance with the Conservatives, and was rewarded with three ministers in the cabinet; all three were soon departed, at least two of them to patronage appointments. The Union Nationale party in Quebec has often been considered to be linked with the Conservatives, chiefly because it became the provincial Conservative party, though not in name; actually it owes its origins to both Liberals and Conservatives, and federal representatives of both parties appear to have had little difficulty in co-operating with it on occasion; it has remained a provincial party with no acknowledged tie with its larger affiliate. It has stayed out of the federal field, while the Progressive Conservatives at the provincial elections conveniently do not contest any seats. Under Duplessis' leadership it was aggressive, nationalist, intolerant, and devoted to the task of defending French Catholic Canada against the machinations of her enemies in the religious, economic, and political fields; Duplessis' successors have been more moderate, possibly as the result of having been relegated to the opposition for six years in 1960 after sixteen years in power, but more likely because of revelations of wide-spread scandals; the party's current leader, Jean-Jacques Bertrand, was obliged to continue a strong pro-Quebec though anti-separatist line, under considerable pressure from a genuinely separatist party under the leadership of René Léves-que. That group, Le Parti québécois, was formed after Mr Lévesque had first tried to turn the provincial Liberal party (one of whose cabinet ministers he was) in a separatist direction; when he failed, he left the Liberals and was successful in forming a coalition from a variety of separatist factions. The party has not so far contested a federal constituency, but one of its leading lights, Gilles Grégoire, left the Social Credit party in the House of Commons to sit as an independent separatist.[18] The reforming zeal of the provincial

16/The recent story of the Social Credit party is succinctly described in Saywell, *Canadian Annual Review for 1960*, and subsequent years.

17/In the 1944 Quebec election the following parties participated: Liberal, Union Nationale, Bloc Populaire, CCF, Labour-Progressive, Canadian, Cardinist, Union des Electeurs. The first four polled 39, 36, 15, and 3 per cent of the total vote, in that order. H. F. Quinn, "Parties and Politics in Quebec," *Canadian Forum*, May 1944.

18/See Saywell, *Canadian Annual Review for 1967*, pp. 63–70 and 123–5; *ibid.*, 1968, pp. 89–90, 94–6; René Lévesque, *An Option for Québec* (Toronto, 1968); Pierre Laporte, *The True Face of Duplessis* (Montreal, 1960).

Liberal party in Quebec after 1960, it should be added, almost qualified it as yet another third party for the province, but its very zeal helped lead to the disarray into which it subsequently fell, before making a sensational comeback in 1970.

The Co-operative Commonwealth Federation was formed in 1932 by members of earlier movements and a section of the old United Farmer (Progressive) organization, who believed that their political interests might be pooled to their mutual advantage.[19] Later the party was able to make a more general appeal to members of all occupations and to record substantial political progress in several parts of the Dominion. It held office in Saskatchewan from 1944 to 1964, has been the official opposition in several other provinces, and always had an active aggressive group in the House of Commons. In 1961 the CCF was merged, with the help of organized labour, into the New Democratic Party (NDP), in an attempt to base the party more broadly on a farmer-labour foundation. The NDP's debut has undoubtedly been successful, including the election of over twenty members in the Dominion elections of 1965 and 1968, and in 1969 the party won a close provincial election in Manitoba under the leadership of Mr Ed Schreyer. The party's appeal generally, and particularly at the federal level, has so far been to the urban and suburban elector.

The NDP's policies constitute a modified and more conservative version of the CCF, which itself watered down its original programme in a reappraisal in 1956. The CCF was born of the depression, and its first manifesto contemplated sweeping economic changes, socialistic in nature. Its purpose was stated in the Regina Manifesto of 1933:

We aim to replace the present capitalist system, with its inherent injustice and inhumanity, by a social order from which the domination and exploitation of one class by another will be eliminated, in which economic planning will supersede unregulated private enterprise and competition, and in which genuine democratic self-government, based upon economic equality, will be possible ... This social and economic transformation can be brought about by political action, through the election of a government inspired by the ideal of a Co-operative Commonwealth and supported by a majority of the people. We do not believe in change by violence. We consider that both the old parties in Canada are the instruments of capitalist interests and cannot serve as agents of social reconstruction, and that whatever the superficial differences between them, they are bound to carry on government in accordance with the dictates of the big business interests who finance them. The C.C.F. aims at political power in order to put an end to this

19/D. Lewis and F. R. Scott, *Make This Your Canada* (Toronto, 1943), pp. 117–19. See also Dean McHenry, *The Third Force in Canada* (Berkeley, 1950); Kenneth McNaught, *A Prophet in Politics: A Biography of J. S. Woodsworth* (Toronto, 1959); Stanley Knowles, *The New Party* (Toronto, 1961); Leo Zakuta, *A Protest Movement Becalmed* (Toronto, 1964); S. M. Lipset, *Agrarian Socialism* (Anchor ed., New York, 1968); Walter D. Young, *The Anatomy of a Party: The National CCF* (Toronto, 1969). Norman Ward and Duff Spafford, eds., *Politics in Saskatchewan* (Toronto, 1968). Works cited in previous footnotes include numerous references to all parties.

capitalist domination of our political life. It is a democratic movement, a federation of farmer, labour, and socialist organizations, financed by its own members and seeking to achieve its ends solely by constitutional methods.

More explicitly the CCF proposed, as part of the planned economic order, the socialization of all financial agencies, transportation, communications, and public utilities generally; a national labour code; social insurance covering old age, illness, accident, and unemployment; freedom of association; socialized health services; crop insurance; removal of the burden of the tariff from the operations of agriculture; parity prices; encouragement of co-operative institutions; amendment of the British North America Act to give the dominion Parliament sufficient powers to carry out measures which are national in scope; and the abolition of the Senate. Some of the ideas underlying some of these proposals have been adopted by the Liberals and Conservatives, and some of the proposals have thus been implemented, at least in part. Others have been modified by the CCF and its successor, the NDP. The party's influence on the policies of the older parties has been considerable, but it is clear that the influence has not been so great as to lead the electorate to conclude that there is no further need for the NDP. The elections since the party's birth suggest the contrary, since the NDP has in three successive elections outpolled the CCF's best showing.

This brief sketch of third parties would not be complete without at least a mention of several more. The Communist party elected one member of Parliament in 1945; his parliamentary career was somewhat abruptly terminated in 1946, when he was convicted of espionage. The Bloc Populaire, a dissident nationalistic group from Quebec, returned two members in 1945. In 1935 the Reconstruction party, an offshoot of the Conservatives, set a record by polling 384,000 votes and electing but one member. (Social Credit in the same election, with less than half as many votes, secured seventeen.) At various times members calling themselves Labour, Liberal Progressive, United Farmers of Ontario–Labour, and Unity have appeared in the House of Commons, without starting any movement towards yet another party.

PARTY DISTINCTIONS

Although both older parties had by the opening years of this century become genuinely national organizations, it would be erroneous to assume that party conflicts from that time on became pitched battles between opposing forces, between those who fought bravely for one set of principles and those who fought no less courageously for principles of an entirely different kind. The parties have, it is true, always disagreed; but they have not always fought their engagements on purely national issues, and it has been by no means uncommon to have the fates of Dominion governments decided by a series of local skirmishes which have borne little real relationship to each other. Nor, when wider and more fundamental questions have been at stake, have the two parties always maintained a consistent attitude to them; and it is rarely possible to examine the course pursued by either party and from that deduce any one philosophy or set of ideas which has been steadily pursued throughout the years.[20] The reasons for this are not hard to find: each party, whatever its point of departure, was always aiming at the same target, enough properly distributed votes to win a majority of seats in the House of Commons. Thus each at the appropriate time has endeavoured to present itself as the party of national unity, the party of national growth, the party with the great national leader, and so forth. "If the successful Canadian party is sometimes the party with the national policy and usually the party which reconciles differences, it is also at times the party which is distinguished chiefly by the personality of its leader."[21] The history of the more successful third parties in recent decades suggests that they are operating on branch lines of the same national system: from zealous and almost evangelical beginnings, both the NDP and Social Credit parties, in seeking to broaden the basis of their appeal to the electorate, have steadily diluted the doctrinaire programmes with which each began, until on an increasing number of points they too become less distinct from recognizable wings of their main rivals. As they do so, of course, they run the risk of failing to satisfy elements within their own ranks; the 1969 convention of the NDP, for example, was marked by a sharp confrontation between the left wing and the "establishment," which the latter won at least temporarily.

Fundamentally all the major parties in Canada do have many common principles, quite apart from their common goal. With variations (some of them very wide) within each party, all of them that are not separatist accept the federal system, the parliamentary system, the party system, the monarchy, the basic freedoms, the necessity for broad welfare programmes, and the desirability of holding off political absorption by the United States (which has so far shown no inclination towards absorbing Canada in any case). All recognize the need for policies which support the Canadian economy, which raise the national standards in education, or promote what is loosely called culture. Where the parties mainly differ is in the emphasis which they place on one or more of the foregoing (and other) points at various times, and on the proper devices to be used to attain the desired ends; on these bases they can be classified from right to left, but only within (by European standards) a narrow spectrum. Recent research has established that the parties vary also in the nature of their internal organization, of their financial support, the economic and social characteristics of their supporters, and the motivations of their workers.[22] Yet another major difference of long duration rests on the remark-

20/A. Brady, *Canada* (Toronto, 1932), pp. 83–7.
21/J. M. Beck and D. J. Dooley, "Party Images in Canada," *Queen's Quarterly*, LXVII (1960), p. 442.
22/See works cited in previous footnotes in this chapter.

able success of the Liberals in attracting civil servants and other administratively minded people into their highest ranks, to the point where "it would
appear to be established that one excellent way of ensuring that one will not
rise to the top of the Liberal party is to start at the bottom."[23]

Historically, it is not at all difficult to find genuine differences between the
older parties; nor, today, between the older parties and the younger. The
Liberals have been traditionally free traders and therefore in favour of a low
tariff, though they maintained an unmistakably protectionist tariff after coming
into office in 1896; the Conservatives were for high tariffs, suitably modified
to placate those parts of Canada which favoured low tariffs. Similarly, both
older parties have vied in supporting the imperial connection while working
towards greater national autonomy, and in variously supporting and opposing
stronger centralized powers for the Dominion as against greater (or less)
provincial autonomy. On public ownership, welfare legislation, conscription,
and indeed almost any controversial subject the older parties can be found
to be divided at least sometimes, though over time neither will be found to
have prized consistency as highly as campaign promises.[24] How far the historical differences between the Liberals and Conservatives have survived into
the 1970s is impossible to determine with precision: the Liberals, for example,
are often accused by Conservatives of being something less than devoted to
the monarchy, and with considerable justice; but it is noteworthy that it is
usually older Conservatives who make these charges, while something remarkably like republicanism has begun to appear at Conservative meetings.[25]

It does no great injustice to the newer parties to suggest that they too, with
some reservations made necessary by both their youthful ebullience and their
inexperience in holding power at Ottawa, fit into this same general pattern.
Both the CCF and Social Credit parties, when young, differed sharply from all
others; both, as they aged, resembled other parties increasingly – partly, of
course, because the other parties tried in some ways to resemble *them*.
Interestingly enough, the holding of power (and conversely the lack of it) can
itself generate party distinctions. Professor John Meisel, in an illuminating
article, has suggested:

A party long in power (and, therefore, increasingly tempted to delusions of
infallibility) apparently comes more and more to think exclusively in national

23/Norman Ward, "The Liberals in Convention" in Thorburn, *Party Politics in
Canada*, p. 96. See also John Meisel, "Recent Changes in Canadian Parties," in
ibid., p. 38.

24/There is a growing literature on differences between the parties, but a great deal
of work clearly remains. See Peter Newman, "How to Tell the Grits from the Tories,"
Maclean's, May 5, 1962; Zakuta, *A Protest Movement Becalmed*, especially pp. 141–52;
J. R. Mallory, "The Structure of Canadian Politics," and Meisel, "Recent Changes in
Canadian Parties" in Thorburn, *Party Politics in Canada*. Again, works cited in
previous footnotes contain a wealth of relevant material.

25/See, for example, "Tories to Retain Pledge to Crown as Loyalists Win," *Globe
and Mail*, March 12, 1969.

terms, particularly if most of the speculation and planning is done not by the party as such, but by Ottawa-based and Ottawa-minded ministers assisted by Ottawa-based and Ottawa-minded civil servants. When the regional interests ultimately come to find the national emphasis no longer tolerable, when they find the national government too intransigent, they turn to a party seemingly more receptive to provincial and regional pressure.[26]

One of the points on which all parties are identical is the insistence of each that it is different from all its rivals. Paradoxically, in that too they are correct. The Social Credit party was clearly in most issues to the right of the others, and the NDP is as clearly to the left; Liberals and Conservatives are demonstrably straddling the same centre, but always offering the electorate different leaders, and different formations of regional support. Regional support is, indeed, one of the major distinctions to be found among the parties, a fact which can be convincingly illustrated by reference to the varying fortunes of the Liberals and Conservatives in Quebec. In the days of Macdonald Quebec was almost invariably Conservative; but it transferred its allegiance in 1891 and since that time has only once failed to send a majority, and frequently an overwhelming majority, of Liberal members to the House of Commons. This may be attributed historically to the greater Liberal sympathy with provincial rights, in part to the leadership of Sir Wilfrid Laurier, Louis St Laurent, and Pierre Elliott Trudeau, and especially, in recent years, to the wider tolerance and sympathy which the Liberals elsewhere in the Dominion have shown to French-Canadian ideas and ambitions even when they did not agree with them. This willingness to allow differences of opinion and to make substantial concessions and alterations in policy in order to obtain a greater measure of agreement had far-reaching consequences in the conscription issue, which in both world wars set the Conservatives against Quebec with disastrous effects on national unity and on the Conservative party. Thus in the four general elections from 1917 to 1926 the Conservatives carried a total of only 11 seats in Quebec out of a potential 260; in the five general elections from 1935 to 1953 the Conservatives carried in Quebec only 12 out of a potential 343 – making a grand total of 23 out of 603, or less than 4 per cent. In the intervening election of 1930 they carried 24 seats and also, incidentally, attained office. In 1957, while winning office, the Conservatives carried only 9 of Quebec's 75 seats, but carried 50 in 1958; in 1962 the party's quota dropped to 14, while the Liberals took 35 and Social Credit 26; since 1962 the Conservatives' Quebec holdings have dropped to 8, and now 4, seats. While the Conservative party has to some degree made a virtue of necessity and for many years tried with some success to turn a weakness into a source of strength by denouncing as excessive the Liberal concessions to Quebec, the

26/"The Formulation of Liberal and Conservative Programmes in the 1957 Canadian General Election," *Canadian Journal of Economics and Political Science*, XXVI, no. 4 (Nov. 1960), p. 573. See also Cairns, "The Electoral System and the Party System in Canada."

awkward fact remains that without some substantial Quebec support it is close to impossible for a party in Canada to obtain office. It is, of course, obvious that a majority in the Commons without any Quebec members is mathematically possible, but the mathematics of politics is not a matter of simple addition: a party that has little appeal in Quebec is unlikely to be able to attract enough support elsewhere to win a majority in the House of Commons. In its endeavours to widen the base of its appeal, the Conservative party has chosen leaders from widely-scattered provinces, while all the Liberal leaders, without exception, have been from Ontario and Quebec.

In a related though sometimes less obvious way the regional basis of their support provides continuing distinctions between the other parties. Prior to 1962 the bulk of the Social Credit members came from Alberta, and those representing the CCF also came predominantly from the west, with particular emphasis on Saskatchewan. The elections of 1962 and after, however, produced groups of parties whose geographical sources seemed to defy all the accepted regional distinctions: 1962, for example, produced a Conservative party which swept the prairies and took a majority of Maritime seats; a Liberal party which drew four-fifths of its support from central Canada and held only two prairie seats; a Social Credit group of twenty-six Québecois, two Albertans, and two British Columbians; and a New Democratic party with no members from the only province where it held power, Saskatchewan, but nineteen urban representatives scattered across the country. A major realignment of party support, not yet firmly established, would seem to be under way, though there can be no doubt of the urban appeal of the Liberal and New Democratic parties.

PARTY COMPROMISES

The foregoing suggests what is probably the primary political generalization about Canadian parties, that no party can go very far unless it derives support from two or more regional areas in the Dominion.[27] and this leads to the further consequence that a national party must take as its primary purpose the reconciliation of the widely scattered aims and interests of a number of these areas. It is chiefly for this reason that the party leaders have been compelled to modify their principles and their policies, to favour the neutral shades rather than the highly satisfying – but politically suicidal – brighter colours. It is no accident that the three prime ministers with by far the longest terms in office – Macdonald, Laurier, and King – possessed to an extraordinary degree

27/See H. McD. Clokie, *Canadian Government and Politics* (2nd ed., Toronto, 1945), pp. 79–90. These areas are broadly the Atlantic provinces, Quebec, Ontario, the Prairie provinces, and British Columbia.

the ability to compromise and to bring together people possessing divergent interests and beliefs.

The differences within the parties are thus frequently more acute than between the parties themselves; and each party, if it is to command anything approaching general support from its members, must work out some kind of consensus within its own ranks. Extremes must be made to accept something far short of what they consider the ideal; the prairies must make concessions to Ontario, Ontario to Quebec, free traders to protectionists, farmers to factory workers, and so on across the Dominion. The inevitable result is that the most successful parties tend to be parties of the centre, swinging gently to right or left, differing about the means, but not the ends, of bilingualism, with a slight urge towards centralization or back towards provincial rights, the pendulum never getting far beyond the point of stable equilibrium.

Political parties in the United States exhibit similar tendencies and for substantially the same reasons. The Republican and Democratic parties

are not in any real sense political parties at all. They do not bring into union people of common fundamental beliefs or philosophies. On the contrary, they attempt to unite elements of the population that are often bitterly antagonistic in their political, social and religious views of life ... They are in point of fact merely loose federations of state and sectional parties ... Small wonder, then, that the two great national parties, attempting as they do to herd together a heterogeneous mixture of irreconcilables, must trim and equivocate on issues and have difficulty in developing true national leadership. Platforms and candidates must be all things to all men, which means very nearly that they must be nothing to anybody.[28]

It is for this reason that the platforms of the older parties particularly tend to be such unsatisfactory documents; for they must always represent the highest common factor in a series of widely divergent terms, and that is apt to be a very small number indeed. The comparative insignificance of this general accord, however, cannot be widely advertised, and inasmuch as there is always a large fringe of voters who might not agree with even this modest statement, the party platform falls back on vague generalizations and ambiguous terms. Platitudes are wrapped up in an elaborate coating of words and symbols in the hope that few voters will attempt to pick them apart and so come to realize to what a small extent the party is committed to definite action. Everyone wants peace, control of pollution, wise measures of social reform, sound immigration policies, scientific conservation of natural resources, improved educational facilities, an adequate system of national defence, measures which will stimulate international trade and widen the markets for Canadian goods; and the parties will promise these and other so-called policies freely. In recent years

28/H. L. McBain, New York Times, June 12, 1932. See Gad Horowitz, "Conservatism, Liberalism, and Socialism in Canada: An Interpretation" Canadian Journal of Economics and Political Science, XXII, no. 2 (May 1966), pp. 143–71.

the use of opinion polls by the parties has led not only to a narrowing of the range of appeals which the parties make to the electorate, but also to a greater similarity in the devices and techniques used to present the appeals. Possibly for this reason Mr Trudeau, conducting his first campaign as prime minister in 1968, broke new ground by making almost no promises.[29]

Another way of widening the appeal is to include in the platform a number of paragraphs, each of which refers to a special area of interest, in the hope that almost everyone will find something to his liking which will catch his eye and perhaps his vote. Thus the platforms have contained paragraphs on labour relations and the St Lawrence Waterway (for the benefit of Ontario and Quebec); on the fisheries, the use of Canadian ports, and Maritime rights (for British Columbia and the Atlantic provinces); on the Hudson Bay railway, freight rates on grain, wheat prices, and the Peace River district (for western Canada); and on veterans' affairs and rehabilitation (to gain the support of the veterans).[30] The absence of sharply defined principles, the softening of those which do exist, and the general attempt to emphasize sectional appeals are apt to produce platforms which bear a close resemblance to one another or, at most, vary only in the matter of emphasis, a not unnatural tendency in view of party performances. If the platforms are drawn up for provincial elections, where the distinction between the parties is often nothing more than a choice between competing sets of persons or between the "ins" and "outs," the differences frequently become so slight as to be farcical.

Professor Hugh Thorburn has written of New Brunswick politics:

For each provincial election both parties draw up platforms. These are remarkable more for their similarities than their differences. For example, in 1952 both parties presented fifteen-point platforms to the electorate. The following points were common to both platforms: industrial development, electric power development, aid to agriculture, greater forestry, mining and fishing development, good roads, promotion of the tourist industry, securing financial assistance from the federal government, a health plan, aid to education, improved labour legislation. The Liberals were exclusive in advocating co-operation with the municipalities, a housing programme, aid for the disabled, penal reform, and a provincial library. The Conservative points of uniqueness were: land settlement, good government, and a promise to try to do away with the 4 per cent sales tax. Obviously, no philosophic difference between the parties can be found by examining these election platforms, and they are typical – merely lists of "bright ideas" that the party hopes will appeal to the public. It is not unusual to find an item (expressed in different words) appearing on four election platforms of the same party in a row. The fact that the party was in power throughout the entire period and might presumably have enacted the required legislation during this time does not seem to occur to those who draw up the platform.[31]

29/See J. M. Beck, *Pendulum of Power* (Toronto, 1968), p. 403; Saywell, *Canadian Annual Review for 1968*, pp. 29–70.

30/Party platforms are collected in D. Owen Carrigan, *Canadian Party Platforms, 1867–1968* (Toronto, 1968).

31/Hugh G. Thorburn, *Politics in New Brunswick* (Toronto, 1961), p. 107.

The newer parties show considerably less inclination to compromise than their more successful rivals, with the CCF and its successor, the New Democratic Party, on the whole showing the greatest rigidity thus far. Unlike the other parties, which are prepared to accept almost anybody as supporter, candidate, or contributor, the NDP continues to have the most formal constitution, the most clear-cut platform, and the strictest requirements for membership and candidacy. But as has been suggested, both the NDP and Social Credit have in recent years shown unmistakable signs of accommodating their campaign utterances to the exigencies of the national political scene; the broader the appeal, in short, the shallower the platform is bound to become.

None of the third parties at the national level has yet had a genuine opportunity to reveal their capabilities in regard to the opportunism at which their older rivals have become so adept. That opportunism, firmly embedded in the Canadian party situation, tends to minimize the importance of the platform and emphasize the importance of the party leaders, who are the ones chiefly responsible for making the adjustments and compromises which are necessary for retaining support. "Our platform is our leader, and our leader is our platform" is sometimes openly avowed, and it is a maxim that is almost always accepted in practice. It follows, therefore, that the leader is the master of the platform, and tends to accept it as a general indication of the way in which the party would like him to move when and if he finds it desirable to do so.[32] And "no man in Canada," Sir John Willison once observed of the older political parties, "has been more inconsistent than the man who has faithfully followed either party for a generation." Both Liberal and Conservative parties have in recent years been experimenting with methods of enlarging the rôles of both their parliamentary caucuses and their extra-parliamentary wings in the formation of policy; it will be interesting to discover how, if at all, Sir John Willison's observation may have to be modified.

32/*Infra*, pp. 488–92.

22 Party organization

A POLITICAL PARTY, however lofty its principles, is as sounding brass unless it can persuade an appreciable number of electors to support it; and hence the election of candidates to office becomes a matter of primary concern, equal and frequently superior in importance to the principles themselves. To succeed in an election on even a small scale demands organization; indeed, the entire effective life of a party as such is closely identified with organization. To keep the party ideas and principles attuned to public opinion; to persuade the voters to seek the realization of their aims through one party rather than another; to stimulate interest; to systematize and consolidate effort before, during, and after an election; to bring the views of the party members to the attention of the parliamentary representatives; to perpetuate and give continuity to endeavour; to enable the voters through the enunciation of common purposes and the selection of representative candidates to become effective participants in one cause – all these aims can be achieved or at least aided by party organization, and the form which the organization will take will be determined in large measure by the zeal with which the members of a particular party desire them.

A party organization in Canada as elsewhere is essentially an empirical device for producing concrete political results, and one of its most obvious characteristics must therefore be its easy adaptability to circumstances. The organization may vary from party to party, although even more striking differences will sometimes be found between one province and another and between rural and urban constituencies within the same province; in Canada, it must be admitted, little is known of party organization in some areas, particularly in Quebec. Constitutions which outline standard forms are very common in the Canadian parties; but they are in many instances suggestive rather than mandatory, and a great deal of local autonomy is permitted and even encouraged, particularly in the older parties. But even in the others, interference from provincial or Dominion headquarters in the activities of the party in the individual constituencies is almost invariably resented by the latter, and even on those occasions when the local organization is torn in internal struggles, the higher party authorities intervene reluctantly and with circumspection. Senior organizations, of course, often assist actively in bringing out suitable candidates at the local level, but these are not imposed on the local organizations, and efforts are made to avoid the appearance of interference. It must be emphasized also that the apparent constitutional structure of a party may be at least in part a façade: no party has been more constitutionally minded than was the old Co-operative Commonwealth Federation but even it, as Professor Zakuta has shown, had an "unofficial leadership" which "was more homogeneous, more spontaneously chosen and, on the whole, more influential than the official set ... Like similar groups in most organizations, this inner circle had neither an official existence nor a formal structure."[1] Parts of the financial organization of most parties, as the Committee on Election Expenses discovered, are commonly so unofficial as to be difficult to find.[2]

All Canadian parties, no matter what form their organization and practices may take, continually pride themselves on their complete identification with democratic procedures, although there is little agreement on what party democracy really involves. Thus the Toronto *Globe* in 1893, in an editorial preceding the first national convention held in Canada, wrote as follows:

The fundamental idea of a freely chosen party convention is the application of the principle of popular government to party institutions. A country may possess all the forms of free government and law-making, and yet the benefit of these will be practically withheld from those who are bound by allegiance to a party despotically governed. A party convention such as that to be held at Ottawa recognizes the right of every member of the party to a voice in the making of its policy, and the means to be adopted to carry it out. As the convention cannot include every member of the party, it is important that it shall be as large as is convenient, and shall be freely chosen and thoroughly representative of the great body of Liberals. Those conditions, we believe, will be fulfilled. In order to be truly popular and democratic it is necessary that the discussion shall be free, and that every delegate shall have a real voice and a real share in the proceedings. We have no fear of this great convention being conducted in any other way. Finally, the publicity of the proceedings enables those who cannot take part to be made fully acquainted not only with the decisions of the convention, but with the discussion leading up to them. There have been unmistakable signs of an awakened interest in public affairs, and we expect that the reports of the convention will be eagerly read and freely commented on.[3]

Yet this convention did nothing more than frame a platform and help its members "go home with their political faith strengthened and their political zeal quickened."[4] It passed, it is true, a resolution of confidence in the leadership of Wilfrid Laurier, but there was no suggestion that it should elect a leader or even confirm Laurier in his position. This function of the party convention has

---

1/Zakuta, *A Protest Movement Becalmed*, pp. 25–6.
2/*Report of the Committee on Election Expenses*, both vols., passim.
3/Toronto *Globe*, May 9, 1893.
4/Oliver Mowat, *Proceedings, Dominion Liberal Convention* (1893), p. 14.

been of later growth: it became fairly common in the provincial field during the opening years of this century, but did not appear in national politics until 1919.

Until recent years, these and other signs of the influence of the party rank and file or the party representative bodies were always sporadic and uncertain in the two older parties, although lip-service was constantly paid to the inherent virtues of so-called democratic control. In actual practice, the extent to which the leaders and their chief assistants felt the need for refreshment or rededication at the source of all party power depended upon the fortunes of the moment. Success at the polls and the control of a government, for example, were usually taken as a sufficient justification and authorization for continued leadership, even although the convention from which the power had been derived and which had laid down a programme was many years removed. The continued success of Mackenzie King thus led the Liberals to ignore the national convention and its legendary prestige and authority for twenty-nine years; while the Conservatives, with little love for conventions but less luck in elections, had no less than three conventions during that period. Under such circumstances, protestations of a belief in the active participation of all members in party affairs began to sound a trifle thin. It is but fair to add, however, that few of the party supporters themselves felt the need to assert their rights in the midst of plenty. A winning team is a good team; and it would be considered sheer foolhardiness to risk a new captain or even new instructions which might quite conceivably break the happy succession of victories. In contrast to this, the organization and practices of the New Democratic party are devoted to the maintenance of a close identification of the party rank and file with its leaders. In recent years other parties have been holding national meetings fairly regularly; in 1960, for example, the Liberals held their first Study Conference on National Problems, and in 1961 their first national convention since 1893 that was not called to select a party leader; meetings or conventions of the national associations of both Liberal and Progressive Conservative parties are now required every two years by their constitutions, and these are frequently supplemented by irregular "thinkers' conferences," at which the parties' long-range aims are discussed.

Through all forms of Canadian party organization runs a current of influences from the United States, clear and persistent, yet not strong enough to be called imitation. There can be no doubt, for example, that much of the belief that conventions should be held and that they should both state a platform and choose a leader, is derived from American examples; and a great part of the procedure at these conventions has also been copied from the same source, although it has been toned down in many respects by a self-consciousness which occasionally asserts itself and partially succeeds in restraining the more phlegmatic Canadian from unseemly exhibitionism. There are other resemblances, both superficial and profound. But differences are also common. Delegates at

Canadian leadership conventions, for example, vote as individuals, and not in provincial blocs. In the United States the frequency and regularity of elections, the enormous number of elective offices, and the common practice of fighting municipal contests on standard party lines, tend to augment the importance of all party machinery to an extent unknown in Canada. Canadian party activity is not nearly as formal or as sustained: there are long gaps between elections; and when the test comes, it is frequently unheralded, and hence must be met by quick improvisation without the benefit of a prolonged preparation which can gradually lead up to an electoral climax on a certain day specified in the constitution. The direct primary has thus made no impression on Canadians. The convention system has never been sufficiently important or corrupt in Canada to create a need for the direct primary as a necessary substitute, nor does the government readily lend itself to the primary device. It could with difficulty be incorporated into a scheme based on uncertain election days; and the one elective office to be filled for each constituency would make a primary an extremely expensive instrument for the achievement of so modest an end as the nomination of one candidate from each party.

Attention has already been drawn to the diversity in the organization and practices of Canadian political parties. The two older parties, however, have so many points in common that they may, so far as these matters are concerned, be conveniently grouped together. The NDP, while using machinery of a similar kind, is run in a different spirit from its older rivals, and it indulges in a kind of ultra-democracy or egalitarianism which is not unusual in parties with radical tendencies. The following description will therefore discuss first the organization and practices of the Liberal and Progressive Conservatve parties, and then indicate the chief points of difference with those found in the NDP. The Social Credit party, it may be added, resembles the older parties more than it does the NDP.

In attempting to follow this programme, however, a further problem arises in dealing with the organization in the provinces, for here locality, custom, and language have tended to introduce variations. Parties in Quebec, for example (except in Montreal and a few other districts), have been more loosely organized than elsewhere, and local and personal influences, in the orthodox French-Canadian tradition, seem to play a much larger part in determining the form of party action in a given area. On the other hand, it is generally true that forms of organization within a particular party will bear a family resemblance from province to province, though even within one province there may be considerable differences within a single party; "this general description," Professor Thorburn writes of his own analysis of party organization in New Brunswick, "applies best to ten of the fifteen counties. The other five differ ..."[5] It is clearly impossible within the scope of one chapter to hope to deal with the forms of organization of even two parties operating within the federal area and in ten

5/Thorburn, *Politics in New Brunswick*, p. 86.

separate provinces as well. A further obstacle is the absence of sufficient information on the subject. Party organization in Canada is no longer the virgin field for study and research that it was until recently; but any general description, to say nothing of analysis and comparison, is still restricted by the limited facts available.[6]

The following pages have thus been confined largely, though not exclusively, to party organization in Ontario, Saskatchewan, and the Dominion. This is fairly typical of that existing elsewhere in Canada, although, speaking very generally, the chosen examples show a more highly developed system than some of the other provinces. Occasional variations in the usual procedures have been indicated from time to time. It should be remembered, of course, that even within the one province no party insists on adherence to a rigid uniformity in such matters. The main objectives are to maintain party harmony and produce the maximum support on election day; and if the party members in one constituency wish to depart somewhat from the normal practice, provincial headquarters will be inclined to regard such idiosyncrasies with a helpful tolerance. Then, too, it must be realized that basically all parties are trying, through their organization, to build substantially the same kind of pyramid: a broadly based system of poll organizations at the bottom, atop which in order are constructed constituency, district or regional, provincial and national associations, culminating in a solitary figure at the apex, the national leader. All democratic parties are, of course, glad to provide copies of their constitutions to interested citizens.

A THE OLDER PARTIES[7]

1 *The poll organization*

It is in a sense misleading to begin a description of party organization with the poll, for the constituency organization is almost everywhere more important. The poll organization, where it exists, is none the less the bottom of the pyramid, the smallest unit in the party organization, and it is built around the individual poll where the votes are cast; its chief and often its only activity is the fighting of an election campaign. Inasmuch as an average constituency will

6/The growing number of studies of elections, political parties, and provincial government is yielding a steady flow of information on party organization, but systematic studies of party organization as such continue to be rare. See Zakuta, *A Protest Movement Becalmed*, especially chap. III; Brian Land, *Eglinton* (Toronto, 1965), especially chap. 2; Meisel, *Papers on the 1962 Election.*

7/Except where otherwise designated, this section refers to organization in Ontario. For a more general description of party organization during a campaign see John Meisel, *The Canadian General Election of 1957* (Toronto, 1962); and see works cited in preceding footnote. I am greatly indebted to Mr Arthur Harnett, executive director of the Ontario Progressive Conservative party, and Mr Jack Heath, assistant to the executive director, Liberal party in Ontario, for letters and material relevant to the next several pages.

have about one hundred and fifty or more polls (a smaller number in the cities, a larger number in rural areas) there will normally be this many party polling sub-divisions or local districts. It is here that the party makes its immediate contact with the voters; here the real work of winning elections is accomplished; here are the rank and file and particularly the non-commissioned officers on whose efforts the final results largely depend. These non-commissioned officers compose the party's committee for the poll, and it includes a handful of the most energetic and helpful workers available, headed by a person known as the poll captain or chairman, who is usually picked by the campaign manager or the candidate. The others may be chosen by a meeting of party members in the polling sub-division, or by a body representing the party in a group of sub-divisions (a township, ward, or smaller area), or they may be informally called together by the captain of the poll, who in turn has been placed there by some higher authority in the party.

One of the chief functions of the poll captain is to maintain an active interested committee. The members of the poll committee are expected to know or to ascertain the political affiliations of all voters in their subdivision; they will check the lists of voters and see that they are revised; they will persuade the party supporters and adherents to go to the poll on election day; they will see that transportation is available to take voters to the poll; they will act as scrutineers at the poll; they will give, in short, whatever assistance the party may require of them within that local area. Some of these workers will be paid by the party a few dollars for their labours on election day; some are paid a little out of public funds because they have been employed as enumerators for the lists of electors. But many serve without immediate remuneration, some for the cause itself, some for the enjoyment of the struggle, some for the sense of importance engendered, some for the more tangible though distant rewards of a rural postmastership, a job in the liquor store, or some other crumb from the patronage table. Parties have often demonstrated that it is possible to run campaigns in particular constituencies relying almost entirely on voluntary unpaid assistants.

Party organization at this lowest level is necessarily irregular and varied, the most disturbing influences being those which flow from the widely different degrees of party support within even a small area, the widely different conditions of city, town, village, and rural district, and, since the war, the extraordinarily rapid growth of, and turnover of population in, the suburban areas. The organization, if it is to function effectively, must be able to adapt itself readily to its environment. This is most evident in the many ways in which the polling sub-divisions will cluster into groups, some quite informal, others regularly organized into a wider association. The purely rural polling area is by force of circumstances cut off from its neighbours, and must do the best it can under its own local officers. If a village has two or three polls, their poll committees will probably merge and the village in effect become the unit. In a small town with eight or ten polls, again the one party executive will supervise the grouped polls and add, perhaps, another seven or eight from the surrounding district. The township in the country and the ward in the city usually become further rallying points; and if circumstances are favourable, they will have their own executives and even permanent associations which administer party affairs at an intermediate level between the poll and the constituency. Similarly, party election officials, usually known as block or district chairmen, will frequently be placed over a number of polls in the city or country respectively, not for the purpose of displacing the poll captains, but of bringing them and their assistants into closer contact with the central constituency organization. The invariable tendency is that as concentration of population mounts, the importance of the individual poll organization diminishes; and the major responsibility will pass from the hands of the poll executive to those of a more widely representative body. The one fact, however, which cannot be over-emphasized, is that party organization at this level knows no arbitrary forms or standards: the successful grouping is that which fits the conditions of the area and the desires of those party members who are most immediately concerned. One generalization that can be safely made is that there are vast differences between rural and urban organizations.

Paid-up memberships are now being sought increasingly by the parties, but annual dues (if any) are small, and smaller in the country than the cities. They are not always essential even so, for while a fee is a formal requirement, party supporters who have paid none may be allowed to serve on committees and in various other capacities. Party orthodoxy is a more stringent requirement than dues, although the primary concern here is to ensure that members have no affiliations with other parties and are generally staunch supporters of the party faith. The fee may be paid to the party organization in either the municipal area or the constituency; but the municipal organization must itself pay an annual levy to the constituency association. Total paid membership varies widely in both older parties. The Conservative party appears to have been more exacting than the Liberal in its insistence on the membership fee, which is one dollar. Each Conservative riding association pays a fee of ten dollars a year to the provincial association, but no affiliation fee is charged for any riding to belong to the Liberal party; some Liberal district associations (see below) do have affiliation fees for ridings.

2   The riding organization

This, as the name indicates, is based on the riding or constituency which elects a member to the legislature. In Ontario the provincial constituencies outnumber the federal 117 to 88 but many are laid out on lines within which the same essential areas are located in corresponding federal and provincial seats. Depending on local circumstances, either the federal or the provincial riding may serve as the basic unit, although the Liberals encourage separate organizations for federal and provincial purposes. The riding association is the key party organization and has many responsibilities, tying in with the higher associations above and overseeing and checking on the poll organization below. Its nominating convention may be the party's most vital representative body; it has the major responsibility for securing the election of its nominees; its vigilance is in large measure essential to secure activity in the polling sub-division, especially in such formal matters as the revision of voters' lists (though the primary responsibility for the accuracy of voters' lists rests with the official returning officer); it transmits opinions, suggestions, and complaints from the party members to the elected representative in Parliament or in the Legislative Assembly, though this function is being superseded in part by the use of private opinion polls. The riding organizations can be active and busy; they can also, if local interest flags for any reason, quickly become moribund. The high mobility of urban and suburban dwellers has faced both poll and riding associations in recent years with serious new problems, and it is not unusual now at party meetings to hear statements like the following, both made at the 1969 annual meeting of the Ontario Progressive Conservative Association: "Some of the local associations are dying of dry rot because they are filled with do-nothings." "Our riding associations are in jeopardy of becoming irrelevant along with the church and the family."[8]

Members may join the riding association directly or indirectly through their local organizations; the Liberals permit a person to join through the provincial party if refused by the riding, which rarely happens. The association is fairly formal in its organization: the Liberal, for example, has its own president, past president, vice-presidents (sometimes called directors), secretary, and treasurer, and a few have honorary officers (notably the federal and provincial party leaders, ex-members of Parliament, etc.) elected at the annual meeting. The executive is composed of the officers, possibly the Liberal candidates in the riding at the last federal and provincial elections in an *ex officio* capacity, and a generous representation from various local groups, including municipal associations (if any) and even at times the polling sub-divisions. (The role of municipal associations has changed markedly in the recent history of the Liberal party, for better communications have made the riding the basic unit everywhere; few municipal associations remain outside the Toronto area, and there they are separate from the riding associations and have their own purpose: the election of Liberals to municipal offices.) The exact personnel of this executive body will depend, however, upon the particular constituency, and especially upon the distribution of rural areas, villages, towns, and cities; different local circumstances once more produce somewhat different solutions. Provisions in the constitution of the riding association ensure that there shall be a minimum number of women and young people as party office-holders.

The riding association as a body makes itself felt chiefly through its general

8/*Globe and Mail* and *Toronto Daily Star*, Dec. 6, 1969.

meetings, which may be special or regular. In the Liberal party, special meetings include annual meetings and nominating conventions at which the party's federal or provincial candidate is chosen; regular meetings comprise any other. The annual or nomination meeting of the riding association may be composed of delegates from all the polling sub-divisions; in the case of the Liberals, it includes all party members in the riding who choose to attend, or else any nomination made is invalidated. Interest in its proceedings is rarely great; two or three hundred is considered to be an excellent attendance. Its main functions are the election of officers (and in a healthy riding all positions are often contested); the discussion of party finances and fund-raising, and the candidate's or member's report; and hearing a guest speaker. Sometimes the meeting is itself a fund-raising activity preceded or followed by a dinner or dance. Riding meetings can be stimulating; they can be, and historically were, insipid affairs, for the practice of passing resolutions of such stirring character as those expressing loyalty to the Queen, welcome to a new governor general, admiration for federal and party leadership, and approval of the party's representative in Parliament was not necessarily conducive to a wild elation; the Liberals have abandoned such resolutions. In recent years party meetings generally seem to have become livelier. Occasionally a meeting, greatly daring, may place on record its opinion on a special measure or policy, but this is uncommon. The opportunity afforded by the annual meeting may on rare occasions be utilized for the ventilation of grievances on such matters as the disposition of patronage (if any), the rejection of proposed names for membership, the control of the party by a clique, the use of dictatorial methods in party business; generally, however, since party associations are continually seeking active members, they try to avoid activities which will discourage those they have. Adversity, none the less, can cause trouble. Liberals in the Toronto area, for example, following a very poor showing in both Dominion and provincial elections, were split in 1945-6 into two separate factions, and the dispute proceeded with such vigour that each faction had its own association in each of the Toronto ridings.[9] Today, by contrast, the highly successful Toronto and District Liberal Association is strong and united.

The normal method of nominating Liberal candidates in Ontario is by a nominating convention; and this is used even in those constituencies where the sitting member is a member of the party and it is generally anticipated that he will again receive the nomination. The convention, however, is regarded as the source of party approval and the member must therefore submit his record and his candidacy to it for vindication. The Progressive Conservative party in Ontario follows a substantially similar procedure. In one district, the city of Toronto, the Conservative constituency organizations have formed a district

9/The Conservative party in 1937 also encountered criticism and serious rebellion in several of the Toronto ridings, although the dissatisfaction was not carried as far as in the Liberal struggle noted above.

association to which has been delegated the power to administer nominating conventions; the district association may refuse permission to a constituency to hold a convention, and it sets the rules under which conventions in Toronto must be conducted. Elsewhere in the province the nomination of candidates remains generally in the hands of the individual constituency associations, although the Ontario Progressive Conservative Association has a rarely-used final authority over nominations. During the Taschereau regime in Quebec the Liberals (and in this they were followed by Quebec Conservatives) went even further than this, and made the arbitrary rule that if the sitting member were a Liberal, he was to be considered the official candidate without a convention, even although the constituency organization was anxious to have a nominating convention called.[10] A similar automatic renomination of Quebec Liberal candidates occurred in the federal election of 1957.

The nominating convention may be a public gathering where everyone present may participate; or it may be open to all party supporters; or it may be closed to everyone except delegates chosen by the polling sub-divisions. Every constituency association in the Conservative party, for example, has its own constitution, and there are marked differences from riding to riding; the Liberals, by contrast, have almost identical nomination rules across Ontario, and for the federal election of 1968 over seventy conventions permitted only association members to vote, while about fifteen were open to anyone present. The decision on this matter is made by the annual meeting of the riding association or by its executive. If the convention is an open one, the official delegates usually sit and vote by themselves, the remainder of the meeting acting as spectators. If the party is very weak and badly organized and sometimes if it is exceptionally strong, the convention may be genuinely public and everyone may take part. The idea is prevalent in some quarters that a public convention is more "democratic" than a closed one, although the reasons for such a curious belief are difficult to surmise. The obvious dangers of the public convention are that opposing parties may gain control of its proceedings and nominate a poor candidate in order to secure later an easy victory in the election (there appear to be no recent instances of this); or that a special faction, or a single

10/The following statement was issued by the Liberal headquarters after consultation with the premier, L. A. Taschereau:

"The Prime Minister has transmitted to the Liberal organization the request made to him for the holding of a convention in St. Lawrence division. This suggestion has been considered and we have come to the conclusion that the holding of such a convention in this division is neither necessary nor useful.

"Mr. Cohen, who has represented the division for the last eight years, has expressed his willingness to present himself again as our standard-bearer. He has rendered valuable service to the party and to the province and he is, therefore, our official candidate. The Liberal organization, and the Prime Minister, urge all Liberals in the division to rally around Mr. Cohen, to assure his success and therefore that of the party in the coming election so that we keep this seat in the Liberal fold." Montreal *Gazette*, Nov. 5, 1935.

See *ibid.*, Aug. 21, 23, 29, Sept. 6, 24, Nov. 5, 1935; Feb. 7, 1936, for other examples of refusals of Liberal and Conservative conventions in Quebec.

candidate, may pack a convention to secure the nomination. (If all constitutional requirements are met, of course, packing is a legitimate activity.) Conventions in city districts are more vulnerable on these points and they therefore tend to be on the closed type. If the membership of a public or open convention is suspect, so that the nomination may be tainted also, the party executive may risk a possible split and call another convention – this time confined to delegates only – and from it obtain a new nomination.

The usual practice in the Liberal party until recent years was to use the delegate system and make the convention a representative body which reflected with some accuracy the opinion of the party members throughout the constituency. Attempts were made to base this representation on the number of party votes cast in each poll at the most recent federal or provincial election, but these efforts introduced complications and do not appear to have been very successful. The common method was to allow each polling sub-division to be represented by a definite number of delegates, usually three or five, including both men and women. A normal attendance is four or five hundred, although one such convention in Saskatchewan reported 1,675 registered delegates. Nowadays, under the general provision that all qualified members may vote, spectacular conventions appear more likely. In Toronto Davenport in 1968, Liberal membership rose in a few weeks from 150 to 5,445, and "here, as elsewhere, the outcome [that is, the nomination] may have been determined by non-residents and ten-year-olds who, under the rules, could not be debarred from voting."[11] The choice of delegates by the executive is still the usual method followed by the Progressive Conservative party in Ontario for closed conventions, the primary purpose being to ensure a fair apportionment of delegates among the polling sub-divisions. The delegates will almost always be formally certified by the proper authorities and will be compelled to present their credentials before being admitted to the convention floor.

The nominating convention, like the annual meeting of the riding association, formerly felt it necessary to pass resolutions pointing with pride to the achievements of its own party and leaders and viewing with alarm the shocking performances and inefficiency of its opponents. These do no harm and in some obscure way add zest to the occasion. The nominating convention rarely, however, attempts anything more than an occasional plank in a platform, and even this is not apt to receive much discussion or consideration. The chief business of the convention is the selection of the party candidate, and the delegates are apt to become impatient if there are too many preliminaries to the main bout. Liberal conventions commonly nowadays get right down to business.

The delegates will as a rule have a fair idea before the convention meets of what candidates are likely to be considered for the nomination. This is partly

11/Beck, *Pendulum of Power*, p. 401. There were a number of other remarkable riding conventions in 1968.

because the number of suitable or even willing candidates is limited (although the 1968 federal campaign saw a large increase in the number of persons seeking Liberal nominations), and also because the riding executive has appointed a committee to receive names and to sound out the possibilities. There appears to be no suggestion that this device is intended to shut out any objectionable candidates; it is designed rather to ensure that suitable men will have been approached and induced to allow their names to be placed before the convention. Instances are on record where, because there was no preliminary canvas, no candidate could be picked, and a second nominating convention had to be called at a later date. If the sitting member comes from the party, this committee may not be appointed, for the delegates will be strongly inclined to place their confidence in one who has already been a winner. The names considered by the nominating committee become fairly general property before the convention meets, and they have therefore already been considered to some degree by the delegates and in the polling sub-divisions. Some of the delegates may be pledged in advance to vote for a certain candidate, or the combined polls in a town may have met together and agreed to give a united support to the same person. Pledged votes are usually effective for only one ballot, the delegates being free thereafter to cast their votes as they please.

The names of those willing to run may be placed before the convention in a report from the nominating committee or each candidate may have his name presented by a delegate who makes a nominating speech reciting the virtues and claims of his nominee. Names of candidates other than those which have come before the committee may also be submitted by any delegate. (A common practice for years, now rare, was for the names of one or two tried party men of long standing to be placed in nomination as a gesture of appreciation for past labours on behalf of the party. In such cases the nomination is made, bedecked with many complimentary remarks; the convention renders the appropriate applause; the nominee responds and declines the honour in a few gracious words; and the delegates thereupon indicate, even more heartily, their approval of such magnanimous conduct and the careful way in which the party courtesies have been observed by all concerned.) After the nominations are declared closed, the candidates will be given an opportunity to speak. This is the invariable practice in Ontario, although it is interesting to observe that in some parts of Canada even the presence of the candidate at the convention has in the past been considered bad form. In Ontario and some other provinces the candidate would actually injure his cause if he were not present and willing to state his views on the outstanding current issues.

The rules of balloting are simple. The successful candidate must receive a majority (not merely a plurality) of votes cast; and balloting continues until this result is obtained. To expedite matters, where there are more than two candidates running, the lowest is dropped after each ballot, although few conventions are compelled to decide between more than two or three candidates. Once the choice is made, one of the defeated contestants will often, although not always, move that the vote be declared unanimous, and this is ordinarily passed with enthusiasm. Candidates are frequently asked in advance of balloting to give a pledge to accept the decision of the convention as final and to support the successful candidate. The Conservative party, while it has no rule on the subject, is strict in demanding that this practice be observed.

The nomination is followed by a speech from the party's new (or rechosen) champion, who uses the opportunity to establish friendly relations with those on whom he must depend in large measure for his success. In some parts of Canada where the convention is closed to everyone except delegates, the latter will adjourn to a larger hall where the general public also can hear the candidate's address. The candidate will outline at this time the main points which he expects to stress in the coming campaign,[12] and the delegates return to their homes presumably filled with enthusiasm and assured of coming victory.

Riding conventions are extremely jealous of their own powers and independence, and they will not tolerate interference from any quarter, particularly from the higher party circles. Thus a mere intimation to one of the outlying constituencies that the Toronto headquarters wanted a delegate convention has been known to be decisive in influencing its choice for an open one. An attempt many years ago to have the Liberals in one riding refuse to make a nomination because it might create possible friction with the Progressives, was ignored by a rebellious convention. A "saw-off" arranged between Liberal and Conservative headquarters in 1937 whereby the former got Frontenac-Addington, and the latter Dufferin-Simcoe, was denounced by both Liberal and Conservative local party organizations, and one convention at least came very close to repudiating its part of the bargain and nominating a candidate. Other circumstances may also break the usual friendly atmosphere of these gatherings. Irregularities in the initial proceedings, attempted packing of the convention, the use of questionable credentials, undue influences exerted by special groups, and unfair practices of any kind will be actively and vigorously resented and denounced. The great solvent of all difficulties is the overriding desire to do nothing to divide or to weaken the party and thereby console and strengthen the enemy. "It shall be the paramount duty of the officials conducting the convention to follow the 'Golden Rule,' " a standard Conservative constitution stated; then, its high principles being tinged with practical candour, it added, "and thus, avoiding discord, ensure united support for the candidate selected." The Liberals' Ontario constitution shrewdly provides that an officer designated by the provincial party may chair any nomination meeting, and this greatly reduces the possibility of questionable procedures.

12/I attended one constituency convention where the chosen candidate's speech was so ridden with clichés that delegates sitting near me were able to complete many of his sentences before he had finished uttering them. [N.W.]

3 *Intermediate organizations*

(a) *Regional (and district) associations.* In Ontario and in a few large cities in other provinces the number of constituencies within a comparatively small area has made it desirable for the party to interpose another body between the riding and provincial organizations.

The Liberals combine from six to ten federal and provincial ridings into a district association, and the districts are in turn organized in four regions. The Conservative constitution permits up to fifteen districts (named, for example, the Northern District No. 1, the Toronto Central Association, and so on) and the executive council of the provincial association is empowered to recognize additional women's district associations and youth district associations. Each district association has its own organization and executive, holds its own meetings, etc.; each includes a group of constituencies. These district associations relieve the provincial body of much work, co-ordinate party activity in the area, transmit the desires of the provincial and federal associations to the riding associations, and render assistance of a general kind on all party matters. The intervention of the district association in local affairs is rare, but circumstances occasionally make it necessary in order to settle disputes in a particular riding. Such intervention is usually along conciliatory lines, but if necessary the superior body may try to impose disciplinary measures, though their effectiveness will depend on the circumstances in the troubled riding.

The Liberal party also has regional associations occupying approximately the same position and discharging substantially the same functions.

(b) *Young people's associations.* Both Liberals and Conservatives in recent decades have paid particular attention to organizations for young party hopefuls, a class of citizen not only formerly neglected, but even scorned. The Young Liberal Federation, which was integrated into the provincial party in 1969 as a standing committee, for years had an establishment which ran vertically parallel with the ordinary hierarchical organization; Ontario is also one of the regions for the organization of the Canadian University Liberal Federation, an allied but separate body. (The party's national leader is honorary president of both.) The primary purpose of organizing young people, whatever form it takes, is to create a body which will interest the younger members of the party and turn their talents and energy into profitable party channels, while, as a by-product, preparing them for later activity in the parent organization.

The Progressive Conservative party also has youth organizations, as yet not integrated into the main party.

(c) *Women's associations.* The Ontario Liberal Women's Association, now also integrated into the party as a standing committee was an effort to construct a women's organization along the same general lines as that for the young people. It also ran vertically through the province with its own groups in small local areas and ridings and its regional, provincial, and Dominion associations.

The women of the Progressive Conservative party are also organized in a separate women's association; and the purposes and general relationships resemble those described above. For some years prior to 1969 the Conservative women were organized as an advisory committee, which gave them an unwanted status as a somehow inferior body; in 1969 they achieved full constitutional recognition. The constitution of the Ontario Progressive Conservative Association requires that three of twelve vice-presidents must be women.

4 *The provincial organization*

Though generalization is difficult it is probably true that the provincial association, if it is effective at all, is the head of each party organization in Canada. There is, as will be seen presently, a national organization also, which used to be no more than a loose federation of autonomous provincial bodies. The national organization has been growing in importance and is of great significance especially where the provincial party is weak, as a source of both direction and money. Poll, village or town or municipality or ward, riding, region or district, and province – these comprise the foundation of the party building proper, and the Dominion organization forms a tower or superstructure, that looms above it. The party as a Dominion organization commonly has contact with the voter primarily through the province and at other lower levels. It would, of course, be conceivable for the party to keep its federal activities apart from those of the party in the province,[13] but this would necessitate the creation of one party organization at the provincial level and another in the Dominion constituencies, a duplication of effort and a confusion of activity which would be both extravagant in terms of expense and effort and utterly bewildering to the voters. The natural alternative is for the party's organizational activities to be conducted through the existing provincial organization if it is strong enough to carry the load; but this cannot be done without a frank recognition of the primacy of the provincial party in the field. Though patronage is so much less important than it formerly was that party workers now question its existence, the acquiescence by the Dominion interests in provincial leadership in some provinces at least may still be given more readily in that the larger part of petty patronage is in the gift of the province, although the balance is to some degree maintained by the Dominion's control over the bulk of the really good jobs. Mutual interest and self-protection can usually be relied upon to keep the two interests working smoothly together, and such incidents as the King-Hepburn feud of the early 1940s illustrate how disastrous can be the results when the party in the Dominion and the party in the province work at cross purposes.

13/The Liberal party in Alberta was at one time organized in a federal and a provincial association. In 1937 these were united and a new constitution for the Alberta Liberal Association adopted. The Conservatives temporarily disbanded their organization in Alberta in 1947. Some allege that this action was taken because they were discouraged; others, that they wished to give the Social Credit party a clear field with the object of co-operating at a later date.

Such incidents also reveal the degree to which relations between the provincial and the national organizations depend on particular circumstances.

The provincial organization, like its counterpart in the ridings, centres about the association and has three formal methods of expression: the executive bodies, the annual and special meetings, and the convention.

The most active members of the Ontario Progressive Conservative Association, designated "delegate members," include (among others) all party candidates in the last provincial and federal elections (or in some cases the candidate nominated for the next election); the party's senators from Ontario; the association's officers; six officers of the Women's Association; six each from the young people's and students' associations; five each from District Associations, District Women's Associations, and District Young Progressive Conservative Associations; delegates-at-large "nominated by the President and approved by the Executive equal in number to not more than one-half the number of Provincial Ridings"; and seven delegates and three alternates from each riding association. There are also "active members" who formerly paid a $1.00 annual fee, but who since 1969 "pay such fees as may be established from time to time." The association's officers, named the "executive," consist of the party leader, the incumbent and immediate past presidents, twelve vice-presidents, a secretary, a treasurer, and two auditors; all of these are elected, and only delegate members may vote. The executive is supplemented by an executive council which consists of the executive itself, plus the presidents of all the party associations named above.

The objects of the association are also defined in the constitution:

(a) To assist, co-ordinate and, where necessary, to initiate thorough political organization throughout the Province of Ontario.
(b) To provide a forum for the membership of the Party to participate in political discussion and to advise with respect to Party policy.
(c) To call and conduct Provincial Conventions and meetings.
(d) To co-operate with and assist Progressive Conservative Associations in the other Provinces and Territories of Canada and the Progressive Conservative Association of Canada.
(e) To help provide good government for the people of Ontario.

The actual operation of the party during an election campaign is not necessarily directed by the association, but more likely by officials appointed by the leader. The election machinery is therefore double-barrelled: the association is responsible to the party's members, the appointed officials to the leader.[14] But the direction of elections apart, the provincial association is an active and indispensable body. Through its executive it does much of the routine work of elections, is a clearing house for advice and information, helps collect funds, and so

14/Letter from Mr. George Hogan, then secretary of the Progressive Conservative party of Ontario, April 30, 1962.

forth. The Liberal party similarly has a provincial association, with the same concentration of executive authority in relatively few hands. In both parties the ordinary party organization may be all but suspended during a campaign, while the candidate, his campaign manager, and his official agent dominate activities in each constituency.

The provincial association of each party holds an annual meeting, the one regular opportunity for delegates to get together in general session. The primary purposes are the election of officers, the appointment of committees, the hearing of reports and speeches, the passage of laudatory resolutions to be sent to party leaders, and the general stimulation of party enthusiasm and morale, all these commonly being brought to a satisfactory climax by the consumption of a dinner. The meeting is usually well attended. Each party, for example, can muster about seven hundred delegates (to say nothing of possible alternate or substitute delegates) and a host of other members and supporters. A gathering of considerably more than 1,500 is not unusual. Before 1969, the meetings of the women's association and of the young people's association in each party convened as a rule a day or so before the main gathering, and the Conservatives still follow such practices.

Aside from the above general statement, it was until recently difficult to indicate what else the annual meeting is expected to do; for the Liberal and Progressive Conservative parties (unlike the NDP) took a long time to decide this question for themselves. It might be considered a fair supposition, for example, that the annual party meeting would meet annually, but this has not by any means been a uniform practice even in Ontario where the provincial associations are unusually virile. Ontario Liberals, to give a striking instance, during one period did not hold an annual meeting for eleven years, despite repeated demands from many prominent supporters that one should be called. A large group in the party was completely out of sympathy with the provincial cabinet and its critical attitude towards the Ottawa government, and the president of the association (who was a member of the Ontario cabinet) declared he would not call a meeting to allow "a lot of hot-heads to lay about them." Certainly there was no reason to suppose that a meeting would have brought about any reconciliation between the conflicting factions, and inaction was apparently considered the most harmless solution. Amendments to the constitution of the Liberal Association were, however, passed at the first opportunity, and these guaranteed annual conventions, made members of the Dominion and provincial legislatures ineligible for the presidency, and gave authority to any four of the twelve vice-presidents to call a special meeting of the association. Both parties now require annual meetings, and the Ontario Progressive Conservative constitution now provides that at every second one all officers are elected except the provincial leader; since 1969, the Executive Council has been empowered to call a leadership convention at any time when the party is not in power. The

Liberal constitution calls for a leadership review within two years of a provincial election.

The matters which may be discussed at a provincial annual meeting, apart from any elections that may take place, naturally depend on the party's morale, its status as government or opposition, the quality of the leader and his relationship with the party, etc. Thus one Liberal meeting went on record as approving an eight-hour day and a five-day week with no reduction in pay; a paid vacation of two weeks a year; equal pay for women for equal work; assistance for needy unemployables; greater Dominion-provincial co-operation in finance; better housing; veterans' preference in the provincial civil service; and other resolutions covering a wide field of provincial activity. Occasionally, at least, such resolutions reflect the interests of organized pressure groups seeking to influence the parties and thus the course of legislation.

While the Liberals in the foregoing resolution may have had an urgent desire to instigate measures of social and economic reform, a factor of at least equal significance was that the Liberals at the time were not in power; "a party in power," as one distinguished Liberal observed at the party's national convention of 1948, "cannot pass resolutions with that fine free careless irresponsible rapture which is characteristic of the opposition." But in opposition any criticism can always be made with impunity; there is apt to be little or no sense of responsibility and no fear that the policies advocated will have to be put into effect. The opposite situation occurred in 1924 when at the Conservative annual meeting in Ontario two members of the legislature introduced a resolution which in effect implied a lack of confidence in the provincial government, which was also Conservative. The resolution was not on the agenda and the chairman did not wish to receive it. The premier thereupon rose and placed the government's position before the convention:

In case anybody might suggest that there was any attempt to throttle the resolution, I ask that it be read. I have not read it myself and I do not know what is in it. But after it is read, I ask you to keep this much in mind. There are certain matters which are purely the matters of Government. They are problems which the Government must consider and must decide for itself, and, having decided, it must take the full responsibility. So far as I or the members of the Government are concerned, we will welcome the fullest discussion of any or all matters of public interest, but I must point out that when it comes to matters of general public policy we, the Government, are the ones who must make the decisions and who must stand or fall by them. We must, and do, assume the fullest responsibility. Perhaps, even, it may mean that the time will come when the people will have to pass upon our decisions, but even in that case it is the Government which must face the answer.[15]

Two years later the same question arose again when the annual meeting proceeded to discuss "in a contentious spirit" the Ontario Temperance Act and other controversial matters. "If we are not here to dictate the policies of the

15/Toronto *Mail and Empire*, Nov. 19, 1924.

Conservative party," said one delegate, "why are we here at all?" "Some of us object to the policies of the Ontario Government," said another speaker, "and now is the time to talk about them. If there is to be any unanimity in the party, we must thresh out these points." A resolution that these matters could be considered by the meeting was carried, although another resolution that recommendations should be made to the government was defeated. Eventually, after a lively discussion and through the combined good offices of the chairman and some of the members of the legislature, the dissentients were calmed down and the controversy was brought to a close.[16] But in succeeding years the Ontario association found it wiser to confine its discussions to more general public questions, which gave ample opportunity for speakers to air their views without involving even an indirect criticism of the government. By 1969 the wheel had turned full circle again, for in that year the party, self-conscious about celebrating twenty-five consecutive years in power, held a brisk convention which overhauled the constitution, and heard stern warnings about the dangers of complacency from ministers themselves.[17]

Such activity at provincial conventions has not been common, although there are signs that all parties are becoming more infused with vitality; but the possibility of a contentious convention has always existed. The Progressive Conservatives in Manitoba, to cite another example, held their first annual meeting in eight years in 1946, attended by some three hundred delegates. Manitoba had had for some years a coalition government, supported by the Progressive Conservatives under the leadership of E. F. Willis, minister of Public Works. The meeting, despite the objections of this minister and many others, proceeded to take what would normally have been a routine motion of confidence in Mr Willis as a serious contest of leadership. A rival contender, complete with a piper in full regalia and supporters bearing placards and leading parades around the hall, was defeated by a two-to-one vote; but it is rumoured that the party leaders were happy to read the clause in the new constitution whereby a two-year interval could elapse between meetings of the association.

The provincial convention, which is held for the purpose of choosing a leader and drawing up a platform, is by far the most colourful of the party organizations in the province by virtue of its size, the greater importance of its functions, its dramatic possibilities, and, most of all, the circus fanfare and artificially stimulated excitement which mark its performances. The theatricalism of the American conventions, which is almost entirely absent from party meetings at the lower levels, bursts into provincial and Dominion conventions, although showing less exuberance than is displayed in corresponding meetings in the United States.

The idea of creating a special body to choose a leader is a fairly recent importation from the United States, and it is sufficiently democratic on the sur-

16/*Ibid.*, March 27, 1926.
17/See especially the Toronto daily newspapers for Dec. 5–8, 1969.

face to make its stay a long one. The practice has now won acceptance in all provinces, and there is no doubt that it is now so firmly entrenched that any other method of choice is in danger of being regarded as exceptional. The earlier method, which was used in all provinces, was for the party members of the legislature to make their own choice; although as the convention idea gained ground, there was a tendency to adopt half-way measures. Thus in 1925 the Conservative leader in Nova Scotia was chosen at a joint meeting of the provincial party executive and the candidates nominated by the party for the coming election; and in 1929 the Liberal leader in British Columbia was chosen by the Liberal members-elect and approved by the executive of the provincial Liberal Association. In 1911 in Ontario the Liberal members notified the meeting of the Reform Association of the resignation of the leader, but the whip "made it clear that the message he bore to the meeting on behalf of the legislative contingent was given as a matter of courtesy and was not by right."[18] Later the same group reported to the association that it had offered the leadership to N. W. Rowell and that he had accepted.

The choice of a leader by the party members in the legislature, undemocratic though it would now be considered, had some merits. The members, though they often represented only limited parts of the province or country, had an active sense of responsibility in the matter for they were themselves most closely affected by the leader's ability to perform his functions. If he proved competent, he probably became premier; if not, he could be quietly asked to resign and make way for a successor similarly chosen. His talents had already been put to the proof in the legislature and party councils where his colleagues could judge their quality; and while wire-pulling and manoeuvring for support by inside cliques were common, at least they were not reinforced by the demagogy and luck which often influence to a substantial degree the choice by the present method.

There is no absolute guarantee that the use of a convention will enable the party to institute a new system of democratic control by breaking away from the official or semi-professional element. In most instances it is the steady party workers who form the mainstay of such meetings. Responsibility for party policies and decisions can thus be lifted from the shoulders of those who should bear it, the party leaders, to those of the convention, which in no way can be considered to have responsibility in any real sense at all. The late John W. Dafoe in his biography of Sir Clifford Sifton stated substantially the same argument as follows:

Sir Clifford knew enough about conventions to know that unless public opinion was vigorously stirred up the convention would fall under the control of the official element in the party ... In theory, the holding of a party convention returns the control of the party as to policy and leadership into the hands of the rank and file; in practice, it often means an opportunity to get an apparent endorsation from the rank and

18/Toronto *Globe*, Nov. 1, 1911.

file for leaders and policies that are ripe for retirement. This perversion is possible owing to the manner in which delegates from the polls are usually chosen – not by a public gathering of electors, but by slimly attended meetings of the local party associations, which are usually made up of workers and members who are keenly interested in the party. A party convention, unless care is taken in the election of delegates, is apt to reflect not the opinions of the great mass of voters, but the wishes and purposes of the ultra-partisans – the "hard-boiled" practitioners of the political game.[19]

Moreover, although a convention is expected to make decisions on two exceptionally difficult matters, each calling for careful consideration, the weighing of various alternatives, and the exercise of dispassionate judgment, neither the qualifications of the delegates nor the conditions under which they must work are at all adapted to the tasks in hand. The time and facilities for gaining information which are at the disposal of the delegates are limited; some, at least, of the candidates are frequently unknown to many of those present; the feverish surroundings are almost certain to react unfavourably on the delegates' capacity to make wise decisions; and there is always a danger that the convention may be rushed off its feet by the emotionalism of the moment. Thus arguments concerning party representative democracy carry but little weight when applied to an over-wrought crowd of fifteen hundred or more people trying to transact business of this nature and importance in the space of a few hours of frantic activity, which commonly also includes a good deal of strenuous partying in the non-political sense. Democratic organizations, like other human institutions, need to be given suitable conditions in which to perform their functions, and by no effort of the imagination could the party convention, provincial or national, be considered wholly suitable. The convention may also throw a heavy burden of expense on people seeking the party leadership, thus excluding some possible candidates, for extensive organization and travelling in the months preceding a convention is increasingly expected of candidates.

The provincial convention (as distinguished from the meeting of the provincial association) was formerly not called at stated intervals, but only when there was a leader to be chosen, and the custom has been steadily growing that a convention should be held to confirm or reject any leader who has been chosen by any other method, and at regular intervals in any event. (The Liberal party of Ontario, indeed, now has constitutional provisions for three separate kinds of conventions: the leadership convention, whose purpose is obvious; the annual meeting, which conducts business and may discuss but not resolve policy; and policy rallies, to be called "once every two years to develop and determine policy." At these rallies, the leader is held accountable for his actions on the decisions of the previous rally or annual meeting.)[20]

19/John W. Dafoe, *Clifford Sifton in Relation to His Times* (Toronto, 1931), pp. 414–18.
20/*Constitution of the Liberal Party in Ontario*, as adopted March 29, 1969, article VII. The Liberals' "accountability rally" of 1970 will see the leader, Mr Nixon, discussing his support of a policy on which the party is divided – separate school grants up to Grade 13.

Where the leadership is involved, a distinction may be drawn between the leader in the House or legislature and the provincial leader of the party; the former being the choice of the party members of the legislature only, the latter of the convention or representative body of the party. Thus in 1929 after Mr T. D. Pattullo was chosen House leader by the Liberal members of the Legislative Assembly of British Columbia, it was carefully announced that "the executive of the British Columbia Liberal Association will assemble in Vancouver to consider the question of the permanent party leadership, which is a matter entirely apart from the choice of a temporary chief to guide the Opposition."[21]

It is, of course, usual for the House leader to be subsequently approved by the convention as the head of the party. An interesting case arose in Ontario in 1942-3. Mitchell F. Hepburn had retired from the premiership and had advised the lieutenant governor to send for G. D. Conant although the latter had not been chosen by even the Liberal members of the House. So great was the general dissatisfaction among the Liberals throughout the province that they demanded a convention[22] to make the choice; and when the meeting was held, the mantle did not fall on Conant. In Ontario and in most of the other provinces the fact that a party leader has not been chosen or confirmed by a convention is now a reproach which can be adequately answered in only one way – approval by a convention called for the purpose.

The responsibility which a leader who has been originally elected by a convention owes to another convention is not fully established, and there are too few precedents from which to generalize. He may feel that if he resigns the leadership, nobody but a convention can accept the resignation, though it is not uncommon for a leader to submit his resignation to the party executive;[23] but only the most acute dissatisfaction, as in the federal Conservative party in 1966-7, could cause a convention to be called to force him out. Open hostility to Premier Anderson in Saskatchewan led to the submission of his resignation to the Conservative convention in 1933 as a way of clearing the party air; and he was thereupon re-elected by the convention with enthusiasm. An effort to avoid this awkward situation appears in the Ontario Progressive Conservative constitution, for, as noted above, it provides for the calling of a

21/*Victoria Times*, Jan. 19, 1929.

22/Both riding and regional associations were instrumental in having this convention summoned; for one association after another passed resolutions demanding such a meeting.

23/"He [H. H. Dewart] was chosen, not by the members as House Leader, but by the delegates to the convention of 1919 as the official chief of the party throughout the province. He may take the ground that only a convention of the party can withdraw the responsibility laid upon him, and that until a convention decides the issue he must remain at the head of the provincial organization and retain the position of Parliamentary Leader." Toronto *Globe*, July 2, 1920 (editorial). Mitchell Hepburn resigned the premiership of Ontario in 1942 (his party being still in office) but he did not relinquish his leadership of the party until a provincial convention formally met the following year.

convention not only "upon the death or retirement" of the leader, but any time the party is in opposition.

The Liberal provincial convention in Ontario is a broadly based affair including most of the personnel qualified to attend meetings, with a strong emphasis on riding representation. The Progressive Conservative convention is also a large and diversified body. It includes, among others, the same kind of personnel described above as delegate members, plus ten delegates and ten alternates from each riding, and delegates-at-large up to one half the number of provincial ridings. The total active membership is thus very large, and will include an additional several hundred alternate delegates. The most interesting feature of this arrangement is the delegate-at-large, nominated by the president and approved by the executive. These, while they may be chosen to sit and speak for some special interest or activity, are, of course, quite unrepresentative in the sense that the other delegates have a representative party character. The Conservative party has also followed the same practice in its national convention; while a Conservative convention in Quebec in 1929 even gave special representation to the three universities in what must be assumed to have been a desperate attempt to present an appearance of wisdom and respectability.[24] The Ontario constitutions of both parties give formal recognition to party clubs in universities and other post-secondary school institutions.

Aside from these and a few other minor differences, the composition and proceedings of provincial conventions of the older parties in Ontario are much the same. The main tasks of the provincial convention, as already stated, are two: to approve a platform for the party and to choose its leader. The convention appoints a resolutions committee to draft the platform; but most of the constructive work will have been done before the convention opens, either by individual effort or by another committee chosen by the executive for that purpose. The riding conventions may suggest resolutions to this committee, but there is no obligation for it to transmit these to the convention, although, of course, amendments or new resolutions may be offered by any delegate on the floor when the proposals come up for approval. Any preliminary thought and study will obviously tend to produce proposals which are not only carefully drafted but which will also prove practicable and likely to gain general acceptance. The consideration given the platform in the convention itself depends entirely upon circumstances, the chief of which are, first, whether the convention is of the same party as the provincial government, and second, the extent to which the convention is absorbed in the companion task of choosing a leader. Thus three consecutive conventions in Ontario followed three different procedures: in one, the platform was discussed at considerable length on the floor; in another, the platform was virtually ignored "so as not to embarrass the new leader" who would also become the premier in a few weeks; and in

24/The nearest Liberal equivalent was the seating at a provincial (Ontario) convention of the editors of Liberal daily papers and "two legal experts" for unexplained reasons.

the third, the excitement over the election of a leader was so intense that every resolution as it came from the resolutions committee was declared carried unanimously without any discussion whatever. The constitution of the Ontario Progressive Conservative Association adopted in 1969 draws a distinction between provincial conventions and annual meetings, and if the latter do indeed continue to be held annually, they may assume a new rôle in the party's organization.

While the convention is called for purely provincial purposes, the party representatives whose interests lie largely in Dominion politics do not and are not expected to remain aloof. In the Liberal convention (and also the Conservative), members in the Dominion Parliament and defeated federal candidates are given seats, and they may form a very powerful group. How openly they may try to influence proceedings will depend on the special conditions at the time. Thus in 1930 Mackenzie King sent a message to the Liberal convention at Toronto advising the delegates against any course which would tend to confuse Dominion and provincial issues, and adding that with this in mind he had decided to stay away from the meeting. Despite this advice, the convention unanimously passed a resolution disapproving of Bennett's actions and proposals at the recent Imperial Economic Conference. Another Liberal convention in 1943 was honoured by the presence of eight Dominion cabinet ministers; and it is rather difficult to suppose that this participation in the selection of a provincial leader was calculated to carry out the "will and wish of every member of the federal Parliament that the convention should not experience restraint of any kind, but carry on its proceedings with a sense of utmost freedom in the direction of sane policies and avoiding extremes."[25] The fact was, of course, that in 1943 the Dominion cabinet could not have regarded with equanimity the selection of a leader who might prove as unsympathetic to the policies of the Dominion government as Mr Hepburn had proved to be in the preceding years. Ottawa had, in effect, its candidate for the Ontario leadership and it was prepared to back him to the limit in the convention. Certainly the tendency for federal organizations to try to influence the choice of provincial leaders continues to be an active one.

The choice of a leader is the main purpose of the convention. Rigid rules are laid down to prevent any one candidate from gaining an unfair advantage. Their names are formally submitted in writing, nominating speeches are usually made, the candidates themselves are allowed to speak for a specified time, and the convention makes its choice by a series of secret ballots, usually with the provision that the lowest man drops out after each ballot until one candidate has received a majority of the votes cast. The first ballot, however, is frequently decisive, for it has become common for candidates whose chances are doubtful to withdraw at the very last moment before the balloting begins and thus make

25/Mackenzie King's statement to the 1930 convention, Toronto *Globe*, Dec. 17, 1930. See Neil McKenty, *Mitch Hepburn* (Toronto, 1967).

the majority immediately possible. The candidates (and, in Conservative conventions, the delegates also) are formally pledged to accept and support the choice, and the leadership is thus always offered by a unanimous vote of the convention.

This bald account gives no hint of the tense excitement that runs through all these proceedings which are reminiscent of both a revival meeting and a football game. Even before the convention opens there is a great display of activity in the lobbying for support, the private conferences, the making of plans of strategy, the bargaining for votes, the attempts to estimate the possible position of wavering delegates after the first ballot, the receptions in the rival committee rooms, the hand-shaking and back-slapping by the candidates themselves who wander about the lobbies in an atmosphere of forced geniality. Pretty girls are at the registration desk to bring to the convention an atmosphere of sweetness and light; buttons and books of matches are issued bearing the pictures of different candidates surrounded by inspiring slogans; signs spell out more reasons for giving support to this or that rival contestant; pipers in full dress (who for some mysterious reason are now considered indispensable at any important party convention) play the bagpipes and parade around the corridors; and an electric organ produces soothing airs in the convention hall when proceedings promise to get out of hand.

There are in attendance delegates from the city, who appear to be very much in their element; delegates from the country, who appear to be very much out of it; and women delegates, most of whom do not feel quite at ease in this troubled environment. There are delegates of distinction – cabinet ministers, hockey players, entertainers, members of the legislature, champion swimmers, mayors, reeves, and others no less noted; there are delegates whose political past is so distant that they are unknown to the great majority of their fellows; there are delegates from the young people's clubs, who are plainly impressed with the gravity of the issues and the great decisions they will be called upon to make within the next forty-eight hours.

The making of speeches is interminable. The temporary chairman delivers a short speech; the permanent chairman delivers a longer one; the mayor of the city welcomes the convention in a few careful sentences; prominent members of the party, under one pretext or another, give long addresses "keynoting" the convention and arousing the delegates to an appreciation of the importance of the occasion. Speeches are made on committee reports; speeches are made on the platform and on other resolutions; then follow the nominating speeches; and then, at long last, the speeches of the rival candidates, each being received with wild demonstrations of enthusiasm. The ballots are cast, and the leader is finally chosen. He thereupon delivers another speech; the delegates give him an ovation; the photographers take endless pictures; the leader and his wife receive the delegates; and the convention is brought to an end by the inevitable banquet.

5 *The national organization*

The permanent national organization of the Liberal party is known as the Liberal Federation of Canada, a name which appropriately suggests the rather loose connection between Dominion and provincial party activities. The membership consists of the ten provincial parties (variously named association, party, or federation), the Northwest Territories association, and the Yukon association, with which are affiliated the national federations of the Liberal Women, the Young Liberals, and the University Liberals (both of which are coeducational), and "such other bodies as the Executive Committee shall recognize from time to time." The Executive Committee, which must meet at least twice a year, consists of the elected officers of the federation (including the president and past president), the national leader, the heads (or their nominees) of the various organizations which compose the Liberal Federation of Canada, and one representative of the federal Liberal caucus. There is also a National Council (which meets at the call of the Executive Committee) which is a larger body including, among others, the officers of the National Liberal Federation, the national and provincial party leaders, a minimum of ten representatives from each province (of whom at least two must be Liberal Women and two Young Liberals) and ten from the federal caucus, and nine representatives of the university Liberal groups; each province is entitled to additional representation at the rate of one member for each three federal constituencies. The Executive Committee is clearly the more authoritative of the two bodies, for it is charged with carrying out the "aims and purposes" of the Liberal Federation.[26]

The federation is instructed to:

1 Seek to achieve a common ground of understanding between the different provinces of Canada;
2 Co-ordinate the efforts of Liberal organizations to create a strong Liberal Federation in Canada;
3 Advocate and support Liberal principles and policies;
4 Provide assistance and leadership to federal Liberal constituency organizations in Canada;
5 Promote the election of candidates of the Liberal Party to the Parliament of Canada.

It is noteworthy that "Liberal principles" are not defined in the constitution; but the federation has standing committees on policy, organization, constitution and party structure, communications and publicity, and finance. Each committee has one English-speaking and one French-speaking co-chairman, appointed by the Executive Committee, and one representative chosen by each of the organizations comprising the federation, "and such other persons as may be appointed thereto by the Executive Committee." The federation maintains a permanent staff which distributes literature, assists the women's and young

26/*Constitution of the Liberal Federation of Canada*, as amended April 4–6, 1968.

people's organizations, and keeps in close touch with the party's headquarters in each province.

The federation, through its Executive Committee and National Council, can be a useful liaison between the parliamentary group and the party throughout the Dominion, and it can keep the former in touch with general trends in public opinion. It thus becomes to some degree a committee of party grievances, and, in the light of recent developments, a potential source of action. The constitution states that "the basic policies of the party shall be established by the Party assembled in policy conferences at least every two years"; and a caucus member appointed by the national leader is required to attend each national meeting or convention and "report upon the consideration given, the decisions made and the reasoning therefore regarding resolutions passed at the previous Convention." The decisions "shall be presumed to be ratified unless there is a contrary decision by the Convention." The convention can thus, presumably, overrule even the cabinet, although such an action would undoubtedly be a vote of want of confidence in the leadership. The term "basic policies," it may be noted, is not defined in the constitution.

The Progressive Conservative central organization bears in all essentials a marked resemblance to its companion body in the Liberal party,[27] though there are interesting variations in detail. The Conservative national organization was originally ahead of the Liberal in stressing less the parliamentary group of the party, though both now provide for limited representation from the federal caucus on the party's national executive, the Conservatives on a notably more generous scale. The functions of the Conservative organization are substantially the same as those of the Liberal; and its relations with other party bodies are likewise consultative and advisory. It also maintains a permanent staff at Ottawa. When the party was in opposition before 1957, its annual meetings were devoted mainly to the enunciation of a party programme, and the Conservative position as the chief opposition party enabled it to pronounce very freely upon topics ranging from price control and old age pensions to the union with Newfoundland. Once in power, however, the party settled down noticeably, and even friendly newspapers found its 1961 annual meeting dull and listless.[28] Its return to opposition in 1963 again produced a spectacular flowering.

When the annual party meeting, whatever form it took, was in its infancy, it had some difficulty securing nourishment, possibly because the upper echelons of both parties included people who were not anxious that their child should thrive. In 1947 the resolutions of the Liberal Federation were buried for three weeks before being given to the public, an interval which was presumably devoted to their revision and possible emasculation by the parliamen-

27/See Williams, *The Conservative Party of Canada*, especially chaps. III–IV; see also *Constitution of the Progressive Conservative Association of Canada*, as amended 1969.
28/Saywell, *Canadian Annual Review for 1961*, p. 79.

tary members. When they finally appeared, even so sturdy a Liberal paper as the *Winnipeg Free Press* gave only half of them in any detail, and the report was tucked away on page 24 of the paper – a treatment which showed either alarm or contempt for the formal opinion of the highest council of the Liberal party. The Progressive Conservative Association in 1947 passed resolutions which did not seem to be particularly startling in any way; but they apparently caused consternation at Ottawa. For although the party had all the scope in these matters which comes from being in opposition, the resolutions were advanced with the astonishing proviso that there was no intention of committing the whole party membership to the association's proposals. The meeting, it was added, was not a policy-making convention, because its sessions were too short to permit of adequate research, consultation, and consideration. Why the national party organization should waste its time in passing resolutions which have no official character and which any party follower or leader can disown at any time was not explained; but the statement almost certainly indicated some uneasiness on the part of the parliamentary group at the prospect of having its hands forced by a rival party body. In the intervening years, however, the party meeting has become increasingly accepted as a useful and indeed necessary element in organization and publicity, though its actual influence on the parties' policies in Parliament is far from clear; certainly the extra-parliamentary wings of both the Liberals and Conservatives are now far louder and more conspicuous than at any previous period of Canadian history.

The national convention is a special and formerly irregular manifestation of party activity called together either to construct a platform, or to plan for the party organization in the Dominion, or to elect a party leader, or to do all three. Its future, like that of its more humble relation in the provinces, is apparently assured, and both older parties are showing a tendency to call more, not fewer, conventions, and at settled intervals. Before 1956 the Liberals had held only three conventions, and only two of those to choose a leader; the Conservatives had held four, all leadership conventions. Since then both parties have held so many meetings, to elect leaders, construct platforms, and think, that it is not always clear what should be classified as a convention and what should not.

The national convention, copied from American practice, was first brought to Canada by the Liberals, who held the first general policy discussion in 1893, and the first leadership convention in 1919,[29] when in a resolute effort to rehabilitate the shattered fortunes of the party and to choose a successor to Sir Wilfrid Laurier they called upon all members to unite in support of the cause of Liberalism. The results in terms of practical politics were as encouraging in 1921 as they had been a quarter of a century before, and the value and prestige of national conventions were greatly enhanced by the convincing manner

29/Conventions had of course been held before these dates. The old Reform party in Upper Canada held conventions in 1859 and 1867, and the Conservatives in 1854.

in which this one had apparently passed the test at the polls. *Post hoc ergo propter hoc* may not carry conviction in an argument; but any political party will gladly accept the sequence of events and forego the logic.

The Conservatives for many years had little liking for or confidence in national conventions, although in 1910, at what appeared to be a very low point in their fortunes, Borden succeeded in securing party consent to a meeting as a source of inspiration and a means of bringing the party leaders into closer touch with their followers. The early Liberal convention furnished the encouraging precedent. "The Liberal party was never so strong," ran an editorial in the *Toronto News*, "as during the three years immediately following the famous convention of 1893. It had ideals worth fighting for. The leader and his aides stood upon firm ground and laid about them in an ecstasy of bludgeoning. They knew the temper of the reserves."[30] The proposed convention, however, was for a variety of reasons postponed; and the electoral success of 1911 removed the most urgent inducement for a Conservative meeting.

Borden had been chosen leader of the Conservative party in 1901 by the usual method of a caucus of Conservative senators and members of Parliament. On his retirement in 1920 his successor was selected by a curious system which was invented for the occasion by Sir George Foster.[31] Each party member of the Senate and House of Commons submitted, as his suggestion, a list of names in order of preference with the reasons for his choice attached; and Sir Robert Borden, having considered these carefully and consulted with his cabinet, was then to make the selection.[32] After much difficulty, frequent discussions with Conservatives outside as well as inside Parliament, a serious divergence of views between ministers and members of Parliament, and the refusal of the position by one candidate, Sir Robert finally selected Arthur Meighen, the popular choice of the caucus, who in a few days became prime minister.

On Meighen's retirement in 1926, his resignation was accepted by a "Conservative Conference" of senators, members-elect of the House of Commons, and defeated candidates; and a temporary successor, Hugh Guthrie, was chosen to lead the party in the House. The disastrous reverse which the Conservatives had just suffered in the election and the contrasting success of the Liberals (who had used the convention system in 1919, also when in a weakened state in opposition) convinced the majority of the conference that some greater effort should be made to identify the Conservative party as a whole with the selection of a new national leader. The obvious way to achieve this end was to hold a national congress of the party. The call was accordingly issued, and the first Conservative national convention assembled at Winnipeg in 1927. R. B.

30/*Toronto News*, Oct. 9, 1909 (editorial).
31/Wallace, *Memoirs of Sir George Foster*, p. 205. See Graham, *Arthur Meighen*, I, chap. II.
32/A detailed account of these different methods of selecting Conservative leaders is given in Dawson, *Constitutional Issues in Canada*, pp. 380–97.

Bennett was chosen leader, and the next election returned the Conservatives to power. Once again, a convention had been followed by victory.

But the system could not guarantee immediate results. On Bennett's resignation, another Conservative national convention met in 1938 and selected Dr R. J. Manion as his successor, only to see the party meet virtual annihilation two years later. After another singularly unsuccessful experiment, involving Meighen again, with a modified version of the old system of choice by Conservative politicians, the party in 1942 turned once more, though with some reluctance and little confidence, to the national convention. But neither the 1942 convention, which chose John Bracken, nor that of 1948, which chose Mr George Drew, was able to produce a winner, and it was not until the choice of Mr Diefenbaker in 1956 that the convention system of choosing a party leader led to the Conservatives, for the second time in five attempts, to victory at the polls: Mr Stanfield's selection in 1967 reduced the odds, temporarily at least, to two out of six. The Liberals have had rather better luck with conventions, choosing winners in King in 1919 and Mr St Laurent in 1948, and a strong contender and finally a winner in Mr Pearson in 1958, and yet another winner in Mr Trudeau in 1968.

It is probably still true that there are a few Liberals and Conservatives who have not yet been fully convinced of the virtues of the system of choosing a national leader by a convention.[33] Most people believe that it is efficacious as publicity device, vote-getter and rouser of enthusiasm, and that a man who can carry a convention successfully is also likely to be the kind of man who can carry an election; but these beliefs were long tinged with a lack of confidence in the reliability of the convention's judgment on men and measures, particularly with the new dimensions added by television. Nor is it possible with the present large loose party organization to "manage" the meeting and bring it under any kind of effective control, although Meighen was apparently the chief instrument in securing the choice of Bracken at the Conservative convention in 1942 and King the one whose influence resulted in the election of Mr St Laurent in 1948. Mr St Laurent, in his turn, was scrupulously careful to choose no favourite as his own successor in 1958, as was Mr Pearson in 1968. Mr Diefenbaker, making an unprecedented bid to succeed himself in 1967, after the Conservative party's extra-parliamentary wing had succeeded in calling a leadership convention against his clearly expressed wishes, did not choose his successor either.[34] But the practice of making selections by the

33/See D. V. Smiley, "The National Party Leadership Convention in Canada: A Preliminary Analysis," Canadian Journal of Political Science, I, no. 4 (Dec. 1968), pp. 373–97. Professor Smiley here quotes a Conservative lawyer who urged a return to the caucus system in 1968.
34/An account of the Conservative national convention of 1942 is given by J. W. Lederle, "National Party Conventions: Canada Shows the Way," Southwestern Social Science Quarterly, Sept. 1944, pp. 118–33; the Liberal convention of 1958 is described

464   THE GOVERNMENT OF CANADA

convention method is not likely to be repudiated in the foreseeable future; for
to do so would be to show an open preference for a restricted method of choice
rather than for one based on the representative and (so it is usually believed)
the democratic principle. No party will willingly expose itself to the reproach
that it is afraid to trust the judgment of its own representative convention.

The usual broad similarities occur in the conventions of the two major parties
as well as the usual minor variations. Space does not permit any extensive
description of these gatherings, and only some of the most prominent features
are indicated below.

The composition of the national convention is bound to be varied and complex, for it is highly desirable to have all elements in the party represented.[35]
However, there has always been a decided tendency to provide generously for
the official section of the party, the members of the Dominion and provincial
cabinets and legislatures. The practice not only gives these members a large
number of seats, but it places them, because of their experience, broad acquaint-

in Norman Ward, "The Liberals in Convention: Revised and Unrepentant," *Queen's
Quarterly*, Spring 1958, pp. 1–11; see also Williams, *The Conservative Party of Canada*.
For an account of the convention that produced the "Diefenbaker Revolution," see
Meisel, *The Canadian General Election of 1957*, pp. 18–33. Additional pertinent material
is in Peter C. Newman, *Renegade in Power: The Diefenbaker Years* (Toronto, 1963)
and *The Distemper of Our Times*; Thomas Van Dusen, *The Chief* (Toronto, 1968);
Patrick Nicholson, *Vision and Indecision* (Toronto, 1968).

35/The constitution of the Liberal Federation provides for the following representation of any national convention:

"1 All the Liberal Members of the Privy Council, of the Senate (including retired
members of the Senate) and of the House of Commons, and where any constituency is
not represented in the House of Commons by an adherent of the Liberal Party, the Liberal
candidate defeated in the last election, or if a new Liberal candidate has been nominated,
such new candidate.

2 The Leaders of the Liberal Party in the ten provinces of Canada.

3 All the members of the Executive Committee of the Liberal Federation of Canada,
the Women's Liberal Federation of Canada, the Young Liberal Federation of Canada
and the Canadian University Liberal Federation.

4 Four members of the Executive of each Association, Federation or Party Organization listed in Clause No. 2-A [that is, the members of the federation].

5 In addition to the president, two other officers of each of the ten provincial
organizations of Liberal Women and of the ten provincial organizations of Young
Liberals.

6 Two representatives of each of the University Liberal Clubs in Canada and of the
five regional organizations of the Canadian University Liberal Federation.

7 The co-chairman of the standing committees of the Federation and the appointed
members of each of the standing committees of the Federation.

8 Six delegates from each federal electoral district at least one of whom shall be a
Liberal Woman and one a Young Liberal, and six alternates, one of whom shall be a
Liberal Woman and one a Young Liberal, who shall be elected at a local meeting, to
be called for that purpose.

9 The Liberal members of each provincial assembly and the Liberal candidates
defeated at the last provincial assembly election in each province or new candidates
nominated, acting jointly, shall have the right to select from among themselves a number
of delegates equal to one-fourth of the total membership of each provincial assembly."

ance, prestige, familiarity with the issues and candidates, and other factors, in a position where they can exercise a great influence over, if not actually dominate, the convention.[36] But this group, based as it is on eleven legislatures across the Dominion, is far from homogeneous and dissension, if it should arise, is not as likely to appear between official and non-official sections as among the political leaders themselves. The presence and influence of this element can, however, scarcely be regretted; they should represent much of the practical wisdom of the party and they certainly constitute the more experienced members; their future lives and conduct will be in large measure determined by the decisions of the convention, a fact which is, admittedly, as likely to lead them to be short-sighted as long. The strong official element will inevitably weaken the influence of the ordinary party or riding delegates. Neither party has apparently considered the possibility of apportioning delegates on a basis of party votes cast.

The resolutions which are passed by the convention and which constitute the party platform are drafted and considered with care, although not necessarily at the convention itself. Any party association may send in suggestions, and a resolutions committee is appointed and at work some days before the convention assembles, sorting out the proposals and preparing the material for consideration by the convention committee on resolutions and the convention itself. (Thus the Conservative convention of 1942 had a resolutions committee of 167 members which was divided into six sub-committees on different subjects. These considered over a thousand suggested resolutions.) The committee eventually reports to the convention, and the platform it proposes is debated and passed, item by item. In many instances, this approval is cursory and largely formal; but in others, the discussion may be keen and amendments may be moved and in rare instances carried. The recent tendency has been to draft long and comprehensive resolutions which lend themselves neither to effective debate nor to ready modification; in 1967, the Conservatives adopted most of their platform from conclusions reached a year before at a conference, while the Liberals in 1968 did not attempt a platform, but concentrated on the leadership. This was perhaps only being realistic, for in all conventions the delegates are much more interested in the election of a leader than in considering a platform, and it is therefore impossible to count on any very prolonged consideration with the election pending; the Liberal convention of 1958, indeed, rejected a proposal to have the new leader elected on the second day of a three-day convention, partly because it was feared too few delegates would remain for the final day. The real platform-maker thus

36/The Liberal convention of 1958 was a particularly conspicuous parade of the party "brass." (See Ward, "The Liberals in Convention: Revised and Unrepentant.") The members of Congress who attend national conventions in the United States are an influential group, but they are relatively a small part of the total membership.

becomes in large measure the resolutions committee, and a genuine effort is therefore made to have it both large and representative of all interests and geographical areas.

The election of a leader by the national convention follows with substantial exactness the procedure already outlined for provincial conventions engaged on the same task. The Liberals in 1919 did not allow the candidates to speak in their own behalf; but the restriction was made almost meaningless by the candidates being given an opportunity to display their wares in the discussion on proposed resolutions. The Conservatives, however, preferred to follow the more common and straightforward practice of allowing candidates to address the convention under a strict time limit. In 1948, 1958, and 1968 the Liberals followed suit and gave each candidate equal time. The election is made by secret ballot – a vast improvement on the American open declarations by states – and the balloting proceeds until a candidate receives a majority. A substantial number of delegates are usually pledged in advance; but there is nothing to show that this is a serious restricting influence in enabling a convention to come to a decision. The same external aids to emotion and general enthusiasm are present as in provincial conventions, and in the 1942 contest one of the candidates did his part by collapsing in the middle of his address. The same pretty girls (on these occasions, both French and English) register the delegates; the same kilted pipers (but in greater numbers) play the same inspiring airs; the same rousing speeches (although ranging over a wider area) go on and on interminably. One important variation, however, occurred in 1942: war shortages compelled the abandonment of the dinner; more variations have appeared with the advent of television, which provides such vivid portrayals of what is going on that delegates now can often be seen, at the site, watching on television the convention they are attending.

The atmosphere of the convention is best given by an eye-witness; the following newspaper account of the concluding stages of the election of W. L. Mackenzie King at the Liberal convention in 1919 is still representative of them all:

The decisive vote was cast and the electric period of waiting begun. There remained a tag end of resolutions to be passed and orators bellowed and perspired in the faces of an audience that was thinking of something else. The great majority was jammed in the corridors, coatless, panting, eating messy ice cream cones, sucking at pop bottles through straws and talking, talking interminably. Here and there a woman delegate, uncurled and damp, talked prohibition or wandered through the crowd. The heart of the assembly was in the Ontario committee room where the scrutineers were translating the will of the assemblage into figures. Outside, a brass band performed amid the dust unregarded.

There were half a dozen false alarms. Bursts of tired cheering from the main hall caused a stampede through the narrow side entrances. But bit by bit the big hall filled as the time drew near. Brown of Alberta was making a rousing speech when the time came, but he might as well have been making it in Cree in his native province, for all the attention he was getting. There was only one thing the audience cared about, and that thing was being rushed in by the door in front of the Quebec delegation. Brown swallowed his peroration and hustled into the background, and a hush fell over the great crowd as Premier Stewart of Alberta stood up with the fateful paper in his hand. There was silence till Mr. King's selection was announced, then pandemonium broke loose. Mr. King had no reason to complain of his reception as leader. There may have been a lack of abandon in the Ontario cheers, but Quebec and the West made up for it. It had to be done all over again when the figures were given.

Then came one of the really nicest incidents of the convention, the motion by Mr. Fielding that the election be made unanimous. While it is the customary thing to do that, it takes real grit, and an innate sporting spirit to do it, as Mr. Fielding did it. Unquestionably, he would have liked to crown his long career with the greatest honour his party had to bestow, but there was not a hint of bitterness, not a shadow of anything but whole-souled sincerity in his short, manly but graceful speech. Mr. Graham followed, back in his old form, mentally debonair as ever, equally eager to offer his services in the ranks ...

Mr. King's speech was adequate and careful, nicely appreciative, duly modest. He omitted nothing; he said nothing he should not have said. He perorated effectively. He did not get across quite as completely as in his speech of the previous night when he was fighting for the prize he had won, but the speech he delivered was quite satisfactory to his audience, or at least to that part of it which was given to satisfaction at all.

The convention came to an end, appropriately enough with "God Save the King." Taking the political interpretation of the National Anthem the crowd sang "send him victorious" with especial fervour. There was a last cheer, a stampede to the platform where the successful candidate underwent the penalty of greatness by shaking a multitude of hands, and the Liberal Convention of 1919 passed into history.[37]

Add buttons, hats, sandwich-boards, walkie-talkies, and microphones and cameras, and one has the 1970s' version of the same thing.

The choice of the convention is frequently narrowed by the operation of what Americans would call "availability," the necessity of choosing not only an able leader, but one whose qualities and background are such that he is likely to appeal to the voters and secure the return of his party to office. Personal integrity is indispensable, but the so-called popular qualities have certainly not been conspicuous in all the leaders chosen in recent years. Political experience in the Dominion rather than in the provincial legislature is one of the most common qualities, but it need not belong (as with Mr Trudeau); and two provincial premiers ran strongly in the Conservative convention of 1967, with one of them emerging as the winner. Racial origin (as between French and British) is unquestionably important, but the significance attached to it is apt to turn primarily on the political situation at the time of choice rather than on any permanent principle. The folly of attaching too much importance to many of these personal factors is best illustrated by the unfortunate fate which overtook Dr Manion. He was a thoroughly likable man, with parliamentary experience; he was a returned soldier and an eloquent speaker; he was a Roman

Catholic from Ontario married to a French wife, a combination which might well have appealed to both Ontario and Quebec; yet although he was the choice of the convention, he led his party to overwhelming defeat.

One of the most important factors in availability today is the province from which the candidate comes. Too close an association with any province – and particularly with some provinces – is a heavy handicap. Thus a provincial premier will not only lack the wider Dominion experience, but he may have so identified himself with his own province that he is as a result disliked in others. But he need not be a premier to have provincial jealousy and distrust rule him out as a serious contender. Thus a candidate from Ontario is likely to be under suspicion from Quebec and from east and west as well; although one from Quebec, particularly if he were of British descent, would not encounter nearly the same opposition. On the whole, considering all the parties together, a maritimer or a westerner, considering the size of his region, seems to have the best chance of success; and the westerner, because of the size of the western vote, would receive a decided preference if there was much likelihood that the West could be induced to give its support. The recent leaning of the West in the direction of the younger parties lengthened the odds for westerners in the party leadership stakes for some time, but Mr Diefenbaker's remarkable success in 1957 and 1958 at least temporarily adjusted them. But none of these observations apply to the Liberals, whose leaders have all been from the two central provinces.

A concluding reflection on the national convention suggests yet another similarity to the conventions which choose the provincial leaders. Although there can be no doubt that the environment is unsuitable, the time for consideration deplorably limited, the delegates' knowledge of the contestants frequently inadequate, the danger of a candidate sweeping a convention off its feet always a grave possibility – despite these and other circumstances working against success, the selective function of the national convention, judged on its record, has been astonishingly well performed. The older parties so far have chosen only ten leaders by convention, but the great majority of them have been men of outstanding ability and character. One would find it difficult to assert with confidence that any other method would have given better results.

B THE NEW DEMOCRATIC PARTY

The Co-operative Commonwealth Federation, from which the NDP was in part formed, prided itself on being "not just another party but ... a new venture in the technique of applied democracy," but the party always showed a sturdy and even conservative interest in the realities of political life, which the NDP appears to have inherited. Certainly the general organization of both CCF and

NDP groups has shown a number of old party characteristics. There are undoubtedly greater differences between the organization of the NDP and that of the other parties than between the organizations of the other parties themselves, but the resemblances in all are many. After all, the general aim of each is to elect candidates to office by inducing the voters to give them vigorous support, and these efforts must be made over a given area under certain conditions: it is therefore not surprising to find that the general machinery each party constructs for this task is very similar. It is true that the CCF and NDP have insisted on their unique character, as indeed have all parties at all times; and they have frequently scorned (again in the best party tradition) the loose organization, and the techniques and spirit of its rivals. In some measure the CCF was able to demonstrate the truth of these contentions, although many of the differences would not appear to be as profound or as significant as the statements of the party would indicate. The NDP, while its organization is clearly the heir of the CCF, is somewhat less unlike the older parties than its honourable ancestor.

The most distinctive feature of CCF organization was the primary assorted grouping of its members at the lowest level, a product of its history rather than of its philosophy. In the early thirties a number of separate protest groups and minor parties came together in a coalition designed to secure more effective political action; but they insisted on maintaining their individuality and making it essentially a co-operative endeavour. After some years these separate parties disappeared; but the CCF remained in local clubs or units (the terms were interchangeable), and other organizations, such as trade unions and farmers' societies, might affiliate for political purposes. The NDP recognizes the importance of supporting groups in a more formal way. The federal constitution of the New Democratic party, first adopted in 1961, provides for two classes of membership: individuals who agree to accept the constitution and principles of the party, and whose application for membership is approved by the appropriate provincial party; and "trade unions, farm groups, co-operatives, women's organizations and other groups and organizations which, by official act, undertake to accept and abide by the constitution and principles of the party." (An attempt to abolish these affiliated members was defeated at the party's 1969 convention.) Individuals pay a small membership determined by each provincial party, of which $1.00 is transferred to the federal party; special arrangements are made for family memberships, and for those on social welfare. Affiliated groups pay five cents per member per month to the federal party, two cents of which is transferred to the appropriate provincial party. The NDP's system of raising funds from trade unions particularly has caused considerable controversy in areas where, for example, trade unions are associated with governments whose legislatures are dominated by other parties; but it should be noted in fairness that the NDP's method of raising funds are at least open to the public for criticism, and that the bulk of the criticism comes from newspapers and other sources associated with the party's opponents. Until the report of the Committee on Election Expenses in 1966, little was known of the sources of funds, or the methods of raising them, used by the other parties.

As with the older parties, the key element in the party's organization is the provincial party, and the basic unit within that is the provincial constituency organization. Thus in Saskatchewan every individual member of the party automatically belongs to a constituency organization, and affiliated groups participate in the activities of the constituency organization on a basis mutually agreed upon. (Any person belonging to an affiliated organization who does not wish to support the NDP can of course contract out.) Each provincial constituency organization has an executive of not less than seven elected from among the party's qualified members (both individual members, and members of affiliated groups). Each federal constituency organization has a similar executive, one of whose chief duties is to co-ordinate the provincial organizations within the federal constituency into an effective unit. In Saskatchewan, where there are thirteen federal seats and fifty-nine provincial, this task can be a complex one; but if the provincial constituency organizations are in good shape, the work is greatly facilitated. Each provincial constituency organization is charged with "the general administration of the affairs ... at all times between conventions, and at the time of the convention or at subsequent meetings [will] divide the constituency into zones and appoint a manager for each zone, and also, if it is considered advisable, appoint workers of any desired number to assist with the organization work."

The governing body of the Saskatchewan NDP (which continued to use "CCF" in its title until 1967) is the Annual Provincial Convention, which has the power to amend the party's constitution and programme, and elects the party's chief officers, including the leader, each year. (As with the CCF, the actual practice is to re-elect the existing leader; but formal machinery for deposing a leader has always existed.) The personnel of the convention, as with all parties, is broadly representative of the party, and includes all members of the Provincial Council; the party's MP s and MLA s; at least ten delegates from each constituency chosen in convention; and delegates from affiliated and young people's organizations. The Provincial Executive, which meets bi-monthly, consists of the officers of the provincial association (that is, the leader, the president and three vice-presidents); five members from the Provincial Council; one from the young people's section, and an appointed secretary-treasurer. The Provincial Council, which meets at least twice-yearly to review the activities of the executive and give directions concerning them, consists primarily of the officers of the provincial association; the presidents of the constituency organizations (or a substitute for them); the province's two members on the party's national council; ten members-at-large elected by the provincial convention; three from the youth section; and one Saskatchewan MP and two MLA s, each elected by their fellows. The Saskatchewan NDP, it will be noted, has no women's organizations as such, the chief reason for this apparently being the dangerous revolutionary doctrine that since women are people, they have the same rights to participate in the party's regular affairs as anybody else.

The preceding mass of detail is necessary to emphasize some peculiarities of NDP organization. The party goes to elaborate lengths to maximize internal party democracy, and to keep the party's politicians as far as possible under some kind of control. The leader is annually elected; no party member while serving as MP or MLA can be elected to other party office, or to the Provincial Council; the Provincial Executive is dominated by ordinary party members, the only political officer being the leader himself. In addition, the party's constitution has a strong article on discipline, which forbids anybody to publish or circulate what purport to be the party's views without the council's approval. Any five members of the party can request disciplinary action against a sixth which may, after a hearing by the appropriate constituency organization, result in admonition, suspension, or expulsion of the erring member by the Provincial Executive; a final appeal lies to the council. The restrictions on publishing party views, and the process of expulsion, it is to be noted, both rest in the hands of the party's lay leaders, not the political. Finally, and most interestingly because of its implications for the principles of responsible parliamentary government, there is the Legislative Advisory Committee, whose description deserves quotation in full:

Article 13: Section 1: An Advisory Committee composed of three members appointed by and from the Provincial Council, shall from time to time advise the members of the Legislature concerning the implementation of the program of the Association.

Section 2: Whenever appointments to a Cabinet are being made, the Political Leader shall submit the names of his proposed Cabinet Ministers to this Committee, which shall act in an advisory capacity, realizing that final responsibility for Ministerial appointments must rest with the Premier.[38]

The final quoted clause reveals as clearly as any single statement could one of the fundamental problems of all party organization in Canada: the reconciliation of some measure – perhaps no more than a façade – of party democracy with recognition of the essentials of responsible government. Responsibility, in the public interest, can only mean responsibility to all the members of a duly elected legislature, not just to the members of a single party; yet the political leadership of a party with what it considers a unique and even indispensable

38/The national organization of the NDP is, *mutatis mutandis*, very similar to that of the Saskatchewan section; but it provides for no Legislative Advisory Committee, and leaves most disciplinary problems to the provincial organizations. The national leader has a two-year term. See next chapter.

programme may find itself caught between the wishes of the party, on the one hand, and the requirements of parliamentary principles on the other. The older parties, despite recent innovations in their constitutions, still solve the potential problem simply by giving, in effect, vast powers to the party's political leadership, powers which are enhanced even more when the leader is a premier or prime minister. The NDP, and before it the CCF, have tried to enlarge the powers of the party *per se*, but in practice appear to have had to accept in one important area a modified but substantially similar version of the older parties' solution. This general problem is referred to again in the next chapter.

23 Party activities and problems

THE PRECEDING CHAPTER on party organization has dwelt almost entirely upon its formal manifestations, the ways in which the active member is able to participate in the party's meetings and decisions on policy and leadership. This participation is by no means unimportant, and it shows every sign of becoming more so as the organization develops and as popular expression through party channels becomes increasingly common. But, as has already been suggested, the success of the party in its major task of winning votes and thereby attaining office does not by any means depend solely on these formal committees and showy gatherings; without discounting the personality of the party leader as a factor in his party's success, a great deal depends upon the prosaic labours of the party canvassers and field workers and their ability to make an impression on the individual voter. The party is above all a fighting organization; and while it must be firmly founded on the opinions and goodwill of its members and must provide occasional open demonstrations that it possesses public interest and support, it must also adopt the army practice of keeping its own counsel on many matters and directing a substantial number of its operations in secret. Thus by far the greater part of the party's labours in organizing the constituencies – in providing canvassers, in checking voters' lists, in adopting means to get its supporters to go to the polls, in raising money, in buying votes (a far rarer method than is generally supposed), in procuring support by promises of special jobs or general employment – is accomplished as unostentatiously as possible and is entrusted to those workers who through inclination or self-interest will give the party unquestioning support. This part of the organization and those who direct and operate it constitute the party "machine," a name which optimistically suggests the mechanical efficiency with which the party is presumed to deliver the vote on election day.

The relationship between this machine at its upper levels, and the parliamentary leader and the caucus, can itself be productive of problems; the chairman of the Progressive Conservative party committee on organization in

1967, recommending major changes in the organization, observed darkly: "The Committee believes that in the past our Party's leaders have had too much responsibility for the 'organization' and unfortunately this responsibility has been coupled with too little knowledge."[1] At lower levels (and the term "lower" can readily be misleading if one forgets that Canada's largest cities are more populous than most of the provinces) new and different problems are arising from the growing tendency of parties to contest municipal elections. In Toronto in 1969, for example, an avowed municipal Liberal party contested seats for the city council, and when its mayoralty candidate lost found itself with a leadership problem, for the absence of the parliamentary system in urban affairs meant that defeated candidates had no official status whatever as an opposition. In the same year, municipal politicians sought formal representation at federal-provincial conferences which, they urged, were inadequately representative if they included no urban spokesmen as such.

The reality of the machine's efficiency is never easy to determine; for while results may be at times impressive, there is no way of analysing them with any certainty, and there is a predilection on the part of defeated candidates to account for their humiliation by throwing the blame on the unscrupulous and regimented activities of the opposing forces. The thoroughness with which an area will be organized in the interests of any party will always depend in large measure upon the party's general position and the circumstances of the time. If the party is strong in a particular constituency, the need for thorough organization and effort is not urgent, and there will be a tendency to direct its attention to the more doubtful districts. Again, if a party has been long in control of a provincial government, it is very likely to have built up an elaborate network of party workers (including civil servants) who will be able to exert considerable weight in an election. A compensating factor, however, will often appear in that many voters dislike a machine which works too efficiently, and from this may come the paradoxical result that a high degree of organization (unless it is kept very much in the background) may bring about unpopularity and defeat. Mr. Diefenbaker's régime at the head of the Conservatives produced a paradox of another sort on the prairies: his dynamic appeal was so great that it was not discovered until after his departure that in many constituencies there was very little organization at all.

Inasmuch as all parties are reluctant to reveal the extent and nature of many of these operations, especially when they are on (or over) the verge of questionable practices, accurate information is not readily obtained. A classic study of the operation of the Liberal machine in Saskatchewan some years ago, while old, still serves as a striking example of the way in which a strongly entrenched party is able to build up and conserve its voting strength.[2] The

---

1/E. A. Goodman, *National Chairman of Organization*, a paper published by the Progressive Conservative Association of Canada, Dec. 7, 1967.
2/Escott Reid, "The Saskatchewan Liberal Machine before 1929," in Ward and Spafford, *Politics in Saskatchewan*, pp. 93–104.

Saskatchewan machine was better organized than most, but there is little reason to suppose that the practices it followed have become obsolete in Canada. Writing in 1965, indeed, Professor Meisel said: "Quite aside from the notorious scandals revealed in the last year or so, and the insouciance with which the cabinet met them, the party has, since 1963, relied as heavily as before on rewarding its friends by the use of patronage and attractive appointments."[3] And since both provincial and federal references here happen to be to the Liberal party, it is only fair to add that there is no known reason for assuming that its chief competitors behave differently.

Each constituency in Saskatchewan had its own organizer, and each polling sub-division its own workers, while in between were a number of liaison or "key" men who kept the organizer informed at all times of the state of each area in the constituency. The voters were all carefully scanned and their political views ascertained; and systematic efforts were made to win over all doubtful voters to the Liberal side. In these and allied endeavours, the Saskatchewan Liberals were simply following normal party practice (by no means confined to the Liberals), although it seems probable that the work may have been done more thoroughly than in most parts of Canada. The provincial organizer, however, seems to have kept in exceptionally close contact not only with the organizers in the ridings but with all party workers throughout the province. Any information likely to be of value came directly to his office, and it was then relayed by him to those chiefly concerned – usually the member or candidate – in the ridings.

The most notable part of the Saskatchewan machine was the close identification of the provincial civil servants and the work of the civil servants with the Liberal party. The highways inspectors, for example, were among the most active of the party workers; and though they did not often discuss politics with the voters, they were most sensitive to any party disaffection in their districts and were a constant source of information for the party authorities. Road supervisors, sanitary inspectors, liquor store managers, and many others were loyal supporters of the party and usually energetic party workers as well. Appointments to the service were made, of course, largely from staunch Liberals; public works, especially roads, were undertaken with a clear eye to party advantage; and the contracts were granted in exchange for party support. The power of the Liberal machine was eventually broken; and although the party later returned to power, its organization was never as highly developed or as successful as in the earlier period. An interesting postscript occurred when the CCF government assumed office in Saskatchewan in 1944. One of its pledges was the elimination of patronage and the institution of a merit system; but the proposal to carry this into execution precipitated a struggle with its own party organization which demanded that patronage should be retained. The reason advanced was the natural but far from original one that the old gang had all the jobs and that the new government would find itself thwarted in its work

3/"Recent Changes in Canadian Parties," p. 46.

by an unco-operative service. A reform act was eventually placed on the statute books, to such good effect that in 1962 the CCF-NDP provincial convention passed a resolution critical of the numbers of civil servants who were not sympathetic enough towards the party.

Party patronage still remains an important adjunct of government throughout Canada, a fact stoutly denied by practically all parties in power. It has certainly not lost its appeal for provincial governments; but neither the Dominion nor any of the provinces (though all are continually seeking improvements) has a complete merit system in the public service. Several provinces have passed statutes which are apparently designed to put up at least a pretence that a merit system is in force.[4] The Dominion service, as noted in an earlier chapter, is in considerable measure under a merit system; but there are those in authority who, while reconciled to a life of virtue, still recall with nostalgic satisfaction the old uninhibited days which, while undoubtedly troublesome and even at times embarrassing, nevertheless had compensating advantages in the constituencies which are not easily forgotten. Thomas Van Dusen, in a revealing paragraph, has described what happened when the newly elected Diefenbaker government attempted to eschew patronage in 1957-8: a number of Conservative members found themselves handicapped in their constituencies while the patronage, gravitating naturally to the civil service level, showed a tendency to benefit Liberals because of traditions established under a long Liberal reign.[5]

Closely allied to the party patronage system is what is known as the "pork barrel," a kind of large-scale patronage and bribery offered to a community in the hope of winning support, an appeal to what President Cleveland called "the cohesive power of public plunder." These promises are not pledges on matters of general policy which the party, if elected, will redeem; they are special concessions dangled before a particular interest or area in exchange

4/The most impressive of the provincial civil services was Saskatchewan's under the CCF; a strong "élite" of well-trained administrators was built up, which in turn helped train other civil servants. The élite group, however, was not unnaturally oriented towards CCF policies and concepts of administration, and when the Liberals returned to power in 1964 there was a large exodus, most of it voluntary, of high-ranking civil servants. Saskatchewan also allows some of its civil servants "full political rights," that is, they may openly support and canvass for any political party; many years' experience with this provision in the law has produced no apparent damage to the province's public service from that source alone, though occasional anomalies appear. Thus a leading figure in the anti-medicare forces during the crisis of 1962 over the government's medical plan was an employee of the Saskatchewan Power Corporation. Later, a Liberal cabinet minister, after an electoral defeat, was appointed as a deputy minister, from which post he subsequently sought another nomination; he did not get it, and continued as deputy minister. the Royal Commission on Provincial Development, 1944, see also Thorburn, Politics the Royal Commission on Provincial Development, 1944; see also Thorburn, Politics in New Brunswick, pp. 159–61; MacKinnon, The Government of Prince Edward Island, chap. IX; M. S. Donnelly, The Government of Manitoba (Toronto, 1963); F. F. Schindeler, Responsible Government in Ontario (Toronto, 1969); J. M. Beck, The Government of Nova Scotia (Toronto, 1957), chap. XIV.

5/Van Dusen, The Chief, p. 36.

for the election of the "right" candidate. In any such bidding, the party in power enjoys a substantial advantage; for it is not only in a position to implement its promises, but it can, if it desires, spend the money first and trust to the collective gratitude of the community to repay the debt on election day. "The 'pork barrel,' " one writer once said in words which still have applications, "dispensed with equal rapacity by all parties and governments since Confederation, has been the worst penalty of our Canadian democracy. It has been the chief source of whatever of corruption has degraded our public life during the past fifty years. It has sinned more than all other agencies combined against efficiency and honesty in politics. And it stands to-day as one of the chief reasons for the extravagance and waste that father taxation and debt."[6]

That statement is probably too strong for much of contemporary Canada, although the chronicles of Mr Duplessis' régime in Quebec indicate that the millennium has not been reached. In older days, tariff protection used to be the most widely used of these inducements, and it still plays a part; but welfare policies and public works of all kinds make the most direct and obvious appeal to the average voter. The list is long, but the public purse is deep. Welfare policies are not commonly considered as "pork" in the usual sense of the word, for they undoubtedly benefit all citizens, and are, equally undoubtedly, very popular; it is often impossible to tell whether individual policies are pork, or are legitimate responses to genuine needs. But public works are generally specifically aimed at a particular constituency, region, or segment of the population. Dry docks, dams, wharves, break-waters, post offices, bridges, armouries, harbour improvements, grain elevators, rifle ranges, free mail delivery, customs houses, increased pay for the civil servants – these are all federal projects, and the party in the provincial field can also offer attractive sweetmeats of its own. Many of these expenditures would normally be denounced by the opposition in Parliament when the estimates are discussed and passed; but they are commonly placed in the supplementary estimates, where they could be slipped through a weary and ill-attended House in the last few days of the session;[7] it is not yet clear whether the Commons' new rules of procedure will significantly alter these practices.

The pork barrel has a closed as well as an open end; for those similarly minded in the opposition can do nothing but make sweeping promises and await the day when it will be their turn to draft estimates and vote them

6/M. Grattan O'Leary, "The Pork Barrel," *Maclean's*, Feb. 15, 1924; reprinted in Dawson, *Constitutional Issues in Canada*, pp. 194–201; see also Saywell, *Canadian Annual Review for 1961*, pp. 53–4; *Task Force on Government Information* (Ottawa, 1969) vol. 1, pp. 28–9; Nicholson, *Vision and Indecision*, p. 333.

7/O'Leary, "The Pork Barrel," pp. 198–201. See also Ward, *The Public Purse*, especially chaps. XIII–XIV. For an account of the "pork barrel" years ago, see *Canadian Annual Review, 1904*, pp. 227 ff.; Skelton, *Life and Letters of Sir Wilfrid Laurier*, II, pp. 265–70; Ward, *A Party Politician*, pp. 11–12, 358–9.

through an acquiescent House. Deserved and necessary improvements in anti-government constituencies are thus frequently neglected, while others with far less justification meet with a ready and even extravagant response; the question ceases to be one of need, but primarily what support for the party in power has been given in the past or is likely to be forthcoming in the future. Frank statements like the following are uncommon, but their relative infrequency is not necessarily proof that the age of pork is over:

Mr. McGibbon: The riding which I have the honour to represent, and which is an important one from the revenue standpoint, has been literally starved for about ten years. We think it is time that members on this side of the House should have some of the requirements of their constituencies considered. We are not pressing for appropriations this year, but we cannot understand the minds of some hon. gentlemen opposite. After having fed so freely from the public estimates for the last ten years they are still hungry ... When the time comes, when we can loosen the strings of the treasury, his [the minister's] first consideration should be those constituencies which have received nothing for some years past.

Mr. Hanbury: Conservative constituencies?

Mr. McGibbon: Yes, Conservative constituencies. I am one of those who believe in being frank about these things. I took my medicine when I was sitting on the other side of the House and could not get anything; we all had to take that medicine ... We take the ground that we are not going to have hon. gentlemen opposite collect the fees while we write the prescriptions. I want to press very strongly upon the Minister that this action be taken, and I do not think any member of this House will object to it. We are all human; we all know what we are here for and most of us are pretty good party people. We follow our party sometimes when we differ from it, because of the greater good to the country, but when the time comes, as we hope it will come, when this depression lifts and the treasury contains a little money, we want the needs of the people in those parts of this country which have been neglected looked after before there are any railway stations built in Temiscouata, or new wharves or anything of that kind.[8]

"Elections," said Israel Tarte with some cynicism and much truth, "are not won by prayers," and one of the instruments of victory is money. All parties therefore possess central campaign funds; and most of them are careful to keep secret the source, the size, and the disposal of its fund and to talk loudly and none too sincerely about the abuses which gather about those of its rivals. The money is used for general party purposes: for campaign literature, radio and television time, the taking of opinion polls, newspaper advertising, lecture halls, billboards, travelling expenses, paid organizers, and assistance to needy candidates and to those running in doubtful constituencies. These and other legitimate outlets dotted across the continent make heavy demands; and any party which is fighting more than two hundred engagements simultaneously will use up ammunition in enormous quantities. An additional reason for the high cost is that it is customary for all those patriots who have something which the parties need at election time to charge generously for their services; thus many newspapers, for example, charge top rates for political advertising

8/*Can. H. of C. Debates,* May 1, 1931, pp. 1191–2.

and, according to a former national party organizer, some newspapers will not cover a candidate's meetings unless he purchases advertising.[9] It is generally accepted that a campaign fund for a national party today needs to be over one million dollars, and possibly four or five, even though it is all spent for quite proper purposes; but the Committee on Election Expenses, appointed by the Pearson government in 1964, obviously believed both that a general scaling down of expenditures was possible, through shorter campaigns and the legal limitation of certain expenses, and that pressures could be taken off both candidates and parties through the provision of several kinds of public assistance.

The committee, faced with an existing electoral law which, based as it was on the assumption that elections were fought only by candidates, and not also by parties, seemed merely farcical in its financial clauses, took a broad view of its terms of reference. Equipped with ample research funds by the government, it made a comprehensive examination of relevant laws and practices at both provincial and federal levels in Canada, and every other country on which it could obtain evidence, and published in 1966 a report buttressed by a thousand pages of studies and surveys, which was in due course referred to the House of Commons' Committee on Privileges and Elections. The report is based on these main considerations:

I Political parties should be legally recognized and, through the doctrine of agency, made legally responsible for their actions in raising and spending funds.

II A degree of financial equality should be established among candidates and among political parties, by the extension of certain services and subsidies to all who qualify.

III An effort should be made to increase public participation in politics, by broadening the base of political contributions through tax concessions to donors.

IV Costs of election campaigns should be reduced, by shortening the campaign period, by placing limitations on expenditures on mass media by candidates and parties, and by prohibiting the payment of poll workers on election day.

V Public confidence in political financing should be strengthened, by requiring candidates and parties to disclose their incomes and expenditures.

VI A Registry under the supervision of a Registrar should be established to audit and publish the financial reports required, and to enforce the provisions of the proposed "Election and Political Finances Act."

VII Miscellaneous amendments to broadcasting legislation should be enacted to improve the political communications field.[10]

The House committee, as this book goes to press, has made no recommendations.

The motivation behind the government's action in appointing the committee is not entirely known, though there can be little doubt that some of the sensational scandals that shook the political world in the early 1960s raised in

9/James Scott, "Political Slush Funds Corrupt All Parties," *Maclean's*, Sept. 9, 1961. A bibliography on the subject is at the end of the first volume of *Report of the Committee on Election Expenses*.

10/*Report of the Committee on Election Expenses*, vol. 1, p. 38.

a frightening form the spectre of sinister elements gaining access to the upper echelons of power.[11] But for years the high costs of electioneering had been a cause for concern, and long before the maw of television had been opened Mr C. G. Power had been moved to say:

The cost of election campaigns is too high and some means must be found to lower it ... Political corruption – wholesale bribery and the distribution of liquor – has to a large extent disappeared from our political morality, usages and customs. It has been succeeded, though, by more modern methods of propaganda and proselytism, which are almost as expensive. Electors, rightly or wrongly, believe that campaign funds are unlimited, and that they are to be dug or gouged out of an almost bottomless purse. As soon as an election is in prospect, candidates, organizers, and supporters get together and decide that their man must have the largest and best-equipped hall in the community. He must have the best brass band, and his advertising must be on the front page. He must have the best and the longest possible time on the radio. His placards and posters must be the most artistic, and if Rembrandt or Titian were alive to-day they would be hired to decorate the fenceposts of the neighbourhood with the portraits of the candidate.[12]

One serious problem which arises out of the party campaign funds (assuming they are legitimately spent) is the source from which they are derived. So far as the NDP is concerned, this has not yet presented any serious difficulty. That party, like its predecessor, although it will receive contributions from anyone in sympathy with its aims, has placed its chief reliance on membership dues and union contributions; its tenets are not likely to appeal to the wealthier part of the community; and, as the late Mr Woodsworth frankly stated of the CCF, "we are too few in number as yet to have come to the attention of some of the men who may be anxious to secure concessions."[13] If no very substantial amount of money is received from any one source, no very substantial obligations can be created; and if this or any other party is able to dispense with large contributions, it will beyond any reasonable doubt be more independent and occupy a much less ambiguous position. It may be noted in passing that the NDP fund, which for the first time approached one million dollars for the election of 1965, so far as it is derived from contributions made by the trade unions, raises a different kind of problem; a member of a union affiliated with the NDP is free to contract out of contributing to the party, but this places him in a position where he must take action to prevent himself from contributing, rather than making the contribution itself voluntary. A heavy reliance on union funds will of course give the unions a large voice in party circles, a fact about which non-union members of the party sometimes complain.

The two older parties have not been favoured with either the happy poverty

11/See Richard Gwyn, *The Shape of Scandal* (Toronto, 1965); Van Dusen, *The Chief*; Newman, *The Distemper of Our Times*.
12/C. G. Power (minister of National Health), *Can. H. of C. Debates*, March 13, 1939, p. 1810; see James Scott, "Political Slush Funds."
13/*Can. H. of C. Debates*, July 31, 1931, p. 4392. See *Report of the Committee on Election Expenses*, both vols., passim.

of the old CCF, or the moderate but orderly prosperity of the NDP. It is customary for large corporations to make donations to both parties, commonly (though not invariably) on a 60-40 basis for the government and opposition parties;[14] and since large businesses are not charitable enterprises, a few of these contributions have led to major scandals. The Pacific Scandal of 1873 is perhaps the most notorious; but the problem is not one which can be dismissed as belonging to a remote and unsavoury past. In 1926 an official inquiry disclosed that various liquor interests in British Columbia had been in the habit of making large contributions to the coffers of both major and minor parties; indeed, certain of the liquor companies seem to have developed so fine a sense of impartiality and public spirit that they insisted on making exactly the same contribution to the Liberals and the Conservatives. In 1929 another investigation showed that a public utility company in Manitoba, which was interested in securing water-power concessions, made generous contributions to all three political parties which were active in the province. In 1931 the Beauharnois inquiry revealed that a company in search of water-power rights on the St Lawrence had contributed well over $700,000 to various campaign funds, individual and collective, in both major parties,[15] although the Liberals, who had happened to be in power in both the Dominion and Quebec, had received by far the greater amount. While there was nothing to indicate that this lavish expenditure by a company, which was expecting very substantial concessions from the governments of Canada and Quebec, made any difference in the actions of these governments, there was also not the slightest doubt that the contributions were made in the expectation that matters in which the company was interested would as a result follow a smoother course. "Gratefulness," said the open-handed president of the Beauharnois Corporation with revealing naïveté, "was always regarded as an important factor in dealing with democratic governments."[16] And both Liberal and Conservative parties, according to the research of the Committee on Election Expenses, have always received most of their funds from a remarkably small number of contributors.

The most recent disclosures have come from the Province of Quebec, though it would be a mistake to assume that other parts of Canada are free of fund-raising chicanery. In Quebec the Union Nationale party early developed a most profitable technique for replenishing its campaign fund.[17] The custom had apparently been long established in the province that tavern keepers on

14/Scott, "Political Slush Funds."
15/The total ascertained payments were, in fact, $864,000, but there is some doubt as to the intended destination of $125,000 of this total. The Conservative central fund received nothing from the Beauharnois Corporation, although $200,000 was offered as a contribution to that fund and was refused. See Ralph Allen, "The Year the Government Sold the St. Lawrence River," *Maclean's*, Sept. 9, 1961.
16/*Can. H. of C. Debates*, July 28, 1931, p. 4260 .
17/Blair Fraser, "Shakedown," *Maclean's*, Nov. 15, 1945; Léon Dion, "Party Politics in Quebec," in Thorburn, *Party Politics in Canada* (1st ed.), pp. 118–29.

obtaining their licences for the first time were expected to make a contribution to the government party; but Mr Duplessis imposed a levy of $500 on many of those who wished to renew their licences for the coming year. In some instances, the renewals were first refused, and the tavern keeper was then given the opportunity of having his licence restored on the payment of $3,000. Other renewals were refused outright because the applicants were supporters of another party. At least one unsuccessful attempt was made to wring tribute from a firm of distillers in Scotland. This firm was asked to advance its price on Scotch whiskey sold to the Quebec Liquor Commission by fourteen shillings a case, and the extra charge was then to be refunded to the party treasury. Such transactions, while not unknown elsewhere in Canada, have been fortunately rather rare. As a footnote to Duplessis' operations, it should be added that the reforming Liberal government which succeeded the Union Nationale in 1960 found its supporters starved for patronage, and its leaders had to work hard to convince some of them that the party "had not fought to replace one corrupt administration by another."[18]

Abuses should not be allowed to obscure the fact that campaign funds are essential in a democracy, for only by spending money can parties promulgate their ideas, whether at elections or at other times. Indeed, the chief objection to having the state itself make grants to all party funds is not that the purpose to be served by these grants would be questionable, but rather that no system of apportionment has been worked out which would be accepted by all parties as satisfactory. Little if any objection can therefore be taken to the practice of members of a party making gifts, and even fairly generous gifts, towards its support and for the attainment of ends in which the donors believe, although the motives which prompt the contributions may, of course, be far from praiseworthy. Gifts from corporations stand in a somewhat different light; for it is by no means obvious that corporate bodies are eager to propagate opinions and ideas apart from the selfish and mercenary ends which they wish to achieve. In Canada, indeed, for many years any corporation (other than those formed for political purposes) was forbidden to make contributions to the support of a candidate or a party; but as this was supposed to be unfair to trade unions,[19] the statute was repealed in 1930. The NDP's device for raising money *via* trade unions has already moved one province to prevent the use of union dues for political purposes, a cure that seems more drastic than the condition it allegedly cures.

Any contributions which are made to more than one party are inevitably suspect. They can scarcely fail to lack sincerity of purpose and are bound to

18/Saywell, *Canadian Annual Review for 1961*, p. 53.
19/The argument here was somewhat unusual. It was difficult to enforce the law to prevent contributions from business corporations because of the secrecy of both the funds and the accounts of the corporations, whereas the trade-union accounts were semi-public and hence more accessible for checking and enforcement. Repeal was effected at the instance of the Labour and Progressive groups. *Can Statutes*, 20–21 Geo. v, c. 16.

raise grave doubts as to the ends which are expected to be served: the primary object is almost certainly to secure what the president of the Beauharnois company called "gratefulness," and hence in due course to gain valuable assistance in obtaining special favours and concessions. The existing law takes no account of these difficulties.[20] The campaign funds are secret; money may be received from any personal or corporate source; and disbursements may be made from the general fund without any accounting or publicity. The recommendations of the Committee on Election Expenses would change much of that. Quebec, it should be added, already has an advanced electoral law limiting expenses and subsidizing candidates.[21]

A problem closely related to party expenses is the absence of effective control over the election expenditures of individual candidates, which may range from $500 to $600 (as reported by one member) to $25,000 or more (as reported by another). Here the existing law has attempted to set certain slight limits and make demands for the publication of exact information.[22] A candidate cannot spend over $2,000 from his own account, and any further payments, while unlimited, must be made through his agent. Claims against the candidate are valid for only a limited time; the agent must keep a record of all contributions received and all expenditures made; and detailed statements of these matters must be sent to the returning officer in the constituency, who must publish a statement, on a form prescribed, in a newspaper published or circulated in the constituency. Superficially, the provisions appear to be fairly adequate, but they are far from being so; for there is a general lack of responsibility for enforcing their terms, and even a candidate who makes no return – and this is a common failing[23] – can avoid the consequences by going before a judge and pleading illness, inadvertence, or other "reasonable cause" and get off scot free. Bennett stated that the efficacy of the Election Act was completely frustrated by the spinelessness of its own provisions:

We provided that if [returns] were not filed certain results would follow. They have not always been filed on time. Extensions have not been granted. Then, on an *ex parte* application, with just an advertisement in a newspaper, you go to a friendly judge and get an order on the ground that you did not think about it ... What is the sense in our passing this legislation if it requires the deposit of a thousand dollars to unseat a member who has relied upon these very things – all the technical machinery of the law, which may be relied upon, through the employment of skilled members of the legal profession? There must be some summary method of dealing

20/The history of the existing law (and of attempts to change it) is in the *Report of the Committee on Election Expenses*, especially chap. II. See also Ward, *The Canadian House of Commons*, chaps. XIV–XV.

21/*Report of the Committee on Election Expenses*, Study no. 7.

22/See R. A. Mackay, "After Beauharnois," *Maclean's*, Oct. 15, 1931, reprinted in Dawson, *Constitutional Issues*, pp. 208–18; Allen, "The Year the Government Sold the St. Lawrence River"; *Can. Statutes*, 8–9 Eliz. II, c. 39; *Report of the Committee on Election Expenses*, chaps. II–III.

23/*Report of the Committee on Election Expenses*, especially Study no. 2; *Can. Statutes*, 8–9 Eliz. II, c. 39, s. 63.

with it, and that summary method must provide that upon proof of contravention of the provisions ... that man must forfeit his seat ... It must not be necessary to deposit a thousand dollars, it must not be necessary to meet all the technical requirements now in the act. The inspector-general of elections should be in a position, at the request of any elector in any constituency, to demand that action be taken and that that action should be summary. A man should forfeit his seat upon proof of an illegal condition existing. If he says he did not know, that is no excuse. It is the job of a candidate to know what is being done ... If we are to prevent the racketeer and the hoodlum, this combination which has been bleeding all parties during the years, from carrying on, we must provide a punishment to fit the crime. If a candidate is likely to lose his seat, he will not have this combination going around handling his election ... The danger lies in the fact that you have this type of person dealing with a situation about which he does not want the candidate to know anything, and about which the candidate does not want to know anything – where the money comes from that runs the election.[24]

The Committee on Election Expenses found Bennett's strictures in general still true, nearly thirty years later.

Party rivalries not unnaturally play an important part in Dominion-provincial relations, although the way in which these are likely to be affected by party bidding for popular support is by no means clear. It can be assumed that normally the maximum co-operation and friendliness can be expected when Dominion and provincial governments are controlled by the same party, although this is by no means certain: one of the leading critics of the Liberal governments of both Mr Pearson and Mr Trudeau in the 1960s was the Liberal premier of Saskatchewan, Mr Thatcher.[25] Any co-operation will include also the granting of any special favours by the Dominion to the province, and Canadian history is full of examples. Thus H. A. Robson, Liberal leader in Manitoba, speaking in 1927 on the subject of an agreement regarding the transfer of the natural resources of Manitoba stated: "We claim to be in a position to have this matter settled satisfactorily with despatch and without any risks of litigation. We hold the advantage of position in this by reason of our affiliations with the federal Liberal Party. From this very important standpoint, the existence in Manitoba of a Government in sympathetic contact with the federal Government will undoubtedly give the province an advantage in all matters of negotiation.[26] Three years later Mackenzie King, speaking in the

24/*Can. H. of C. Debates*, April 5, 1938, pp. 2030–2.
25/When Dominion and provincial members of the same party fall out, the dispute can become doubly bitter because of the family connection. Thus the Liberal Government of Ontario under the leadership of Hepburn carried its dislike of the Liberal Government at Ottawa under King to such lengths that it moved a resolution of censure on the latter's war policies. Many of Hepburn's followers disapproved of the quarrel, and the effects of these disagreements were soon reflected in the standing of the Liberal party in Ontario. The Saskatchewan Liberal party of the 1960s also had internal divisions over federal-provincial matters, and the Quebec wing of the party has commonly been an almost autonomous body.
26/*Manitoba Free Press*, April 25, 1927.

Dominion Parliament, accepted the same principle in his famous "five-cent speech," and after a few years re-stated it in a somewhat milder form:

So far as giving money from this federal treasury to provincial governments is concerned, in relation to this question of unemployment as it exists to-day, I might be prepared to go a certain length possibly in meeting one or two of the western provinces that have Progressive premiers at the head of their governments, but I would not give a single cent to any Tory government ... May I repeat what I have said? With respect to giving moneys out of the federal treasury to any Tory government in this country for these alleged unemployment purposes, with these governments situated as they are to-day, with policies diametrically opposed to those of this government, I would not give them a five-cent piece.[27]

A guarantee of provincial co-operation is to be found in the fact that, save in one province out of nine, Liberal Governments are already in office ... It would seem that this is the kind of national Government the people of Canada really want; a Government, in the Dominion and provinces alike, that will be able to give expression to the will of the people as unmistakably expressed at the polls.[28]

However natural such a stand may be, and leaving aside the questionable ethics on which it is based, an avowal along these lines is of doubtful political value. Certainly there is a strong probability that many people will be antagonized by the idea that considerations of party advantage will materially affect Dominion-provincial arrangements, which, they like to believe, are thought out on a higher plane and are determined by principles and not by expediency.[29] There can be little doubt, for example, that the "five-cent speech" heavily handicapped the Liberals in the election which followed almost immediately.

The curious and paradoxical aspect of this Dominion-provincial party relationship is that despite what has been stated above about friendly co-operation when the Dominion and provincial governments belong to the same party, it is by no means certain that a party is better off in the constituencies when it is in power in both places. Under such circumstances the dominant party cannot shift the blame for inaction, mistakes, or unpopuar policies, for it is clearly bound to accept responsibility through its control of both Dominion and provincial governments; whereas any unfortunate consequences which may occur under a separation of party control can usually be ascribed to the neglect or the errors committed by the other side. It has even been said that Sir John Macdonald believed that there was no disadvantage in having his opponents in power in the provinces, but the care which Sir John took to keep his provincial fences intact does not seem to justify such a statement. Certainly Sir Wilfrid Laurier paid exceptional attention to the party fortunes in the provinces

27/Can. H. of C. Debates, April 3, 1930, pp. 1227–8.
28/Quoted in ibid., Oct. 19, 1945, p. 1295.
29/Such ideas can be readily corrected by a study of the Dominion-provincial negotiations of 1946 and 1947, and of Maxwell, Federal Subsidies to the Provincial Governments in Canada.

and he never doubted that solid provincial support was a great bulwark for the party in the Dominion.

The reverse, however, may not be true. While it may be advantageous for a Dominion government to have its own party in power in the provinces, it may well be that a provincial government is more secure if it is politically opposed to the party in power in Ottawa. Here and there, no doubt, a provincial government in such a situation may lose through a lack of federal cordiality and assistance; but even in these circumstances, fate, working through the Dominion government, has placed a magnificent electoral weapon in the hands of the provincial cabinet which it can scarcely fail to use to its advantage. The election issues which have always been most successful in the Canadian provinces have been those which were directed at the encroachments of the Dominion, and these can be urged without restraint if the provincial cabinet is not handicapped in advance by belonging to the same party as its federal adversary. Unity of party control may arouse, indeed, the suspicion in the province that its ministers are unduly acquiescent in Dominion policies and that they are afraid of antagonizing their friends in Ottawa by fighting fearlessly for the rights of the province. This was the opinion, for example, voiced by a western paper in the following editorial:

These western provinces have had sharp conflicts with Ottawa in an endeavour to secure full equality with the other provinces in Confederation, and are still suffering in a very considerable degree from discrimination in federal legislation. Too close relationship between federal and provincial parties in the past has been a potent factor in preventing the removal of this discrimination, and undoubtedly the maintenance of such relationship will prove a handicap in the future. It may be difficult at times to maintain a clear-cut distinction, but the needs of this country will be better served if provincial parties as far as possible adhere to provincial matters and avoid those relationships with federal parties which have proved to be detrimental to the welfare of these western provinces.[30]

That a provincial electorate may be little moved by a desire to choose a government of the same party as the federal cabinet receives a substantial degree of confirmation in the records, and elections down to fairly recent years have often shown cyclic party movements which follow a pattern. First, the great majority of the Dominion and provincial governments will belong to the same political party; second, the provincial governments will begin to fall away to the opposition party or parties until these are in a majority; third, there is an overturn in the Dominion Parliament which brings it once more into sympathy with the provinces, whereupon the cycle begins anew. No sure conclusions can be drawn from these sequences, and the pattern is not a consistent one; but one generalization seems possible. The records suggest at least that provincial electorates have shown a decided tendency to fall away from the party which gains control of the Dominion Parliament.[31]

30/*Grain Growers Guide*, quoted in *Canadian Annual Review, 1923*, pp. 715–16.
31/These generalizations are, of course, subject to some qualifications. For an analysis

While normally provincial elections are fought on provincial issues, questions which involve Dominion-provincial relations (and particularly financial relations) have been very common, although these two may be considered to be provincial issues. There are also numerous instances where Dominion issues have virtually forced the provincial questions out of the field, especially when either party has felt it would gain by such a manoeuvre and turn attention from less popular topics. Thus the Saskatchewan Liberal government, wishing to capitalize on the popularity of reciprocity in that province as shown in the 1911 federal election, fought the provincial election in the following year on the same question. "The issue in the election," said the Liberal leader, "will be the trade question"; and in his manifesto of sixteen paragraphs, the one dealing with reciprocity was given as much space as the other fifteen combined. A second manifesto, proclaimed just before the election, declared that reciprocity was "the whole issue."[32] In 1925 the premier of Nova Scotia announced: "The one and really great issue in this [provincial] election is to lift from this province the weight of an oppressive tariff visited upon us to our damage by a closely organized body of manufacturers a thousand miles away."[33] The Conservative leader not unnaturally refused the challenge, promised to give Nova Scotia a purely "business government," and stressed especially the great need to divorce provincial from Dominion politics. He (Mr Rhodes) "would hew to the line, let the chips fall where they may."

Yet Premier Rhodes presided at the Winnipeg National Conservative Convention in 1927. In the federal election of 1930 the whole weight of his government was thrown in the Conservative interest. During a campaign visit to Nova Scotia by R. B. Bennett the premier spoke from his platform, and "subscribed" to his policies. His minister of Mines, speaking from the same platform as Bennett, said "if one is in agreement with the principles of the Conservative Government in Nova Scotia, it is impossible not to be a Conservative in federal politics as well." While there are sound reasons for local and federal politics being "divorced" the fact remains that they are not. Mr Rhodes' first lieutenant, the minister of Mines, said, "I am not of those who believe in divorcing federal and provincial politics in their entirety. It cannot be done. One cannot be a political chameleon."[34] Nor is it unknown for a provincial issue to loom large in a Dominion election: the medical care insurance plan introduced by the government of Saskatchewan in 1961-2 was an influential factor in the province in the federal election of 1962, and NDP supporters outside Saskatchewan also used the issue during the campaign.[35] The low sales of wheat and the federal

---

of relevant material see Howard A. Scarrow, "Federal-Provincial Voting Patterns in Canada," *Canadian Journal of Economics and Political Science*, xxxvi, no. 2 (May 1960), pp. 289-98.

32/*Canadian Annual Review, 1912*, pp. 561-6.
33/*Ibid., 1925-6*, pp. 402-3.
34/*Queen's Quarterly*, Winter 1929, pp. 161-3.
35/See Ward and Spafford, *Politics in Saskatchewan*.

government's white paper on taxation, both national matters, were lively issues in all three prairie provinces in 1969–70.

Party candidates, Dominion and provincial, commonly but not always support one another on the hustings; it is often (but again not always) mutually advantageous for them to make the party supporter a consistent voter in both fields. "Political chameleons" clearly do not make for party solidarity and reliability. The same reciprocal exchange of talent does not extend so commonly to Dominion and provincial cabinet ministers although it is by no means unknown. The support of members of a provincial cabinet in the past was given freely and eloquently in a Dominion election; and it was appreciated and not infrequently recognized by appointment to the federai cabinet.[36] Federal ministers, however, do not participate in provincial elections with anything like the same frequency; for such intervention is apt to be misconstrued and resented as an interference in provincial affairs.[37] It is becoming increasingly common too for provincial leaders to hold themselves aloof from federal campaigns for prolonged periods, commonly because of a desire not to damage their province's position in the complex of Dominion-provincial relations.

Some consideration has been given in earlier pages to the methods used to draw up a party platform and to choose a party leader; and it was seen that all parties are now generally agreed that these two functions should be exercised by party meeetings chosen for the purpose. But there is little agreement – particularly between the older parties and the NDP – beyond this point; and such things as the nature of the platform, the relation of the members of the legislature to the platform, and the continuing relation between the leader and the party organization have been the occasion for the adoption of different practices and much controversy. These and allied questions have been already raised under the head of party organization; but they deserve a fuller discussion.

The nature of the platform and its influence on party measures are in some respects still a matter for disagreement. Certainly the older parties do not regard their platforms with the same apparent respect as does the NDP, which follows in this regard its predecessor. Some significance may attach to the prominence which each party gives to its own formal pronouncements. The Liberals have not hesitated to publish the proceedings of their conventions and with them the full statement of their programmes. The Conservatives, who had derived great enjoyment and possibly some political advantage from sniping at

36/Thus Wilfrid Laurier's first cabinet in 1896 included no less than three provincial premiers – Mowat, Fielding, and Blair. Bennett in 1930 made the premier of Nova Scotia a federal minister; the premier of Ontario, the high commissioner for Canada in London.

37/A most exceptional intervention was that of Dominion ministers in the Quebec election of 1939; but this could be attributed to the serious emergency caused by the Quebec premier's demand for popular support against participation in the war. On that occasion the four French Canadians in the federal cabinet announced that a victory for the Quebec Union Nationale party (under the premier) would be followed by their withdrawal from the Dominion government, and they threw their influence wholeheartedly into the provincial struggle with conspicuous success.

the Liberals with their 1919 principles, deliberately avoided presenting their enemies with the same kind of ammunition when their national programme was drafted in 1927, for in a published report running to 436 pages they were unable to find room for a verbatim statement of the platform. Other Conservative national conventions were not even honoured with a souvenir book of pictures; in 1957, indeed, the mass of resolutions passed at the party's 1956 convention was not only not used as a coherent platform, but was reportedly ordered burned by the party leader. In 1966 Prime Minister Pearson announced that he considered resolutions passed at party conferences as guidelines only.[38] The CCF party had the courage – or foolhardiness – to publish the proceedings of their conventions, provincial and national, in detail, and the most conspicuous section was that which gave the impressive list of resolutions which had been proposed and considered.

The NDP, like the CCF, is willing to be explicit in its general aims and in many of the measures which it puts forward. This may be due in part to its realization that the opportunity to carry these into execution is still remote, but it arises chiefly from the system it uses and the remarkable fertility of its conventions at all levels in producing proposals of infinite number and variety. The older parties are inclined to be more cautious, and until recently their constitutions said literally nothing about the formulation of the party platform, or the leader's responsibility in regard to it; both national associations now have standing committees on policy, and provisions for regular policy meetings have been added to their constitutions. It has already been pointed out that the Canadian situation frequently leads both these parties to follow contradictory policies in the drafting of platforms: some sections are kept very general in order to avoid antagonizing different groups of voters, while others deal with a wide variety of particular topics on the assumption that each of these will appeal to a special element or area in the Dominion. Even so, both the older parties admit the desirability of phrasing all paragraphs, with few exceptions, in vague terms, so that when the party eventually goes into action it will have the advantage of flexibility in interpretation and not find itself hampered by bonds which it itself has tied. The following comment by a friendly newspaper of the Conservative platform of 1927 gives a somewhat cynical statement of this attitude which still has validity:

The Conservative convention has apparently listened with at least one ear to the wise advice which came to it from all over the country not to attempt to write a "platform." The loose and unrelated collection of resolutions which it has adopted – commonly with little discussion and even less consideration – come as near as such a flood of words possibly could to being the absolute zero in the way of "platforms."

38/John Dafoe, "How the Tories Fared on the Way to Democracy," *Globe and Mail*, March 15, 1969; Newman, "How to Tell the Grits from the Tories," *Maclean's*, May 5, 1962. See also Meisel, "The Formulation of Liberal and Conservative Programmes in the 1957 Canadian General Election," *Canadian Journal of Economics and Political Science*, XXVI, no. 4 (Nov. 1960), pp. 565–74.

Most of them are notable for what they leave out; and yet some of them could with profit have left out more ... The convention has got the right idea, i.e., that the best platform for a hurried, haste-driven and heterogeneous gathering to adopt is either a blank piece of paper or one to which even the most cantankerous Grit could not take exception.[39]

Even when the platform is fairly specific, the official party leaders, when they attain power, will use their discretion as to how much of it shall be enacted or executed and whether the time or the occasion for action has yet arrived. This might fairly be dubbed the "chart and compass" theory, for the metaphor was used by Mackenzie King at the time of his election as leader, and he reverted to it on several later occasions. King insisted that the 1919 platform of the Liberal party was given to him and the leaders for guidance only; and that if elected to office he would not attempt to follow it literally but would exercise a wide discretion.[40] The great majority of Liberals and Conservatives would adopt such a position with little hesitation. They acknowledge an obligation to observe in general fashion Liberal and Conservative principles (although these may at times become a trifle elusive), and they accept broadly the party platform,[41] though it is not to be construed as mandatory as to time or extent. Leaders of both parties have generally since the inception of the national leadership convention in 1919 been in the position of having been selected *after* the platform has been settled, which candidates for the leadership rarely try to influence; Mr Diefenbaker's stout opposition to the "two nations" concept at the Conservative convention of 1967, at which he was seeking re-election, was a notable exception.

On the other hand, members of these older parties will support with reasonable certainty the party manifesto which the leader issues to the country immediately before an election or at least did until the campaign of 1968, when the nature of the Liberal leader's pronouncements, particularly, made it difficult to determine whether a manifesto had been issued or not. The manifesto in effect tended to supplant the platform, and this emphasizes yet again the dominating position of the party leader.[42] The manifesto was drafted by him, usually with assistance from those in his immediate confidence, and it stressed those issues on which the leader counted to win the election. The manifesto (which has no doubt not disappeared) usually drew heavily from the formal platform; but its great merit was its timeliness and its close association with the immediate problem of how the electorate will vote. No platform can anticipate accurately matters of this kind; and even the CCF party, which was most in-

39/*Montreal Daily Star*, Oct. 12, 1927 (editorial).
40/*Can. H. of C. Debates*, May 23, 1923, p. 3048.
41/Even this is not to be taken too literally. W. S. Fielding, a past and then a later minister of Finance, said he had not voted for the tariff section in the Liberal platform, that he had never concealed his disapproval of it, and that it was not discussed at his election. *Ibid.*, June 6, 12, 1922, pp. 2529–30, 2851.
42/*Supra*, pp. 190–2.

clined to glorify the platform as an inspired pronouncement, did not dispense with a manifesto before the election although it insisted that this be approved by the convention or, failing that, by the national (or provincial) council.

The Conservative party has been both the chief sufferer and beneficiary in recent years from the dominant position which the leader has acquired over the party policies and, indeed, over many of the accepted party principles. Time and again the Conservative leaders have cut loose from traditional Conservative parties – not without some justification, but frequently at the cost of creating a disunited and dissatisfied element in the party following. Sir Robert Borden's nationalist tendencies in the later years of the First World War, Meighen's ill-starred Hamilton speech in which he advocated a general election before any troops should be sent abroad to fight another war, Bennett's endorsement of a programme of social legislation, and Bracken's departure in the direction of freer trade, are all outstanding examples of how far a Conservative leader has led, or attempted to lead, his party from the well-worn traditional path; and Mr Diefenbaker had to survive many suspicions that he was a dangerous prairie radical, both before and after his choice as leader; and in the end he did not survive, but became, in a singularly moving convention, the first leader to be publicly rejected by his own party. Two contemporary comments from the Conservative press will indicate the shock which some of these pioneering adventures administered to many loyal Conservatives:

Our own view is that since the party came into power in 1911 Conservative leaders have at times taken a little too much on themselves in the matter of shaping policy. The policy of the Conservative party is delivered to the leader, and it is his business to do what he can to carry it out, not to presume to add to it or subtract from it.[43] When Sir Robert Borden was leader and Prime Minister he exceeded his warrant in laying down the doctrine of Canada's status as an independent member of the family of nations, free to vote against the mother country in international conferences. He had no proposition of Conservative policy that he could refer to by way of explaining his taking the long step he took for the separate diplomatic representation of Canada at Washington. He was not carrying out any article of Conservative policy when he took his stand against the Sovereign's conferring titles on Canadians for services deserving of such recognition ...

Meighen did more than his duty as a party leader when he stated in his Hamilton speech that, should Britain again find herself in a crisis similar to that of 1914 no troops would be allowed to leave the country to aid her until a general election should be held and the people's consent by that means obtained.

When leaders go against the grain of their party's traditional sentiments and expressed policy, they should be pulled up and required to keep within the party charter. Few of the party leaders this country has ever had, whether Conservative or Liberal, have not at moments gone somewhat beyond their latitude. For that they ought to be checked, not deposed unless they are very wrong-headed.[44]

The Prime Minister [Bennett] to-night is to continue his series of broadcasts and

---

43/This is itself as unorthodox a piece of Conservative doctrine as the ideas which are being criticized.

44/Toronto *Mail and Empire*, Sept. 18, 1926 (editorial).

is to take the public, including the members of the Conservative party and not excluding, probably, his colleagues in the Government, a little further into his confidence. No doubt he will have a large audience. He has already, in his address of Wednesday evening, startled and shocked the Canadian people, and more especially those of Conservative leanings, by informing them that he proposes to "reform" the business of the country by means of a policy of intervention, regulation and control. He has stated that the old order has passed, never to return, that corrections are imperative and that the right time to bring about the changes has come. Reform means intervention and he nails the flag of "progress" to the masthead. All of which is very strange talk from a Conservative Prime Minister, strange because it does violence to every Conservative principle, and strange because it is glaringly illogical.

It is not pretended, or, at any rate, it is not stated, that this policy of so-called reform is the policy of the cabinet as a whole, and it most certainly cannot be represented as the policy of the Conservative party, since the party has been given no opportunity of saying whether or not it is disposed to fly the flag of Socialism side by side with the historic banner under which Conservatism heretofore has always made its appeal to responsible, sober-minded Canadians.[45]

The clear answer to criticism of this kind is that if the party solidarity and support are to be maintained, a closer liaison between leader and party must be established and continually maintained; and today both the Liberal and the Progressive Conservative parties are making an effort to bridge the gap by means of more frequent meetings of their national representative bodies. "The Prime Minister," Mr Dalton Camp wrote in 1966, in a critical mood which has become increasingly representative of the older parties, "recently told his party supporters ... that he would stay on, so long as his strength and health were maintained, as if continuing his leadership were a matter between himself and his Maker, and not between himself and his supporters."[46] Mr Camp was then national president of the Progressive Conservative Association, and one of the leaders of a movement which may revolutionize two fundamental relationships in the Liberal and Conservative parties: that between the leader and the party, and that between the leader and the platform. Both parties, as noted above, have begun at least to attempt the enlargement of the rôle of the extra-parliamentary wing in policy formation, and the practice of meeting more frequently cannot help but encourage that. Both parties also now have constitutional provisions for a regular review of the leadership. The Liberal constitution says simply: "A resolution calling for a Leadership Convention shall be placed automatically on the Agenda of the Biennial Convention next following a Federal General Election. If such resolution is duly adopted by secret ballot the Executive Committee shall call a Leadership Convention to take place within one year."[47] The Conservative provisions are more cautious, for when the

45/Montreal *Gazette*, Jan. 4, 1935 (editorial).
46/*Globe and Mail*, Sept. 21, 1966.
47/*Constitution of the Liberal Federation of Canada*, as amended at the National Convention, 1968, clause 9, H.

party is in power "no resolution calling for a leadership convention may be put unless the office is then vacant through death or resignation or unless the chairman of caucus shall certify that the leader has lost the support of that body by a regular vote of caucus on the question of confidence." When the party is in opposition, the first general meeting after an election is to be asked: "Do we wish to have a leadership convention next year?" but the question cannnot be put "following any election where the party increased its standing in the House by more than 20 percent."[48]

These constitutional limitations on the absolute majesty of party leaders, sensible (and even innocuous) though they may seem, are major departures for the older parties; for the NDP, as for the old CCF, such limitations are routine. The NDP constitution reads starkly: "The Convention shall be the supreme governing body of the Party and shall have final authority in all matters of federal policy, program and constitution ... The Convention shall elect the following officers: (a) a Leader."[49] No CCF or NDP leader has been deposed when seeking re-election, but on at least two occasions (in Ontario and Manitoba in 1968) provincial conventions became genuine leadership battles. Such contests can produce bitter divisions within parties, and it is common for the victor in any party leadership race to seek to placate or otherwise accommodate his unsuccessful rivals; but it is not easy for a leader to take a charitable view of a colleague who has openly tried to overthrow him.

The NDP conventions, like their CCF predecessors give a frequent opportunity to the party rank and file to review the work of the leaders and to stimulate them, if need be, by criticism and suggestion; the idea that underlies the acceptance of the convention as "the supreme governing body of the Party" is fundamentally healthy, and if the process of review is used with common sense, should benefit leaders and ordinary workers alike. Certainly the provincial annual meetings of the older parties as commonly conducted are almost entirely routine affairs which arouse no interest either within or without the party, although it is becoming increasingly common for provincial leaders to seek affirmations of support from them, which presumably implies a willingness to step down. The Conservative meetings which led up to the calling of a federal leadership convention when the leadership was not vacant have no precedent in Liberal or Conservative history, but the NDP is heir to a lively tradition. In 1945 in Ontario, for example, the CCF leader accused the provincial government of operating a Gestapo, and the government was vindicated at the polls. One of the resolutions submitted to the next CCF convention questioned the wisdom both of precipitating an election and of making the charges, and it constituted a virtual vote of want of confidence in the leader, E. B.

48/*Constitution of the Progressive Conservative Association of Canada*, as amended March, 1969, article XII.
49/*Constitution of the New Democratic Party*, as amended November, 1969, articles IV and VI.

Jolliffe. The convention went into closed session, the leader spoke an hour and a half in his own defence, and the whole matter was debated at length, resulting in the vindication of Mr Jolliffe by the convention. The NDP's national convention of 1969 was a controversial affair, pitting a strong left-wing group against the established leadership.

Given the basic principles of parliamentary government, a convention's power must be used with restraint, and it was never entirely clear whether the CCF party as a whole had appreciated what this involved. There was, for example, the emphasis placed on the convention's power to pass resolutions supposedly binding on all members of the party and particularly on those who sit in the legislature. While it is true that these resolutions were first discussed to some extent by groups and meetings at a lower level and then discussed by the convention itself, this latter consideration was almost always of a most cursory nature and in many instances could not fail to be based on insufficient information. Thus one Ontario CCF convention was expected to pronounce upon the merits of no less than 199 proposals dealing with almost every subject under the sun including the National War Labour Board, cattle, tourist trade, the atomic bomb, old age pensions, immigration, the CCF constitution, publications, nursery schools, religious freedom, university scholarships, Dominion-provincial relations, sewage disposal, sale of war assets, arts and crafts, and Palestine. To accept the opinion of local units on many of these questions as authoritative is on the face of it preposterous, and to accept the collective opinion of the convention as being of any greater value is even more so, for the time which the convention was able to devote to these resolutions was quite literally on an average not more than three or four minutes each.[50] The resolutions passed by the conventions of the other parties are obviously open to attack on the ground that they frequently receive the most casual consideration by the delegates; but they are few in number, are usually general in character, and are rarely expected to be binding immediately and in detail on the party leaders.

The outpouring of collective wisdom by any convention cannot prove very embarrassing as long as the party remains in opposition; but accession to power and acceptance of office may increase rather than stem the flood, to the potential discomfiture of the premier and his cabinet. The only province to have a CCF government was Saskatchewan, and the experience there was instructive, for it revealed clearly the paradox that a party leadership can become involved in when it is responsible both to a legislature, in accordance with the country's constitution, and also to a non-legislative body, under the party's constitution.[51]

50/The minutes of a Dominion convention in 1946, which was faced with 127 resolutions covering an extremely wide range, give this time with some exactness. Early resolutions apparently received a moderate allotment of time; but on the last day they were passed at the rate of at least thirty an hour, or an average of two minutes to each resolution.
51/See Evelyn Eager, "The Paradox of Power in the Saskatchewan C.C.F., 1944–1961,"

The party convention was apparently willing to issue a multiplicity of orders to its ministerial representatives and demand that they be implemented without delay. On a few issues, indeed, the Saskatchewan cabinet and members of the legislature balked at implementing immediately the dictates of the convention, and their prior responsibility to the legislature as a whole had to be insisted upon. That the NDP has once more inherited from the CCF was indicated in 1962 when the Saskatchewan provincial convention of the party passed, among many others, two resolutions requiring the dropping of the legal drinking age to correspond to the voting (that is, from 21 to 18), and a loosening of the religious restrictions surrounding the adopting of children. Whatever else might be said for the merits of these proposals, they were at the time politically explosive and, when added to the convention's criticisms of the political attitudes of the civil service cited above, aroused considerable unfavourable comment at a time when the government was already deeply engaged in the medical care dispute.

Since the CCF government in Saskatchewan lasted twenty years, the demands of parliamentary government and party democracy would not seem to be irreconcilable, though the questioning of the former by zealots who believe in the latter seems to be an inevitable by-product of any serious conflict; it was an element in the NDP's 1969 convention. From the point of view of parliamentary government, it must be conceded that the assertion of what may easily be an immature and ill-informed judgment over the more careful and considered opinion of the leading representatives of the party, in the name of democracy, contains dangers. Procedure of this kind does not necessarily permit reasoned discussion; it fails to utilize the expert knowledge and judgment of a civil service which is trained in what may be a highly specialized field; it ignores administrative and other difficulties which are frequently of decisive importance; it is not designed to produce deliberate and tentative progress towards a desired end; it disregards authority and decision by those who are best informed and who are willing to be judged by their record and performance, and substitutes ill-informed verdicts and instructions by those who have no responsibility and have little to lose by failure. The CCF party always asserted, and the NDP would undoubtedly agree, that the vital considerations in all these matters were the principles and the policies and that the persons who carry them out are entirely secondary; but human institutions can work successfully only if they are being operated by people who are able to devote their utmost efforts and best talents and judgment to their task. In the words of Professor Finer:

The rank and file of employers and employees and of members of the liberal professions have, however, a rather limited personal experience. Think of the railway ticket-collector, the postman, the grocer, the bank clerks, of the bus driver, the miner, the textile worker, and multitudes of others who constitute the modern com-

in J. H. Aitchison, ed., *The Political Process in Canada* (Toronto, 1963), pp. 118–35, for an excellent treatment of this problem.

munity, and ask, what would they know of any fruitful use to government, even of a rural district council, if no external agencies existed to discover and report to them the things they do not and cannot otherwise know? Save for the help of a few, we should be at a standstill. Wants which are largely the issue of instinctive dispositions could be expressed; the immediate self-regarding interest of each group would be well understood and claimed; but how to prevent these from causing collisions with undesirable consequences, how to attain them in an order of priority which would neither balk the desire nor kill the possibility of satisfaction, whether the satisfaction is in any degree possible – these things are not to be learned in the appropriate degree from the common experience of the average man. It requires years of close and constant application to master even a single branch of public affairs.[52]

Those words are no doubt unacceptable to the ultra-democrat; and it is also true that the CCF–NDP procedures are unquestionably more democratic than those of the other parties. That democratic practices can be accommodated to the realities of responsible leadership is suggested by the constitution of the NDP's Legislative Advisory Committee in Saskatchewan, cited in the last chapter; and that the CCF–NDP combination in Saskatchewan lasted twenty years, not only without serious breaks between the political leadership and the party as a whole, but with repeated votes of confidence in the leader at annual conventions, suggests that the problems which an internally democratic party may thrust upon its leaders are not necessarily insurmountable. To think otherwise, indeed, is to raise profound questions about whether democratic government in Canada, with or without parties like the NDP, is possible at all.

On the surface, at least, the common factor underlying all the attempts at control of party leaders and platforms, which were as common with the Progressives and United Farmers as with the CCF and NDP, and have now appeared in Liberal and Conservative ranks, appears to be distrust of organized authority. This has a positive side: another common factor is a firm belief in the validity of the opinions of the ordinary citizen. It is undoubtedly true, as Professor Laski argued years ago, that "The business of the modern citizen is not to ask, what shall I do? But rather, whom shall I trust?"[53] But those words were written before the rise of the modern state, with its complex technical and welfare programmes and the inevitable aggrandizement of executive authority. The modern citizen must add to Laski's admonition at least two other pragmatic questions: "How shall I trust those I trust? And how can I ensure that my trust is not abused?" The CCF and NDP, following in the footsteps of earlier radical movements in Canada, have one answer to these questions. But the other parties, too, have been gradually meeting a new political environment by increasingly complex national organizations which meet oftener, and more systematically, than their predecessors. A decade ago, the leader of the opposi-

52/H. Finer, *The Theory and Practice of Modern Government* (rev. ed., New York, 1949), pp. 262–3.
53/*New Republic*, July 16, 1919.

tion told his party's Study Conference on National Problems that "politics in Canada is becoming a contest for a single category of citizen, the 'liberally-minded' man." One may argue about what a "liberally-minded man" is, but the validity of the underlying assumption that parties must be ready to adapt themselves to changing conditions has never been more obvious than it is now. The parties, it should not be forgotten, are continually seeking control of those changing conditions.

Appendices

Appendix A

THE BRITISH NORTH AMERICA ACT, 1867*

Consolidated with amendments
as of January 1, 1967

An Act for the Union of Canada, Nova Scotia, and New Brunswick, and the Government thereof; and for Purposes connected
therewith.

29th March, 1867.

WHEREAS the Provinces of Canada, Nova Scotia and New Brunswick have expressed their Desire to be federally united into One
Dominion under the Crown of the United Kingdom of Great
Britain and Ireland, with a Constitution similar in Principle to
that of the United Kingdom:

And whereas such a Union would conduce to the Welfare of the
Provinces and promote the Interests of the British Empire:

And whereas on the Establishment of the Union by Authority of
Parliament it is expedient, not only that the Constitution of the
Legislative Authority in the Dominion be provided for, but also
that the Nature of the Executive Government therein be declared:

And whereas it is expedient that Provision be made for the
eventual Admission into the Union of other Parts of British
North America:[1]

I *Preliminary*

1 This Act may be cited as The British North America Act, 1867. Short title

2 Repealed.[2]

• •

*30 and 31 Victoria, c. 3.

1. The enacting clause was repealed by the *Statute Law Revision Act,
1893*, 56–57 Vict., c. 14 (U.K.). It read as follows:
Be it therefore enacted and declared by the Queen's Most Excellent Majesty, by
and with the Advice and Consent of the Lords Spiritual and Temporal, and Commons, in this present Parliament assembled, and by the Authority of the same, as
follows:

2. Section 2, repealed by the *Statute Law Revision Act, 1893*, 56–57
Vict., c.14 (U.K.), read as follows:
2. The Provisions of this Act referring to Her Majesty the Queen extend also to *Application*
the Heirs and Successors of Her Majesty, Kings and Queens of the United Kingdom *of Provisions*
of Great Britain and Ireland. *referring to
the Queen*

II   *Union*

3   It shall be lawful for the Queen, by and with the Advice of Her   Declaration
Majesty's Most Honourable Privy Council, to declare by Proclama-   of Union
tion that, on and after a Day therein appointed, not being more
than Six Months after the passing of this Act, the Provinces of
Canada, Nova Scotia, and New Brunswick shall form and be One
Dominion under the Name of Canada; and on and after that Day
those Three Provinces shall form and be One Dominion under
that Name accordingly.[3]

4   Unless it is otherwise expressed or implied, the Name Canada   Construction
shall be taken to mean Canada as constituted under this Act.[4]   of subsequent
                                                                   Provisions of
                                                                   Act

5   Canada shall be divided into Four Provinces, named Ontario,   Four
Quebec, Nova Scotia, and New Brunswick.[5]   Provinces

6   The Parts of the Province of Canada (as it exists at the passing of   Provinces of
this Act) which formerly constituted respectively the Provinces of   Ontario and
Upper Canada and Lower Canada shall be deemed to be severed,   Quebec
and shall form Two separate Provinces. The Part which formerly
constituted the Province of Upper Canada shall constitute the
Province of Ontario; and the Part which formerly constituted the
Province of Lower Canada shall constitute the Province of
Quebec.

• •

3. The first day of July, 1867, was fixed by proclamation dated May
22, 1867.

4. Partially repealed by the *Statute Law Revision Act, 1893*, 56–57
Vict., c. 14 (U.K.). As originally enacted the section read as follows:
   4. The subsequent Provisions of this Act shall, unless it is otherwise expressed or
implied, commence and have effect on and after the Union, that is to say, on and
after the Day appointed for the Union taking effect in the Queen's Proclamation;
and in the same Provisions, unless it is otherwise expressed or implied, the Name
Canada shall be taken to mean Canada as constituted under this Act.

5. Canada now consists of ten provinces (Ontario, Quebec, Nova
Scotia, New Brunswick, Manitoba, British Columbia, Prince Edward
Island, Alberta, Saskatchewan and Newfoundland) and two territories
(the Yukon Territory and the Northwest Territories).
   The first territories added to the Union were Rupert's Land and the
North-Western Territory, (subsequently designated the Northwest Ter-
ritories), which were admitted pursuant to section 146 of the *British
North America Act, 1867* and the *Rupert's Land Act, 1868*, 31–32 Vict.,
c. 105 (U.K.), by Order in Council of June 23, 1870, effective July 15,
1870. Prior to the admission of these territories the Parliament of
Canada enacted the *Act for the temporary Government of Rupert's
Land and the North-Western Territory when united with Canada*
(32–33 Vict., c. 3), and the *Manitoba Act* (33 Vict., c. 3), which provided for the formation of the Province of Manitoba.
   British Columbia was admitted into the Union pursuant to section
146 of the *British North America Act, 1867*, by Order in Council of
May 16, 1871, effective July 20, 1871.

7   The Provinces of Nova Scotia and New Brunswick shall have the   Provinces of
     same Limits as at the passing of this Act.   Nova Scotia
                                                                      and New
                                                                      Brunswick

8   In the general Census of the Population of Canada which is hereby   Decennial
     required to be taken in the Year One thousand eight hundred and   Census
     seventy-one, and in every Tenth Year thereafter, the respective
     Populations of the Four Provinces shall be distinguished.

III   *Executive Power*

9   The Executive Government and Authority of and over Canada is   Declaration
     hereby declared to continue and be vested in the Queen.   of Executive
                                                                     Power in
                                                                     the Queen

10   The Provisions of this Act referring to the Governor General ex-   Application
     tend and apply to the Governor General of the Time being of   of Provisions
     Canada, or other the Chief Executive Officer or Administrator for   referring to
                                                                         Governor
     the Time being carrying on the Government of Canada on behalf   General
     and in the Name of the Queen, by whatever Title he is designated.

11   There shall be a Council to aid and advise in the Government of   Constitution
     Canada, to be styled the Queen's Privy Council for Canada; and   of Privy
     the Persons who are to be Members of that Council shall be from   Council for
                                                                        Canada
     Time to Time chosen and summoned by the Governor General

• •

     Prince Edward Island was admitted pursuant to section 146 of the
British North America Act, 1867, by Order in Council of June 26, 1873,
effective July 1, 1873.
     On June 29, 1871, the United Kingdom Parliament enacted the
British North America Act, 1871 (34–35 Vict., c. 28) authorizing the
creation of additional provinces out of territories not included in any
province. Pursuant to this statute, the Parliament of Canada enacted
The Alberta Act, (July 20, 1905, 4–5 Edw. VII, c. 3) and *The Saskatchewan Act,* (July 20, 1905, 4–5 Edw. VII, c. 42), providing for the
creation of the provinces of Alberta and Saskatchewan respectively.
Both these acts came into force on Sept. 1, 1905.
     Meanwhile, all remaining British possessions and territories in North
America and the islands adjacent thereto, except the colony of Newfoundland and its dependencies, were admitted into the Canadian Confederation by Order in Council dated July 31, 1880.
     The Parliament of Canada added portions of the Northwest Ter-
ritories to the adjoining provinces in 1912 by *The Ontario Boundaries
Extension Act,* 2 Geo. V, c. 40, *The Quebec Boundaries Extension Act,
1912,* 2 Geo. V, c. 45, and *The Manitoba Boundaries Extension Act,
1912,* 2 Geo. V, c. 32, and further additions were made to Manitoba by
The Manitoba Boundaries Extension Act, 1930, 20–21 Geo. V, c. 28.
     The Yukon Territory was created out of the Northwest Territories
in 1898 by *The Yukon Territory Act,* 61 Vict., c. 6, (Canada).
     Newfoundland was added on March 31, 1949, by the *British North
America Act, 1949,* (U.K.), 12–13 Geo. VI, c. 22, which ratified the
Terms of Union between Canada and Newfoundland.

and sworn in as Privy Councillors, and Members thereof may be from Time to Time removed by the Governor General.

12   All Powers, Authorities, and Functions which under any Act of the Parliament of Great Britain, or of the Parliament of the United Kingdom of Great Britain and Ireland, or of the Legislature of Upper Canada, Lower Canada, Canada, Nova Scotia, or New Brunswick, are at the Union vested in or exerciseable by the respective Governors or Lieutenant Governors of those Provinces, with the Advice, or with the Advice and Consent, of the respective Executive Councils thereof, or in conjunction with those Councils, or with any Number of Members thereof, or by those Governors or Lieutenant Governors individually, shall, as far as the same continue in existence and capable of being exercised after the Union in relation to the Government of Canada, be vested in and exerciseable by the Governor General, with the Advice or with the Advice and Consent of or in conjunction with the Queen's Privy Council for Canada, or any Member thereof, or by the Governor General individually, as the Case requires, subject nevertheless (except with respect to such as exist under Acts of the Parliament of Great Britain or of the Parliament of the United Kingdom of Great Britain and Ireland) to be abolished or altered by the Parliament of Canada.[6]

All Powers under Acts to be exercised by Governor General with Advice of Privy Council, or alone

13   The Provisions of this Act referring to the Governor General in Council shall be construed as referring to the Governor General acting by and with the Advice of the Queen's Privy Council for Canada.

Application of Provisions referring to Governor General in Council

14   It shall be lawful for the Queen, if Her Majesty thinks fit, to authorize the Governor General from Time to Time to appoint any Person or any Persons jointly or severally to be his Deputy or Deputies within any Part or Parts of Canada, and in that Capacity to exercise during the Pleasure of the Governor General such of the Powers, Authorities, and Functions of the Governor General as the Governor General deems it necessary or expedient to assign to him or them, subject to any Limitations or Directions expressed or given by the Queen; but the Appointment of such a Deputy or Deputies shall not affect the Exercise by the Governor General himself of any Power, Authority or Function.

Power to Her Majesty to authorize Governor General to appoint Deputies

15   The Command-in-Chief of the Land and Naval Militia, and of all Naval and Military Forces, of and in Canada, is hereby declared to continue and be vested in the Queen.

Command of armed Forces to continue to be vested in the Queen

16   Until the Queen otherwise directs, the Seat of Government of Canada shall be Ottawa.

Seat of Government of Canada

●●●

6. See the notes to section 129, *infra*.

IV   *Legislative Power*

17   There shall be One Parliament for Canada, consisting of the Queen, an Upper House styled the Senate, and the House of Commons.

Constitution of Parliament of Canada

18   The privileges, immunities, and powers to be held, enjoyed, and exercised by the Senate and by the House of Commons, and by the Members thereof respectively, shall be such as are from time to time defined by Act of the Parliament of Canada, but so that any Act of the Parliament of Canada defining such privileges, immunities, and powers shall not confer any privileges, immunities, or powers exceeding those at the passing of such Act held, enjoyed, and exercised by the Commons House of Parliament of the United Kingdom of Great Britain and Ireland, and by the Members thereof.[7]

Privileges, etc. of Houses

19   The Parliament of Canada shall be called together not later than Six Months after the Union.[8]

First Session of the Parliament of Canada

20   There shall be a Session of the Parliament of Canada once at least in every Year, so that Twelve Months shall not intervene between the last Sitting of the Parliament in one Session and its first Sitting in the next Session.[9]

Yearly Session of the Parliament of Canada

THE SENATE

21   The Senate shall, subject to the Provisions of this Act, consist of One Hundred and Two Members, who shall be styled Senators.[10]

Number of Senators

● ●

7. Repealed and re-enacted by the *Parliament of Canada Act, 1875*, 38–39 Vict., c. 38 (U.K.). The original section read as follows:

18. The Privileges Immunities, and Powers to be held, enjoyed, and exercised by the Senate and by the House of Commons and by the Members thereof respectively shall be such as are from Time to Time defined by Act of the Parliament of Canada, but so that the same shall never exceed those at the passing of this Act held, enjoyed, and exercised by the Commons House of Parliament of the United Kingdom of Great Britain and Ireland and by the Members thereof.

8. Spent. The first session of the first Parliament began on November 6, 1867.

9. The term of the twelfth Parliament was extended by the *British North America Act, 1916*, 6–7 Geo. v, c. 19 (U.K.), which Act was repealed by the *Statute Law Revision Act, 1927*, 17–18 Geo. v, c. 42 (U.K.).

10. As amended by the *British North America Act, 1915*, 5–6 Geo. v, c. 45 (U.K.), and modified by the *British North America Act, 1949*, 12–13 Geo. vi, c. 22 (U.K.).
The original section read as follows:

21. The Senate shall, subject to the Provisions of this Act, consist of Seventy-two Members, who shall be styled Senators.

The *Manitoba Act* added two for Manitoba; the Order in Council admitting British Columbia added three; upon admission of Prince

22   In relation to the Constitution of the Senate Canada shall be Representa-
tion of
Provinces
in Senate
deemed to consist of Four Divisions:—
1   Ontario;
2   Quebec;
3   The Maritime Provinces, Nova Scotia and New Brunswick,
and Prince Edward Island;
4   The Western Provinces of Manitoba, British Columbia, Saskatchewan, and Alberta;
which Four Divisions shall (subject to the Provisions of this Act)
be equally represented in the Senate as follows: Ontario by
twenty-four senators; Quebec by twenty-four senators; the Maritime Provinces and Prince Edward Island by twenty-four senators,
ten thereof representing Nova Scotia, ten thereof representing
New Brunswick, and four thereof representing Prince Edward
Island; the Western Provinces by twenty-four senators, six thereof
representing Manitoba, six thereof representing British Columbia,
six thereof representing Saskatchewan, and six thereof representing Alberta; Newfoundland shall be entitled to be represented in
the Senate by six members.

In the Case of Quebec each of the Twenty-four Senators representing that Province shall be appointed for One of the Twenty-
four Electoral Divisions of Lower Canada specified in Schedule A.
to Chapter One of the Consolidated statutes of Canada.[11]

23   The Qualification of a Senator shall be as follows: Qualifications
of Senator
1   He shall be of the full age of Thirty Years:
2   He shall be either a natural-born Subject of the Queen, or a
Subject of the Queen naturalized by an Act of the Parliament of
Great Britain, or of the Parliament of the United Kingdom of
Great Britain and Ireland, or of the Legislature of One of the
Provinces of Upper Canada, Lower Canada, Canada, Nova Scotia,

• •

Edward Island four more were provided by section 147 of the *British
North America Act, 1867*; *The Alberta Act* and *The Saskatchewan Act*
each added four. The Senate was reconstituted at 96 by the *British
North America Act, 1915*, and six more Senators were added upon
union with Newfoundland.

11. As amended by the *British North America Act, 1915*, and the
British North America Act, 1949, 12–13 Geo. VI, c. 22 (U.K.). The
original section read as follows:
22. In relation to the Constitution of the Senate, Canada shall be deemed to Representa-
tion of
Provinces
in Senate
consist of Three Divisions:
    1. Ontario;
    2. Quebec;
    3. The Maritime Provinces, Nova Scotia and New Brunswick;
which Three Divisions shall (subject to the Provisions of this Act) be equally
represented in the Senate as follows: Ontario by Twenty-four Senators; Quebec by
Twenty-four Senators; and the Maritime Provinces by Twenty-four Senators, Twelve
thereof representing Nova Scotia, and Twelve thereof representing New Brunswick.
    In the Case of Quebec each of the Twenty-four Senators repesenting that Province
shall be appointed for One of the Twenty-four Electoral Divisions of Lower Canada
specified in Schedule A. to Chapter One of the Consolidated Statutes of Canada.

or New Brunswick, before the Union, or of the Parliament of Canada, after the Union:

3   He shall be legally or equitably seised as of Freehold for his own Use and Benefit of Lands or Tenements held in Free and Common Socage, or seised or possessed for his own Use and Benefit of Lands or Tenements held in Franc-alleu or in Roture, within the Province for which he is appointed, of the Value of Four thousand Dollars, over and above all Rents, Dues, Debts, Charges, Mortgages, and Incumbrances due or payable out of or charged on or affecting the same:

4   His Real and Personal Property shall be together worth Four thousand Dollars over and above his Debts and Liabilities:

5   He shall be resident in the Province for which he is appointed:

6   In the Case of Quebec he shall have his Real Property Qualification in the Electoral Division for which he is appointed, or shall be resident in that Division.

24   The Governor General shall from Time to Time, in the Queen's Name, by Instrument under the Great Seal of Canada, summon qualified Persons to the Senate; and, subject to the Provisions of this Act, every Person so summoned shall become and be a Member of the Senate and a Senator. *Summons of Senator*

25   Repealed.[12]

26   If at any Time on the Recommendation of the Governor General the Queen thinks fit to direct that Four or Eight Members be added to the Senate, the Governor General may by Summons to Four or Eight qualified Persons (as the Case may be), representing equally the Four Divisions of Canada, add to the Senate accordingly.[13] *Addition of Senators in certain cases*

27   In case of such Addition being at any Time made, the Governor General shall not summon any Person to the Senate, except upon a further like Direction by the Queen on the like Recommendation, to represent one of the Four Divisions until such Division is represented by Twenty-four Senators and no more.[14] *Reduction of Senate to normal Number*

• •

12. Repealed by the *Statute Law Revision Act, 1893*, 56–57 Vict., c. 14 (U.K.). The section read as follows:

25. Such Persons shall be first summoned to the Senate as the Queen by Warrant under Her Majesty's Royal Sign Manual thinks fit to approve, and their Names shall be inserted in the Queen's Proclamation of Union. *Summons of First Body of Senators*

13. As amended by the *British North America Act, 1915*, 5–6 Geo. v, c. 45 (U.K.). The original section read as follows:

26. If at any Time on the Recommendation of the Governor General the Queen thinks fit to direct that Three or Six Members be added to the Senate, the Governor General may by Summons to Three or Six qualified Persons (as the Case may be), representing equally the Three Divisions of Canada, add to the Senate accordingly. *Addition of Senators in certain cases*

14. As amended by the *British North America Act, 1915*, 5–6 Geo. v, c. 45 (U.K.). The original section read as follows:

27. In case of such Addition being at any Time made the Governor General shall not summon any Person to the Senate, except on a further like Direction by the Queen on the like Recommendation, until each of the Three Divisions of Canada is represented by Twenty-four Senators and no more. *Reduction of Senate to normal Number*

28 The Number of Senators shall not at any Time exceed One Hundred and ten.[15]   Maximum Number of Senators

29 (1) Subject to subsection (2), a Senator shall, subject to the provisions of this Act, hold his place in the Senate for life.   Tenure of Place in Senate
2   A Senator who is summoned to the Senate after the coming into force of this subsection shall, subject to this Act, hold his place in the Senate until he attains the age of seventy-five years.[15A]   Retirement upon attaining age of seventy-five years

30 A Senator may by Writing under his Hand addressed to the Governor General resign his Place in the Senate, and thereupon the same shall be vacant.   Resignation of Place in Senate

31 The Place of a Senator shall become vacant in any of the following Cases: Disqualification of Senators
1   If for Two consecutive Sessions of the Parliament he fails to give his Attendance in the Senate:
2   If he takes an Oath or makes a Declaration or Acknowledgment of Allegiance, Obedience, or Adherence to a Foreign Power, or does an Act whereby he becomes a Subject or Citizen, or entitled to the Rights or Privileges of a Subject or Citizen, of a Foreign Power:
3   If he is adjudged Bankrupt or Insolvent, or applies for the Benefit of any Law relating to Insolvent Debtors, or becomes a public Defaulter:
4   If he is attainted of Treason or convicted of Felony or of any infamous Crime:
5   If he ceases to be qualified in respect of Property or of Residence; provided, that a Senator shall not be deemed to have ceased to be qualified in respect of Residence by reason only of his residing at the Seat of the Government of Canada while holding an Office under that Government requiring his Presence there.

32 When a Vacancy happens in the Senate by Resignation, Death, or otherwise, the Governor General shall by Summons to a fit and qualified Person fill the Vacancy.   Summons on Vacancy in Senate

33 If any Question arises respecting the Qualification of a Senator or a Vacancy in the Senate the same shall be heard and determined by the Senate.   Questions as to Qualifications and Vacancies in Senate

●●●

15. As amended by the *British North America Act, 1915,* 5–6 Geo. v, c. 45 (u.k.). The original section read as follows:
28. The Number of Senators shall not at any Time exceed Seventy-eight.   Maximum Number of Senators

15A. As enacted by the *British North America Act, 1965,* Statutes of Canada, 1965, c. 4 which came into force on the 1st of June, 1965. The original section read as follows:
29. A Senator shall, subject to the Provisions of this Act, hold his Place in the Senate for Life.   Tenure of Place in Senate

34   The Governor General may from Time to Time, by Instrument under the Great Seal of Canada, appoint a Senator to be Speaker of the Senate, and may remove him and appoint another in his Stead.[16]

Appointment of Speaker of Senate

35   Until the Parliament of Canada otherwise provides, the Presence of at least Fifteen Senators, including the Speaker, shall be necessary to constitute a Meeting of the Senate for the Exercise of its Powers.

Quorum of Senate

36   Questions arising in the Senate shall be decided by a Majority of Voices, and the Speaker shall in all Cases have a Vote, and when the Voices are equal the Decision shall be deemed to be in the Negative.

Voting in Senate

THE HOUSE OF COMMONS

37   The House of Commons shall, subject to the Provisions of this Act, consist of Two Hundred and sixty-five Members of whom Eighty-five shall be elected for Ontario, Seventy-five for Quebec, Twelve for Nova Scotia, Ten for New Brunswick, Fourteen for Manitoba, Twenty-two for British Columbia, Four for Prince Edward Island, Seventeen for Alberta, Seventeen for Saskatchewan, Seven for Newfoundland, One for the Yukon Territory and One for the Northwest Territories.[17]

Constitution of House of Commons in Canada

38   The Governor General shall from Time to Time, in the Queen's Name, by Instrument under the Great Seal of Canada, summon and call together the House of Commons.

Summoning of House of Commons

39   A Senator shall not be capable of being elected or of sitting or voting as a Member of the House of Commons.

Senators not to sit in House of Commons

40   Until the Parliament of Canada otherwise provides, Ontario, Quebec, Nova Scotia, and New Brunswick shall, for the Purposes of the Election of Members to serve in the House of Commons, be divided into Electoral Districts as follows:
1   *Ontario.* Ontario shall be divided into the Counties, Ridings of

Electoral districts of the Four Provinces

• •

16. Provision for exercising the functions of Speaker during his absence is made by the *Speaker of the Senate Act*, R.S.C. 1952, c. 255. Doubts as to the power of Parliament to enact such an Act were removed by the *Canadian Speaker (Appointment of Deputy) Act, 1895,* 59 Vict., c. 3 (U.K.).

17. As altered by the *Representation Act,* R.S.C. 1952, c. 334, as amended by S.C. 1962, c. 17. The original section read as follows:
37. The House of Commons shall, subject to the Provisions of this Act, consist of the One hundred and eighty-one Members, of whom Eighty-two shall be elected for Ontario, Sixty-five for Quebec, Nineteen for Nova Scotia, and Fifteen for New Brunswick.
See now the *Electoral Boundaries Readjustment Act*, Statutes of Canada, 1964–65, c. 31.

Counties, Cities, Parts of Cities, and Towns enumerated in the First Schedule to this Act, each whereof shall be an Electoral District, each such District as numbered in that Schedule being entitled to return One Member.

2 *Quebec.* Quebec shall be divided into Sixty-five Electoral Districts, composed of the Sixty-five Electoral Divisions into which Lower Canada is at the passing of this Act divided under Chapter Two of the Consolidated Statutes of Canada, Chapter Seventy-five of the Consolidated Statutes for Lower Canada, and the Act of the Province of Canada of the Twenty-third Year of the Queen, Chapter One, or any other Act amending the same in force at the Union, so that each such Electoral Division shall be for the Purposes of this Act an Electoral District entitled to return One Member.

3 *Nova Scotia.* Each of the Eighteen Counties of Nova Scotia shall be an Electoral District. The County of Halifax shall be entitled to return Two Members, and each of the other Counties One Member.

4 *New Brunswick.* Each of the Fourteen Counties into which New Brunswick is divided, including the City and County of St. John, shall be an Electoral District. The City of St. John shall also be a separate Electoral District. Each of those Fifteen Electoral Districts shall be entitled to return One Member.[18]

41   Until the Parliament of Canada otherwise provides, all Laws in force in the several Provinces at the Union relative to the following Matters or any of them, namely,—the Qualifications and Disqualifications of Persons to be elected or to sit or vote as Members of the House of Assembly or Legislative Assembly in the several Provinces, the Voters at Elections of such Members, the Oaths to be taken by Voters, the Returning Officers, their Powers and Duties, the Proceedings at Elections, the Periods during which Elections may be continued, the Trial of controverted Elections, and Proceedings incident thereto, the vacating of Seats of Members, and the Execution of new Writs in case of Seats vacated otherwise than by Dissolution,—shall respectively apply to Elections of Members to serve in the House of Commons for the same several Provinces.

Continuance of existing Election Laws until Parliament of Canada otherwise provides

Provided that, until the Parliament of Canada otherwise provides, at any Election for a Member of the House of Commons for the District of Algoma, in addition to Persons qualified by the Law of the Province of Canada to vote, every Male British Subject, aged Twenty-one Years or upwards, being a Householder, shall have a Vote.[19]

● ●

18. Spent. The electoral districts are now set out in the *Representation Act*, R.S.C. 1952, c. 334, as amended. See also the *Electoral Boundaries Readjustment Act*, Statutes of Canada, 1964–65, c. 31.

19. Spent. Elections are now provided for by the *Canada Elections Act*,

42 Repealed.[20]

43 Repealed.[21]

44 The House of Commons on its first assembling after a General Election shall proceed with all practicable Speed to elect One of its Members to be Speaker.

As to Election of Speaker of House of Commons

45 In case of a Vacancy happening in the Office of Speaker by Death, Resignation, or otherwise, the House of Commons shall with all practicable Speed proceed to elect another of its Members to be Speaker.

As to filling up Vacancy in Office of Speaker

46 The Speaker shall preside at all Meetings of the House of Commons.

Speaker to preside

47 Until the Parliament of Canada otherwise provides, in case of the Absence for any Reason of the Speaker from the Chair of the House of Commons for a Period of Forty-eight consecutive Hours, the House may elect another of its Members to act as Speaker, and the Member so elected shall during the Continuance of such Absence of the Speaker have and execute all the Powers, Privileges, and Duties of Speaker.[22]

Provision in case of Absence of Speaker

48 The Presence of at least Twenty Members of the House of Commons shall be necessary to constitute a Meeting of the House for the Exercise of its Powers, and for that Purpose the Speaker shall be reckoned as a Member.

Quorum of House of Commons

• •

s.c. 1960, c. 38; controverted elections by the *Dominion Controverted Elections Act*, R.S.C. 1952, c. 87; qualifications and disqualifications of members by the *House of Commons Act*, R.S.C. 1952, c. 143 and the *Senate and House of Commons Act*, R.S.C. 1952, c. 249.

20. Repealed by the *Statute Law Revision Act, 1893*, 56–57 Vict., c. 14 (U.K.). The section read as follows:

42. For the First Election of Members to serve in the House of Commons the Governor General shall cause Writs to be issued by such Person, in such Form, and addressed to such Returning Officers as he thinks fit.

Writs for First Election

The Person issuing Writs under this Section shall have the like Powers as are possessed at the Union by the Officers charged with the issuing of Writs for the Election of Members to serve in the respective House of Assembly or Legislative Assembly of the Province of Canada, Nova Scotia, or New Brunswick; and the Returning Officers to whom Writs are directed under this Section shall have the like Powers as are possessed at the Union by the Officers charged with the returning of Writs for the Election of Members to serve in the same respective House of Assembly or Legislative Assembly.

21. Repealed by the *Statute Law Revision Act, 1893*, 56–57 Vict., c. 14 (U.K.). The section read as follows:

43. In case a Vacancy in the Representation in the House of Commons of any Electoral District happens before the Meeting of the Parliament, or after the Meeting of the Parliament before Provision is made by the Parliament in this Behalf, the Provisions of the last foregoing Section of this Act shall extend and apply to the issuing and returning of a Writ in respect of such vacant District.

As to Casual Vacancies

22. Provision for exercising the functions of Speaker during his absence is now made by the *Speaker of the House of Commons Act*, R.S.C. 1952, c. 254.

49   Questions arising in the House of Commons shall be decided by a   Voting in House of Commons
Majority of Voices other than that of the Speaker, and when the
Voices are equal, but not otherwise, the Speaker shall have a Vote.

50   Every House of Commons shall continue for Five Years from the   Duration of House of Commons
Day of the Return of the Writs for choosing the House (subject to
be sooner dissolved by the Governor General), and no longer.

51   1   Subject as hereinafter provided, the number of members of the   Readjustment representation in Commons
House of Commons shall be two hundred and sixty-three and the
representation of the provinces therein shall forthwith upon the
coming into force of this section and thereafter on the completion
of each decennial census be readjusted by such authority, in such
manner, and from such time as the Parliament of Canada from
time to time provides, subject and according to the following
rules:

I   There shall be assigned to each of the provinces a number of   Rules
members computed by dividing the total population of the
provinces by two hundred and sixty-one and by dividing the population of each province by the quotient so obtained, disregarding,
except as hereinafter in this section provided, the remainder, if
any, after the said process of division.

II   If the total number of members assigned to all the provinces
pursuant to rule one is less than two hundred and sixty-one, additional members shall be assigned to the provinces (one to a
province) having remainders in the computation under rule one
commencing with the province having the largest remainder and
continuing with the other provinces in the order of the magnitude
of their respective remainders until the total number of members
assigned is two hundred and sixty-one.

III   Notwithstanding anything in this section, if upon completion
of a computation under rules one and two, the number of members to be assigned to a province is less than the number of senators
representing the said province, rules one and two shall cease to
apply in respect of the said province, and there shall be assigned to
the said province a number of members equal to the said number
of senators.

IV   In the event that rules one and two cease to apply in respect of
a province then, for the purposes of computing the number of
members to be assigned to the provinces in respect of which rules
one and two continue to apply, the total population of the provinces
shall be reduced by the number of the population of the province
in respect of which rules one and two have ceased to apply and the
number two hundred and sixty-one shall be reduced by the number
of members assigned to such province pursuant to rule three.

V   On any such readjustment the number of members for any
province shall not be reduced by more than fifteen per cent below
the representation to which such province was entitled under rules
one to four of this subsection at the last preceding readjustment of
the representation of that province, and there shall be no reduction

in the representation of any province as a result of which that province would have a smaller number of members than any other province that according to the results of the then last decennial census did not have a larger population; but for the purposes of any subsequent readjustment of representation under this section any increase in the number of members of the House of Commons resulting from the application of this rule shall not be included in the divisor mentioned in rules one to four of this subsection.

VI   Such readjustment shall not take effect until the termination of the then existing Parliament.

2   The Yukon Territory as constituted by chapter forty-one of the statutes of Canada, 1901, shall be entitled to one member, and such other part of Canada not comprised within a province as may from time to time be defined by the Parliament of Canada shall be entitled to one member.[23]

Yukon Territory and other part not comprised within a province

• •

23. As enacted by the *British North America Act, 1952*, R.S.C. 1952, c. 304, which came into force on June 18, 1952. The section, as originally enacted, read as follows:

51. On the Completion of the Census in the Year One Thousand eight hundred and seventy-one, and of each subsequent decennial Census, the Representation of the Four Provinces shall be re-adjusted by such Authority, in such Manner, and from such Time, as the Parliament of Canada from Time to Time provides, subject and according to the following Rules:

Decennial Re-adjustment of Representation

1 Quebec shall have the fixed Number of Sixty-five Members.
2 There shall be assigned to each of the other Provinces such a Number of Members as will bear the same Proportion to the Number of its Population (ascertained at such Census) as the Number Sixty-five bears to the Number of the Population of Quebec (so ascertained):
3 In the Computation of the Number of Members for a Province a fractional Part not exceeding One Half of the whole Number requisite for entitling the Province to a Member shall be disregarded; but a fractional Part exceeding One Half of that Number shall be equivalent to the whole Number:
4 On any such Re-adjustment the Number of Members for a Province shall not be reduced unless the Proportion which the Number of the Population of the Province bore to the Number of the aggregate Population of Canada at the then last preceding Re-adjustment of the Number of Members for the Province is ascertained at the then latest Census to be diminished by One Twentieth Part or upwards:
5 Such Re-adjustment shall not take effect until the Termination of the then existing Parliament.

The section was amended by the *Statute Law Revision Act, 1893*, 56–57 Vict., c. 14 (U.K.) by repealing the words from "of the census" to "seventy-one and" and the word "subsequent".

By the *British North America Act, 1943*, 6–7 Geo. VI, c. 30 (U.K.) redistribution of seats following the 1941 census was postponed until the first session of Parliament after the war. The section was re-enacted by the *British North America Act, 1946*, 9–10 Geo. VI, c. 63 (U.K.) to read as follows:

51. (1) The number of members of the House of Commons shall be two hundred and fifty-five and the representation of the provinces therein shall forthwith upon the coming into force of this section and thereafter on the completion of each decennial census be readjusted by such authority, in such manner, and from such time as the Parliament of Canada from time to time provides, subject and according to the following rules:—

1 Subject as hereinafter provided, there shall be assigned to each of the provinces a number of members computed by dividing the total population of the provinces by two hundred and fifty-four and by dividing the population of each province by the quotient so obtained, disregarding, except as hereinafter in this section provided, the remainder, if any, after the said process of division.
2 If the total number of members assigned to all the provinces pursuant to rule one is less than two hundred and fifty-four, additional members shall be assigned to the provinces (one to a province) having remainders in the computation under rule one commencing with the province having the largest remainder and continuing

51A Notwithstanding anything in this Act a province shall always be entitled to a number of members in the House of Commons not less than the number of senators representing such province.[24]   Constitution of House of Commons

52 The Number of Members of the House of Commons may be from Time to Time increased by the Parliament of Canada, provided the proportionate Representation of the Provinces prescribed by this Act is not thereby disturbed.   Increase of Number of House of Commons

MONEY VOTES; ROYAL ASSENT

53 Bills for appropriating any Part of the Public Revenue, or for imposing any Tax or Impost, shall originate in the House of Commons.   Appropriation and Tax Bills

54 It shall not be lawful for the House of Commons to adopt or pass any Vote, Resolution, Address, or Bill for the Appropriation of any Part of the Public Revenue, or of any Tax or Impost, to any Purpose that has not been first recommended to that House by Message of the Governor General in the Session in which such Vote, Resolution, Address, or Bill is proposed.   Recommendation of Money Votes

55 Where a Bill passed by the Houses of the Parliament is presented to the Governor General for the Queen's Assent, he shall declare, according to his Discretion, but subject to the Provisions of this Act and to Her Majesty's Instructions, either that he assents thereto in the Queen's Name, or that he withholds the Queen's Assent, or that he reserves the Bill for the Signification of the Queen's Pleasure.   Royal Assent to Bills, etc.

56 Where the Governor General assents to a Bill in the Queen's Name, he shall by the first convenient Opportunity send an authentic Copy of the Act to one of Her Majesty's Principal Secretaries of State, and if the Queen in Council within Two Years after Receipt   Disallowance by Order in Council of Act assented to by Governor General

● ●

with the other provinces in the order of the magnitude of their respective remainders until the total number of members assigned is two hundred and fifty-four.
3 Notwithstanding anything in this section, if upon completion of a computation under rules one and two, the number of members to be assigned to a province is less than the number of senators representing the said province, rules one and two shall cease to apply in respect of the said province, and there shall be assigned to the said province a number of members equal to the said number of senators.
4 In the event that rules one and two cease to apply in respect of a province then, for the purpose of computing the number of members to be assigned to the provinces in respect of which rules one and two continue to apply, the total population of the provinces shall be reduced by the number of the population of the province in respect of which rules one and two have ceased to apply and the number two hundred and fifty-four shall be reduced by the number of members assigned to such province pursuant to rule three.
5 Such readjustment shall not take effect until the termination of the then existing Parliament.
(2) The Yukon Territory as constituted by Chapter forty-one of the Statutes of Canada, 1901, together with any Part of Canada not comprised within a province which may from time to time be included therein by the Parliament of Canada for the purposes of representation in Parliament, shall be entitled to one member.

24. As enacted by the *British North America Act, 1915,* 5–6 Geo. v, c. 45 (U.K.).

thereof by the Secretary of State thinks fit to disallow the Act, such Disallowance (with a Certificate of the Secretary of State of the Day on which the Act was received by him) being signified by the Governor General, by Speech or Message to each of the Houses of the Parliament or by Proclamation, shall annul the Act from and after the Day of such Signification.

57   A Bill reserved for the Signification of the Queen's Pleasure shall not have any Force unless and until, within Two Years from the Day on which it was presented to the Governor General for the Queen's Assent, the Governor General signifies, by Speech or Message to each of the Houses of the Parliament or by Proclamation, that it has received the Assent of the Queen in Council.

<small>Signification of Queen's Pleasure on Bill reserved</small>

An Entry of every such Speech, Message, or Proclamation shall be made in the Journal of each House, and a Duplicate thereof duly attested shall be delivered to the proper Officer to be kept among the Records of Canada.

v   Provincial Constitutions

EXECUTIVE POWER

58   For each Province there shall be an Officer, styled the Lieutenant Governor, appointed by the Governor General in Council by Instrument under the Great Seal of Canada.

<small>Appointment of Lieutenant Governors of Provinces</small>

59   A Lieutenant Governor shall hold Office during the Pleasure of the Governor General; but any Lieutenant Governor appointed after the Commencement of the First Session of the Parliament of Canada shall not be removeable within Five Years from his Appointment, except for Cause assigned, which shall be communicated to him in Writing within One Month after the Order for his Removal is made, and shall be communicated by Message to the Senate and to the House of Commons within One Week thereafter if the Parliament is then sitting, and if not then within One Week after the Commencement of the next Session of the Parliament.

<small>Tenure of Office of Lieutenant Governor</small>

60   The Salaries of the Lieutenant Governors shall be fixed and provided by the Parliament of Canada.[25]

<small>Salaries of Lieutenant Governors</small>

61   Every Lieutenant Governor shall, before assuming the Duties of his Office, make and subscribe before the Governor General or some Person authorized by him Oaths of Allegiance and Office similar to those taken by the Governor General.

<small>Oaths, etc., of Lieutenant Governor</small>

• •

25. Provided for by the *Salaries Act*, R.S.C. 1952, c. 243 as amended by s.c. 1963, c. 41.

62   The Provisions of this Act referring to the Lieutenant Governor   Application of
extend and apply to the Lieutenant Governor for the Time being   provisions
of each Province, or other the Chief Executive Officer or Adminis-   referring to
trator for the Time being carrying on the Government of the   Lieutenant
Province, by whatever Title he is designated.   Governor

63   The Executive Council of Ontario and of Quebec shall be com-   Appointment
posed of such Persons as the Lieutenant Governor from Time to   of Executive
Time thinks fit, and in the first instance of the following Officers,   Officers for
namely,—the Attorney General, the Secretary and Registrar of   Ontario and
the Province, the Treasurer of the Province, the Commissioner of   Quebec
Crown Lands, and the Commissioner of Agriculture and Public
Works, with in Quebec the Speaker of the Legislative Council and
the Solicitor General.[26]

64   The Constitution of the Executive Authority in each of the Prov-   Executive
inces of Nova Scotia and New Brunswick shall, subject to the   Government
Provisions of this Act, continue as it exists at the Union until   of Nova Scotia
altered under the Authority of this Act.[26A]   and New
Brunswick

65   All Powers, Authorities, and Functions which under any Act of   Powers to be
the Parliament of Great Britain, or of the Parliament of the United   exercised by
Kingdom of Great Britain and Ireland, or of the Legislature of   Lieutenant
Upper Canada, Lower Canada, or Canada, were or are before or   Governor of
at the Union vested in or exerciseable by the respective Governors   Ontario or
or Lieutenant Governors of those Provinces, with the Advice or   Quebec with
with the Advice and Consent of the respective Executive Councils   Advice, or
thereof, or in conjunction with those Councils, or with any Number   alone
of Members thereof, or by those Governors or Lieutenant Governors individually, shall, as far as the same are capable of being
exercised after the Union in relation to the Government of Ontario
and Quebec respectively, be vested in and shall or may be exercised
by the Lieutenant Governor of Ontario and Quebec respectively,
with the Advice or with the Advice and Consent of or in conjunction with the respective Executive Councils, or any Members
thereof, or by the Lieutenant Governor individually, as the Case
requires, subject nevertheless (except with respect to such as exist
under Acts of the Parliament of Great Britain, or of the Parliament
of the United Kingdom of Great Britain and Ireland,) to be

● ●

26. Now provided for in Ontario by the *Executive Council Act*, R.S.O.
1960, c. 127, and in Quebec by the *Executive Power Act*, R.S.Q.
1964, c. 9.

26A. A similar provision was included in each of the instruments
admitting British Columbia, Prince Edward Island, and Newfoundland.
The Executive Authorities for Manitoba, Alberta and Saskatchewan
were established by the statutes creating those provinces. See the footnotes to section 5, *supra*.

abolished or altered by the respective Legislatures of Ontario and Quebec.[27]

66 The Provisions of this Act referring to the Lieutenant Governor in Council shall be construed as referring to the Lieutenant Governor of the Province acting by and with the Advice of the Executive Council thereof.

Application of Provisions referring to Lieutenant Governor in Council

67 The Governor General in Council may from Time to Time appoint an Administrator to execute the Office and Functions of Lieutenant Governor during his Absence, Illness, or other Inability.

Administration in Absence, etc., of Lieutenant Governor

68 Unless and until the Executive Government of any Province otherwise directs with respect to that Province, the Seats of Government of the Provinces shall be as follows, namely,—of Ontario, the City of Toronto; of Quebec, the City of Quebec; of Nova Scotia, the City of Halifax; and of New Brunswick, the City of Fredericton.

Seats of Provincial Governments

LEGISLATIVE POWER

1 ONTARIO

69 There shall be a Legislature for Ontario consisting of the Lieutenant Governor and of One House, styled the Legislative Assembly of Ontario.

Legislature for Ontario

70 The Legislative Assembly of Ontario shall be composed of Eighty-two Members, to be elected to represent the Eighty-two Electoral Districts set forth in the First Schedule to this Act.[28]

Electoral districts

2 QUEBEC

71 There shall be a Legislature for Quebec consisting of the Lieutenant Governor and of Two Houses, styled the Legislative Council of Quebec and the Legislative Assembly of Quebec.

Legislature for Quebec

72 The Legislative Council of Quebec shall be composed of Twenty-four Members, to be appointed by the Lieutenant Governor, in the Queen's Name, by Instrument under the Great Seal of Quebec, One being appointed to represent each of the Twenty-four Electoral Divisions of Lower Canada in this Act referred to, and each

Constitution of Legislative Council

● ●

27. See the notes to section 129, *infra.*

28. Spent. Now covered by the *Representation Act,* R.S.O. 1960, c. 353, as amended by S.O. 1962–63, c. 125, which provides that the Assembly shall consist of 108 members, representing the electoral districts set forth in the Schedule to that Act.

holding Office for the Term of his Life, unless the Legislature of Quebec otherwise provides under the Provisions of this Act.[29]

73 The Qualifications of the Legislative Councillors of Quebec shall be the same as those of the Senators for Quebec.[30]

Qualification of Legislative Councillors

74 The Place of a Legislative Councillor of Quebec shall become vacant in the Cases, *mutatis mutandis*, in which the Place of Senator becomes vacant.

Resignation, Disqualification, etc.

75 When Vacancy happens in the Legislative Council of Quebec by Resignation, Death, or otherwise, the Lieutenant Governor, in the Queen's Name, by Instrument under the Great Seal of Quebec, shall appoint a fit and qualified Person to fill the Vacancy.

Vacancies

76 If any Question arises respecting the Qualification of a Legislative Councillor of Quebec, or a Vacancy in the Legislative Council of Quebec, the same shall be heard and determined by the Legislative Council.

Questions as to Vacancies, etc.

77 The Lieutenant Governor may from Time to Time, by Instrument under the Great Seal of Quebec, appoint a Member of the Legislative Council of Quebec to be Speaker thereof, and may remove him and appoint another in his Stead.[31]

Speaker of Legislative Council

78 Until the Legislature of Quebec otherwise provides, the Presence of at least Ten Members of the Legislative Council, including the Speaker, shall be necessary to constitute a Meeting for the Exercise of its Powers.

Quorum of Legislative Council

79 Questions arising in the Legislative Council of Quebec shall be decided by a Majority of Voices, and the Speaker shall in all Cases have a Vote, and when the Voices are equal the Decision shall be deemed to be in the Negative.

Voting in Legislative Council

80 The Legislative Assembly of Quebec shall be composed of Sixty-five Members, to be elected to represent the Sixty-five Electoral Divisions or Districts of Lower Canada in this Act referred to, subject to Alteration thereof by the Legislature of Quebec: Provided that it shall not be lawful to present to the Lieutenant Governor of Quebec for Assent any Bill for altering the Limits of any of the Electoral Divisions or Districts mentioned in the Second

Constitution of Legislative Assembly of Quebec

● ●

29. Spent. Now covered by the *Legislature Act*, R.S.Q. 1964, c. 6 as amended by S.Q. 1965, c. 11; the membership remains at twenty-four, representing the divisions set forth in the *Territorial Division Act*, R.S.Q. 1964, c. 5, as amended by S.Q. 1965, c. 12.

30. Altered by the *Legislature Act*, R.S.Q. 1964, c. 6, s. 7, which provides that it shall be sufficient for any member to be domiciled, and to possess his property qualifications, within the Province of Quebec.

31. Spent. Now covered by the *Legislature Act*, R.S.Q. 1964, c. 6.

Schedule to this Act, unless the Second and Third Readings of such Bill have been passed in the Legislative Assembly with the Concurrence of the Majority of the Members representing all those Electoral Divisions or Districts, and the Assent shall not be given to such Bill unless an Address has been presented by the Legislative Assembly to the Lieutenant Governor stating that it has been so passed.[32]

3 ONTARIO AND QUEBEC

81   Repealed.[33]

82   The Lieutenant Governor of Ontario and of Quebec shall from Time to Time, in the Queen's Name, by Instrument under the Great Seal of the Province, summon and call together the Legislative Assembly of the Province.

Summoning of Legislative Assemblies

83   Until the Legislature of Ontario or of Quebec otherwise provides, a Person accepting or holding in Ontario or in Quebec any Office, Commission, or Employment, permanent or temporary, at the Nomination of the Lieutenant Governor, to which an annual Salary, or any Fee, Allowance, Emolument, or Profit of any Kind or Amount whatever from the Province is attached, shall not be eligible as a Member of the Legislative Assembly of the respective Province, nor shall he sit or vote as such; but nothing in this Section shall make ineligible any Person being a Member of the Executive Council of the respective Province, or holding any of the following Offices, that is to say, the Offices of Attorney General, Secretary and Registrar of the Province, Treasurer of the Province, Commissioner of Crown Lands, and Commissioner of Agriculture and Public Works, and in Quebec Solicitor General, or shall disqualify him to sit or vote in the House for which he is elected, provided he is elected while holding such Office.[34]

Restriction on election of Holders of offices

84   Until the Legislatures of Ontario and Quebec respectively otherwise provide, all Laws which at the Union are in force in those Provinces respectively, relative to the following Matters, or any of

Continuance of existing Election Laws

● ●

32. Altered by the *Legislature Act*, R.S.Q. 1964, c. 6 as amended by S.Q. 1965, c. 11 and the *Territorial Division Act*, R.S.Q. 1964, c. 5 as amended by S.Q. 1965, c. 10; there are now 108 members representing the districts set out in the *Territorial Division Act*.

33. Repealed by the *Statute Law Revision Act, 1893*, 56–57 Vict., c. 14 (U.K.). The section read as follows:

81. The Legislatures of Ontario and Quebec respectively shall be called together not later than Six Months after the Union.

First Session of Legislatures

34. Probably spent. The subject-matter of this section is now covered in Ontario by the *Legislative Assembly Act*, R.S.O. 1960, c. 208, and in Quebec by the *Legislature Act*, R.S.Q. 1964, c. 6.

them, namely,—the Qualifications and Disqualifications of Persons to be elected or to sit or vote as Members of the Assembly of Canada, the Qualifications or Disqualifications of Voters, the Oaths to be taken by Voters, the Returning Officers, their Powers and Duties, the Proceedings at Elections, the Periods during which such Elections may be continued, and the Trial of controverted Elections and the Proceedings incident thereto, the vacating of the Seats of Members and the issuing and execution of new Writs in case of Seats vacated otherwise than by Dissolution,—shall respectively apply to Elections of Members to serve in the respective Legislative Assemblies of Ontario and Quebec.

Provided that, until the Legislature of Ontario otherwise provides, at any Election for a Member of the Legislative Assembly of Ontario for the District of Algoma, in addition to Persons qualified by the Law of the Province of Canada to vote, every male British Subject, aged Twenty-one Years or upwards, being a Householder, shall have a vote.[35]

85   Every Legislative Assembly of Ontario and every Legislative Assembly of Quebec shall continue for Four Years from the Day of the Return of the Writs for choosing the same (subject nevertheless to either the Legislative Assembly of Ontario or the Legislative Assembly of Quebec being sooner dissolved by the Lieutenant Governor of the Province), and no longer.[36]
   Duration of Legislative Assemblies

86   There shall be a Session of the Legislature of Ontario and of that of Quebec once at least in every Year, so that Twelve Months shall not intervene between the last Sitting of the Legislature in each Province in one Session and its first Sitting in the next Session.
   Yearly Session of Legislature

87   The following Provisions of this Act respecting the House of Commons of Canada shall extend and apply to the Legislative Assemblies of Ontario and Quebec, that is to say,—the Provisions relating to the Election of a Speaker originally and on Vacancies, the Duties of the Speaker, the Absence of the Speaker, the Quorum, and the Mode of voting, as if those Provisions were here re-enacted and made applicable in Terms to each such Legislative Assembly.
   Speaker, Quorum, etc.

• •

35. Probably spent. The subject-matter of this section is now covered in Ontario by the *Election Act*, R.S.O. 1960, c. 118, the *Controverted Elections Act*, R.S.O. 1960, c. 65 and the *Legislative Assembly Act*, R.S.O. 1960, c. 208, in Quebec by the *Elections Act*, R.S.Q. 1964, c. 7, the *Provincial Controverted Elections Act*, R.S.Q. 1964, c. 8 and the *Legislature Act*, R.S.Q. 1964, c. 6.

36. The maximum duration of the Legislative Assembly for Ontario and Quebec has been changed to five years by the *Legislative Assembly Act*, R.S.O. 1960, c. 208, and the *Legislature Act*, R.S.Q. 1964, c. 6 respectively.

4 NOVA SCOTIA AND NEW BRUNSWICK

88 The Constitution of the Legislature of each of the Provinces of Nova Scotia and New Brunswick shall, subject to the Provisions of this Act, continue as it exists at the Union until altered under the Authority of this Act.[37]

Constitutions of Legislatures of Nova Scotia and New Brunswick

89 Repealed.[38]

6 THE FOUR PROVINCES

90 The following Provisions of this Act respecting the Parliament of Canada, namely,—the Provisions relating to Appropriation and Tax Bills, the Recommendation of Money Votes, the Assent to Bills, the Disallowance of Acts, and the Signification of Pleasure on Bills reserved,—shall extend and apply to the Legislatures of the several Provinces as if those Provisions were here re-enacted and made applicable in Terms to the respective Provinces and the Legislatures thereof, with the Substitution of the Lieutenant Governor of the Province for the Governor General, of the Governor General for the Queen and for a Secretary of State, of One Year for Two Years, and of the Province for Canada.

Application to Legislatures of Provisions respecting Money Votes, etc.

VI *Distribution of Legislative Powers*

POWERS OF THE PARLIAMENT

91 It shall be lawful for the Queen, by and with the Advice and Consent of the Senate and House of Commons, to make Laws for the Peace, Order, and good Government of Canada, in relation to all Matters not coming within the Classes of Subjects by this Act

Legislative Authority of Parliament of Canada

• •

37. Partially repealed by the *Statute Law Revision Act, 1893*, 56–57 Vict., c. 14 (U.K.) which deleted the following concluding words of the original enactment:

and the House of Assembly of New Brunswick existing at the passing of this Act shall, unless sooner dissolved, continue for the Period for which it was elected.

A similar provision was included in each of the instruments admitting British Columbia, Prince Edward Island, and Newfoundland. The Legislatures of Manitoba, Alberta and Saskatchewan were established by the statutes creating those provinces. See the footnotes to section 5, *supra*.

38. Repealed by the *Statute Law Revision Act, 1893*, 56–57 Vict., c. 14 (U.K.). The section read as follows:

5 *Ontario, Quebec, and Nova Scotia.* 89. Each of the Lieutenant Governors of Ontario, Quebec and Nova Scotia shall cause Writs to be issued for the First Election of Members of the Legislative Assembly thereof in such Form and by such Person as he thinks fit, and at such Time and addressed to such Returning Officer as the Governor General directs, and so that the First Election of Member of Assembly for any Electoral District or any Subdivision thereof shall be held at the same Time and at the same Places as the Election for a Member to serve in the House of Commons of Canada for that Electoral District.

First Elections

assigned exclusively to the Legislatures of the Provinces; and for greater Certainty, but not so as to restrict the Generality of the foregoing Terms of this Section, it is hereby declared that (notwithstanding anything in this Act) the exclusive Legislative Authority of the Parliament of Canada extends to all Matters coming within the Classes of Subjects next herein-after enumerated; that is to say,—

1   The amendment from time to time of the Constitution of Canada, except as regards matters coming within the classes of subjects by this Act assigned exclusively to the Legislatures of the provinces, or as regards right or privileges by this or any other Constitutional Act granted or secured to the Legislature or the Government of a province, or to any class of persons with respect to schools or as regards the use of the English or the French language or as regards the requirements that there shall be a session of the Parliament of Canada at least once each year, and that no House of Commons shall continue for more than five years from the day of the return of the Writs for choosing the House: provided, however, that a House of Commons may in time of real or apprehended war, invasion or insurrection be continued by the Parliament of Canada if such continuation is not opposed by the votes of more than one-third of the members of such House.[39]

1a The Public Debt and Property.[40]

2   The Regulation of Trade and Commerce.

2a Unemployment insurance.[41]

3   The raising of Money by any Mode or System of Taxation.

4   The borrowing of Money on the Public Credit.

5   Postal Service.

6   The Census and Statistics.

7   Militia, Military and Naval Service, and Defence.

8   The fixing of and providing for the Salaries and Allowances of Civil and other Offices of the Government of Canada.

9   Beacons, Buoys, Lighthouses, and Sable Island.

10 Navigation and Shipping.

11 Quarantine and the Establishment and Maintenance of Marine Hospitals.

12 Sea Coast and Inland Fisheries.

13 Ferries between a Province and any British or Foreign Country or between Two Provinces.

14 Currency and Coinage.

15 Banking, Incorporation of Banks, and the Issue of Paper Money.

● ●

39. Added by the *British North America (No. 2) Act, 1949*, 13 Geo. VI, c. 81 (U.K.).

40. Re-numbered by the *British North America (No. 2) Act, 1949*.

41. Added by the *British North America Act, 1940*, 3–4 Geo. VI, c. 36 (U.K.).

16 Savings Banks.
17 Weights and Measures.
18 Bills of Exchange and Promissory Notes.
19 Interest.
20 Legal Tender.
21 Bankruptcy and Insolvency.
22 Patents of Invention and Discovery.
23 Copyrights.
24 Indians, and Lands reserved for the Indians.
25 Naturalization and Aliens.
26 Marriage and Divorce.
27 The Criminal Law, except the Constitution of Courts of Criminal Jurisdiction, but including the Procedure in Criminal Matters.
28 The Establishment, Maintenance, and Management of Penitentiaries.
29 Such Classes of Subjects as are expressly excepted in the Enumeration of the Classes of Subjects by this Act assigned exclusively to the Legislatures of the Provinces.

And any Matter coming within any of the Classes of Subjects enumerated in this Section shall not be deemed to come within the Class of Matters of a local or private Nature comprised in the Enumeration of the Classes of Subjects by this Act assigned exclusively to the Legislatures of the Provinces.[42]

• •

42. Legislative authority has been conferred on Parliament by other Acts as follows:

1. The *British North America Act, 1871*, 34–35 Vict., c. 28 (U.K.).

2. The Parliament of Canada may from time to time establish new Provinces in any territories forming for the time being part of the Dominion of Canada, but not included in any Province thereof, and may, at the time of such establishment, make provision for the constitution and administration of any such Province, and for the passing of laws for the peace, order, and good government of such Province, and for its representation in the said Parliament. *Parliament of Canada may establish new Provinces and provide for the constitution etc., thereof*

3. The Parliament of Canada may from time to time, with the consent of the Legislature of any Province of the said Dominion, increase, diminish, or otherwise alter the limits of such Province, upon such terms and conditions as may be agreed to by the said Legislature, and may, with the like consent, make provision respecting the effect and operation of any such increase or diminution or alteration of territory in relation to any Province affected thereby. *Alteration of limits of Provinces*

4. The Parliament of Canada may from time to time make provision for the administration, peace, order, and good government of any territory not for the time being included in any Province. *Parliament of Canada may legislate for any territory not included in a Province*

5. The following Acts passed by the said Parliament of Canada, and instituted respectively,—"An Act for the temporary government of Rupert's Land and the North Western Territory when united with Canada"; and "An Act to amend and continue the Act thirty-two and thirty-three Victoria, chapter three, and to establish and provide for the government of "the Province of Manitoba," shall be and be deemed to have been valid and effectual for all purposes whatsoever from the date at which they respectively received the assent, in the Queen's name, of the Governor General of the said Dominion of Canada." *Confirmation of Acts of Canada, 32 & 33 Vict. (Canadian) cap. 3; 33 Vict., (Canadian) cap. 3*

6. Except as provided by the third section of this Act, it shall not be competent for the Parliament of Canada to alter the provisions of the last-mentioned Act of the said *Limitation of powers of*

EXCLUSIVE POWERS OF PROVINCIAL LEGISLATURES

92　In each Province the Legislature may exclusively make Laws in relation to Matters coming within the Classes of Subject next herein-after enumerated; that is to say,— Subjects of exclusive Provincial Legislation

1　The Amendment from Time to Time, notwithstanding anything in this Act, of the Constitution of the Province, except as regards the Office of Lieutenant Governor.

2　Direct Taxation within the Province in order to the raising of a Revenue for Provincial Purposes.

3　The borrowing of Money on the sole Credit of the Province.

4　The Establishment and Tenure of Provincial Offices and the Appointment and Payment of Provincial Officers.

5　The Management and Sale of the Public Lands belonging to the Province and of the Timber and Wood thereon.

6　The Establishment, Maintenance, and Management of Public and Reformatory Prisons in and for the Province.

7　The Establishment, Maintenance, and Management of Hospitals, Asylums, Charities, and Eleemosynary Institutions in and for the Province, other than Marine Hospitals.

8　Municipal Institutions in the Province.

9　Shop, Saloon, Tavern, Auctioneer, and other Licences in order to the raising of a Revenue for Provincial, Local, or Municipal Purposes.

10　Local Works and Undertakings other than such as are of the following Classes: (*a*) Lines of Steam or other Ships, Railways, Canals, Telegraphs, and other Works and Undertakings connecting the Province with any other or others of the Provinces, or extending beyond the Limits of the Province; (*b*) Lines of Steam Ships between the Province and any British or Foreign Country;

● ●

Parliament in so far as it relates to the Province of Manitoba, or of any other Act hereafter establishing new Provinces in the said Dominion, subject always to the right of the Legislature of the Province of Manitoba to alter from time to time the provisions of any law respecting the qualification of electors and members of the Legislative Assembly, and to make laws respecting elections in the said Province. Parliament of Canada to legislate for an established Province

The *Rupert's Land Act, 1868*, 31–32 Vict., c. 105 (U.K.) (repealed by the *Statute Law Revision Act, 1893*, 56–57 Vict., c. 14 (U.K.)) had previously conferred similar authority in relation to Rupert's Land and the North-Western Territory upon admission of those areas.

2. The *British North America Act, 1886*, 49–50 Vict., c. 35, (U.K.).

1. The Parliament of Canada may from time to time make provision for the representation in the Senate and House of Commons of Canada, or in either of them, of any territories which for the time being form part of the Dominion of Canada, but are not included in any province thereof. Provision by Parliament of Canada for representation of territories

3. The *Statute of Westminster, 1931*, 22 Geo. v. c. 4, (U.K.).

3. It is hereby declared and enacted that the Parliament of a Dominion has full power to make laws having extra-territorial operation. Power of Parliament of a Dominion to legislate extra-territorially

(c) Such Works as, although wholly situate within the Province, are before or after their Execution declared by the Parliament of Canada to be for the general Advantage of Canada or for the Advantage of Two or more of the Provinces.

11   The Incorporation of Companies with Provincial Objects.

12   The Solemnization of Marriage in the Province.

13   Property and Civil Rights in the Province.

14   The Administration of Justice in the Province, including the Constitution, Maintenance, and Organization of Provincial Courts, both of Civil and of Criminal Jurisdiction, and including Procedure in Civil Matters in those Courts.

15   The Imposition of Punishment by Fine, Penalty, or Imprisonment for enforcing any Law of the Province made in relation to any Matter coming within any of the Classes of Subjects enumerated in this Section.

16   Generally all Matters of a merely local or private Nature in the Province.

EDUCATION

93   In and for each Province the Legislature may exclusively make Laws in relation to Education, subject and according to the following Provisions:— *Legislation respecting Education*

1   Nothing in any such Law shall prejudicially affect any Right or Privilege with respect to Denominational Schools which any Class of Persons have by Law in the Province at the Union:

2   All the Powers, Privileges, and Duties at the Union by Law conferred and imposed in Upper Canada on the Separate Schools and School Trustees of the Queen's Roman Catholic Subjects shall be and the same are hereby extended to the Dissentient Schools of the Queen's Protestant and Roman Catholic Subjects in Quebec:

3   Where in any Province a System of Separate or Dissentient Schools exists by Law at the Union or is thereafter established by the Legislature of the Province, an Appeal shall lie to the Governor General in Council from any Act or Decision of any Provincial Authority affecting any Right or Privilege of the Protestant or Roman Catholic Minority of the Queen's Subjects in relation to Education:

4   In case any such Provincial Law as from Time to Time seems to the Governor General in Council requisite for the due Execution of the Provisions of this Section is not made, or in case any Decision of the Governor General in Council on any Appeal under this Section is not duly executed by the proper Provincial Authority in that Behalf, then and in every such Case, and as far only as the Circumstances of each Case require, the Parliament of Canada may make remedial Laws for the due Execution of the Provisions of

this Section and of any Decision of the Governor General in Council under this Section.[43]

UNIFORMITY OF LAWS IN ONTARIO, NOVA SCOTIA AND
NEW BRUNSWICK

94 Notwithstanding anything in this Act, the Parliament of Canada may make Provision for the Uniformity of all or any of the Laws relative to Property and Civil Rights in Ontario, Nova Scotia, and New Brunswick, and of the Procedure of all or any of the Courts in Those Three Provinces, and from and after the passing of any Act in that Behalf the Power of the Parliament of Canada to make Laws in relation to any Matter comprised in any such Act shall, notwithstanding anything in this Act, be unrestricted; but any Act of the Parliament of Canada making Provision for such Uniformity shall not have effect in any Province unless and until it is adopted and enacted as Law by the Legislature thereof. *Legislation for Uniformity of Laws in Three Provinces*

• •

43. Altered for Manitoba by section 22 of the *Manitoba Act*, 33 Vict., c. 3 (Canada), (confirmed by the *British North America Act, 1871*), which reads as follows:

22. In and for the Province, the said Legislature may exclusively make Laws in relation to Education, subject and according to the following provisions:— *Legislation touching schools subject to certain provisions*
  1 Nothing in any such Law shall prejudicially affect any right or privilege with respect to Denominational Schools which any class of persons have by Law or practice in the Province at the Union:
  2 An appeal shall lie to the Governor General in Council from any Act or decision of the Legislature of the Province, or of any Provincial Authority, affecting any right or privilege, of the Protestant or Roman Catholic minority of the Queen's subjects in relation to Education:
  3 In case any such Provincial Law, as from time to time seems to the Governor General in Council requisite for the due execution of the provisions of this section, is not made, or in case any decision of the Governor General in Council on any appeal under this section is not duly executed by the proper Provincial Authority in that behalf, then, and in every such case, and as far only as the circumstances of each case require, the Parliament of Canada may make remedial Laws for the due execution of the provisions of this section, and of any decision of the Governor General in Council under this section. *Power reserved to Parliament*

Altered for Alberta by section 17 of *The Alberta Act*, 4–5 Edw. VII, c. 3 which reads as follows:

17. Section 93 of The British North America Act, 1867, shall apply to the said province, with the substitution for paragraph (1) of the said section 93 of the following paragraph:— *Education*
  1. Nothing in any such law shall prejudicially affect any right or privilege with respect to separate schools which any class of persons have at the date of the passing of this Act, under the terms of chapters 29 and 30 of the Ordinances of the Northwest Territories, passed in the year 1901, or with respect to religious instruction in any public or separate school as provided for in the said ordinances.
  2. In the appropriation by the Legislature or distribution by the Government of the province of any moneys for the support of schools organized and carried on in accordance with the said chapter 29 or any Act passed in amendment thereof, or in substitution therefor, there shall be no discrimination against schools of any class described in the said chapter 29.
  3. Where the expression "by law" is employed in paragraph 3 of the said section 93, it shall be held to mean the law as set out in the said chapters 29 and 30, and where the expression "at the Union" is employed, in the said paragraph 3, it shall be held to mean the date at which this Act comes into force."

Altered for Saskatchewan by section 17 of *The Saskatchewan Act*, 4–5 Edw. VII, c. 42, which reads as follows:

17. Section 93 of the British North America Act, 1867, shall apply to the said province with the substitution for paragraph (1) of the said section 93 of the following paragraph:— *Education*

OLD AGE PENSIONS

94A The Parliament of Canada may make laws in relation to old age _{Legislation}
pensions and supplementary benefits, including survivors' and dis- _{respecting old age}
ability benefits irrespective of age, but no such law shall affect the _{pensions and}
operation of any law present or future of a provincial legislature _{supple-mentary}
in relation to any such matter.[44] _{benefits}

AGRICULTURE AND IMMIGRATION

95 In each Province the Legislature may make Laws in relation to _{Concurrent}
Agriculture in the Province, and to Immigration into the Province; _{Powers of Legislation}
and it is hereby declared that the Parliament of Canada may from _{respecting}
Time to Time make Laws in relation to Agriculture in all or any of _{Agriculture, etc.}
the Provinces, and to Immigration into all or any of the Provinces;
and any Law of the Legislature of a Province relative to Agriculture or to Immigration shall have effect in and for the Province as
long and as far only as it is not repugnant to any Act of the Parliament of Canada.

● ●

    1. Nothing in any such law shall prejudicially affect any right or privilege with
respect to separate schools which any class of persons have at the date of the passing
of this Act, under the terms of chapters 29 and 30 of the Ordinances of the North-
west Territories, passed in the year 1901, or with respect to religious instruction in any
public or separate school as provided for in the said ordinances.
    2. In the appropriation by the Legislature or distribution by the Government of
the province of any moneys for the support of schools organized and carried on in
accordance with the said chapter 29, or any Act passed in amendment thereof or in
substitution therefor, there shall be no discrimination against schools of any class
described in the said chapter 29.
    3. Where the expression "by law" is employed in paragraph (3) of the said section
93, it shall be held to mean the law as set out in the said chapters 29 and 30; and
where the expression "at the Union" is employed in the said paragraph (3), it shall
be held to mean the date at which this Act comes into force.

Altered by Term 17 of the Terms of Union of Newfoundland with
Canada (confirmed by the *British North America Act, 1949*, 12–13
Geo. VI, c. 22 (U.K.)), which reads as follows:

    17. In lieu of section ninety-three of the British North America Act, 1867, the
following term shall apply in respect of the Province of Newfoundland:
    In and for the Province of Newfoundland the Legislature shall have exclusive
authority to make laws in relation to education, but the Legislature will not have
authority to make laws prejudicially affecting any right or privilege with respect to
denominational schools, common (amalgamated) schools, or denominational colleges,
that any class or classes of persons have by law in Newfoundland at the date of Union,
and out of public funds of the Province of Newfoundland, provided for education,
    (*a*) all such schools shall receive their share of such funds in accordance with scales
        determined on a non-discriminatory basis from time to time by the Legislature for
        all schools then being conducted under authority of the Legislature; and
    (*b*) all such colleges shall receive their share of any grant from time to time voted for
        all colleges then being conducted under authority of the Legislature, such grant
        being distributed on a non-discriminatory basis.

    44. Added by the *British North America Act, 1964*, 12–13, Eliz. II,
c. 73 (U.K.). Originally enacted by the *British North America Act,
1951*, 14–15 Geo. VI, c. 32 (U.K.), as follows:

    "94A. It is hereby declared that the Parliament of Canada may from time to time
make laws in relation to old age pensions in Canada, but no law made by the Parliament of Canada in relation to old age pensions shall affect the operation of any law
present or future of a Provincial Legislature in relation to old age pensions."

VIII   *Judicature*

96   The Governor General shall appoint the Judges of the Superior,   Appointment
     District, and County Courts in each Province, except those of the   of Judges
     Courts of Probate in Nova Scotia and New Brunswick.

97   Until the laws relative to Property and Civil Rights in Ontario,   Selection of
     Nova Scotia, and New Brunswick, and the Procedure of the Courts   Judges in
     in those Provinces, are made uniform, the Judges of the Courts of   Ontario, etc.
     those Provinces appointed by the Governor General shall be
     selected from the respective Bars of those Provinces.

98   The Judges of the Courts of Quebec shall be selected from the Bar   Selection of
     of that Province.   Judges in
                                                                          Quebec

     1   Subject to subsection two of this section, the Judges of the   Tenure of
     Superior Courts shall hold office during good behaviour, but shall   office of
     be removable by the Governor General on Address of the Senate   Judges
     and House of Commons.
     2   A Judge of a Superior Court, whether appointed before or   Termination
     after the coming into force of this section, shall cease to hold office   at age 75
     upon attaining the age of seventy-five years, or upon the coming
     into force of this section if at that time he has already attained that
     age.44A

100 The Salaries, Allowances, and Pensions of the Judges of the   Salaries etc.,
     Superior, District, and County Courts (except the Courts of Pro-   of Judges
     bate in Nova Scotia and New Brunswick), and of the Admiralty
     Courts in Cases where the Judges thereof are for the Time being
     paid by Salary, shall be fixed and provided by the Parliament of
     Canada.45

101 The Parliament of Canada may, notwithstanding anything in this   General Court
     Act, from Time to Time provide for the Constitution, Mainte-   of Appeal,
     nance, and Organization of a General Court of Appeal for Canada,   etc.
     and for the Establishment of any additional Courts for the better
     Administration of the Laws of Canada.46

● ●

44A. Repealed and re-enacted by the *British North America Act, 1960*,
9 Eliz. II, c. 2 (U.K.), which came into force on the 1st day of March,
1961. The original section read as follows:
     99. The Judges of the Superior Courts shall hold Office during good Behaviour, but   Tenure of
shall be removable by the Governor General on Address of the Senate and House of   office of
Commons.   Judges of
                                                                                       Superior
                                                                                       Courts

45. Now provided for in the *Judges Act*, R.S.C. 1952, c. 159, as amended
by S.C. 1963, c. 8, 1964–65, c. 36 and 1966–67, c. 76.

46. See the *Supreme Court Act*, R.S.C. 1952, c. 259, and the *Exchequer
Court Act*, R.S.C. 1952, c. 98.

VIII   *Revenues; Debts; Assets; Taxation*

102   All Duties and Revenues over which the respective Legislatures of Canada, Nova Scotia, and New Brunswick before and at the Union had and have Power of Appropriation, except such Portions thereof as are by this Act reserved to the respective Legislatures of the Provinces, or are raised by them in accordance with the special Powers conferred on them by this Act, shall form One Consolidated Revenue Fund, to be appropriated for the Public Service of Canada in the Manner and subject to the Charges in this Act provided.

Creation of Consolidated Revenue Fund

103   The Consolidated Revenue Fund of Canada shall be permanently charged with the Costs, Charges, and Expenses incident to the Collection, Management, and Receipt thereof, and the same shall form the First Charge thereon, subject to be reviewed and audited in such Manner as shall be ordered by the Governor General in Council until the Parliament otherwise provides.

Expenses of Collection, etc.

104   The annual Interest of the Public Debts of the several Provinces of Canada, Nova Scotia, and New Brunswick at the Union shall form the Second Charge on the Consolidated Revenue Fund of Canada.

Interest of Provincial Public Debts

105   Unless altered by the Parliament of Canada, the Salary of the Governor General shall be Ten thousand Pounds Sterling Money of the United Kingdom of Great Britain and Ireland, payable out of the Consolidated Revenue Fund of Canada, and the same shall form the Third Charge thereon.[47]

Salary of Governor General

106   Subject to the several Payments by this Act charged on the Consolidated Revenue Fund of Canada, the same shall be appropriated by the Parliament of Canada for the Public Service.

Appropriation from Time to Time

107   All Stocks, Cash, Banker's Balances, and Securities for Money belonging to each Province at the Time of the Union, except as in this Act mentioned, shall be the Property of Canada, and shall be taken in Reduction of the Amount of the respective Debts of the Provinces at the Union.

Transfer of Stocks, etc.

108   The Public Works and Property of each Province, enumerated in the Third Schedule to this Act, shall be the Property of Canada.

Transfer of Property in Schedule

109   All Lands, Mines, Minerals, and Royalties belonging to the several Provinces of Canada, Nova Scotia, and New Brunswick at the Union, and all Sums then due or payable for such Lands, Mines, Minerals, or Royalties, shall belong to the several Provinces of Ontario, Quebec, Nova Scotia, and New Brunswick in which the

Property in Lands, Mines, etc.

• •

47. Now covered by the *Governor General's Act*, R.S.C. 1952, c. 139.

same are situate or arise, subject to any Trusts existing in respect thereof, and to any Interest other than that of the Province in the same.[48]

110   All Assets connected with such Portions of the Public Debt of each Province as are assumed by that Province shall belong to that Province.
Assets connected with Provincial Debts

111   Canada shall be liable for the Debts and Liabilities of each Province existing at the Union.
Canada to be liable for Provincial Debts

112   Ontario and Quebec conjointly shall be liable to Canada for the Amount (if any) by which the Debt of the Province of Canada exceeds at the Union Sixty-two million five hundred thousand Dollars, and shall be charged with Interest at the Rate of Five per Centum per Annum thereon.
Debts of Ontario and Quebec

113   The Assets enumerated in the Fourth Schedule to this Act belonging at the Union to the Province of Canada shall be the Property of Ontario and Quebec conjointly.
Assets of Ontario and Quebec

114   Nova Scotia shall be liable to Canada for the Amount (if any) by which its Public Debt exceeds at the Union Eight million Dollars, and shall be charged with Interest at the Rate of Five per Centum per Annum thereon.[49]
Debt of Nova Scotia

115   New Brunswick shall be liable to Canada for the Amount (if any) by which its Public Debt exceeds at the Union Seven million Dollars, and shall be charged with Interest at the Rate of Five per Centum per Annum thereon.
Debt of New Brunswick

116   In case the Public Debts of Nova Scotia and New Brunswick do not at the Union amount to Eight million and Seven million Dollars respectively, they shall respectively receive by half-yearly Payments in advance from the Government of Canada Interest at Five per Centum per Annum on the Difference between the actual Amounts of their respective Debts and such stipulated Amounts.
Payment of interest to Nova Scotia and New Brunswick

117   The several Provinces shall retain all their respective Public Property not otherwise disposed of in this Act, subject to the Right of Canada to assume any Lands or Public Property required for Fortifications or for the Defence of the Country.
Provincial Public Property

● ●

48. The four western provinces were placed in the same position as the original provinces by the *British North America Act, 1930*, 21 Geo. V, c. 26 (U.K.).

49. The obligations imposed by this section, sections 115 and 116, and similar obligations under the instruments creating or admitting other provinces, have been carried into legislation of the Parliament of Canada and are now to be found in the *Provincial Subsidies Act*, R.S.C. 1952, c. 221.

118   Repealed.⁵⁰

119   New Brunswick shall receive by half-yearly Payments in advance   Further
from Canada for the Period of Ten Years from the Union an addi-   Grant
tional Allowance of Sixty-three thousand Dollars per Annum; but   to New
as long as the Public Debt of that Province remains under Seven
million Dollars, a Deduction equal to the Interest at Five per

• •

50. Repealed by the *Statute Law Revision Act, 1950*, 14 Geo. VI, c. 6
(U.K.). As originally enacted, the section read as follows:

118. The following Sums shall be paid yearly by Canada to the several Provinces for   Grants to
the Support of their Governments and Legislatures: Provinces

	Dollars
Ontario	Eighty thousand.
Quebec	Seventy thousand.
Nova Scotia	Sixty thousand.
New Brunswick	Fifty thousand.

Two hundred and sixty thousand;
and an annual Grant in aid of each Province shall be made, equal to Eighty Cents per
Head of the Population as ascertained by the Census of One thousand eight hundred
and sixty-one, and in the Case of Nova Scotia and New Brunswick, by each subsequent
Decennial Census until the Population of each of those two Provinces amounts to Four
hundred thousand Souls, at which Rate such Grant shall thereafter remain. Such
Grants shall be in full Settlement of all future Demands on Canada, and shall be paid
half-yearly in advance to each Province; but the Government of Canada shall deduct
from such Grants, as against any Province, all Sums chargeable as Interest on the
Public Debt of that Province in excess of the several Amounts stipulated in this Act.

The section was made obsolete by the *British North America Act,
1907*, 7 Edw. VII, c. 11 (U.K.) which provided:

1. (1) The following grants shall be made yearly by Canada to every province,   Payments
which at the commencement of this Act is a province of the Dominion, for its local   to be made
purposes and the support of its Government and Legislature:—   by Canada to
(a) A fixed grant—   provinces
    where the population of the province is under one hundred and fifty thousand, of
    one hundred thousand dollars;
    where the population of the province is one hundred and fifty thousand, but does
    not exceed two hundred thousand, of one hundred and fifty thousand dollars;
    where the population of the province is two hundred thousand, but does not
    exceed four hundred thousand, of one hundred and eighty thousand dollars;
    where the population of the province is four hundred thousand, but does not
    exceed eight hundred thousand, of one hundred and ninety thousand dollars;
    where the population of the province is eight hundred thousand, but does not ex-
    ceed one million five hundred thousand, of two hundred and twenty thousand
    dollars;
    where the population of the province exceeds one million five hundred thousand,
    of two hundred and forty thousand dollars; and
(b) Subject to the special provisions of this Act as to the provinces of British Columbia
    and Prince Edward Island, a grant at the rate of eighty cents per head of the
    population of the province up to the number of two million five hundred thousand,
    and at the rate of sixty cents per head of so much of the population as exceeds
    that number.
(2) An additional grant of one hundred thousand dollars shall be made yearly to
the province of British Columbia for a period of ten years from the commencement of
this Act.
(3) The population of a province shall be ascertained from time to time in the case
of the provinces of Manitoba, Saskatchewan, and Alberta respectively by the last
quinquennial census or statutory estimate of population made under the Acts establishing those provinces or any other Act of the Parliament of Canada making provision
for the purpose, and in the case of any other province by the last decennial census for
the time being.
(4) The grants payable under this Act shall be paid half-yearly in advance to each
province.
(5) The grants payable under this Act shall be substituted for the grants or subsidies (in this Act referred to as existing grants) payable for the like purposes at the
commencement of this Act to the several provinces of the Dominion under the provisions of section one hundred and eighteen of the British North America Act 1867,   30–31 Vict.,
or of any Order in Council establishing a province, or of any Act of the Parliament   c. 3
of Canada containing directions for the payment of any such grant or subsidy, and
those provisions shall cease to have effect.
(6) The Government of Canada shall have the same power of deducting sums
charged against a province on account of the interest on public debt in the case of the

Centum per Annum on such Deficiency shall be made from that Allowance of Sixty-three thousand Dollars.[51]

120 All Payments to be made under this Act, or in discharge of Liabilities created under any Act of the Provinces of Canada, Nova Scotia, and New Brunswick respectively, and assumed by Canada, shall, until the Parliament of Canada otherwise directs, be made in such Form and Manner as may from Time to Time be ordered by the Governor General in Council.

Form of Payments

121 All Articles of the Growth, Produce, or Manufacture of any one of the Provinces shall, from and after the Union, be admitted free into each of the other Provinces.

Canadian Manufactures, etc.

122 The Customs and Excise Laws of each Province shall, subject to the Provisions of this Act, continue in force until altered by the Parliament of Canada.[52]

Continuance of Customs and Excise Laws

123 Where Customs Duties are, at the Union, leviable on any Goods, Wares, or Merchandises in any Two Provinces, those Goods, Wares, and Merchandises may, from and after the Union, be imported from one of those Provinces into the other of them on Proof of Payment of the Customs Duty leviable thereon in the Province of Exportation, and on Payment of such further Amount (if any) of Customs Duty as is leviable thereon in the Province of Importation.[53]

Exportation and Importation as between Two Provinces

124 Nothing in this Act shall affect the Right of New Brunswick to levy the Lumber Dues provided in Chapter Fifteen of Title Three of the Revised Statutes of New Brunswick, or in any Act amending

Lumber Dues in New Brunswick

● ●

grant payable under this Act to the province as they have in the case of the existing grant.

(7) Nothing in this Act shall affect the obligation of the Government of Canada to pay to any province any grant which is payable to that province, other than the existing grant for which the grant under this Act is substituted.

(8) In the case of the provinces of British Columbia and Prince Edward Island, the amount paid on account of the grant payable per head of the population to the provinces under this Act shall not at any time be less than the amount of the corresponding grant payable at the commencement of this Act, and if it is found on any decennial census that the population of the province has decreased since the last decennial census, the amount paid on account of the grant shall not be decreased below the amount then payable, notwithstanding the decrease of the population.

See the *Provincial Subsidies Act*, R.S.C. 1952, c. 221, *The Maritime Provinces Additional Subsidies Act*, 1942–43, c. 14, and the Terms of Union of Newfoundland with Canada, appended to the *British North America Act, 1949*, and also to *An Act to approve the Terms of Union of Newfoundland with Canada*, chapter 1 of the statutes of Canada, 1949.

51. Spent.

52. Spent. Now covered by the *Customs Act*, R.S.C. 1952, c. 58, the *Customs Tariff*, R.S.C. 1952, c. 60, the *Excise Act*, R.S.C. 1952, c. 99 and the *Excise Tax Act*, R.S.C. 1952, c. 100.

53. Spent.

that Act before or after the Union, and not increasing the Amount of such Dues; but the Lumber of any of the Provinces other than New Brunswick shall not be subject to such Dues.[54]

125   No Lands or Property belonging to Canada or any Province shall be liable to Taxation.

Exemption of Public Lands, etc.

126   Such Portions of the Duties and Revenues over which the respective Legislatures of Canada, Nova Scotia, and New Brunswick had before the Union Power of Appropriation as are by this Act reserved to the respective Governments or Legislatures of the Provinces, and all Duties and Revenues raised by them in accordance with the special Powers conferred upon them by this Act, shall in each Province form One Consolidated Revenue Fund to be appropriated for the Public Service of the Province.

Provincial Consolidated Revenue Fund

IX   Miscellaneous Provisions

GENERAL

127   Repealed.[55]

128   Every Member of the Senate or House of Commons of Canada shall before taking his Seat therein take and subscribe before the Governor General or some Person authorized by him, and every Member of a Legislative Council or Legislative Assembly of any Province shall before taking this Seat therein take and subscribe before the Lieutenant Governor of the Province or some Person authorized by him, the Oath of Allegiance contained in the Fifth Schedule to this Act; and every Member of the Senate of Canada and every Member of the Legislative Council of Quebec shall also, before taking his Seat therein, take and subscribe before the Governor General, or some Person authorized by him, the Declaration contained in the same Schedule.

Oath of Allegiance, etc.

129   Except as otherwise provided by this Act, all Laws in force in Canada, Nova Scotia, or New Brunswick at the Union, and all

Continuance of existing Laws, Courts, Officers, etc.

● ●

54. These dues were repealed in 1873 by 36 Vict., c. 16 (N.B.). And see *An Act respecting the Export Duties imposed on Lumber*, etc., (1873) 36 Vict., c. 41 (Canada), and section 2 of the *Provincial Subsidies Act*, R.S.C. 1952, c. 221.

55. Repealed by the *Statute Law Revision Act, 1893*, 56–57 Vict., c. 14 (U.K.). The section read as follows:

127. If any Person being at the passing of this Act a Member of the Legislative Council of Canada, Nova Scotia, or New Brunswick to whom a Place in the Senate is offered, does not within Thirty Days thereafter, by Writing under his Hand addressed to the Governor General of the Province of Canada or to the Lieutenant Governor of Nova Scotia or New Brunswick (as the Case may be), accept the same, he shall be deemed to have declined the same; and any Person who, being at the passing of this Act a Member of the Legislative Council of Nova Scotia or New Brunswick, accepts a Place in the Senate, shall thereby vacate his Seat in such Legislative Council.

As to Legislative Councillors of Provinces becoming senators

Courts of Civil and Criminal Jurisdiction, and all legal Commissions, Powers, and Authorities, and all Officers, Judicial, Administrative, and Ministerial, existing therein at the Union, shall continue in Ontario, Quebec, Nova Scotia, and New Brunswick respectively, as if the Union had not been made; subject nevertheless (except with respect to such as are enacted by or exist under Acts of the Parliament of Great Britain or of the Parliament of the United Kingdom of Great Britain and Ireland,) to be repealed, abolished, or altered by the Parliament of Canada, or by the Legislature of the respective Province, according to the Authority of the Parliament or of that Legislature under this Act.[56]

130   Until the Parliament of Canada otherwise provides, all Officers of the several Provinces having Duties to discharge in relation to Matters other than those coming within the Classes of Subjects by this Act assigned exclusively to the Legislatures of the Provinces shall be Officers of Canada, and shall continue to discharge the Duties of their respective Offices under the same Liabilities, responsibilities, and Penalties as if the Union had not been made.[57]   *Transfer of Officers to Canada*

131   Until the Parliament of Canada otherwise provides, the Governor General in Council may from Time to Time appoint such Officers as the Governor General in Council deems necessary or proper for the effectual Execution of this Act.   *Appointment of new Officers*

132   The Parliament and Government of Canada shall have all Powers necessary or proper for performing the Obligations of Canada or of any Province thereof, as Part of the British Empire, towards Foreign Countries, arising under Treaties between the Empire and such Foreign Countries.   *Treaty Obligations*

133   Either the English or the French Language may be used by any Person in the Debates of the Houses of the Parliament of Canada and of the Houses of the Legislature of Quebec; and both those Languages shall be used in the respective Records and Journals of those Houses; and either of those Languages may be used by any Person or in any Pleading or Process in or issuing from any Court of Canada established under this Act, and in or from all or any of the Courts of Quebec.   *Use of English and French Languages*

The Acts of the Parliament of Canada and of the Legislature of Quebec shall be printed and published in both those Languages.

● ●

56. The restriction against altering or repealing laws enacted by or existing under statutes of the United Kingdom was removed by the *Statute of Westminster, 1931*, 22 Geo. v, c. 4 (U.K.).

57. Spent.

ONTARIO AND QUEBEC

134 Until the Legislature of Ontario or of Quebec otherwise provides, the Lieutenant Governors of Ontario and Quebec may each appoint under the Great Seal of the Province the following Officers, to hold Office during Pleasure, that is to say,—the Attorney General, the Secretary and Registrar of the Province, the Treasurer of the Province, the Commissioner of Crown Lands, and the Commissioner of Agriculture and Public Works, and in the Case of Quebec the Solicitor General, and may, by Order of the Lieutenant Governor in Council, from Time to Time prescribe the Duties of those Officers, and of the several Departments over which they shall preside or to which they shall belong, and of the Officers and Clerks thereof, and may also appoint other and additional Officers to hold Office during Pleasure, and may from Time to Time prescribe the Duties of those Officers, and of the several Departments over which they shall preside or to which they shall belong, and of the Officers and Clerks thereof.[58]

Appointment of Executive Officers for Ontario and Quebec

135 Until the Legislature of Ontario or Quebec otherwise provides, all Rights, Powers, Duties, Functions, Responsibilities, or Authorities at the passing of this Act vested in or imposed on the Attorney General, Solicitor General, Secretary and Registrar of the Province of Canada, Minister of Finance, Commissioner of Crown Lands, Commissioner of Public Works, and Minister of Agriculture and Receiver General, by any Law, Statute, or Ordinance of Upper Canada, Lower Canada, or Canada, and not repugnant to this Act, shall be vested in or imposed on any Officer to be appointed by the Lieutenant Governor for the Discharge of the same or any of them; and the Commissioner of Agriculture and Public Works shall perform the Duties and Functions of the Office of Minister of Agriculture at the passing of this Act imposed by the Law of the Province of Canada, as well as those of the Commissioner of Public Works.[59]

Powers, Duties, etc. of Executive Officers

136 Until altered by the Lieutenant Governor in Council, the Great Seals of Ontario and Quebec respectively shall be the same, or of the same Design, as those used in the Provinces of Upper Canada and Lower Canada respectively before their Union as the Province of Canada.

Great Seals

137 The words "and from thence to the End of the then next ensuing Session of the Legislature," or Words to the same Effect, used in

Construction of temporary Acts

● ●

58. Spent. Now covered in Ontario by the *Executive Council Act*, R.S.O. 1960, c. 127 and in Quebec by the *Executive Power Act*, R.S.Q. 1964, c. 9 as amended by 1965, c. 16.

59. Probably spent.

any temporary Act of the Province of Canada not expired before the Union, shall be construed to extend and apply to the next Session of the Parliament of Canada if the Subject Matter of the Act is within the Powers of the same as defined by this Act, or to the next Sessions of the Legislatures of Ontario and Quebec respectively if the Subject Matter of the Act is within the Powers of the same as defined by this Act.

138 From and after the Union the Use of the Words "Upper Canada" instead of "Ontario," or "Lower Canada" instead of "Quebec," in any Deed, Writ, Process, Pleading, Document, Matter, or Thing, shall not invalidate the same. *As to Errors in Names*

139 Any Proclamation under the Great Seal of the Province of Canada issued before the Union to take effect at a Time which is subsequent to the Union, whether relating to that Province, or to Upper Canada, or to Lower Canada, and the several Matters and Things therein proclaimed, shall be and continue of like Force and Effect as if the Union had not been made.[60] *As to issue of Proclamations before Union, to commence after Union*

140 Any Proclamation which is authorized by any Act of the Legislature of the Province of Canada to be issued under the Great Seal of the Province of Canada, whether relating to that Province, or to Upper Canada, or to Lower Canada, and which is not issued before the Union, may be issued by the Lieutenant Governor of Ontario or of Quebec, as its Subject Matter requires, under the Great Seal thereof; and from and after the Issue of such Proclamation the same and the several Matters and Things therein proclaimed shall be and continue of the like Force and Effect in Ontario or Quebec as if the Union had not been made.[61] *As to issue of Proclamations after Union*

141 The Penitentiary of the Province of Canada shall, until the Parliament of Canada otherwise provides, be and continue the Penitentiary of Ontario and of Quebec.[62] *Penitentiary*

142 The Division and Adjustment of the Debts, Credits, Liabilities, Properties, and Assets of Upper Canada and Lower Canada shall be referred to the Arbitrament of Three Arbitrators, One chosen by the Government of Ontario, One by the Government of Quebec, and One by the Government of Canada; and the Selection of the Arbitrators shall not be made until the Parliament of Canada and the Legislatures of Ontario and Quebec have met; and the Arbitrator chosen by the Government of Canada shall not be a Resident either in Ontario or in Quebec.[63] *Arbitration respecting Debts, etc.*

● ●

60. Probably spent.

61. Probably spent.

62. Spent. Penitentiaries are now provided for by the *Penitentiary Act*, s.c. 1960–61, c. 53.

63. Spent. See pages (xi) and (xii) of the Public Accounts, 1902–03.

143   The Governor General in Council may from Time to Time order that such and so many of the Records, Books, and Documents of the Province of Canada as he thinks fit shall be appropriated and delivered either to Ontario or to Quebec, and the same shall thenceforth be the Property of that Province; and any Copy thereof or Extract therefrom, duly certified by the Officer having charge of the Original thereof, shall be admitted as Evidence.[64]   *Division of Records*

144   The Lieutenant Governor of Quebec may from Time to Time, by Proclamation under the Great Seal of the Province, to take effect from a Day to be appointed therein, constitute Townships in those Parts of the Province of Quebec in which Townships are not then already constituted, and fix the Metes and Bounds thereof.   *Constitution of Townships in Quebec*

145   Repealed.[65]

XI   *Admission of Other Colonies*

146   It shall be lawful for the Queen, by and with the Advice of Her Majesty's Most Honourable Privy Council, on Addresses from the Houses of the Parliament of Canada, and from the Houses of the respective Legislatures of the Colonies or Provinces of Newfoundland, Prince Edward Island, and British Columbia, to admit those Colonies or Provinces, or any of them, into the Union, and on Address from the Houses of the Parliament of Canada to admit Rupert's Land and the North-western Territory, or either of them, into the Union, on such Terms and Conditions in each Case as are in the Addresses expressed and as the Queen thinks fit to approve, subject to the Provisions of this Act; and the Provisions of any Order in Council in that Behalf shall have effect as if they had been enacted by the Parliament of the United Kingdom of Great Britain and Ireland.[66]   *Power to admit Newfoundland, etc., into the Union*

• •

64. Probably spent. Two orders were made under this section on the 24th of January, 1868.

65. Repealed by the *Statute Law Revision Act, 1893*, 56–57 Vict., c. 14, (U.K.). The section reads as follows:

X *Intercolonial Railway*
   145. Inasmuch as the Provinces of Canada, Nova Scotia, and New Brunswick have joined in a Declaration that the Construction of the International Railway is essential to the Consolidation of the Union of British North America, and to the Assent thereto of Nova Scotia and New Brunswick, and have consequently agreed that Provision should be made for its immediate Construction by the Government of Canada: Therefore, in order to give effect to that Agreement, it shall be the Duty of the Government and Parliament of Canada to provide for the Commencement, within Six Months after the Union, of a Railway connecting the River St. Lawrence with the City of Halifax in Nova Scotia, and for the Construction thereof without Intermission, and the Completion thereof with all practicable Speed.   *Duty of Government and Parliament of Canada to make Railway herein described*

66. All territories mentioned in this section are now part of Canada. See the notes to section 5, *supra*.

147 In case of the Admission of Newfoundland and Prince Edward As to Rep-
Island, or either of them, each shall be entitled to a Representation resentation of New-
in the Senate of Canada of Four Members, and (notwithstanding foundland and Prince
anything in this Act) in case of the Admission of Newfoundland Edward
the normal Number of Senators shall be Seventy-six and their Island in Senate
maximum Number shall be Eighty-two; but Prince Edward Island
when admitted shall be deemed to be comprised in the Third of
the Three Divisions into which Canada is, in relation of the Constitution of the Senate, divided by this Act, and accordingly, after
the Admission of Prince Edward Island, whether Newfoundland
is admitted or not, the Representation of Nova Scotia and New
Brunswick in the Senate shall, as Vacancies occur, be reduced
from Twelve to Ten Members respectively, and the Representation of each of those Provinces shall not be increased at any Time
beyond Ten, except under the Provisions of this Act for the Appointment of Three or Six additional Senators under the Direction
of the Queen.[67]

67. Spent. See the notes to sections 21, 22, 26, 27 and 28, *supra*.

Appendix B

THE STATUTE OF WESTMINSTER, 1931*

An Act to give effect to certain resolutions passed by Imperial Conferences held in the years 1926 and 1930.

11th December, 1931

WHEREAS the delegates to His Majesty's Governments in the United Kingdom, the Dominion of Canada, the Commonwealth of Australia, the Dominion of New Zealand, the Union of South Africa, the Irish Free State and Newfoundland, at Imperial Conferences holden at Westminster in the years of our Lord nineteen hundred and twenty-six and nineteen hundred and thirty did concur in making the declarations and resolutions set forth in the Reports of the said Conferences:

And whereas it is meet and proper to set out by way of preamble to this Act that, inasmuch as the Crown is the symbol of the free association of the members of the British Commonwealth of Nations, and as they are united by a common allegiance to the Crown, it would be in accord with the established constitutional position of all the members of the Commonwealth in relation to one another that any alteration in the law touching the Succession to the Throne or the Royal Style and Titles shall hereafter require the assent as well of the Parliaments of all the Dominions as of the Parliament of the United Kingdom:

And whereas it is in accord with the established constitutional position that no law hereafter made by the Parliament of the United Kingdom shall extend to any of the said Dominions as part of the law of that Dominion otherwise than at the request and with the consent of that Dominion:

And whereas it is necessary for the ratifying, confirming and establishing of certain of the said declarations and resolutions of the said Conferences that a law be made and enacted in due form by authority of the Parliament of the United Kingdom:

And whereas the Dominion of Canada, the Commonwealth of Australia, the Dominion of New Zealand, the Union of South Africa, the Irish Free State and Newfoundland have severally requested and consented to the submission of a measure to the Parliament of the United Kingdom for making such provision with regard to the matters aforesaid as is hereafter in this Act contained:

Now, THEREFORE, BE IT ENACTED by the King's Most Excellent Majesty, by and with the advice and consent of the Lords Spiritual and Temporal, and Commons, in this present Parliament assembled, and by the authority of the same, as follows:—

*British Statutes, 22 George V, Chapter 4.

1. In this Act the expression "Dominion" means any of the following Dominions, that is to say, the Dominion of Canada, the Commonwealth of Australia, the Dominion of New Zealand, the Union of South Africa, the Irish Free State and Newfoundland.

2. 1. The Colonial Laws Validity Act, 1865, shall not apply to any law made after the commencement of this Act by the Parliament of a Dominion.
2. No law and no provision of any law made after the commencement of this Act by the Parliament of a Dominion shall be void or inoperative on the ground that it is repugnant to the law of England, or to the provisions of any existing or future Act of Parliament of the United Kingdom, or to any order, rule, or regulation made under any such Act, and the powers of the Parliament of a Dominion shall include the power to repeal or amend any such Act, order, rule or regulation in so far as the same is part of the law of the Dominion.

3. It is hereby declared and enacted that the Parliament of a Dominion has full power to make laws having extra-territorial operation.

4. No Act of Parliament of the United Kingdom passed after the commencement of this Act shall extend or be deemed to extend, to a Dominion as part of the law of that Dominion, unless it is expressly declared in that Act that that Dominion has requested, and consented to, the enactment thereof.

5. Without prejudice to the generality of the foregoing provisions of this Act, sections seven hundred and thirty-five and seven hundred and thirty-six of the Merchant Shipping Act, 1894, shall be construed as though reference therein to the Legislature of a British possession did not include reference to the Parliament of a Dominion.

6. Without prejudice to the generality of the foregoing provisions of this Act, section four of the Colonial Courts of Admiralty Act, 1890 (which requires certain laws to be reserved for the signification of His Majesty's pleasure or to contain a suspending clause), and so much of section seven of that Act as requires the approval of His Majesty in Council to any rules of Court for regulating the practice and procedure of a Colonial Court of Admiralty, shall cease to have effect in any Dominion as from the commencement of this Act.

7. 1. Nothing in this Act shall be deemed to apply to the repeal, amendment or alteration of the British North America Acts, 1867 to 1930, or any order, rule or regulation made thereunder.
2. The provisions of section two of this Act shall extend to laws made by any of the Provinces of Canada and to the powers of the legislatures of such Provinces.
3. The powers conferred by this Act upon the Parliament of Canada or upon the legislatures of the Provinces shall be restricted to the enactment

of laws in relation to matters within the competence of the Parliament of Canada or of any of the legislatures of the Provinces respectively.

8. Nothing in this Act shall be deemed to confer any power to repeal or alter the Constitution or the Constitution Act of the Commonwealth of Australia or the Constitution Act of the Dominion of New Zealand otherwise than in accordance with the law existing before the commencement of this Act.

9. 1. Nothing in this Act shall be deemed to authorize the Parliament of the Commonwealth of Australia to make laws on any matter within the authority of the States of Australia, not being a matter within the authority of the Parliament or Government of the Commonwealth of Australia.

2. Nothing in this Act shall be deemed to require the concurrence of the Parliament or Government of the Commonwealth of Australia, in any law made by the Parliament of the United Kingdom with respect to any matter within the authority of the States of Australia, not being a matter within the authority of the Parliament or Government of the Commonwealth of Australia, in any case where it would have been in accordance with the constitutional practice existing before the commencement of this Act that the Parliament of the United Kingdom should make that law without such concurrence.

3. In the application of this Act to the Commonwealth of Australia the request and consent referred to in section four shall mean the request and consent of the Parliament and Government of the Commonwealth.

10. 1. None of the following sections of this Act, that is to say, sections two, three, four, five and six, shall extend to a Dominion to which this section applies as part of the law of that Dominion unless that section is adopted by the Parliament of the Dominion, and any Act of that Parliament adopting any section of this Act may provide that the adoption shall have effect either from the commencement of this Act or from such later date as is specified in the adopting Act.

2. The Parliament of any such Dominion as aforesaid may at any time revoke the adoption of any section referred to in sub-section (1) of this section.

3. The Dominions to which this section applies are the Commonwealth of Australia, the Dominion of New Zealand, and Newfoundland.

11. Notwithstanding anything in the Interpretation Act, 1889, the expression "Colony" shall not, in any Act of the Parliament of the United Kingdom passed after the commencement of this Act, include a Dominion or any Province or State forming part of a Dominion.

12. This Act may be cited as the Statute of Westminster, 1931.

Select bibliography

A SELECT BIBLIOGRAPHY, like an anthology, always raises weighty questions about the inclusion of some items and the omission of others, and I should like to make clear that the following short bibliography (which partially overlaps the longer one in the footnotes) is intended to support a teaching text being used by students. Acting on the assumption that anyone competent to teach a course that uses this book is probably also competent to collect his own reading list for his own and his students' purposes, I have included below only sources likely to be readily available in an average library; many of these books in turn contain further and more extensive bibliographies, and many more such works can be found in footnotes to the text. I have omitted specific references to such learned journals as the *Canadian Journal of Economics,* the *Canadian Journal of Political Science*, the *Canadian Historical Review, Canadian Public Administration*, and the *Canadian Bar Review*, on the further assumption, based on considerable experience, that students will benefit more from exploring these admirable periodicals than from being given the titles of isolated articles to look up; in any event, numerous articles are cited in the footnotes to the preceding text, and a large number of the best of them are contained in books of readings listed below.

The need to supplement a book on the government of Canada through the reading of a general history of Canada seems to me so obvious that I have not selected a history for inclusion; Canada's centennial helped generate several excellent new volumes. The *Canadian Annual Review,* in both its old and revived forms, is an invaluable commentary on contemporary political issues. The *Canada Year Book,* an annual compendium of facts prepared by the Dominion Bureau of Statistics, and the debates and committee reports of the Senate and House of Commons of Canada, are the main indispensable sources of official origin. The Royal Commission on Bilingualism and Biculturalism was responsible for a veritable library of relevant reports, some of them published, others deposited in the National Library and available through inter-library loan.

Chief among general works I would select:

ALEXANDER BRADY, *Democracy in the Dominions* (3rd ed., Toronto, 1958).
J. A. CORRY and J. E. HODGETTS, *Democratic Government and Politics* (3rd ed., Toronto, 1959).
W. L. MORTON, *The Canadian Identity* (Toronto, 1961).
JOHN PORTER, *The Vertical Mosaic: An Analysis of Social Class and Power in Canada* (Toronto, 1965).
PETER RUSSELL, ed., *Nationalism in Canada* (Toronto, 1966).
FRANK H. UNDERHILL, *In Search of Canadian Liberalism* (Toronto, 1960).
MASON WADE, ed., *Canadian Dualism/ La Dualité canadienne* (Toronto, 1960).

A special category of books which cuts across almost any type of classification into which one might attempt to fit a bibliography is the political biography, a species happily on the increase in Canada:

Robert Laird Borden: His Memoirs (Toronto, 1938).
J. M. S. CARELESS, *Brown of the Globe*, I (Toronto, 1959); II (Toronto, 1963).
RAMSAY COOK, *The Politics of John W. Dafoe and the Free Press* (Toronto, 1963).
DONALD CREIGHTON, *John A. Macdonald*, I (Toronto, 1952); II (Toronto, 1955).
R. MACG. DAWSON, *William Lyon Mackenzie King, I, 1874–1923* (Toronto; 1958).
ROGER GRAHAM, *Arthur Meighen*, I (Toronto, 1960); II (Toronto, 1963).
KENNETH MCNAUGHT, *A Prophet in Politics: A Biography of J. S. Woodsworth* (Toronto, 1959).
BLAIR NEATBY, *William Lyon Mackenzie King, II, 1924–1932: The Lonely Heights* (Toronto, 1963).
PETER C. NEWMAN, *Renegade in Power: The Diefenbaker Years* (Toronto, 1963).
— *The Distemper of our Times* (Toronto, 1968).
J. W. PICKERSGILL, ed., *The Mackenzie King Record, I, 1939–1944* (Toronto, 1960).
J. W. PICKERSGILL and D. F. FORSTER, eds., *The Mackenzie King Record, II, 1944–1945* (Toronto, 1968).
SIR JOSEPH POPE, ed., *Correspondence of Sir John A. Macdonald* (Toronto, 1921).
J. T. SAYWELL, ed., *The Canadian Journal of Lady Aberdeen* (Toronto, 1960).
JOSEPH SCHULL, *Laurier* (Toronto, 1965).
O. D. SKELTON, *Life and Letters of Sir Wilfrid Laurier* (Toronto, 1921); reissued in the Carleton Library, nos. 21–2, edited by DAVID M. L. FARR.
DALE C. THOMSON, *Alexander Mackenzie: Clear Grit* (Toronto, 1960).
— *Louis St. Laurent: Canadian* (Toronto, 1967).

NORMAN WARD, ed., *A Party Politician: The Memoirs of Chubby Power* (Toronto, 1968).
THOMAS VAN DUSEN, *The Chief* (Toronto, 1968).

The following books are grouped to correspond to the major sections into which the text is divided; this necessitates some repetition.

I CONSTITUTIONAL DEVELOPMENT
Parliamentary Debates on Confederation of British North American Provinces (Quebec, 1865, reprinted Ottawa, 1951).
SIR REGINALD COUPLAND, *The Quebec Act* (Oxford, 1925).
DONALD CREIGHTON, *The Commercial Empire of the St. Lawrence, 1760–1850* (Toronto, 1937).
— *The Road to Confederation* (Toronto, 1964).
LORD DURHAM, *Report of the Affairs of British North America*, edited by SIR C. P. LUCAS (Oxford, 1912); reissued in the Carleton Library, no. 1, edited by GERALD M. CRAIG.
A. B. KEITH, *The Governments of the British Empire* (London, 1935).
W. P. M. KENNEDY, *Statutes, Treaties, and Documents of the Canadian Constitution, 1713–1929* (Toronto, 1930).
— *The Constitution of Canada, 1534–1937* (2nd ed., London, 1938).
KLAUS EUGEN KNORR, *British Colonial Theories, 1570–1850* (Toronto, 1944, reprinted 1963).
W. L. MORTON, *The Critical Years: The Union of British North America, 1857–1873* (Toronto, 1964).
Ontario Advisory Committee on Confederation, *Background Papers and Reports* (Toronto, 1967).
SIR JOSEPH POPE, ed., *Confederation: Being a Series of Unpublished Documents Bearing on the British North America Act* (Toronto, 1895); reissued in the Carleton Library, no. 40, edited by G. P. BROWNE.
J. H. S. REID, KENNETH MCNAUGHT, and HARRY S. CROWE, *A Source-Book of Canadian History* (Toronto, 1959).
LOUIS SABOURIN, *Le Système politique du Canada* (Ottawa, 1968).
A. SHORTT and A. G. DOUGHTY, eds., *Documents Relating to the Constitutional History of Canada, 1759–1791* (Ottawa, 1918).
P. B. WAITE, *The Life and Times of Confederation* (Toronto, 1962).
W. M. WHITELAW, *The Maritimes and Canada before Confederation* (Toronto, 1934).

II THE CONSTITUTION
J. M. BECK, *The Government of Nova Scotia* (Toronto, 1957).
R. MACG. DAWSON, *Constitutional Issues in Canada, 1900–31* (Toronto, 1933).

— *The Development of Dominion Status, 1900–1936* (Toronto, 1937).

M. S. DONNELLY, *The Government of Manitoba* (Toronto, 1963).

DAVID M. FARR, *The Colonial Office and Canada, 1867–87* (Toronto, 1955).

PAUL FOX, ed., *Politics: Canada* (Toronto, 1970).

P. GÉRIN-LAJOIE, *Constitutional Amendment in Canada* (Toronto, 1950).

W. P. M. KENNEDY, *Statutes, Treaties, and Documents of the Canadian Constitution, 1713–1929* (Toronto, 1930).

— *The Constitution of Canada, 1534–1937* (2nd ed., London, 1938).

BORA LASKIN, *Canadian Constitutional Law: Cases, Text and Notes on Distribution of Legislative Power* (Toronto, 1969).

FRANK MACKINNON, *The Government of Prince Edward Island* (Toronto, 1951).

EDWARD MCWHINNEY, *Judicial Review* (4th ed., Toronto, 1969).

J. R. MALLORY, *Social Credit and the Federal Power in Canada* (Toronto, 1954).

J. A. MAXWELL, *Federal Subsidies to the Provincial Governments in Canada* (Cambridge, Mass., 1937).

J. PETER MEEKISON, ed., *Canadian Federalism: Myth or Reality* (Toronto, 1968).

MAURICE OLLIVIER, *Problems of Canadian Sovereignty* (Toronto, 1945).

Reports of the Royal Commission on Bilingualism and Biculturalism (Ottawa, 1965 *et seq.*).

Report of Royal Commission on Constitutional Problems (Quebec, 1957).

Report of the Royal Commission on Dominion-Provincial Relations (Ottawa, 1940).

JOHN T. SAYWELL, *The Office of Lieutenant-Governor* (Toronto, 1957).

FRED SCHINDELER, *Responsible Government in Ontario* (Toronto, 1969).

F. R. SCOTT, *Civil Liberties and Canadian Federalism* (Toronto, 1959).

Senate of Canada, *Report on the British North America Act* (1939).

B. L. STRAYER, *Judicial Review of Legislation in Canada* (Toronto, 1968).

L. H. THOMAS, *The Struggle for Responsible Government in the North-West Territories, 1870–1897* (Toronto, 1956).

P. E. TRUDEAU, *Federalism and the French Canadians* (Toronto, 1968).

III and IV THE EXECUTIVE AND THE ADMINISTRATION

J. H. AITCHISON, ed., *The Political Process in Canada: Essays in Honour of R. MacGregor Dawson* (Toronto, 1963).

KEITH B. CALLARD, *Advanced Administrative Training in the Public Service* (Toronto, 1958).

TAYLOR COLE, *The Canadian Bureaucracy* (Durham, NC, 1949).

R. MACG. DAWSON, *The Civil Service of Canada* (Toronto, 1929).

— *The Conscription Crisis of 1944* (Toronto, 1962).

— *The Principle of Official Independence* (London, 1922).

JAMES EAYRS, *The Art of the Possible* (Toronto, 1961).

EUGENE A. FORSEY, *The Royal Power of Dissolution of Parliament in the British Commonwealth* (Toronto, 1943).

PAUL FOX, ed., *Politics: Canada* (Toronto, 1970).

J. E. HODGETTS, *Pioneer Public Service* (Toronto, 1955).

J. E. HODGETTS and D. C. CORBETT, eds., *Canadian Public Administration* (Toronto, 1960).

JOHN E. KERSELL, *Parliamentary Supervision of Delegated Legislation* (Toronto, 1960).

LLOYD D. MUSOLF, *Public Corporations and Accountability: The Canadian Experience* (Cambridge, Mass., 1959).

Organization of the Government of Canada (Ottawa, semi-annually).

FRANK W. PEERS, *The Politics of Canadian Broadcasting: 1920–1951* (Toronto, 1969).

MAURICE POPE, *Soldiers and Politicians* (Toronto, 1962).

Report of the Royal Commission on Government Organization (Ottawa, 1962–3).

NORMAN WARD, *The Public Purse: A Study in Canadian Democracy* (Toronto, 1962).

A. M. WILLMS and W. D. K. KERNAGHAN, *Public Administration in Canada: Selected Readings* (Toronto, 1968).

V THE LEGISLATURE

SIR J. G. BOURINOT, *Parliamentary Procedure and Practice in the Dominion of Canada*, edited by T. B. FLINT (3rd ed., Toronto, 1903)

ROBERT M. CLARK, ed., *Canadian Issues: Essays in Honour of Henry F. Angus* (Toronto, 1961).

W. F. DAWSON, *Procedure in the Canadian House of Commons* (Toronto, 1962).

ELMER A. DRIEDGER, *The Composition of Legislation* (Ottawa, 1957).

PAUL FOX, ed., *Politics: Canada* (Toronto, 1970).

JOHN E. KERSELL, *Parliamentary Supervision of Delegated Legislation* (Toronto, 1960).

R. A. MACKAY, *The Unreformed Senate of Canada* (London, 1926).

NORMAN WARD, *The Canadian House of Commons: Representation* (2nd printing, Toronto, 1963).

— *The Public Purse: A Study in Canadian Democracy* (Toronto, 1962).

VI THE JUDICIARY

PAUL FOX, ed., *Politics: Canada* (Toronto, 1970).

VINCENT C. MACDONALD, *Legislative Power and the Supreme Court in the Fifties* (Toronto, 1960).

EDWARD MCWHINNEY, *Judicial Review* (4th ed., Toronto, 1969).

F. R. SCOTT, *Civil Liberties and Canadian Federalism* (Toronto, 1959).

B. L. STRAYER, *Judicial Review of Legislation in Canada* (Toronto, 1968).

VII POLITICAL PARTIES

J. M. BECK, *Pendulum of Power* (Toronto, 1968).

S. D. CLARK, *Movements of Political Protest in Canada, 1640–1840* (Toronto, 1959).

CATHERINE CLEVERDON, *The Woman Suffrage Movement in Canada* (Toronto, 1950).

PAUL G. CORNELL, *The Alignment of Political Groups in Canada, 1841–1867* (Toronto, 1962).

J. L. GRANATSTEIN, *The Politics of Survival: the Conservative Party of Canada, 1939–1945* (Toronto, 1967).

GEORGE HOGAN, *The Conservative in Canada* (Toronto, 1963).

GAD HOROWITZ, *Canadian Labour in Politics* (Toronto, 1968).

JOHN A. IRVING, *The Social Credit Movement in Alberta* (Toronto, 1959).

J. A. LAPONCE, *People vs Politics: A Study of Opinions, Attitudes, and Perceptions in Vancouver-Burrard, 1963–1965* (Toronto, 1969).

S. M. LIPSET, *Agrarian Socialism* (Anchor Books Ed., 1968).

DEAN MCHENRY, *The Third Force in Canada* (Berkeley, 1950).

C. B. MACPHERSON, *Democracy in Alberta* (Toronto, 1953).

J. R. MALLORY, *Social Credit and the Federal Power in Canada* (Toronto, 1954).

JOHN MEISEL, *The Canadian General Election of 1957* (Toronto, 1962).

W. L. MORTON, *The Progressive Party in Canada* (Toronto, 1950).

MICHAEL OLIVER, ed., *Social Purpose for Canada* (Toronto, 1961).

J. W. PICKERSGILL, *The Liberal Party* (Toronto, 1962).

HERBERT F. QUINN, *The Union Nationale* (Toronto, 1963).

L. G. THOMAS, *The Liberal Party in Alberta* (Toronto, 1959).

HUGH G. THORBURN, ed., *Party Politics in Canada* (Toronto, 1963).

— *Politics in New Brunswick* (Toronto, 1961).

NORMAN WARD and DUFF SPAFFORD, eds., *Politics in Saskatchewan* (Toronto, 1968).

JOHN R. WILLIAMS, *The Conservative Party in Canada, 1920–1949* (Durham, NC, 1956).

WALTER D. YOUNG, *The Anatomy of a Party: The National CCF, 1932–61* (Toronto, 1969).

Index